THE ORIGINS OF THE KOREAN WAR

STUDIES OF THE EAST ASIAN INSTITUTE OF COLUMBIA UNIVERSITY

The East Asian Institute of Columbia University was established in 1949 to prepare graduate students for careers dealing with East Asia, and to aid research and publication on East Asia during the modern period.

The Studies of the East Asian Institute were inaugurated in 1962 to bring to a wider public the results of significant new research on modern and contemporary East Asia.

THE ORIGINS
OF THE
KOREAN WAR

Liberation and the
Emergence of Separate Regimes
1945-1947

Bruce Cumings

PRINCETON UNIVERSITY PRESS
PRINCETON, NEW JERSEY

Copyright © 1981 by Princeton University Press

Published by Princeton University Press, Princeton, New Jersey
in the United Kingdom, Princeton University Press, Oxford

All Rights Reserved

Third printing, 1989

Library of Congress Cataloging in Publication Data will be
found on the last printed page of this book

Publication of this book has been aided by a grant from the
Whitney Darrow Publication Reserve Fund of Princeton University Press

This book has been composed in Linotype Baskerville

Clothbound editions of Princeton University Press books
are printed on acid-free paper, and binding materials are
chosen for strength and durability

Printed in the United States of America

9   8   7   6   5   4

For
Bonnie and Jackie

Contents

Abbreviations used in text:

CC	Coalition Committee (*Chwa-u hapjak wiwŏnhoe*)
CCRRKI	Central Council for the Rapid Realization of Korean Independence (*Taehan tongnip ch'oksong chungang hyŏbŭi-hoe*)
ch'iandae	Peace Preservation Corps
Chŏnnong	National League of Peasant Unions (*Chŏn'guk nongmin chohap ch'ong yŏnmaeng*)
Chŏnp'yong	National Council of Korean Labor Unions (*Chosŏn nodong chohap chŏn'guk p'yŏng'ŭi-hoe*)
CIC	Counter-Intelligence Corps
CPKI	Committee for the Preparation of Korean Independence (*Chosŏn kŏn'guk chunbi wiwŏnhoe*)
DNF	Democratic National Front (*Minjujuŭi minjok chŏnsŏn*)
ENC	Emergency National Council (*Pisang kungmin hoeŭi*)
JC	U.S.-Soviet Joint Commission
JCS	Joint Chiefs of Staff
KCP	Korean Communist Party (*Chosŏn kongsandang*)
KDP	Korean Democratic Party (*Han'guk minjudang*)
KMT	Kuomintang
Kŏnmaeng	Korean Independence League (*Chosŏn kŏn'guk tongmaeng*)
KPG	Korean Provisional Government (*Taehan min'guk imsi chŏngbu*)
KPR	Korean People's Republic (*Chosŏn inmin konghwa'-guk*)
KVA	Korean Volunteer Army (*Chosŏn ŭiyŏng-gun*)
MG	Military Government
NKC	New Korea Company
NKCP	North Korean Communist Party (*Puk-Chosŏn kongsandang*)
NKIPC	North Korean Interim People's Committee
NKWP	North Korean Worker's Party (*Puk-Chosŏn nodongdang*)
NPA	National Preparatory Army
NSRRKI	National Society for the Rapid Realization of Korean Independence
PC	People's Committees
RPU	Red Peasant Union

SDP   Social Democratic Party (*Sahoe minjudang*)
SKIG   South Korean Interim Government
SKILA   South Korean Interim Legislative Assembly
SMRC   South Manchurian Railway Company
SWNCC   State-War-Navy Coordinating Committee
USAFIK   United States Armed Forces in Korea
USAMGIK   United States Army Military Government in Korea

Abbreviations used in notes and bibliography:

FRUS   *Foreign Relations of the United States*
"HUSAFIK"   "History of the United States Armed Forces in Korea"
"HMGK"   "History of the United States Army Military Government of Korea"
THMGS   *Taehan min'guk-sa* (History of the Republic of Korea)

In 1953 the Korean peninsula was a smoldering ruin. From Pusan in the south to Sinŭiju in the north, Koreans buried their dead, mourned their losses, and sought to draw together the shattered remains of their lives. In the capital at Seoul, hollow buildings stood like skeletons alongside streets paved with weird mixtures of concrete and shrapnel. At American military encampments on the outskirts of the capital, masses of beggars waited to pick through the garbage that foreign soldiers tossed out. In the north, modern edifices scarcely stood anymore; P'yŏngyang and other cities were heaps of bricks and ashes, factories stood empty, massive dams no longer held their water. People emerged from a mole-like existence in caves and tunnels to find a nightmare in the bright of day. Moreover, Koreans were not alone. Descending upon the peninsula was the force of three great powers, who had clashed to the point of world war and who had raised the specter of nuclear destruction before the Korean people. All this, and still the war that ended in 1953 resolved nothing; only the status quo ante had been restored. All this, and yet three decades later the problem remains.

In 1945 another war had ended, one that had barely touched Korea in its heated phase. From the perspective of that year, however, even the most misanthropic doomsayer could not have conjured the fate of the Koreans in 1953, for 1945 was a year of liberation, of deliverance. And this was true for more than just Koreans; the other antagonists in the war ending in 1953 had also been allies in the previous war. How did 1945 turn into 1953? Where should we begin to seek the origins of the Korean War?

Attention has focused, for the most part, on events in the weeks and months prior to June 25, 1950, whether in Moscow, Washington, P'yŏngyang, or Seoul. The literature has sought to assess responsibility for the outbreak of conventional fighting. Both South and North Korean official accounts state that the *casus belli* occurred on the morning of June 25, when one side attacked the other—not a simple attack, but an unprovoked, surprise attack, different from previous skirmishes. Official American accounts also claim surprise and an absence of provocation. Officially the north was blamed for the attack, but the assumption of key decision makers was that Joseph Stalin was behind it. As President Harry S. Truman put it:

Communism was acting in Korea just as Hitler, Mussolini, and the Japanese had acted fifteen and twenty years earlier. . . . If this was allowed to go unchallenged it would mean a third world war, just as similar incidents had brought on the second world war.[1]

The secondary literature generally agrees that the point of this war is who started the shooting and that the answer is to be sought in the narrow confines of 1950. David Rees argues that Stalin had "a grand Korean design"; Adam Ulam remarks that "no sane person could doubt the ultimate Soviet responsibility for the attack";[2] Glenn Paige's interesting analysis of the American decision to intervene in the war basically accepts the official American position on the responsibility for the opening of the war and devotes but one page to the internal Korean situation before 1950.[3] I. F. Stone long ago contributed the best-known critique of the American position, arguing that the war's origins were murky and that many important questions remained unanswered. According to Stone, the hypothesis should at least be entertained that the south provoked the war or encouraged it through a conspiracy of silence and that high American officials such as John Foster Dulles and General Douglas MacArthur may have connived with Syngman Rhee in this. His concern, however, is also limited to events occurring in 1950.[4] Scholarly literature of more recent vintage has been less comfortable with the argument that Stalin directed the events, but it retains the supposition that the North Koreans started the war.[5] In general, the literature on the war continues to range through themes that have been with us since 1950—from rumination on Soviet responsibility, to plots of military skirmishes along the thirty-eighth parallel, to analyses of decisions in high places, and finally to theories of conspiracy that, from opposite points of view, mimic each other.

This study proceeds from different premises. I maintain that the origins of the Korean War must be sought primarily in the events of the period 1945 to 1950 and secondarily in forces descending upon Korea in the period of colonial rule that left their peculiar stamp on the interwar years in Korea. This interlude—which began with liberation from Japanese rule, continued through the establishment of separate Korean states, and ended with the roar of artillery in 1950—constituted an historical unit with the prime distinguishing characteristic being revolution. In August 1945 all of Korea was thrown into an era characterized by widespread demands for thoroughgoing political, economic, and social change. Demands for political change expressed themselves in the creation of a host of new organizational forms: political parties, "people's committees," labor unions, and mass organizations of peasants, youths, and women. Demands for social and economic change accompanied this explosion of political participation, focusing on a land situation inherited from Japanese rule in which most peasants were enmeshed in a system of tenancy dominated by landlords. That is to say, when we study Korean politics in 1945, we deal, in a residual and fundamental sense, with the relationship of lord to peasant in a time of cataclysmic change. This was the essential characteristic of Korean society as it left the Japanese grip.

The basic issues over which the war in 1950 was fought were apparent immediately after liberation, within a three-month period, and led to open fighting that eventually claimed more than one hundred thousand lives in peasant rebellion, labor strife, guerrilla warfare, and open fighting along the thirty-eighth parallel—all this before the ostensible Korean War began. In other words, the conflict was civil and revolutionary in character, beginning just after 1945 and proceeding through a dialectic of revolution and reaction. The opening of conventional battles in June 1950 only continued this war by other means.

Although the conflict was primarily civil, Korea did not exist in a vacuum, but in a vortex of contending great powers and supranational forces. Neither north nor south Korea had emerged pristine at liberation; both had had a Japanese gestation, a colonial integument of long standing that burst asunder with stunning abruptness. Furthermore, as latent contradictions in Korean society became manifest in 1945, Koreans sought to solve them not alone, but in the presence of the two new great powers that were to dominate the postwar era— the Soviet Union and the United States—and in the presence of two ancient nations—China, involved in its own revolution, and Japan, watching as its empire crumbled to the ground. Thus Korea, which for four decades had been linked tightly to the fortunes of the Japanese empire, escaped that embrace only to be split in two in the immediate aftermath of the Pacific War. A striated and complex set of connections to Japan and to Manchuria was torn apart summarily, and the question that played upon the peninsula in the ensuing five-year period was which way new loyalties would run—to Moscow, to Washington, to Peking? Or would Koreans fulfill their ideal of an independent, unified, self-reliant nation that could choose its own relationship to the world? The war was also about these matters.

These domestic and international contingencies defined the agenda for liberated Korea and shaped the choices that Koreans made. These were the contingencies that remained unresolved in the period from 1945 to 1950 and gave the ostensible solutions forced upon Korea by the great powers (national division, alter regimes) a distinctly temporary quality in the minds of all Koreans.

This volume, the first of a planned two-volume study of the origins of the Korean War, deals primarily with the first year or so after liberation. The second will deal with the period from 1947 to 1950. The study is biased toward the first year of the interwar period because that was the year in which the basic structural framework for both the southern and northern Korean states was laid and the one in which the seeds of war were sown. This year, and in some cases even the entire period to 1948, has been largely ignored as analysts rush up to 1950 and to judgment on the nature of the war—as if not much of consequence had happened before 1948 or 1949, or as if the three-year period of American occupation in the south merited but brief mention. Yet the establishment of separate northern and southern regimes in 1948 was only the final expression of patterns forged in 1945 and 1946, and the Korean War was the denouement of struggles ensuing over the preceding five years. There is, in short, an unbroken chain of critical events linking August 1945 with June 1950.

The interlude from 1945 to 1950 had its own background as well—in a thirty-six-year colonial period that put an end to the old Korean order and in so many ways prepared and shaped the new one that appeared when Japan's empire collapsed. Japanese rule deeply affected the class structure of Korean society, by accelerating change here and retarding it there. It encouraged, for example, the emergence of a Korean working class and discouraged the development of entrepreneurial elements. As the Japanese modernized the peninsula in the interests of the metropole, and after 1931 as they sought to integrate Korea and Manchuria, they laid a structure of roads, railroads, ports, and communications facilities; in the northern part, they built major industrial installations. All of this gave Korea an overdeveloped quality; such modern facilities bore little correspondence to the actual strengths (or weaknesses) of the Korean social structure. Korean society resisted its transformation at Japanese hands, with peasants fighting back against tenancy arrangements, aristocrats withdrawing to patient educational efforts or private contemplation, and nationalist and communist guerrillas attacking the Japanese along the periphery or in the interstices of their empire. The imperial authorities responded by utilizing a highly articulated, penetrative state apparatus to develop the colony and to channel and control Korean resistance, thereby grossly distorting the traditional role of the state in Korea and leaving the postwar period with a ponderous, overgrown bureaucracy that greatly affected the course of politics in the interwar period.

Agrarian and industrial change left its mark most clearly on the Korean peasantry, the most numerous of the Korean classes and the class that gave the liberation period its dual characteristic of extensive participation and widespread resistance. Of particular importance in this regard was the extraordinary level of population mobility during the colonial years, caused by changes in land tenure, the rise of international marketing arrangements, widespread social mobilization, and the conscious, activist, direct mobilization of Koreans in service to the war effort that marked the last years before the Japanese demise. Thus masses of Korean peasants were uprooted and shipped abroad or into industry. Such events are most disruptive when they happen abruptly, extensively, and for the first time. In Korea, a sedentary population of long standing was shaken out of its old routine and then loosed upon society at the precise time that the colonial enterprise was coming to an end, so that the effect was much greater after the Japanese had retired to their islands. It was these peasants—or worker-peasants, soldier-peasants, and the like—who provided the raw force behind the extraordinary levels of popular participation in the liberation era.

The changes wrought by the colonial era were felt most acutely in the weeks just after liberation, when the Japanese were ineffective but before the Allied armies had established full occupation. This was thus a Korean period, and one of rapid flux; it was dominated by emergent, left-leaning political organizations such as the Committee for the Preparation of Korean Independence, the Korean People's Republic, and the people's committees, labor unions, youth groups, and peasant associations that were the provincial offshoots of the central organizations. During this period there emerged the idea of a "people's republic," a new thing to all Koreans, and the actuality of hundreds of self-governing organizations. This liberation regime and its fate then became the central, if sometimes unspoken, issue of Korean politics for the remaining years up to 1950. The conflicts of this period, when foreign power had yet to make itself fully felt, are crucial elements in the specifically *Korean* and civil genesis of later conflict. It was more the case that the Americans and the Soviets arrayed themselves around existing Korean cleavages, nourishing one at the expense of the other, than that Koreans chose sides in American-Soviet conflicts.

The circumstances in which the United States and the Soviet Union came to have the major responsibility for the fate of the Korean peninsula have never been clear, and for the Soviet side they must remain so. In the absence of necessary documentation, this volume can do little more than speculate on Soviet motives. The wealth of documentation released from the American side in recent years, however, now makes it possible to probe the earliest but least understood of America's postwar Asian entanglements. The reader should bear in mind this fact; for whatever else he may conclude about the Americans after digesting such documentation, he cannot gainsay the democratic spirit embodied in the retrospective opening of top secret documentation to any and all interested parties. Not only does it speak to the individual's right to know, but it suggests that people can learn from their past: both radical ideas in the world in which we live.

The documentation reveals that within two years after Pearl Harbor the United States had reversed its longstanding policy of noninvolvement in Korean affairs, had begun to define the peninsula as important to American security concerns, and had evolved a quintessential internationalist device to handle Korea's problems at war's end: a multilateral trusteeship, embracing the four great powers that the Americans thought would straddle the postwar world. The emphasis on involving many powers and accommodating diverse interests persisted as a current in United States policy toward Korea thereafter, eventually showing up in the United Nations Command by which American intervention in the Korean War was known. From the beginning, as at the end, this current also had an anticommunist impulse, one that sought not direct confrontation but a means to confine and contain the adversary in multiple, crisscrossing arrangements that would hamstring him and render his insurgent impulses manageable. The adversary, of course, was Stalin, and the policy took shrewd account of his desires for Russian great power status. But it did not take account of Korean revolutionary nationalism, and it is upon this that it foundered.

As American power confronted Korean rather than Soviet revolutionaries, the internationalists melted into the background and a different sort of American policy emerged, one that was nationalist in its own way and sought through unilateral actions to build a bulwark against communism in Korea. This current sought its national solution in a separated southern Korean state, behind which could be drawn lines of containment and confrontation and within which could be shaped a society whose main *raison d'être* would be anticommunism. This is, of course, nothing more than the story of the Cold War on a world scale. The interesting thing about Korea is that it all came so early—within three months of the Japanese defeat. From September through December 1945, the American Occupation made a series of critical decisions: it revived the Government-General bureaucracy and its Korean personnel; it revived the Japanese national police system and its Korean element; it inaugurated national defense forces for south Korea alone; and it moved toward a separate southern administration. These actions were unilateral, usually proceeding without knowledge of similar decisions in the north, and often proceeding in opposition to established American policy in Washington. It is only in this last point that occupation in Korea bore any resemblance to the one in Japan; otherwise, it was a complete contrast to the reformist and at times radical bent of American policy in Japan, at least until the "reverse course" in 1948. In Korea, the reverse course started immediately. The events of the first few months of occupation severely skewed and biased future possibilities, whether those advocated by policy makers in Washington or those agreed upon in negotiations with the Soviets, for resolution of the division of Korea. This was because doing differently, or doing better, would require undoing the work of the last three months of 1945. As it happened, the decisions were never undone, so this period becomes the crucible of American policy toward Korea, the time when most of the fundamental choices were made.

Such choices occurred in a cauldron where Korean desires were almost always at variance with what the Americans wanted, save those of a small Korean element that could not stand alone. For workers, peasants, students, and others returning to native places after Japanese mobilization, the liberation regime was one worth fighting for, and this they did in countless engagements that grew more extensive as time passed. The unrest proved to be greatest in the regions where the Japanese impact had been deepest, in provinces and counties where population change and agrarian disorder went hand in hand, where favorable geography provided time to organize and establish roots.

North Korea, by contrast, was an island of tranquility. Soviet policies had encouraged rapid mobilization of the Left[6] and, under Korean leadership, a thoroughgoing, but not terribly violent social revolution. After an initial period of undisciplined rampage, the Soviets retreated to the background and gave Koreans their head, an effective and low-cost policy that proved quite successful in the short run. In the long run, of course, the Soviets failed to create a docile satellite state, a complete contrast with the situation to this day in several Eastern European countries; this was because the Soviets sponsored a group of radical nationalists who had cut their teeth in anti-Japanese conflict and who chafed at Soviet controls. This story will be more the concern of the second volume of this study; newly available archival materials on the north are much better for the period between 1947 and 1950. The current volume benefits from the dominance of the south just after 1945, however, which contained the capital city, the major share of the Korean population, and occupation by the world's premier power. In the immediate aftermath of liberation, the south was more the locus of determining events. But the northern pattern of politics was widespread in the south as well in the first year, so in this sense, once we grasp the pattern of leftist politics in the south, we open a window on the north as well.

The second part of this study will examine the period from 1947 to 1950 during which the array of political and social forces in Korea underwent significant, if not fundamental, change. As the Cold War deepened, the United States attempted to escape the worst effects of previous actions by again seeking multilateral backing for its Korean policy, this time through the auspices of the United Nations. With the emergence of the Republic of Korea in 1948, the Americans also sought to distance themselves from the perceived volatility of this regime and its leader, Syngman Rhee. Troops were withdrawn and, at times, the regime was placed at arm's length; questions about the American commitment to South Korea were raised and used to discipline the regime. It will be argued, however, that the American commitment to defend the ROK was never cut, for the simple reason that this regime was so clearly the responsibility of the United States, a result of measures taken by Americans in the aftermath of liberation. It was more an American creation than any other postwar regime in Asia.

The relationship between the two Korean sides also changed during the later period, as a potent mass politics of the Right appeared in the south, fed by uprooted and aggrieved refugee families from the north. With the continuing strength of the Left in the north, the possibility of a peaceful unification of the peninsula evaporated. The resultant near extinction of the Left in south Korea, after an uproarious summer in 1947, led to a guerrilla movement that was mostly indigenous to the south and based in regions of earlier people's committee strength. Thus the civil conflict entered a phase of unconventional warfare, consuming the mountainous regions and the whole of Cheju Island. Southern counterinsurgent forces expanded their capabilities in response; upon his assumption of power, Syngman Rhee placed predominant influence within the army in the hands of officers of northern origin with experience in the Japanese military. At the same time, the north Korean military expanded in a Manchurian cocoon, as tens of thousands of Koreans did battle as part of the People's Liberation Army in the Chinese civil war.

The guerrilla struggle continued until the end of 1949, punctuated by engagements along the thirty-eighth parallel. This phase ended, however, with the virtual defeat of the southern partisans, an outcome, it will be argued, that then skewed the north-south conflict toward a conventional military solution. With the efficient virtues of large-scale conventional warfare shown decisively in the final reckoning of China in 1949, the Korean struggle moved into this phase as well. A period of waiting and testing ensued in early 1950, however, as both sides sought backing from their respective guarantors for a conventional assault. This story must await a second volume; the events of 1950 may still hold surprises for us.

Another concern of the present volume will be the considerable evidence in the Korean case that bears on the origins of the Cold War. A quintessential Cold War relationship marked Soviet-American interactions from day one in Korea, the only country in Asia where the United States confronted Soviet power directly after the end of the world war. A policy of containment was pursued from the beginning, even if it had not yet won sanction in Washington; and at several critical junctures in the first year after liberation, containment thinkers on the scene in Seoul won the endorsement of such figures as John J. McCloy, Averell Harriman, and George Kennan. Korea was a minor backwater to Americans in 1945, yet it showed the way to a future that other countries and regions would later traverse. Adventuresome and preemptory policies in Seoul would, after vacillation and recrimination in Washington, eventually find favor and support. It was as if Seoul rather than Washington were in the lead. Another way of making the point is to say that what seemed wrong from Washington's standpoint in 1945 or 1946 simply seemed early and prescient by 1947 or 1948. In 1950, of course, Korea moved front and center, its refractory effect definitive as Washington's policy shifted on a global scale in response to perceived Soviet aggression in Korea. But the leverage to force events and decisions seemed to have been present from the beginning.

There is also the matter of Asian revolution, in which Korea is again a neglected case. The Korean peninsula was ripe for revolution in 1945. Even if the Soviets and the Americans had not entered Korea, revolution would have overtaken the country in a matter of months. Korea had Asia's oldest communist movement, with a plethora of experienced leaders. And land conditions and relationships, especially in the south, augured revolution. Yet Korea did not develop on the Vietnam pattern of communism in the north and a rooted insurgency in the south. Why this was so will be another major concern of this study.

The hallmarks of politics in postwar Korea express themselves in nouns of conflict: violence, cleavage, disorder, change. In this small peninsula, the grand conflict of our epoch—that between two world views and two great powers—was played out with peculiar intensity. In such a politics of crisis, no one can remain neutral; no pure objectivity is possible. Anyone who immerses himself in historical materials knows that daily choices must be made; no fact is free from preconceptions, assumptions, and considerations of context and relevance. In politics it is worse. Overnight an event is woven into a tapestry of special pleading, lies, and mystification. Power disrespects truth, and therefore the scholar's only concern must be for truth, regardless of the consequences. This study will not please the guardians of orthodoxy in North or South Korea, but that is as it should be. While I can never fully appreciate the Korean experience, my perspective as an outsider and the freer atmosphere in which I work may have some compensation. The terrible conflicts of the Koreans repeat themselves in the literature time and again, as both Koreas erase history and subject the opposing sides to relentless calumny. Reading the literature, one comes to respect even more those Koreans who have had the courage and insight to reject orthodoxy and seek truth.

This study was also conceived during a time of turmoil in the United States, which extended to the disciplines of Asian studies and political science. As a member of the Committee of Concerned Asian Scholars, and later as an editor of the *Bulletin of Concerned Asian Scholars,* I played a minor role in these controversies. In retrospect, I realize that I could not have had a better education in politics: living in interesting times, having the freedom to pursue disciplined inquiry, and participating in political events and in discussions with people who shared both a warm regard for each other and a rare willingness to engage in withering debate and criticism. Such experiences lead to a recognition, often melancholy but also exhilarating, of the consequent nature of politics: politics is choice and inescapable responsibility for choice.

The course of this study has led me to an absolute fascination with the Korean experience in this century and with the Korean-American relationship since 1945. In the United States, in spite of three decades of intense involvement with Korean affairs, the country remains for the most part an unknown nation; even for the makers of American foreign policy, it is an afterthought, important mostly for its relation to something else. Most Americans associate Korea only with a nasty war that happened sometime in the misty past. When my wife and I were bound for Korea in 1967, people in the university town in southern Illinois where she grew up seemed to call up but one common observation, a remark by a Korean War veteran that Korea "was nine hundred years behind us." This same region produced the commander of the American Occupation, John R. Hodge. No one to whom I talked remembered that Hodge had ruled fifteen million Koreans for three critical years. Today in the United States the number of Americans who profess any expertise on Korea is exceedingly small, and ludicrously so when compared with the millions of Americans who have been active in Korea in the past decades. Korea is just not a place that Americans think about very often. The United States means something quite different to Koreans, however. It is the country that has defined South Korea's existence since 1945. And in North Korea, it remains a daily concern, thirty years after the war, with much of the society structured by reference to a constant threat from American imperialism.

The immense gap between American and Korean perceptions of their relationship has carried over into studies of the Korean War. For most Americans, scholars included, the war remains a thunderclap that burst in the summer of 1950, a sudden hot war in a distant and unexpected place amid a Cold War focused in Europe. The idea that this war had origins long before 1950, or that this same Cold War had been fought in Korea since 1945, or that the United States was entirely responsible for the existing brand of southern politics, rarely if ever penetrated comment on the war; and it still seems difficult to grasp. In Korean histories of the war, however, the beginning year is usually 1945. Those who live with a particular history have a finer sense of its dimensions. As I have pursued this inquiry, I have become aware of the debt that I owe the Korean people, who have taught me much.

This study has had additional benefactors, however, and it is a pleasure to acknowledge their support. James Palais is one of those treasured friends and colleagues who always has time to discuss important questions and comment on work in progress. This study has benefited both from his detailed commentary at every stage and from countless conversations and debates over lunch. James Kurth is a friend who has taught me more about politics than any teacher ever did in a classroom, showing that intense and serious discussion is the preferred pedagogy. Frank Baldwin and Michel Oksenberg supported from the beginning the part of this study that developed as a dissertation at Columbia University, providing critical and insightful commentary as it progressed. Gari Ledyard has been a constant source of warm encouragement and, like Oksenberg, has provided detailed written commentary on the entire dissertation. Steven Levine likewise has commented helpfully on the dissertation and gave particular aid in structuring chapters. Dorothy Borg was always ready for a spirited discussion, seeking (but often failing) to get me to pin my speculations down in the realm of hard fact. I learned more than she can guess from those encounters. Gregory Henderson has been encouraging and helpful all along, pointing me toward useful sources, drawing enthusiastically on his own extensive knowledge of the period and people under consideration, and treating with aplomb and toleration my occasional barbs directed at his own work. Others who helped to guide my thinking and writing at the dissertation stage include Herb Bix, Donald Hellmann, John Kotch, Donald MacDonald, James Morley, Jim Peck, Han T'ae-su, James Townsend, Donald Treadgold, and Edwin Winkler.

I would like to express special appreciation of two individuals who have done so much to build the field of twentieth-century Korean studies, Chong-sik Lee and Dae-sook Suh. Their books are treasure troves of information and argument; and both men have been generous with their time and expertise, even when they disagreed with the substance of my work. Professor Lee, in particular, has provided me with rare newspapers and other research materials, and I am most grateful. Ilpyong Kim also deserves thanks for his warm encouragement of my interest in Korea.

Jon Halliday has also been a continual source of inspiration and warm support. Among others who have commented upon or discussed with me various aspects of this manuscript I wish to thank in particular Perry Anderson, Edward Baker, Barton Bernstein, Daniel Chirot, Thomas Ferguson, Edward Friedman, Charles Goldberg, Peter Gourevitch, Edwin Gragert, Robert Kaufman, Theodore Kloth, John Merrill, Mark Paul, Elizabeth Perry, Samuel Popkin, Michael Robinson, Kenneth Sharpe, Martin Sherwin, Rinn-sup Shinn, and William Stueck. Two anonymous readers for Princeton University Press also deserve thanks for their extensive comments.

During my stay in the Republic of Korea, numerous individuals shared their experiences with me, pointed me toward research materials, and encouraged my work. I remember especially the many booksellers throughout the country who, when learning of my interests, would often disappear into a back room and return with a dusty but valuable old volume. Many librarians aided my studies, especially those at the Korean Research Center, the Asiatic Research Center, and the Central National Library. For reasons that will be understandable to some readers, I choose not to thank them by name. I would also like to thank Eugene Chai of the East Asian Library of Columbia University and K. P. Yang of the Library of Congress for their kind and continuous help.

Among the many archivists who gave of their time and expertise, John Saunders of the National Records Center and John Taylor of the Modern Military History Division of the National Archives deserve special thanks. I also wish to thank William Lewis and James Miller of the National Records Center, Hannah M. Zeidlik of the Office of the Chief of Military History, Kathie Nicastro of the Modern

Diplomatic History Division of the National Archives, the friendly and helpful staff in the National Archives reading room, and archivists at the MacArthur Memorial in Norfolk and the Hoover Institution in Stanford.

From my colleagues in Korean studies I ask indulgence. Only those who have sought to order and interpret Korea's colonial experience, or the liberation period, or the Korean War, can appreciate how much remains to be done. If questions and challenges have been raised that spur the curiosity of others, enough will have been done for now. My method in this volume also required an integration of various disciplines, and I hope that in so doing I have not completely violated the canons of any particular field of inquiry.

A Columbia University Traveling Fellowship aided my preliminary research in Washington, D.C. in 1971. A Foreign Area Fellowship granted by the Social Science Research Council allowed a year's stay in Seoul and subsequent research and writing in the U.S. The East Asian Institute of Columbia University provided travel funds to visit archival holdings, enabled me to spend a pleasant year in residence as a research associate in 1974-1975, and subsequently saw fit to include this book in their list of sponsored research, for which I am most grateful. A grant from the Joint Committee on Korean Studies of the Social Science Research Council, and from the Swarthmore College Summer Research Fund, supported my summer studies in 1975 and 1976. The Henry M. Luce Foundation has provided support for research and writing in the period 1977-1980, through a grant for the study of Korean-American relations. In an issue of concern to me if not to the reader, I wish to state that no money from official or unofficial sources in South or North Korea has supported this study. David Satterwhite and Michael Robinson deserve thanks for their research assistance. The final manuscript was typed with impeccable professionalism by Karen Hannan, while Leila Charbonneau made the maps and Tammy An helped with the index. I thank Dr. Kenneth Pyle, Director of the School of International Studies of the University of Washington, for providing their services.

I also wish to thank Sandy Thatcher and especially Tam Curry of Princeton University Press for tireless, painstaking, intelligent, and above all pleasant help with editing. Finally, full responsibility for errors and interpretations is, of course, mine.

All Korean names are given according to the McCune-Reischauer system of transliteration except for Syngman Rhee's and Kim Il Sung's, which are given in their own idiosyncratic renderings.

Part I

SETTING

Chapter One

CLASS AND STATE IN
COLONIAL KOREA

IMAGINE a Korean from, let us say, the fifteenth century, strolling the streets of Seoul in 1875. He would notice the greater population, the relative variety of goods for sale, perhaps an increase in the number of officials. But little or nothing would startle him. He would be, for the most part, at home with the clothing people wore, with the configuration of the houses, with the classes of people he would meet. It is only in 1945 that he would give a start at the physical aspect of Seoul, with its colonial architecture, bustling trolley cars, modern factories, and widened streets. And it is only in about 1965 that he would be taken aback at the social aspect of Seoul, with its uproarious commerce, its hurrying bureaucrats, its massed laborers, and its shack-lined hillsides.

Now if we imagine an American strolling these same streets in 1875, we can begin to trace the vast gulf separating the two peoples. To such an American, Korea would lack most of the presumed requisites of nineteenth-century society.[1] Its cities, such as they were, betrayed few hints of commerce, no evidence of a commercial class, and everywhere hindrances to such pursuits: narrow alleys and walls that inhibited association, rudimentary transportation facilities, masses of people seemingly idling away their time, and a government whose first inclination was to inhibit business intercourse, at home and abroad. This bucolic backwater would be utterly alien to an American. It is only in around 1970 that our American would begin to feel at home, or at least recognize features common to his own society.

In these conjurings we begin to apprehend the contours of the Korean-American interaction. The one was an agrarian bureaucratic kingdom of a half-millennium's duration in its Yi dynastic incarnation, whose people thought in terms of class and state, lord and peasant, land and its product, cultured excellence and barbarian ignorance. The other was a capitalist democracy of a century's duration, whose people thought in terms of individuals and representatives, freeholders and farmers, commerce and industry, dynamic growth and stagnant indolence. This yawning chasm in social forms was the result of centuries of continuity in the one and change in the other; and it had not significantly narrowed in 1945 when Americans arrived to oc-

3

cupy Korea, or in 1950 when they arrived to make war. But the gap had begun to narrow, and as it did so, it set off millennial changes in Korean society—changes with which we must begin if we hope to understand the origins of the Korean War.

The first agency of change was Japan, so it is appropriate to begin there. Japan in the mid-nineteenth century resembled Korea in its isolation from the Eurocentric world system, its sense of closeness to Chinese civilization, and its concern for land and its products. It was also similar in that the vast change it was about to experience was to be set off by external forces—that is, contact with the West. The difference was that Japan had a feudal structure—in a strict sense, the only pure and indigenous feudalism outside the European (or Carolingian) heartland.[2] Although lively debate continues regarding feudalism's contribution to subsequent Japanese development, there seems little doubt that the feudal mode bequeathed to Japan a productive agricultural system, extensive commercialization, a useful martial spirit, and a literate, educated population, before it was swept away in the wake of the Meiji Restoration.[3]

In chronological time Japan's evolution may have been quick, but in world time it was late. Japan developed, in both a real and a symbolic sense, within one of the few remaining interstices of the nineteenth-century world system, with newly risen industrial powers knocking at its door. For a time these powers cast long glances at Japan but rested their eyes mostly on China—thereby providing a "breathing space" within which Japan could mobilize its resources. Imperialist inattention provided both the opportunity and the rationale for quickened Japanese development.[4] To compete, Japan husbanded and nurtured its resources at home and began to search for a hinterland, a periphery, a region with raw materials and labor such as those the industrial powers possessed.[5] Thus competition with the West dictated immediate restructuring at home and suggested eventual restructuring abroad.[6]

One result of this restructuring was the creation of a strong state as the essential ally of industrialization. Although there is currently some debate on the role of the Meiji state,[7] it seems irrefutable that Japan provided a classic example of Alexander Gerschenkron's argument regarding the advantages of "backwardness" in countries undergoing "defensive" modernization. The persistence of feudalism into the nineteenth century, he argues, prevented these countries from industrializing on the English pattern, a slow process that was accompanied by liberal political correlates such as the extension of the franchise and the rise of parliamentarianism. Other countries, which began industrialization later, had scarce and diffuse private capital, a lack of entrepreneurial elements, distrust of commercial or industrial activities, and the threat implied by the existence of earlier industrializers.[8] But feudal disabilities become advantages when a country begins to develop industries such as iron, steel, and railways, with greatly enhanced capital and organizational requirements. In this phase, power is cast upward; in countries like Germany and Japan, a strong state emerges as the great ally, stimulator, and organizer of industrialization. The state, in other words, substituted itself in the "classic," entrepreneurial role ordinarily assumed by a rising bourgeoisie; but the substitution was not without costs. David Landes writes of Japan:

> It was the State that conceived modernization as a goal and industrialization as a means, that gave birth to the new economy in haste and pushed it unrelentingly as an ambitious mother her child prodigy. And though the child grew and developed its own resources, it never overcame the deformity imposed by this forced nurture.[9]

Recognizing these birthmarks and deformations is essential to understanding the role of the Japanese state, within and without Japan. At home, the state bureaucracy spawned by Meiji developed interests of its own, as is usually the case, and became, in E. H. Norman's words, "the dominant instrument in Japanese political life" after 1885. The Home Ministry and the police constituted the bureaucracy's "general headquarters," with the Home Minister being "almost invariably a man of the darkest reaction and autocratic temper."[10] The bureaucracy provided an effective means, also, for extracting surpluses from the peasantry, a policy that caused a general decline in the number of small and middle peasant proprietors in the 1880s and 1890s, with an accompanying concentration of land in landlord hands. Norman likened the process to the English enclosures of the sixteenth and eighteenth centuries.[11] Such interpretations are questioned in some Japanese and American scholarship, as might be expected; but it is difficult to argue over the intended function of the Meiji state when it was projected onto Korea in the form of a colonial apparatus with enormous strength, autonomy, and resulting extractive and manipulative powers. Were we to suggest that the Japanese people paid bearable, even acceptable, costs exacted from them by the Meiji state in the interests of rapid industrialization and competition with the West, we could not say the same of the Koreans. The costs rankled in Korea —and subsequently in Manchuria and China proper.

Korea was annexed and made Japan's colony in 1910, but the critical year was 1905, when Japan subdued Russia to climax three decades of imperialist conflict over the disposition of the Korean peninsula. The actual colonization of Korea seems a wearisomely familiar, even repetitious exercise to anyone cognizant of European colonial practice. It was far from the *sui generis* phenomenon depicted in so much Korean historiography. But certain aspects of Japanese colonization were indeed unique.

If it is proper to speak of a defensive Japanese industrialization, we may also speak of its defensive colonialism. In its colonial experience, too, timing and context were important. Just as the onset of Japan's development was late in comparison with the great world powers, so was its colonization of Taiwan and Korea. Japan hardly acted differently than the European powers in turn-of-the-century Asia in seeking to carve out a Japanese sphere in the East Asian hinterland; but it entered a modern world that had had hundreds of years of colonial experience and that, in the most advanced countries such as England and the United States, was beginning to feel the pressures of anti-imperialist dissent at home and incipient nationalism abroad. From the beginning, Japan had to suffer the condemnation of British socialists and American liberals; within a few years of its annexation of Korea, it faced both Wilsonian idealist pressures for self-determination in the colonies and the more formidable Leninist analysis of imperialism and Bolshevik support for colonized peoples. Japan's colonial enterprise became, rather quickly, anachronistic in the eyes of many (not the least being socialists and liberals within Japan). Yet the anachronism of Japanese colonialism is inexplicable apart from the anachronism of its introduction into the modern world. Japan sought territorial acquisition both because it was resource poor at home and because such activity was thought to be an essential accoutrement for competition with the advanced industrial nations of the West.

We can understand Japan's position in another way if we conceive of the world in the late nineteenth century as being structured by a Euro-American core of advanced industrial societies, with the rest of the world constituting a periphery or semi-periphery.[12] This structure was founded in unevenly distributed development, such that a division of labor on a world scale obtained and the condition of advantage in the core meant disadvantage in the periphery. The system worked in such a way that a slight edge in one period translated into a gross disparity in a subsequent period, as surpluses extracted from the periphery by the core enabled the flourishing of towns and cities, functional specialization and differentiation, and the liberation of commercial and laboring classes. The core-periphery structure was transnational in its essence; national boundaries counted much less than economic intercourse regulated by bureaucratic state systems.[13]

Japan was "semi-peripheral" in the late nineteenth century; it was in a state of contingency between the promise of core status and the threat of peripheral status.[14] And if the examples of China and Southeast Asia were any guide to Japan's predicament, a future beckoned of dependency on the core if not outright colonization. The successes of Meiji enabled Japan to forestall dependency and to entertain the notion of being a junior partner in the core societies. But if it could widen its own sphere in Northeast Asia, it could perhaps create an alternative core-periphery structure of its own.

This did not happen, but we can say so only in the light of Japan's defeat in 1945. Until that time, the possibility was alive that Japan would succeed in establishing a new core-periphery structure including much of Asia. Korea was the best integrated area within this transnational system and came to have most of those characteristics that are associated with the underdevelopment of the periphery. Capitalism, as it develops, abhors national boundaries. And the development of Japanese capitalism shows successive moves outward, as if in concentric circles, first encompassing its "internal colony," meaning primarily the Japanese peasantry;[15] then substituting Korea for this internal colony as the former's potential was exhausted (or as the Japanese peasantry differentiated); then enrolling Manchuria in the 1930s to assume Korea's place, thus establishing a new periphery and giving certain semi-peripheral qualities to Korea. The apparatus of the state, essential to development at home, was transplanted to Korea in the colonial form, and thence to Manchuria. In each case, the state mobilized resources to serve the interests of the core and provided the conditions and supports necessary for the development of modern market relations. The uniqueness rests not in the enterprise itself, which was modeled on European practice and is closely comparable to it, but in the timing and the context. Japan got off the mark late, in the context of existing core-periphery relations on a world scale; both circumstances frustrated and eventually defeated Japan's attempt to constitute itself as an alternative core to the Euro-American heartland.

A second unique, related, and perhaps more remarkable characteristic of Japanese imperialism was the contiguity of the colonial territories to Japan itself. Japan's lateral expansion, or "development in width,"[16] occurred because most of the other appropriate regions (China proper and Southeast Asia) were taken or untakeable and because a weak and wobbling Russia was no match for Japan. Thus Japan became the only world power to colonize its contiguous neighbors. It could maximize its power close to home, providing a relative advantage over far-flung empires. It could carve out a geographic sphere, or unit, in a region where territorial boundaries were already well defined (unlike, say, Africa). Contiguity could also facilitate the settling of metropolitan citizens close to the mother country, especially important to an insular and homogeneous people like the Japanese. Above all, contiguity raised the possibility of an integral coordination and tying of the colonies to the metropole such that exchange time in market relations was extraordinarily rapid, with railroads rather than sea lanes as the prime medium.[17]

A third noteworthy characteristic, unique in degree if not in kind, was the highly conscious, planned, and anticipatory nature of the Japanese colonial enterprise. Although much of the planning was derivative of European colonial experience, Japan's posthaste coloni- zation imparted an architectonic, structured and structuring, quality to the enterprise. It seemed to proceed so much from the minds of its leadership that, in retrospect, Japanese policy statements about what they were doing in Korea and elsewhere seem worse (or, from an al- ternative viewpoint, more promising) than were the realized policies themselves. In other words, this was a Platonic colonialism. The West- ern threat and the pursuit of autonomy through expansion concen- trated the Japanese mind.

If Japan sought autonomy, Korea got dependency. The condition of Japan's relative success was Korea's loss of sovereignty and a general skewing of Korean development toward Japanese needs. To say this is to say nothing new, nor to differentiate Korea's colonial experience from others. What is unique and distinctive, however, is that Korea had existed for more than a millennium before 1910 as an independ- ent, self-governed nation. Unlike many other colonial experiences, the metropolitan power did not carve a new nation out of a welter of geographic units divided along ethnic, racial, religious, or tribal lines; it imposed its control upon an ancient political system with stable, well-established geographical boundaries and an astonishing homo- geneity in language, culture, and ethnicity. Such conditions had pro- vided Korea with most of the prerequisites of nationhood long before the peoples of Europe attained them. The Japanese, in colonizing Ko- rea, had to co-opt, pension off, or destroy the rulers of an agrarian bureaucratic dynasty that had administered Korea for five hundred years and that had long considered itself superior to Japan. Japanese aggression was not new to Koreans, either; for three centuries, Korean tots had heard tales of the invasions of 1592 and 1597 when an earlier world-revising Japanese leader, Hideyoshi Toyotomi, had sought and failed to subordinate Korea as a first step in the conquest of the Asian mainland. Thus Japanese colonial policies did not have the usual ef- fect of creating both a new nation and a new elite among the colonized that then became conscious of the potentialities of nationhood. A distinct sense of Koreanness, if not nationalism, had set Koreans apart from Japanese all along; and it stimulated the Korean resistance to Japanese colonialism at the time of the Annexation, in the 1919 independence movement, and in the tenancy disputes, worker and peasant unions, and exile movements of the 1920s and 1930s.

Throughout the colonial period, Koreans could and did maintain that their nation was not a gift created by the colonizer, but something that the Japanese, in league with traitorous Koreans, had snatched away. Japan and the feeble ancient regime could be blamed for the debacle of lost sovereignty, and continuing resistance at home and abroad could be the repository of hopes for recovery. In short, Koreans were less able than some other colonial peoples to grant the legitimacy of colonial rule. This did not mean that Koreans always and in all places resisted the Japanese—they did not—but it did mean that the Japanese had perhaps a more difficult time imposing and sustaining their rule in Korea than did European powers in their colonies.[18]

Instead of colonial creations in Korea, there were colonial substitutions: a colonial bureaucracy in place of the ancient regime, a Japanese elite for a Korean elite, the Japanese language in place of Korean (the latter reflecting a linguistic unity that had existed for centuries), Japanese landlords for Korean landlords. This business of substitution rather than creation made the ethnic cleavages that typically develop under colonial rule all the more intense. We must remember, however, that the substitutions occurred in an agrarian bureaucratic, rather than a feudal setting. This was a fundamental difference between Korea and Japan and goes a long way toward explaining Korea's failure to resist imperialist encroachment in the late nineteenth century.

The traditional Korean state was very nearly the opposite of the new Meiji state. The Yi state assumed responsibilities in the economy primarily to raise revenue, but always to levels of adequacy rather than surplus, and never with the intention of using surpluses for economic growth. The Yi was in this sense comparable to the traditional Chinese state, and to other bureaucratic regimes whose major task was short-run maintenance and adaptation.[19] The Yi system was adaptable, even supple, in the context of the marginal changes necessary to maintain an equilibrium of conflicting forces over time and the minor adjustments necessary to maintain a steady-state, autarkic economy.[20] Contrary to recent studies that depict the old Korean state as highly centralized and therefore very strong in relation to society,[21] James Palais has shown this state to have been weak, dominated by society in the manifestation of a landed aristocracy: "the ostensible centralized and autocratic structure was merely a facade that obscured the reality of aristocratic power."[22] The aristocracy used state power to preserve privilege; this occurred up to and including the years just prior to the Japanese annexation.[23]

Aristocracy and state in Korea competed for available surplus resources, with the latter often losing out. The bureaucratic structure was adapted to aristocratic needs and therefore lacked the autonomy and the extractive capacity usually associated with strong states. What traditional Korea had instead was strong class structure, a "fusion of aristocratic status with private landownership" that almost resembled "a bona fide feudal nobility" in its capacity to resist the encroachments of central government.[24] The Yi was inured to fighting losing battles with the aristocracy over a relatively static pool of wealth; how then could it conceive of the modern distinction between public and private realms or understand that the public realm might intervene to stimulate the accumulation of wealth in the interests of overall growth?[25] Instead there was a kind of political involution, analogous to agricultural involution,[26] whereby the state found new ways to get, or redoubled its efforts to get, more out of existing resources.

The Yi state was, then, superficially strong at the center, but with weak and tenuous links to the periphery. The landed class used the state to perpetuate itself and to dominate a peasant mass. But the domination was incomplete; the connections could be snapped, and therefore peasant rebellions were a recurrent phenomenon.[27] At the end of the nineteenth century, this state proved utterly incapable of responding to the encroachments of newly risen industrial powers, whether Japan or Western nations, a story too familiar to need repeating here. What might be emphasized instead is that the very success of the landed aristocracy in utilizing the state to perpetuate its dominance fatally weakened the Korean nation itself in its capacity to resist outside pressure.

THE COLONIAL STATE

The colonial state was a far cry from the decrepit Yi. It soon came to possess a comprehensive, autonomous, and penetrating quality that no previous Korean state could possibly have mustered. One scholar, indeed, has called it totalitarian.[28] The label is less interesting, however, than the function of this state, which was to organize, mobilize, and exploit Koreans in the interests of the metropole. One way Japan achieved this was by shrewdly manipulating tensions within the Korean upper class, finding important collaborators within the old bureaucracy and mobilizing others into pro-Japanese organizations such as the *Ilchin-hoe*. After Annexation some 84 aristocrats were pensioned off along with 3,645 bureaucrats, "selected with a detailed knowledge of the Korean upper class and its fractions."[29] In the early years of the colony, the state apparatus had a distinct military cast, its governor-general recommended by the Meiji *Genro* Yamagata Aritomo, who chose high-ranking military officers from his Choshu clique to rule Korea.[30] After the 1919 uprisings against colonial rule, it was possible for a civilian to be appointed governor-general, but none ever was.[31] From Tokyo's standpoint, the governor-general was largely free to administer Korea as he pleased, and indeed answered only to the emperor until 1919.

The role of the Meiji state in developing the Japanese core provided an obvious analogue in the colonial periphery. Thomas C. Smith has concluded, regarding the Meiji state, that "in developing modern industry the government had no choice but to act as entrepreneur, financier, and manager . . . private capital was too weak, too timid, and too inexperienced to undertake development."[32] The opinion of Tōgō Minoru, an important specialist on colonial agriculture, was almost identical: "He believed that [the state] . . . had to take an active part in the financing, management, and planning of the colonies because the investments could not be expected to make quick returns." The private sector, he thought, could not do it alone.[33] Such judgments were much more true of the Korean than the Japanese private sector, given the differences in class structure between the two countries. And whereas in Japan the state was at least endogenous, in Korea the state was exogenous, its source being the metropole. Therefore, the substitutions and distortions attendant to a strong role for the state in industrialization were all the more acute in the Korean specific.

The colonial state stood above Korean society, exercising authoritative and coercive control. It possessed connections to only the fringe Korean upper class and colonial parvenus—aristocrats, landlords, bureaucrats—and even those ties were tenuous at best, designed to co-opt and to thwart dissent, not to provide meaningful participation in the affairs of state. In general, the Japanese sought to strengthen central bureaucratic power in Korea, as a means of shifting the balance of forces and providing the wherewithal to mobilize and extract resources on an unprecedented scale. Instead of a weak bureaucracy with brittle links at the periphery, there evolved imperative coordination penetrating from top to bottom.

If we compare the Korean situation with that of colonial Vietnam, we find that while in 1937 the French ruled a population of 17 million

Vietnamese with 2,920 administrative personnel, supplemented by 10,776 regular French troops and about 38,000 indigenous personnel in the administration and in militia organizations, the Japanese ruled about 21 million Koreans in the same year with some 246,000 Japanese in public and professional positions that Andrew Grajdanzev classifies as part of the colonial apparatus and some 63,000 Koreans in like but subordinate positions. Upwards of 42 percent of the Japanese population in Korea in 1937 were in government service. By comparison, the French in Vietnam occupied a thin stratum indeed. And yet resistance leaders like Ho Chi Minh often noted the large French presence in Vietnam, in contrast to British rule in India.[34] Japan was responsible for an extreme skewing of Korean bureaucratic power in the direction of ponderous, overgrown centralization; it bequeathed to postwar Korea a formidable bureaucratic weapon that could rapidly accelerate or severely retard new forms of political participation.[35]

Rails Lead the Way

Heinrich Heine, in 1843, registered the effect of railway systems on every day life in the following manner:

> What changes must now occur, in our way of looking at things, in our notions! Even the elementary concepts of time and space have begun to vacillate. Space is killed by the railways, and we are left with time alone. . . . Now you can travel to Orleans in four and a half hours, and it takes no longer to get to Rouen. Just imagine what will happen when the lines to Belgium and Germany are completed and connected up with their railways! I feel as if the mountains and forests of all countries were advancing on Paris. Even now, I can smell the German linden trees; the North Sea's breakers are rolling against my door.[36]

Among all the advanced industrial powers in the late twentieth century, Japan remains the one with the most rapid, efficient, and comfortable railway transportation: we might be tempted to call it the preeminent nation of the rails. The extension of the rails into Korea and Manchuria facilitated Japanese development of these colonies, a circumstance unique in colonial relationships and made possible because Japan colonized its next-door neighbors rather than faraway lands. The rails served to link core and periphery; to ease the extension of marketing relations; to cut the time involved in production, transaction, and consumption of goods; and to make possible the rapid movement of troops. The colonial railways also enhanced Japan's self-image as a progressive modernizer and provided the people of Korea and Manchuria with a harbinger of unprecedented change and a symbol of Japanese power. This was nowhere more evident than in a ubiquitous poster of the 1930s by which the South Manchuria Railway Company advertised itself. It portrayed a powerful, jet-black locomotive, "the Asia Express," trailing wisps of smoke, with a map of Japan's Manchurian railway network superimposed on it. The pattern of this rail network (see figure 1) offers its own testimony of the degree to which Japan succeeded, for a time, in carving out its own transnational unit in East Asia.

Eric J. Hobsbawm writes the following about the development of railways in England between 1830 and 1850:

> In every respect this was a revolutionary transformation. . . . It reached into some of the remotest areas of the countryside and the centers of the greatest cities. It transformed the speed of movement —indeed of human life . . . and introduced the notion of a gigantic, nation-wide complex and exact interlocking routine symbolized by the railway time-table (from which all subsequent 'time-tables' take their name and inspiration). It revealed the possibilities of technical progress as nothing else had done.[37]

In France, too:

> The penetration of many parts of the countryside by the new railway network was foreshadowing a real social revolution. . . . With their completion the isolation of the rural village became a thing of the past. Men, ideas, products, could at last flow into and out of the villages.[38]

Railways in Korea and Manchuria had this same penetrative and integrative effect, replacing the A-frame carrier, oxcart, and meandering path with the most up-to-date and rapid means of conveyance. With a concomitant laying of roads and highways and opening of ports, Japan came to have a "mighty trio" of railway, highway, and sea transportation linking the three regions together, bringing them closer.[39] Before the division of Korea in 1945, it was possible to embark from Pusan and travel all the way to Paris on a modern coach. The rails symbolized permanence and integrity—the permanence of industry (if not of Japan), and the integrity of the Japanese empire, within which national boundaries were increasingly less relevant. But above all, railway development in Korea and Manchuria advanced the commercialization of agriculture and drew the two regions not just into market relations with the Japanese metropole but into the world market system.[40] Japan used the rails to break the traditional isolation of Korea and integrate it with the world economy. The rails became the entrails and sinews of this small nation, connecting it first to To-kyo and then to the rest of the advanced world; in so doing, the rail traffic took villages like Taejŏn and transformed them into cities.

In any process of industrialization, railroad development requires tremendous outlays of capital, which implies a strong role for the state, even if only to exercise rights of eminent domain to obtain the necessary land. In Japan the state played a large part in railway construction, as we would expect; but in the Asian hinterland, state railways were the spearhead of colonial policies and, in the 1930s, were the leading sector of colonial industrialization.[41] In 1906 the Japanese had set up the South Manchuria Railway Company (SMRC), "the first of the great semi-official companies organized to promote Japanese economic and political interests on the Asiatic continent."[42] The SMRC was in effect an organ of state, its capital subscribed by the great Japanese banks and industrial and commercial houses. After Japan achieved control of Manchuria in 1931, it took over existing lines built by Russians, Chinese, and Japanese (a total of about 5,800 kilometers of lines), and within a decade, it had nearly doubled the total length through new construction. In 1933 the Korean network was given over to the SMRC. The SMRC also had charge of harbor and road construction, which meant that it possessed coordinated control of "all the modern means of transportation by land and water."[43] An early report, written when the SMRC was still confined to the Kwantung leased area, said the following:

> This great company is in fact playing the part of both master and servant in Manchuria. . . . The traveler journeys in the company's cars and stops at the company's hotels, which are heated by coal from the company's own electric works. . . . If unfortunate enough to fall sick on the way, [the traveler] is certain to be taken to one of the company's hospitals.[44]

The rails linked the Manchurian expanse with ports in northern Korea like Najin (Rashin), which grew from "a mere village of 500 people in 1927 to a bustling port of 26,000 inhabitants a decade later."[45] By the 1940s Manchuria was integrated with industry in Japan and northern Korea. The SMRC also served as a means of moving Koreans into Manchuria; it set up Korean village settlements, protected by its own railway police. Thus the rails were the means, and Koreans the movable human capital, for the penetration of Manchuria.

This "New Deal"[46] in transport facilities in Manchuria and Korea was of importance not simply for its transformation of communications but also because the period of the transformation was com-

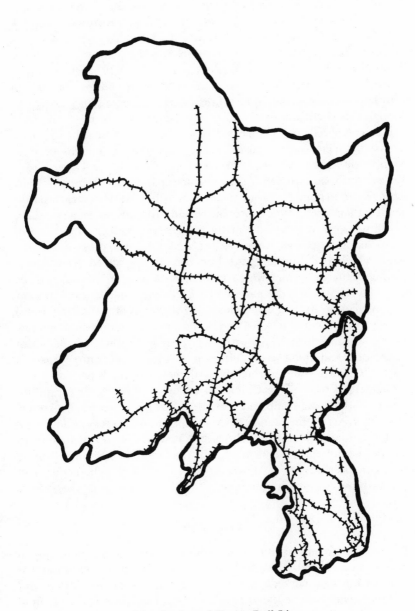

1. Manchuria and Korea, Rail Lines

pressed such that development proceeded, not in phases one following on another (as in England, for example), but in union with vast change throughout the society. Until this century, Korea was "one of the most roadless countries in the world."[47] But by 1945 there were extensive bus and truck routes crisscrossing the peninsula and some 6,200 kilometers of railroad (slightly more than half of which was in south Korea). There were 24 kilometers of roads and 3 kilometers of railroads for every 100 square kilometers of Korea's territory.[48] Although this is not impressive in comparison with advanced countries, it is so compared with China or Vietnam in 1945. China had perhaps 21,700 kilometers of railroad in 1945, about three-fourths of it in Manchuria and much of it in disrepair. In their peak year, 1943, Korea's railroads carried 128.47 million passengers, compared with China's pre-1949 peak year of 265.01.[49] In other words, Korea, a nation smaller than some Chinese provinces, had railroads 30 percent as long as China's, carrying half as many passengers. Furthermore, the railroads in China proper were concentrated along the coast, as in Vietnam, which had but one rail line meandering down from Hanoi through Hue to Saigon. Korea had lines running to all major cities; only the isolated middle part of the East coast and the mountainous regions had no lines at all. Road network followed a similar pattern. China was estimated to have had about 100,000 "serviceable" kilometers of roads in 1950, again with most of them in the east and northeast. Korea had about 53,000 kilometers of auto and country roads in 1945.[50] This works out to roughly 2 kilometers of roads per 100 square kilometers of territory in China (based on a total area of 5.9 million square kilometers), compared with Korea's 24 per 100 square kilometers. This exercise in comparative transportation ecology should serve to differentiate Korea from China and Vietnam in infrastructural capacity; the difference helps to explain the fate of rural political movements in postwar Korea, especially southern Korea where the roads and railways were most extensive.

COMMERCE

It was Korea's misfortune to be colonized by a power like Japan, flushed with the recent success of its modernization program, and to have within it a markedly weaker entrepreneurial impulse than that in Japan, which made the virtues of state initiative seem all the more appropriate to the colonial power. Thus existing weaknesses in the Korean class structure were perpetuated well into the twentieth century. And perhaps as important, when bourgeois elements did appear, they did so at the sufferance of, or with the aid of, the colonial regime, and thus were tainted in the eyes of a people that, after all, had never had much use for commerce to begin with.

The class structure of early twentieth-century Korea followed reasonably closely Barrington Moore's portrayal of the agrarian-bureaucratic route to modernity. Instead of a landed aristocracy that turned to commercialized agriculture, a leisured class relied on a central bureaucratic apparatus to sap agricultural surpluses. Instead of independent yeoman-farmers, there were, for the most part, peasant-tenants. Instead of a burgeoning commercial class, insistent on its rights and possessing its own ideology, there were itinerant peddlers, small shopkeepers, and errant aristocrats who had begun to invest in things like small banks.[51] In no sense was this a commercial class strong enough to make an alliance with the landed class ("exchanging the right to rule for the right to make money"), as in Japan and Germany.[52] Korea more closely resembled China. In fact, it may even accord with Moore's model better than China, because the landed class was, if anything, more entrenched in Korea than in China and because the commercial impulse was weaker. The result, had indigenous development run its course, should have been a peasant revolution. But Japan's intrusion rendered Korean development discontinuous, and much more so in 1945 when it ended than in 1910 when it began.

Commerce within Korea was growing in the eighteenth century, especially in Kaesŏng and Suwŏn; and some recent Korean historiography has made much of this and other developments as indicative of the first spontaneous stirrings of capitalism.[53] But this prelude, however interesting, had no sequel and no sustenance. After Korea was opened in 1876, the Kaesŏng and Suwŏn merchants were nowhere in evidence;[54] they thus become interesting primarily as exceptions that prove the rule. The Yi did not view commerce as a source of government revenue, or even as an essential activity. In the face of economic debility, the first recourse was to frugality, not expansion. Korea in the second half of the nineteenth century had neither a market nor a money economy; its limited domestic trade was conducted under state supervision. The center of its external economic intercourse was Japan House in Ch'oryang, first established in 1408 and the sole point of contact with Japan since 1609. Six military checkpoints controlled access to the tall stone walls that surrounded it; and to get through the gates, one had to submit to a thorough search.[55] Nothing could better symbolize the encapsulated commerce of nineteenth-century Korea.

Even after the opening of ports to Japan and the West, Korean traders in the 1880s and 1890s remained small, weak, unsupported, and generally, unwealthy. Foreign competition did many of them in. These were not the people, let alone the class, to provide the yeast to transform old Korea. The general observation was that these merchants "were an undistinguished lot, despised socially by the upper classes, perennially worrying about the preservation of their monopoly rights, and mistrusted by the general populace."[56]

In the late 1800s there were a few Koreans who might be called entrepreneurs. Generally speaking, they were aristocrats who translated landed wealth into commercial property or errant types who rose to economic prosperity through foreign connections. An example of the former would be Kim Chong-han. Born into an aristocratic family in 1844 and classically educated, he passed the prestigious *munkwa* examination in 1877, whereupon he entered the state bureaucracy; in the 1890s he established one of the first indigenous Korean banks. An example of the latter would be Pak Ki-jŏng. Born into a poor family in Pusan in 1839 and lacking in formal education, he learned Japanese, became an interpreter for Japanese traders, and eventually helped open Korea's first indigenous railway company.[57] Even such relatively successful entrepreneurs, however, received little or no support from the Yi state; they had to rely either on their own capital, which was weak, or on foreign capital. Thus most of the entrepreneurial talent came from outside the country before the Annexation; and in 1910 the Japanese passed laws inhibiting the formation of indigenous Korean firms. Even at that time, foreign predominance in established firms was pronounced: Japanese-owned firms constituted 70.1 percent of the total; joint Japanese-Korean firms, 10.5 percent; and wholly Korean-owned firms, only 17.8 percent.[58]

The situation changed somewhat after 1920 when Japan inaugurated its "cultural policy" in the wake of the 1919 uprisings, loosening restrictions on Korean commercial activity. Certain individual entrepreneurs emerged who subsequently played important roles in liberated Korea, and considerable capital found its way to Korean hands. Whether such people grew wealthy independently or through Japanese midwifery is another matter—as is the question of whether anything like a bourgeoisie, conscious of itself and its prerogatives, emerged at all.

Until recently, Koreans tended to argue that they were systematically excluded from commercial roles during the entire colonial period. A careful Korean observer in the 1930s, Hoon K. Lee, argued:

> The Koreans are poor merchants. Their historical development shows this plainly. At the present time a relatively small number of Korean business men carry on enterprises which are efficient enough to vie with those of Japanese and Chinese competitors. There are wholesalers, retailers, brokers, inspectors, commission merchants,

shippers, etc.; but in the rural sections the retailers are mostly ped-
dlars who move from one market place to another, without shops.
Their capital and business turnover are small.[59]

Commerce, he thought, was "almost monopolized by Japanese merchants." Korean industrialists were few and could not compete with
their Japanese rivals "because they have only little capital and limited
experience." Korean industry consisted mostly of handicraft and cottage work; and even that was being "swept away" by the introduction
of Japanese factory systems, causing increased unemployment in the
rural areas.[60]

In 1928, according to Government-General figures, Japanese owned
93 percent of the total capital invested in manufacturing enterprises,
representing 76 percent of the total manufacturing output. Koreans,
however, owned 2,751 factories, compared to 2,425 Japanese, and employed about 30 percent of the factory work force, compared to the
Japanese figure of 67 percent.[61] On the one hand, this reflected the
undercapitalization and the smaller size of Korean firms; but on the
other, it suggested the degree to which Korean factory ownership had
grown under Japanese rule.

Korea's cities, according to Lee, hardly presented that bustling aspect that a thriving commerce lends:

> The cities of Korea . . . are largely centers of administrative activ-
> ity. . . . Not a single city in Korea is busy and brisk like a trading
> center of the Western world, or Tokyo or Shanghai; Seoul, the larg-
> est, has a population of less than 370,000, and even here everything
> seems at a standstill and quiet.[62]

The few seats of commerce were the new railway centers and rice-
exporting seaports.

Other sources report more change than suggested above. One analyst found that during the 1920s the "social prestige attached to entrepreneurial activities increased significantly" and that there occurred
"a tremendous increase in the number of Korean entrepreneurs." Still
he noted that only 3 percent of firms with more than 250,000 yen in
paid-up capital were owned by Koreans.[63] At the aggregate level, it
seems that until the early 1930s we cannot speak of a significant Korean commercial class. What about in the later years, when rapid industrialization began?[64]

The rather substantial industrialization of the Korean peninsula in
the 1930s and 1940s was accomplished primarily by a trio of big institutions: the Government-General, including "national public companies,"[65] such as the Oriental Development Company and the SMRC;

the central banks, such as the Bank of Chōsen and the *Shokusan Ginkō* or Industrial Bank; and the great *zaibatsu* houses of Japan, such as Mitsubishi, Mitsui, and Sumitomo.[66] Again, the mechanism of change was exogenous to the Korean class structure. The colonial state and the banks provided the Japanese with various subsidies, access to credit, and guarantees of certain levels of annual return. Some of these operations were huge on a world scale; the Korean Nitrogen Fertilizer Corporation, for example, established the world's second largest fertilizer works in Hŭngnam. Paid-up industrial capital increased approximately ninefold in the decade from 1929 to 1939, but the Korean-owned element continued to be miniscule.[67]

It is likely that Koreans with capital to spare found most profit in investments in land and its products, although the research necessary to demonstrate the point remains to be done. Since land speculation, rural moneylending, and usury had long been established, this would be the expected development. Hoon K. Lee notes that most of the Koreans engaged in commerce were wholesalers, brokers, and merchants in grain transactions and that this activity mushroomed in such newer port cities as Kunsan, Mokp'o, and Pusan. Land registration records during the 1920s show that many Koreans had money to lend and mortgages to provide. In some cases, Koreans were even more active than Japanese.[68] Many Korean landlords graduated from simple reliance on rent to marketing and shipping grain for the export trade. Very few of these invested their returns in industry, however; indeed, it was probably far more profitable for them not to do so, given the competition with Japanese firms that had full government and bank backing.

Some recent Korean research has sought to depict the rise of a "national bourgeoisie" during the colonial period as part of a general interest in the depth and import of Korean nationalism. This phenomenon, to the extent that it existed at all, occurred after the 1919 uprisings and in the context of Japan's "cultural policy," which was designed to hold the hope of Korean independence at some fairly distant future point and to encourage Koreans to take the moderate path of lesser resistance—the lengthy work of preparing, educating, and nurturing the Korean people for that day when they would be free of Japanese rule. Although in my view no class of national bourgeois arose, the appearance of these individuals and the cleavages that they (and Japanese policy) caused among Koreans were extremely important. It is in this post-1920 period that the fissures that divided the elite in liberated Korea began to emerge—in political, cultural, and social spheres. The figures touted as members of a national bourgeoisie are critical to this development.

Among such Korean bourgeois, there were again two types.[69] The first were those who invested landed capital in commercial and industrial activities; this group derived from both new and old landlord backgrounds. The second type derived from commoner or despised (*ch'ŏnmin*) backgrounds; these figures moved onward and upward through sheer enterprising talent. It is among the latter that we find the classic Schumpeterian entrepreneurial virtues of foresight, daring, and creativity; it is also, however, this latter group who could expect little reinforcement from the structure of Korean prestige and who thus clung to the Japanese. Their national or patriotic character was, in most cases, as questionable as their origins were obscure. It was among what one scholar calls the "landlord-entrepreneurs" (*chiju kiŏpga-dŭl*) that the nationalist stamp was more visible.[70] These were the individuals who had the rooted stability and security in Korean society necessary to resist unseemly closeness to the Japanese master.

The Honam area of southwestern Korea, rich in rice and land and containing the rice-exporting cities of Kunsan and Mokp'o, was preeminently the place of origin of the landed entrepreneurs; and preeminent among these was Kim Sŏng-su. Kim became the core figure in a group of Honam people who subsequently played key roles in postwar Korea. Born into a landed family that had been prominent for many generations, on an enormous estate in Koch'ang, North Chŏlla, he founded among other things the *Tonga ilbo*, the leading Korean newspaper after 1921; the Kobu school in Chŏlla, and Posŏng College in Seoul (later named Korea University); and the Kyŏngsŏng Textile Company, which became the largest Korean-owned enterprise during the colonial period. His brother, Kim Kye-su, aided him in some of these enterprises and in the 1930s invested heavily in textiles and other manufacturing and in schools for Koreans in Manchukuo.[71] Kim Sŏng-su had gone to college in Japan and during this time formed close ties with classmates who remained his associates thereafter, including Song Chin-u, Yun Sang-un, Kim Pyŏng-no, Hyŏn Chun-ho, Chang Tŏk-su, and the most famous of Korean nationalist writers, Yi Kwang-su.

After returning to Korea, Hyŏn Chun-ho, Kim Pyŏng-no, and Yun Sang-un, all from wealthy landed families, worked with Kim Sŏng-su to found the Honam Bank and Kyŏngsŏng Textile Company. The bank was part of a general effort to build up indigenous and self-reliant Korean capital and soon drew investments from major Korean landlords throughout the Chŏlla provinces.[72]

Other landlord-entrepreneurs in the Honam area, all from substantial landholding backgrounds, would include the following: Cha Nam-jin, another founder of the Honam Bank; Cho Kye-hyŏn, who helped set up the Maedong Bank and several companies; Chŏng Yong-ch'ŏl, a Mokp'o area landlord involved with the Honam Bank and the Mokp'o Rubber Company; Kim Sang-byŏn, in banking, grain, and rubber enterprises in Mokp'o; Kim Sŏng-gyu, who helped set up the Kwangju Agricultural and Industrial Bank and was thought to have the largest landholdings in the Mokp'o area in 1930; Kim Wŏn-hŭi, involved in grain warehousing and shipping; and Mun Chae-ch'ŏl, also in grain trading.[73] In the Taegu area, similar Korean activities were evident; landlords Chŏng Chae-hak, Ch'oe Chun, and Yi Il-u established the Taegu Bank, and Chang Chik-sang was associated with the Kyŏng-il Bank.[74]

Among the early Korean entrepreneurs of the 1920s who did not have landlord backgrounds, but rather rose through their own enterprise and talent, the most important figure is Pak Hŭng-sik. From commoner background, he scraped enough money together to open a printing shop in Yonggang, in South P'yŏng'an Province. Shortly thereafter, at age twenty, he went to Seoul and established the Hwasin Department Store; he subsequently helped to found several large enterprises, including one that manufactured airplane parts for Japanese planes during the Sino-Japanese War. Pak was thought to be one of the richest men in Korea in 1945 and remains an important corporate figure in South Korea today. A similar individual was Pang Ŭi-sŏk, a commoner and an associate of Pak's during the 1930s and 1940s.[75]

In the case of these last two, it is difficult to argue that they had any nationalist leaning at all. Both had very close ties to the Japanese. In the 1940s Pang was on the Central Advisory Council, a collaborationist body of the first degree, and both Pang and Pak were widely thought of as unseemly collaborators after liberation. The case of the landlord-entrepreneurs is more complex. Many of them, like Kim Sŏng-su, are not perceived to have been collaborators by the South Korea of today, even though Kim and Chang Chik-sang, for example, were also on the Central Advisory Council in the 1940s. The nationalist color of these groups was at least in question during the last years of Japanese rule, however, and in comparison with other Korean nationalists, the path they took enabled them to maintain substantial wealth. Furthermore, their hopes for patient Korean nurturing proved illusory, although the failure of the tutelary cultural rule period was not their doing but the result of the abrupt change that occurred when Japan embarked upon aggressive war in 1937. After this point, and until 1945, the Japanese forced the most prominent Koreans to actively and publicly support their rule and their war. Thus they ruined the position of those moderate nationalists who sought to work under the Japanese system from 1920 to 1937. In any case, the nationalist color of these individuals, or lack of it, is not really the issue here. We should be focusing our attention instead on the term "landlord-entrepreneur." Surely that is precisely what they were, a first generation of Koreans in transition from one form of property and activity to another. Korean development was interrupted, however, as the Japanese period aborted abruptly in 1945; this left its mark on all Korean classes. The Honam group and ones like it were in a contingent status—as intent on maintaining their landed holdings and the derived prerogatives as on pursuing commercial or industry activity.

Thus this national bourgeoisie may or may not have been "national"; and in any case, it was not a bourgeoisie but only something embarked on the path toward that end.[76] The path was trod in a society remarkably resistant to seeing virtue in capitalism. Confucian doctrine and practice militated against commercial activities, a point made so many times as to become hackneyed. It is true; but it is also a truism, and one that hides the fact that all societies had to be dragged kicking and screaming into capitalist relations. All precapitalist societies viewed capitalism and capitalists with varying measures of disdain.[77] It is better in the Korean case to emphasize how neither class nor state during the Yi had much notion of development or stirrings of acquisitive drive, of things changing for the better in the future, or of how people could shape such a future. As Alexander Gerschenkron puts it:

> To break through the barriers of stagnation in a backward country, to ignite the imaginations of men, and to place their energies in the service of economic development . . . even the classical daring and innovative entrepreneur needs a more powerful stimulus than the prospect of high profits. What is needed to remove the mountains of routine and prejudice is faith—faith, in the words of Saint-Simon, that the golden age lies not behind but ahead of mankind.[78]

No entrepreneurial class in Korea had such faith in itself before the 1960s. During the colonial period and for years thereafter, the general Korean judgment was that commerce and industry were not the sorts of activities one should engage in or be rewarded for. In postwar north and south Korea, the colonial era was often referred to as a "capitalist" period, a term meant to signify not an epoch but a thirty-five-year imposition of an alien system. The system was as alien as the auspices of its introduction for most Koreans; those wealthy, enterprising individuals who assisted the Japanese colonization of Korea, even if they did not directly harm other Koreans, were perceived as servitors of alien influence, as "internal foreigners."[79] Hongkee Karl provides a representative example when he says that Korean capitalists had "denationalized" themselves, in the sense that "they have been in close cooperation with the invading imperialism and the alien capitalists in the land, while [the] only salvation of the Korean masses lies in their liberation from the exploitation of these bourgeois forces."[80]

Such attitudes die hard. Similar views were still dominant in *South* Korea in the mid-1960s, when an authentic Korean capitalism was just beginning to emerge. An international conference of scholars held in Seoul in 1965 produced a record that is remarkable for what it says about both Korean and American attitudes toward capitalist virtues.[81] It barely distorts the record to say that none of the distinguished Korean economists and philosophers present viewed Korean capitalists as anything more than profiteering crooks, whereas none of the distinguished Americans understood the entrepreneurial impulse to be anything less than the talisman of modernity. For example, after a Korean scholar disparaged Korean conglomerates for excessive profiteering, Marion Levy interjected that "a radically asymmetrical" distribution of income leads of necessity to forced savings and that this can be done in many ways, including profiteering; what counts is what is done with the capital "after it is extracted." Later, after presentation of a paper by a Korean scholar arguing that there were no entrepreneurial elements in traditional Korea, Professor Levy said that he could not believe that "an entrepreneurial category, a class of trained people opportunistically looking for the main chance," did not exist during the Yi. After a similar paper, Lucien Pye criticized the Korean author for leaving out of his presentation those people (who must have existed) "who have the capacity to destroy while being constructive in the process." He went on to describe the entrepreneur as "a man who really creates something . . . who conceives something big and carries it through. This requires a very strange mixture of qualities—ruthlessness (he has to believe in what he wants at all costs), the ability to persuade other people to come along. . . ."

In general, the Korean scholars argued that capitalism was foisted on Korea by the Japanese; that Korean capitalists during the colonial period used surpluses for leisure and the education of their sons; that with but a handful of exceptions all such capitalists were "pro-Japanese"; and that the situation remained essentially the same in the 1960s in South Korea, where there were no entrepreneurs, only those who profited from speculation in commodities or collusion with the government. One of the Korean scholars remarked, "we have never had any entrepreneur in the true sense of that word." This prompted the following response from Professor Levy:

> I don't care whether you call it exploitation it can ultimately have the effect of expanding the economy. The question is not whether you like it or not, but whether, if it is going to happen, you can . . .

control and direct it . . . it is not a question whether you can eliminate it, and do other things entirely.

There is, in these unguarded exchanges, no better example of the Marxian judgment that class ethos cannot appear in the absence of the class itself. It is as if the conference were a distillery, reducing an entire complex of assumptions to a residue of slogans—accumulate capital! throw it into industry! have no qualms!—or to the winnowed Korean assumptions—capital accumulation is barely disguised thievery; profits are something of a disgrace; not an iota of legitimation for the activity can be mustered.[82]

Of course, both the Korean and the American scholars speaking at this conference shared the common assumption that capitalism historically grew through the private activities of talented individuals and classes, when in fact reliance on speculation in commodities or "collusion" with governments was a common means to growth, even if capitalist virtue did not dignify such activities. Furthermore, the Korean scholars do exaggerate the weakness of commercial elements in their country. People like Kim Sŏng-su and his allies were unheard of in many colonies (for instance, in Java or Burma); there was more space for such Korean endeavor under the Japanese. It is the taint of the alien auspices and alliances behind such developments that offends the Koreans and leaves this a largely unresearched aspect of the colonial period. Still, the general verdict seems clear. We find in Korea, perhaps until the mid-1960s,[83] but certainly in 1945, a society that had produced no vibrant commercial class; an ethos so suffused with Confucian doctrine that it could place no blessing on capitalist pursuits; a colonial period perceived to have constituted an imposition of alien capitalist forms from without; and, perhaps less clearly perceived but no less important, an experience in which a strong and foreign state intruded and substituted itself for "natural" processes. We can perceive how wrenching this experience was, and how compressed in time; structure became a graft onto a foreign body, ideology appeared lacking in all subtlety, and assumptions emerged with no complexity. In other words, in ideology as in reality, Korea has been a harsh battleground where great and modern forces have clashed with naked abandon.

A Mobilized Working Class

In the following passage from *Darkness at Noon*, Arthur Koestler gives a memorable illustration of the difference between industrial work and all previous forms:

"I," said Gletkin in his usual correct voice, "was sixteen years old when I learnt that the hour was divided into minutes. In my village, when the peasants had to travel to town, they would go to the railway station at sunrise and lie down to sleep in the waiting room until the train came, which was usually at about midday. . . . In all other countries, the peasants had one or two hundred years to develop the habit of industrial precision and of the handling of machines. Here they only had ten years."

Industry calls for routine, for regularity, for pace, for precision, and for discipline. It is the antithesis of peasant life, timed to an agricultural cycle that exacts a tyrannous routine only at certain points during the year. People do not spontaneously or lightly choose to give up the one for the other; they have to be pushed and prodded to do so. They must first be loosed from the land and made mobile, then the tie to the land must be cut, and then they must be molded to the skills and disciplines of the industrial milieu. In Korea the process began under foreign auspices and was compressed into little more than a decade; then as suddenly as it began, it ended, and workers were thrown back into their previous occupations. In Korea under Japanese rule, peasants became workers only to be faced with being peasants again, in a rush that changed the lower reaches of the class structure at a rate much greater than it changed the upper reaches.

At the time of the Annexation, Korea's occupational distribution reflected its agrarian structure, with 84 percent of all households engaged in agriculture and a tiny 0.81 percent engaged in mining and manufacturing.[84] But by 1936 heavy industry accounted for 28 percent of total industrial production, and more than half a million Koreans were employed in industry. These numbers continued to grow rapidly through 1944, with the Korean industrial force nearly tripling (see table 1). The total of 1.3 million Korean workers in 1941 compared

TABLE 1

KOREANS EMPLOYED IN INDUSTRY WITHIN KOREA, 1923 TO 1943

Year	Number of Persons	Index of Increase
1932	384,951	100
1934	483,396	126
1936	594,739	154
1938	585,589	152
1940	702,868	183
1942	1,171,094	304
1943	1,321,713	343

SOURCE: *Chosŏn t'onggye nyŏn'gam*, pp. 26-32 (excludes mining and transportation figures; all data from official Government-General compilations).

with the figure of about 2 million for all of China in 1933 (and it was probably little higher a decade later).[85] Industry expanded in Korea at double or triple the rate of that in the Taiwan colony.[86] Furthermore, figures for Korea proper grossly underrate the total number of Koreans working in industrial circumstances, since hundreds of thousands were at work in Japan and Manchuria. Thus Korea's industrial revolution began in earnest during the last fifteen years of Japanese rule, providing a stark contrast with the experience of other colonies.

In 1945 Korea had an incipient working class, and occupational concentration was moving steadily away from agrarian bases. This working class was a spurious one, however, because swelling had been so rapid, yet there was little continuity in the development after the colony ended. Much of the Korean working class came from the rice-producing southern regions; they were displaced peasants who hoped to return to agricultural cultivation, or who had the recent memory of leaving the land. Thus they were not quite workers; but then they were not really peasants anymore either. Like the landlord-entrepreneurs, they were hybrids, touched but not transformed by industrial circumstances.[87]

Koreans found themselves in industry chiefly as a result of two mobilization processes. The first ensued during the 1920s and early 1930s and was largely the result of increasing concentration of landholdings. As peasants lost their land, they faced either unemployment or the necessity of migrating out of their native locale; although higher wages and better work opportunities drew a portion of the rural population off the land up until the late 1930s, the greater influence on peasants was the push off the land caused by more concentrated holdings. This we can call mobilization "from below." The second mobilization effort came from above, as colonial authorities sought to organize nearly every aspect of Korean life to serve the war that began in China in 1937. Korean laborers became the human capital to be moved hither and yon according to the dictates of Japan's industrial and military policies. Koreans, like the Japanese at home, were subject to the National General Mobilization Law (the basic enabling act for labor control), various forms of conscription, forced participation in work details, "patriotic" organizations, and the like.[88] Japanese and Koreans were to become one under the *naisen ittai* (Japanese-Korean unity) policy, their bodies, minds, and spirits mobilized jointly to serve Japanese needs. In 1937 the Korean League for the General Mobilization of the National Spirit was established, with branches at province, county, township, and workplace levels. The next year, a Special Volunteers Corps gathered youths for military service, and colonial authorities established the Korean Anti-Communist Association

(*Chōsen bōkyō kyōkai*) with allied branches in every province, local offices at police stations, and associated groups in villages, factories, and companies.[89] Participation in anticommunist "spiritual" discussion became compulsory in workplaces and elsewhere, a measure of the degree to which socialism had become attractive; recalcitrant Koreans, whether leftist workers or intellectuals, had improper ideas winnowed out of their heads through totalitarian methods of interrogation until they were ready to confess their sins in writing and join associations for those who had "reformed their thoughts" (branches in every province).[90] Communist apostates were first created and then marched before the Korean public as examples worthy of emulation.

After Pearl Harbor, the general mobilization of Korea was stepped up. In 1942 budget expenditures for the national mobilization movement quadrupled those of 1937, and doubled again in 1943.[91] Colonial authorities passed the Korean Youth Special Training Law in 1942, and shortly there were some 3,245 "youth organizations" divided among all of the provinces, cities, counties, and townships in Korea, with a total membership of two and a half million.[92] Such groups provided labor, among other things, for widespread work camps. This was part of a huge labor mobilization effort in which, according to Korean historians, 4,146,098 Koreans were conscripted for labor inside Korea.[93]

Edward Wagner's discussion of the *Naisen kyōwakai* (Japan-Korea Harmony Society), which was set up in Japan in 1936, is particularly revealing in its portrayal of the intense, total nature of the mobilization organizations: "The activities of the *kyōwakai* pervaded every aspect of the daily lives of Koreans, and touched every Korean individually, following his every action and (sometimes) word."[94] Korean laborers were grouped into units of ten; four such units constituted a patrol; three patrols constituted a "self-discipline unit." At the next level up, occupation-related branches were supervised by *kyōwakai* district offices, which were in turn supervised by the central office. All Koreans in Japan had to register with the *kyōwakai* and carry its identification card. It controlled all their necessary employment and travel documents. Among Koreans in Manchuria there were the same *kyōwakai*, "Youth Protective Corps," "Patriotic Labor Corps," and so on— means both of mobilizing labor and of getting Koreans to watch Koreans. Members of the youth corps, for example, served as wardens for groups of Korean householders; families harboring "political suspects" were the prime targets.[95]

Koreans, including women and children, were sent to Japan in droves during the war, so that by January 1945 they made up 32 percent of the entire labor force. In 1941, of some 1.4 million Koreans in

Japan, 770,000 were in the labor force; of these, 220,000 were in construction work, 208,000 in manufacturing, 94,000 in mining, and the remainder in agriculture, fishing, and other occupations. Yet more than half a million more Koreans were sent to Japan between 1941 and 1945, about half of whom were put to work in the mines. Some 136,000 Koreans worked Japanese mines in early 1945. The total figures are staggering—unprecedented in other colonial experiences.

We might pause here to imagine what the quality of the life must have been for these Korean workers or peasants thrown into a coal mine during these years. The dirty, harsh, and risky nature of coal mining made it an occupation that was socially shunned in Korea, like butchery during the Yi Dynasty; thus miners must have often felt that they belonged to the lowest stratum of society.[96] How much more demeaning could it be for a peasant stripped of his modest landholdings only to find himself working in a coal pit? Furthermore, during the war, protective legislation for workers in Japan was abolished. In the place of free labor contracting, a military command system was substituted so that capital and labor would "sincerely unite" to serve the war.[97] Japanese mines used little machine power, thus human labor was in great demand. The dirtiest work was in the pits—and there, during the war, Koreans constituted 60 to 70 percent of the pit force. Work began at 5:30 A.M., with miners lining up to march off in formation to start the day. Official sources put the work day at twelve hours and cited increased accident rates and "accumulated exhaustion" of miners during the latter war years, as production was expanded to the limit and the daily ration for miners was cut to 700 grams of staples per day, with no supplementary food such as fish or fruit.[98]

The labor mobilization process was harsh and divisive. When a request for laborers would come into the Government-General Ministry of the Interior, provincial quotas would be established on the basis of population. After that stage, the process tended to be haphazard, with orders depending on the whims of local government and police officials.[99] The Japanese limited themselves to supervisory roles at this level so that the process would "appear to be a Korean operation." Labor offices were usually located in local police stations, where policemen and labor officials were well rewarded for passing their quotas; "these same Korean officials were the most hated men in their communities."[100]

Such colonial labor policies intensified the already significant changes occurring as the Korean class structure differentiated. By milking labor in the short run (most of the laborers had two- or three-year contracts, whereupon they returned to Korea), the Japanese mortgaged human capital instead of investing in it. They pulled peasants away from their villages but failed to create new moorings in industrial structure; they raised peasant consciousness of the horrors of modern industry but failed to integrate them into it. To this was added ethnic cleavage; colonial authorities exploited what they took to be an inferior race and stimulated intra-Korean hatreds and rivalries that long outlasted the colony.

During the early part of the colonial period, a fairly uniform parallelism between ethnicity and official position existed, as the Japanese substituted themselves for the Korean elite. During later decades, however, the parallelism began to break down as incongruities between ethnicity and privilege emerged. This occurred first among the Korean landed class, which found out in the 1920s, if not earlier, that the Japanese were quite willing to tolerate and encourage their privileges. But it was really in the post-1931 period of industrialization that the coincidence of ethnicity and position waned; as class antagonisms and socialist ideology spread, the Japanese, like other colonial powers, recognized the uses of divide-and-rule techniques.[101] As the colonial regime penetrated and mobilized more Koreans, the artifice of pitting Koreans against Koreans spread. The extension of the bureaucracy, as offices proliferated, opened more of it to Koreans. Koreans could no longer simply blame the foreign race for the misfortunes that befell them, since the regime often presented itself in the person of a Korean official.

The Korean officials, too, were in a "structural bind." The more they cut themselves off from their own people, the more they were rewarded by the colonial power. But the more they rose in the colonial bureaucracy, the more they recognized the limits to their own aspirations for upward mobility because of their race, which then suggested their own solidarity with exploited Koreans.[102] The point of such colonial practice was to set up a multitude of crisscrossing ties and cleavages, thus breaking down the coincidence between ethnicity and class or status and confusing the colonial situation so that a Korean laborer was as likely to strike out at a Korean country magistrate as at a Japanese gendarme.

Within the working class itself, there were clear racial divisions as well. Japanese workers doing the same job that Korean workers were doing were paid two or three times more than the Koreans, a form of discrimination not nearly as severe in the Formosa colony. A Japanese joiner in 1937 received 1.97 yen per day in Japan, 2.00 per day in Formosa, and 2.15 per day in Korea. A Formosan joiner received 1 yen per day, and a Korean joiner, .66 yen per day.[103] A similar wage structure prevailed throughout the colonial system.

It was in the colonial police that the contradictions between ethnicity and status reached their zenith. This self-contained national force, appointed by and responsive to the center in Seoul, was a particularly effective agent of what was, in essence, a forced national integration. Because about half of its membership was Korean, the police tended to aggravate intra-Korean tensions. Everywhere the Japanese used Koreans in the harsher forms of police work. Labor mobilization was directed by local police offices and boxes. In Manchukuo a "considerable number" of Koreans were employed in the police force and acquired "an especially bad name for brutality and venality." The mobile detachments used to suppress Korean and Chinese guerrillas "were particularly dreaded, since they were composed mainly of Japanese *soshi*, or thugs, and low class Koreans."[104] Many Korean officers got their first military training in Manchukuo in antiguerrilla operations. The Japanese also utilized Koreans as prison guards in Allied POW camps during the Pacific War, giving the Koreans a nasty reputation that outlived the end of the war.

Thus we apprehend the bitter legacy that colonial divide-and-rule strategies have left everywhere, and left acutely in Korea. As a Korean climbed upward in the bureaucracy, he had increasingly to distance himself from his own people. To prove his mettle, he had to demonstrate ability to "handle Koreans." As he grew more distant from his people, he came to further identify with and depend upon the Japanese master and, perhaps, to experience more self-hatred and masochistic lashing out at others. Koreans in the police were the colonial collaborators *par excellence*, and in their heart of hearts they knew it. The fate of the Korean element of this force went a long way toward determining the politics of liberated Korea.

The overall effect of Japanese policy was not just to pit Koreans against each other but to strip legitimacy from dominant Korean groups and classes. Whether it was a landlord controlling his tenants, a policeman mobilizing laborers, a bureaucrat assessing taxes, or an intellectual lecturing on the virtues of the Greater East Asia Coprosperity Sphere, the experience has gnawed at the Korean national identity ever since. Had the colony not ended, or ended less abruptly, the Korean elite of the 1930s and 1940s might today be the self-confident masters of a less tightly Japan-linked Korea. They flipped their nickle in the air, thinking it would land heads up; but in 1945 it fell tails down.

THE RESISTANCE

Direct Japanese mobilization presented Koreans with political choices: join the anticommunist group, labor in a mine, fight the war, hate

Japan's enemies—or resist and take the consequences. Thus political consciousness emerged, especially among peasants for whom government had long been an abstraction. Politics was brought to the lowest levels of Korean society, and peasants and workers began to understand a politics of choice. At a minimum, Japanese propaganda suggested that there *was* a choice, that there were Koreans in resistance. Insurgents in the Korea-Manchukuo border regions were the last organized resistance within the transnational unit in the late 1930s; these were people that the Japanese called communists, people that Koreans were told daily to hate. Communists, both Chinese and Korean, led the anti-Japanese resistance in north China, in pockets not yet integrated into the developing Japanese sphere. Thus for many Koreans, leftism and communism became synonymous with opposition to Japan. The resistance took on a nationalist, patriotic aura. Daesook Suh is eloquent on this point:

> [The communists] succeeded in wresting control of the Korean revolution from the Nationalists; they planted a deep core of Communist influence among the Korean people, particularly the students, youth groups, laborers, and peasants. Their fortitude and, at times, obstinate determination to succeed had a profound influence on Korean intellectuals and writers. To the older Koreans, who had groveled so long before seemingly endless foreign suppression, communism seemed a new hope and a magic torch. . . . For Koreans in general, the sacrifices of the Communists, if not the idea of communism, made a strong appeal, far stronger than any occasional bomb-throwing exercise of the Nationalists. The haggard appearance of the Communists suffering from torture, their stern and disciplined attitude toward the common enemy of all Koreans, had a far-reaching effect on the people.[105]

Such identifications also were part of the Japanese legacy, stimulating mass sympathy with the left in Korea throughout the period from 1945 to 1950.

The resistance around the time of Annexation, the so-called *ŭibyŏng* or "righteous army," engaged the Japanese in scattered quasi-guerrilla skirmishes during the years from 1907 to 1910. As in Vietnamese resistance to the French, it was led by aristocrats.[106] The beginnings of Korean nationalism, however, are usually dated from the aftermath of the 1919 uprisings; it was also in this period that the first communists appeared. The nationalists were split between those who remained within Korea and those who went into exile abroad; and within each of these groups there were splits between advocates of armed struggle and those who urged a gradualist path of preparing

Korea for independence through cultural, educational, social, and political activities.[107] This last group was particularly vulnerable to Japanese manipulation, since the existence of moderate Korean nationalists, willing to make accommodations to Japanese rule, painted the less moderate groups in extreme colors; the colonial authorities could repress the "extremists," who naturally were a much greater threat, while nurturing the moderates and giving them the impression that, through their activities, one day an independent Korea would emerge. The result was that the Japanese allowed considerable freedom in intellectual circles until the late 1930s, as long as such groups presented no overt challenge to their rule. The conflicts that such policies set up persisted into the postwar period; the Left-Right conflicts of the late 1940s had their genesis two decades earlier.

Within Korea some groups of individuals continued to seek direct confrontation, in the form of tenant struggles, strikes, and occasional acts of violence. Thousands of Koreans ended up in jail for these activities in the 1930s, not to reappear until the Pacific War had ended. The majority of them were leftists and communists of various stripes; and through their struggles, the Left gained ascendancy in the anti-Japanese struggle after about 1925.[108] There evolved essentially four aspects to Korean communism: a so-called "domestic" group within Korea, including some of Korea's first and most influential communists; activists in the Soviet Union, which became one of the important refuge points for dissident Koreans after the Bolshevik Revolution; activists in China who, in the early 1940s, grouped in Yenan and other base areas with the Chinese Communists; and partisans in the Sino-Korean border region. Generally speaking, the communist movement (if it could be called that) was splintered and continually being reorganized, the result primarily of sophisticated Japanese police methods of suppression and control. Thousands of Koreans, however, had truly remarkable careers of resistance, spanning decades, and played important roles in the revolutionary tides sweeping Asia after World War I. Furthermore, too much has been made of the alleged factionalism, cliquishness, and immaturity of the Korean communists. Were anyone to do a systematic comparison of the Korean and Vietnamese movements from about 1920 to 1945, for example, they would find, I believe, that the movements show remarkable similarities and that the Koreans were at least as active and had at least as many successes when the differences in Japanese and French colonialism are taken into account.[109] In the 1930s, in particular, organizers within Korea and in Manchuria succeeded in reorienting activities toward the peasantry and the agrarian situation; and they achieved fair success in creating Red Peasant Unions and stimulating unrest among peasants within Korea and in establishing small guerrilla base areas in border regions in Manchuria and winning several skirmishes with the Japanese.[110]

The establishment of the puppet state of Manchukuo[111] and the effects of the worldwide depression, which forced many Koreans to migrate to Manchuria, precipitated a rapid swelling of anti-Japanese guerrilla and bandit groups in the Sino-Korean border region. Upwards of 160,000 insurgents occupied this area in the early 1930s, including communists, nationalists, and secret societies, the most important of which was the "Big Sword Society" (*Ta Tao Hui*).[112] The Japanese *Kwantung* Army mounted "bandit suppression" campaigns, one after another, in which they denied food to rebel base areas, fashioned "protective villages," organized capitulated guerrillas to hunt down their former comrades, and sought to supplant communist cell organizations with mirror-image "white cells" of anticommunists.[113]

Much of the Manchurian guerrilla activity in the 1930s occurred in a region that was simultaneously remote and backward yet important to Japanese needs. Ienaga Saburo has suggested that China, especially North China and Manchuria, constituted the core of the Pacific War, which he dates from 1931. The "tenacious resistance" of anti-Japanese partisans bogged down the Asian mainland war effort; and the quagmire in Manchuria and North China undid Japanese designs and produced frustrations that led to the suicidal attack at Pearl Harbor.[114] Within this core area or "main war theater" as Ienaga terms it, the so-called Tungbientao[115] region was critical. Japanese officers thought that in the event of war with the Soviet Union, this Sino-Korean border area "would serve as the strategic and material base for army operations."[116] A research expedition in 1933 had disclosed that Tungbientao was rich in natural resources, especially coal and iron. The hope was that these resources could be linked with the massive Yalu River hydroelectric facilities then being constructed (including the Suiho Dam, second largest in the world at the time); the town of Tunghua was to be the hub distribution center for the region. Toward that end, the Japanese extended rail lines to Tunghua in the late 1930s.[117]

The problem was that Tungbientao and adjacent prefectures were core base areas for Manchurian guerrillas, Chinese and Korean, with a local population that was living in dire poverty and was deeply resistant to Japanese intrusion. The region was also mountainous and heavily forested, with the sparse population farming in the narrow valleys by "coarse and primitive" methods or pursuing slash-and-burn cultivation in the remote hills.[118] In the late 1930s the Japanese sought to pacify and develop Tungbientao by extending an infrastructure of railways, "security highways," and police and military communications; police reports continually referred to the uses of such facilities in suppressing guerrillas.[119]

Tungbientao was full of Korean migrants who were "influenced by strong nationalist and Communist movements of long duration."[120] And neighboring Chientao, a province in which guerrillas were also active, had 530,000 Koreans in 1940, or 70 percent of the total population.[121] There and in Tungbientao, Japanese authorities set up "Concordia" associations (*kyōwakai* in Japanese, *hyŏpjohoe* in Korean), ostensibly to foster racial concord, but in fact "to use loyal Koreans to destroy recalcitrant Koreans."[122] Many of the members were former partisans who had had their "thoughts" cleansed; they were drafted into "Special Operations" sections to fight against Korean insurgents.

Tungbientao and contiguous prefectures harbored guerrillas throughout the 1930s. But after murderous suppression campaigns mounted in the wake of the establishment of Manchukuo, guerrilla and bandit numbers were reduced to about 2,000 in 1936. At that time a Chinese guerrilla, Yang Ching-yu, reorganized the remnants into the Northeast Anti-Japanese United Army (NEAJUA), an umbrella military organization that included a number of disparate Chinese and Korean guerrilla groups. It was in this milieu that Kim Il Sung (Kim Il-sŏng), the current North Korean leader, emerged as a prominent partisan fighter. Born Kim Sŏng-ju in a town near P'yŏngyang in 1912, he migrated to Manchuria as a youth and probably began organized guerrilla activity in 1932. In the NEAJUA, Kim commanded a unit of several hundred Korean partisans; they scored a number of victories in skirmishes with the Japanese in the period from 1937 to 1940, both in Manchuria and in northern Korea. The best known of these was an attack in 1937 on Pojŏn, a village in Korea (now renamed Poch'ŏnbo) in which various public buildings were destroyed and a number of Japanese policemen killed.[123] By 1939 Japanese police reports judged Kim to be the equal of Yang Ching-yu; each had about 400 partisans under their command. (Ch'oe Hyŏn, subsequently another important North Korean leader, had command of an additional 100 partisans, and assorted other Korean and Chinese partisan bands brought the total in the Sino-Korean border region to 1,200.[124]) The Japanese set up a "Kim Special Activities Unit" to track down Kim Il Sung and his allies, made up of fifty capitulated insurgents, mostly Koreans, and led by a Korean.[125]

One of Kim's postwar advantages was that he rose to prominence in the last decade of a four-decade-long resistance struggle; when other leaders were dead, in prison, or had given up, he was able to establish a reputation for himself, preserve his strength, and situate himself and his followers profitably as liberation approached. Around the time of Pearl Harbor, he and his allies apparently retreated to the border between Manchuria and the Soviet Far East (probably to the vicinity of Khabarovsk) to await the inevitable result of Japan's decision to wage war on a world scale. Kim was a battler, but also a survivor with a shrewd instinct for self-preservation and for timing.

From the beginning Kim also seems to have sought that most elusive of Korean political ideals, unity. During the 1930s he was an opponent of factionalism, a believer in united front tactics, and an adept at mixing nationalism with revolution. He was one of the few Koreans who joined forces both with Chinese and Soviet communism yet still seemed to keep a patriotic image and the loyalty of Korean comrades. This could be (and certainly has been) called opportunism; but in fact, it is simply good politics. Kim, like Syngman Rhee, was a shrewd practitioner of a skill in great demand in smaller countries, the ability to play greater powers off to one's own benefit.

Another key element in Kim's later success was that the Japanese never captured him. Thousands of other Korean revolutionaries fell into the hands of the colonial police, where ruthless methods, including torture, were used to obtain information about their comrades and to seek recantations of belief; no one emerged from the process unscathed. Of some 934 political prisoners released in Korea in 1934, 375 are said to have renounced communism.[126] Most of those imprisoned found it difficult to convince their allies that they had not been broken, a feeling that the Japanese police encouraged. Questions did not arise only among those who stayed free. In 1945 this was an important asset to Kim Il Sung and a handful of other Korean resisters.

Also important in Kim's rise to power was that before 1945 he had come to the attention of all the important forces in postwar Korean politics: the Japanese, the Korean people themselves, the Soviets, and even the American State Department. He was, of course, regularly mentioned in Japanese police and intelligence reports after 1935. A fascinating, tantalizing, but unverified report on him as late as November 1944, says the following in part:

> Kim Il-Song at present is at the Oganskaya Field School near Vladivostok, busily training insurgent Koreans for activities in Manchuria. According to the information recently received, Kim is preparing to dispatch agents to important points along the Korean-Manchurian border area in order to destroy railroads in coordination with the air raids of the United States Air Force in the same area.[127]

Within Korea, reports of Kim's exploits appeared in newspapers and in the November 1938 issue of the magazine *Samch'ŏlli*; he was described, in Scalapino and Lee's paraphrase, as "a robust young man of 27, with a wealth of experiences in guerrilla warfare."[128] Dae-sook Suh has argued that Kim was not known to the Russians before 1941;[129] but there is an important reference to him in the Soviet journal, *Tikhii Okean* (Pacific Ocean) in 1937. In this article, V. Rappaport refers to Kim Il Sung most favorably. Of far more importance, however, is the fact that this particular article was translated within the United States State Department in 1945, before the fall of Japan, at the request of George McCune of the Japan Affairs Division[130] (In this translation Kim is referred to as "Kim-Ni-Chen," an English rendition of a Russian transliteration from the Japanese, Kin Nichi-sei):

> In the course of combat with Japanese imperialists great and talented leaders have had the opportunity to distinguish themselves. . . . Among them the detachment of Kim-Ni-Chen stands out, especially. The men in this detachment are very brave. All the most dangerous operations are carried out by this detachment. Its actions are usually well planned, quick and precise. Two heavy machine guns in the possession of the detachment make it possible to withstand serious encounters with the Japanese troops. The unsuccessful hunt for the detachment of Kim-Ni-Chen by the Japanese has already been in progress for a year.

The article also detailed the exploits of the remarkable woman leader of Korean guerrillas in Manchuria who died in battle in 1935, Yi Hong-gwang.[131]

Thus Kim Il Sung was an important and recognized resistance fighter by the time the final struggle of the Pacific War was joined. It is a sad irony that this hardy but lucky survivor should be virtually the only individual given credit in the North Korea of today for the courageous exploits of the Manchurian resistance, which claimed the lives, the health, the minds, or the place in history of thousands of others.

Recognition of the Manchurian resistance episode is critical to an appreciation of the specificities of Korean communism. The activities of Kim Il Sung, Ch'oe Hyŏn, Yi Hong-gwang, and their allies occurred late in a struggle that began around the time of the Annexation. The longevity of the resistance movement, combined with the ruthless but often successful repression by the Japanese, meant that by the mid-1930s many of the older leaders had been destroyed or discredited, opening the way to a new generation of activists. Even minimal Korean success in the harsh Manchurian milieu would guarantee a place in postwar Korean leadership for the resistance, and the successes of Kim and his allies were more than minimal. Furthermore, they operated close to or within Korea, while other exiled activists struggled in the Chinese heartland. Their very proximity to Korea, however, rendered them remote from American or Western concerns; Manchuria may have been a critical arena of conflict with Japan, but not for the West. Thus, unlike the Chinese Communists at Yenan or Ho Chi Minh and his allies in Vietnam, the Manchurian resistance had no contact with the West—none of the broadening experience of Vietnamese communists under the French—and remained on the far periphery of Western concerns. Even today in the West, there is almost no knowledge of the history of this resistance movement; basic research remains to be done, and the North Koreans have not helped by making a national myth of Kim's resistance and ignoring everything else. The result is that Kim Il Sung remains for most Westerners a poseur at best and an imposter at worst, and there is no understanding of the Manchurian gestation of the subsequent North Korean leadership.

One other element of this Manchurian experience deserves special mention. Kim and the other guerrillas were not hunted by the Japanese alone; the Japanese found willing Koreans to stalk and kill them. Hundreds of Koreans participated in counterinsurgency operations, as foot soldiers and low-ranking officers, and a few even achieved high rank, such as Kim Sŏk-wŏn, a swashbuckling colonel who sported a Kaiser Wilhelm moustache. Owing to his "brilliant war record in the China theater," he was portrayed as a hero in the early 1940s to attract Koreans into the Japanese armed forces.[132] His heroics included command of the special Korean detachment of the Japanese Army that was assigned to suppress Kim Il Sung and his guerrillas in 1937; the confrontation of the two Korean leaders was played up in Japanese newspapers.[133] As the Korean War approached in 1950, the confrontation was renewed. Kim Sŏk-wŏn, by then a division commander of the southern forces, became famous for his assertion that if the South Korean Army attacked North Korea, it would have breakfast in Wŏnsan, lunch in P'yŏngyang, and dinner in Sinŭiju.[134] The actual sequence in June 1950 worked rather differently than Kim Sŏk-wŏn expected, but this should not obscure the civil genesis of the war. The origins of the conflict ran deep into the colonial period. The Japanese sowed the wind; Koreans reaped a whirlwind.

Chapter Two

LORD AND PEASANT IN
COLONIAL KOREA

A new way of life spread over the planet with a claim to universality unparalleled since the age when Christianity started out on its career, only this time the movement was on a purely material level. Yet simultaneously a countermovement was on foot. This was more than the usual defensive behavior of a society faced with change; it was a reaction against a dislocation which attacked the fabric of society.

Karl Polanyi

THE history of land relationships in Korea poses a remarkable example of a rare continuity in social forms, with lord and peasant interacting in ways that remained intact for centuries. It would be difficult indeed to pinpoint the origins of Korean agrarian relations. We might start with the beginnings of the Yi Dynasty in 1392, but as Edward Wagner argues, the Yi "more nearly represented a renovation than a new construction." The composition of the dominant *yangban* class underwent little change in the transition from Koryŏ to Yi.[1] In any case, in the early Yi we already find *yangban* landowners with peasant subordinates, just as we do in the nineteenth century.[2] This is not, of course, to say that the early Yi was a feudal society. But by the early eighteenth century, for which substantial documentary evidence is available, the land tenure system had established the pattern it was to maintain until 1945—large private or state-owned landholdings cultivated by tenants, with the larger holdings clustered in the Kyŏngsang and Chŏlla regions. The ubiquity of tenancy was evident in the last major land survey undertaken by the Yi administration (1898-1904), where one study of the results suggested that perhaps 75 percent of Korean peasants rented all or part of their land.[3]

The conditions of tenant life were penurious, often in the extreme, with stiff rents paid in kind and a general insecurity of tenure.[4] Peasant rebellions occurred frequently, the uprisings tending to happen, as we might expect, when the peasants were pushed below their typical subsistence level by things like additional taxes or usury.[5] The *yangban* landowners, on the other hand, fused aristocratic privilege with private landownership in a most potent mix. Their great power is evident, for example, in the general infrequency of land surveys. One held in 1820 was the first in a century, although the statutes called for them every twenty years. A state that had mastery over landed power would examine and classify land in search of revenue much more frequently. But the Yi state danced to landlord tunes. Nineteenth-century Korean scholar-officials themselves acknowledged that landed wealth wielded greater power in Korea than in China; the *yangban* were so entrenched that classical Chinese land reforms could not work.[6]

Anthropological studies have documented this historical pattern in microcosm. A study of three Korean villages indicates that landed families dominant in the 1940s had been so since the Hideyoshi invasions, if not earlier. A Pak clan in the Miryang district of South Kyŏngsang, for example, traced its substantial landholdings back to the period after Hideyoshi and claimed that the lineage itself had its origin with Pak Hyokkose, the Silla king of 57 B.C. Commoners in the village had long depended on this clan for their livelihood and were expected to render personal services in return. In another village near Koch'ang in North Chŏlla, six wealthy landlords from the dominant clan also traced their origins to the post-Hideyoshi period. They tended to fill local government positions as well and to maintain control over moneylending activities.[7]

In recent years some Korean scholars, such as Kim Yŏng-sŏp, have argued that the structure of late Yi Dynasty land relations deteriorated with the emergence of so-called managerial peasants, tenant-entrepreneurs, and the like. Like Thomas Smith's analysis of changes in Tokugawa Japan, their argument maintains that these new entrepreneurial elements within the peasantry began an indigenous process of commercializing agriculture. Kim Yŏng-sŏp notes that a substantial number of commoners (*sangmin*) and even outcasts (*ch'ŏnmin*) moved upward into *yangban* status and commensurate landholding by dint of their own efforts; thus land relationships were not fixed. But possibilities for establishing a native Korean commercial agriculture were ruined, according to Kim, by the intrusion of Japanese and Western capital and goods after 1876, which threw the agricultural village economy into bankruptcy and gave *yangban*s and bureaucrats the opportunity to throw peasants off the land and concentrate their holdings.[8]

The problem with such interpretations, apart from the desire to blame the Japanese for colonial land conditions, is that when compared to Japan in the eighteenth century, or England in earlier periods, Korea produced nothing on the scale of the Japanese peasant-entrepreneur or the English yeoman-farmer.[9] Furthermore, the Korean landlord class, as a class, did not emerge out of the peasantry. A handful of isolated individuals who rose to landlord status, or a regional pocket of permanent tenure arrangements, do not constitute an emerging class. Finally, of course, no one has maintained that the essential feature of eighteenth-century Japan, the rise of the market and the commercialization of the agrarian sector, was fully in evidence in late Yi Korea.[10] Instead the structure of land relations remained at the end of the nineteenth century what it had been for hundreds of years: private land was concentrated "in the hands of a few large landowners," with peasant cultivators who "were either smallholders, tenants, or agricultural laborers."[11]

COLONIAL AGRICULTURE

The Japanese Annexation in 1910 did not cause abrupt changes in the structure of Korean land relations. Instead, the dominant impression is the degree of continuity with the past. The Yi aristocracy lost its official component and its control over the central bureaucracy, but to say that the old ruling class disappeared is simply to ignore the persistence of Korean landholding patterns.[12] Rather, Japanese rule rooted the aristocracy even more firmly to the land, for land was the last bastion of its strength. The peerages and emoluments granted to thousands of former Yi officials, for example, were in the main invested in land. Some Korean scholars have argued that this transformed the Yi scholar-official class into a new landlord class.[13] This was true perhaps of the element that had possessed no land before and had therefore relied on bureaucratic position alone to maintain itself, but it was not true of the traditional landholding class, which persisted through the changes wrought by colonialism.

The first major program begun by Japanese colonial authorities was an exhaustive cadastral survey, carried out from 1910 to 1918. Like European colonial powers, Japan recognized the uses of rationalizing traditional land relationships by setting up a system of private property with identifiable rights and privileges, reinforced by codified law, and coupled with a modern administrative apparatus capable of extracting crop surpluses and tax revenue on an unprecedented scale.[14] The survey recorded for every plot of land in Korea the details of its ownership, type, quality, and value. The result was the fixing of a new land tax in 1918; and by 1930, the state was able to extract two and one-half times as much revenue as in 1910. In 1930 the land tax accounted for 45 percent of all government revenues.[15] The survey had thus vastly improved the colonial bureaucracy's ability to check the old tax dodges such as chronic underreporting or false reporting of crop yields; illicit, improper, or disguised ownership registrations; and hidden resources.[16] But the cadastral survey had other results as well.

Gunnar Myrdal noted that colonial authorities in Southeast Asia "had an obvious stake in producing a firm administration cheaply . . . [which] necessitated an accommodation with the inherent indigenous power structure." Moreover, administrative authority over titles to land "was a powerful weapon that could be turned either to punishing those who were hostile to the colonial regime or to rewarding those who cooperated."[17] Although much study remains to be done on the cadastral survey, it appears to have been a prime factor in mollifying opposition to and rewarding support of colonial policies. The land registration laws allowed Koreans from the *yangban* class, as well as Korean bureaucrats and clerks in the old Yi and the new colonial administrations, to establish title to lands or put their holdings on a legal contractual basis. Peasants, on the other hand, often were dispossessed through ignorance of the new laws or purposeful misinformation. It was in the aftermath of this reform that the first great migrations of Korean peasants began. But the Japanese also exacted a price from Korean landholders: the maintenance of landed privilege was contingent upon collaboration with Japanese efforts.

The county (*kun*) committees set up to administer the land tax reform were made up of more or less equal numbers of Japanese and Koreans.[18] Such officials were responsible for interpreting and implementing the land reform regulations. The actual trigonometric survey was conducted by technicians accompanied by an armed policeman, a Korean interpreter, and prominent local Korean landlords. The result was a rationalization of landholdings and dispossession of thousands of weak Korean peasants; but another result was an accommodation with existing Korean landlords. Thus in 1922, for example, 426 Koreans possessed more than 100 *chŏngbo* (1 *chŏngbo* = 2.45 acres), compared with 490 Japanese.[19] The Japanese later made the same accommodation with Manchurian landlordism.[20]

By placing landlord-tenant relations on a modern, or legal-rational, footing, ancient and customary reciprocal obligations were eroded. Tenant rights became less secure as landlords became more aware of the possibilities for profit in changing one tenant for another; thus whatever informal ties existed that may have given some measure of stability to the old system began to disintegrate. The fixing of land values and prices meant that land became a more negotiable asset; it could be used for securing loans and mortgages. And the weakening of traditional proscriptions meant that few barriers remained to those seeking land defaults and dispossession. In fact, landlords, moneylenders, and other intermediaries develop a positive interest in default under such circumstances.[21]

The Japanese increased the productivity of Korean agriculture through innovations in irrigation, scientific advances in crop strains and yields, and the like. But the consequences of the cadastral survey and the rise of market relations led to rapidly increasing concentration of landownership in the hands of a few and corresponding degradation of smallholders into tenants, thus creating a tenancy situation "with few parallels in the world."[22] The Japanese were not unlike other colonial powers who recognized that "an agrarian situation heavily weighted with tenancy and burdened with debt does provide devices useful in extracting marketable foodstuffs."[23]

Two land surveys conducted in Korea around 1930 indicate that nearly 80 percent of the Korean population were tenant-farmers. Hoon K. Lee's survey finds that when part-owners/part-tenants are included, "almost four out of every five Korean farmers (were) tenants." An American missionary-conducted survey reports that three-fourths of Korean peasants were renting all or part of the land they farmed.[24] Studies at later dates bear out these findings, while marking steady increases in numbers of tenants (see table 2).[25]

TABLE 2

INCREASES IN TENANCY DURING THE COLONIAL PERIOD
IN PERCENTAGES OF FARMING HOUSEHOLDS

Year	Landlords	Self-Cultivators	Self-Cultivators/ Tenants	Tenants
1913	3.1%	22.8%	32.4%	41.7%
1918	3.1	19.7	39.4	37.8
1924	3.8	19.4	34.6	42.2
1930	3.6	17.6	31.0	46.5
1932	3.6	16.3	25.3	52.8
1936		17.9	24.1	51.8
1939*		19.0	25.3	55.7
1943†		17.6	15.0	65.0
1945‡		14.2	16.8	69.1

SOURCE: Kobayakawa, *Chōsen nōgyo hattatsu-shi*, appendix table 3; except (*) Suh, *Growth and Structural Changes*, p. 81; (†) *Chosŏn t'onggye nyŏnbo*, pp. 42-43; and (‡) figures for south Korea only as of December 1945, USAMGIK, Department of Agriculture survey, XXIV Corps Historical File.

A system that fosters land tenancy is not inherently oppressive or exploitative: farmers who rent can be prosperous and productive. But it is exploitative when there is insecurity of tenure, widespread debt and usury, various forms of labor required without compensation, and resulting poverty and insecurity for the farming household. In Korea, population growth and increasing concentration of landholdings caused a growing pool of potential tenants, which gave landlords the leverage—the threat of replacement—to press their tenants to the limit.[26] Astounding levels of transfers of tenant rights thus developed. Lee estimates that 20 to 40 percent of all tenant-farmed lands in southern Korean provinces changed hands annually, while Wolf Ladejinsky puts the figure for all Korea at about 30 percent.[27] That this situation was more attributable to general agrarian class structure than to rifts between the Japanese and the Koreans is revealed in statistics showing that among Japanese landowners, the same relationship between landlord and tenant held true.[28]

Smallholders and tenants hoping to retain rights to their land faced mounting debt and rent burdens. The prevalent rent in 1930 for tenants was about 50 percent of the harvest in kind—so-called *t'ajak* rent based on annual yield. It approached 90 percent, however, in lush and productive paddy lands of North Chŏlla, South Kyŏngsang, and certain other regions.[29] This may be compared to the worst tenancy situations in China, which had similar rents.[30] Most peasants had to secure loans at some point in the agricultural cycle to enable them to survive. A stratum of moneylenders and other intermediaries, seeking profit from such misery, charged 60 to 70 percent interest annually on loans.[31] Tenants faced other exactions as well, "lest they be deprived of the lease." These included unpaid extra labor, gifts to landlords at the New Year, and in some cases, payment of the land tax in addition to the tenancy rent.[32] All this further burdened tenants who, on the average, worked tiny plots barely sufficient to maintain the annual needs of a peasant household.

Korean newspapers during the 1930s depicted the harsh plight of Korean peasants, especially in the period of "spring suffering":

> How can the hunger-stricken peasants live? In Tŏg'wŏn county alone, there are twenty thousand starving peasants. Over two thousand have wandered away, because they could not wait for death by staying at home. The irrational system of rural economy in Korea has cursed the peasant class to such an extent that the villages are devastated. . . . In spite of continued damage to the crops by the forces of nature, the peasant-tenants were deprived of such farm products as they had by merciless landlords and by iron-hearted usurers in the early autumn. They have been suffering from lack of food. By eating grass roots and tree bark they barely escape immi-

nent death. . . . The situation is hopeless. They have to wander away from the villages with their little children on their backs and arms.[33]

The Government-General itself reported in 1938 that about three million households, or 80 percent of the farming population, were tenants:

> Most of [these] in spring every year have been short of food and had to maintain life by searching for edible weeds, roots, and barks [sic] on the hillsides, a condition without hope that led to indolence and lack of interest in work.

This report also acknowledged their "crushing debts."[34]

Many Korean peasants came to prefer the insecurities of isolated, slash-and-burn (*hwajŏn*) agriculture in the mountains to tenancy.[35] Agrarian life for the mass of Korean peasants thus meant "extreme poverty [that] can hardly be imagined by the outsider."[36] Moderate scholars like Lee and Andrew Grajdanzev agreed that Korea's land situation was hopeless without radical change. Grajdanzev thought that far-reaching reforms should come with liberation from Japanese rule. He argued forcefully for redistribution of land to those who worked it, without recompense to the owners, and for measures to prevent "the danger of class government" by Korea's landlords, whom he termed "an almost purely parasitic group of the population."[37]

Who were these Korean landlords as the colonial period drew to a close? There has been little systematic study of Korean landlordism during the Japanese period. Conservative Korean historiography tends to downplay the holdings of Korean landlords, as opposed to Japanese, and to suggest that, unlike their Japanese counterparts, they lived harmoniously with their tenants.[38] But statistics show the persistence of a distinct Korean landed class throughout the colonial period. And while it would be hard to demonstrate, it is also hard to imagine that Korean landlords would have exploited their tenants less than did the Japanese, although ethnic sentiments may have led tenants to prefer Korean overlords.

Korean scholars tend to call anyone who owned more land than he could work himself (perhaps 5 *chŏngbo*) a landlord but distinguish as "big landlords" those with 50 or more *chŏngbo* (approximately 123 acres). Available figures indicate that in the 50-100 *chŏngbo* category, there were roughly twice as many Koreans as Japanese; in the 100-200 *chŏngbo* category, the numbers were about equal; and in the 200-plus *chŏngbo* category, the number of Japanese tended to be double or triple the number of Koreans, depending on the year (see table 3).

TABLE 3

LANDLORDS BY NATIONALITY AND SIZE OF HOLDING, 1921 TO 1942

Year	200+ Chŏngbo		100-200 Chŏngbo		50-100 Chŏngbo	
	Koreans	Japanese	Koreans	Japanese	Koreans	Japanese
1921	66	169	360	321	1650	519
1926	66	177	325	366	1689	676
1930	50	187	304	361	1566	676
1936	49	181	336	380	1571	749
1942*	116	184	429	402	1628	733

SOURCE: Kobayakawa, *Chōsen nōgyo hattatsu-shi*, appendix table 4; except (*) *Chosŏn kyŏngje nyŏnbo, 1948*, p. I-30 (1 chŏngbo = 2.45 acres).

By 1942, however, it appears that Koreans in the 200-plus category approximated two-thirds of the Japanese number. Table 4, giving a breakdown by province of the number of Korean landlords in 1942,

TABLE 4

KOREAN LANDLORDS BY PROVINCE, 1942

Province	200+ Chŏngbo	100-200 Chŏngbo	50-100 Chŏngbo
Kyŏnggi	13	85	317
N. Ch'ungch'ŏng	2	7	66
S. Ch'ungch'ŏng	2	30	116
N. Chŏlla	4	30	143
S. Chŏlla	13	48	117
N. Kyŏngsang	2	19	98
S. Kyŏngsang	4	15	74
Hwanghae	44	76	267
N. P'yŏng'an		18	112
S. P'yŏng'an	24	30	139
Kangwŏn	4	62	120
S. Hamgyŏng	4	6	53
N. Hamgyŏng		3	8

SOURCE: *Chosŏn kyŏngje nyŏnbo, 1948*, p. I-30-31.

demonstrates the higher incidence of landlordism in southern Korea provinces. We can better understand this when we realize that labor-intensive, wet-paddy farming with correspondingly higher land values was prevalent in the south, while dry field, grain farming was prevalent in the north. The incidence of absentee landlordism was also quite high in the south, with 30 to 46 percent of landlords in all southern provinces except Kangwŏn living in some other region.[39]

There are no reliable statistics on the numbers of Korean landlords in the years immediately succeeding liberation. The situation was

complicated by widespread destruction of land titles, informal transfers of Japanese-held land to Koreans (particularly to Korean agents
of Japanese landlords), and the rather quick dispossession of landlords
in north Korea and in some regions in the south. The United States
Military Government Department of Agriculture estimated that there
were 47,021 landlords in the south in December 1945, but it is not
known what basis was used for defining the label "landlord." Writing
in 1946, In Chŏng-sik estimated that there were about 30,000 "big
landlords" and "absentee landlords" in the south.[40] It seems fair to
assume that the number of landlords with large holdings in south
Korea swelled considerably after liberation because of transfers of
Japanese land to Koreans and because of an influx of landlords from
north Korea who, although dispossessed, remained conscious of the
prerogatives of their class and hoped one day to recover their holdings.

Korean landlords did differ in certain respects from Japanese landlords. They tended to have less access to capital and thus, in general,
less land and smaller capital investments in their land. Japanese landlords also had better information on how and where to obtain land
and generally superior expertise and technique in obtaining high
yields and surpluses. But there is no evidence to suggest that Korean
landlords were any less exploitative or "parasitic" than Japanese landlords. In fact, the reverse may have been true. Whether landlordism
is exploitative or not, it is often suggested, depends on whether the
landlord performs essential functions in the productive process, such
as supplying tools and implements, seeds, technical expertise. As Barrington Moore puts it, "the contributions . . . must be obvious to the
peasant, and the peasants' return payments must not be grossly out of
proportion to the services received." In other words, a determination
of whether exchanges of goods and services are reciprocal or not, helps
distinguish progressive landlordism from parasitic varieties.[41]

Jeffrey Paige argues that progressive landlords used economic sanc-
tions and inducements and entrepreneurship to maintain their positions, whereas "bureaucratic" landlords relied on political means and
coercion.[42] Whichever definition we use, we must classify Korean landlords in the backward category. They tended to rely on the colonial
bureaucracy to preserve and enhance their status; and the strong state
—especially the police and the courts—gave them a degree of backing
they never had from the old Yi. With their bargaining power thus
enhanced, Korean landlords were able to transfer more of the costs of
production to tenants, including responsibility for providing tools,
seeds, fertilizer, and other essentials.[43]

The entrepreneurial function, in the form of scientific, innovative,
and technical planning, was in the hands of "a large army" of colonial

administrators and technicians who were spread throughout Korea and who controlled agricultural production.[44] Furthermore, there was little incentive for Koreans to invest in commercial or industrial capital and thereby change to a more progressive form of capitalism; instead a low, fixed land tax and high rates of return on investments in land combined to encourage Korean landlords to consolidate landholdings. The rate of return on paddy land was 8.0 percent in 1937, while that on dry fields was 8.5 percent; this may be compared with the rate of return on common stocks of 6.5 percent and that on paddy land in Japan in the same year of 4.89 percent.[45] This was part of a colonial policy—to make landlords the key both to rural stability and the extraction of rice for export. With landholding made attractive and few incentives to diversify, Korean landlords, like native lords under European colonialism in Southeast Asia, "managed to enjoy the prerogatives of a capitalist landlord without giving up the privileges of a feudal chief."[46]

The primary effect of Japanese rule was thus to perpetuate, not eliminate, Korea's traditional landed aristocracy. This was not unique in colonial situations in Asia; in fact, the agrarian structure in French-ruled Vietnam showed patterns of continuity and change remarkably similar to those in Korea.[47] But the picture of a colonially exploited Korean society, encompassing all elements, is a simple myth.

The Korean Peasantry and the Rise of the Market

As Karl Polanyi has noted:

> A market economy must comprise all elements of industry, including labor, land and money. . . . But labor and land are no other than the human beings themselves of which every society consists and the natural surroundings in which it exists. To include them in the market mechanism means to subordinate the substance of society itself.[48]

Most Koreans were peasants before the Japanese came and remained peasants after they left. Yet in the decade preceding liberation, the peasant class lost upwards of 10 percent of its members, mostly to industry; and many more than this had been touched by the force of the world market system. It was the simultaneity of the coming of the market and the rise of industry that was so critical to shaping the fate of Korea under the Japanese and thereafter. This was, in essence, the onset of Korea's capitalist revolution.

There can be no understanding of the peasant apart from the society in which he lives. The essential element of peasant society is "a structure of authority governing the allocation, disposition and use of the basic resource: land."[49] Typically this structure is hierarchical; more than in most social relationships, structure in peasant society is that of imperative coordination by rulers over ruled—although the ruled classes may be more variegated than they appear at first glance and the ruling class or classes may be open to limited social mobility. But subsistence peasants, such as those in Korea, were not like farmers, producing crops for profit in a market economy; instead they utilized their entire household as a unit of production geared to an agricultural cycle.[50] The goal of their labor was to meet the consumption needs of the household and the "enforced dues" of those who held political, social, and economic power.[51] In R. H. Tawney's image, subsistence peasants were like people standing in water up to their noses, such that the least ripple in their fortunes could drown them.[52]

Social classes, and social esteem or prestige, in Korea were defined by relationships to the land. While the greatest prestige and power was of course attached to landownership, working land in someone else's interests or being a tenant placed one above those who had no land to work or who labored with their hands at some other occupation. Distinctions within the peasantry are important to keep straight; peasants who owned and worked their land differed in their behavior from subsistence tenants. It is the latter group that possessed what George Foster aptly called "an image of limited good,"[53] believing that all that is good in life is perennially in short supply; that the next year may well be worse than the present year, so resources must be husbanded; and that one never gets something for nothing, but only gets something at someone else's expense. In other words, the world of the subsistence peasant was one of zero-sum perspectives and struggles. The majority of Korean peasants were this way until the 1920s when the Japanese completed their cadastral survey and thus linked the mass of Korea's peasants with not only Japan but with the world market system as a whole.

In recent years, the best studies of peasant politics have placed emphasis, quite properly, on the transformative effects of the world market system on agrarian relations.[54] It is not so often recognized, however, the degree to which such analyses rest on the shoulders of two social theorists, Karl Marx and Karl Polanyi. For Marx, the penetration of the market mechanism into rural areas was the essential cause of the disruption of peasant life; it separated the peasants from their property, destroyed the old agrarian relationships, and created a "free mass of living labor," which, as capitalism developed, became lodged in modern factory production. What Marx called "primitive accumulation," was an essential process in any capitalist revolution, such that one cannot speak of mature capitalism until it happens.[55] Nearly a century later, after the market had spread and deepened, Polanyi analyzed the process of uprooting peasants both in Europe and in the colonial areas of the world. His emphasis was on the dialectic between market and society: the one penetrating and attempting to subordinate the other; the other reacting and protecting itself as best it could:

> Our thesis is that the idea of a self-regulating market implied a stark utopia. Such an institution could not exist for any length of time without annihilating the human and natural substance of society; it would have physically destroyed man and transformed his surroundings into a wilderness. Inevitably, society took measures to protect itself.[56]

Whether in England or elsewhere, market economy produced "an avalanche of social dislocation;" and it was the peasantry more than any other class that was shaken loose from its ties to the land and "made free." Fundamentally, the market substituted the motive of gain in the agrarian sector for that of subsistence. It took an economy that had been subordinate to society, to social relations, to typical mechanisms for maintenance such as practices of reciprocity and redistribution, and reversed the relationship: now it was economy that would dominate society. For the old periodic rural markets, which Polanyi called "an adjunct of local existence," a world market system was substituted with its base in the city.[57] Polanyi placed critical emphasis on the rate at which this substitution took place. Was it slow, encompassing decades and centuries, so that society had time to accommodate the change? Or was it fast, so that society was laid waste? In the end, it becomes a matter of how quickly the market system "is foisted upon an entirely differently organized community." In the colonial regions, the process had three phases: first, commercialization of the agrarian sector; then, increases in the production of food; and then, exporting the surplus to the metropole.[58] Marx also emphasized rates of change, arguing that revolutionary "above all" are those moments "when great masses of men are suddenly and forcibly torn from their means of subsistence, and hurled as free and 'unattached' proletarians on the labour-market."[59] It remained for Moore, then, to examine society's reaction to market penetration and commercialization and to analyze how differing class structures changed in reaction and what political structures resulted.[60] It remains for us to explore the peculiarly potent and explosive impact of the entry of world market relations into regions of irrigated rice production, such as those that pertained in most of Korea.[61]

We have begun to grasp the process of commercialization in Korea in its general features: the establishment of contractual bases for land; the fixing of a price in world terms for its product; the utilization of landlord and bureaucratic domination for the extraction of rice; and the use of the surplus for investment elsewhere (Korean cities, Manchurian factories) or to feed the metropole. The result was a clustering of forces at the extremes: accumulation, wealth, diversity at the one end, whether in the colonial city or the metropole; primitive accumulation, poverty, and homogeneity at the other.

In the seven years succeeding the completion of the cadastral survey, Korean rice accounted for 47 percent of Japanese imports. In the next five years (1926-1930), it accounted for 57 percent; and in the next five, 65 percent. Then the percentage began to drop off; indeed, even in certain of the last five years, such as at the height of the depression, imports dropped drastically.[62] Yet throughout the period, Korean rice production climbed steadily. In other words, exports were determined entirely by Japan's need for Korean rice, rather than by the production of increasing surpluses in Korea. Per capita consumption of rice dropped steadily in Korea from the 1915-1919 figure of 0.71 *koku* to the depression (1930-1933) figure of 0.45 *koku*.[63] After 1931 Koreans were fed with millet from Manchukuo to make up for rice exports, an excellent example of a core/semi-periphery/periphery relationship. As Japan expanded its war effort in 1940, it was able to incorporate a new periphery, southeast Asia; thus, almost overnight Korean rice exports to Japan dropped, replaced by exports from Indochina. Whereas the Japanese imported 1.7 million metric tons of rice from Korea in 1938, in 1940 they imported only 66,000 metric tons from Korea but 1.3 million metric tons from Indochina.[64]

As such market and export mechanisms develop, they have profound effects on agrarian class structures. Peasants tend to be homogenized into a common mass, although enterprising individuals, often those closer to new marketing cities and ports, may rise into rich peasant or landlord status. For smallholding peasants and tenants working small plots, the market can raise or lower the standard of living, but more important is the fluctuation and cycling that the market brings. For peasants up to their noses in water, in Tawney's image, the market simply makes the waves larger and more devastating. Many peasants are forced into debt, into watching their holdings contract, or into outright dissolution. Rates of rural conflict rise. And indeed, we find that tenancy disputes and small-scale jacqueries in Korea increased rapidly in the late 1920s and early 1930s, coinciding with the onset of the depression.

It is during these depression years that the Korean agrarian economy really nose-dived, intensifying peasant misery and setting off mass migrations from the land. Upwards of 80 percent of the peasants suffered a reduction in per capita consumption of food grains, and land concentration and peasant dissolution increased rapidly. The living conditions during the depression illustrate the general fact that it was the Korean peasant who suffered the worst effects of linkages with the world market, and enjoyed few of the benefits. Rice for the export trade was extracted by the colonial state and its landlord allies; it was not marketed by peasants. Indeed, Korean peasants did not even hull their own rice, as did peasants in Japan; the unhulled rice was taken to large rice mills and then introduced into the export trade.[65] Yet these same peasants were subject to the fluctuations of the world market in rice.

The landholding classes feel the effects of the market as well. Some continue to sit back and reap surpluses, to use profits to engage in speculation and moneylending, to absent themselves to the cities, and so on.[66] Let us call such people "type A" landlords, a generally backward variety. Then there is "type B," the landlords who become deeply involved in commercialized export agriculture—as entrepreneurs who reinvest their returns in expanded production, or as rice mill owners, shippers, warehousemen. It is in this second group that we find the incipient commercialization of a landed class that points the way toward a capitalist transformation.[67] Marx, Paige, and others argue that we can expect more tolerance of peasants' and workers' rights and organization among "type B" landlords, since the concept of free labor implies freer politics—they see that it is in their interest; they grasp the possibilities of an expanding economic pie in ameliorating sharp class conflict. "Type A" landlords, however, share the peasant's zero-sum perception of the world; they are less likely to grant political rights and more likely to use repression in the face of dissidence. Such landlords will also likely seek to prevent peasant access to markets, since this lessens their control and enhances the bargaining position of the peasants.[68]

In Korea there was just such class differentiation. Some Korean landlords became buyers and transporters of their tenants' grain, millers and warehousemen in the export cities, or speculators in grain futures in the major rice markets of the 1930s, such as Kunsan, Mokp'o, Pusan, Taegu, Seoul, Wŏnsan, Sinŭiju.[69] But because so much of the agrarian change was exogenous, stimulated by the Japanese, these landlords were in the minority. Change was imposed by colonial authorities who were primarily interested in the extraction of rice rather than the progressiveness of Korean landlords. As Suh notes, because extraction for the export trade was the main objective, the Japanese sought "to obtain complete control of the distribution of output so as to maximize the surplus" to be transferred to Japan. They used the landlords to pressure and control peasants, and neither landlord nor peasant had much incentive to foster innovation in agricultural production. Most of the rice collected as rent went to the export trade, and upwards of 60 percent of exports came from the large-scale landholdings.[70] Japanese controls were much more extensive in Korea than those of most colonial powers in their colonies; the whole country rather than a few export enclaves was integrated with the metropole. This control inhibited the Korean private sector in agriculture.

In addition, until 1945 it was in keeping with tradition and also patriotism for Korean landlords to shun entrepreneurial pursuits, for thereby they did not involve themselves in unseemly, day-to-day activities with the Japanese. They could go up to Seoul, take their ease, study the classics or the native language, and await the day when Japan would be gone. Especially among the *yangban* landlords this was the pattern. For the Korean parvenus, though, prospering under Japan and freed from the prejudices and lack of opportunity of the old Korean class structure, commercial enterprise held more interest. In both cases, wealth and privilege were guaranteed by the colonial bureaucratic structure that enforced such land relations, just as they had been by the Yi state in the past. When the colonial state crumbled in August 1945, the supports were abruptly pulled out from under Korean landlords, casting them on their own resources, which, politically speaking, were slim. The substitution of Japanese for Korean skills and infrastructure, however, guaranteed that postwar Korea would be left with mostly "type A" landlords. Agricultural development had gone on in the interests of the core; it had been in the hands of Japanese administrators, Japanese landlords, Japanese capital.

The Korean Population Hemorrhage

The effects of the new market relations, the rise of industry in the 1930s, and the mobilization policies of the colonial regime were so powerful that we can say with little hesitation that few if any societies ever were subject, in such a relatively short time period, to the immense population shifts and dislocations that Korea was under the Japanese. The phenomenon was all the more disruptive in Korea because of the ancient stability of provincial population distribution there. Radical changes occurred particularly in the later years of Japanese rule. Not only was the natural population increase among Koreans very high but the indirect and direct (forced) mobilization of Koreans by the Japanese led to astonishing levels of population movement. Mass migrations occurred both within Korea and from Korea to Japan and Manchuria. By 1944 fully 11.6 percent of all Koreans were residing outside Korea, "a proportion unequalled by other Far Eastern populations and rarely matched in other parts of the world."[71] Perhaps 20 percent of all Koreans were either abroad or in provinces other than those in which they were born.[72]

There is excellent data with good internal consistency on the extent of Korean population growth and movement in the later decades of Japanese rule. Figures on internal (interprovincial) migration are better than those on external migration, however, which is unfortunate since the latter was much larger. According to these figures, the overall Korean population increase during the colonial period was high, averaging between 25 and 30 percent in each decade. The figures also show that urbanization proceeded rapidly, particularly in the 1930s and early 1940s as industrialization ensued. From 1932 to 1942, cities like Seoul, P'yŏngyang, and Wŏnsan nearly tripled their populations, while Pusan and Taegu doubled theirs. Some north Korean cities, like Najin, increased fourfold in the same period.[73] In fifteen short years, the percentage of the total population living in urban areas jumped from 3 to 10 percent. Cities experienced a fourfold population increase, while counties grew by only 15 percent (see table 5).[74]

TABLE 5

City and County Population Growth, 1925 to 1940
(In Millions)

Division	1925	Percent 1925-1929	1930	Percent 1930-1934	1935	Percent 1935-1939	1940
Cities	.6	46.4%	.9	40.0%	1.2	91.0%	2.4
Counties	18.4	6.2	19.5	7.2	20.9	1.0	21.2

Urbanization was obviously significant, with far reaching implications for a sedentary peasant population. More significant, however, was interprovincial and transnational Korean migration. Japanese policies caused literally millions of Koreans to leave their home counties and move into cities, to other provinces, or out of Korea altogether. Migration to Japan, Manchuria, and Russia was substantial before 1920, but its causes remain unclear. After the cadastral survey and the rise in landless peasants, however, "a huge army of indigent persons grew up on Korea, for their land was gone and there was no industry to absorb them."[75] Until the mid-1930s, these landless peasants accounted for most of the Koreans migrating to Japan and Manchuria. Wagner finds that the 400,000 Koreans who migrated to Japan from 1921 to 1931 were mostly surplus agricultural households and individuals. A survey made in Kobe in 1936 indicates that some 90 percent of Koreans had been peasants before coming to Japan.[76] Irene Taeuber notes that 90 percent of the Koreans in Manchuria in 1930 were employed in agriculture.[77] By 1940, however, burgeoning industry in northern Korea and in Manchuria (Manchukuo) had begun to utilize surplus agricultural labor. In 1940 only 69 percent of the 1.45 million Koreans in Manchuria were employed in agriculture: "Manchukuo became an industrial and urban frontier for the Koreans."[78] As the large Japanese, heavy-industrial infrastructure in north Korea grew, workers were found from among the surplus peasant population of southern Korea. Figures 2 and 3 give an indication of the degree of interprovincial migration occurring in 1930 and 1940. Figure 4 demonstrates the role of industrialization in the north in siphoning labor from the south.[79] Almost all of the increases in employment in the northern provinces were the result of growth in manufacturing and industry, mining, and commerce.

Much of this internal and external migration involved peasants from the provinces of southern Korea. North Kyŏngsang had a particularly acute population loss resulting from migration to north Korea and Japan. In the years 1931 to 1945, for instance, while the population of certain north Korean provinces was increasing by as much as 35 percent, North Kyŏngsang lost 3 percent. Moreover, general migration figures for North and South Kyŏngsang take into account the significant increases in the populations of Taegu and Pusan.[80] External migration figures, or aggregate population losses, for the provinces do not complete the picture of total population movement, however. South Korean provinces had significant inflows of population as well, and annual population movement could reach as high as 29 percent of total provincial population (see table 6). This was because so much of the interprovincial and international migration was short-term. Like many other colonial powers, Japan did not attract labor into industry through high wage incentives but used coercion and compulsion to secure maximum labor output in the short run.[81] After a few years of squeezing labor out of people who were working for pittances under wretched conditions, they discarded them and brought new people in. Thus the total number of Koreans remaining outside Korea or in non-native provinces in 1945 was far smaller than the actual

TABLE 6

INCREASES IN POPULATION DENSITY, 1930 TO 1946
BY PROVINCE, IN PERSONS PER SQUARE KILOMETER

Province	1930-1940	1930-1944	1944-1946	1930-1946
Kyŏnggi*	33.33%	43.45%		
N. Ch'ungch'ŏng	4.96	9.09	13.64%	23.97%
S. Ch'ungch'ŏng	13.45	20.47	13.11	36.26
N. Chŏlla	6.25	10.80	20.51	33.52
S. Chŏlla	13.10	17.26	7.61	26.19
N. Kyŏngsang	2.36	7.87	21.90	31.50
S. Kyŏngsang	3.45	12.64	31.63	48.28
Kangwŏn*	14.93	24.56		
all Korea	15.79	23.16		

SOURCE: Derived from *Chosŏn kyŏngje nyŏnbo, 1948*, p. III-19.
* 1946 figure is for area south of thirty-eighth parallel only.

number of Koreans who had been uprooted from their agrarian circumstances. The large flows of Koreans to Japan were matched by
large flows back to Korea. From 1917 to 1929, for example, 1.8 million
Koreans were admitted to Japan and .9 million Koreans returned to
Korea. In 1939/40, 400,000 Koreans returned home. Many Koreans
only remained in Japan for a year or so.[82] The same probably held
true for migration to northern Korea and Manchuria, although industry there may have retained Koreans for longer periods. It is impossible to present an exact figure for the total number of Korean
peasants who left agricultural cultivation in Korea for similar work
abroad or for labor in industry; but it seems clear that more than
four million Koreans worked in Japan at some point during the colonial period, and the figure would be at least two million for
Manchuria.

At the end of the colonial period, most Koreans who had been
displaced to Japan, Manchuria, and north Korea returned to their
native homes. Table 7 illustrates the population influx into south
Korea after official repatriation facilities were set up in October 1945.
Although these figures represent the number who returned before the
end of 1947, the greater proportion had returned by mid-1946. Furthermore, informal repatriation before October 1945 was very substantial. Wagner estimates that 300,000 to 500,000 Koreans returned from
Japan between January and August 1945, and that another 550,000 or
so returned informally between August 15 and the end of November.[83]
Figures on informal repatriation from Manchuria are unavailable.

We can make certain generalizations about this extraordinary return of the Korean population after liberation, although returning

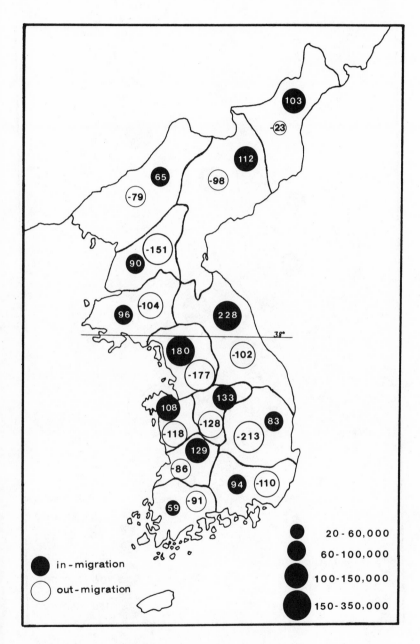

2. Interprovincial Migration, 1930 (in thousands)

SOURCE: Based on Trewartha and Zelinsky, "Population Distribution and Change," fig. 10.

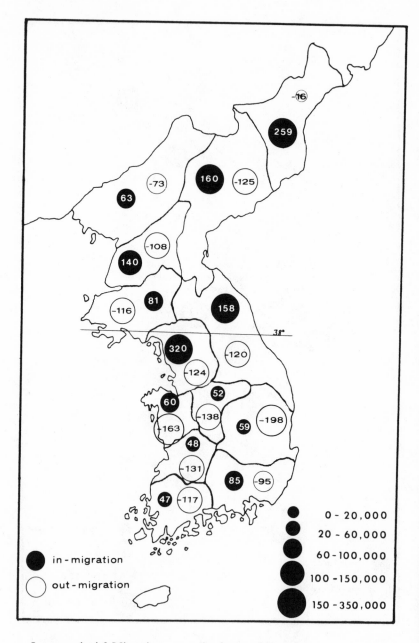

3. Interprovincial Migration, 1940 (in thousands)

SOURCE: Based on Trewartha and Zelinsky, "Population Distribution and
Change," fig. 11.

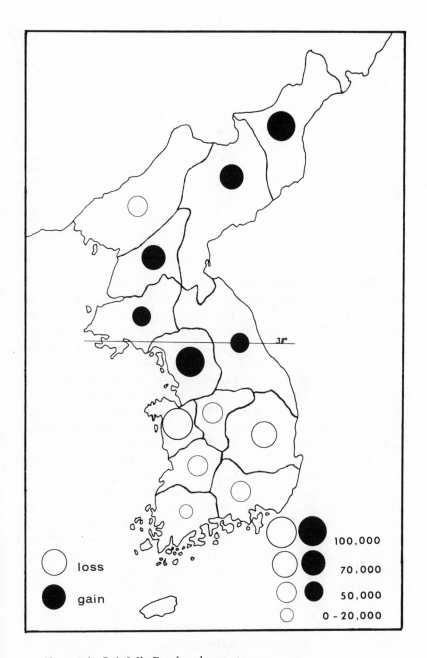

4. Changes in Gainfully Employed, 1930 to 1940

SOURCE: Based on Trewartha and Zelinsky, "Population Distribution and Change," fig. 9.

TABLE 7

POPULATION INFLUX, SOUTH KOREA, OCTOBER 1945 TO DECEMBER 1947

Origin of Influx	Number of Returnees	Returnees as Percent of South Korean Population*
North Korea†	859,930	5.4%
Manchuria	304,391	1.9
Japan	1,110,972	7.0
China	71,611	0.5
Other	33,917	0.2

SOURCE: Derived from *Chosŏn kyŏngje nyŏnbo, 1948,* p. III-19, using official USAMGIK repatriation figures.

* Using an estimate of 15,800,000 for population of Korea south of thirty-eighth parallel, May 1945.

† 388,694 termed refugees from north Korea, rest (60%) returning to homes in southern Korea.

individuals naturally differed in terms of occupation, status, and class.[84] The vast majority were peasants who, through loss of land and the pressures of surplus population, left their native residences.[85] Their loss of land or economic utility, or their misfortune in being mobilized into conscripted work details, had social as well as economic disadvantages. In Korea, as in other peasant societies, the possession of land or the right to work the land placed a person above those who engaged in wage labor in industry. To lose land in Korea only to end up working in mines in Japan thus added status loss to economic loss. Many Koreans, particularly those who were abroad for only a short time, or for less than one generation, returned with severe status and property losses and deep grievances. They became ready recruits for those who called for dividing up the land and ousting former colonial officials; many of the latter were instrumental in dispatching Koreans abroad in the first place. In general, the significance of the growing numbers of Koreans employed in industry in Korea and elsewhere during the colonial period was not that a new proletariat had been created, but that peasants in new work circumstances had developed a new awareness of themselves, and a sense of their marginality. Or as Eric Wolf puts it:

> It is probably not so much the growth of an industrial proletariate as such which produces revolutionary activity, as the development of an industrial work force still closely geared to life in the villages.[86]

Koreans returning from abroad and from north Korea were also directly affected by political ideologies. Those who returned from Japan tended to be influenced by leftist ideology, because the Japanese Communist Party was one of the few groups in Japan that was sympathetic to Korean liberation and called attention to the abysmal conditions of Koreans in Japan. Some 350,000 returnees from Japan went to north Korea after liberation, even though many of them had been southerners originally.[87] Those returning to south Korea tended to congregate in North and South Kyŏngsang provinces. The influx from north Korea in the fall of 1945 and early 1946 was a mixture of dispossessed classes with grievances against the Left and peasants returning from labor in northern industry.[88] Communists were also quite active in the Korean population in Manchuria, affecting worker and peasant elements. Returnees from Manchuria, however, also included the element that occupied an intermediate position between the Japanese and the resident Chinese, including bureaucrats in the Manchukuo administration and commercial elements who followed in the Japanese wake; it also included the displaced and *lumpen* elements who were camp followers of Japanese troops or worked in the agencies of public order and antiguerrilla activities. Still, the majority of Koreans returning from Manchuria were displaced peasants. In a single generation, millions of them had been pushed from the land by alien colonial and economic forces into the unfamiliar and inhospitable circumstances of industry.

Mobilization and Revolt

It is much easier to lay out figures on mobilization and population displacement than it is to explain how such aggregate growth and change affected the individuals concerned. This is particularly true of peasants, among whom change often remains unarticulated, and sometimes beyond the grasp of scholarly inquiry. As Leon Trotsky put it, however, peasants have a way of voting with their feet. And the sounds of their footsteps were heard throughout the liberation period in Korea—running to take over the estates of landlords, smashing land records and county offices, fighting pitched battles with police, and organizing for political action.

It is generally recognized that pronounced growth and differentiation in peasant economies and rapid growth or uprooting of peasant populations are central factors in breaking peasant ties to tradition and stimulating new forms of political participation. Within American political science, such change has come to be called "social mobilization," and in the following paragraphs will briefly examine the essentials of this process.

In Karl Deutsch's definition, social mobilization is "the process in which major clusters of old social, economic, and psychological commitments are eroded or broken and people become available for new patterns of socialization and behavior." It involves "change of residence, of occupation, of social setting, of face-to-face associates, of institutions, of roles. . . ." Social mobilization is a two-stage phenomenon: the first stage forces people from the land, breaks old habits, provides new life chances, and may be plotted by reference to a variety of indicators—industrialization, urbanization, increases in literacy—which do not necessarily grow or change at the same *rate*, but do grow in the same *direction*. The second stage is less easy to plot or specify; here Deutsch postulates the political effects of the first stage. The cumulative impact of the changes in the first stage somehow affects the political behavior of the individual. In countries in which the mass of the population has remained largely outside the framework of political activity, "social mobilization brings with it an expansion of the politically relevant strata of the population." People are displaced, impoverished, disoriented, made marginal, influenced, coerced, made to vote; and "the increasing numbers of the mobilized population . . . tend to translate themselves, albeit with a time lag, into increased political participation."[89]

Samuel Huntington writes that people swept up in the social mobilization process "become increasingly aware of themselves as groups and of their interests and claims in relation to other groups." "Most striking" is "the increased consciousness, coherence, organization, and action which [social mobilization] produces in many social forces." It gives rise "to enhanced aspirations and expectations which, if unsatisfied, galvanize individuals and groups into politics."[90] Of particular interest for the Korean situation and its land relations is Huntington's suggestion that "social mobilization . . . increases awareness of inequality and presumably resentment of it. The influx of new ideas calls into question the legitimacy of the old distribution. . . . Hence, social mobilization turns the traditional economic inequality into a stimulus to rebellion."[91] It is not generally recognized that Huntington has here linked a more or less quantifiable concept from the American school of political development, social mobilization, with the critical question of Marxian analysis, consciousness as an agent of social change and social conflict. Huntington is saying that increases in communications, population displacement, and class differentiation caused by industrialization work a transformation upon classes and groups in inferior positions, making them aware of their interests in changing "the old distribution." Or, in Marxian terms, objective interest is translated into subjective interest and a class "in itself" becomes a class "for itself." In any case, we have gone beyond Deutsch's passive and instrumental formulation in which socially mobilized people "become available" for new forms of political participation (on the assumption that "others" must bring such people into participation), to a more dynamic formulation indicative of changes *within* the class that stimulate new and different political behavior.

Marx used the term "class" not as a static, descriptive category, but as an analytical one that expressed a dynamic relationship between those at different places in the social hierarchy.[92] This is evident in the distinction he made between a class "in itself" and a class "for itself." The former represents an observer's judgment that one class exists in a structural relationship with other classes and that each has an objective class interest. The objective interest of a disadvantaged class, according to Marx, is to overthrow advantaged classes. But activity toward that end does not occur until a class recognizes its interest and becomes a class "for itself." Or, in Ralf Dahrendorf's useful reformulation, "classes do not constitute themselves as such until they participate in political conflicts as organized groups."[93] Thus the conversion of objective interests into subjective ones is a definition of the development of political consciousness.[94]

For Marx, the development of class consciousness was contingent on relative ease of communications between members of a class. He was well aware that oppressed classes could exist for centuries without attempting to change their fate. Robert Michels phrases Marx's point this way: "it is not the simple *existence* of oppressive conditions, but it is the *recognition of these conditions by the oppressed*, which in the course of history has constituted the prime factor of class struggles."[95] Not just recognition, we might add, but also a perception of the chance for change. Marx thought that the proletariat could become a class for itself under the conditions of modern factory production, where workers were brought together and, through ease of communications, could become conscious of their collective interests. Peasants, however, existed apart from each other; therefore, their objective grievances could not become collective ones. In Marx's famous image, the French peasantry was "formed by simple addition of homologous magnitudes, much as potatoes in a sack form a sack of potatoes." Stated differently:

> In so far as millions of families live under economic conditions of existence that separate their mode of life, their interests and their culture from those of other classes, and put them in hostile opposition to the latter, they form a class. In so far as there is merely a local interconnection among these small-holding peasants, and the

identity of their interests begets no community, no national bond and no political organization among them, they do not form a class.[96]

This is, among other things, a statement on the problems of communicating among peasants and the consequent problems of stimulating political consciousness and organization. It is an accurate statement under conditions where peasants are not thrown together by external processes. But peasant interests are not always to be condemned to latency. As Teodor Shanin points out, "the peasantry would appear as a social entity of comparatively low 'classness,' which rises in crisis situations."[97] The "classness" appears in situations that create among peasants homogeneity, solidarity, collectivity, an identification of narrow individual interests with the common good, and a horizontal rather than vertical direction of those interests.

Marx notes that "the advance of industry . . . replaces the isolation of laborers, due to competition, by their revolutionary combination, due to association."[98] Unfortunately for Marx's world view, however, a revolutionary combination occurs only rarely and depends not only on a concentration of laborers but also on the adaptability and resiliency of the owning classes. In Korea in the 1930s and early 1940s, masses of peasants were brought together in industries of significant size and concentration. Our assumption would be that such concentration would break down a peasant's narrow focus on his own family, clan, and native village and enhance a horizontal direction of peasant interests. The possibility of a common struggle deriving from common interests would replace a family-based struggle for subsistence rights and sustenance. Peasants that formerly fought with each other for marginal advantage, and that were tied to richer peasants and landlords through varieties of crisscrossing associations (through tradition, custom, or clan), would come to a broader sense of their situation and its remedies. An industrial clock would replace the older agrarian cycle, which had demanded a tyrannous routine only at various points in the year and made peasants extremely careful in the husbanding of scarce resources (it was this that made peasants "conservative," not a putative peasant mentality). Likewise, the former emphasis on possessing a small plot of land as the basic security for the family—also imparting a conservative bias—would lessen as peasants lost their land and wound up in industry. And the weaker the tie to the land or the possibility of owning land, the more former peasants would be available for collective movements.

The possibility of upward mobility also affects such a situation.[99] If a peasant tenant or smallholder is even slightly successful, his interests will be directed vertically; he will identify his interests with those above him. Subsistence peasants will often make any sacrifice to gain on fellow peasants. A rapid fall in social and economic status, along with bleak prospects for improvement, however, such as occurred in colonial Korea, would presumably place an emphasis on collective rather than individual mobility.

The nature of the landed class affects all of these considerations. If mobilized peasants were to return to a native place where landlords were willing to give up control of the land in the general interest of maintaining dominance by other means—that is, were these to be our "type B" landlords—they might find their grievances quickly satisfied with a new plot of land. If, on the other hand, landlords were to seek to hold on to land and to rule through political, coercive means rather than through economic means (which provide incentives for peasants to return to cultivation), a volatile, rebellious situation would likely develop. Jeffrey Paige's model of brittle landlords and peasants who had become proletarians would also apply, the result presumably being revolution.[100] Korea in the 1940s unfortunately spites this neat model, however, because the result was so mixed. Some landlords had moved toward commerce and industry, toward becoming "type B" landlords, while others had not. Peasants in some regions (especially those in the Kyŏngsang provinces) had moved out of their native homes *en masse*, while others remained tied to the land. Some regions were barely touched at all by the processes of change. Still, this approach has merit in its focusing attention not on a presumed "peasant mentality," but on peasants as responsive to interest and conflict situations that vary greatly, on individual versus collective mobility, and on the nature of the landed class.

Finally, the existence of political organization that appeals to and directs peasant grievances would be an indispensable ally, one that can skew the preceding model in various ways. Analyses of the situation in China have shown how political organization emerged in regions where landlord control was weak or had been broken and directed peasants in a multistage process leading toward authentic peasant revolution. Mao Tse-tung and his allies brought the peasants from antitraitor movements, to "speak bitterness meetings," to settling accounts with landlords, and finally to the organization of peasant unions and local administrations; they used a mixture of incentives and a set of procedures that utilized a dialectic between each stage and between old and new, never letting peasants slide back to the old. The prime role of organization, as William Hinton puts it, was to provide "a concept of justice linked to the possible."[101] Thus, when speaking of peasant activity, organization may not be the determining factor, but it is certainly necessary.

Conclusions

During Korea's colonial period, masses of peasants migrated away from their villages. Most were young, most were poor, most were aggrieved. At the end of the world war, when these masses returned, they were still young, still poor, still aggrieved. But they were no longer quite peasants and yet not quite workers; they were somewhere in between. They had been cast into roles as workers, miners, soldiers; but more important, they had been exposed to the world outside the village. It surely had not occurred to them before they migrated that human society could take different form than that which they knew. By 1945, however, their vision was not so limited. For peasant-workers, the end of the war brought a new beginning. For radical organizers, it brought a mass of new raw material.

The Japanese left Korea with many of the trappings of the modern world when they withdrew in 1945. They left it with a relatively advanced transportation network, and with links to the world market system. They left its population with modern skills. They bequeathed to the ancient homogeneities of Korea the physical essentials of modern national integration, not the least of which was a highly articulated bureaucracy. They left a highly dispersed population—one that had been mobilized "from below," through the host of processes set in motion by the entry of the market and the beginnings of industrialization, and "from above," through the conscious, forced policies of the war years. But most significant, the Japanese simply left Korea; the colonial overlordship dissolved abruptly in 1945, and the pressure that had been building in Korea was unleashed.

Yet the fundamental fact to remember about the colonial period is not the degree of Japanese-fostered change, although that change was substantial enough. The point of note is that the changes did not run their course. Peasants were not torn from the land, destroyed as a class, and integrated into industry (as in England, for example, with the enclosures and the emergence of factory production); instead they were introduced to industry and then spewed back upon Korean villages. Landlords did not turn into commercial and industrial entrepreneurs, but remained to varying degrees somewhere between entrepreneurship and tradition. Korean bureaucrats were not integrated into the career patterns of modern, or rational-legal bureaucracy so much as used as ethnic interlopers in a foreign administration, setting them against their Japanese superiors and their own Korean brethren.

Even in the Korean resistance, both nationalist and communist, fissures developed, setting one faction against another with effects that long outlasted the colony itself. Finally, the abrupt denouement of the war shattered and sundered even that grandest of Japanese creations, the incipient transnational unit carved out of northeast Asia.

The end of the war divided the Korean nation itself, into northern and southern halves. In the process, railroad, road, and sea networks were severed, trailing off into wilderness or emptied of purpose. The Japanese defeat thus destroyed an integral and delicate structure that had linked metropole to periphery. The southern half of Korea was left with a disabled economy and chaotic politics that could only fester until new associations were formed. The colonial bureaucracy, for instance, remained at its center in Seoul, with its ponderous but effective agencies and with only half of a nation to worry about. The northern half remained integrated with Manchuria for a time after liberation, but its ties to the south and to the east were cut. Thus was set up the contingency that played upon liberated Korea in the years between 1945 and 1950: would the linkages be intra-Korean, in a unified peninsula; or would they run north to Moscow or Peking, in a socialist transnational system, or to Tokyo and Washington, in another transnational system?

Thus, whether we speak of the Korean nation or of the class structure, the great shifting and reintegration occasioned by the Japanese defeat had critical consequences. Korea had been put through a ringer, but it was a "modern" one, with colonialism, industrialization, war, and great power conflict loosing political and social forces upon the peninsula that tore Korean society apart. It is this context of abortive, fractured "development" that must be the touchstone for evaluating the politics of liberated Korea and the origins of the Korean War.

Chapter Three

AUGUST TO SEPTEMBER 1945:
REVOLUTION AND REACTION

> Evils which are patiently endured when they seem inevitable become intolerable when once the idea of escape from them is suggested.
>
> _Alexis de Tocqueville_

> Human history is like palaentology. Owing to a certain judicial blindness even the best intelligences fail to see things which lie in front of their noses. Later, when the moment has arrived, we are surprised to find traces everywhere of what we failed to see.
>
> _Karl Marx_

> There is a Korean word, _sinparam_, that expresses the pathos, the inner joy, of a person moved to action not by coercion but by his own volition. _Param_ is the sound of the wind; if a person is wafted along on this wind, songs burst from his lips and his legs dance with joy. A _sinparam_ is a strange wind that billows in the hearts of people who have freed themselves from oppression, regained their freedom, and live in a society of mutual trust. This word, redolent with a shamanistic mystique, has a talisman-like appeal for Koreans.
>
> _Chŏng Kyŏng-mo_

T HE war that ended in 1945 was a world war, with worldwide conse-
quences. Just as the prosecution of the war consumed the passions of people everywhere, so its end released forces that touched people everywhere and held a common fate for a diverse world. The unprecedented dislocation and jumbling of relationships that followed in the war's wake made people's lives of a common piece. The exhilaration of a resistance fighter in France was echoed by a guerrilla in Vietnam. The presentiments of doom of a Quisling in Norway touched puppets in Manchuria. Awakened peoples determined that the past was past, and a new era dawned; as reborn people sought to forge a new fate, a revolutionary contagion swept the earth.

Emperor Hirohito's rescript declaring the Japanese surrender was broadcast in Korea on August 15, 1945, provoking spontaneous, emotional celebrations; and Liberation Day became the most important day in the lives of an entire generation of Koreans. In this atmosphere of exhilaration, a revolutionary era began that did not end for years, making liberation not just a day, but an entire period of great flux, an era of mass participation virtually unprecedented in Korean history and unequaled since. The demise of the Japanese brought Koreans to rediscover their heritage—their history, their culture, their language, their rights as a people. If in this awakening the Koreans asserted their rights in ways that seemed excessive to others, that made them no different from Frenchmen, Greeks, or Vietnamese. In August 1945, Korean revelry and self-assertion came as a breath of fresh air after decades of discipline.

We would make a mistake, however, to see in the bacchic celebration of Korean manumission only an aimless pursuit of the moment. Those who danced naked on table tops[1] woke up the next morning with sober concerns. For some, these were the positive concerns of building new institutions and a new nation; for others they were apprehensive fears of the new order. From this milieu emerged a politics of crisis to which conflict is intrinsic. Strong forces for change, symbolized and led by the supporters of a "people's republic" in north and south, clashed with less strong but critically placed opponents of change. The former augured revolution, which may be defined for our purposes here as "a violent, fundamental, and abrupt change of incumbent elites, status and class relations, institutions, values, symbols, and myths," or more simply, "an act of destruction willed against a whole ruling class."[2] The latter stood for all that is implied by the term "counterrevolution."

The End of the Japanese Colony

A curious reciprocity in the master-subject relationship of colonialism is evident in the following statement made by an unidentified Japanese: "[This] was too unbearable for us . . . Koreans treat us as if we were foreigners."[3] It is essential for his dominance that the master establish the fundamental separateness of the subject from himself: the subject is different, he is inferior, he is base and given to violence, he cannot run his own affairs. Otherwise, what possible justification exists for the colonial relationship? Such dehumanizing illusions are necessary for most people to dominate others, since few can tolerate oppression without reference to rationalization or to a higher purpose. No means yet devised can separate the subject from his humanity, however, and in some recess of the mind, the master recognizes this and the knowledge never leaves him. The nagging questions remain: what human being would stand for such arrangements? What might the subject do to the master were he free? What if the tables turn? The answer to such questions is clear, thus in the master's mind, two images of the subject coexist. One is of the passive, docile, obedient subject who is prevented from lifting a finger in his own defense; the other is of that subject free to take righteous retribution. The latter image strikes terror in the heart. This is the one small victory that every colonial subject wins; by the smallest gesture of sullen compliance he can set the image in the master's mind. The subject succeeds in projecting a sense of his remnant humanity and a threat of potency that may be quite beyond his real capabilities.[4]

Therefore, although the Japanese colony in Korea had by 1945 nearly four decades of consolidation behind it, and although the Korean population had only the narrowest forms of resistance left to it and could not in itself threaten Japanese armed force, Japanese in Korea experienced "great uneasiness" and "terror" at the thought of being caught in a liberated Korea in August 1945.[5] The assimilationist policies of the previous twenty-five years had not borne fruit; Koreans remained incorrigibly Korean and they held in their hearts an enmity for Japan that would long outlive the Japanese regime. Some 30,000 prisoners in colonial jails, a majority of them political, or "thought" cases, offered their own testimony to the depth of Korean resistance and the failure of Japanese policy.[6]

The Japanese thus had good reason to fear Korean reprisal. Accordingly, when the surrender was only a few days away, colonial authorities began to approach influential Koreans about an interim administration to preserve law and order and to allow the Japanese to leave Korea unscathed. On August 9 four Japanese high officials met with Song Chin-u at an unidentified Japanese home.[7] They told Song that they hoped he would organize an "administrative committee" to preserve the peace and prepare for Korean independence. He refused this entreaty and several others in the days from August 10 to 13. The officials told Song he could have access to newspapers, radio, and other means of communication, and to various transportation facilities, if he would just cooperate. Song's supporters say he refused the Japanese offers because (1) he realized that any Korean administration would have to await the sanction of incoming Allied forces and (2) he believed the Korean Provisional Government (KPG) in Chungking was the legitimate government of Korea. They also say Song did not want to give the Japanese the benefit of cooperation in their time of need.[8] Another source, however, indicates that Song told the Japanese he was too ill to accept such responsibilities.[9] It is likely that Song, because of his wealth and because of the pressures to collaborate that the Japanese placed on him throughout the war, could not have avoided the taint of collaboration had he worked with the colonial administration at this point. In the face of Song's continuing opposition, the Japanese tried on August 14 to reach him through his close associate, Kim Chun-yŏn. But Kim would do nothing without Song, thus the Japanese were forced to turn elsewhere.[10]

The Japanese next approached Yŏ Un-hyŏng. Yŏ, aware of the earlier proposition made to Song Chin-u, heard on August 14 that the Japanese would ask him to form a peace-keeping administration.[11] He determined to accept such an offer and did so when he met with Endō Ruysaku, the Governor-General's Secretary for Political Affairs, in the early morning hours on August 15.[12] Endō reportedly told Yŏ, "Japan is now defeated. It will be announced today or tomorrow. At that time we must keep the peace. From now on, the preservation of our lives depends on this." Before he agreed, Yŏ made the Japanese accept five demands: (1) Release all political and economic prisoners immediately throughout the nation; (2) Guarantee food provisions for the next three months; (3) Absolutely no interference with the maintenance of peace or with Korean activities for the sake of independence; (4) Absolutely no interference with the training of students and youths; (5) Absolutely no interference with the training of workers and peasants.[13]

These demands went far beyond what the Japanese had hoped for —indeed they raised the specter of just what the colonial master wanted to avoid—but there were few choices left on the morning of August 15. Oda Yasuma, an aide of the Governor-General, later said that Yŏ had been approached because his "somewhat radical views" made him popular with students. Since the Japanese very much feared Korea's students, they hoped that Yŏ's cooperation might help rein in student demonstrations. Oda also said that on August 15 the Japanese expected the Russians eventually to occupy all of Korea; placing a "somewhat radical" Korean out front might aid them in gaining Russian cooperation.[14] The Japanese followed similar policies at the end of the war in Southeast Asia, sponsoring radicals and nationalists who might be hoped to adopt an independent, thus anti-Western, stance. The assumption that such men would not only work for independence but would also uphold Japanese interests, however, proved false, in Southeast Asia as in Korea.

THE COMMITTEE FOR THE PREPARATION OF KOREAN INDEPENDENCE

Shortly after Yŏ left his early morning meeting with Endō, he gathered several leaders at his home in Unni-chŏng to discuss the agreement he had made with Endō and to prepare for subsequent organizing activities.[15] Yŏ asked rhetorically if "peace-keeping" was the only concern of Koreans; he advocated a much broader political movement lest pro-Japanese Koreans seize power. Such a movement, he felt, should act as an interim administrative authority, pending the entry of the Allied armies and the return of exiles from abroad.[16] Thus he and the men present decided to form the *Chosŏn kŏn'guk chunbi wiwŏnhoe*, or Committee for the Preparation of Korean Independence (CPKI).

Yŏ had apparently been thinking about forming such a body for several days prior to the surrender, for on August 11 he had drawn up a draft of a four-point agreement that he hoped to submit to the incoming Allied forces. It expressed Korea's gratitude for Allied assistance in gaining liberation from the Japanese, but stressed that Korea must be for the Koreans. The Allies must observe "strict neutrality" in Korean internal political affairs. This, he hoped, would avoid the problems of *sadae*[17] and the use of foreign influence in domestic political struggles. On the same day Yŏ directed one of his lieutenants to draft a Korean Declaration of Independence, to be based on the one issued in 1919, but to include specific advocacy of democracy and an ousting of pro-Japanese collaborators. Otherwise, there would be an "absolutely equal reconciliation" of Koreans at home and abroad.[18]

The demands in these two documents for immediate Korean independence without foreign interference and for preventing collaborators with Japan from exercising power enunciated two themes that struck a resonant note in Korean history and that came to dominate political discourse in the liberation period. Both themes harked back to the period before the Japanese Annexation, when Korean groups like the *Ilchin-hoe* had aided and abetted the Japanese takeover. In 1945 many Koreans worried that similar groups might make an unprincipled alliance with foreign power and thus frustrate Korean independence once again. Koreans like Yŏ Un-hyŏng and his supporters tended to link Koreans who had been in league with the Japanese war effort in the 1940s with traitors at the time of the Annexation. They were determined that the suffering of anti-Japanese patriots and revolutionaries at home and abroad would not go unrequited after liberation.[19] Although they were not specific about the fate that would await collaborators, they felt that allowing them to maintain power would represent gross injustice.

Events followed quickly upon each other in the next couple of days, making it difficult to present in a precise chronology. CPKI headquarters were set up in Kyedong, and "from daybreak [every day] notables from the worlds of culture, thought, economics, and education continuously streamed in and out."[20] Teams of propagandists were sent to the countryside under the general direction of Yi Yŏ-sŏng and Kim

Se-yong. On August 16 some 5,000 Koreans heard Yŏ call for the unity of all Korean groups and urge that there be no bloodletting. An Chae-hong, vice-chairman of the CPKI, asked Koreans to protect Japanese citizens and property.[21] These rather moderate speeches seemed in line with what the Japanese expected of Yŏ and An, a co-operative relationship for maintaining the peace. The relationship was emphasized by a picture in the August 16 *Maeil sinbo* (Daily News) of Yŏ standing with Endō.[22]

That relationship deteriorated rapidly, however, with the release of political and economic prisoners throughout the country on August 16. Since many of the dedicated, nonapostate communists had remained in jail until the end of Japanese rule, the prisoner release quickly added a radical tinge to CPKI activities. It also added a patriotic aura, and made it clear that the CPKI was not simply a Japanese-sponsored peace-keeping body.[23] These released prisoners quickly became active in organizing CPKI branches (*kŏn'guk chibang chibu*) and other groups throughout the nation. It seems that a total of about 16,000 prisoners were freed in southern Korea; some 10,000 were released in Seoul alone, 1,600 in Taegu, and so on.[24] Moreover, about 15,000 Korean soldiers were demobilized from the Japanese Army, many of them students and youths who had been forcibly conscripted.[25] To this corps of people may be added unknown thousands of young people released from Japanese youth groups, labor camps, and work details. Thus within days, tens of thousands of Koreans were free and available for peace-keeping duties and political mobilization.

On August 17 Koreans throughout the country learned formally of the establishment of the CPKI and five days later saw a long list of the Koreans leading it. But the news had traveled far and wide before that by informal communications: couriers, word-of-mouth, telephone calls. CPKI branches and associated organizations sprouted everywhere overnight. Some 145 branches existed in north and south Korea by the end of August.[26] That was but one aspect of the explosion of participation that struck Korea in these halcyon days, however. A heretofore quiescent population, controlled by a dictatorship with seeming ease for several decades, suddenly leapt into political action and organization. Gerald Brenan's eloquent description of Spanish peasant anarchists in Andalusia fits liberated Korea as well:

> An extraordinary ferment, as sudden and apparently as causeless as a religious revival, swept over the country districts. In the fields, in the farms and wayside inns only one subject was discussed and always with intense seriousness and fervour. In the midday rests and at night, after supper, groups were formed to listen to a laborer

reading aloud from one of the Anarchist papers. Then came speeches and comments. It was what they had known and felt all their lives. How could they shut their ears to it?[27]

In these heady days it was possible to believe that truth and justice would triumph, indeed *had* triumphed. The foreign usurper had been cast down: did not the millennium beckon?

Such political activity does not, of course, develop overnight. In Korea it existed in latent form during the previous decade and was made particularly acute by the existence of a communist movement and workers' and peasants' unions and the intensive penetration of Korean society at all levels by Japanese-sponsored patriotic and anti-communist groups. Thus by 1945 millions of Koreans had had some experience with modern forms of political mobilization.[28]

On August 16 several CPKI leaders including Chang Kwŏn and Ch'oe Yong-dal organized a *Kŏn'guk ch'ŏngnyŏn ch'iandae* (CPKI youth peace preservation corps) with its headquarters at P'ungmun School in Seoul. They mobilized some 2,000 youths and students to direct traffic and keep the peace and sent about 100 more to the countryside to organize local *ch'iandae*.[29] The central body also gave its sanction to the functioning of many other local peace-keeping groups, going by the names of *haktodae, ch'ŏngnyŏndae, chawidae*, and *nodongdae*.[30] This was preeminently a youth and student movement, often led by judo and physical education teachers.[31] *Ch'iandae* headquarters later stated that 162 branches were organized throughout the country, by representatives sent from the central body and by local groups later sanctioned by the center. On September 2 the headquarters in Seoul was officially designated as the Bureau of Peace Preservation (*Kŏn'guk ch'ianbu*), with Chang Kwŏn as bureau chief.[32] Other leaders included Chŏng Sang-yun, Chang Il-hong, and Song Pyŏng-mu.

The formal organization of the peace-keeping groups suggests coherence and direction that rarely existed in the harried days after liberation. Certainly the groups that came together under the bureau umbrella were eclectic. Both groups that later allied with the Left and those that later allied with the Right functioned as peace-keeping bodies. For example, the *Chosŏn hakpyŏng tongmaeng* (Korean student-soldier's league) joined the *ch'iandae* on September 1; its initial slogans had no political content other than vague patriotic exhortations, but it eventually moved to the Right.[33] The spontaneity and lack of central coordination with which many of these groups sprang up is evident in Richard Kim's reminiscence of his native home in north Korea after liberation, where his father was selected to chair the local peace-keeping committee primarily because he was perceived to have resisted the Japanese to the end.[34]

To what extent did the *ch'iandae* succeed in supplanting the existing colonial police force? We will have occasion to explore this question in greater detail in later chapters; the success of the *ch'iandae* varied widely from region to region. Taking the nation as the unit, however, it seems fair to say that by the end of August *ch'iandae* units had made considerable progress in forging an alternative police force. This was more true of the north, where Soviet support for local peace-keeping organizations and for activities directed against the colonial force led to a mass exodus of Japanese and Korean police. In the south the Japanese maintained tight control of cities like Seoul, Pusan, Kaesŏng, and Ch'unch'ŏn and ports like Inch'ŏn and Mokp'o, which were essential for the Japanese retreat from Manchuria and northern Korea and return to Japan. Thus *ch'iandae* activities in the south flourished for the most part in provincial regions that were no longer important to the Japanese.

But even in the south *ch'iandae* supplanted the Korean element of the colonial police force on a wholesale basis. An official source reported that while some 90 percent of Japanese police officers remained at their posts from August 15 to September 8, in the same period about 80 percent of the Korean officers stopped working, were ousted, or simply fled.[35] Since Koreans constituted about 50 percent of the colonial police force, this represented a significant diminution of police potency. Furthermore, the majority of policemen who remained at their posts did little more in the pursuit of law and order than protect their own persons and interests.

Thus the *ch'iandae* did play an important role in maintaining the peace in August of 1945. It is a tribute to the individuals who staffed these groups and to the Korean people themselves that so little violence occurred. Even the Japanese had to admit that the *ch'iandae* performed admirably.[36] The *New York Times* later reported, "Korean sources estimate that thirty-five Koreans have been killed by Japanese police since August 15, but not one Japanese has been killed by a Korean as far as is known."[37] There were, however, reports indicating a widespread pattern of violence against the Korean element of the colonial police force. Korean policemen were beaten and thrown in jail and had their homes occupied or wrecked in many towns in the Seoul/Inch'ŏn/Suwŏn area, for example. In some cases, these activities were attributed to *ch'iandae*, and in others, simply to spontaneous outrage on the part of villagers.[38] The general level of violence would have been much higher, though, had not Korean policemen and other colonial officials decided that discretion was the better part of valor.

Many of them simply fled or went into hiding. On the whole, Koreans did very well in containing violence in the highly volatile atmosphere after liberation, especially when compared to similar situations elsewhere, as in France.[39]

A number of military and quasi-military organizations appeared in Korea in the days and weeks after August 15, with soldiers and officers demobilized from the Japanese Army playing a major role. It is likely that whole units left the army *en bloc* and simply adopted a new name. After the American entry in September, these organizations split into myriad private armies and youth groups. During August, however, most of them were under the CPKI wing. Some acted as *ch'iandae*, but the majority were part of the *Chosŏn kukkun chunbidae* (National Preparatory Army—NPA), a military organization formed by officers and soldiers dismissed from the Japanese Army who met on August 17 to plan a way of aiding the CPKI in peace preservation. At the end of the month, the NPA title was adopted and headquarters were established in Myŏngdong in downtown Seoul. The leaders were Yi Hyŏk-ki, formerly a second lieutenant in a Japanese Army student-soldier's brigade (*hakpyŏng*), and Pak Sŭng-han, who later went to north Korea and became an Air Force vice-commander.[40] In the provinces, CPKI and NPA branch leadership was sometimes conterminous. Thus, in North Kyŏngsang, O Tŏk-jun led both organizations and had under him some 700 men.[41] Although little information exists on the NPA, it appears to have done some remarkable organization. According to one official (and hostile) source, the NPA established detachments in every province in south Korea, enlisted some 60,000 recruits, and gave 15,000 of them at least a modicum of training; thus it "had stronger organization than any other unofficial military body."[42]

The most impressive organizational effort of all, however, was the establishment in August of embryonic mass organizations of workers, peasants, youths, and women. The Japanese truly opened a Pandora's box when they acquiesced to Yŏ Un-hyŏng's demand that they not interfere with mass mobilization, for within weeks, these unions and mass organizations emerged on a wide scale, most of them associated with the Left. Communists and leftists had achieved some success in organizing workers and peasants in the 1930s; moreover, the introduction of modern mass politics into Korea was largely the work of leftists, who took their cues from counterparts in the Soviet Union, China, and Japan. Conservative Koreans, of course, left mass politics to others for the most part. Factory owners and landlords made few appeals that would be likely to win the allegiance of workers and peasants. At a deeper level, many conservatives simply failed to recognize the importance of mass organization. When the conservative Korean in 1945 thought about political organization, he envisioned a council of well-educated notables who would gather in Seoul and make the important decisions. When he thought about workers and peasants, he thought of control and thus turned to police and bureaucratic organs, not to unions and other mass organizations.

Most of the mass organizations became visible in November and December 1945 when representatives from the provinces met in Seoul and formed national organizations designed to unify provincial bodies at all levels. From that time on, the organization of workers and peasants was directed more from the top. But in August and September it had a spontaneous quality, having come into being through the efforts and commitment of the general population.

Shortly after August 15, workers' unions (*nodong chohap*)[43] were organized in factories and workplaces all over Korea. Many of them succeeded in taking over plants and factories from Japanese and Korean owners. In some instances, *chohap* members actually ran the factories, while in others, they solicited bids from potential managers and then contracted out managerial positions to those with the requisite expertise.[44] An American officer who subsequently had access to Labor Department records said that "virtually all of the larger factories" were taken over in these ways. Koreans said that no labor movement in the world ever grew so rapidly.[45] *Nodong chohap* were particularly strong in South Kyŏngsang Province where workers "freely managed the factories" from August to November 1945.[46] Where unions did not succeed in actually taking over workplaces, they sometimes called strikes and work slowdowns; a noteworthy example was the strike at the Kyŏngsŏng Textile Factory in Seoul begun on August 31.[47]

Peasant unions (*nongmin chohap*)[48] also developed in these weeks. When the Americans occupied the provinces in the fall of 1945, they found such unions everywhere. Some were quite radical and quickly tried to dispossess Japanese and Korean landlords, while others were moderate and worked for a rationalization of tenancy relationships, rents, and so on. Many peasant unions also organized rice collection, storage, and distribution during the autumn harvest. By the end of 1945, peasant unions were probably stronger in terms of sheer numbers than any other organizational form in Korea.

Worker and peasant unions had antecedents in organization work done in the 1920s and 1930s. Scattered workers' unions were organized in the aftermath of the March First Movement in 1919. Then in 1924 Koreans who had been deeply influenced by the success of the Bolsheviks in Russia organized the *Chosŏn no-nong tongmaeng* (Korean

Worker-Peasant League) in hopes of uniting disparate unions in the localities. In 1926 and 1927 this league split into two organizations, the *Chosŏn nodong ch'ong tongmaeng* (General League of Korean Workers) and the *Chosŏn nongmin ch'ong tongmaeng* (General League of Korean Peasants).[49] The workers' league was particularly successful in initiating a three-month-long strike in Wŏnsan in 1929. Workers' unions were forced underground, however, after the Japanese suppressed a strike in Ch'ŏngjin that had been organized as a protest against the Manchurian Incident in 1931. Peasant unions sometimes claimed to be successors to the *Tonghak*;[50] but more important in establishing their legitimacy was their relative success in leading tenancy disputes in the late 1920s and early 1930s. Red Peasant Unions (*Chŏksaek nongmin chohap*) set down roots in numerous counties throughout Korea and provided organization that could be revived in 1945.

There seems little question that in August and September 1945 worker and peasant unions mushroomed in a spontaneous, decentralized manner. There is no evidence that any central organization was behind union growth. When leaders in Seoul finally established national mass organizations and central offices in November and December, the whole process had a *post hoc* quality, like cooks removing cakes from an oven and putting the icing on. In truth, these leaders lagged behind the mass movement, to put it in Marxist jargon. They themselves said that *chohap* in the provinces "came to be organized on a broad scale in a natural and dispersed fashion," that they had "developed separately," in "scattered," "local," "unplanned" fashion.[51] Since by acknowledging all this these leaders did not place themselves in a particularly good light, there is reason to accept their analysis.

The successes of the various groups discussed above occurred for the most part in the provinces. But it is nearly impossible to obtain useful, detailed information on provincial developments in August and early September. Only after the American occupation of the provinces does such material become available. In part, this gap reflects the difficulties of information gathering anywhere under conditions of chaos and confusion accompanying the end of a war. But it also indicates where Korean interests lie. It appears that when Koreans sit down to write about politics, they want to write about Seoul, and they want to write about factions among leaders in Seoul. Thus the investigator finds a fairly complete account in Korean documents of all the factions that made up the CPKI and the groups that came to oppose it and is in effect forced to deal with these accounts. But events in Seoul must be kept in perspective. The CPKI's primary role was to light a spark that set a fire. An analysis of the groups that led the CPKI says very little about the character of the movements in the provinces.

Nonetheless, it is important to understand something of the workings of the CPKI. Two basic factions existed among CPKI leaders in Seoul, although each side was further divided into subfactions of differing political sympathies and loyalties. One faction was loyal to Yŏ Un-hyŏng and was largely noncommunist; the other was made up mostly of communists.[52] Yŏ's faction was based on an organization that he had founded on August 10, 1944, called the *Chosŏn kŏn'guk tongmaeng* (Korean Independence League—known as *Kŏnmaeng* for short).[53] Initial *Kŏnmaeng* leaders included Cho Tong-ho, a former associate of Yŏ's who had gone to China with him in 1914. Others who later joined the group included Kim Se-yong, Yi Man-gyu, and Yi Yŏ-sŏng. The platform of the *Kŏnmaeng* called for independence, expulsion of the Japanese, and a *taedong tan'gyŏl*, or "great union," of the Korean people, excluding only "pro-Japanese" Koreans and "traitors." Yŏ and his supporters claimed that their organization participated in quite a number of anti-Japanese activities in the year before liberation, but there is little independent confirmation that much activity took place. Yŏ also had the loyalty of nationalists, like the Methodist minister Yi Kyu-gap, Ham Sang-hun, and the well-known An Chae-hong; and of communists in the so-called *Sŏngdae-p'a* (Keijo Imperial University group), such as Yi Kang-guk, Ch'oe Yong-dal, and Pak Mun-gyu. These last three had formed a Marxist study group at the university in 1932 and later worked together in labor organization in Wŏnsan.[54] The other major group in the CPKI was the so-called *Changan* faction; it took its name from the Changan Building in Seoul where a meeting was held on August 16 to found a new Korean Communist Party. Leaders of this group included Yi Yŏng, Ch'oe Ik-han, Chŏng Paek, and Hong Nam-p'yo.[55] Most of these were old-line "domestic" communists who had been associated with one faction or another in the late 1920s and 1930s.

The presence of these two main factions is clear in the initial rosters of CPKI leaders, published on August 17 and 22.[56] Yŏ had about eleven of his supporters on the August 22 list, *Changan* had between five and eleven, and another twelve could not be identified.[57] Perhaps ten of these leaders were self-proclaimed communists who held important responsibilities, such as organization and inspection. Does this mean that the CPKI was communist-dominated as of August 22, as has so often been charged?

The answer is a categorical no, since no disciplined, strongly organized communist party existed in Korea at this time. The *Changan* faction dominated little if anything in August 1945. It managed to place a slight majority of its members on the August 22 roster, but its influence had almost dissipated by the end of the month. Moreover, the *Changan* faction was not a disciplined party. In truth, it was little more than a club of intellectuals who spent the next several months trying to figure out what "historical stage" Korea was at in 1945.[58] The individuals who met at the Changan Building on August 16 were simply those old-line communists who happened to be in Seoul (or in Seoul's prisons) on that day. In the rush of liberation, they acted hastily, trying to form a communist party in the absence of numerous other communist leaders. Yet in the end, the *Changan* faction could not even control its own members, let alone anything else.

It is not possible to explain the presence of the numerous communists in the CPKI, and later in the People's Republic, through the perspective of hindsight. We must step out of the categories that Korea's subsequent division imposes on the mind and see Korea as Koreans saw it in 1945.[59] For years those opposed to Japan had turned to communism, while the nationalist camp had been severely weakened and compromised by the collaboration of many of its leaders with the Japanese. When communists emerged from hiding or from prison on August 15, they had unimpeachable patriotic credentials. The prime test of political legitimacy in liberated Korea was a person's record under Japanese rule; and communists generally passed this test with ease. Many of the old nationalist leaders in Korea did not measure up as well and thus remained inactive until early September. This is why so many communists appeared in the CPKI.[60] Not one active CPKI leader was ever seriously charged with being a collaborator or "pro-Japanese." In fact, virtually all the identifiable individuals on the August 22 list had spent varying lengths of time in Japanese prisons. Such people prevailed in August 1945, because of their own records and because there were few if any viable alternatives.

The August 22 roster also reflects events that took place in the days immediately preceding its publication. On August 19 or 20 Kim Pyŏng-no and Paek Kwan-su visited CPKI headquarters and urged that the CPKI be broadened to include more nationalists and conservatives.[61] They also recommended that it renounce its claims to being a government and organize a simple peace-keeping force.[62] There is much that does not meet the eye in this entreaty, however. Around August 15 Yŏ Un-hyŏng and Chŏng Paek had tried to get Song Chin-u and Kim Pyŏng-no to join them in organizing the CPKI. Yŏ apparently tried to gain their cooperation several other times in succeeding days, without success.[63] In the days between August 15 and

August 20, the Japanese had turned against the CPKI. They charged that it had "strayed from [its] original mission" and had made "terrible mistakes." Japanese authorities had hoped that the CPKI would act in their interests; but at a minimum, they expected a moderate and pliable organization. Around August 18 they demanded that the CPKI reduce its functions to limited peace-keeping. Moreover, Japanese Army headquarters authorized the distribution of weapons to "trustworthy Koreans."[64] On August 18 terrorists attacked Yŏ and he apparently retired to his country home for a few days to recuperate.[65] It is impossible to determine if the attack came from rightists or leftists; but the effect was to make cooperation between Right and Left more difficult.

Thus when Kim Pyŏng-no and Paek Kwan-su presented themselves at CPKI headquarters, they appeared to be urging the CPKI to do the very thing that the Japanese wanted. Moreover, their arrival on the day after Yŏ's beating raised questions. Days earlier they had rejected Yŏ's requests to work together. Now they appeared asking for cooperation when Yŏ was absent and the more congenial An Chae-hong acted in his stead. It is not surprising that leftists within the CPKI, who viewed Song Chin-u and his group as bourgeois gentlemen if not collaborators, felt threatened by their suggestions. Indeed, a leftist source indicated that precisely this entreaty introduced the issue of what to do about "bourgeois rightists" and "impure elements" (implying collaborators). It said that men who had resisted the Japanese to the end were not about to aid those who had benefited under Japanese rule and do things for them now that they could not do for themselves. It went without saying that Korea's leadership would now come from anti-Japanese fighters.[66] Japanese opposition to the CPKI confirmed this view. The August 22 roster was thus a specific rejection of the Kim/Paek approach and a signal to the Japanese that the CPKI would call its own shots.[67]

THE KOREAN PEOPLE'S REPUBLIC

Until late August it appeared that the Soviet Army might take the Japanese surrender throughout Korea. In mid-August Japanese Army units skirmished with Soviet forces in northmost Korea, delaying the Russian move southward. Russians did not appear near the thirty-eighth parallel until the last week in August. It is difficult to determine how the prospect of Soviet occupation affected the political situation in south Korea. The Japanese may have hoped that the presence of the CPKI, with many communists in its leadership, would somehow cushion the Soviet entry. Fear of the Soviets was probably behind the significant monetary contributions that wealthy Koreans made to the CPKI as well.

It is not at all clear that communists and leftists in south Korea welcomed a Soviet move southward, although one might at first think otherwise. For one thing, they probably recognized that the Soviets would have their own ideas about future Korean leadership, especially since the Comintern had never had an effective relationship with communists inside Korea. For another, these individuals felt ashamed that they themselves had not liberated Korea, after years of trying, and thus hoped to recoup their honor by building a Korean government on their own.[68] For communists and leftists who had cut their teeth in anti-Japanese struggle, nationalism came before internationalism. Finally, no one had any idea how long the Soviets might stay if they did enter the south, nor could anyone know if they would come alone or if they might be joined by the forces of the other Allied powers.

By the last week in August, however, the news was abroad that the Soviets had halted their push southward and that the Americans were coming. This news profoundly affected the developing political situation in the south. The Japanese got some breathing space; but more important, they sensed an opportunity to extend their influence over Korea somewhat longer. Koreans on the Left now recognized a necessity to broaden the base of the CPKI. Koreans on the Right no longer felt a need to try to work through or to influence the CPKI; instead they began to think of organizing on their own behalf.

Because the Russians accepted the American initiative to partition Korea at the thirty-eighth parallel, and because the Americans lacked the resources to move occupation forces into Korea until early September, the Japanese unexpectedly gained about three weeks to marshal their withdrawal. They used this time to bequeath to Koreans gifts quite befitting the character of their colonial rule. They destroyed inventories, printed inflated money, and distributed "imperial gifts" (*ŭnsagŭm*) to favored Koreans.[69] They sacked warehouses and sold the contents, whether food, oil, cloth, or whatever. They sold factories, homes, furnishings—anything that they could not carry back to Japan.[70] In their rush to liquidate their assets, the Japanese nearly ruined the south Korean economy. In a few weeks, they printed some three billion yen against an estimated five billion yen in circulation on August 15.[71] Then at the end of August, Japanese colonial authorities established contact with American occupation forces and fed them tales of communist treachery and civil disorder, hoping thereby to gain American sympathy.

On August 28 a CPKI proclamation appeared that demonstrated that the organization had moved far from its original emphasis on peace-keeping and toward the establishment of a new government.[72] The CPKI was to be a temporary, transitional organ pending the establishment of a national government; the latter would be formed through "a people's committee elected by a national conference of peoples' representatives." In other words, the CPKI would be a "midwife" on the path to Korean sovereignty. The statement carried revolutionary implications for Korea. It called for "complete independence and true democracy," a "sweeping out of feudal remnants," and for "mass struggle against the anti-democratic and reactionary forces . . . [who] colluded with Japanese imperialism and committed crimes against the nation." The latter people would have no place in the new government; there would be no "unprincipled unity" with them.

There is no way of telling whether this proclamation emanated from Yŏ's faction or from the *Changan* faction. Its language would seem to accord more with the *Changan* extremists, until we realize that such strongly worded statements had great appeal in the radical atmosphere of August 1945 and were little different from statements issued by nationalists in the KPG in Chungking.[73] Since by August 28 the word was out that American forces would occupy south Korea, however, and since rightists began organizing on that day, this proclamation probably was designed by the Left to throw down the gauntlet to the Right and to quicken the process of establishing a government before the Americans arrived.

In the first days of September, steps were taken toward establishing a Korean government. The prime movers in this effort were Yŏ Un-hyŏng, Hŏ Hŏn, and Pak Hŏn-yŏng. Hŏ Hŏn was a lawyer who, like Yŏ, leaned to the Left but was not a communist.[74] Pak Hŏn-yŏng was described in 1945 as "the greatest leader of Korean communism."[75] In late August, Pak returned to Seoul from the provinces and found that his old rival, Yi Yŏng, had already begun to organize a communist party around his *Changan* faction.[76] Pak viewed this activity as not only premature but, as an affront to his own prestige. His influence was such that he was quickly able to win away many of Yi Yŏng's supporters and, on September 8, to organize the so-called Reconstructed Korean Communist Party (*Chaegŏn Chosŏn kongsandang—KCP*).[77] Among those who left the *Changan* group to join Pak were Hong Nam-p'yo, Cho Tong-ho, and Ch'oe Wŏn-t'aek, all former Tuesday Association activists.[78] Pak also won over Yi Kang-guk and Ch'oe Yong-dal, who had been working closely with Yŏ and his *Kŏnmaeng*.[79] Pak also seems to have succeeded in weeding out most of the *Changan* activists from the CPKI, which demonstrated *Changan* weakness as much as Pak's strength.

On September 6 several hundred CPKI activists from Seoul and the provinces gathered at Kyŏnggi Girl's High School and announced the formation of the Korean People's Republic (*Chosŏn inmin konghwa'guk*—KPR).[80] The main reason for this hasty action was the impending arrival of American occupation forces. CPKI leaders wanted to establish an ostensible Korean government, both to show that Koreans could run their own affairs and to forestall either a prolonged American tutelage or the installation in power of other Koreans who might gain American favor.

The KPR was also a product of the heady atmosphere and revolutionary fervor of liberation. Following the classic "drill" of the French Revolution, KPR organizers called a representative assembly, proclaimed a republic, and scheduled future elections to ascertain the popular will. Patterning itself after another revolution, the September 6 assembly chose fifty-five leaders to staff the interim administration pending general elections. Unlike the American Constitutional Convention, however, KPR leaders proclaimed a social revolution as well; "a second liberation" was at hand.[81]

Very little is known about the origin of the KPR in the first week in September. Anticommunist accounts say that a decision to form the KPR came out of a secret meeting between Yŏ Un-hyŏng, Hŏ Hŏn, Pak Hŏn-yŏng, and Chŏng Paek on September 4.[82] The problem with this analysis is that Chŏng Paek (a leader of the *Changan* faction) had just been replaced in the CPKI organization department by Yi Kang-guk; moreover, Pak Hŏn-yŏng's name did not even appear on the KPR roster published on September 6. A substantial number of *Chaegŏn* KCP leaders did appear on this roster, however, so it is probable that Pak was directly involved in KPR planning. It also seems that the split in the CPKI between Yŏ's *Kŏnmaeng* adherents and communists continued in the KPR; for example, *Kŏnmaeng* leaders wanted the name of the new organization to be *Chosŏn konghwa'guk* (Korean Republic) rather than *Chosŏn inmin konghwa'guk* (Korean People's Republic).[83] But cooperation rather than conflict seemed to be the order of the day, and the moderate influence of Yŏ and Hŏ Hŏn was evident in the leaders selected on September 6. Yŏ, Hŏ, and others appear to have recognized that the imminent American arrival and the requisites for Korean unity necessitated a real broadening of CPKI/KPR leadership to include revolutionaries and anti-Japanese fighters at home and abroad, regardless of whether they were communists or nationalists, leftists or rightists. The KPR roster embraced Korean leaders from all walks of life; it went much further than subsequent rightist initiatives ever did in reaching out across ideological lines in the interests of unity and coalition.

The September 6 assembly selected a total of eighty-seven leaders. Fifty-five were selected for the central People's Committee (*inmin wiwŏnhoe*), twenty for the candidate committee, and twelve as advisors (see Appendix A). An analysis of the backgrounds of these individuals gives an interesting picture of Korean leadership in 1945. Of the sixty-two whose backgrounds are known, fully thirty-nine or about 63 percent had been in colonial prisons for political crimes. Many of these people (particularly the communists) had just emerged from prison on August 15. Only a handful of the eighty-seven had ever cooperated with the Japanese to the extent that their patriotism might be questioned. This was, then, a patriotic and revolutionary leadership, full of men with hard and bitter experience at the hands of the Japanese. Some of the elder patriots like Syngman Rhee, Kim Ku, Yŏ Un-hyŏng, Kim Kyu-sik, O Se-ch'ang, Kwŏn Tong-jin, and Kim Ch'ang-suk had grown to manhood in the last decades of the Yi Dynasty and provided in their own persons a link with Korean resistance to the Japanese Annexation. O and Kwŏn were among the thirty-three signers of the Korean Declaration of Independence in 1919, and Hong Myŏng-hui had had a hand in writing it. Exile leaders like Rhee, Kim Ku, Kim Wŏn-bong, Mu Chŏng, and Kim Il Sung[84] were accorded leading places, despite their absence, in recognition of their struggle against Japan.

The KPR roster, however, betrays a generation gap that followed political lines. The average age of nationalists and rightists was sixty-six, while that of leftists and communists was forty-seven. This striking difference clearly delineates the tendency of young Korean patriots in the 1920s and 1930s to turn to communism as a remedy for their country's predicament. In sheer numbers, the September 6 roster was obviously weighted to the Left. Of the fifty-five leaders who are known to have had backgrounds of political activity during the Japanese period, forty-two had been associated with the Left or communism. Only thirteen were nationalists or rightists. This distribution, it might be added, did not unfairly distort the respective contributions of communists and nationalists in the last two decades of anti-Japanese struggle.

But there are real problems with these labels. Self-proclaimed communists like Yi Kang-guk and Hyŏn Chun-hyŏk should be designated leftists or fellow-travelers; neither exhibited much understanding of communist ideology.[85] The same could be said of many other KPR leaders. Even extreme communist critics of the KPR in September 1945 betrayed a puerile grasp of Marxism-Leninism.[86] The erudite Kim Kyu-sik could probably have offered a better exposition of the materialist view than many of his "communist" opponents.[87] Another distinct problem in labeling of this sort is that the Japanese affixed most of the labels. Japanese colonial police and intelligence agencies captured, interrogated, and labeled Korean recalcitrants; and their exhaustive reports are still used almost exclusively in studies of Korean communism before 1945. Although the Japanese were thorough and precise in such investigations, they also tended to merge and blur the distinction between communists and simple opponents of Japanese rule. More important, by their constant harping on the menace of communism, they led Koreans to identify communism with Korean resistance. Yet the initial nationalistic impulse toward communism should not be used to misconstrue the commitment of these Koreans to the social revolution that Marxism implied for Korea. As they became aware of the social content of the doctrine, they saw that the implications for Korea went deeper than simply ridding their nation of the Japanese.

It is extremely difficult for an American, with inbred assumptions about society and the good life, to understand or appreciate Korean political and social conflicts in 1945. An American's understanding of communism in the United States held little relevance for understanding communism in Korea. Whereas in the United States communists had never succeeded in winning mass support, in Korea in 1945 they had it dropped in their laps by virtue of their staunch resistance to Japan and the mass appeal of their programs.

Communism in Korea in 1945 did not signify a deeply held world view, or adherence to an authority residing in the Kremlin, or commitment to Marxist internationalism. It was a specifically Korean communism. Its adherents could scarcely be distinguished from nationalists and conservatives in their belief in the uniqueness of the Korean race and its traditions and the necessity to preserve both, or in their understanding that a unique Korea required unique solutions.[88] What did distinguish Left from Right was: (1) a commitment to a thoroughgoing extirpation of Japanese influences in Korea, with all that this implied for Korean society and for Koreans who had profited from colonial rule; (2) a commitment to mass politics and mass organization and to the social equality that this implied; (3) a commitment to the reform of Korea's "feudal" legacy, feudalism being a code word for gross inequalities in the allocation of resources, particularly land. It was disputes over these issues that divided Koreans and that help to explain the consistency in political sides among Korean leaders from about 1920 on. Although international influences have involved themselves from time to time on one side or another, the prevailing cleavage has been a Korean one, and fought over Korean issues.

The KPR leadership roster reflects an attempt to bridge the two sides while maintaining a predominance of the Left. It did not exclude leading exile politicians, even though they were abroad and might not return for months. It did not exclude domestic conservatives like Kim Sŏng-su and Kim Pyŏng-no. In fact, it gave the leading KPR position to the man who soon became the pillar of the Right, Syngman Rhee; although KPR leaders knew Rhee only as a long-lost exile, and may have suspected that he had already won American sympathies, they still made this magnanimous gesture, something that Rhee himself never would return.

On September 8 the KPR published a list of the cabinet members that went still further toward genuine coalition of Left and Right:[89]

Chairman: Syngman Rhee (Yi Sŭng-man)
Prime Minister: Hŏ Hŏn
Education: Kim Sŏng-su
Interior: Kim Ku
Justice: Kim Pyŏng-no
Vice-chairman: Yŏ Un-hyŏng
Foreign Minister: Kim Kyu-sik
Economics: Ha P'il-wŏn
Finance: Cho Man-sik
Communications: Shin Ik-hŭi

These men seem to have been chosen on the basis of their specialty: Kim Kyu-sik, for instance, was widely known as a well-traveled, cultivated man, fluent in several languages; Kim Sŏng-su was the founder of what later became Korea University; Kim Pyŏng-no was a famous jurist; Kim Ku's reputation as a terrorist and assassin no doubt commended him for duty concerning domestic law and order. Some see this cabinet as having been a communist plot, with the real power being retained by Korean communists then on the scene in Seoul.[90] And on the one hand, it is true that KPR leaders like Yŏ and Hŏ Hŏn did not plan to retire to the countryside and let Rhee, Kim Ku, Kim Sŏng-su, and the others take over. But on the other hand, the atmosphere of liberated Korea had not yet been so poisoned that magnanimity had no place and cooperation no virtue. Leftist leaders of the KPR felt that they operated from a position of strength and could afford to give their opponents some positions in the KPR and the considerable publicity that went with them, in the interests of unity and coalition.

The revolutionary thrust behind the KPR was evident in the platforms and proclamations that it put out in the week following the inaugural assembly. KPR leaders, like those in so many other countries in the aftermath of the war, saw themselves as part of a world tide of democracy rising on the ashes of imperialism and fascism. A political liberation had been won; now the task was to give meaning to a second, social liberation. The distinction between liberation, pure and simple, and social liberation precisely delineated the difference between Korean nationalism, pure and simple, and Korean revolutionary nationalism. As with so much else during the liberation period, this crucial distinction can be traced back to the formative period after the March First Movement in 1919.[91]

The KPR declaration of September 14 stated:

> We are determined to demolish Japanese imperialism, its residuary influences, antidemocratic factions, reactionary elements, and any undesirable foreign influence in our state, and to establish our complete autonomy and independence, thereby anticipating the realization of an authentically democratic state.[92]

A twenty-seven point platform followed, directed at the residual influences of imperialism and "feudalism." It called for the confiscation without compensation of lands held by the Japanese and by "the national traitors" (*minjok panyŏk-cha*) and for free distribution of the lands to the peasants who worked them; unconfiscated land would have tenancy rent rationalized on a "3-7" basis (rent in kind would be no more than 30 percent of the crop). Major industries such as mines, factories, railways, shipping, communications, and banking would be nationalized, while "middle and small" commerce and industry would be allowed to function in private hands under state supervision. A major program of rapid industrialization was promised.

The platform also guaranteed the fundamental freedoms of speech, assembly, and faith. It gave the franchise to all males and females over eighteen years of age, excluding again the national traitors. It pledged the "abrogation of all privileges and prerogatives and maintenance of absolute equality," including the "complete emancipation of women." It took a reformist position toward labor, promising an eight-hour day, prohibition of child labor, and a minimum wage. It obligated the state to provide compulsory elementary education. Finally, regarding Korea's foreign posture, the platform urged "establishment of close cooperation with U.S.A., U.S.S.R., England and China, and positive opposition to any foreign influences interfering with the domestic affairs of our state."[93]

The demands contained in this platform gave the KPR a momentum that quickly came to overshadow the specific personalities, factions, and political viewpoints that made it up. They defined the agenda for the future government and delineated the terms of social and political debate for the next three years in Korea. Here, KPR leaders thought, was the means to lift an ancient nation, one that in their view had had its progress in the twentieth century fettered by an anachronistic colonialism, into the ranks of the world's advanced nations. For the next three years, demands for land reform, reform of working conditions, and for the political participation implied in the guarantees of fundamental rights dominated political discourse. The term "people's republic" came to symbolize for many Koreans the means for attaining these ends and quite transcended the specific origins of the KPR itself.

The platform pledge of "positive opposition to any foreign influences interfering with the domestic affairs of our state" was important because of what it said about Korea's history as a nation among nations, and for what it presaged in the developing American-Korean relationship. Uppermost in the minds of KPR leaders had been Korea's history as a passive actor in the great power diplomacy of the several decades that led up to the Annexation. Yŏ acknowledged in his speech to the September 6 assembly that the imminent American arrival in south Korea had occasioned the "emergency" conditions in which the KPR was proclaimed. Whatever its faults, the KPR would at least symbolize Korean sovereignty and, they hoped, prevent yet another round in Korea's five-hundred-year history of dependency on foreign power.[94]

Although Yŏ admitted that Korea's final liberation had been won by foreign powers, he saw no reason to entrust Korea's future to them. Koreans had been fighting Japan at home and abroad since 1910; they had every right, therefore, to self-determination. The Allies should respect this history and take a neutral position of noninterference in Korean affairs. Yŏ struck a responsive chord among Koreans. It was the shame of a generation of patriots that they had not won Korea's liberation themselves; did they not at least have the right to try to win the peace? Would they have to sit still while foreign powers framed and defined a future Korean government?[95] Yi Kangguk echoed Yŏ's position when he said, "although Korea's liberation was not achieved independently through our own efforts, it was natural that Koreans should demand an independent government." Independence, he thought, "was not something given to us by the Americans or the Soviets. It is something that can be achieved only by gathering together the revolutionary forces within Korea . . . through our own efforts and our own blood."[96]

This was the other side of the hurried, and in the eyes of some observers, opportunistic establishment of the KPR. As Yŏ later put it:

> We believed that we must construct a country which, through
> standing for true and progressive democracy, would receive without
> hesitation recognition from the rest of the nations of the world . . .
> and we thought of course the [American] Military Government
> would wholly aid in setting up such a government and follow the
> path to independence.[97]

There was much that could be criticized about the manner in
which the KPR was established. Because the Left was much more
willing to air grievances and criticism than were its opponents, a general critique of the KPR is available mainly in leftist literature from
the period. Some pictured the September 6 assembly as hastily convened, and "rash and thoughtless."[98] A communist newspaper said
that such an assembly should have been preceded by a campaign of
mass propaganda and mobilization designed to link the leaders and
the masses, and to link the center with the localities. Instead, there
was little "direct mass participation" in the September 6 meeting;
indeed, there was no difference between it and "an isolated, bourgeois
bureaucratic organ." The KPR platform showed no "revolutionary"
point of view. Thus a new mass assembly was needed, under "the
hegemony of the proletariat." But, pending that, the KPR must be
supported because it was opposed by "the landed bourgeoisie."[99]
Another source stated that the "impatient" leaders of the CPKI and
KPR

> failed to mobilize the revolutionary masses and separated the masses
> from vanguard leadership. They placed too little value on the work
> of wiping out the remnants of Japanese imperialism. Not only were
> they vague about the basic provisions for the establishment of the
> people's sovereignty, but they also attached too much importance to
> [simply] establishing power and neglected international considera-
> tions.[100]

Some found the KPR to have been "dogmatic and arbitrary" in its selection of leaders,[101] while others criticized the undisciplined spontaneity of "the people's movement."[102]

The faults of the KPR, however, lay as much with its communist
leaders as with the more moderate, "bourgeois" leaders. The CPKI
and the KPR were the objects of rash power grabs by communists.
Far from being conspiratorial or devious, these communists openly
sought political position; they made no effort to conceal their intentions. In August and September it often seemed as if the communists
were engaged in a free-for-all, with every man for himself; they certainly had no disciplined, united party that could be used as a tool of

organization. There is some truth in the later north Korean critique of the factionalism, "splittism," and immaturity of the communist effort in the south. It was of a piece with the pre-1945 effort.

In general, all the KPR leaders had much to learn about forging an enduring organization and little experience with a political movement having strong roots in the countryside. They focused their efforts on the urban areas, and Seoul in particular, trying to link up with other factions or parties. The peculiar irony was that by indulging in the tired politics of Seoul, they weakened the movement that they themselves had spawned in the provinces. To put it another way, they revived traditional politics at the expense of modern politics, if the latter is defined as mobilizing and bringing into national political life the rural masses and establishing strong links between the center and the periphery.

Having said all this, it remains true that the leaders of the KPR did far better than any other Koreans in the south in laying the groundwork for sovereignty, in terms of organization, mobilization, and the delineation of national goals. The *ch'iandae* kept the peace for three weeks under extremely volatile conditions. CPKI authorities managed and protected essential food provisions stocks and aided in the harvest of a bumper crop of fall rice. Labor leaders and workers managed numerous factories and enterprises. Provincial organizers helped develop people's committees and peasant unions that inaugurated a year of mass political participation in the provinces that eventually rivaled any in Korea's history in depth and import. All this proceeded in spite of the opposition of Japanese, and subsequently American, central authorities. Without foreign intervention, the KPR and the organizations it sponsored would have triumphed throughout the peninsula in a matter of months.

OPPOSITION TO THE REPUBLIC

As Robert Michels argued:

> A society which lacks a lively faith in its own rights is already in its political death-agony. A capacity for the tough and persevering defense of privilege presupposes in the privileged class the existence of certain qualities, and in especial of a relentless energy, which might thrive, indeed, in association with cruelty and unconscientiousness, but which is enormously more prosperous if based upon a vigorous faith in its own rectitude.[103]

August 1945 was not a good month for Koreans who still had some measure of power, wealth, and influence. All Koreans, of course, welcomed liberation, except perhaps for a tiny minority of Japanese sympathizers. But those who had benefited from Japanese rule were highly apprehensive of the post-colonial order. Would reprisals follow? Trials? Who would prevail? It is these considerations that elicited the mixed reaction of elation and enervation, hopefulness and despair, relief and anxiety with which privileged Koreans greeted the end of colonial rule. Landlords, in particular, had the unfortunate fate in 1945 of looking backward toward a past in which their class had been dominant for centuries and looking forward to a future that, even in their own eyes, held little utility for them. By the end of the colony, any Korean who possessed significant landed wealth had paid a fateful price to the Japanese for such privilege. The obvious part of the price was active support of colonial policies. The more subtle, but the greater, part of the price was the irremediable tearing of the fabric of consensus that had legitimated Korea's privileged classes' very right to rule. Koreans of position had been so tainted by their association with the Japanese that they had lost and could not call forth the old legitimations. More than that, they no longer believed in themselves. The Japanese legacy was the destruction of the essential self-confidence necessary to preserve privilege amidst cataclysmic change. It is against this background that we must examine the precarious and faltering organizational efforts of the Korean Right in the weeks after liberation.

In these weeks, wealthy and influential Koreans were faced with a popular movement to share the wealth and punish collaborators. In the provinces, peasant radicalism led to the forcible dispossession of Japanese and Korean landlords. The CPKI controlled the national press, radio, and other communications facilities for a time and railed against collaborators. Japanese and Koreans crossed the thirty-eighth parallel with tales of people's trials and dispossession in the north. Koreans who had held high office, and especially those who served in the Japanese police, dispersed and often went into hiding. Their privileges seemed gone for good. Some lesser collaborators and landlords, however, succeeded in joining or even leading local CPKI branches. Many wealthy Koreans contributed funds to the CPKI.[104] Conservatives like Song Chin-u and Kim Sŏng-su, as we have seen, tried to win the CPKI to their purposes. Others, with fewer scruples, apparently accepted Japanese offers of aid and weaponry in the interests of self-preservation. But in the last week in August, the news came that the United States would occupy southern Korea. This news provided the critical factor in enabling the establishment of embryonic organizations of the Right.

On August 28 a group of men described only as "patriots" held a preparatory meeting for the founding of a Korean Nationalist Party

(*Chosŏn minjokdang*). This group included Kim Pyŏng-no, Paek Kwan-su, Cho Pyŏng-ok, Yi In, Kim Yong-mu, Wŏn Se-hun, Ham Sang-hun, and Pak Ch'an-hŭi.[105] They soon discovered that another faction of conservatives had the same idea. The other group wanted to form a Korean Nationalist Party (*Han'guk kungmindang*) as well, and included Paek Nam-hun, Kim To-yŏn, Chang Tŏk-su, Ku Cha-ok, Hŏ Chŏng, Ch'oe Yun-dong, and Yi Un.[106] On September 1 two more groups appeared—An Chae-hong's *Chosŏn kungmindang*, and a group around Song Chin-u calling itself the "Preparatory Committee for Welcoming the Return of the Korean Provisional Government."[107] The first two groups gathered on September 4 to hold a preparatory meeting in the interests of developing a "democratic" political party. On September 7 Song Chin-u's group reorganized as the "Preparatory Committee for a National Congress" (*Kungmin taehoe chunbi wiwŏn-hoe*). Joining Song in this were Kim Sŏng-su, Chang T'aek-sang, and Kim Chun-yŏn, among others.[108] On September 8 these three organizations sponsored their first joint publication, a leaflet entitled "Down with the KPR" and released to coincide with the American entry. On September 16 they united to form the Korean Democratic Party (*Han'guk minjudang*—KDP). Cho Pyŏng-ok, Yi In, Chang Tŏk-su, Wŏn Se-hun, and Paek Nam-hun spoke at this founding meeting, held in the Ch'ŏndogyo Hall in downtown Seoul.[109]

The Korean Democratic Party became the pillar of the Right in the first few months after liberation and remained the strongest single rightist party throughout the American Occupation. It was self-described as a party of "patriots, notables, and various circles of the intellectual stratum," a characterization that contained a measure of truth as well as an indication of its elitist values.[110] Leftists and moderates viewed it as a mixture of propertied men and intellectuals, patriots and collaborators, "pure" and "impure" elements.[111] The more acceptable leaders appeared out front, but they were widely perceived to be a shield for landlords who hoped to preserve their holdings and collaborators and traitors who hoped to avoid punishment or perpetuate their influence in the transition from Japanese to Korean rule.[112] American sources later said the KDP was "composed predominantly of large land owners and wealthy businessmen"; and an American present at the inaugural KDP meeting noted the fine dress of those in attendance and decided that "this was the party of wealth and respectability."[113]

A mainstay of the KDP was the collection of landlord, manufacturing, and publishing interests led by Kim Sŏng-su, Song Chin-u, and others. This Honam group, as it was often called, consisted precisely of those landlord-entrepreneurs whom we discussed in chapter one.

These individuals had been part of the reformist and gradualist resistance to Japanese rule in the 1920s, an impulse that dissipated after the Sino-Japanese War began and colonial authorities began to apply intense pressure on them to collaborate. Whether this group could be termed collaborationist would depend on the definition and the eye of the beholder. A man like Song Chin-u had perhaps not irremediably tarnished the bedrock of traditional legitimacy that justified his standing. There were undocumented charges that he actively served the Japanese war effort; and what resistance he did put up consisted at best of peculiarly effete and passive acts of feigned illness and forced inaction. This latter activity, however, such as it was, was probably viewed as patriotic and befitting of his status by conservative and traditional Koreans. There is no question that Kim Sŏng-su actively aided the Japanese in the early 1940s, through speeches and contributions, and through his membership on the Central Advisory Council (*Chūsuin*).[114] Still, Yŏ Un-hyŏng tried several times to secure the cooperation of these men in forming the CPKI.[115] It is probably fair to say that their *participation* in postwar Korean politics would have been accepted by most Koreans at home and abroad who had been more staunch in their resistance but that their *dominance* of postwar affairs would be unseemly and something to be opposed. This expressed the widely held sentiment that it was one thing for an individual to have succumbed to Japanese pressures, and quite another for him to fail to reflect (*pansŏng*) on his transgressions and simply come out after liberation as if his honor were untarnished.[116]

Some leaders of the KDP had undeniable, and less readily forgivable, collaborationist records. Chang Tŏk-su, a professor at Posŏng College, had given many speeches during the war in service to the Japanese and had appeared publicly with such prominent collaborators as Yi Kwang-su, Hugh Cynn (Shin Hŭng-u), Ch'oe In, and Ch'oe Nam-sŏn.[117] He had apparently led a "People's Volunteer Corps" in Kyŏnggi Province as well. When he was assassinated in 1947, his slayer accused him of having been an advisor to Japanese Army headquarters in Korea and a leader of a "reeducation institute" for Korean political and "thought" criminals.[118] Leonard Bertsch, the American in the Occupation perhaps most knowledgeable of Korean politics, once said that Chang "cooperated heartily with the Japanese, speaking violently against the American barbarianism, and now [1946] cooperates heartily with the Americans and would in turn cooperate heartily with the Russians."[119] Another KDP leader, Kim Tong-hwan, was also a leading speechmaker and organizer in service to the Japanese war effort.[120] Other KDP leaders who were charged with varying degrees of collaboration included Kim Tong-wŏn, Paek Nak-chun

(George Paik), Pak Yong-hŭi, Yi Hun-gu, Yu Chin-o, and Sŏ Sang-il.[121] Although by no means all KDP leaders had collaborationist backgrounds, the KDP's patriotic credentials were lacking when compared to those of the KPR.

Even wealthy Koreans who had not openly and actively supported colonial policies tended to be linked in the public mind with the Japanese. As we noted earlier, both colonialism and capitalism symbolized to many Koreans alien intrusions that had disrupted and destroyed the placid self-sufficiency of the traditional Korean economy and society. The Japanese period was often distainfully termed Korea's "capitalist stage," and Korean capitalists themselves appeared as parvenu opportunists and servitors of alien influences. Opposition to capitalism could thus bring together both tradition-minded reactionaries who sought the restoration of a tranquil, self-contained economy and progressives who sought remedies in socialism. Such popular attitudes placed heavy burdens on Koreans trying to perpetuate capitalist forms of ownership in liberated Korea.

KDP rosters included men who had been leading figures in Korean manufacturing and industry, education, and in the colonial apparatus itself.[122] Kim To-yŏn had been the director of the Korean Industrial Company. Cho Pyŏng-ok, an early nationalist leader, had managed the Poin Mining Company from 1937 to 1945. Min Kyu-sik had been a leader of the Chohŭng Bank, one of the two or three leading financial institutions in Korea. Kim Tong-hwan (mentioned above) owned the Taedonga Company. Cho Chong-guk had been a major figure in drug manufacturing. Kim Tong-wŏn owned the P'yŏng'an Commercial and Industrial Company. Chang Hyŏn-jung had run the Tonga Enterprise Company. Leading educators in the KDP were Kim Sŏng-su, Paek Nak-chun, Yi Hun-gu, Paek Nam-hun, and many others. Many Koreans who had held high office in the colonial administration worked closely with the KDP, as we will see in later chapters, though in the fall of 1945 they did not openly identify with it, for obvious reasons. The KDP did openly count among its members the following Japanese-appointed councilors on provincial and city advisory boards: Yi Pong-gu, Pae Yŏng-ch'un, Ch'ŏn Tae-gŭn, Chŏng Sun-sŏk, Yi Chong-gyu, and Yi Chong-jun. Most of these men were also landlords. Indeed, virtually all KDP members mentioned in biographical lists compiled by American Intelligence were landlords, industrialists, or businessmen of one sort or another.

Until 1945 only a tiny percentage of educated Koreans had studied in the West. Except in rare instances, a Western education was in itself an indication of substantial wealth. A number of KDP leaders had studied in the West, however, among them, Chang Tŏk-su (Columbia University), Chang Myŏn, Chang T'aek-sang (a graduate of Edinburgh College in England), An Ho-sang (a philosophy Ph.D. from Jena University in Germany), and Ku Cha-ok, Kim Chun-ok, and Cho Pyŏng-ok (graduate studies at Columbia University).

Some KDP leaders seem to have emerged from the Japanese period with their patriotism still intact. Yi In, for example, was a famous lawyer and scholar who had been imprisoned by the Japanese and who had defended Korean resisters of all political stripes on numerous occasions. Myŏng Che-se had been imprisoned for his activities in the March First Movement; in August 1945 he left the CPKI to join the KDP. Wŏn Se-hun was a highly regarded patriot who led a moderate faction in the KDP. Kim Chun-yŏn and Kim Yak-su were communist apostates who had spent long years in Japanese prisons. Like the KPR, the KDP embraced in its leadership rosters elder patriots such as O Se-ch'ang and Kwŏn Tong-jin. But unlike the KPR, the KDP never tried to reach across Korea's political divisions and include Koreans on the Left. Its initial cabinet included only the rightist leaders of the exile KPG, Syngman Rhee and Kim Ku; it excluded the moderate Kim Kyu-sik and the leftist Kim Wŏn-bong. The rest of the cabinet was as follows:[123]

Chairman: Song Chin-u
General Affairs: Wŏn Se-hun, Kim Tong-wŏn, Paek Nam-hun, Cho Pyŏng-ok, Paek Kwan-su, Sŏ Sang-il, Kim To-yŏn, Hŏ Chŏng
Secretariat: Na Yong-gyu
Foreign Affairs: Chang Tŏk-su
Finance: Pak Yong-hŭi
Information: Pak Ch'an-hŭi
Education: Kim Yong-mu
Inspection: Yu Chin-hŭi
Bodyguards: Kim Chŏn-gwang, Sŏ Sang-ch'ŏn, et al.
Party Affairs: Yi In
Organization: Kim Yak-su
Propaganda: Ham Sang-hun
Industry/Agriculture: Hong Sŏng-ha
Welfare: Yi Un
Liaison: Ch'oe Yun-dong
Supervision: Kim Pyŏng-no

The KDP, unlike the KPR, offered Koreans no well-articulated outline of its goals and no programmatic appeals. Instead, the KDP seemed from the beginning to be obsessed with opposing the People's Republic and the groups associated with it. A reading of early KDP publications suggests that this was almost its sole *raison d'être*.[124] On September 8, the day of the American entry into Korea, the "Preparatory Committee" of the KDP issued a broadside entitled "Down with the KPR." This document said the CPKI and the KPR were the work of a tiny clique of "running dogs of Japanese imperialism" who, with the aid of the Japanese, had gotten control of radio stations, newspapers, transportation facilities, and so on and used them to "disturb the public order." This "treacherous handful" established the "laughable" KPR and even went so far as to steal the names of Korea's "men of repute" (*chimyŏng insa*). But now, the "righteous sword" of the KDP would "carry out resolutely the great, noble undertaking of smashing the evil and laying bare the right."[125]

The KDP thus established a litany of abuse that would long outlive the KPR itself. Its primary case against the People's Republic was that it was the seed of postwar Korea's disunity, that it had usurped sovereignty that rightfully belonged to others, that it was solely made up of communists, and that it was pro-Japanese.[126] CPKI activities in August, according to the KDP, consisted of unlawful seizures of factories, businesses, stocks of grain and fuel, cars and trucks, and so on. *Ch'iandae* units did not keep the peace, but disturbed it. The Japanese aided the CPKI with funds and other resources as part of a plot to perpetuate their power. CPKI and KPR transgressions also included their telling "the farmers that the land was theirs, the workers that the factories were theirs, the clerks that the shops were theirs." For all these reasons, "righteous leadership could not be established in Seoul" in August and early September.[127] But from September 8, according to one of its primary leaders, the KDP's "great task" became the overthrow of the CPKI, the KPR, and the organizations that succeeded it.[128]

KDP platforms and programs consisted of vague, opaque generalities about the promotion of world peace and national culture, "the enhancement of the livelihood of the working masses," and "rational reorganization of the land system."[129] KDP publications were specific primarily in reference to the People's Republic. The reason for this befogged and cryptic agenda for Korea's future is not hard to find: a group did not win popularity in Korea in 1945 by urging the maintenance of landlordism, private ownership of industry, little or no punishment for collaborators, and the continuation in power of those Koreans who had influence under the Japanese. Robert Michels once wrote that "a party of the landed gentry which would appeal only to the members of its own class and to those of identical economic interests," or a "conservative candidate who should present himself to his electors by declaring to them that he did not regard them as capable of playing an active part in influencing the destinies of the country," would evince incomparable sincerity but political insanity.[130]

For a political party to have any hope of success, it must present its own selfish interests as universal. Few parties have paid less fealty to this principle than the KDP. But widespread demands for land reform compelled the KDP to address this issue; and its position evolved into one of *yusang* reform, or reform with compensation to landowners. Land would be bought from landlords and redistributed to those who tilled it; the burden of payment would thus fall on peasants in the form of long term, annual installments.[131] From this we might deduce that the KDP had maximum and minimum goals. Its maximum goal would have been to perpetuate the form and structure of land relations existing before 1945. A much more realistic, minimum goal— one quite in keeping with the evolving character of the advanced sector of Korea's landed class—would be to perpetuate the existing structure of social domination that allowed landlords and other Korean elite differential and superior *access* to get what there was to get, whether land or other forms of capital.

Another essential point in the KDP platform was that the establishment of any Korean government must await the return of the Korean Provisional Government from Chungking as well as the entrance into Korea of the Allied armies. Since the KDP could not hope to win a mass constituency on its own, a perceived tie to the KPG was most useful.[132] Once the KPG returned, however, one of the first acts of those members who were associated with Kim Ku was the assassination of the KDP chairman, Song Chin-u; but by that time, it mattered little that no tie existed between the KPG and the KDP, for the KDP had forged a much more important relationship with the incoming Americans.

KDP spokesmen acknowledged with candor that Song Chin-u and his supporters did not begin their organizational efforts until the end of August, "the time when [they] had been told with certainty that the Allied Armies would arrive in Seoul on September 7."[133] Song's biographers too say he acted only after he was certain that the Americans were coming.[134] And other Korean and American sources are in agreement on this point as well; the official history of the Occupation even suggests that the actual founding of the KDP on September 16 was done at American urging.[135] Cho Pyŏng-ok wrote that the KDP faced not only the opposition of a strong People's Republic in Seoul but people's committees organized "in every nook and cranny of the land" in north and south Korea and supported by the Soviets; the only hope of KPR opponents lay with the incoming Americans.[136]

Self-preservation is the first law of politics. There is nothing morally or ethically wrong with the KDP's seeking the succor of the Americans. But the KDP need to do so is revealing. The leaders of the People's Republic, as we have seen, saw no such need.[137] Lacking the KPR's positive and appealing program, its superior organizational capabilities, and much chance of securing a constituency among Koreans, though, the KDP had no choice but to rely on the incoming foreign power.

CONCLUSIONS

Within weeks after liberation, it was apparent that Korea lacked the very requisites of political order. A vast chasm divided the political elite over such elemental issues as the circumstances of ownership and allocation of basic resources, appropriate social forms, distribution of life chances, and the rules of the game governing political conflict. As conflicts over these issues—in truth, over the appropriate forms of domination for postwar Korea—developed in succeeding months, it became clear that instead of a political spectrum, Korea had two sides that were divided on virtually everything of importance. Rather quickly, politics came to be fought largely on the streets. Here was the endgame to which C. Wright Mills alluded when he remarked that in the final analysis political power is a matter of one person beating another over the head.[138]

The Korean Democratic Party in 1945 was a council of social notables who knew little about the process of creating and enrolling constituencies. They focused their efforts in Seoul, almost entirely overlooking provincial organization. When they did turn their attention to the localities, it was with the intention of enlisting provincial officials, county magistrates, and local police, not building a mass rural base. These were individuals who feared people *en masse*; in their politics, if not always in their persons, they provided a link with the later decades of the Yi Dynasty. The elder generation of the 1940s mimicked the techniques of the 1890s.[139] Eric J. Hobsbawm wrote that English elite have a preference for sticking old labels on new bottles, "maintaining the *form* of old institutions with a profoundly changed content."[140] Precisely the opposite characterized the politics of the elder Korean generation; their inclination was to preserve content while changing form, that is, to adapt the old Yi pattern of utilizing the state bureaucracy to protect class privilege and call it democracy. The difference in the 1940s was that the Japanese bequeathed a state far more potent than the old Yi.

When Americans entered southern Korea in 1945, they found on one side a small, tenuous holding operation, a congeries of individuals and factions with no provincial, or mass, base, groups of people who murmured vaguely about democracy. On the other side, they found revolutionary organizations that claimed the mantle of Korean sovereignty and bolstered the claim with extensive penetration of the countryside. They found revolutionaries who posited their right to rule on the charismatic basis of resistance to the Japanese, and conservatives who based their claim to legitimacy in tradition: they had ruled before, they would rule now—that is to say, if the Americans would have them.

Chapter Four

CRUCIBLE OF POLICY: CONTENDING FORCES IN AMERICAN PLANNING FOR KOREA, 1943-1945

Korea is the place . . . there you will see diplomacy in the raw, diplomacy without gloves, perfume, or phrases.
William W. Rockhill

The internationalists were America's version of China's Confucianists, elitist but humane, believers in harmony rather than struggle, hostile to the military but conservative, and supremely and arrogantly confident that their way of life was the only conceivable one which guaranteed men "happiness, wealth, and long life," as the old Chinese saying goes.
H. Franz Schurmann

A s THE Japanese transnational creation in Northeast Asia aborted in 1945, it set off explosive social forces within Korea. Of greater importance, however, were the shocks it caused the international configuration of power in the region. As this system came apart, it loosed contingencies that remained unresolved until 1950 (or perhaps we should say 1953): would a new transnational system replace the old? Would there be another integration of the peninsula into some larger unit? Or would Korea assume a unified, national form? However much Koreans may have wished differently, their country did not stand alone and isolated, but existed amid a maelstrom of international forces. During the interwar period, from 1945 to 1950, the peninsula remained in an indeterminate status, the extremes of which ran from complete autarky to complete integration.

To say that this reality was only dimly perceived by Americans fighting a world war on two fronts, however, is only to begin to appreciate how little Korea meant to most Americans before 1945. This ancient nation, so critical to the peace of Northeast Asia in any era, was little more than an afterthought, or a minor ganglion to a secondary enemy for most Americans. Yet in spite of American ignorance of things Korean during the world war, American foreign policy planning did have a place of gloved diplomacy and perfumed phrases; but it also had one of "diplomacy in the raw." Domestic American forces, which we will call nationalism and internationalism, also played themselves out in Korea, as in so many other places on the globe.

American planners had relatively little to say about Korea before the Japanese surrender; this will come as no surprise to the reader. This is not to say, however, as so many have, that the United States had *no* policy toward Korea, nothing beyond vague intentions to make Korea independent after Japan succumbed. Korea was never important to Americans as a unique entity. But it did figure prominently in the general context of American thought regarding the postwar disposition of former colonial areas; that particular problem exercised Americans as much at the end of the Second World War as it had a generation earlier at the end of the First World War. Japan's defeat would loose the bonds of control in Korea, but also in Manchuria, Taiwan, Indochina, Malaya, Indonesia, and elsewhere. The defeat of the European Axis powers would liberate colonies in Africa. Would the colonies gain independence? Would they be divided among victorious allies? Would they remain with their old masters? How could American desires for a stable, tractable postwar world be reconciled with pledges in the Atlantic Charter and elsewhere to encourage the independence and self-determination of colonized peoples?

The American response to this problem was mixed. At the pinnacle was President Franklin Delano Roosevelt, architect of a grand vision for the postwar world, one that would embrace and incorporate forces as diverse as communism, capitalism, and anticolonial nationalism. In the State Department, planners with more mundane concerns attempted to implement a presidential vision that most of them did not understand and were frustrated by a lack of direction and close consultation. In the American military, officers proposed policy with an eye to the postwar fortunes of their particular branch of the military, and with a realistic concern for the limits of American power. Thus at one level, there were bureaucratic struggles over policy; but at another and more significant level, there was a struggle between alternative visions of the American role in the world. One vision placed emphasis on the capitalist virtues of free trade, open systems, the workings of the world market, and on the progressive virtues of representative democracy, aid to the downtrodden, and a generous if paternal sharing of American blessings. The other emphasized a more rough-hewn American impulse toward asserting national interest, carving territorial spheres and national economies, and confronting enemies of the American way. The first was transnational, incorporative, and global in scale; the second was national, exclusive, and regional.[1] Roosevelt was the preeminent exponent of the first view and dominated Korean policy to a remarkable degree.

The touchstones of internationalist policy toward Korea were two: the attempt to forge a multilateral trusteeship from 1943 to 1946; and the use of the United Nations to seek a resolution of the Korean problem from 1947 to 1950. The trusteeship idea was intended to provide a benevolent condominium that would succor postcolonial peoples toward independence while maintaining an American foot in the door. The colonies would be held in trust by the great powers until such time as they were deemed ready to handle their own affairs. Multilateral trusteeship would replace unilateral colonialism, and the colonies would be started on the road to independence gradually. This was a quintessential Rooseveltian idea. The president was always at his best when discussing trusteeships; they were pet projects that befitted this benevolent grandee, who hoped to do for colonial peoples what, so it seemed, they could not do for themselves. All that was required was simply that postcolonial nations not orient themselves against American interests, as conceived in the broadest terms. H. Franz Schurmann has written that Rooseveltian imperialism "is the phenomenon of one very powerful country . . . organizing large spaces of territory in the world for purposes of security of a sort that will bring progress to the poor but also subject them to controls that will guarantee stability."[2] It is also an imperialism that thinks in "both-and" rather than "either-or" terms, maintaining that the benefit of the greatest can be that of the smallest as well. It is this having-one's-cake-and-eating-it-too syndrome that dominated American internationalist postwar diplomacy[3] and that was so characteristic of Roosevelt himself.

The trusteeship concept was thus a fundamental element of Roosevelt's vision, which was, in Willard Range's words, a "grand design for a new world order . . . aimed at nothing less than the creation of a new system of international relations."[4] A grand design he had, but it is an ahistorical error to attribute it to Roosevelt alone.[5] What was unique about FDR was that he presided over the world's most powerful nation at the time when old-world colonialism was collapsing; and unlike his predecessors, such as Woodrow Wilson, he was poised and situated to seek to implement his vision. The dream itself is as old as the United States; it is a liberalism that, in Louis Hartz's words, "elicits an impulse to impose Locke everywhere," a liberalism that rests "on miles of submerged convictions."[6] In its twentieth-century incarnation, the vision has roots in the Open Door policy, something much less significant as a policy than as an idea, or as a metaphor for American involvement abroad. The open door symbolized an expansionism that flowed freely, filled vacuums, abhorred obstacles, rejected the concept of a world divided into isolated spheres. This mode of transnational capitalism emphasized unfettered exchange relations and was deeply antithetical to the older, garden-variety imperialism.[7]

After World War I, open door thinking as it was applied to the colonies resulted in the mandate system, a means to render the colonial enterprise rational and humane and to open colonies to commercial interests at large. For the colonial peoples, it meant disinterested tutelage toward a distant independence; for the great powers, it meant freedom of access.[8] The trusteeship idea in the 1940s was close enough to the mandate system and Wilsonian diplomacy that one can say of Roosevelt what has been said about Woodrow Wilson:

> Wilsonian anti-imperialism emerges as a limited form of international reformism. That is to say, Wilson opposed traditional exploitive imperialism involving territorial annexations, armed force, protectionism, and war. . . . Wilson's basic concern, inspired both by the expansive needs of American capitalism and by his own liberal-internationalist ideology, was to make more rational and humane the existing world economic and social relationships. The mandate system . . . was a classic example of his paternalistic orientation.[9]

The difference in the 1940s was that the rise of revolutionary nationalism and the struggles of colonial peoples had made a novel idea of the 1920s into something of an anachronism; few postcolonial nations were willing to contemplate yet another round of great power tutelage toward independence. Furthermore, a new open door would not simply maintain an entry for a weak or reticent America in a world of power politics. Now the United States would emerge the most powerful nation in the world and could well expect to dominate multilateral arrangements. This was a fact of which all the Allies were well aware, and it shaped their responses to American wartime proposals.

MARCH 1943: TRUSTEESHIP EMERGENT

The trusteeship idea foundered almost from the first day it was broached in international discussions. In a meeting held in Washington on March 24, 1943, between President Roosevelt and British Foreign Secretary Anthony Eden, Roosevelt mentioned Korea and Indochina as areas for which postwar trusteeships would be particularly appropriate. Eden remarked that "the President was being very hard on the French," but accepted an American draft on trusteeships for further study.[10] This was the first of many occasions during the war when Allied opposition to or reticence about the trusteeship idea was brushed aside by the Americans. Secretary of State Cordell Hull wrote, "Eden indicated that he was favorably impressed with this proposal"; Eden later wrote, however, that he did *not* like the trusteeship idea "when Roosevelt brought it up in Washington in 1943."[11] In any case, after much prodding, Eden gave his formal response to the trusteeship draft in August 1943, a response that spoke volumes for the British attitude. According to Hull's account: "To be perfectly frank, [Eden] had to say he did not like our draft very much. He said it was the word "independence" that troubled him. He had to think of the British Empire system, which was built on the basis of Dominion and colonial status."[12]

Eden thereby joined the issue; and British—not to mention French —opposition to trusteeship marked all further wartime discussions. The British and the French did not like the implications of this idea for their colonial holdings, to be sure.[13] The Americans, as the above quotation indicates, felt, and no doubt hoped to imply, that parochial national interests were behind Allied opposition to trusteeship, while the Allies, the British in particular, understood that the intention of the trusteeship idea was the furthering of American interests. Eden clearly stated the British view: "[Roosevelt] hoped that former colonial territories, once free of their masters, would become politically and economically dependent upon the United States and had no fear that others might fill that role."[14] It is fair to conclude that the trusteeship concept barely saw the light of day in 1943 before stimulating rather substantial opposition.[15]

In spite of British opposition, American planners within the State Department went ahead with proposals for postwar trusteeships. Liberal internationalists sought to give coherence to FDR's ideas, and in so doing, set a pattern for internationalist thinking on Korea that lasted for years. The trustee powers, according to documents drafted in early 1943, would "prepare and educate" the "dependent peoples" for self-government; they would "protect them from exploitation" and "promote their economic development and social justice." In addition, the following would be done by the trustees "in the interests of the world": the powers would maintain "nondiscriminatory commercial treatment," "promote equal economic opportunity," and "contribute to general security." The trust powers for Korea, it was thought, would be China, the United States, and the Soviet Union.[16]

The Cairo Conference: Independence "In Due Course"

On December 1, 1943, the three participants in the Cairo Conference, the United States, Great Britain, and China, published a declaration that contained the first great power pledge of support for Korean independence since the Annexation:

The aforesaid three great powers, mindful of the enslavement of the people of Korea, are determined that in due course Korea shall become free and independent.[17]

Koreans welcomed the pledge, but worried about the implications of the proviso "in due course." They grasped the intent—that Koreans would not be ready to govern themselves at the end of the war—and took it as a judgment on specifically Korean weaknesses; as one exile publication put it:

> Some Americans and Europeans who are not acquainted with the Koreans' historical background, question—"Can they govern themselves?" Koreans are of an old nation. When the ancestors of northern Europe were wandering in the forests, clad in skins and practicing rites, Koreans had government of their own and attained a high degree of civilization.[18]

Koreans had had a wealth of experience with similar Japanese legitimations for control of Korean affairs. Thus for the next two years, Koreans filled their exile publications with self-justification.[19] But the participants at Cairo had no knowledge of postwar Korean potentialities. The proviso reflected only the paternalistic, gradualist element of the trusteeship idea that deemed no colonial people fit to run their own affairs without a period of tutelage.

The context of the Cairo Conference, indeed its *raison d'être*, was Roosevelt's desire to build up China as one of the Big Four powers, partially as a· means of invigorating China's resistance to Japan, but also as an essential part of his own vision of postwar East Asian power relationships.[20] Churchill thought it naive and illusory, even whimsical, to expect that China could play a positive role in the stability of postwar Asia.[21] James Peck has suggested, however:

> The emphasis on China should not be reduced to a naive or romantic gesture on Roosevelt's part. A stable, "democratic" (pro-Western) China was almost a prerequisite for a stable, peaceful Asia *if* Japan were to be demilitarized (emphasis in original).[22]

If China were too weak or unstable to play a key role in postwar Asia, the United States might have to take on more responsibilities than it planned and might have to revise its thinking about the postwar role of Japan.[23] A strong China might be expected to reassert its traditional paternal interest in Korea. A weak or divided China could not exert any significant influence in Korea, and this strategic peninsula might again become the focus of great power disputes. Roosevelt thought he could secure Chinese commitment to the stability of postwar Asia by implying an augmented role for China in Korean affairs, at the expense of immediate Korean independence. He remarked at Cairo that "China had wide aspirations which included the reoccupation of Manchuria and Korea." He thought that at a minimum Generalissimo Chiang Kai-shek would want Chinese participation in any postwar trusteeship in Korea.[24] The record of the Cairo Conference shows only that the Chinese expressed the hope that Korea would be independent after the war;[25] but Roosevelt's perceptions are what counted.[26]

China could also be relied upon to side with the Americans in most postwar disputes, thus giving the United States another major vote in any multilateral arrangement (such as a trusteeship).[27] Internationalism of this sort thereby embodied a practical core—shrewd pursuit of American interests, thus accumulating what Churchill once called "faggot votes" on the American side. This was another prime reason for Roosevelt's constituting a weak and divided China as a great power.

Roosevelt apparently did not consult the State Department experts on East Asia before the Cairo Conference, for they played no part in composing the Cairo Declaration and in fact read it only when it was published on December 1.[28] The Korean section of the declaration went through several drafts. The first rendering was in an American draft of November 24, 1943, which said Korea should become independent "at the earliest possible moment." The next day Roosevelt amended that phrase to read, "at the proper moment." Then a succeeding British draft produced the eminently British flourish, "in due course."[29] These revisions were not trivial. There is a difference between independence at the earliest possible moment and independence at the proper time. The first implies that independence is the paramount goal; the second implies that other considerations take precedence over immediate independence. The latter is precisely what Roosevelt intended to imply.

Roosevelt's personal interventions in policy making were not capricious, but they often suggested to observers, as Anthony Eden put it, a "cheerful fecklessness":

> He seemed to see himself disposing of the fate of many lands, allied no less than enemy. He did all this with so much grace that it was not easy to dissent. Yet it was too like a conjurer, skillfully juggling with balls of dynamite, whose nature he failed to understand.[30]

Perhaps the British resented Roosevelt's lectures to them on world politics, such as the one he gave to Churchill at Cairo:

> Winston, this [the trusteeship concept] is something which you are just not able to understand. You have 400 years of acquisitive in-

stinct in your blood and you just don't understand how a country might not want to acquire land somewhere if they can get it. A new period has opened in the world's history, and you will have to adjust yourself to it.[31]

Roosevelt relished his view of himself as the champion of independence and self-determination pitted against the old-world prejudices of British imperialists. He also possessed a sophisticated and shrewd understanding of the intolerance that the world would have for acquisition and annexation after the war ended; he hoped it would tolerate access. If it would tolerate access, the Americans would prevail. What FDR failed to grasp was the mood of colonial peoples, especially those in Asia, as liberation beckoned. This most accomplished of strategists was blind to the Asian peoples' impatience for full restoration of their independence. It was a peculiarly American blindness, deriving from a flawed perception of America's tutelary and proprietary colonial policies in the Philippines. This perception of fifty years of American benevolence toward Filipinos inspired paternal sympathies for the strivings of Asian colonial peoples; Roosevelt used this Philippine analogy time and again in discussions of trusteeship.[32] But the analogy overlooked the darker aspects of the American record in the Philippines, particularly the three years of counterinsurgency necessary to establish American dominance in the first place. It also overlooked the simple fact that the peoples of Indochina, Korea, Malaya, and elsewhere did not contemplate a patient wait for independence after Japan's defeat. *Noblesse oblige* would not suffice.

When Roosevelt told Marshal Stalin about the Cairo discussions when they met shortly thereafter at Teheran, he

> referred to one of his favorite topics, which was the education of the peoples of the Far Eastern colonial areas, such as Indo-China, Burma, Malaya, and the East Indies, in the arts of self-government; he pointed with pride to the American record in helping the people of the Philippines to prepare themselves for independence.[33]

The President specifically linked the Philippine experience with trusteeships for Indochina and Korea. According to the American account of his conversations with Stalin at Teheran:

> [Roosevelt] said that Chiang Kai-shek had told him China had no designs on Indochina but the people of Indochina were not yet ready for independence, to which he replied that when the U.S. acquired the Philippines, the inhabitants were not ready for independence which would be granted without qualification upon the end of the war against Japan.[34]

Roosevelt apparently told Stalin that he and Chiang had discussed a trusteeship for Indochina, "which would have the task of preparing the people for independence within a definite period of time, perhaps twenty or thirty years. Marshal Stalin completely agreed with this view."[35] Roosevelt later said that at Teheran Stalin had also agreed with him that "the Koreans are not yet capable of exercising and maintaining independent government and that they should be placed under a 40-year [*sic*] tutelage."[36]

Yalta and Potsdam: Trusteeship in the Balance

As the end of the war appeared on the horizon and as postwar considerations came to dominate the thinking of all the Allies, the essentially political character of trusteeship and the deep opposition it aroused in the European Allies became all too apparent. As the Americans faced this opposition, they also confronted internal ambiguities and contradictions concerning the postwar role of the United States —which led, in the Korean case, to planning for outright military occupation.

In informal discussions with Stalin on February 8, 1945, during the Yalta Conference, Roosevelt again spoke warmly of America as the tutor of the Filipinos, and again applied the analogy to Korea. Since the Philippines had required fifty years of tutelage, Roosevelt said, Korea should have a trusteeship of twenty to thirty years. Stalin replied by saying that the shorter the period of trusteeship, the better.[37] The American ambassador to the Soviet Union, W. Averell Harriman, was present at this meeting and later quoted Stalin as asking why a trusteeship was necessary if the Koreans could produce their own government, which Harriman assumed to mean a Soviet-style government.[38] The official transcript of the meeting does not show this, however. In any case, the Americans and the Soviets reached no firm agreement on a postwar trusteeship for Korea.

The next day Allied discussions on the trusteeship idea brought forth a vituperative attack from Churchill. According to the American account:

> Under no circumstances, [Churchill] declared hotly, would he ever consent to the fumbling fingers of forty or fifty nations prying into the life's existence of the British Empire. As long as he was Prime Minister, he declared, he would never yield one scrap of Britain's heritage.[39]

Churchill's attack apparently pleased Stalin, for he "got up from his chair, walked up and down, beamed, and at intervals broke into applause."[40] Stalin enjoyed seeing the American and British Allies at each other's throats, of course, but perhaps he also appreciated Churchill's immediate grasp of the fundamental issues at stake, which no trusteeship could paper over. Churchill's thrusts forced the issue: the Americans had to capitulate and grant that the machinery of trusteeship "was not intended to refer to the British Empire."[41]

Within weeks the Americans also capitulated to the French when Secretary of State Edward R. Stettinius told French representatives to the San Francisco United Nations Conference that "the record is entirely innocent of any official statement of this government questioning, even by implication, French sovereignty over Indochina."[42] The deliberations of the American side leading up to the United Nations Conference show clearly that trusteeship was no longer intended to apply to the colonial empires of the Allies. In a draft memorandum of March 17, 1945, the Interdepartmental Committee on Dependent Areas developed the basic formula for trusteeships that eventually was written into the United Nations Charter: the concept would apply only to territories still under the League of Nations mandate system; to areas detached from the Axis powers; and to territories *voluntarily* placed under the trusteeship system by the responsible states. The memorandum also allowed for the designation of certain territories as "strategic areas," thereby enabling the responsible power to fortify or to create bases on the territory. The latter formula reflected demands, primarily from the United States Navy, that the United States retain sole control of and have the right to fortify mandated islands in the Pacific that it had captured from the Japanese. The formula also demonstrated the elasticity of the trusteeship concept when applied to areas in which the United States had a direct interest.[43]

Some scholars have suggested that, after Roosevelt's death in April 1945, the new Truman administration subverted his sincere commitment to anticolonialism. This is especially true of those scholars critical of America's subsequent role in Indochina.[44] For them, Roosevelt's idealism raised hopes and, like a faint bell tinkling in the night, suggested that somehow things might have been different. Roosevelt's opposition to British and French colonialism was real, but his rhetoric about colonial peoples rang with the naive optimism of the Progressive Era and seemed uncomprehending and anachronistic in the 1940s.[45] It is also true, however, that in his last months Roosevelt fought a battle with nationalist elements in the military and elsewhere, a conflict that remained unresolved when he died. For example, in March 1945, when informed that the American military wanted all Japanese islands north of the equator designated as "strategic areas," FDR responded as follows: "What is the Navy's attitude in regard to the territories? Are they trying to grab everything?"[46] A subsequent memorandum of April 9, 1945 from Stettinius to FDR noted that the military wanted "complete control" over certain designated areas and stated that such activity would "prejudice all possibility of international trusteeship." A few days later, Stettinius referred to the military as having "a policy of annexation."[47] James Forrestal and Henry Stimson urged on the State Department "a system of defense in the Pacific," rather than vague plans for trusteeships, and urged "full control" of necessary territories. Stettinius, however, continued to seek a policy that would allow for strategic bases in the Pacific and still escape charges that the United States had "annexation[ist] and expansionist policies."[48]

Roosevelt's internationalism was nonterritorial and opposed to unilateral control of any country or region; Americans would prevail without such means. It did not seek to oppose anticolonial nationalism, but to channel and corral it through American tutelage and in the interests of world commerce. And it was not anticommunist in a direct and frontal sense, seeking instead to embrace and envelop the Soviet Union in a host of multilateral arrangements that would hamstring it and render its insurgent impulses manageable. By the time of his death, FDR had retreated from his opposition to the return of French rule in Indochina and from his plans for an Indochina trusteeship. This was less because of chastened idealism, however, than because his idealism was always a useful vehicle for a policy designed both to end unilateral colonialism and to prevent, or at least shape, the emergence of communism. As Walter LaFeber has argued, when forced to choose between the two in Indochina, FDR chose France.[49]

Harry S Truman succeeded to the presidency in April 1945, a politician grossly inexperienced in foreign affairs and "temperamentally a nationalist." With Truman at the helm, postwar American policy was skewed more toward nationalism, and the nationalists among FDR's advisors suddenly gained a hearing.[50] The Americans still pressed for Allied agreement on a trusteeship for Korea, however. An internal memorandum in mid-May 1945 acknowledged that the subject had been "discussed only orally at Yalta" and that clarification of Soviet intentions was required.[51] In May 1945 President Truman sent FDR's close advisor Harry Hopkins to Moscow to try to firm up postwar commitments made by the Russians before Roosevelt died. Hopkins urged a four-power trusteeship for Korea: "it might be twenty-five years; it might be less, but it would certainly be five or ten." According to the American transcript, Stalin replied that he "fully agreed" with this proposal.[52] But again this was no more than an informal, verbal understanding.

The lack of detailed, written agreement on the postwar status of Korea distressed State Department policy planners, particularly since, under the Yalta Agreement, the Soviet Union would play a dominant role in neighboring Manchuria. Therefore, they determined that at the Potsdam Conference in July 1945 there should be "a detailed discussion" of a postwar trusteeship for Korea.[53] American planners sought, as a "maximum objective," Allied—and particularly Soviet—agreement on joint actions relating to trusteeship; and as a "minimum objective," Soviet adherence to the Cairo Declaration. They thought either would prevent unilateral action by any of the Allies designed to set up "a 'friendly' government,"[54] which was a code phrase for Sovietization. Other planning documents indicated that the Americans viewed Soviet adherence to the Cairo Declaration as implied, formal approval of a trusteeship for Korea.[55]

The Soviets also hoped for an exchange of views on a trusteeship for Korea at Potsdam. On July 3, 1945, Harriman wired Truman from Moscow concerning Stalin's talks with the Chinese representative T. V. Soong, saying that "with reference to Korea, Stalin confirmed to Soong his agreement to establish a 4-power trusteeship. Molotov interjected that this was *an unusual arrangement with no parallel* and that therefore it would be necessary to have *a detailed understanding*" (emphasis added).[56] In a meeting at Potsdam of the Allied heads of state on July 22, 1945, Stalin began discussions on trusteeships by recommending that they begin with Korea. Churchill, however, began talking about the disposition of Italian colonies in Africa. When Stalin then asked which powers would participate in a trusteeship over Italian colonies like Libya, "Churchill said he did not see what their Soviet Allies wanted. Did Stalin wish to put forward a claim to one of these Italian colonies." Churchill went on to say that "he had not considered the possibility of the Soviet Union desiring to acquire a large tract of the African shore."[57] Amid such recriminations and accusations of bad faith, plans to discuss postwar Korea dissolved. Further discussions had to be put off until a later Council of Foreign Ministers meeting, which did not come until December 1945 (see chapter seven).

Churchill and Stalin had no difficulty in grasping the political implications of the trusteeship concept. Such things came as second nature to them. Certain Americans, however, not only had trouble comprehending the Rooseveltian internationalist vision that underlay the idea but also, quite rightly and realistically, questioned whether the United States could expect adherence to the concept from Allies with very different sets of interests. As Secretary of War Henry Stimson put it, no Allied discussions of trusteeship could usefully proceed without a consideration of the specific areas to be trusteed. Immediately the subject is introduced, the various powers would certainly consider the subject in the light of how it would affect the areas in which they are interested or which they covet.[58]

This is precisely what happened every time the issue appeared in wartime Allied discussions. It is possible, however, that a bilateral agreement on Korea between the United States and the USSR could have been worked out at some point in 1945 before the war ended. An essential aspect of the Roosevelt world vision was to incorporate the Soviet Union into an Anglo-American partnership, acknowledge its interests, and give it responsibilities for maintaining the peace.[59] The Korean peninsula, as a state contiguous to the USSR, required, even demanded, full Soviet participation in any postwar arrangements; with American recognition of this fact, some formula to neutralize Korea might have been possible. This could have taken the form of mutual pledges to respect Korean sovereignty and a truly joint Soviet-American occupation of the peninsula to receive the Japanese surrender, followed by a quick withdrawal of all foreign troops. Such an idea may sound preposterous three decades after the fact, yet there is no evidence that either Roosevelt or Stalin saw overriding strategic interests in the Korean peninsula. Perhaps the ideal time to pursue such an option would have been during the Potsdam Conference when, as we will see, it was not clear that either American or Soviet military imperatives required an entry into Korea.

Such an option was not pursued, however, because, among other reasons, the view had taken hold within the military and the State Department that trusteeship arrangements were not a sufficient hedge against potential Soviet duplicity on a peninsula increasingly defined as essential to the security of the postwar Pacific. From late 1943 on, State Department planners began to worry about a Korea in Soviet hands; and from early 1944 on, they began to plan for a partial or full military occupation of Korea. Much of this planning was done in territorial subcommittees of the State Department, the membership of which included officers who came to play important roles in Korean policy throughout the 1940s, among them: Hugh Borton, John Carter Vincent, William R. Langdon, and H. Merrell Benninghoff. It was also at this time that a set of assumptions about Korea were enunciated, ones that would later prove to be quite consistent: Korea was important to postwar American security concerns; a Korea entirely in hostile (that is, Soviet) hands was a threat to that security; Korea could not govern itself after Japan's defeat; multinational administration of Korea was preferable to unilateral means, unless American predominance was in jeopardy; trusteeship arrangements were the preferable means for handling postwar great power conflicts over Korea, but partial or full military occupation of Korea might be necessary to assure an American voice.

In November 1943 a territorial subcommittee paper noted that "the security of the North Pacific will be of concern to the US"; Korea will also be of concern, since "Korea's political development may effect this security."[60] At about the same time, Benninghoff, Vincent, Borton, and Alger Hiss, among others, prepared and reviewed a paper containing the following statement:

> Korea may appear to offer a tempting opportunity to apply the Soviet conception of the proper treatment of colonial peoples, to strengthen enormously the economic resources of the Soviet Far East, to acquire ice-free ports, and to occupy a dominating strategic position in relation both to China and to Japan. . . . A Soviet occupation of Korea would create an entirely new strategic situation in the Far East, and its repercussions within China and Japan might be far reaching.[61]

The reader should be reminded that this was a time when the Soviets were still pressing the Americans to open a second front in Europe. In terms of traditional American security concerns, to include Korea implied a great leap forward in American expansionism. What created "an entirely new strategic situation in the Far East" was not that Russia was interested in Korea—it had been for decades—but that the United States was interested.

State Department planning in March 1944 envisioned an American occupation of Korea and noted the importance for American postwar aims of United States participation in whatever military operations took place in Korea:

> The assumption by the United States of a major part in civil affairs and in international supervision of an interim government would be greatly facilitated by the participation of the United States in such military operations as take place in and around Korea.[62]

This paper also raised the possibility of a military government, a short one it was to be hoped, but potentially one of "considerable duration." The planners of this paper thought the Soviet Far East harbored 35,000 Koreans, "thoroughly indoctrinated with Soviet ideology and methods of government." They expected the Soviets to be "in occupation of considerable portions of Koreas" but that the occupation was not to be zonal; American forces were to cooperate with the Soviets in administering Korea prior to the imposition of a trusteeship.[63] This analysis recommended occupation first, trusteeship later, because actual occupation was a surer course were the Soviets to prove uncooperative, or were they to utilize their "thoroughly indoctrinated" Koreans. Another paper dated two months later stated that if Soviet forces occupied Korea alone, "the United States might consider such a development as a threat to the future security of the Pacific."[64] Such early expectations of Soviet bad faith may have had the effect of willing it into existence and thereby tainting subsequent American responses to Soviet activities.

State Department plans for occupying Korea spoke in the same breath of cooperation and conflict with the Soviets, of simple American participation in occupation arrangements and American dominance. In an important study developed for the Yalta Conference, State Department planners wrote:

> It is the view of the department that the problems of Korea are of such an international character that with the completion of military operations in Korea, (1) there should be, so far as practicable, Allied representation in the army of occupation and military government in Korea; (2) such representation should be by those countries which have a real interest in the future status of Korea, such as the United States, Great Britain, and China and the Soviet Union if it has entered the war in the Pacific; (3) the representation of other states should not be so large as to reduce the proportionate strength of the United States to a point where its effectiveness would be weakened.[65]

Again it was suggested that Korea should be administered "as a single unit and not as separate zones." But the key point was that American strength should be large enough to ensure "effectiveness"—the United States "should play a leading role in the occupation and military government."[66]

A subsequent planning paper for the Potsdam Conference said:

> It is possible that the Soviet Union will make strong demands that it have a leading part in the control of Korean affairs. If such demands required the establishment of an administrative authority in which powers other than the Soviet Union had only a nominal voice, it might be advisable to designate Korea as a trust area and to place it under the authority of the United Nations organization itself.[67]

This paragraph stated succinctly the essential problem, "control of Korean affairs," and laid out three means to achieving that end: an administrative authority [occupation], trusteeship, and the use of the fledgling United Nations organization to realize American political goals. The Americans could turn from one to the other, as one became more or less effective in enabling them to control Korea, or a part of it. The sequence established above was followed in Korea from 1945 to 1948, and some even recommended its virtues for securing American interests in China.[68]

We must recognize the unprecedented expression of ambition contained in the preceding paragraphs. Until 1943, the United States had never expressed much interest in the security of the Korean peninsula. Indeed, it had given its blessing to Japanese plans for Korea in 1905, and had not challenged them thereafter. Now here it was proposing to project its power onto the Asian mainland and to challenge the Soviet Union in a country that touched Soviet borders, one in which the Russians had long had an interest. For these American planners, trusteeship amounted to just one means among many capable of securing American interests; it was not simply an artful device meant to secure certain minimum interests and recognize those of the Soviets as well. Instead of "both-and" thinking, they favored "either-or" thinking. Roosevelt had excluded the State Department from much of his postwar planning, especially regarding trusteeships. He did not trust the department's planners to understand his program.[69] They, in turn, were forced to plan policy without much presidential guidance. There is no evidence that the plans discussed above had any impact on Roosevelt's ideas; but after his executive leadership was gone, bureaucratic power was cast upward, and the plans of 1943 and 1944, and the planners themselves, became more relevant than they might have been had Roosevelt lived. In any case, as will be argued throughout this study, we can discern a consistent set of assumptions about Korea that emerged in 1943 and continued up to 1950.

The complexities, contradictions, and ambiguities of American wartime planning for Korea persisted until Japan's defeat. That there was not a unanimous State Department view, but a mélange of competing views, is evident from a remarkable document compiled in the summer of 1945, which laid out alternatives that bear little resemblance to the subsequent record of the American Occupation. That is to say, the actions taken by the Occupation were in fact *choices* made between competing visions. This paper, entitled, "An Estimate of Conditions in Asia and the Pacific at the Close of the War in the Far East and the Objectives and Policies of the United States," pledged "the right of all peoples to choose the form of Government under which they will live."[70] It bordered on being anti-imperialist, speaking of the historical extension of Western sovereignty in Asia "by war, threat of war, and exploitation of ignorance." It demonstrated an excellent grasp of the agrarian situation within Korea at the end of Japanese rule, noting that the majority of Korean farmers were tenants, subject to "extortionate treatment" by Japanese and Korean landlords; it said these farmers would "undoubtedly expect sweeping agrarian reforms and may take definite steps to destroy the control of the landlords both Japanese and Korean." The paper refused to prejudge potential Soviet actions in Korea. Although it noted that the Soviets might want to set up a "friendly" government, such a regime, it said, "might easily receive popular support . . . [since] the economic and political situation in Korea would be conducive to the adoption of communist ideology." The paper ended its section on Korea by recommending that the United States "participate in both the military government and the interim administration of Korea" and assist Koreans in establishing "a strong, democratic, independent nation." The paper did not specify, however, how anti-imperialism was to be wedded to American postwar aims in East Asia, or how sweeping agrarian reforms would correlate with American interests and definitions of democracy, or how the United States and the Soviet Union were to set up compatible regimes in Korea. The resolution of these ambiguities awaited future events.

The First Postwar Act of Containment: The Partition of Korea in August 1945

The development of the war in the Pacific did not augur well for significant American participation in Korean affairs in the summer of 1945. The American military planned an invasion of the Japanese home islands (Kyushu) to commence around November 1, 1945, and only after the homeland was secured would attention turn to Korea. At the Potsdam Conference in July 1945, the military situation could not be ignored, and the invasion of Korea was left, in effect, entirely to Soviet military operations. The record at Potsdam clearly shows the unanimity of American military planners on the need for Soviet entry into the war against Japan. A key document said, "with reference to clean-up of the Asiatic mainland, our objective should be to get the Russians to deal with the Japs in Manchuria (and Korea if necessary)."[71] The parenthetical contingency regarding Korea was clarified in a Tripartite Military Meeting of July 24, when George C. Marshall, Chief of Staff of the United States Army, informed the Russians, in response to their query on the prospect of joint American-Soviet operations against Korea, that American amphibious landings "had not been contemplated, and particularly not in the near future"; he said that "there were no additional assault ships which would permit a landing in Korea . . . [and] the possibility of an attack on Korea would have to be determined after the landings on Kyushu."[72]

Secret American estimates of Japanese armed strength in June 1945 in Manchuria and Korea had put the total at 875,000 men (and Americans had a high opinion of the Japanese Kwantung Army in Manchuria). The estimate for Kyushu was 300,000.[73] Although these estimates later proved to be exaggerated, American thinking about Korea and about Soviet participation cannot be judged today except in terms of their expectations in July 1945. At that time, they seemed to expect losses incurred in invading the Japanese homeland to be exceedingly high, but those incurred in invading Manchuria and Korea to be even higher. The Americans wanted to leave the latter operation, and the attendant losses, to the Soviet land armies. And for this, they were willing to pay a high price. General Douglas MacArthur had spelled out the consequences some months earlier: the Soviets "would want all of Manchuria, Korea and possibly part of North China. This seizure of territory was inevitable; but the United States must insist that Russia pay her way by invading Manchuria at the earliest possible moment."[74] At Potsdam the American military was still ready to grant the Soviets their (putative) goals as a quid pro quo because, it thought, "the impact of Russian entry on the already hopeless Japanese may well be the decisive action levering them into capitulation."[75]

The American military did not anticipate Japan's virtual overnight collapse, however. They could not, even in the first week of August, predict the effects of the atomic bombing of Nagasaki and Hiroshima or those of the rapid Soviet engagement of Japanese forces on the Asiatic mainland. It is likely that the Soviets were in the same situation in these weeks. Thus Soviet Army Chief of Staff, Alexey Antonov, may have accurately stated anticipated Russian goals when he said at Potsdam, "the objective of the U.S.S.R. in the Far East was the destruction of the Japanese troops in Manchuria and the occupation of the Liaotung Peninsula."[76]

Given the military situation, it is conceivable that an agreement to neutralize Korea could have been reached at Potsdam, as we have suggested. Certainly any agreement would have had to account for the fact that military operations in Korea had been left to the Soviets. Had the subject been broached, the Soviets might have argued for a free hand in Korea in return for entry into the war. On the other hand, they might have agreed to stay out of Korea in return for American assurances of nonintervention in Korean affairs. At Potsdam—and indeed throughout discussions of the use of military power

1. Kim Il Sung (center) during his guerrilla days in the 1930s

2. Yŏ Un-hyŏng greeting young people on August 16, 1945

in Korea, up to and including the Blair House conferences in June 1950—the United States military consistently maintained the position that the Korean peninsula had no strategic value to the United States in time of general world conflict.[77] For the United States to take on responsibilities for the defense of Korea would strain resources to the limit; a better place could be found to make a stand. However much certain liberal internationalists may wish to blame the American military for decisions taken in Korea in the 1940s, the responsibility rests with political planners. At Potsdam it was these officials, close advisors to the president and the president himself, who determined in the middle of the conference that the successful testing of the atomic bomb at Alamogordo, New Mexico, provided an opportunity to abjure diplomacy, draw the Pacific War to a quick close, and exclude the Soviets from significant participation in postwar East Asian affairs— in effect, to contain the Russians.[78] The United States dropped atomic bombs on Hiroshima and Nagasaki on August 6 and 9, Soviet forces quickly and unexpectedly engaged Japanese forces on the Asian mainland, and Japan collapsed. In the immediate aftermath of these events, Korea was divided at latitude 38° North, into American and Soviet occupation zones.

The initial decision to draw a line at the thirty-eighth parallel was wholly an American action, taken during a night-long session of the State-War-Navy Coordinating Committee (SWNCC), on August 10-11, 1945. There are several versions of this meeting, one of which follows:

> About midnight, August 10-11, 1945, Colonel Charles H. Bonesteel and Major Dean Rusk . . . began drafting part of a General Order that would define the zones to be occupied in Korea by American and Russian forces. They were given thirty minutes to complete their draft, which a State-War-Navy Coordinating Committee was waiting for. The State Department wished the dividing line to be as far north as possible, while the military departments, knowing that the Russians could overrun all of Korea before any American troops could land there, were more cautious. Bonesteel and Rusk wanted to follow provincial boundary lines north of Seoul, which would violate political divisions as little as possible and would place the capital city in the American zone. The only map immediately available was a small-scale wall map of the Far East, and time was pressing. Bonesteel noted that the 38th Parallel passed north of Seoul and almost divided Korea into two equal parts. He seized on it as the proposed zonal boundary.[79]

An eyewitness account by Dean Rusk generally agreed with the above rendering. Rusk wrote that he and Bonesteel were asked by John J.

McCloy (representing the Army in SWNCC) "to retire to an adjoining room and come up with a proposal which could harmonize the political desire to have U.S. forces receive the surrender as far north as possible and the obvious limitations on the ability of the U.S. forces to reach the area."[80] It is important to note in both of these accounts that the character of the decision was essentially political and that representatives of the State Department advocated the political virtues of partition into spheres, while representatives of the military cautioned that the forces necessary to secure a foothold in Korea might be lacking.

Rusk commented that the thirty-eighth parallel was "further north than could be realistically reached . . . in the event of Soviet disagreement"; and when the Soviets agreed to the proposed division, he was "somewhat surprised." Another account stated that after the American proposal was communicated to the Russians, "there was a short period of suspense" in anticipation of the Russian reply, accompanied by suggestions that American troops be rushed into Pusan if the Russians refused to accept the American proposal.[81] Thus the selection of this line represented an explicit test of Soviet intentions. Would they halt their march south? The test went rather well. Soviet forces entered Korea almost a full month before American forces, with the whole peninsula theirs for the taking; yet they honored the agreement.[82] American troops were later able to occupy the portion of Korea that included its capital, two-thirds of its population, most of its light industry, and the greater part of its agricultural capacity. It is also comforting to note the presence in the deliberations of Dean Rusk, an archetypal containment thinker who twenty years later would stubbornly insist "on restoring the inviolability of the 17th parallel in Vietnam."[83]

Stalin probably chose to honor the agreement because he interpreted the parallel as designating a strict, sphere-of-influence quid pro quo. The Russians and the Japanese had discussed dividing Korea at the thirty-eighth parallel in 1896 and again in 1903.[84] Stalin made explicit references in 1945 to recovering interests lost to the Japanese in the Russo-Japanese War (1904-1905).[85] Like the Americans, the Soviets might have preferred a unified, friendly Korea, but a divided Korea would well serve the basic security interest of the Soviet state—assurance that the Korean peninsula would not provide venue for an attack against Russia. As William Morris argues, Stalin probably also limited Soviet actions in Korea out of a desire to maintain Allied cooperation.[86] Whatever the reason, Stalin permitted joint action in a region where he had the power to take full control.

Japan's collapse thus provided an unexpected opportunity for

American forces to move into a country that had been all but conceded to the Russians only days earlier at Potsdam. In that short time, the ambiguities inherent in two years of American planning for postwar Korea were resolved: occupation was the surer method, joint measures or trusteeship arrangements being unreliable, so American troops were rushed into the breach. Although the decision was taken quickly, even rashly, in the hectic days of mid-August, it was a logical result of previous planning that, as early as October 1943, had linked control of the Korean peninsula to the security of the Pacific. A Korea wholly in Soviet hands was seen as a threat to that security. Relating the decision "only" to the acceptance of the Japanese surrender (the official American apology for the actions since 1945) obscures what was, in fact, the point: the developing power relationship in East Asia was contingent on who received the surrender and where; this was based on the principle that "military victory would define local politics."[87]

Thus the first round on Korea went to the nationalists. Had the State Department not defined this peninsula, previously in the far periphery of American concerns, as essential to postwar Pacific security, internationalism might have prevailed. As we have seen, military planners, always the realists when the chips are down, knew they did not have the forces to occupy Korea if the Soviets resisted. State planners urged the military to run up the peninsula as far as possible, for the political purpose of staunching the Russian flow southward. Instead of having one's cake and eating it too, August 1945 brought only half the cake.

Okinawa to Seoul: The "Scramble"

It is a strange fate that brought a one-time farm boy from Golconda, Illinois, to rule over the fortunes of fifteen million Koreans. John Reed Hodge, commander of the XXIV Corps of the United States Tenth Army, became Commanding General, United States Armed Forces in Korea (USAFIK), largely because in August 1945 his forces could be moved most quickly into the perceived vacuum on the Korean peninsula caused by Japan's rapid collapse. Although the United States had made no firm decision to occupy southern Korea until the SWNCC meetings of August 10-11, the General Headquarters of the American Forces in the Pacific under General Douglas MacArthur had developed certain contingency plans in May 1945 for an invasion of Japan that implied an eventual occupation of Korea. On July 16 MacArthur's headquarters issued Operation Blacklist, providing detailed instructions for the occupation of Japan and, if possible, Korea.[88] The portion of Operation Blacklist dealing with Korea was designated Operation Baker. It envisioned a three-phase occupation: phase one would cover the occupation of the Seoul/Inch'ŏn region; phase two, the Pusan region; phase three, the Kunsan region. It allocated three infantry divisions under the XXIV Corps of the United States Tenth Army to the occupation.[89]

On June 23, 1945, General MacArthur had appointed General Joseph W. Stilwell as Commander of the Tenth Army.[90] At some point in mid-August, however, the XXIV Corps was withdrawn from the Tenth Army and placed under MacArthur's direct command.[91] Apparently Generalissimo Chiang Kai-shek had objected to a Stilwell command over any American occupation forces landing on the China coast or in Korea. Washington acquiesced to Chiang.[92] Although it is unclear whether Stilwell would have assumed direct command of the occupation of Korea had the XXIV Corps remained in his jurisdiction, it is fair to assume that Chiang's intervention had the desired effect of removing Stilwell's influence.

General MacArthur then appointed John R. Hodge, the XXIV Corps commander, as Commanding General, USAFIK.[93] In many ways, Hodge was reminiscent of Stilwell. He was "a soldier's soldier," noted for his simple, blunt, direct approach; he was quite "without pose or affectation."[94] Born in the gently rolling farmlands of southern Illinois, Hodge came up through the military the hard way. He was not a West Point graduate; instead he pursued his military education at the Command and General Staff School and at the Army War College. His rank of lieutenant general, attained at the war's end, came largely from his distinguished record in the Pacific War. He was wounded during the Bougainville campaign, where he commanded the newly formed Americal Division. Thereafter, he commanded forces at Guadalcanal, Leyte, and in the bloody, difficult Okinawa fighting that became "the last battle."[95] For his heroism in these campaigns, he was awarded the Legion of Merit and the Distinguished Service Medal.[96] His aggressive warfare led war correspondents to designate him "the Patton of the Pacific,"[97] but his lack of pomp and pretense and his popularity with the troops were more suggestive of Stilwell. Unlike Stilwell, however, Hodge had no experience with Asian culture or politics.

In August 1945 the XXIV Corps on Okinawa was a battle-weary, drained, depleted force. Because of heavy losses in the Okinawa campaign, a significant percentage of its rank and file soldiers were green recruits just out of boot camp. But it was a well-officered corps, its higher ranks consisting of confident, battle-tested veterans.[98] The XXIV Corps drew duty in Korea because of its relative proximity to the peninsula, not because of any obvious proficiency for administering Korean affairs. Much has been made of this allegedly strange criterion for choosing an occupation force, as if Korea were the only place where such considerations applied, and as if a choice based on proximity reflected poor planning and half-hearted commitment to postwar Korea.[99] In fact, proximity was the criterion applied in selecting initial occupation contingents for all American-occupied territories. Infantry divisions like those of the XXIV Corps were to implement the initial phase of occupation (so-called tactical occupation) and were to be replaced by military government teams as soon as possible. A relative abundance of such teams replaced XXIV Corps tactical units rather quickly in Korea, as we will see. Thus perceived failures in the occupation of Korea cannot be blamed on the unpreparedness of Hodge and his XXIV Corps any more than perceived successes in the occupation of Japan can be attributed to the quality of American planning and personnel there. Responsibility for failure and success rested at a higher level.

In August 1945 American planners in Washington thought of military occupation as an extension of political policy and infantry troops as the agents of policy implementation. The XXIV Corps and other infantry divisions were used as mobile resources, to fill vacuums, to staunch the flow of alien ideologies and political movements, and to be the general shock forces in redrawing the strategic lines of great power politics. That such infantry forces might be ill-prepared and uncomprehending was of little moment. In fact, it was a given in the situation. The point was just to get them there.

Four days before the Japanese surrender, Ambassador Harriman in Moscow urged that infantry forces move into Korea and the Kwantung peninsula.[100] Truman's close personal advisor and representative concerning reparations Edwin Pauley also urged from Moscow that American troops "occupy quickly as much of the industrial areas of Korea and Manchuria as we can."[101] Planners at SWNCC in Washington had a better understanding of the limits of American troop movement capabilities and hoped that Russian acquiescence in General Order No. 1 would allow occupation of southern Korea at least. But "if the Russians failed to accept the proposal, and if Russian troops occupied Seoul, General [George A.] Lincoln suggested that American forces move into Pusan."[102] Some of these helter-skelter suggestions filtered down to officers of the XXIV Corps on Okinawa, who can be excused if they failed to make adequate preparations for occupying Korea, Manchuria, the Kwantung Peninsula, Japan, or Tientsin.[103] Even after the announcement on Okinawa on August 11 that the XXIV Corps would occupy south Korea, there was a brief period when it looked like they would not enter Korea at all.[104] And once a firm decision to move the XXIV Corps into Korea was made, the date of entry was moved up three times. On August 12, it was decided that the entry date would be "V-J day plus twenty-seven," which everyone expected would mean an entry sometime late in September. Japan's surrender on August 14 (American time) moved the date up to September 11. On August 27 it was decided that an initial contingent of troops would be sent into Korea on September 7; then shortly thereafter, Hodge narrowed that to "a small advance party" to arrive by September 4.[105] Small wonder that Hodge later referred to "that scramble move" from Okinawa to Seoul.[106]

The reason for this scramble into Korea was not that the Japanese enemy was putting up strong resistance or engaging in depredations in Korea, as some might think. The date of American entry was moved up repeatedly because of the rapid Russian advance into Manchuria and Korea.[107] One of MacArthur's officers said: "A rapid movement into Korea has the backing and direction of the President. Numerous radios have been exchanged with the War Department in which the priority of the Keijo [Seoul] area has been greatly stressed."[108] The Joint Chiefs of Staff cabled MacArthur on August 24 saying, in reference to the need to move rapidly into Korea, "There is no certain assurance that the Soviets will not continue their occupation movements southward in Korea until such time as they meet US forces."[109] Within the State Department, Far Eastern staffers "concluded that the major factor in the Korean question was no longer the necessity of tutelage, but the prevention of a Soviet sponsored regime." One of them suggested that American forces have no specific time limit on their stay in Korea but instead remain "as long as necessary," or until Korea was enmeshed in a system of international security.[110]

An entry in the XXIV Corps Journal dated August 25 reads, "Truman anxious to have Korea occupied promptly."[111] Official historians on the scene in Okinawa reported that "the possibility of Russian movement south [of the thirty-eighth parallel] continued high in the minds of the American staffs."[112] MacArthur sent supplementary instructions to Hodge on August 29 saying that he should proceed into Korea, even if the Russians were occupying Seoul, unless "international complications" would result, in which case the landing would be delayed.[113] But the Russians never proceeded further south than Kaesŏng, just below the thirty-eighth parallel; and they withdrew from there well before the American entry.[114] A month after Korea was nearly conceded to the Russians at Potsdam, the United States was sponsoring a rush into Korea and had acquired, so it seemed, a commitment to defend at least a part of Korea against Soviet encroachments or a Soviet-sponsored regime. The scramble into Korea, and this commitment, had the support of virtually all government agencies concerned with the matter, from the presidency on down.

POLICY AND PLANNING BEFORE DEPARTURE

In the existing literature, the XXIV Corps is depicted as having been a virtual *tabula rasa* upon its entry into Korea. Gregory Henderson has written that the occupation forces "had no selfish aims; indeed, they did not have any aims at all, lacking policy."[115] We should examine this claim more closely, however: first, what did the XXIV Corps understand of United States policy toward Korea; second, did the occupation have aims? Hodge and his troops met their first difficulty in that the assumption underlaying almost all military planning for postwar occupations was that defeated, not liberated nations would be occupied. Article 43 of the Hague Convention, the primary statute of international law governing military occupation, gave hostile occupations virtually unlimited power, whereas pacific occupations were to be governed by agreements covering the specific rights and duties of the occupant. It made a big difference whether the citizens of occupied territory were deemed hostile or peaceful, defeated or liberated, enemies or friends.[116] Another crucial assumption of American planning was that the war itself was a struggle against lawlessness and that after victory "the rule of law" must prevail.[117] The perceived lawlessness of the fascist powers would require a thorough revamping of their institutions; otherwise, what had the war been about?

So, had Korea been defeated or liberated? Were Koreans enemies or friends? The Cairo Declaration in 1943 referred to Korean "enslavement," acknowledging by implication that Korea was not an enemy, but rather the first victim of Japanese aggression. General Stilwell sent a radio message to Okinawa on August 14 declaring that the occupation of Korea was to be regarded as "semi-friendly"; that is, "all but about five per cent of the population who are Japanese" were to be considered friendly.[118] And at the end of August, MacArthur directed the XXIV Corps to treat Koreans as "liberated people."[119] But on September 4, General Hodge instructed his own officers that Korea "was an enemy of the United States" and therefore "subject to the provisions and the terms of the surrender."[120] Official occupation sources later reported that "government and its activities and attitudes were modelled upon the experience in enemy countries and on the usual instructions and training of an army in a hostile country."[121] Southern Korea was subjected to a hostile occupation possessing the full panoply of powers of a victor in enemy territory; and the Occupation did not relinquish these powers until August 15, 1948. Yet occupation officers had been told that Korea was to be liberated. What happened?

It appears that the Occupation command on Okinawa hearkened more to Japanese definitions of the *mise en scene* in Korea than to whatever passed for established American policy on Korea. On August 29 the colonial Government-General got the following message through to Okinawa:

> The condition in northern Korea has taken a sudden turn for the worse since 23 August and the lives and property of the Japanese residents are exposed to imminent danger. This deplorable situation, if left unremedied, will in all probability spread to southern Korea. . . .
>
> Accordingly, the local Japanese authorities eagerly await for the arrival of the Allied Forces which are to take [over] the maintenance of peace and order from the Japanese forces in southern Korea, and urgently desire that the Allied forces will fully take into consideration the actual conditions on the spot before proceeding with the disarmament of Japanese forces and *the transfer of administrative organs from the Japanese hand* (emphasis added).[122]

MacArthur's covering memo referred to this message and in effect gave General Hodge *carte blanche* to do as he saw fit: "You will take such action on this matter in southern Korea as future events may justify."[123]

After some difficulty, the XXIV Corps established direct radio contact with Seoul on August 31, and "a flood of messages poured through in both directions."[124] Lieutenant General Kozuki Yoshio radioed from Seoul on September 1, "there are communist and independence agitators among Koreans who are plotting to take advantage of the situation to disturb peace and order here." In other messages on that day and the next two, Kozuki warned of possible sabotage of the American landing in Korea by "Red" labor unions and told of "Korean mob violence against the police, theft of munitions, and strikes." He asserted that his position was difficult and that he "was eagerly awaiting the arrival of the Americans."[125]

Kozuki's messages had a direct influence on Hodge. On September 1 Hodge told Kozuki to maintain order and preserve the existing machinery of government. He ordered some 300,000 leaflets dropped over southern Korea from September 1 to 5, which said essentially the same thing (see Appendix 3). On September 1 he also sent a message to MacArthur, saying in part:

> In view of the situation peculiar to Korea, where revolutionary forces may acquire Japanese arms and start serious trouble, request authority to destroy or render completely inoperative any and all weapons turned over by the Japanese armed forces.

MacArthur approved this request.[126] Hodge later reported that the Japanese had been his best sources of information and that they had greatly aided the American entry into Korea.[127]

Americans from SWNCC on down desired to block the southward flow of Soviet power in Korea; this dictated the occupation in the first place. Hodge and the XXIV Corps understood the imperatives behind their rush from Okinawa to Korea. But by early September, they knew better than Washington that they would confront not only the Soviets but indigenous revolutionaries as well. Thus Hodge and his officers cooperated with and utilized the Japanese in ways that would subsequently appear unseemly to Americans of higher authority in the distant and comfortable confines of Washington. In doing so, a pattern was set that would continue for years, whereby Hodge would go beyond the bounds of his authority, force issues, and end up in embarrassing predicaments. Hodge always did with directness and dispatch whatever he found necessary to do to secure American interests in Korea. As he did so, however, events originating in Korea swayed policy in Washington.

In August and September of 1945, Koreans changed to quasi-enemies, and Japanese to friends, in the eyes of the American Occupation, because changing evaluations of the wartime Soviet ally directly affected American perceptions of Korea and the imperatives of occupation and control. This, however, was not the supreme irony. That accolade goes to the astonishing fact that Korea got the occupation designed for Japan. In early September, MacArthur and others decided to utilize the existing administration in Japan, meaning that no real military government would be established. From 1942 on, some 2,000-plus army and navy officers had trained for duty in the occupation of Japan. But when it became apparent that military government (or "civil affairs") teams would do little real governing in Japan, but rather would supervise the Japanese administrators, the majority of these teams were transferred to the occupation of Korea. Korea became "the one country in the Pacific Theater over which a real military government was established."[128] Some twenty-eight military government companies were transferred from Japan to Korea, resulting in "a super-abundance" of such teams; 87 officers and 247 enlisted men who had been trained for civil affairs had entered Korea with the first wave of American forces on September 8, and by September 27, 450 of the 600 military government officers then deemed necessary were either in Korea or on their way. About half of the total number of officers working in military government bureaus in the fall of 1945 had training or experience in military government. Ultimately, nearly 2,000 officers staffed the American Military Government (MG) in Korea, leading some to describe it as a "general's government." These officers did not know the Korean language (many *had* studied Japanese), but that hardly makes this operation different from any other in Asia since 1945.

What did the XXIV Corps and the civil affairs teams know of Korea? They had with them on Okinawa a massive, detailed study entitled "Joint Army-Navy Intelligence Study of Korea" (JANIS-75), a remarkably accurate source on Korea in 1945.[129] It noted the strong desires of Koreans for independence and their long history of self-rule and said that Koreans "would prefer the initial inefficiencies of administrative inexperience to the danger of extended control by some successor to Japan." The benefits of Japanese rule, it stated, had fallen mostly to the aristocratic minority, whereas tenant-farmers were badly oppressed. This document was so voluminous that the XXIV Corps officers, far from having nothing to study, probably had too much.[130]

On September 3 H. Merrell Benninghoff, State Department liaison and political advisor to Hodge, arrived on Okinawa. The official history of the occupation stated that he had "been given the briefest of instructions in Washington and added little to the sum total of knowledge on overall policy towards Korea."[131] In fact, Benninghoff received substantial briefing; he had been a prominent figure in State Department planning for Korea from 1943 on. The problem was that he had been briefed on the trusteeship idea and the basic instruments of surrender in Korea, both of which seemed to lose relevance, as Americans learned more about domestic events in Korea. The occupation forces, then, did have aims, and they did have policy; the problem was in the "fit" of policy established in Washington to circumstances that they found upon landing in Korea. Local events made the internationalist vision seem inapplicable to Korea, while the nationalist view came to seem the essence of sweet reason.

CONCLUSIONS

Roosevelt's policy toward Korea, as toward Indochina, was trusteeship. This quintessential internationalist device was meant to accommodate postwar American security concerns, open the colonies to

American commerce and tutelage, and corral communist and anticolonial revolution. In Korea, where from at least 1943 on most United States planners thought American and Soviet power would meet, Roosevelt assumed that a multilateral trusteeship would involve the Soviets and recognize their interests in this country contiguous to their border, but also limit their power. He believed that by committing the Soviets to a new international system, he could render them ineffectual, or at least "responsible," checked by the United States and its allies among the other trust parties. For FDR this was a containment policy toward the Soviets; but instead of drawing lines in the dirt, this sort of containment policy embraced and enrolled the adversary in mutually beneficial relationships.

This was a policy that required a deft touch and the confident assurance that the United States would be likely to dominate any sort of security arrangement after the war ended. Trusteeship was a typical example of the supreme confidence with which this American aristocrat approached politics, domestic and international. FDR had a penchant for ambiguity and an easy assurance that no matter how things came unglued at the war's end, the United States would emerge on top. Alone among scholars of Roosevelt's presidency, Franz Schurmann has understood that FDR was a dynamic executive, the analogue in the state of Joseph Schumpeter's entrepreneur in the economy. Roosevelt remade the American state during the New Deal years and sought to remake the world in the 1940s according to his global vision.[132] This vision, in turn, was not an emanation of one creative personality, but a response both to the challenges of the postwar era and the certainty that the United States would, once the peace was won, play a hegemonic global role. FDR thus was a person who looked after the whole, not the parts; like a shrewd stockholder, he was a 51 percenter. The man who succeeded him, a courageous but limited former haberdasher named Harry Truman, was an 85 percenter,[133] a person who looked after the parts, a man with a penchant for clarity. Roosevelt dominated Korean and trusteeship policy until early 1945, but his vision could not outlast him and his political skills. The vision was resisted by the wartime Allies time and again and it had a weak base in the foreign policy bureaucracy which FDR had long ignored.

FDR's internationalism was a matter of means, not ends; the goal was American hegemony in the postwar world. Yet means make a difference, and with Roosevelt gone, the balance shifted toward those who preferred classic nationalist methods: the use of military force and occupation, direct confrontation with the Soviets, and the establishment of definite territorial boundaries. Trusteeships and other internationalist devices remained the preferred methods of an increasingly isolated set of foreign policy elite. In the case of Korea, this policy of containing the Soviets and anticolonial nationalism through multilateral means was put aside in the harried weeks following Potsdam in favor of a unilateral policy of rushing troops into a peninsula virtually conceded to the Russians in mid-July. The result was a divided nation, and the first postwar act of containment.

Part II

POLITICS AT THE CENTER, 1945-1947

Chapter Five

FORGING A NEW ORDER:
THE ENTRY OF AMERICAN FORCES AND
POLICIES TOWARD THE BUREAUCRACY,
THE POLICE, AND THE MILITARY

In all periods of reconstruction the eye may rest either on the
creative forces which are building a new world, or on the debris
of the old which encumber the ground, and amid which the
masons must stumble to their task.

R. H. Tawney

It is this business of destruction and creation which goes to the
heart of the problem. For the point of departure of great revolutionary thought everywhere else in the world has been the
effort to build a new society on the ruins of an old one, and
this is an experience America has never had.

Louis Hartz

In general, the XXIV Corps had to be benevolently what more
than half a million Japanese had done tyrannically.

A XXIV Corps historian

T HE decisions made by the Americans in the three months following
their arrival in Korea substantially determined the fundamental
political structure of postwar south Korea. Policies emerged regarding
"the classical instruments of rule: army, police, bureaucracy, judi-
ciary."[1] Americans chose the structures and the people to fill them.
They also chose not to do certain things, such as recognize the People's Republic; and negative "decisions" proved to be as important as
positive ones.[2] The essence of policies and decisions is choice. The
Occupation made critical choices in the last months of 1945 that
shaped the conditions in which a rightist autocracy could emerge
triumphant more than two years later.

The essential political condition in Korea that defined American
thinking in these months was the revolutionary thrust from the Left.
The existence of the People's Republic, with its allied people's committees, labor unions, and peasant organizations throughout the peninsula, deeply politicized the Occupation and became the touchstone
against which all policies and decisions were evaluated.[3] Measures
were taken or not taken according to whether they could be expected

to hinder or aid the progress of revolution. Soon after their entry into Korea, the American masons stumbled to their task, seeking a separate force to displace, or to provide a counterforce to, the organizations of the Left. Their goal was to build a bulwark to stem the tide of Soviet-inspired and domestic revolution. This "bulwark" metaphor is fitting. As events proceeded in Korea in the late 1940s, no image was more descriptive of the effort in the south. It is a containment metaphor (or in French an *endiguement*, "a network of dikes to hold in onrushing flood waters"[4]). It is also the antithesis of open door metaphors, and by comparing the two, we discern a key to differing American conceptions of postwar Korea.

Established policy in late 1945 remained the pursuance of a multilateral trusteeship embracing the whole peninsula, with significant, substantial, perhaps even equal, Soviet participation; this was the internationalist path. But on the scene in south Korea, nationalists significantly outnumbered internationalists, whether American or Korean and regardless of State Department or military affiliation. Americans in Korea tasted the atmosphere of liberation and found it wanting; those in Seoul found themselves on an island of stasis in a sea of unrest, conjuring a variety of images which we will encounter shortly: sitting atop an abyss, perched on the rim of a volcano, treading thin ice. Within the rubric of internationalist policy, thus, nationalists carved out, *de facto*, a quite different policy. By examining concrete actions, we begin to perceive the activist, conscious, dynamic nature of an American policy of seeking a Korea (or a part of Korea) oriented toward and responsive to American interests. Moreover, by probing a bit beneath American policy statements designed for public consumption, we find that such a policy had definitive statement. The official history of the Occupation said that the "basic principle" guiding the American effort in Korea was that "an orderly, efficiently operated *and politically friendly* Korea was more important than pleasing and winning the enthusiastic cooperation of all the Korean people" (emphasis added).[5] Another official study indicated on its very first page that the United States had a more basic goal in occupying Korea than the publicly stated ones: "This was physically to occupy a part of Korea and to assure (itself) thereby that no other power would control the situation exclusively."[6]

These goals were consistent with the intent of that element of State Department planning for Korea that since 1943 had emphasized the danger that could come to American (or Pacific) security were the peninsula to fall wholly to the Soviets. Effective control of Korea or a part of it was a common denominator in these plans; this established a theme that would later appear to be quite consistent, running from the wartime months of 1943 through the entire course of the Occupation. These goals diverged from the ostensible goals of trusteeship, however. The result was that a small cadre of liberal internationalists, most of them associated with the State Department, came to oppose Occupation policies, because the Occupation resolved ambiguities in presurrender American planning in ways that affronted some policy makers in Washington. But did the policies do any injustice to the intent and goals of American planning? Or were they simply premature, harbingers of a developing Cold War that caused American internationalism to lose relevance around the world?

INCH'ŏN AND SEOUL: NEW FRIENDS AND ENEMIES

Hodge and his XXIV Corps weighed anchor in typhoon conditions off Okinawa on September 5, in a convoy of twenty-one ships proceeding in five close columns. A complete blackout concealed its presence, and a flotilla of destroyers protected its flanks against an errant Japanese submarine captain who might hope to take yet more Americans down with his fallen empire.[7] But the three-day journey proved uneventful. The ships negotiated the treacherous tides of Inch'ŏn harbor in the dawn hours of September 8, a warm, clear, late-summer day of the sort that renders Korea especially beautiful and makes one think the sky is nowhere higher.

The arrival of these ships had a real and symbolic significance for Korea comparable to that of Commodore Perry's "black ships" for Japan in 1853. The American-Korean relationship had begun in earnest, sixty-three years after the original treaty making the United States Korea's benefactor from afar had been signed. Now the benefactor had arrived.[8] It was, so it happened, the first of two Inch'ŏn landings for the Americans, the second to come five years later (nearly to the day) when (North) Korean defeat would be snatched from the jaws of victory by another victorious general.

When the Americans began disembarking at 1:00 P.M., they found black-coated Japanese police with fixed bayonets lining the streets of Inch'ŏn. The atmosphere was tense, since two Koreans had been killed earlier in the day during demonstrations to welcome the incoming Americans.[9] It was an ironic, "hostile" entry, made worse by insensitive remarks attributed to General Hodge. After landing at Inch'ŏn, Hodge apparently congratulated the Japanese for their cooperation in preserving order, and told an American correspondent:

There have been a few incidents between the Koreans and the Japanese, including one in which some Japanese shot into a group of Koreans attempting to welcome us at the docks. I had ordered civilians kept away because they would hinder the landing operation.[10]

He also was widely quoted as calling Koreans "the same breed of cat" as the Japanese.[11] Although Hodge asserted that he was misquoted, and others reported that he referred only to those Koreans who had collaborated with the Japanese,[12] his remarks infuriated Koreans and betrayed a remarkable insensitivity to Korean aspirations.

On the morning of the next day, the Americans marched into Seoul in silence. Again Japanese troops lined the streets; there was no triumphal parade or cheering throng.[13] High-ranking American officers established living quarters at the Chosŏn Hotel, while the rest went to the Bando (*Pando*) Hotel to set up XXIV Corps Headquarters. That afternoon Hodge accepted the formal surrender of Japanese forces at the capitol building. Thereafter, great crowds of Koreans went wild, snake dancing through the streets. *Ch'iandae* units bearing dummy rifles now took command of the city. That night the Americans instituted a dusk-to-dawn curfew.[14]

Shortly after the surrender ceremony on September 9, Hodge announced that the Government-General would continue to function with all of its Japanese and Korean personnel, including Governor-General Abe Nobuyuki. In a speech to Koreans, he urged that they be patient, and added:

> By your conduct in the months ahead, you can demonstrate to the democratic nations of the world and to me as their representative your capacities and abilities as a people and your readiness to accept an honored place in the family of nations.[15]

Koreans were less than enchanted by this vintage paternalism, however; one editorial asserted that Koreans would rather be governed by "some chief from Borneo" than by Abe and alleged that it was the Japanese who should be celebrating the American arrival.[16] Even official American sources stated that this action "seemed to have the effect of aligning the Japanese and Americans against the Koreans."[17]

Such feelings were reinforced by a distressing show of camaraderie between American and Japanese officers.[18] In part, this behavior resulted from simple relief that the war was over and that the Japanese had been compliant and cooperative. Yet this early association of American officers with the Japanese set in motion prejudices that persisted throughout the Occupation. Although any generalizations along these lines must be impressionistic and hazarded with care, it does seem that from the beginning many Americans simply liked the Japa-

nese better than the Koreans. The Japanese were viewed as cooperative, orderly, and docile, while the Koreans were seen as headstrong,
unruly, and obstreperous. These characterizations cropped up repeatedly in the literature and probably had their origin in initial American
responses to Korea in the fall of 1945.

In Washington the State Department reacted strongly to Hodge's
retention of Japanese officials, and the *New York Times* reported that
"the State Department . . . disclaimed any part in military orders
leaving the Japanese in office temporarily. . . . It was evidently a decision by the local theater commander."[19] On September 14, the
department communicated their disapproval to MacArthur:

> For political reasons it is advisable that you should remove from
> office immediately: Governor-General Abe, Chiefs of all bureaus of
> the Government-General, provincial governors and provincial police
> chiefs. You should furthermore proceed as rapidly as possible with
> the removal of other Japanese and collaborationist Korean ad-
> ministrators.

MacArthur had already radioed Hodge on September 11 that Japanese
officials would have to be removed forthwith.[20]

On September 12 Hodge replied that he had arrived at similar conclusions himself, but that he felt this "reversal" of policy might lead
to chaos.[21] Official sources offer little explanation for Hodge's initial
retention of high Japanese officials. We might suggest that there are
two possible reasons for such action, however: (1) MacArthur's decision to operate through existing arrangements in Japan may have
strengthened similar inclinations among XXIV Corps officers in Korea
(this might explain why MacArthur's radio message of September 11
represented a "reversal" of policy); and (2) a People's Republic had
been proclaimed two days before the American entry and might assume power if the Japanese were run out. It is probably this revolutionary situation that caused Hodge to murmur about chaos and work
closely with the Japanese. In any case, there began a slow erosion
of the immense good will Koreans felt for their American liberators.

On September 12 Major General Archibald V. Arnold replaced Abe
as Governor-General.[22] Two days later, Endō Ryusaku and all Japanese bureau chiefs were removed from office, and the title of the administration was changed from Government-General to "Military
Government," because the former denoted "a colonial status."[23] English became the official language of the Occupation.

Arnold announced on September 14, "the present police organization in Korea is to continue until it will be replaced by the Koreans."
It would be placed under his command; and he would replace Japa-

nese employees as soon as "meritorious Koreans" could be trained.[24] When the Americans dismissed Japanese officials, however, they often continued to call on them as unofficial advisors.[25] One of Abe's key aides, Oda Yasuma, became a prime American informant in these early weeks. He helped the Americans secure interpreters, gave interviews, and wrote memorandums on the situation in Korea since August 15. The Americans spent much of their time in consultation with Japanese officials. The latter offered some 350 separate memorandums in English to the MG in the period August to October 1945.[26] Officers of Military Government team no. 3, assigned to Seoul city government, spent their first few days in lengthy conversations with the Japanese mayor. As the relationship with the Japanese proceeded, the first contacts with Korean leaders began.

The Americans had an introduction to Korean politics before they even landed. In the morning hours of September 8, while the American convoy deployed offshore at Inch'ŏn, three Koreans were received aboard the command ship *Catoctin*. The men were Yŏ Un-hong (younger brother of KPR leader Yŏ Un-hyŏng), Paek Sang-gyu, and Cho Han-yong. They had been bobbing in the water off Inch'ŏn for three days and claimed to represent the CPKI.[27] Their basic interest, as recorded by a friendly source, was in warning the Americans of Japanese treachery and explaining that the CPKI was meant to be a transitional authority pending the establishment of a Korean government.[28] But they presented the Americans with two lists—the first naming "loyal, trustworthy" Koreans, and the second listing "pro-Japanese" Koreans. The first of these raised questions about precisely whom the three men really represented. Of course, this first list included the three men making the presentation. In addition, it named Yŏ Un-hyŏng and two of his loyal supporters, Yi Man-gyu and Hwang Chin-nam. Of the remaining eleven people on the list, however, at least eight were early members of the Korean Democratic Party (KDP).[29] And the leading leftists in the CPKI, like Yi Kang-guk and Hŏ Hŏn, were not mentioned. The suspicion is strong that these three men represented little more than themselves. Yŏ Un-hong's own background as a collaborator[30] would have militated against his selection in the first place, and indeed, the second list that they presented demonstrated a narrow and restrictive definition of collaboration.[31] At best, this bold approach was a remarkable display of opportunism, a humorous attempt to curry favor with the new American regime.

This episode would be relatively unimportant had the American response to it been less revealing. But in an April 1946 interview, Hodge said he had refused to meet the delegation because "they were sponsored by the Japanese" and he had not wanted to appear to favor any one political group.[32] Hodge engaged in a little history by hindsight here. Only the KDP charged that the CPKI was Japanese-sponsored, so Hodge could not have known this in the waters off Inch'ŏn. Moreover, the G-2 report for September 8 said nothing about Japanese sponsorship; it deemed the three men "fairly reliable" and said they "recognized fully the military government and volunteered to serve in a liaison capacity between that government and the people."[33] The *Seoul Times* reported that the three men did indeed meet Hodge, and Hodge himself later told reporters that he had met at least one member of the delegation.[34] Finally, had Hodge known Kim Sŏng-su and Chang Tŏk-su, listed as "loyal, trustworthy" Koreans, he would have welcomed the approach for within days he had made similar judgments himself.

The ties that developed between Americans and Koreans in the first weeks of Occupation offer a case study in American responses to political conflict in unfamiliar settings, and in Korean responses to the presence of foreign power. Overnight, the Americans found themselves involved with the most conservative of Koreans, albeit with somewhat different aspirations. It is a principle of military occupation that "no local personalities nor organized political groups . . . should have any part in determining the policies of the military government."[35] Yet within days, the XXIV Corps had formed a relationship with the Korean Democratic Party that colored American views of other political groups from then on.

On September 10 three KDP representatives, Cho Pyŏng-ok, Yun Po-Sŏn, and "T.Y. Yun" (possibly Yun Chŏng-yong), met MG officers and told them that the KPR had been organized by "a group of pro-Japanese collaborating Koreans" and that Yŏ Un-hyŏng was "well-known to the Korean people as [a] pro-Japanese collaborator and politician."[36] For the next ten days, virtually all Korean informants cited in daily G-2 reports were KDP leaders, including Song Chin-u, Kim Sŏng-su, Chang Tŏk-su, Sŏ Sang-il, Sŏl Ŭi-sik, Kim Yong-mu, and Kim To-yŏn, among others.[37] KDP supporters like Louise Yim (Im Yŏng-sin) and Pak In-dŏk also gained a hearing in the American camp in these days.[38] Yi Myo-muk, a KDP supporter and soon to become Hodge's personal interpreter, made an important speech to MG officers at a September 10 gathering at the famous Myŏngwŏlgwan Restaurant. He told the Americans that Yŏ and An Chae-hong were well-known "pro-Japs" and that the KPR had "communistic leanings."[39] An official KDP history later related that the aim of its activities in these days was to convince the Americans that the KPR was pro-Japanese, communist, and a "traitor to the Korean nation."[40]

Since the end of August, the Japanese had been telling the Americans that the CPKI and KPR were also communist; but somehow the contradiction implied in calling the KPR both "pro-Japanese" and "communist" did not seem to faze the XXIV Corps officers. Instead, they took the malicious propaganda of Seoul politics as gospel. The KDP was fighting for its life and, lacking the popular support and organizational know-how of the KPR, could only respond in the traditional idiom of Yi Dynasty factional infighting. The Americans, in their ignorance, could not know that many KDP leaders had barely cleared their throats from anti-American speeches in service to the Japanese war effort before excoriating stalwart opponents of Japan like Yŏ Un-hyŏng, Hŏ Hŏn, and An Chae-hong.[41] But the root problem was not American ignorance; the KDP leaders accurately gauged American political parameters and told them what they wanted to hear and wanted to believe.

Thus American opposition to the KPR was patent from the day after the ships landed. Hodge would not receive Yŏ Un-hyŏng until October 5,[42] and when he did, confronted him with questions like "What connections have you with the Jap?" and "How much money did you receive from the Jap?" Hodge demonstrated how beholden he was to KDP propaganda, although it must be said that this was one of the few allegedly "pro-Japanese" things to which Hodge ever objected. Yŏ later remarked gently, "I can truly say that the A.M.G. from its very beginning did not have tender sentiments for me."[43]

KDP informants not only convinced the Americans (to the extent that they needed to be convinced) that the KPR was communist and traitorous but that the KDP itself was the leading force for democracy in south Korea. After talking with Sŏ Sang-il, Sŏl Ŭi-sik, Kim Yong-mu, and others on September 11, the G-2 chief, Colonel Cecil Nist, wrote that these men were "well-known and respected businessmen and leaders" and that the KDP was the party "most representative of the general Korean public and contains the largest number of conservatives, competent and well-thought-of Korean leaders and businessmen."[44] A week later, Nist had concluded that the KDP was "*the* major democratic party, representing the great majority of the Korean people" (emphasis in original).[45] Such judgments soon informed the thinking of General Hodge, Merrell Benninghoff, and other key policy makers in the Occupation. They had a profound influence on de facto American policy making in succeeding weeks.

The KDP managed to forge the prime link necessary to its own survival, the succor and support of resident foreign power; now its leaders could concentrate on cultivating American sympathies toward their ultimate goal, control of the highly centralized political system bequeathed by the Japanese. Toward this end, they were willing to suffer, at least temporarily, the outrage and calumny of less fortunate Koreans.[46] The KDP had greater success than it thought possible, perhaps, because it convinced the Americans not only that it was a reliable ally but that it was a democratic ally; and this was something that even certain KDP leaders might not have conceded. The Americans, for their part, needed loyal allies who could be counted upon to stem the tide of domestic revolution in Korea.[47] In the early months of Occupation, the KDP seemed ideally suited for this task and willy-nilly would have to be deemed democratic, whether it was or not, to salve an American conscience that viewed itself as a liberator, not an oppressor.

The American-KDP relationship was prominent in the important initial political reports forwarded to Washington by H. Merrell Benninghoff, State Department political advisor to General Hodge. In his first report, dated September 15, Benninghoff began by describing the Korean political situation:

> Southern Korea can best be described as a powder keg ready to explode at the application of a spark.

> There is great disappointment that immediate independence and sweeping out of the Japanese did not eventuate. Although the hatred of the Koreans for the Japanese is unbelievably bitter, it is not thought that they will resort to violence as long as American troops are in surveillance.

> The removal of Japanese officials is desirable from the public opinion standpoint, but difficult to bring about for some time. They can be relieved in name but must be made to continue in work. There are no qualified Koreans for other than the low-ranking positions, either in government or in public utilities and communications. Furthermore, such Koreans as have achieved high rank under the Japanese are considered pro-Japanese and are hated almost as much as their masters. . . . It is believed that the removal of the Governor General and the Director of the Police Bureau, both Japanese, accompanied by wholesale replacements of police personnel in the Seoul area will mollify irate Koreans even though the government itself is not strengthened thereby.

> All [political] groups seem to have the common ideas of seizing Japanese property, ejecting the Japanese from Korea, and achieving immediate independence. Beyond this they have few ideas. . . . Korea is completely ripe for agitators.

He then went on to allude to the incipient association between the Occupation and the KDP:

The most encouraging single factor in the political situation is the presence in Seoul of several hundred conservatives among the older and better educated Koreans. Although many of them have served with the Japanese, that stigma ought eventually to disappear. Such persons favor the return of the "Provisional Government" and although they may not constitute a majority they are probably the largest single group.[48]

This frank admission of American sympathies accurately represented the views of many key officers in the American command. It simply embellished the intelligence reports of Colonel Cecil Nist. Both Nist and Benninghoff were so anxious to embrace any handful of men calling themselves both democratic and pro-American that the tiny KDP, acknowledged to exist only in Seoul and to be made up of many men who served the Japanese, could in the space of one paragraph be transformed from "several hundred conservatives" to the "largest single group," or in Nist's phrase, the group "representing the great majority of the Korean people." Yet in truth, it was the largest single group that the Americans could count on. The other major group, which Benninghoff identified as the "radical" or "communist" group, was perceived to have ties to the Soviet Union:

Communists advocate the seizure *now* of Japanese properties and may be a threat to law and order. It is probable that well-trained agitators are attempting to bring about chaos in our area so as to cause the Koreans to repudiate the United States in favor of Soviet "freedom" and control. Southern Korea is fertile ground for such activities because USAFIK lacks sufficient troops to expand its area of control rapidly (Benninghoff's italics).[49]

Within the space of a week (September 8-15), leading American officers in Korea seemed to think that their main source of support would come from Koreans who had done Japanese bidding, and their main opposition, from a pro-Soviet fifth column. Can we explain this by the relative inexperience of Benninghoff, Hodge, and Nist? Apparently not, for no less an authority than the late diplomatic historian Herbert Feis referred to this report as "a farsighted description and analysis of the situation."[50] It seems, then, that we are dealing not with naive planning or anomalous thinking, but with widely held, deeply rooted assumptions that say much about American responses to political conflict in unfamiliar settings. Benninghoff, Hodge, and the others also had the virtue of being able to set down their thoughts simply and bluntly, thereby cutting through clouds of rhetoric and providing a harbinger for the developing Cold War itself.

Further on in his September 15 report, Benninghoff complained of a lack of policy guidance from Washington and related Hodge's wish for "high-powered officers for my staff who are experienced in governmental affairs and who know orientals." Benninghoff ended the report by suggesting the germ of a new policy, one to which we will return shortly: "[Hodge asks that] consideration be given to returning the Chungking Government in exile to Korea as a provisional government under Allied sponsorship to act as figureheads during occupation and until Korean people stabilize to where there can be an election."[51]

Two weeks later, Benninghoff's thinking had evolved. He now saw a fundamentally polarized south Korea:

> Seoul, and perhaps southern Korea as a whole, is at present politically divided into two distinct groups; each is composed of several smaller components, but each follows its own distinct school of political philosophy. On the one hand, there is the so-called democratic or conservative group, which numbers among its members many of the professional and educational leaders who were educated in the United States or in American missionary institutions in Korea. In their aims and policies they demonstrate a desire to follow the western democracies, and they almost unanimously desire the early return of Dr. Syngman Rhee and the "Provisional Government" at Chungking.[52]

The largest element in this group was the KDP, which, according to Benninghoff, "consists of well-educated business and professional men as well as community leaders in various parts of the country." The other side consisted of "the radical or communist group," its main strength lying in the People's Republic:

> The radicals appear to be better organized than their Democratic [*sic*] opponents . . . their publicity material in the press has behind it a definite program and probably trained direction.

> The guiding genius of the organization is Yuh Woon Hyung [that is, Yŏ Un-hyŏng]. . . . The people do not know how to judge him at present, however, because his political beliefs have apparently changed from Christian to communist.[53]

Benninghoff dropped the qualification "apparently" in the next paragraph; now Yŏ was simply "the communist." He then offered his analysis of the People's Republic since August 15:

> Yuh Woon Hyung and his adherents considered themselves the government; they released political prisoners, and assumed responsibility for public safety, food distribution, and other government

functions. This was perhaps the peak of power enjoyed by the Committee [CPKI], which rapidly lost influence because of the disaffection of the more conservative members following the ascendancy of the communist elements.

Meanwhile, the Japanese learned that the United States was to occupy southern Korea; they also learned that Yuh was not going to follow their dictates. They transformed the Committee into a Public Safety Committee in order to reduce its power, and added three thousand Japanese soldiers to the police force of Seoul by giving them civil status overnight. . . . Yuh, however, was not to be suppressed. He seized on the American privilege [?] of free political endeavor and on September 5, reconstituted his group as a political party with the object of forming a Korean Peoples Republic. . . . The less aggressive conservatives, claiming the adherence of a majority of the people, were forced to organize for their own protection and in behalf of their anti-communist pro-democratic beliefs. The radicals . . . are better organized and more vocal; the nature and extent of actual communist (Soviet Russian) infiltration cannot be stated with certainty, but it may be considerable.[54]

Benninghoff reported that the radicals were "vague as to the manner they will receive [*sic*] aid and guidance in rehabilitating their country." He ended this report by assuring Washington:

The attitude of the American forces toward these political developments is one of aloofness as long as peace and order is maintained. There seems to be no other policy to adopt, as USAFIK cannot afford to support any one particular group.[55]

American aloofness was questionable at the time Benninghoff wrote this report (September 29), however. On September 12 the Occupation command organized a meeting of political leaders, during which Cho Pyŏng-ok, a key KDP organizer, arose and denounced communism and the People's Republic, provoking a storm of protest from others present. On September 21 the Americans allowed Song Chin-u, the chairman of the KDP, to attack the KPR as communist and pro-Japanese over the official radio station, JODK.[56] Then on September 27 the Americans authorized the formation of a committee to prepare an official welcome for the American Occupation. This committee was chaired by the elderly Kwŏn Tong-jin, with Kim Sŏng-su as vice-chairman and Cho Pyŏng-ok as managing director.[57]

Benninghoff's report of October 9 discussed the first organizational effort designed to bring KDP leaders into the Military Government, the so-called Advisory Council:

On October 5th, Major General Arnold, Military Governor, appointed an Advisory Council composed of 11 carefully chosen prominent Koreans including educators, lawyers, business men, "patriots" as well as the leaders of the two leading political groups (Left Wing or Radical and Conservative). General Arnold told them that they were selected to give him advice on Korean matters on an honest and non-partisan basis, having in mind only the good of the country and not personal or party gain. The 11 men accepted appointment on that basis and in secret session chose one of their number, Kig (Kim) Sung Soo by name, to act as chairman.[58]

Benninghoff erred in saying that all eleven men accepted their appointments. One man named to the Council who did not participate was Cho Man-sik, a famous nationalist who led the north Korean branch of the CPKI in August 1945 and later founded the *Chosŏn minjudang* (Korean Democratic Party; not affiliated with the KDP). Someone had apparently wrongly informed the Americans that Cho was in the south and wished to participate in the Advisory Council.[59] The other, Yŏ Un-hyŏng, the one representative chosen from the Left, never participated in the council. When Arnold requested his participation on October 5, Yŏ refused, saying that the arrangement would "reverse the fact of who is guest and who is host in Korea." Yŏ then reversed his decision at Hodge's specific request. When he was ushered into the first council session, however, and saw that the nine other Koreans present were all members of the KDP, he promptly quit and walked out, asking Hodge if a nine to one advantage was his idea of working together.[60]

The nine men who participated in the council were Kim Sŏng-su, Kim Yong-mu, Kim Tong-wŏn, Song Chin-u, Yi Yong-sŏl, Kim Yong-sun, O Yŏng-su, Kang Pyŏng-sun, and Yun Ki-ik.[61] The first four men, as we have seen, were principal organizers of the KDP. There is no independent confirmation that the remaining five men were KDP leaders or members. Their names do not appear on KDP listings, and their political affiliations, if any, remain unknown. Official American sources, however, reported that all nine men were "prominent, conservative Koreans."[62]

The Advisory Council was the first of several abortive attempts to secure high-level Korean participation in the Occupation on terms distinctly favorable to the Right. A nine-to-one ratio of rightists to leftists virtually reversed the actual distribution of political influence and popular support disposed of by the Right and the Left in south Korea in the fall of 1945. For that reason, the plan was unworkable and had to be dropped. Moreover, the very idea smacked of Japanese practices. As Benninghoff put it on October 9, "So far the public announcements concerning the creation of the Council have not received much public reaction or comment in the press, perhaps because of similar council under Japanese auspices (recently dissolved) was regarded as a gathering of collaborationists."[63] The fact that the council chairman, Kim Sŏng-su, had also been a member of the dissolved Government-General Central Advisory Council no doubt reinforced such feelings.[64] The Americans were victims of the Koreans they chose to advise them; around September 22 one "Kim Dong-sung" had suggested to Occupation intelligence officers that good results could be had from reconstituting the Japanese advisory apparatus with "patriotic Koreans."[65]

In spite of the lack of public acceptance of the council, the Occupation reported that it accepted council recommendations for the appointment of "suitable" Koreans to be provincial governors and to staff similar advisory councils at all administrative levels throughout south Korea.[66] It is likely that such advice came from informal groupings of conservatives and KDP leaders rather than from the council itself, however, as we will see.

The Occupation command was not pleased with Yŏ's refusal to join the council and attributed his action to the continuing KPR claim that it was the legitimate government of Korea. In response, on October 9 General Arnold drafted a vitriolic condemnation of the KPR and ordered it published on the first page of all newspapers on October 10. In it Arnold accused KPR leaders of being childish, "venal" men, "so foolish as to think they can take to themselves and exercise any of the legitimate functions of the Government of Korea."[67] Benninghoff noted that "the statement carried a clear implication that force would be used if necessary to put a stop to activities maliciously designed to disturb peace and order."[68] This statement was extremely demeaning to KPR leaders, many of whom were not only Arnold's elders but vastly more politically experienced than he was. Virtually the entire south Korean press corps criticized the statement, and the *Maeil sinbo* refused to print it.[69] Nothing an American said in 1945 offended Koreans as much as this attack, if we can judge by the number of times it was mentioned. Moreover, since the Advisory Council had supported Arnold's statement,[70] it was tainted even more in the eyes of Koreans who felt that their national honor was at stake.

The KPR response to Arnold's blast was the publication of a famous pamphlet entitled "The Traitors and the Patriots." It charged that Arnold's statement was "so insulting that we cannot publish it in our newspapers." It deemed the KPR the "duly constituted organ of the people" and said Americans do not recognize this because they are advised by pro-Japanese Koreans who "again try to oppress the masses under the shelter of an alien power." If the Americans wished to find really "venal" men, they should look at Kim Sŏng-su, who in a speech made on November 5, 1943, proclaimed, "The new order in East Asia is in the process of being built," and this is "the time to die for royal justice [that is, Japanese imperial righteousness]." The pamphlet went on to quote from similar wartime speeches, some of them viciously anti-American, delivered by KDP leaders Chang Tŏk-su, Ku Cha-ok, and Paek Nak-chun, and by Yi Yong-sŏl of the Advisory Council. It gave citations for each speech taken from the *Maeil sinbo* from 1941 to 1945.[71] Immediately after the appearance of this pamphlet, the Occupation banned the publication and distribution of political handbills and pamphlets. American officers cited "Communist faction handbills" as the reason for this order.[72] The order had little effect, however.

During this tumultuous week, the Americans also took action in a significant case of labor unrest in Seoul. Pak Hŭng-sik, whom we discussed in chapter one, had watched his Hwasin Department Store be taken over after liberation by a self-rule committee of employees led by Mun Sŏk-t'ae. On October 4 the committee began formal negotiations with Pak concerning its demands for the reorganization of the store. The negotiations failed, however, and on October 12 four American MPs, accompanied by two Japanese police advisors and two Japanese interpreters, entered the store and arrested Mun Sŏk-t'ae.[73] Thereafter, Pak regained his store, and established a close relationship with several high-ranking American officers.

By mid-October it had become apparent that the KPR had no future under the American Occupation. We could say that conflict with the KPR was inherent in the situation from the beginning, given the ideological incongruities between the Americans and the KPR and the ethnocentric assumptions Americans brought with them to Korea. But the Advisory Council brouhaha offered proof positive, as far as the Americans were concerned, that KPR leaders were "uncooperative." It also demonstrated that the main source of positive support for American plans was the KDP. That Occupation officers had come to such conclusions is clear in Benninghoff's report of October 10. He said of the KPR:

> There is evidence that the [KPR] group receives support and direction from the Soviet Union (perhaps from Koreans formerly resident in Siberia). In any event, it is the most aggressive party; its newspaper has compared American methods of occupation [with Soviet methods] in a manner that may be interpreted as unfavorable to the United States.

The KDP, according to Benninghoff, was most supportive of American plans—even to the point of sacrificing Korean independence:

> The Conservative Group, which is much less aggressive but which is believed to represent the thought of the majority of thinking Koreans, are willing to cooperate with Mil Govt. Many of them have stated that they realize that their country must pass through a period of tutelage, and that they would prefer to be under American rather than Soviet guidance.[74]

Benninghoff supported KDP requests for the return of Syngman Rhee and other KPG leaders, if they were "prepared to work with Mil Govt and sit on the Advisory Board on the same terms as the present Council members." Koreans "from Yenan or elsewhere" should be told that although they are welcome to return, "the Mil Govt finds it necessary for the time being to limit the number of Koreans who can return."

KDP support of American tutelage was revealing. Although some might excuse the Americans on grounds of ignorance for not seeing how divisive this issue would become, the Koreans could not have mistaken its implications. Tutelage conjured up all the old Japanese justifications for ruling Korea, and KDP support of it suggested to most Koreans an unprincipled compromise with foreign power. Some years later, Cho Pyŏng-ok admitted that the KDP supported tutelage as a means of preventing the communization of the peninsula.[75] Moreover, newspapers at the time hinted at such KDP thinking, and the Korean Communist Party's *Haebang ilbo* (Liberation Daily) came right out and charged Song Chin-u and Kim Pyŏng-no with advocating the continuation of the Occupation "for a certain period" so that Koreans could learn administrative and other skills. The KCP called this *sadae* thinking and said that although the United States should be lauded for its "long struggle against Japan," the only justification for its presence in Korea was the disarmament of the Japanese Army.[76]

On October 20 an official welcoming ceremony for the American forces was held, which served to highlight publicly the degree of American-KDP camaraderie. Cho Pyŏng-ok chaired the ceremony. His appointment as Korean director of the Korean National Police was timed to coincide with it.[77] Kwŏn Tong-jin and Yi In gave speeches, which Chang T'aek-sang (soon to be named director of the Seoul Metropolitan Police) translated. Yi and Chang were early organizers of the KDP. The ceremony also heralded the return of Syngman Rhee to Korea. Cho and General Hodge gave fulsome welcomes to Rhee; and Rhee used the occasion to condemn, among other things, the "slavery" of the north Koreans under the Soviets.[78]

This and other examples of unseemly American favoritism toward KDP leaders caused much protest from Koreans, as well as from some Americans in the Occupation and in Washington. William Langdon, another State Department advisor in Seoul, responded to such criticism in the following manner:

> As for favoring plutocracy in, and excluding popular left wingers from, Military Government, it is quite probable that at the beginning we may have picked out a disproportionate number of rich and conservative persons. But how were we to know who was who among unfamiliar people? For practical purposes we had to hire persons who spoke English, and it so happened that these persons and their friends came largely from moneyed classes because English had been a luxury among Koreans. But Military Government long ago realized the unrepresentative character of its Korean structure and is fast broadening the social base of that structure.[79]

This cable was for internal consumption; Langdon was protesting innocence to his superiors in Washington. He was, consciously or unconsciously, trying to deceive them, however, for Yŏ Un-hyŏng also spoke English; his brother, Yŏ Un-hong, was a graduate of Wooster College in Ohio; and many other leftist leaders spoke English. Moreover, as we shall see, by the end of November the Occupation had acted to solidify rather than dismantle what Langdon called "the unrepresentative character" of the Koreans employed by the Military Government.[80]

REVIVING THE BUREAUCRACY

In 1945 there were, at the most general level, two residual roles of the state bequeathed to Korea. The first derived from the old Yi, a weak state bureaucracy uninterested in stimulating the economy as a path to national wealth and power, but useful as a holding operation for landed privilege. The other was, of course, derived from the colonial state, a strong bureaucracy that intervened continuously in economy and society and that had few qualms about subordinating people and alternative political conceptions to colonial goals. The Japanese had also rationalized Korean bureaucracy in the Weberian sense, introducing modern forms of recruitment, a complete civil service apparatus, salaries that did not invite corruption, and so on. The emphasis was on imperative coordination, through a Government-General that was centralized and overgrown but extremely effective at control and domination. This structure was bequeathed intact, minus the Japanese element.

Most Koreans who were able to preserve their wealth and influence through the colonial period had done so through landholdings in the countryside; there had been no hope of real power at the center. The period after liberation therefore witnessed, on the part of landed Koreans, a casting upward of power toward the central bureaucracy, a recentralization in the wake of the undoing of the colonial integument. This was also a reassertion of Korean political tradition, a casting backward to Yi Dynastic patterns; the colonial period had so rearranged the Korean social situation, however, that the post-1945 reorganization had the flavor of a last-ditch stand, an alpenglow of the old order.[81]

The Americans obtained central control of what they called this "giant bureaucratic octopus" by virtue of Soviet acquiescence to their occupation of Seoul. The entire structure south of the thirty-eighth parallel fell into American hands. And with the departure of the Japanese overlords, the Americans would have immense patronal power—that is, if they chose to utilize existing structures to govern south Korea. The point to be remembered is that the Americans had a choice here. Planning for occupation, as we have seen, envisioned an American-staffed military government; the colonial apparatus, recognized as oppressive and a means of foreign control of Korea, was to be dismantled. Moreover, the Americans had the example of the Russians in the north, who had ousted the Japanese and their Korean employees, dismantled the Government-General, and turned over day-to-day administration to the province and lower-level people's committee structure.

Official Occupation sources wrote that the Government-General was "reduced to a phantom" after August 15. The Governor-General's acceptance of Yŏ Un-hyŏng's five demands "was almost tantamount to an abdication."[82] When the Americans arrived in Seoul, they found department after department in nearly complete disarray. Public services had been suspended. Absenteeism approached 90 percent of the bureaucratic work force. Korean employees refused to take orders from Japanese superiors. Korean police officers had fled in droves; those that remained were afraid to carry out their duties. Jails and prisons were nearly empty. The courts did not function.[83] The initial American response to this predicament was the attempt not only to revive the colonial apparatus itself but to utilize Japanese officials from the highest levels on down. When that approach met immediate and massive opposition from Koreans and from American superiors in Tokyo and Washington, the Occupation tried to appease criticism with forced public removals of Japanese officials; but they retained some as advisors in unofficial capacities. Japanese advisors then played key roles in suggesting Koreans for high personnel appointments.[84] In general, the Americans followed a policy of moving Korean bureaucrats up to fill posts held by departing Japanese, following the existing hierarchical rankings.[85] At the top of each department, the Occupation appointed an American and a Korean director; the Koreans selected were, for the most part, either former Japanese Government-General employees or members of the Korean Democratic Party.

Although American personnel appointments greatly influenced the developing configuration of the postwar south Korean bureaucracy— Lee Won-sul estimates that the Americans eventually filled some 170,000 positions[86]—perhaps more important was the decision to preserve the bureaucratic structure itself. Nowhere in the existing scholarly literature on postwar Korea can we find an appreciation of the implications of this act. Official Occupation sources wrote that the Americans "utilized the existing administrative machinery of the Government General." They made cosmetic changes, such as changing bureaus (*kuk*) to departments (*pu*) and departments to bureaus.[87] But they retained the ponderous bureaucracy, designed for colonial exploitation, until 1948 and even expanded some of the departments (notably the police). Think of the difference from occupation policies in Japan. There, the United States *weakened* the state, an appropriate remedy for the ills of Japanese development.[88] In Korea, however, the state was strengthened. Any Korean regime interested in preserving its power and in rapid industrialization would have done the same; this was, shall we say, an appropriate remedy for the pattern of Korean historical development, if we can somehow disregard the effects of colonial imperative coordination. We cannot, of course, nor can we overlook the main question, the uses to which this state was put. It was used not for rapid change and development, nor for channeling the highly motivated population into forward-looking pursuits, but for the maintenance of outmoded privilege. The postwar south Korean state was a walking anachronism, if a potent one.

Ralf Dahrendorf has written:

> As a medium and instrument of domination, bureaucracy stands at the disposal of anyone who is called upon to control it. As a constant in political conflict it accompanies and supports whatever group is in power by administering its interests and directives dutifully and loyally.[89]

The Korean colonial bureaucracy would have constituted a powerful organizational weapon in the hands of any political group, but in 1945 the issue of Korean collaboration with the Japanese added life-and-dimensions to the prospects facing Korean bureaucrats who had staffed the colonial government. The Russians and their Korean allies did a thorough housecleaning in the north in the fall of 1945; and the implications for south Korea were clear and continually reinforced by the infusion of ousted officials from the north. Therefore, although in theory any bureaucracy is neutral about whose interests it serves, Korean bureaucrats at the higher levels were a bit less neutral than most. High Korean officials, if they were allowed to retain their positions, were precisely situated to prevent renovation in the south.

How many Korean officials are we talking about? Among high colonial officials (*chokunin* and *sonin* ranks), the Korean element fluctuated between 18 and 22 percent in the last decade of colonial rule; in absolute numbers, there were 442 high Korean officials in, for example, 1942. In the police, the number of ranked officers fluctuated between 251 and 210 in the last decade, or between 13 and 19 percent. The percentages of Korean prosecutors and judges were in the same range.[90] With the division of Korea in 1945, however, most northern officials fled south, perhaps doubling the number of officials available for service in the revamped Government-General, or Military Government.

In the fall of 1945, Korean colonial bureaucrats found willing allies in the American command and the Korean Democratic Party; and in a rather large number of cases, KDP leaders came to control key elements of the bureaucracy:[91]

Cho Pyŏng-ok, Korean National Police
Chang T'aek-sang, Seoul Metropolitan Police ("Division A")
Kim Yong-mu, Chief Justice of the Supreme Court
Yi In, Chief Prosecutor
Kim Ch'an-yŏng, Prosecutor
Ch'oe Pyŏng-sŏk, Department of Justice, Korean Director
Ku Cha-gwan, Director, Criminal Bureau of Department of Justice
Yun Po-sŏn, Department of Agriculture and Forestry, Korean Director
Yu Ok-kyŏm, Department of Education, Korean Director
Yi Tong-jae, Korean Commodity Company, Korean Director
Pak Chong-man, Department of Communications, Acting Assistant Director
Im Pyŏng-hyŏn, Program Director, Central Broadcasting Company
Yi Hun-gu, Korean Agricultural Association, President
Paek Nak-chun, Seoul National University, President
Yi Sun-t'ak, Head Statistician, Planning Section of Secretariat
Yi Un, Chief, Civil Affairs Section, Seoul City Government
Chŏng Il-hyŏng, Director, Civil Service Section of Secretariat
Kim Chun-yŏn, Kim To-yŏn, Hong Sŏng-ha, three of five members from KDP on National Labor Mediation Board

Available information on provincial appointments in 1945, although limited, provides a similar picture of KDP control:

Ku Cha-ok, Provincial Governor, Kyŏnggi
Kim Hong-sik, Chief, Kyŏnggi Department of Mining and Industry
Kim Myŏng-sŏn, Chief, Kyŏnggi Department of Public Health
Yi Kyŏng-hŭi, Mayor of Taegu
Sŏ Min-ho, Mayor of Kwangju

Information on political affiliations of American-appointed county magistrates exists for only one province, South Chŏlla. In early 1946, it was reported that seventeen of twenty-one magistrates were members of the KDP.[92]

There can be no gainsaying the significance of the Occupation's placing the coercive police and justice apparatus in the hands of leading members of the KDP. Cho Pyŏng-ok, Chang T'aek-sang, Kim Yong-mu, and Yi In all held their positions until 1948 and became dominant figures in suppressing the Left in the south. In spite of the assurances Langdon offered his superiors about changing the "unrepresentative character" of Korean appointees, and in spite of repeated advice from within the Occupation that Cho, Chang, and the others be replaced, they were never removed. And when a KDP member like Ch'oe Pyŏng-sŏk was relieved of his duties in early 1946, he was replaced by Kim Pyŏng-no, another early KDP leader.[93] It is clear that General Hodge and his closest advisors felt that no other Koreans could be entrusted with the agencies of law and order.

KDP influence over other governmental departments was not as clear and consistent; moreover, certain people like Yi Hun-gu had impressive qualifications that would have merited high position in any administration.[94] Also, we have dealt above with only a portion of all appointments made in 1945. American favoritism toward the KDP would be mitigated were it possible to show that the Americans had appointed Koreans from other political groups. Yet this writer could not find a single instance in which the Americans appointed a leftist Korean to any responsible position. Rather, most non-KDP appointees appear to have been Koreans who had served in the colonial apparatus or Koreans prominent during the colonial period. The first mayor of Seoul, Yi Pŏm-sŭng, had been provincial governor in Hwanghae Province for nine years and was apparently chosen on the advice of Chang U-sik, a vice-president of the Chohŭng Bank.[95] Yi Sang-gi, appointed as a justice of the Korean Supreme Court, had been in the Japanese court system in Taegu.[96] Im Mun-mu, made chief of Home Affairs in South Chŏlla, and Kim Tae-u, made provincial governor in North Kyŏngsang, had both been high officials under the Japanese.[97] The

American-appointed mayor of Kunsan, Kim Yong-ch'ŏl, had been on the Kunsan Advisory Council.[98] It is thus doubtful that a case could be made for the absence of partisan considerations in American appointments were additional information on the backgrounds of appointees to become available.

As we suggested earlier, KDP leaders cared little for the stuff of modern politics—mobilizing mass support, creating responsible ties between leaders and led, representing constituencies, forging positive programs. All this paled before the political power that would issue from access to and control of the bureaucracy. Here was a classic case of what the Vietnamese call *trum men*: the representatives of the old order abdicate the formulation of new societal goals and retreat into the use of police and administration to gain their ends.[99] It is scarcely an exaggeration to say that American appointments in 1945 allowed the KDP to seize "actual political, economic, and social power."[100] Although the Americans may not have understood the power of bureaucratic position in Korean society, and may have overestimated their capability to control appointees and underestimated the tenacity of KDP functionaries, the KDP did not mistake the opportunity provided it.

Little information is available on the specific mechanisms of Occupation personnel selection for the mass of appointments. Official sources reported that some 75,000 Koreans were either retained or newly appointed in the last three months of 1945.[101] Given time limitations, the vast majority of these appointments must have represented retention of existing officials. Appointments at the highest levels, however, were the logical outgrowth of American reliance on KDP-affiliated informants in September and October. The role of George Z. Williams, an advisor to Hodge and the Korean-born son of a missionary, was particularly important here.[102] He was known for his close ties to KDP leaders and played the key role in selecting a KDP man to head the national police. He reportedly called on the KDP chairman, Song Chin-u, on October 17 and asked that Song suggest someone for the job. According to Cho Pyŏng-ok's account, Williams told Song and others present:

> As you all know, in north Korea the communist army has established itself. Even though the communist doctrine is transparent and anticommunist thought is thoroughly established [in Korea], if there are no patriots in Korea who will meet this situation by putting [anticommunism] into practice, coping thoroughly with it may be difficult. Since General Hodge has asked for the recommendation of such patriots who will cooperate with the MG for the sake of Korea, I

3. Citizens welcoming prisoners released from colonial jails,
   August 16, 1945

4. Syngman Rhee speaking at the Welcoming Ceremony for American forces,
   October 20, 1945; General Hodge is sitting to his right

hope you gentlemen will give this the most serious thought and give me your recommendation.[103]

The next day, Song convinced Cho to take the job. Williams then arrived at KDP headquarters in the Tonga ilbo building and escorted Song and Cho to a meeting with General Hodge. Hodge told Cho that he would have to resign his position with the KDP. But Cho refused, and it was agreed that he could remain a member but not a leading officer of the KDP.[104]

Williams had very definite views on Korean politics. In an interview on October 13, 1945, he complained to an Occupation historian that he was tired of opposition to his personnel selections. After consulting "many prominent and trusted Koreans," he had appointed one "Chung Soong Yung" to some post. Immediately thereafter, Koreans charged that Chung had contributed large sums of money to a "notorious" Japanese reform school for Koreans and that he headed a narcotics ring. Williams thereupon determined that neutrality was impossible in postwar Korea: there were only two groups, "the rank radicals and the democrats," and one must choose between them.[105] A more enlightened American officer, Leonard Bertsch, told me that few Americans cared much about the preliberation background of Koreans. He himself operated on the principle of "letting anyone seek his own level."[106] This was not, however, the way that most Koreans viewed the issue. And Cho Pyŏng-ok, Chang T'aek-sang, and the others were not just allowed to seek their own level; rather, they were placed in position where they had a virtual monopoly on the means of violence. In this manner, a small holding operation on the Right was established at the very seat of political power.

AGENCIES OF LAW AND ORDER

The Americans on the scene in Korea had made most of the fundamental decisions regarding the agencies of law and order—the Department of Justice, the courts, and the national police—by the end of 1945. This was where "Koreanization," as the policy came to be known, occurred earliest. According to official sources, this Koreanization was complete in the Department of Justice by November 1945, with Americans functioning thereafter only as advisors to Korean personnel.[107] In other words, Koreanization consisted of little more than turning over Japanese agencies of justice to Korean hands; no basic changes in structure or Korean personnel were made through the end of the Occupation.

The Japanese court system in Korea consisted of local and district

courts, regional courts of review, and a supreme court. At the apex
stood the large and highly centralized Department of Justice. These
were agencies of colonial justice and thus had functions in addition
to those generally associated with the preservation of peace and order.
For example, the chief judges of district courts exercised "strict supervision" over local land registrar's offices, where transfers of title took
place. The Americans also found that prosecutors had to be told not
to assume detailed police functions, but to confine themselves to legal
analysis.[108]

As far as can be determined, the Occupation retained all Koreans
employed in the Japanese Bureau of Justice even though, as American
sources acknowledged, they were generally viewed as collaborators.[109]
New appointments were made on the advice of the National Bar Association that had existed during the colonial period, while appointments to high positions, such as to the Supreme Court or the courts
of review, required that the appointees have ten or more years experience as judges or prosecutors, or fifteen or more years as lawyers or
professors of law.[110] Appointees to the most responsible positions came
from the Korean Democratic Party: Yi In, Kim Yong-mu, Ch'oe
Pyŏng-sŏk, Kim Pyŏng-no, Ku Cha-gwan. Perhaps the most important
Korean in the MG Department of Justice was the executive assistant
to the American director, Kim Yŏng-hŭi, a Yale Ph.D. who had been
secretary of the National Bar Association during the last years of the
colonial period.[111] It is not known if he too was a member of the KDP.
But leftist and moderate sources continually charged that the MG
system of justice was largely a creature of the KDP.[112]

The system of law codes and precedents used during the Occupation
was a combination of Japanese law and the special or extraordinary
law deriving from the inherent powers of a military occupant. The
Americans used their special powers to repeal many oppressive and
obnoxious colonial laws, such as those requiring emperor worship,
those that dealt differentially and prejudicially with Koreans on the
basis of race, those that gave the police extraordinary powers in cases
of political crimes, and so on.[113] Yet they retained many Japanese laws
and special military powers that later came to be used against Koreans
who opposed the Occupation or its arrangements. Thus Ordinance no.
21 of November 2, 1945 stated:

> Until further ordered, and except as previously repealed or abol-
> ished, all laws which were in force, regulations, orders, notices, or
> other documents issued by any former government of Korea having
> the force of law on 9 August 1945 will continue in force until re-
> pealed by competent authority.[114]

This ordinance allowed Cho Pyŏng-ok to suggest in the fall of 1946 that a 1912 Japanese law be used as the basis for massive preemptive arrests of potential political dissidents.[115] It also meant that other objectionable Japanese laws continued in force, such as the Military Criminal Code of 1908, the Act Prohibiting Political Meetings of 1910, the Inflammatory Document Controlling Ordinance of 1936, even Peace Preservation Law no. 2 of 1907. None of these were repealed until April 8, 1948.[116] A compendium of MG legal opinions indicates that Japanese colonial law was used frequently as a source of precedents for cases tried during the Occupation.[117] The Occupation, however, generally relied more heavily on its inherent powers as an occupant of territories deemed "hostile" than on Japanese law in order to suppress dissidence. The Occupation dealt with political problems by exercising its powers to censor publications (even mail), to require the registration of all political parties (see Ordinances nos. 55 and 72, discussed in chapter seven), and in general, to prevent anything deemed "inimical" to the Occupation.[118]

The Korean press constantly voiced criticism over court cases and procedures. A. Wigfall Green, a judge advocate and a president of the Judicial Board of Review during the Occupation, was also highly critical of the MG system of justice, citing a total lack of *habeus corpus*, the prominence of political favoritism, and an efficiency rating system that required unusually high percentages of convictions.[119] Major George A. Anderson, executive officer in the Department of Justice, contended that Koreans in the department were incessantly involved in political activities. He also related incidents in which the American director of the department, Emery Woodall, toured Seoul police stations handing out summary sentences to prisoners who had been arrested but not yet convicted.[120] Paradoxically, in no other MG department were there more widely experienced officers. Ernst Fraenkel, a leading authority on military government, served as legal advisor to the Department of Justice and wrote many MG legal opinions. He was assisted by Charles Pergler, a well-known expert on international law.[121] Their expertise became irrelevant, however, with the Department of Justice in the hands of Koreans with political axes to grind.

The tragedy of the liberation period and the depth of American responsibility are most evident in the history of the Korean National Police (KNP) during Occupation. A highly centralized, arbitrary, self-contained national force was placed in the hands of collaborators and rightists and used on a daily basis as a quintessentially counterrevolutionary force: "the spearhead of the nation" would abjure passive peace-keeping:[122]

The task and mission of the Korean police has not been like that of the various democratic nations, of preserving the peace passively by maintaining public order and protecting life and property; in Korea's situation such passive peace-keeping could not prevent the killings, destruction, and guerrilla warfare of the communists. So the police took up arms and fought actively to preserve the independence and freedom of the nation.[123]

For servants of Japan facing an uncertain fate, and for rightists lacking the organizational and popular resources of their opponents, the police structure was an indispensable resource in political conflict. Moreover, it is an inescapable fact that the Americans in Korea who made policy regarding the police saw its uses in essentially the same manner.

The first Supreme Command, Allied Powers (SCAP) report on Korea stated that the police in Korea had "been thoroughly Japanized and efficiently utilized as an instrument of tyranny."[124] Presurrender intelligence reports available to the XXIV Corps on Okinawa also recognized the totalitarian character of the police in Korea. In mid-October the Occupation received the following SWNCC "Basic Initial Directive":

Criminal and ordinary police agencies, and such others as you may consider proper to be retained under appropriate supervision, will be progressively purged of undependable and undesirable elements, and in particular, of Japanese and Koreans who collaborated with the Japanese.[125]

Historians of the Occupation wrote that "the Japanese police in Korea possessed a breadth of function and an extent of power equalled in few countries in the modern world."[126] These functions included, among other things, the registration, control, and observation of all political groups and political meetings; prior censorship of printed matter, newspapers, moving pictures, and other forms of communication; the supervision of and participation in rice and other grain collections; a highly developed system of secret police spies and informants; and functions subsumed by the term "thought control."

Such functions were dispatched through a centrally controlled, highly integrated system that penetrated to the lowest levels of Korean society. The national police had headquarters in Seoul and subordinate provincial headquarters in every province, supplemented by a separate headquarters ("Division A") for the Seoul metropolitan area. Below that were 132 county offices in south Korea alone. Then followed stations, substations, and boxes in towns and villages. All police officers were responsible to the provincial headquarters, which were in turn responsible to the headquarters in Seoul, not to the provincial governors.[127] The national system had its own communication and transportation facilities. The only system that approximated local or community controls was police interaction with county magistrates and local influentials, especially landlords.

When the American forces arrived in Korea, as we have seen, they found the Korean element of the Japanese force in near total disarray, with absenteeism approaching 80 or 90 percent. In most areas, *ch'iandae* units kept the peace, units responsive largely to local people's committees rather than to a central organization in Seoul. Brigadier General Lawrence Shick, the American most directly involved with police affairs in the first months of the Occupation, stated on September 13 that the police (Japanese and Korean) were "almost powerless."[128] Shick was probably instrumental in Hodge's initial decision to continue the police force in power, with all of its Japanese and Korean personnel intact. When superiors in Washington and Tokyo overruled Hodge's actions regarding the police, he and his closest advisors decided to remove the Japanese element from the force but also to resuscitate the Korean element in its entirety and retain the existing national structure. At the top, the Americans placed two important KDP organizers, Cho Pyŏng-ok and Chang T'aek-sang. As we noted earlier, Cho, recommended by Song Chin-u, was appointed head of the national police by Hodge on October 18, 1945. Chang was officially appointed chief of "Division A" on January 16, 1946, but he actually assumed his position on October 7, 1945.[129] His position was hardly less important than Cho's, for "Division A" included one-third of all police employed in south Korea.[130]

The reason that the Americans chose to retain the KNP structure and its Korean personnel was simply that there were no other forces that were at once cohesive and determinedly opposed to the Left. Korean policemen who had served Japan were highly conscious of their common interest in preventing the rise to power of political groups bent on ousting or punishing collaborators. Such an interest gave them a cohesion that few other Korean groups could match. Cho Pyŏng-ok stated bluntly in his biography that he and Hodge believed that only the national police were capable of disbanding the People's Republic and the people's committees throughout south Korea.[131] American sources agreed. The official history stated that "in the absence of an army, the police were the only instrument of power." Moreover, "the disordered state of the country demanded a large flexible force which could be moved quickly wherever it was needed." A national, centrally controlled force would allow the "breaking of local ties [which] would minimize the joining of resistance groups" and the transference of police officers who "had become too deeply rooted in one community."[132]

Americans have resisted a national police force like this in their own country for the duration of its existence. But they justified its use in Korea because of the threat from the Left. Occupation historians wrote that although the KNP could hardly be called democratic, and although in theory the police in any locality should be "answerable to the people of that community," in Korea "a national police was deemed essential, as offering the following advantages":

1. During emergencies and disasters any number of policemen could be mobilized and moved to the scene without delay.
2. Jurisdictional disputes and petty quarrels between police were thus avoided.
3. Political influence was eliminated.
4. Uniform training and impartial law enforcement was guaranteed.
5. The possibility of police, either individually or collectively, joining any [political] group was lessened.
6. Maximum protection for many communities was made available.
7. Intelligence information on subversive movements was not lost in the files of a local organization, but it was evaluated and passed along.[133]

We would be remiss in not asking if Japanese justifications for such a force could have been much different. The irony, of course, is that the national police in Japan was abolished during the Occupation, through reforms "based on the correct assumption that the old system of a national police divorced from popular local controls had been too easily used as an instrument of authoritarian oppression."[134] But in Korea such reform was prevented by fear of the Left, and by a certain American callousness exemplified in the reported statement of Colonel William Maglin, American director of the KNP: "we felt that if [the Korean element of the KNP] did a good job for the Japanese, they would do a good job for us."[135]

American and Japanese military accouterments were added to the existing resources of the KNP. As Donald S. McDonald described it:

> The most drastic centralization was in the police force. The provincial police chief was made responsible, not to the provincial governor, but to his department chief in Seoul; all police in the country were integrated into a single machine, equipped with U.S. Army vehicles, Japanese Army rifles, bayonets, and machine guns, and their own private telephone and radio network.[136]

Such self-contained systems of communications were "especially needed in a country where riots were commonplace." By mid-1946, the KNP had thirty-nine radio stations and 22,700 kilometers of telephone lines in operation.[137]

As point seven in the list of advantages of a Korean national police would suggest, the Occupation came to rely on the KNP for much of their information concerning political groups. Korean sources state that the Americans allowed the police to continue in operation the "intelligence section" of the KNP, responsible for spying and thought control. The Americans reportedly told the Koreans that this apparatus would now function "in the interests of the Korean people."[138] Official American sources, however, reported that although American officers ordered the KNP to abolish its "thought" and secret police sections, "time and time again" the police had to be told not to collect political information, not to seize books for examination and censorship, and so forth. According to American accounts, the police "were unwilling to give up any of their original power." The metropolitan division, for example, maintained an "observation section" with responsibility for "all the political activities, news, magazines, public morality, strikes, foreign affairs,[139] and religious activities." According to the Americans, "some police thought that the main interest of Military Government was the suppression of Leftists." Police power to issue permits for demonstrations served as a political weapon "to prevent meetings, parades, publications, and even theatrical performances by Leftists. . . . They even precensored moving pictures."[140]

The Occupation's inability, or unwillingness, to abolish such practices reflected both American difficulties in controlling the activities of Korean charges and the admitted American need to use police sources of information. Given the fact that criticism of police practices was voiced constantly within the Occupation force and in the Korean press, American officers responsible for police policies cannot be excused on the grounds of ignorance. Moreover, to my knowledge, the Americans never did more to correct police excesses than periodically force a handful of resignations and issue statements promising reforms at some undetermined future date. Nothing was ever done about the basic KNP structure or the use of collaborationist personnel.

American personnel policies regarding the police were delineated by Colonel Maglin in an interview with Mark Gayn in October 1946:

> When we took over last year, 12,000 out of the 20,000 men in the police force were Japanese. What we did, after sending the Japs home, was to push the Koreans up, and then build up the force by incorporating all the young men who had been helping the police.

5. Members of the Korean Provisional Government, Seoul, 1945 (Kim Ku, front center, with Kim Kyu-sik on his left)

6. Chang T'aek-sang (center) in 1946

In this manner, we have brought up the police strength from 20,000 to 25,000 men.[141]

What Maglin failed to note here is that the figure 20,000 represented police strength for the entire Korean peninsula, not just for south Korea. The Americans nearly doubled the number of employees that had been in the colonial force in southern Korea, demonstrating the increased requisites of control in the highly mobilized political setting.[142]

Initially, the Americans said that only those who had police or military training under the Japanese would be accepted into the MG police force. But this requirement had to be rescinded owing to the storm of protest it provoked. Soon, however, the Americans again "ceased to pay attention to pro-Japanese charges,"[143] and the result was a wholesale reemployment of Koreans from the colonial force. In November 1946 Maglin reported to the Korean-American Conference that of the 8,000 Koreans who had been in the colonial force in north and south Korea, 5,000 were still in the MG police force; the latter constituted the "nucleus" around which the MG force was built. Because the Americans rewarded those with long police experience, fully 80 percent of officers above the rank of patrolman had served the Japanese.[144] The percentages of officers who had been in the colonial force were highest at the upper levels of the KNP (see table 8).

TABLE 8

FORMER COLONIAL POLICE OFFICERS REMAINING
IN KOREAN NATIONAL POLICE, NOVEMBER 1946

Position	1946 Total	In Colonial Police	Percentage
Superintendent	1	1	100%
Division Chiefs	8	5	63
Provincial Chiefs	10	8	80
Inspectors	30	25	83
Captains	139	104	75
Lieutenants	969	806	83

SOURCE: Derived from minutes of Col. William Maglin's briefing to the Korean-American Conference, November 1, 1946; in XXIV Corps Historical File.

Many colonial police officers from north Korea, after fleeing or having been ousted from their jobs in the north, came south to join the MG police force. This process was detailed by Ch'oe Nŭng-jin ("Danny Choy"), chief of the KNP Detective Bureau, in a remarkable statement submitted to the Korean-American Conference on November 20, 1946. He called the KNP "the refugee home for Japanese-trained police and traitors," including "corrupt police who were chased out of North Korea by the Communists." Such policemen received sums of money from the Japanese in P'yŏngyang after August 15; then "with this money, these officers came to Seoul, using it to obtain jobs in the police force." Other policemen came to Seoul after being forced from their jobs in the provinces of south Korea; according to Ch'oe, they "cannot go back to their own parts of the country as people will confiscate their property." He gave as examples one Kim Hu-wŏn, who was kicked out of Kaesŏng, and Yi Ku-bŏm, "a famous Japanese [*sic*] detective in Korea . . . [whose] home was wrecked after the liberation and he came here [Seoul]." Yi became chief of a major ward police station in Seoul. Ch'oe said that he and Cho Pyŏng-ok differed over the issue of utilizing collaborators: "He opposes me constantly because I want to use patriotic men and independence movement workers in the department." Ch'oe charged that "everyday men are arrested without any evidence at all because of personal feelings. Someone just says the man is no good, and the man is put in jail and beaten." Ch'oe thought that "the police department is rotten and is an enemy of the people. 80% of the Koreans will turn Communist if this condition persists." Ch'oe was relieved of his duties after submitting this statement.[145]

Scattered information on the backgrounds of high KNP officers supports the picture presented above. Chang Pyŏng-in, the head of the KNP Organization and Planning Section in 1946, had been the head of the General Affairs and Mobilization sections of the Government-General police in a county in North Ch'ungch'ŏng Province. Cho Chu-yŏng, chief of the KNP Administrative Bureau from 1945 on, had been an attorney in the Tokyo provincial court system from 1927 to 1936; he was also president of the Wŏndong Trading Company from 1942 to 1945. Concurrently with his KNP position after 1945, Cho held the post of inspector in the Chohŭng Bank. Chu P'yŏng-no, a KNP official and subsequently the Korean director of the Bureau of Home Affairs in South Chŏlla Province (1947), had been chief of the Nationalism Unit of the Manchukuo Cooperative Society in Manchuria from 1938 to 1941 and subsequently the secretary of the Manchukuo Central Agricultural Improvement Cooperation Association from 1941 to 1945.[146] No Tŏk-sul, reviled by Gregory Henderson as a "Japanese police torturer," was a prominent figure in the "Division A" police and a former inspector and Peace Preservation Section head in the preliberation North P'yŏng'an Province police department.[147] Another key advisor to Chang T'aek-sang in the "Division A" police was Ch'oe Yŏn, section chief of the Kyŏnggi Province Criminal Department in the last years of Japanese rule. Yi Ik-hŭng, also of "Division A," had been chief of police in Pakch'ŏn, North P'yŏng'an Province under the Japanese.[148] The assistant director of the KNP, Ch'oe Kyŏng-jin, had been an official in the Training Section of the Government-General Secretariat.[149]

Some American advisors put great effort into trying to reorient former colonial policemen. Americans like Horace H. Underwood gave lectures on how to be a democratic policeman. American advisors replaced Japanese police slogans with a new one, *pul-pyŏn pu-dang* (impartial and nonpartisan); they attempted to inculcate ideals of public service and civic responsibility. They tried, in short, to make over colonial policemen in their image of American policemen. At any given time, however, only about twenty Americans were assigned to the KNP. Although all of them had police experience in the United States, their small numbers, if nothing else, dictated that day-to-day police affairs would be in the hands of Koreans.[150] The language problem meant that when the old Japanese Police Academy was reopened on October 15, 1945, Japanese instructors had to be used at first. They were then replaced by Korean instructors who had been in the colonial force.[151] In effect, then, "Koreanization" of police training and the KNP itself began almost immediately. It is also true that no amount of American training could have convinced colonial police officers that they had to be impartial and nonpartisan. They had life-and-death interests in the outcome of the political struggles of liberated Korea. Like anxious and threatened men everywhere, once given the opportunity, they acted to protect their interests.

There were also plenty of Americans willing to justify such a police force. Colonel H. E. Erickson, an advisor to the KNP, said in 1947:

> In recent months the National Police has proven itself, as an organization, to be truly democratic. . . . This change has been gradual but consistent, and the time is now here when the slight-left, slight-right, or even mild pink, understands that he can go about his business without fear of molestation from the police.[152]

Other Americans rationalized police excesses as "the way Orientals do things."[153] Yet this justification obscured the undeniable American role in installing in the KNP Koreans with a particular experience in an oppressive police force.

Could the Americans have done anything but employ the KNP structure and the Korean element of the colonial force? In September 1945, Hodge and his advisors had with them instructions to purge the police of collaborationist Koreans. As early as September 14, an officer within the Occupation suggested doing away completely with existing police.[154] Yet even after the autumn uprisings in the fall of 1946, Hodge refused to make even limited personnel changes at the top ranks of the KNP, and no consideration was given to changing the KNP structure. Americans had to rely on the KNP as long as they perceived the People's Republic, the people's committees, and the other organizations of the Left as threats to American plans for Korea. From a purely *Realpolitik* standpoint, Hodge and his close advisors were correct in seeing the KNP as the only cohesive and reliable instrument of power in south Korea. Attempts to utilize less cohesive forces such as the Constabulary (see below) proved disastrous. In the end, Hodge was vindicated in his determination to resist purges and changes in the KNP, because the superior organizational and technical resources of the KNP proved to be the prime factor in the demise of leftist organizations in the south.

The costs of such a policy were great, however. The perceived virtues of the KNP—its self-contained organizational and communications systems, its lack of local ties and loyalties, its information-gathering and surveillance capacities—would fit many definitions of totalitarianism. Totalitarian theory emphasizes processes by which cohesive and highly integrated organization breaks down secondary associations, locally rooted political organizations, and intermediate bodies of all types, leaving the mass of a population at its mercy. If, as Henderson suggests, contemporary South Korea resembles a "mass society," perhaps the history of the KNP offers part of the explanation for how it got that way.[155]

THE EMERGENCE OF NATIONAL DEFENSE FORCES

The Korean National Police possessed, at least on paper, resources sufficient to maintain order throughout south Korea. But it was not until 1947, at the earliest, that the KNP attained levels of efficiency necessary to handle threats to its hegemony in the south. In the fall of 1945, police officers were severely demoralized and often had to be accompanied on their rounds by Americans. Even minor disorders in the provinces required support of the police by American tactical troops. Therefore, in October 1945 the Americans decided to establish Korean military forces that could serve as an auxiliary and back-up resource for the KNP. Hodge later remarked:

> I was very interested in establishing a Korean Army from the beginning of the Occupation, not only to relieve American troops of many details in handling Korean security, but to get a start for the future when we accomplished our mission of setting up a Korean Government. I met much opposition at higher levels.[156]

The immediate stimulus for this creation of army forces was the Namwŏn Incident of October 15, in which elements of the Namwŏn people's committee and a branch of the National Preparatory Army

(NPA) clashed with Korean police and American tactical troops (see chapter nine). In the wake of this incident, Reamer T. Argo, an American advisor to the KNP, met with Kim Ŭng-jo, chief of police in North Chŏlla Province, and proposed the creation of a "Police Standing Reserve" (*kyŏngch'al sangbi-dae*) to aid the KNP in maintaining order. Kim responded that such an organization should be made the kernel of a national army. Argo said they could not give the body such a title: "Since Korea is under the dual occupation of the U.S. and the U.S.S.R., how can we unilaterally establish a national army?" Argo also advised Kim that Korea was to be placed under a multilateral trusteeship and would be prevented from organizing an army for the duration. Kim left this meeting unsatisfied, and determined to organize an antitrusteeship movement among North Chŏlla police officers.[157]

Americans in Seoul had a broader view of the situation in the provinces and saw the Namwŏn Incident as part of a general pattern of KPR resistance to American-imposed arrangements. The existence of the KPR-linked NPA and other private armies was particularly frightening to military men like Hodge and Brigadier General Schick. They therefore decided to ignore the Soviet presence in the north and American plans for a trusteeship and to establish the beginnings of a national army. They hoped that such a body could both back up the KNP and provide a vehicle to either enroll or disband existing private armies.[158] Schick, who had been instrumental in reviving the KNP, wrote a memorandum entitled "Plan for the National Defense of Korea" on October 31, which claimed there was a necessity for creating a force capable of "quelling internal disturbances" and suitable for defending south Korean borders. Ordinance no. 28 of November 13 thereupon created the "Office of the Director of National Defense," with jurisdiction over the police and "a new Bureau of Armed Forces comprising Army and Navy Departments." The plan envisioned an army and air force of about 50,000, a navy and coast guard of 5,000, and a national police force of 25,000. Each body would be equipped with surplus American and Japanese military stocks. Hodge approved this plan on November 20, and MacArthur forwarded it to Washington, seeking the judgment of the State Department and the Joint Chiefs of Staff.[159] On November 13, however, the KNP had already been merged with the Office of the Director of National Defense; and the next day the Occupation stated publicly that Korean national defense forces would be created to aid the police in keeping order.[160]

The Occupation had no mandate to set up a Korean military force. American civil affairs training schools had never even considered the prospect of establishing native national defense forces in occupied areas.[161] Hodge had no instructions for such an action from SWNCC.

There is no evidence, either, that the Soviets had taken such action in the north. The earliest American G-2 report of Soviet activities possibly directed toward building an army came nearly six months after the American initiative.[162] Soviet authorities in north Korea even disarmed Korean forces in the Chinese Eighth Route Army when they tried to return to Korea in the fall of 1945.[163] Furthermore, because the Russians maintained a consular office in Seoul until mid-1946, they could not have been unaware of the American creation of national defense forces; in a staff meeting of November 5, 1945, an American officer suggested that such developments might make the Russians think that the United States was building an army to attack north Korea.[164] Perhaps for reasons such as the above, on January 9, 1946, the Joint Chiefs of Staff wired MacArthur as follows:

> The matter of establishing "Korean National Armed Forces" is closely allied to unsettled problems connected with international commitments for implementing Korean independence. Action to establish such force will therefore be deferred.[165]

There is no indication that either the lack of approval from Washington in November and December, or its explicit disapproval in January, had much impact on Hodge's determination to build a Korean army, however. It was not until June 1946 that the Office of the Director of National Defense was renamed the Department of Internal Security, and the Bureau of Armed Forces became the Bureau of the Constabulary (the army force was thereafter known as the Korean Constabulary [*Chosŏn kyŏngbi-dae*]).[166] In December 1945 the Occupation drew up plans for the defense of south Korea (or Korea?) known as plans "Alpha" and "Bamboo," the contents of which remain unknown.[167] Selection and training of Korean military officers began in early December. Recruitment of Korean infantrymen began on January 14.[168] What was the reason for this precipitate and, in a technical sense at least, insubordinate action?

The Korean history of the development of the army said simply, "the MG utilized the Government-General administrative apparatus which it found, but there was no [existing] military apparatus," thus one had to be created.[169] But as we have seen, the Occupation had no precise mandate to revive the Government-General, let alone to create a military force. Rather, the development of national defense forces was part of the Occupation's response to the revolutionary conditions it found in south Korea. By mid-October, if not earlier, reports from the provinces had sensitized Hodge to the ubiquitous existence of people's committees, peasant unions, and other leftist organizations throughout the south. This weighed on his mind and convinced him that he could not wait passively for his superiors to grasp the gravity of the situation. He told staff officers at a meeting on November 12, "we are walking on the edge of a volcano,"[170] and later forwarded a remarkable report to MacArthur saying:

> The U.S. occupation of Korea under present conditions and policies is surely drifting to the edge of a political-economic abyss from which it can never be retrieved with any credit to United States prestige in the Far East. Positive action on the international level or *the seizure of complete initiative in South Korea by the U.S. in the very near future is absolutely essential to stop this drift* (emphasis added).[171]

Hodge had a knack for imagery that captured the American predicament and a pragmatic concern for American interests in Korea that led him again and again to act on the principle, "better safe than sorry."

Perhaps most unnerving to a military man like Hodge was the presence of a number of unofficial or private Korean armies, the strongest of which was the NPA. At some point in late October, Hodge directed Cho Pyŏng-ok to use KNP to disband all private military bodies. Cho refused to do this until the MG came up with a plan to incorporate them into a sanctioned military body: "When the MG resolves the problem of the military, then we will disband the private military organizations."[172] Cho later said that he had viewed the early establishment of a national army as essential to Korean independence.[173] More important in October 1945 was his unwillingness to disband rightist military groupings then aiding the KNP and the KDP. These included a group of Korean officers from the Japanese Army led by Yi Ŭng-jun and another group of Koreans from the Japanese Kwantung Army led by Wŏn Yong-dŏk.[174] The latter group was specifically cited for playing "a leading role as a right-wing organization protecting law and order" in the days following the American entry.[175] Cho apparently won Hodge over to his view, which demonstrates his great influence within the Occupation. The MG then selected leaders of private military groupings "who agreed with the plan" to be the new leaders of the Constabulary.[176] Soon thereafter, according to official Korean sources, "some thirty military organizations were disbanded and the majority of the right-wing organizations ended up entering the Constabulary, one after the other."[177]

On December 26 and 27, the KPR's National Preparatory Army held a meeting in Seoul, attended by some 300 members from the local Seoul detachment and 160 representatives from the countryside. During the meeting, Kim Il Sung, Kim Wŏn-bong, Yi Ch'ŏng-ch'ŏn, and Mu Chŏng were elected as titular leaders. The actual leader of the NPA, Yi Hyŏk-ki, served as chairman of the assembly.[178] There is no indication that the MG in Seoul requested NPA participation in the Constabulary, although NPA detachments in the Kyŏngsang provinces later became a part of the Constabulary regiment there. In early January the KNP and American Military Police units raided the NPA headquarters in Seoul and its training school in Yangju County. They arrested Yi Hyŏk-ki and several other NPA leaders. After the release on January 20 of an ordinance requiring all private military bodies to disband, an American military court used its provisions to sentence Yi to three years in prison and gave two-year sentences to five other NPA leaders.[179]

On December 5, 1945, a Military English Language School (*Kunsa yŏngŏ hakkyo*) was established to train officers destined for the Constabulary in the language of the Occupation. Many of the original sixty officers selected for the first class eventually came to dominate the top levels of the Republic of Korea Army (ROKA) after 1948, thus this class took on an importance that may not have been perceived in 1945. The sixty officers came from three groups: twenty from the Japanese Army, twenty from the Japanese Kwantung Army, and twenty from the KPG- and Kuomintang-aligned *Kwangbok Kun* (Restoration Army).[180] During World War II, some 50,000 Koreans served in the Japanese military. Nearly all of these were conscripted. Several hundred Koreans attained officer rank, and about twenty graduated from the elite Japanese Military Academy. A somewhat larger group graduated from the less prestigious Preparatory Officers Training School. Korean officers associated with the Kwantung Army in Manchuria had usually attended the Manchukuo Military Institute and then joined an auxiliary force with the prime task of suppressing Korean and Chinese anti-Japanese guerrillas.[181] But the number of Koreans with officer rank in the Japanese military was very small; they represented a miniscule pool from which to select officers for the Constabulary.

The Kwangbok Army was established in Chungking on September 17, 1940. Official South Korean sources describe it as having been 5,000 strong in 1945 and as the *only* body of Koreans that fought the Japanese during the war.[182] But these assertions are not backed up with details on, for example, Kwangbok detachments or regiments, or the dates and circumstances of engagements with the Japanese forces in China. An independent source said some 200 Koreans were associated with the Kwangbok Army at its inception.[183] An American Office of Strategic Services (OSS) officer who observed this army in Chungking in August 1945 and who was most sympathetic to its cause estimated its total numbers to be around 600, of which fully 200 were "officers." It had three detachments of 200 men each and planned two more comparable detachments to bring the total up to 1,000.[184] Other observers in Chungking said the Kwangbok forces were made up mostly of intellectuals and students.[185]

Apparently the Chinese Nationalist Ministry of War hoped that, with the Japanese surrender in August, Koreans in the Japanese Army in China could be enrolled into the Kwangbok Army:

> This decision is in line with the greatly improved cooperation which has been accorded the [Korean] Provisional Government by the KMT [Kuomintang] and the [Chinese] Central Government following the entry of the Soviet Union into the Pacific War and, particularly, the advance of Soviet troops into both Manchuria and Korea.[186]

The difficulties that the Chinese Nationalists encountered in taking the Japanese surrender in China meant that such plans could not be carried out, however. An undetermined number of demobilized Koreans did join, at least loosely, the Kwangbok forces, but a much larger number either returned to Korea on their own or joined with other Koreans fighting in the Chinese Eighth Route Army.[187]

Kwangbok Army people began straggling back to south Korea in November 1945. They apparently told some tall tales to American officers, for an Occupation historian wrote that the Kwangbok had "a 200,000-man, all-Korean army in China to fight with Chiang's forces." He also averred that "one must assume that the Soviets were fully cognizant of this infiltration of the Kwang Bok Army into South Korea and its relation to the Kuomintang and Kim Koo."[188] Although the Soviets perhaps knew little and cared less about the ineffectual Kwangbok forces, American perceptions such as the above are important. By November 1945, Hodge had decided that he was fighting the same battle in Korea that Chiang was in China. Like Chiang, he hoped to use the KPG and the Kwangbok Army to attain his ends (see next chapter). Unfortunately for Hodge, the Kwangbok forces proved not just to number only in the hundreds, or even tens, but to be reticent about participating in American arrangements in south Korea.

In general, as we will see, the return of KPG and Kwangbok people to Korea in late November and early December emerges as a key factor both in American de facto policy making and in the subsequent failures of these policies. The Americans had hoped that the return of such patriots would give legitimacy to other American employees, particularly those in the fledgling national defense force, who were widely viewed as collaborators. However, even extreme rightist Koreans like Yi Pŏm-sŏk, a Kwangbok leader and one-time officer in the Kuomintang "Blue Shirts," refused to participate in the Constabulary. When the Americans sent a special mission to Shanghai in February 1946 to ask Yi to join, he reportedly said, "What idiot's military organization is this, this 'Constabulary' under a military government? Before organizing a military we must recover our national sovereignty."[189] Kwangbok people who had returned to Korea did not want to participate in the Constabulary with officers from the Japanese military who were "widely stigmatized as pro-Japanese."[190] Those who did participate became "a vociferous and discontented minority," resentful of the "collaborators."[191] The Americans responsible for the Constabulary also found Kwangbok people to be lacking in rudimentary military training. Thus most of the original twenty Kwangbok officers selected for the language school did not go on to attain high position in the Constabulary.[192] Moreover, because the Americans stipulated that no Constabulary personnel could have records of imprisonment by the Japanese, Korean resisters at home and abroad were excluded. Thus the Constabulary and the subsequent ROKA became the preserve of "those officers with a Japanese [military] background."[193]

The eclipse of the Kwangbok people was probably inevitable from the time that the Americans began to rely on Koreans who had ranked high in the Japanese military. The most important of these was Yi Ŭng-jun, who advised and aided the Americans in developing plans for national defense forces in November 1945. Yi was apparently recommended to the Americans by Cho Pyŏng-ok.[194] He had been a colonel in the Japanese Army and became a prominent figure in the selection of entrants to the language school; he later became an advisor to General Schick, the director of the Office of National Defense. Yi was the first ROKA chief of staff in 1948.[195] Irma Materi probably referred to him when she discussed a certain "Lee" who "had seen a great deal of action with the Japanese troops in China," and who, with his jackboots and riding crop, "retained some of the arrogance of the Jap military."[196] Also influential in the selection of officers to lead the Constabulary was Wŏn Yong-dŏk, a lieutenant colonel in the Kwantung Army who became the first commander of the Constabulary.[197] Yu Chae-hŭng, a major in the Japanese Army who had been chief of a Japanese arsenal, was another who played an important role in the development of the Constabulary.[198] Other Korean officers from the Japanese military who were members either of the first class of the language school or the first two classes of the Constabulary officers' training school in 1945-1946 and who later played important roles in the ROKA under Syngman Rhee or in the military coup of 1961 in-

cluded: Ch'ae Pyŏng-dŏk, Chang To-yŏng Ch'oe Ch'ang-un, Ch'oe
Kyŏng-nok, Chŏng Il-gwŏn, Kang Mun-bong, Kim Chae-gyu (assassin
of President Park Chung Hee in 1979), Kim Hong-jun, Kim Paeg-il,
Kim Sŏk-pŏm, Kim Tong-ha, Paek Sŏn-yŏp, Pak Chŏng-hŭi (Park
Chung Hee, ROK President, 1963-1979), Pak Im-hang, Pak Ki-yong,
Yang Kuk-chin, Yi Chong-ch'an, Yi Chu-il, Yi Han-nim, and Yun
T'ae-il.[199] The Constabulary in 1945 and 1946 thus produced the lead-
ing ROK military elite that its organizers hoped it would, although to
be more accurate we might say that it eased the transfer of military
elite from the Japanese Army to the ROKA.

During the Pacific War, the Japanese military served as one of the
few routes of upward mobility open to Koreans. Japanese successes
in the Pacific no doubt made a military career all the more attractive.
Thus the Japanese had no difficulty building up Korean officers like
Kim Sŏk-wŏn into heroes and models to young Koreans (for Kim
Sŏk-wŏn's activities, refer back to chapter one). Many Koreans perhaps
did not know that they might end up fighting their own countrymen
in Manchuria. In any case, the Japanese lost and the spoils went to
their opponents. In Japan, the American Occupation tried and executed a number of high Japanese and Korean militarists as war criminals and made "automatic purgees" of "all former commissioned officers of the regular army, navy, and volunteer reserves."[200] Yet in
Korea, such commissioned officers were rewarded with control of the
Constabulary.[201]

The strange ironies of such developments touched even the Japanese-
trained Korean officers themselves. When Reamer Argo approached
Yi Hyŏng-gŭn to obtain his aid in building the Constabulary, Yi reportedly declined, saying, "How can those who served in the Japanese
Army participate in building a [Korean] army?" Argo replied, "If
experienced men like yourself do not participate, who will?"[202] Other
Koreans, like the swashbuckling Kim Sŏk-wŏn, were also reticent about
joining the Constabulary. In early 1946, Hodge met with Kim and
others and reportedly said:

> The Constabulary is going along well now, using American-style
> training, and when a government is set up, it will become the
> national army. . . . You have had your experience in the Japanese
> military, but now you must have a new beginning in a democratic
> military.[203]

Americans complained that Korean training methods conflicted with
United States Army doctrine, as in "banzai charges against an enemy
position."[204] But language problems prevented the implementation of
American training methods.[205] A more serious limitation on effective

training derived from the uses to which the Constabulary was put, however. Instead of training a force that could defend south Korea's borders, the Americans emphasized techniques of riot suppression. The Occupation feared internal disorder and viewed the Constabulary as an essential police reserve.[206] Americans responsible for the Constabulary saw tactical training opportunities in "civil disorders and guerrilla-like activities by Communist elements" in south Korea; they were able to inculcate "the principles of village fighting" in actual operations. Thus, the Constabulary and the KNP became the two prime weapons to be used against the severe disorders that dotted south Korea from 1946 to 1950. The Constabulary was never authorized to make arrests, but "it consistently ignored this lack of legal right, making arrests at will and searching without warrants." It gained "valuable experience" fighting guerrillas on Cheju Island and suppressing rebels in Yŏsu and Sunch'ŏn in 1948.[207]

But the use of the Constabulary for counterinsurgency proved to be a fateful mistake. The objects of these counterinsurgency efforts quickly came to see the Constabulary as a political weapon that, in their own hands, could effectively serve their purposes. Thus, unlike the KNP, the Constabulary quickly came to include many leftists. By October 1946 American Counter-Intelligence Corps (CIC) investigators deemed such people "a threat to American control of the Army."[208] In the South Kyŏngsang Province regiment, O Tŏk-chun, who led the local NPA detachment, joined the Constabulary and brought most of his men in with him.[209] The same thing happened in the North Kyŏngsang regiment, where the NPA leader Ha Chae-p'al brought in his followers, who were termed "all communists."[210] As a result, the Kyŏngsang branch of the Constabulary proved largely worthless in suppressing the leftist uprisings in the fall of 1946. Elsewhere pitched battles occurred between the KNP and the Constabulary.[211] The final failure of American policies toward the Constabulary became evident when the refusal of the 14th Regiment to embark for Cheju Island to fight guerrillas there erupted into the bloody Yŏsu-Sunch'ŏn Rebellion of 1948.

Koreans involved with the Constabulary thought that these problems could be remedied by thought control. Thus, although professed leftist military groups were automatically prevented from entering the language school, still members of rightist groups "had their qualifications checked and their thoughts examined in order to block the entrance into the school of the left wing."[212] After that, Koreans requested of American officers that new recruits have their thoughts examined. But the Americans "did not understand Korea's situation" (meaning that a strong Left threatened south Korea from within as well as from without) and thus refused. This "great mistake" allowed leftist "infiltration" of the Constabulary.[213]

Koreans were wrong to think that the Americans did not fear the Left within the south, however. As we have seen, such fears led Hodge and his advisors to embrace any group, regardless of its background, that could be counted upon to oppose the Left. But in supporting police and military officers who had done Japanese bidding, the Americans cast themselves down a path with few returns and few outlets. A momentum developed that increasingly tended to close off alternatives. Patriots would not work with collaborators. Collaborators wanted to examine the thoughts of others. Americans wanted to turn collaborators into democrats. The tail wagged the dog. As contradiction piled upon contradiction, Hodge and his advisors decided to opt for a new policy that would at once give a patriotic cast to their Korean employees and move toward "the seizure of complete initiative in South Korea by the U.S." This policy will be the subject of the next chapter.

TOWARD A SEPARATE
SOUTHERN GOVERNMENT

When I return, the Government of Korea returns.
Kim Ku

I have no children, but all young Koreans are my sons and
daughters.
Syngman Rhee

W E HAVE examined the pattern of de facto American policies regarding the fundamental instruments of political power—bureaucracy, police, army—that emerged in Korea in the weeks and
months following the initial American entry. These policies implied
that Korea was effectively a divided nation and that no cooperation or
complementarity in policy was possible between the American and the
Soviet zones of responsibility. The Soviets, unlike the Americans, had
recognized the People's Republic shortly after occupying northern Korea; therefore, the two foreign powers operated through entirely different structures, allied with Koreans at the opposite ends of the political spectrum.

The Americans, however, were at a distinct disadvantage because
many of their Korean allies were tainted by past affiliations with the
Japanese and seemed incapable of building popular support or viable
political organization outside the MG bureaucracy. Thus, the goal
of the American command became the enlistment of patriotic and reliable Koreans who might lend their nationalist credentials to American efforts. These individuals and their supporters could be installed
in executive positions atop the revived bureaucratic structures, placing a stamp of legitimacy on the existing arrangements. Much of
American policy from the end of 1945 through 1948 was, in fact, concerned with a search for acceptable Korean leaders who could command the revived bureaucracy. Here, too, Hodge found himself at
odds with superiors in Washington.

THE RETURN OF THE KPG AND THE "GOVERNING COMMISSION"

In 1945 Hodge and his advisors thought that the Korean Provisional
Government and the Koreans associated with it, like Syngman Rhee

and Kim Ku, had the popular support and legitimacy that could aid the American effort. We noted earlier that on September 15 H. Merrell Benninghoff had passed along Hodge's recommendation that KPG leaders be returned to Korea as figureheads for the Occupation. The acting political advisor to MacArthur in Japan, George Atcheson, pushed this idea again in mid-October, after a conversation with Hodge:

> For some time I have delayed recommending that [the State] Dept seriously consider whether situation in Korea is not such that we should commence to use some progressive, popular and respected leader, or small group, to act as a nucleus of an organization which in cooperation with and under the direction of our military government could develop into an executive and administrative governmental agency. Such nuclear organization would not need to be called "The Korean Provisional Government," but might be given some title as "National Korean Peoples Executive Committee," and the Advisory Council which General Hodge has set up could either act as advisors to such committee or, if circumstances should so dictate, might in due course be integrated into the Committee.[1]

He then suggested three men who might head this committee: Syngman Rhee, Kim Ku, and Kim Kyu-sik, all KPG leaders. He acknowledged that such a proposal was "contrary to past American thinking" but maintained, "unless positive action is taken . . . our difficulties will increase rather than diminish, and the Communistic group set up and encouraged by the Soviets in northern Korea will manage to extend its influence into southern Korea with results which can be readily envisaged."[2] What was the KPG, and what had been "past American thinking" regarding it?

The leaders who organized the provisional government in 1919 worked together only until 1921. After that the group, riven with factions, was described as "almost defunct."[3] In the late 1920s in Shanghai, Kim Ku even had trouble meeting the rent on KPG headquarters.[4] The KPG revived a bit after Pearl Harbor, and in the latter stages of the war, the rightist faction under Kim Ku allied temporarily with moderate and leftist factions led by Kim Kyu-sik and Kim Wŏn-bong. But the KPG had no ties with the homeland Korean population and existed only at the sufferance of the Kuomintang in Chungking.[5] After seven years of war in China with Japan, KPG leaders still remained uncertain as to how they might participate in the Allied war effort, as can be seen in the May 1944 conversation between Clarence E. Gauss, United States Ambassador to China, and Cho (Tjo) So-ang of the KPG:[6]

TJO: With recognition [of the KPG] we might be able to prevent
        Koreans from being drafted into the Japanese Army.
GAUSS: How?
TJO: Well, what would you suggest as a possible action?
GAUSS: Have any Koreans been able to obtain military intelligence
        on Korean [*sic*], Manchuria, or Japan and pass it on to
        the UN?
TJO: No.
GAUSS: Has there been attempt to do it?
TJO: No. But that is difficult without money. There might be
        opportunities for propaganda because a recent man who
        reached Chungking from Korea reported that at home there
        is no knowledge of the Cairo Declaration and little of
        the KPG.

In this same meeting, Cho told Gauss that although the KPG's Kwangbok Army consisted of only 500 unarmed men and officers, there were
large numbers of partisans in Manchuria—meaning, of course, forces
such as those led by Kim Il Sung.

The KPG was self-styled and in no way comparable to, say, the
Polish government-in-exile in London, which was recognized by the
British and the Americans and which fielded some 90,000 soldiers during the war. The KPG politicians were, as the Europeans used to say,
in partibus infidelium, or in the land of the infidels and without a
constituency. In spite of this, Syngman Rhee, ousted from the KPG in
1925 yet still calling himself "Minister Plenipotentiary and Envoy
Extraordinary [of the KPG] to the United States," sought during the
early 1940s to obtain official American recognition of the KPG as the
legitimate government of all Korea.[7] Rhee met and corresponded with
State Department officials beginning in 1942, when he solicited the
aid of a Brooklyn publisher named M. Preston Goodfellow.[8] By June
1944 Rhee was telling American officials, who thought that they had
joined and nearly won the ultimate conflict, that a new conflict was
on the horizon—one between communism and democracy: "The only
possibility of avoiding the ultimate conflict between the United States
and the Soviet Union is to build up all democratic, not communistic
elements wherever possible." He urged recognition of the KPG, thereby "to eliminate the possibility of civil war in Korea."[9] When recognition was not forthcoming, Rhee and his American backers chose to
blame it on communist influence within the State Department:

[Communist] groups have been and still are receiving the cooperation of some officers of the State Department.

This seems to confirm our belief that the State Department has been delaying recognition of the Korean Provisional Government in order to give the Korean Communists a chance to form a Lublin government.[10]

The State Department was not persuaded. As early as 1942, according to Rhee's biographer,

Rhee was flatly informed by Dr. [Stanley] Hornbeck that in the opinion of the State Department he was wholly unknown inside Korea and the provisional government was no more than a self-constituted club with limited membership among a group of expatriates.[11]

Later the Department found KPG leaders "personally ambitious and somewhat irresponsible" and said that the KPG's following was limited "even among exiles."[12] In the summer of 1945, American officials found no Korean body "which might be considered really representative of the Korean people."[13] Such judgments fully accorded with the history and present status of the KPG, and were particularly important since, as we have seen, the State Department had been worried about possible Soviet possession of the Korean peninsula from 1943 on.

Such State Department thinking about the KPG was included in the SWNCC "Basic Initial Directive" that was received at MacArthur's headquarters at approximately the same time Atcheson forwarded his recommendations about the KPG to Washington. The directive said: "You will not extend official recognition to, nor utilize for political purposes, any self-styled Korean provisional government or similar political organizations."[14] Although the directive included an apparent loophole regarding the KPG when it said "You will utilize the services of such organizations as individuals when desirable without commitment as to the organizations," it also said: "You will establish liaison with the Russians and seek through that liaison to achieve the maximum uniformity of procedures and policies in the control of Korea, consistent with the purposes of this directive."[15] Since the Russians had made no commitments to the KPG, "uniformity of procedures and policies" could not be established by setting up KPG leaders as figureheads. But the KPG was the least of the problems involved in seeking uniformity in administering north and south Korea in mid-October 1945. The Occupation had not worried about such considerations when establishing the Advisory Council or reviving the police and it remained undeterred in its determination to make use of the KPG.

The director of the State Department Office of Far Eastern Affairs, John Carter Vincent, said in answer to Atcheson's cable that he opposed using the KPG in Korea; but his statement revealed the essential conflict in American policy between idealism and reality. Vincent agreed that there was "need for some kind of responsible Korean leadership to counter-balance the activities of the Communist elements" but went on to say:

> This Government has consistently advocated a policy that nothing be done by this Government or by the Commander in Korea to give any group, such as the Kim Koo group [KPG] . . . or any individual, such as Dr. Rhee, the impression that we were supporting such a group or individual as against any other Koreans.[16]

Vincent and his colleagues in Washington had long been impatient with Rhee's antics; moreover, Vincent probably hoped to maintain continuity between presurrender and postsurrender American policy regarding the KPG. But he viewed Korea from the comfortable confines of Foggy Bottom. Hodge and his State Department advisors on the scene in Korea had actually confronted the revolutionary ferment of liberation. Would Washington be willing to resolve the ambiguities of its presurrender Korean planning by taking the high road of impartiality and paternal tutelage toward independence if it meant a victory for the Left? Hodge could not simply manufacture both "responsible" and anticommunist Korean leadership. He had to find his allies where he could. The burden of convincing the State Department of this reality fell to Assistant Secretary of War John J. McCloy, whose memorandum, written in response to Vincent's, argued:

> Vincent's memorandum seems to me to avoid in large part the really pressing realities facing us in Korea. . . . From talking with General Hodge I believe that his concern is that the communists will seize by direct means the government in our area. If this were done, it would seriously prejudice our intention to permit the people of Korea freely to choose their own form of government. There is no question but that communist action is actively and intelligently being carried out through our zone. . . . It would seem that the *best way to approach it in the over-all is to build up on our own a reasonable and respected government* or group of advisors which will be able under General Hodge to bring some order out of the political, social, and economic chaos that now exists south of the 38th parallel and so provide a basis for, at some later date, a really free and uncoerced election by the people (emphasis added).

After listing various allegations about Russian actions in the north, McCloy continued:

> To get back to Vincent's memorandum—does it not add up to asking us to tell Hodge that we really repose little confidence in him, that we are not prepared to let him do the few things which he, on the spot—and what a spot—feels can be useful towards achieving our aims. . . . Let us ask him, by all means, for more information on the communist problem and his thoughts as to how to keep it from wrecking our objectives, but let us also let him use as many exiled Koreans as he can, depending on his discretion not to go too far.[17]

McCloy here clearly stated the contradictions in American policy toward Korea and agreed with the Occupation: the Americans must build up a government on their own. McCloy, of course, was not a minor official in a distant backwater, but a central figure in postwar American foreign policy. The Occupation had thus won a formidable ally in its struggle with the State Department.

The Occupation's determination to establish a government unilaterally was most clearly stated in William Langdon's cable of November 20, 1945. He began by saying that the trusteeship idea should be dropped:

> After one month's observation in liberated Korea and with background of earlier service in Korea, I am unable to fit trusteeship to actual conditions here or to be persuaded of its suitability from moral and practical standpoints, and, therefore, believe we should drop it. It is thought wrong because the Korean people have always been a distinct nation except for 35 years of Jap rule and have high literacy, cultural and living standards judged by Asiatic and Middle Eastern standards. . . . The fact seems to be that all Koreans want their country to themselves in their life time and will not have any form of foreign tutelage [in order] to attain an alien standard of nationhood.

Since Kim Ku's group "has no rival for first government of liberated Korea," he went on, the return of the KPG "offers United States an opportunity for attempting a constructive Korean policy that can hardly be resented or traduced. In broad outline this policy might be as follows":

> (1) The Commanding General directs Kim Koo to form a council in MG representative of the several political groups to study and prepare the form of government of Korea and to organize a Gov-

erning Commission; MG provides facilities, advice and working funds for such commission.

(2) The Governing Commission is integrated with MG (presently rapidly being built up as an all Korean organization).

(3) The Governing Commission succeeds MG as interim government, with Commanding General retaining power of veto and of appointing such American supervisors and advisors as he deems necessary.

(4) Three other powers concerned [Great Britain, China, the Soviet Union] are requested to supply some supervisors and advisors in Governing Commission in place of American.

(5) Governing Commission hold[s] selection of head of state.

(6) Government formed by elected head of state [is] recognized, treaties made with and missions accredited to it, and Korea admitted to UNO [that is, United Nations]. Note: Somewhere in the transition, perhaps between (4) and (5), *negotiations to be signed with Russia* for mutual withdrawal of troops and *extension to Russian zone of Governing Commission's authority.* Russia should be informed in advance of above plan and invited to further it by allowing persons in Russian zone nominated to Governing Commission *by council* to proceed to Seoul, but *if Russian participation is not forthcoming plan should be carried out for Korea south of 38th parallel.*

The old native regime internally was feudal and corrupt but the record shows that it was the best disposed toward foreign interests of the three Far Eastern nations, protecting foreign lives and property and enterprises and respecting treaties and franchises. I am sure that *we may count on at least as much from a native government evolved as above,* although we may be justified in expecting much more considering the progress of the people and country since [the demise of the old regime] and the leavening there will be of foreign supervisors. . . . As for the quarter of the population [*sic*] in the Northern Zone, I believe the Korean people too homogeneous to be so estranged by political and social innovations to the point where they would not welcome a national government (emphasis added).[18]

Langdon ended this remarkable paper with a pointed reference to Ordinance No. 28 of November 13, "which has as aim, organizing, training and equipping armed Korean military and naval forces."

Langdon's cable has been quoted nearly in its entirety because it was the most important document to appear during the first year of the Occupation. It elaborated a policy that resulted in the Representative Democratic Council of February 1946, the South Korean Interim Government of 1947, and the eventual assumption of power by the Rhee government in 1948. The basic difference between Langdon's proposal and the actual course of events was that the United Nations was brought in at (5) rather than at (6), when it was used to sanction the National Assembly elections of May 1948. Also, of course, Rhee won over Kim Ku. Apart from these alterations, though, the plan was followed nearly point-by-point to its conclusion.

The War Department held a conference in regard to Langdon's plan on December 4, with Colonel Charles Bonesteel, General Archer Lerch, and Benninghoff present. Bonesteel's memorandum of the conversation noted that Langdon's policy would "obviate the need of a trusteeship." Furthermore, it continued, the "Langdon plan for granting Korean independence utilizes the Chungking Provisional Government, yet concurrently takes into consideration present Korean lack of experience in governing themselves." The memo then related the plan to the basic goals of American policy in Korea, stated as follows: "The major US interest in facilitating Korean independence is that Korea shall become truly free, democratic, friendly to the US, and not unduly dependent on any of its three major neighbors."[19]

The governing commission proposal was a classic expression of "nationalist," containment policy. It abjured more sophisticated policies designed to win Soviet adherence to and participation in American arrangements, saying to the Soviets, in essence, "cooperate with us on our terms or there will be no cooperation." Internationalist thinkers like Vincent therefore opposed the plan. He, Hugh Borton, and other internationalists in the State Department responded to the governing commission telegram of November 20 by saying that the State Department was considering this new policy, but that the established trusteeship policy "may still be necessary to secure the elimination of the barrier of the 38th parallel." Merrell Benninghoff, then in Washington, signed this telegram and returned to Seoul a few days later. Yet on December 12 Langdon sent another salvo to the State Department, saying, "We have already submitted a plan to cover the transition to full independence (I refer to my telegram dated 20 November). Will this be in accord with Russian policy?" Langdon argued that if agreement with the Russians was impossible along the lines he had suggested, then it is imperative that the U.S. act as the situation requires on its own, even though these actions may sound *national in character* . . . [only such definite actions will] convince the Korean leaders that our intentions of their independence are genuine and in this way we can win their support in fighting Communism, unrest, and hostility of the masses toward us (emphasis added).[20]

Those already in Seoul were in a position to implement policy regardless of opposition in Washington, however; and there was near unanimity on the scene, whether we speak of Hodge, his State Department advisors, MacArthur in Tokyo, or prestigious visitors like John J. McCloy. Americans in Seoul thought that the Soviets had created their own government in the north by this time (they had not; see chapter eleven); they saw the whole People's Republic apparatus as a creature of Soviet designs. More important in these plans, however, American alliances with rightist groups had influenced Occupation thinking with respect to the KPG. As we noted in the previous chapter, the Korean Democratic Party advocated the return of the KPG even before the Americans arrived. On September 14 Cho Pyŏng-ok and Wŏn Se-hun of the KDP wrote to KPG leaders in Chungking asking that they return to Korea forthwith (see Appendix C). KDP advocacy of an early KPG return was reflected in Merrell Benninghoff's report of September 15.

Perhaps of equal importance to Occupation views on the KPG was a secret report prepared by Clarence Weems, Jr., who had recently come to Korea from Chungking.[21] According to Weems, the KPG was "the God-head of the Korean movement and its presence in Korea will help influence leaders and people to act wisely and patriotically." Furthermore, he said, "a substantial body of technically and professionally trained Korean personnel is available in China and many of these people could be brought back to Korea by the Provisional Government." The leaders of the KPG "oppose communism," Weems said, but they oppose "the spread of foreign control" even more: "If the Provisional Government has its way, Korea will have a democratic form of government which is absolutely opposed to domination of Korea by any foreign power, and which will have relations of sincere friendship with the United States." KPG leaders felt that American missionaries and businessmen had made good impressions in Korea, and thus "temporary American supervision" of Korea would aid in the achievement of democratic government. Weems said that Koreans like Yŏ Un-hyŏng, Song Chin-u, Kim Sŏng-su, Chang Tŏk-su, Cho Man-sik, and Yun Ch'i-ho favored the return of the KPG; as for the

KPG leaders, they were "unqualified in their admiration for Yŏ Un-hyŏng . . . his character is beyond reproach."[22] Weems detailed some of the extreme factional rivalries of the KPG—Kim Ku hated Kim Kyu-sik, neither could stand Syngman Rhee, and so on—and then concluded as follows:

> The presence of this revolutionary Godhead in Korea at this time would unquestionably aid the process of developing a sound Korean administration. It favors American influence over that of any other power, as do the people within Korea if they are free to choose. It is fearful of the effects of Russian occupation.

The first fruit of the Occupation's determination to utilize the KPG was the return of Syngman Rhee on October 16, 1945. Rhee was flown into Seoul on one of MacArthur's airplanes after discussions in Tokyo between MacArthur and Hodge on October 12 through 15. Although official American sources reported that Hodge urged Rhee's return and hoped to use him and other KPG leaders as the nucleus of an interim government,[23] the circumstances of Rhee's homecoming are rather more complex. The State Department had blocked Rhee's passport because he insisted upon calling himself "High Commissioner [of the KPG] to the United States Returning to Korea."[24] Rhee apparently had better luck with the War Department and the Office of Strategic Services (OSS). During the war, as we have seen, Rhee befriended M. Preston Goodfellow, who soon rose to the rank of deputy director of the OSS. In general, the OSS was a place where "every eccentric schemer with a harebrained plan for secret operations (from phosphorescent foxes to incendiary bats) would find a sympathetic ear."[25] Rhee had a scheme to send Koreans behind Japanese lines, and "through Goodfellow's intercession, the War Department accorded Rhee limited recognition as liaison with the OSS in recruiting a group of young Koreans for behind-the-scenes service in the Far East."[26] Nothing came of this plan, perhaps because Rhee had no such Koreans under his control, but it appears that other schemes tied him to his American supporters. Like Yi Dynasty kings, Rhee offered Americans certain concessions in Korea in return for favors. For example, in March 1945, he appointed Samuel H. Dolbear to be "Minerals Advisor" to the KPG. In return, Dolbear wrote letters to the State Department urging recognition of the KPG.[27] Rhee apparently had similar arrangements with Goodfellow; for in mid-1946 when Rhee's deals with both Dolbear and Goodfellow for concessions of Korea's resources became public, Goodfellow was forced to leave Korea.

In August and September 1945 Goodfellow, as an OSS official, interceded with the State Department on Rhee's behalf. He told them that "Dr. Rhee has more of the American point of view than other Korean leaders."[28] In spite of continuing State Department opposition, but perhaps because of his liaison status with the War Department, Rhee managed to get the venerable head of the State Department passport section, Mrs. Ruth Shipley, to approve his credentials for travel to Japan.[29]

After Rhee arrived in Tokyo, MacArthur sent a cable back to the War Department entitled, "Attention Col. Goodfellow from Col. [sic] Rhee from SCAP to WAR." Its contents stated, "Arrived safely October 12th at 11 A.M. Will rest tonight and make contact tomorrow."[30] There is no other record of Rhee's stopover in Tokyo. It is difficult to believe that Rhee did not meet with MacArthur and Hodge; and it is inconceivable that Hodge did not at least discuss with MacArthur his hopes regarding Rhee's return to Korea. Yet Hodge later told his staff that Rhee's arrival in Seoul surprised him.[31] Other evidence suggests that Hodge was less than candid, however. In a letter of October 21, 1945, Rhee said, "General Hodge came to Tokyo to meet me," and confided, "Hodge and I had agreed not to announce my arrival [in Seoul] until we are ready."[32] Let us be frank: Hodge, MacArthur, Goodfellow, and Rhee conspired against established State Department policy. In so doing, they returned to Korea not simply a nationalist, containment thinker but one of the prime advocates of a new strategy for dealing with the communists, liberation or rollback.[33] The Occupation quartered Rhee in a suite at the Chosŏn Hotel, then reserved as a billet for the highest American officers. In succeeding days, crowds of curious Koreans milled around the hotel, hoping to glimpse a legendary patriot. Who was this Syngman Rhee?

Perhaps Rhee's greatest advantage in 1945 was that few Koreans and fewer Americans knew anything about him. Syngman Rhee (Yi Sŭng-man) was born in 1875 in Hwanghae Province into an impoverished *yangban* family. Some 400 years earlier, an ancestor had had some connection with royal blood, which is perhaps the reason that Rhee's father worked as a scholar of genealogy. Rhee failed the civil service examinations several times between 1887 and 1893. He then entered the Paejae School in 1894 and began to study English.[34] In 1898 he was loosely associated with the famed Independence Club as a minor follower of Sŏ Chae-p'il (Philip Jaisohn). Shortly thereafter, he was imprisoned for political activities; he remained incarcerated until 1904. In 1905 Rhee left for the United States and entered George Washington University as a sophomore. He graduated in 1907 and then went on to achieve an M.A. at Harvard (1908) and a Ph.D. at Princeton (1910).[35] He was thus the first Korean to receive a doctorate from an American university, which became no small part of his prestige among older Koreans. Rhee returned briefly to Korea in 1910. He then embarked again the next year for the United States where he remained until 1945.

During his more than three decades in the United States, Rhee became a quintessential exile politician. It seems he was never gainfully employed, but supported himself through contributions from other Koreans. He haunted the corridors of the State Department, claiming to be a friend and student of Woodrow Wilson and petitioning in vain for American intervention on behalf of Korean independence. The character trait that stands out above all others, though, was Rhee's monumental obstinacy. He was the original *kojip jaengi* (stickler, dogmatist). KPG leaders accused him of dogmatism and usurpation of authority in 1919 and ousted him from the KPG in 1925.[36] His struggles with expatriate Koreans in the United States were legendary. In 1943 the Korean National Association in the United States denounced him for "misuse of hard-earned Korean cash," "personalized publicity," and "uncompromising stubborness."[37]

Rhee's opponents, particularly those in north Korea, called him an "American-Korean"[38] who had lost his Korean heritage. But Rhee grew to manhood in the last quarter-century of the Yi Dynasty and was hardly changed or broadened by his years in the United States. It was in Korea that Rhee mastered the traditional Korean art of cultivating the weaknesses of foreigners toward Korean ends and the manipulative and instrumental skills of "low determines high" diplomacy.[39] In 1945, despite his advanced age (he was seventy), these skills and his pluck and determination made Rhee a formidable figure for Americans like Hodge who were seeking patriotic yet cooperative Koreans to serve as figureheads for a troubled Occupation.

Koreans across the political spectrum welcomed Rhee back as a long-lost patriot—not as the *only* exile who had devoted his life to Korean independence, but as one of a handful of Koreans linked to the original opposition to the Japanese Annexation. As Hŏ Hŏn of the KPR put it, "When I was twelve or thirteen years old, Dr. Rhee started his career with Yi Sang-jae. Because he has been fighting for our country all his life, we selected him as President of the KPR."[40] The KCP's *Haebang ilbo* also heralded the return of this "revolutionary" who devoted his career to Korea. But the issue for the KCP, and for all other political groups, was which groups Rhee would support: "Dr. Rhee will not and must not betray the expectations of the people."[41]

In the first few days after his return, Rhee succeeded in portraying himself as a unifying figure between Right and Left. Under the vague slogan, *tŏp'ŏ nok'o mungch'i* (willy-nilly or all-inclusive grouping or unity), he rallied the KDP, the KCP, a few KPR leaders, and other groups into a body called the Central Council for the Rapid Realization of Korean Independence (*Taehan tongnip ch'oksŏng chungang hyŏbŭi-hoe*—CCRRKI).[42] But on October 20, at the Welcoming Ceremony for the Occupation, he denounced Russia and Russian policies in the north. He also refused entreaties to join the KPR or work with it.[43] As a result, leftists and many moderates came to see Rhee's "unity" as an "unprincipled" one, embracing pro-Japanese Koreans and "feudal remnants" but excluding anti-Japanese fighters on the Left.[44] Leading leftists like Pak Hŏn-yŏng and Yŏ Un-hyŏng attended the founding session of the CCRRKI on October 23 but had left it by the time of its second meeting on November 2.[45]

And indeed, even as he preached political unity, Rhee allied with the Korean Democratic Party. The CCRRKI committee that nominated new members, for example, was made up of Song Chin-u, Paek Nam-hun, Kim Tong-wŏn, Hŏ Chŏng, and Wŏn Se-hun, all KDP leaders.[46] Han T'ae-su wrote that Rhee was one of the few anti-Japanese patriots who would work with the KDP, though even he did not join it because he frowned on its collaborationist element.[47] But Rhee could not ignore the KDP's newly won power within the Occupation; and KDP leaders needed Rhee to give them some legitimacy as patriots. The result was a tempestuous marriage of convenience.

Rhee further squelched the hopeful and cooperative atmosphere that had characterized his initial relations with south Korean political organizations with a series of denunciations of the People's Republic and the Left in general, beginning with a radio broadcast over JDOK on November 7.[48] His public statements dismayed the Occupation command. That such statements were made over MG-controlled radio "was no doubt a contributing factor to putting a damper on relations with the Russians."[49]

Rhee, instrumental in convincing Hodge and his advisors to bring KPG leaders back from Chungking, confided in his letter of October 21 to Robert Oliver, "We are planning to bring Kim Koo and several others from Chungking with the exception of the Kongsan [communist] group." He also claimed that Hodge had shown him copies of cables sent to Washington urging a change in American policy and an early return of the KPG. Apparently, the Chinese Nationalists had the same idea. Although one Chinese official had told the OSS in May 1945 that "both the so-called Korean government which operates under Chinese sponsorship and with Chinese subvention in Chungking, and all the Korean nationalist leaders in the U.S. have no roots and no following in Korea," in September 1945 Dr. K. C. Wu relayed the following message to American officials in Chungking:

> Generalissimo [Chiang Kai-shek] considers that it would be advisable that members of the Korean Provisional Government in Chungking be flown to Korea as possible appointees to administrative positions of the [Korean] government.[50]

In a staff meeting on November 2, Hodge announced that Kim Ku and his element in the KPG would soon return to Korea and described Kim as "the salt needed for the stew."[51] Ten days later, Hodge informed his staff that Kim's return was a top-secret matter and added:

> We are walking on the edge of a volcano . . . the political affairs in Korea simply mirror political affairs throughout the Far East, particularly China. Chiang Kai-shek is fighting communism in China and he wants a democratic Korea on his flank. He is therefore backing Kim Koo and this fact is well known to Korean radicals. The point at issue now is whether or not the entire Far East will go communism [*sic*].[52]

Hodge specifically requested that the rightist faction under Kim Ku be sent back to Seoul before the other factions under Kim Kyu-sik and Kim Wŏn-bong.[53] Because of continuing State Department opposition to the return of the KPG qua "government," the Occupation also made Kim Ku sign a pledge that the KPG would not act as a government before air transportation was approved. Thus, Kim Ku and fourteen or fifteen of his supporters returned to Seoul on November 23, followed by Kim Kyu-sik, Kim Wŏn-bong, and about twenty of their supporters on December 3.[54]

Shortly after the return of the KPG, Seoul was awash with rumors that the Occupation intended to set it up as a Korean government under American supervision. Some reports spoke of a coalition between the KPG and other groups, while others said that the Americans would simply recognize the KPG and allow it to take over.[55] Han T'ae-su, who was not aware of the Langdon proposal, thought that the KDP and Syngman Rhee were behind the clamor to set up the KPG as the government of Korea.[56] The rumors had merit, since Kim Ku's group received the protection of American MPs, Kim's personal bodyguards were allowed to carry weapons (those of other political groups were not), and the Occupation provided a residence and transportation facilities.[57] The KPG held "Councils of State" in December, with the participation of Syngman Rhee.[58]

Unfortunately for General Hodge and his advisors, Kim Ku and his followers proved even less useful and trustworthy than Syngman Rhee. The Occupation learned the hard way that the State Department had been right about the KPG: it was but one small exile group among many; it was a congeries of factions rather than an effective political organization; its leaders could be willful and erratic. These facts came out during the trusteeship imbroglio, after which all hope of utilizing the KPG foundered (see next chapter). Hodge later remarked that when the KPG leaders returned, "their popularity was not as great as they [*sic*] had expected" and that "they could not coalesce with anybody, except a group of wealthy men that they wanted to have support them."[59] Moreover, the KPG personages did not like what they found in south Korea. They refused to join in Rhee's denunciations of the People's Republic.[60] Perhaps most important, like the Kwangbok officers, they had contempt for the collaborators within the MG bureaucracy and for the KDP's opportunism in seizing so many important governmental positions. Such views were expressed in a private memorandum written by Sin Ik-hŭi, one of Kim Ku's lieutenants:

> We will have to discharge all officials appointed by the interpreters of Military Government. After August 1945 all pro-Japanese and national traitors under the Japanese first went into hiding . . . and later came out to buy off the interpreters so that they would get positions in the provincial governments, the district governments, and the police. We must clean out all these people, and at the same time stop this spirit of dependence on foreign countries.[61]

OPPOSITION TO THE LEFT

The background to and touchstone of American policy making in Korea in the fall of 1945 was a strong Left that, as the weeks progressed, appeared to thrive rather than weaken under the Occupation. In September the People's Republic may have seemed like a minor problem that could be overcome if the Americans supported the conservative opposition in Seoul; but as Occupation troops filtered into the provinces and began sending back reports, the extent of the KPR's influence became apparent to the Occupation command. The People's Republic loomed before them as a ubiquitous and powerful organization. It was not just a group of bickering, "venal" old men in Seoul. Suddenly Seoul appeared to be teetering on the edge of an abyss, or sitting precariously atop a smoldering volcano, as Hodge variously described the situation. Hodge received information that showed the KPR to be "organized into a government at all levels," whereas the KDP was "poorly organized or unorganized in most places" and seemed to have nothing to offer the people. He was told that "without Military Government intervention in [its] favor, no other party would be allowed to flourish."[62] Thus, as a corollary to and a consequence of its policy making in other areas, the Occupation developed policies to uproot the formidable Left. Hodge later confessed in a letter to an unidentified friend that,

> Flatly stated, one of our missions was to break down this Communist government [the KPR] outside of any directives and without benefit of backing by the Joint Chiefs of Staff or the State Department.[63]

The basic de facto policy followed by the American command and its Korean employees was to break up organizations oriented to the Left, creating a void, and hope that with police and Constabulary support, rightist groups would be able to take their places. We will have occasion to examine this policy as it was applied in the provinces in chapter nine, but here and in the next chapter we will be concerned with events in Seoul.

As we have seen, the Americans solicited Yŏ Un-hyŏng's participation in the Advisory Council as an individual on October 5 and were incensed when he refused. When General Arnold then issued his blast against the KPR and Yŏ, virtually all of Seoul's journalists criticized the statement. The Occupation command thereupon decided to suppress the *Maeil sinbo*, which had been sympathetic to the KPR since August and which had declined to print Arnold's statement. This action was to be a lesson to the south Korean press corps. In an interview on October 13, George Williams set the scene for this decision by charging that Seoul's reporters were "a grubby, ill-educated, and irresponsible lot" and that all but one of its newspapers were "irresponsible rank radical sheets." He accused the *Maeil sinbo* of being run by a committee of workers "under communist control" and called upon the conservatives to "bestir themselves and publish a paper that would give the other side."[64] In the first week of November, an investigation of the *Maeil sinbo* was ordered:

> The purpose of this investigation was to discover some flaw which could be used as a legitimate reason for controlling the paper if it seemed advisable. "It was like getting Al Capone for his income tax," said one of the officers charged with the investigation.

"The ax fell" on November 10 when *Maeil* presses were ordered to cease.[65] Ostensibly it was closed for having its accounts in arrears, but the real reason was obviously its general radicalism and its refusal to print Arnold's October 10 statement. The entire Korean press corps protested this closure.[66]

In the fall of 1945, there were only three modern printing presses in Seoul capable of producing thousands of newspapers on a daily basis. Two of these presses had printed the *Maeil sinbo* and the Japanese-language *Keijo nippo* (Seoul Daily). The third, called the Chōsen Printing Company, was already taken over by the MG for its own publications. Other newspapers were printed by small jobbers with comparatively primitive equipment. The *Maeil sinbo* was reorganized as the *Seoul sinmun* (Seoul News) and placed under the management of Ha Kyŏng-dŏk, a KDP leader. On November 16, Song Chin-u's group was granted use of the *Keijo nippo* presses and authorized to publish the *Tonga ilbo*, which had been closed by the Japanese in 1940 on the pretext of management irregularities.[67] Other KPR newspapers were allowed to continue publishing, but they no longer had access to efficient printing presses.

At about the same time, the Occupation achieved its first political coup when it caused Yŏ Un-hyŏng and his supporters to reorganize as the People's Party (*Inmindang*—PP). They did not leave the KPR, but they implicitly consented to Hodge's demand that the KPR drop its claims to being a government and call itself a political party. Yŏ founded the party on November 11, a week before a scheduled three-day meeting of the KPR in Seoul. The People's Party was a carry-over from the *Kŏn'guk tongmaeng*. It had a thirty-point platform much like that of the KPR, aiming at "the complete liberation of the working masses," and distinguished itself from the KDP and the KCP in the following manner:

> The KDP is the class party representing the capitalists, the KCP represents the proletariat, but the People's Party is a mass party representing all the people, including workers, farmers, small bourgeoisie, capitalists, and landlords; it excludes only the reactionary [and pro-Japanese] elements.[68]

The formation of this party weakened the KPR by siphoning off its more moderate elements and thus making it easier for People's Republic opponents to picture it as an extremist organization. It was never really clear just how separate the KPR and the PP were, however, and in February 1946 they were again aligned together in the Democratic National Front. Yŏ probably hoped that his conciliatory gesture would wean the Occupation command away from the KDP and the KPG; but it had no such effect. The Americans, for their part, thought that the PP would be a "tractable" party; but difficulties with Yŏ in early 1946 convinced them that it was just another communist front group.[69]

Political events in Seoul came to a climax of sorts in the third week of November. For the KPR, the imminent return of the KPG leaders posed a significant threat, especially if, as rumor had it, the Americans might set up the KPG as an interim or provisional government. For the Americans, continuing KPR claims to be a government confronted Occupation plans, largely secret, to set up another would-be government in its stead. The above mentioned national meeting of people's committee representatives (chŏn'guk inmin wiwŏn-hoe taep'yoja taehoe) in Seoul held from November 20 to 22, had as its main purpose the framing of a response to Hodge's demands that the KPR drop the word konghwaguk ("republic") from its title and reorganize as a political party. Some 600 representatives from provincial, county, and township committees and from various KPR organizations in Seoul attended the sessions, which were chaired for the most part by Hŏ Hŏn.[70] The question was debated for three days. In the end, those present refused to give in to Hodge's demands, although they expressed their support for the Occupation and recognized its authority south of the thirty-eighth parallel.[71]

The KPR representatives arrived at this decision for four reasons. First, the Occupation did not object to the KPG's use of characters meaning "government."[72] Second, they felt that the Americans could not unilaterally require the KPR to drop its claims to be a government. The KPR apparatus had been used by the Soviets in the north, thus the Russians should be a party to any resolution of the KPR's status.[73] Third, provincial and county people's committee representatives had made it clear that "the national name" and governmental status were essential to their continued functioning. Many of them were governing counties in the name of the KPR, and if they gave up the designation they might suddenly appear as illegitimate usurpers of authority and be subject to prosecution.[74] Fourth, those at the meeting felt that the Americans had come to oppose the KPR because of the advice of "traitors" and pro-Japanese elements, and in spite of repeated KPR statements that it would cooperate with and support the MG in its main mission in Korea—to disarm and remove the Japanese. This last point prompted some of those present to say, "we felt as though we were again [experiencing] the decisive moment that decided the fate of Korea 36 years before."[75]

From the third point, it appears that KPR leaders in Seoul were not entirely aware of the extent of the movement in the provinces until the November meeting, after which they saw that people's committees were organized nearly everywhere in north and south Korea. They therefore determined to increase liaison between the center and the provinces.[76] It also seems, however, that leaders at the center were more willing to give up KPR claims to being a government (perhaps because they were not governing anything in Seoul). The Seoul People's Committee passed a resolution stating that "as long as the American Military Government exists in Korea south of the thirty-eighth

parallel, the Republic cannot and will not act as a government."⁷⁷
This did not represent an abandoning of the "republic" designation,
but it apparently went further than provincial representatives were
willing to go.

Three days after the meeting ended, Hodge sent a cable to Mac-
Arthur which said:

> Recent convention in Seoul of the Korean People's Republic failed
> to comply with my request that they stop the use of Chinese char-
> acter "republic" in their name which denotes a going government.
> This political party is the most powerful Communist backed group
> in Korea and has some connections with Soviet politics. Includes also
> considerable number of Leftists, not true Communists; new, it was
> formed before our arrival here. In the past their use of characters
> to indicate government . . . has caused considerable confusion among
> the people and gained them many followers among the uneducated
> and laboring classes, and has fostered radical actions in the prov-
> inces under the guise of orders from the Korean People's Republic.
> I have worked hard on the leaders to remove the name and misun-
> derstandings at the recent convention. Although the consensus of
> meetings, as reported by my representatives attending, was that they
> will render full support and aid to US efforts in Korea, I cannot
> be sure of this support until such time as I can see result from a
> changed attitude. If future attitude is unchanged based on results,
> it is believed essential to denounce this party group in their status
> of terminology as a government and go on record to the people as
> opposing the party. This will constitute in effect a "declaration of
> war" upon the Communistic elements in Korea, and may result
> in temporary disorders. It will also bring charges of political dis-
> crimination in a "free" country, both by local pinko and by pinko
> press [*sic*]. If activities of the Korean People's Republic continue
> as in past, they will greatly delay time when Korea can be said to
> be ready for independence. Request comment.⁷⁸

MacArthur replied on the same day, giving Hodge *carte blanche* as
he had in the past: "Use your own best judgment. . . . I am not sufficiently familiar with the local situation to advise you intelligently,
but I will support whatever decision you may take in this matter."⁷⁹
On December 12 Hodge publicly denounced the KPR and declared
its activities to be "unlawful." Thereafter, in the words of the official
history, the KPR people became "public enemies."⁸⁰

During November and December, KPR-affiliated mass organizations
also held national meetings in Seoul, and also became objects of suppression. On November 5 and 6 various representatives of labor unions

(*nodong chohap*) from throughout north and south Korea came together in Seoul with the object of unifying the scattered unions into one body. The central organ that emerged from the meeting was the National Council of Korean Labor Unions (*Chosŏn nodong chohap chŏn'guk p'yŏngŭi-hoe*), led by Hŏ Sŏng-t'aek and known by its shortened title *Chŏnp'yŏng*.[81] Other leaders included Hyŏn Hun, Mun Ŭn-jung, Kim Hwal-yŏng, Pak Se-yŏng, and Ch'oe Chŏl. All ten members of the *Chŏnp'yŏng* executive committee had done time in Japanese colonial prisons for political crimes. The *Chŏnp'yŏng* platform included demands for an eight-hour work day, improvement of wages and working conditions, prohibitions on child labor, and so on. Its newspaper expressed support for the KPR and for communists like Pak Hŏn-yŏng; but it had little Marxist content and devoted as much space to the British Labor Party as to reports from the communist world.[82] Table 9 presents a *Chŏnp'yŏng* organizational breakdown.

TABLE 9

Chŏnp'yŏng Strength, August 1946

Industry	Branches (*Chibu*)	Chapters (*Punhoe*)	Members
Metals	20	215	51,364
Chemicals	18	167	49,015
Textiles	16	121	30,368
Printing	16	65	4,368
Transportation	28	140	58,041
Foodstuffs	23	108	23,523
Construction	17	127	59,118
Electric	14	54	15,742
Lumber	2	125	30,722
Fishing	9	50	35,653
Mining	9	123	64,572
Communications	9	40	10,215
Railroads	14	117	62,439
General	14	107	17,065
Seamen	7	9	4,720
Shipbuilding	10	38	5,549
Total	235	1,676	574,475

Source: Official *Chŏnp'yŏng* figures, in *Chŏson haebang illyŏn-sa*, p. 158.

According to Stewart Meacham, Hodge's labor advisor, *nodong chohap* in south Korea were "for a short period . . . in almost complete control of those plants which had been Japanese-owned." *Chŏnp'yŏng* was the only labor organization in the south until mid-1946 and remained the strongest union until after the autumn uprisings.[83]

Reports from other American observers in the provinces generally supported such assessments (see chapter nine). *Chŏnp'yŏng* seemed to have branches *(chibang p'yŏngŭi-hoe)* in every industrial town and city.[84]

Many Americans within the MG recognized that *Chŏnp'yŏng* and its *nodong chohap* affiliates were representative of Korean workers and largely reformist in character. One memorandum on "Labor Section Policy" stated:

> The Worker's Committees, which have in many cases taken affairs into their own hands by throwing out the Jap owners, can be better controlled through regularly-constituted unions than by outright suppression. The policy of Military Government [should be] to foster truly representative unions and thus weed out leaders who are irresponsible agitators with only a vague program of kicking out former owners and no positive plan to open up the plants. . . . [Americans should not] jump to conclusions that every Worker's Committee is communist-dominated . . . most of the so-called Communist groups have turned out to be pretty mild.[85]

What was reformist to Americans, however, was revolutionary in the Korean context. As the official history put it, "in some cases the police merely retained the Japanese police idea that all farmers' and laborers' organizations were communist."[86] In addition, Occupation alignment with rightist groups and Japanese-employed Korean police took the issue of policy toward labor unions out of American hands. The result, intended or unintended, was that *Chŏnp'yŏng* became the object of widespread attempts at suppression.

At first, the Occupation sought to control labor unions through nonviolent, lawful means. It instituted compulsory arbitration between workers and managers in October 1945 as a means of dealing with strikes in Seoul, Taejŏn, and elsewhere.[87] Section II of Ordinance no. 19 of October 30 stated, "the right of any individual or group of individuals to accept employment and to work unmolested shall be respected and protected." The legal scholar Ernst Fraenkel later ruled that this right-to-work law "does not offer protection from discharge to employees; the provision prohibits third persons from interfering with the labor relations between individual employers and employees." Thus, "protection of labor" under the ordinance came to mean "protection from being involved in open labor conflicts."[88] Meacham commented wryly that the ordinance "consisted of a declaration to protect the right of labor to work under those terms specified by business and professional people. Korean labor had enjoyed this 'right' during the entire Japanese regime."[89]

On December 8 Ordinance no. 34 was issued, prohibiting strikes and establishing the National Labor Mediation Board. As we noted earlier, three of the five board members were KDP leaders. Soon thereafter similar boards were established in the provinces: "Koreans appointed to these boards were in no instance industrial wage earners or their representatives . . . [but] for the most part business men, professional men, and employers."[90] In truth, the boards were little more than employers' associations, the typical device for translating economic influence into political power. During the Occupation, these boards had the right "to inflict punishments for contempt" just as if they were courts of law.[91]

Another important device used to secure Occupation control of unions and the plants that many of them managed was to vest Japanese property in the Occupation, to be held in trust until a Korean government was established. Thus, the Occupation was able to appoint some 375 plant, factory, and business managers by February 1946.[92] The immense corruption attendant to such appointments is commonly remarked upon in the literature of the period. George McCune stated that the appointed Korean managers were usually former high-ranking employees of the Japanese-owned enterprises.[93] After the Rhee regime was established, most of them ended up as outright owners of the enterprises; the entrepreneurial elements of postwar south Korea, such as they were, thus continued the pattern of relying on connections with the bureaucracy rather than on their own hard efforts. The Americans, however, were not interested in putting an entrepreneurial class on its feet; instead the rationale for this policy, as with most others, was political. Edwin Pauley, advisor to President Truman, stated it unequivocally after his tour of Korea in 1946:

> Communism in Korea could get off to a better start than practically anywhere else in the world. The Japanese owned the railroads, all of the public utilities including power and light, as well as all of the major industries and natural resources. Therefore, if these are suddenly found to be owned by "The People's Committee" (The Communist Party), they will have acquired them without any struggle of any kind or any work in developing them. This is one of the reasons why the United States should not waive its title or claim to Japanese external assets located in Korea until a democratic (capitalistic) form of government is assured.[94]

In early February 1946 the national police raided *Chŏnp'yŏng* headquarters in Seoul and arrested eleven people, allegedly for possession of illegal weapons. Later on, Meacham visited factories throughout the south and found "systematic suppression" of *Chŏnp'yŏng* leaders and activities.[95] But this union had deep roots and was not easily overturned. It remained strong until the general strike in the fall of 1946. Like many people's committees in the provinces, it flourished until met with naked force.

On December 8 in Seoul representatives of provincial peasant unions and other political leaders formed the National League of Peasant Unions (*Chŏn'guk nongmin chohap ch'ong yŏnmaeng*), led by Kim Chin-yŏng and known as *Chŏnnong*. One friendly source claimed that some 239 peasant unions sent 545 representatives, including 84 from north Korea, to this meeting.[96] *Chŏnnong* expressed support for the People's Republic and particularly for the KPR land reform platform. Although peasant unions were widespread in south Korea, it appears that *Chŏnnong* was less successful than *Chŏnp'yŏng* in linking together disparate unions and other peasant organizations in the provinces. The same was true of the KPR-related Korean Democratic Youth League (*Chosŏn minju ch'ŏngnyŏn tongmaeng*), formed on December 11 in Seoul, and the Women's League (*Chosŏn puryŏ ch'ong tongmaeng*), formed ten days later.[97] In the case of these last two, both had Seoul-based organizations stronger than comparable organizations on the Right (rightists had many youth groups but, so far as can be determined, no peasant organizations), but they do not appear to have forged strong links between Seoul leaders and provincial bodies. Locally entrenched peasant unions perhaps resisted the imposition of central controls. A key reason for the development of *Chŏnnong* and the Youth League, no doubt, was the KPR's need for supportive organizations in Seoul in the wake of Hodge's "declaration of war."

POLICIES TOWARD LAND AND RICE

Perhaps nothing as clearly demonstrates the peculiar combination of warm-spirited good will, benevolent naiveté, and arrogant ethnocentrism that the Americans brought with them to Korea as the record of policies adopted toward land and rice. Within a month of its arrival, the Occupation had acted both to reform an oppressive land rental system in the interests of tenants and to disrupt a carefully regulated rice economy in the interests of parochial American economic assumptions. Such self-defeating effort also characterized the sincere attempt by American officers to end land relationships of "semi-enslavement," even as the Occupation command formed political ties with Koreans hoping to preserve such land relationships. The end result was a catastrophic economic situation that deeply affected the politics of the Occupation and even American-Soviet relations.

In 1945, as we have seen earlier in this study, Korea had a rice-based colonial economy that was tightly controlled both in the interests of creating rice surpluses to feed Japan and in the interests of providing profits for Japanese and Korean landlords. Southern Korea, in particular, was an agrarian region with consistent and bountiful grain surpluses, but also with oppressive tenancy conditions. When the Americans landed in September, however, they found that Japanese controls had been loosened or abolished altogether. Japanese officials and landlords had fled by the thousands; Korean landlords had been dispossessed in some provincial regions; and agencies of the Government-General concerned with agricultural management and crop collection were largely inactive. Leaders of the People's Republic managed food stocks; and according to later American accounts, "after the Koreans drove the Japanese police out [the KPR leaders] took over the rice collection machinery and were operating it successfully when the Americans arrived."[98] The fall rice harvest proved to be a bumper crop, with predictions that a one million bag surplus would be available for export from south Korea.[99]

Upon arrival in Korea the Americans also found a nearly universal clamor for the reform of existing land relationships. All political groups advocated land reform, although as we have seen, the KDP and the KPR had quite different ideas on the desirable extent of reform. The Occupation issued two important ordinances on October 5 in response to problems with land conditions and the rice economy. Ordinance no. 9 stated:

> A national emergency in Korea is hereby declared to exist by reason of oppressive rents and interest rates payable under existing contracts by tenants of farm lands and the resulting semi-enslavement and a standard of living below the standard which is the object of the Military Government. . . . The maximum rent in kind, money, or in any form payable by any type of tenant to any person . . . will hereafter not exceed one-third (1/3) of the total of the natural crops, produce and fruits of such land cultivated and tended by any such tenant and thereafter harvested by anyone from such land.[100]

This ordinance also prohibited landlords from voiding contracts with tenants "except for just cause." The second ordinance (designated "General Notice No. 1") established a free market in rice: "all laws and regulations having the force of law . . . are hereby abolished to the end that Korea may have a free market in rice." It struck down all laws and provisions prohibiting "the private and free sale of rice," or requiring the sale of rice to government agencies, or limiting in any way "the freedom of prices in the purchase and sale of rice to anyone" (except Japanese nationals and agencies).[101] This notice was followed shortly by one establishing a "free commodity market" in all goods except those managed by government monopolies (tobacco, salt, opium, ginseng, sugar, and medicines) and those which the MG might deem to be "in critical demand." In other words, "free market conditions will be maintained so far as practical."[102] Ordinance no. 19 argued:

> [The MG is] restoring the principle of a free market, giving to every man, woman, and child within the country equal opportunity to enjoy his just and fair share of the great wealth [with] which this beautiful nation has been endowed.[103]

The limitation on tenancy rent proved to be very popular. Although it conformed in its essentials to the KPR's "3/7" system, the Americans probably adopted it in response to genuine concern over existing conditions and because of similar Russian policies in the north. Unfortunately, the ordinance had no effective enforcement mechanism, and accordingly was widely violated by landlords.[104] The ordinance did have some effect on the ability of some tenant households to move up into the part-tenant/part-owner category during the Occupation.[105]

The attempted institution of the free market was an unmitigated disaster from start to finish. This policy decision apparently came about through natural American inclinations toward allowing the free play of economic forces of supply and demand as well as opposition to a colonial system that often amounted to forced confiscation of the producer's output. As the quotation from Ordinance no. 19 might suggest, the Americans also felt that a free market would demonstrate the worth of the American way and provide a contrast to Soviet methods in the north. It seems that KDP advisors also had some influence on the decision, since it was later reported that they favored lifting price controls and allowing free transactions in rice.[106]

The free market plan stands as a classic example of the costs of an unthinking imposition of assumptions and models developed in one setting onto another alien and radically different setting. The vast majority of Korean peasants were concerned with subsistence cultivation and were accustomed to having surpluses extracted by landlords and their agents rather than exchanged in market transactions. They were not entrepreneurs who would benefit from price rises by putting the proceeds into investment, but typical subsistence peasants who would react to the loosening of controls by working less and consuming more of their product. But most Korean landlords were not the capitalists who would turn increased profits from the sale of rice into substantial investments, either. In general, they were accustomed to sapping surpluses and giving very little in return. How could they suddenly turn into "rational economic man" on the Western model?[107] Instead of a free market, then, landlord-dominated marketing arrangements persisted, but without the administrative structure that had previously controlled them. Thus the predictable result of the MG's free market was an orgy of speculation, hoarding, and overconsumption. The autumn harvest surplus disappeared quickly. Through its free market policy, the MG lost the main strong point of the south Korean economic system—its ability to extract large surpluses of grain—and caused in its stead spiraling inflation, near starvation in early 1946, and a general economic breakdown.

The price of a bushel of rice increased from 9.4 yen in September 1945 to a staggering 2,800 yen in September 1946.[108] Landlords, police and other government officials, and wealthy individuals engaged in speculation on a wholesale basis. Richard Robinson reported that a top police official "made a private fortune by shipping rice illegally into Seoul and selling it at enormous prices." Robinson also alleged that "a flourishing smuggling trade" in rice developed between south Korea and Japan that may have eaten up one-fourth of the 1945 harvest.[109] Official sources reported that provincial MG appointees were widely engaged in speculation and that at one point smugglers were shipping 300 bags of rice a day to Japan.[110] Most of the rice supply in South Ch'ungch'ŏng Province was shipped out of the province by speculators during the winter of 1945/46. In one incident, a Korean from Pusan purchased ten railroad cars full of rice on a siding in Nonsan.[111] During the free market period, the Department of Agriculture authorized "certain entrepreneurs" to take over and operate Japanese rice warehouses on the condition that they would sell the rice at fixed prices to the poor; instead they sold it at "tremendous profits."[112]

By February 1946 the MG had not only rescinded the free market but had ordered rice rationing at the rate of one hap per person per day, or half the Japanese allowance during the war.[113] Starvation reports began to occur frequently in rice-poor provincial areas, so the MG soon had to begin to import surplus American cereals to feed Koreans in the south.[114] American-Soviet relations were seriously strained when the Americans reported that no surplus grain would be available for shipment to the north in the spring of 1946. Perhaps the greatest cost of all, however, was that the Americans were forced to revive and utilize the old Japanese system of agricultural management and rice collection. The official history of the Occupation stated that the only remedy for the disasters of the free market policy was to put the old rice collection system back into effect, thereby "virtually reestablishing the Japanese system."[115] The MG first "revivified" various governmental and quasi-governmental colonial agencies.[116] These included the Chōsen Food Company, the Oriental Development Company, the Chōsen Import Materials Control Corporation, and other trucking, oil, and coal monopolies. The titles of these companies were changed to Korea Commodity Corporation, New Korea Company, Materials Control Company, and so on; but all Koreans in these companies formerly employed by the Japanese were retained.[117]

The Korea Commodity Corporation was given responsibility for buying up much of the annual rice harvest and distributing it at fixed prices. But as one American wrote, Koreans viewed it as "a huge exploitative organization determined to take all and give nothing."[118] As a result, they resisted its reimposition upon the rice economy and refused to sell to it.[119] Soon the corporation buyers had to be accompanied by police.

The New Korea Company (NKC) was created by Ordinance no. 52 of February 21, 1946, but the organization had been functioning since November 1945.[120] It supervised and controlled all land that had belonged to the Oriental Development Company (ODC), additional land that had belonged to some 102,000 Japanesse companies and individuals, and 19 industrial, engineering, and mining companies. According to the MG organizational manual, the NKC "attend[ed] to all such details as fertilizer and reclamation, land registration, signing of contracts for land leases and raising of foodstuffs."[121] The ODC, like other Japanese agencies for colonial exploitation, was a highly centralized bureaucracy controlled from Seoul; the NKC retained this efficient organization. During the Occupation, the NKC managed 24.1 percent of all land worked by the south Korean farming population. When Japanese Oriental Development Company functionaries returned to Japan, the Americans moved ODC Korean employees into the top jobs of the new agency. Only about twenty Americans worked in the NKC at any given time.[122]

The NKC proved to be one of the more successsful and efficient agencies of the MG during the Occupation. Unlike other agencies, it had relatively little trouble with rice collections. NKC/ODC "tenant supervisors" in the provinces performed the "valuable functions of the landlord": providing seeds, fertilizer, and general supervision to tenants.[123] Thus, the NKC functioned much as it had under the Japanese, as a technically proficient and effective organization for extracting surpluses from tenants who were working barely subsistence-level plots. Because of the loss of Japanese expertise, however, the NKC had more irregularities and corruption than did the ODC.[124]

In late January 1946 the Occupation placed provincial, non-NKC rice collections back in the hands of village elders and local notables, city, county, and township officials, and in the hands of the police.[125] Local boards, "appointed with American approval and composed of high police officials, village elders, businessmen, and large landowners," set rice quotas for peasants. The boards allowed no appeals on the quotas, and peasants were often jailed when they failed to fulfill them.[126] Rice collection functions that had been taken away from the Korean National Police in the fall of 1945, were restored in the wake of the failures of the free market policy. The KNP proceeded to establish "rice details" to accommodate this duty, in which policemen either worked alone or with non-police rice collection officials. Police were punished and even dismissed for not meeting their collection quotas, on the assumption that they were skimming rice for their personal use.[127] Thus, they were harsh in their methods of collecting rice and tended to single out peasants who were associated with people's committees or peasant unions. According to the official history, "farmers who refused to give up their rice were taken to police headquarters and kept in jail with no food except that bought from the police at exorbitant prices."[128] Ch'oe Nŭng-jin told the Korean-American Conference in late 1946:

> I have gone around to farmers and have been informed by them that during the summer, policemen went out to the farms blindly, without knowing what the quota assignment was and attempted to force the farmers to turn over their rice. If they did not, the police handcuffed them and took them to the police station where they were held all day, sometimes without food.[129]

The 67th MG Company in North Ch'ungch'ŏng sent in a report in May 1946 entitled "Rice Raid in Umsong" in which rice collection teams, here called "raiding parties," consisted of "Korean police and civil officials with U.S. troops maintaining peace and order." The 68th Company in Kyŏnggi reported that peasants in Kwangju blocked rice collections by Korea Commodity Company agents; "old people cast themselves in front of the [Company] truck."[130] Perhaps it was such experiences that prompted Hodge to tell General Albert Wedemeyer that in Korea "when the other fellow has the weapons and the ration cards he has control of everything."[131]

In the winter of 1945/46, the Occupation tried other devices to aid in rice collection. On December 11 General Arnold announced that a "Patriots Committee" made up of fifty businessmen had been asked to tour the provinces, talk to peasants, and try to convince them to give up the rice that they had been hoarding.[132] Nothing came of this, however. When the committee met at the offices of the Materials Control Corporation on December 13, it turned out that most of its members were wealthy landlords with ties to the KDP. They had formed an organization called the "Korean Economic Contributor's Association," which was less interested in aiding rice collections than in bank-rolling Syngman Rhee and other KPG leaders. Later they reportedly toured the provinces in American jeeps, seeking contributions for Rhee from rich individuals.[133]

This organization is important, both for its make-up and for its ties to Rhee and other politicians. It was a group of landlords, bankers, businessmen, and entrepreneurs, many of whom could be described as the landlord-entrepreneurs we discussed earlier. The group organized in the aftermath of two critical events: the returns of Syngman Rhee and Kim Ku; and certain actions taken by the Occupation regarding banks. On December 8 the Occupation merged the remaining branches of Japanese banks with "Korean" banks. That is, the Chōsen Commercial Bank was authorized to take over the Seoul branch of the Teikoku Bank, the Chohŭng Bank took over a branch of the Yasuda Bank, and so on.[134] Yet these ostensibly Korean banks had been Japanese banks until August 15; it is not clear from available materials exactly how Koreans came to manage or own various banks that had been important elements of colonial financial operations. In any case, on that same day, December 8, the contributor's association met and decided to ask various banks to provide a loan of 20 million yen (between $.4 million and $1.3 million, depending on whether we use the official exchange rate of 15 yen to $1, or the black market rate of 50 to one) to the association, which would then be given to Rhee and Kim Ku for their uses.[135] Such loans had to be approved by the Occupation at some level, however, and the manner in which this was achieved casts the honor of the Occupation command in doubt.

Rhee's American benefactor M. Preston Goodfellow had by that time arrived in Seoul, through rather questionable channels, as some sort of an advisor to the Occupation.[136] A letter from Rhee found in Goodfellow's papers refers to "the ten financiers' contributions of ten million *yen* to our cause" and goes on to say:

> The ten men made a signed statement, denying any knowledge of the money coming from the MG. All that they knew about it was that *you secured permit from the MG* allowing the bank to furnish a loan of twenty million yen on the securities they have given (emphasis added).

In another letter to Goodfellow, Rhee said:

> The ten million yen given by the ten men was to be left entirely in my hands to be used for the independence movement and I have their signatures to that effect.[137]

Goodfellow became a charter member of Rhee's tiny lobby in the United States after his return, as we will discuss in more detail later on. One of the elements binding this group together was the hope of gaining concessions, trading rights, and so on, were Rhee to emerge on top in the south. Thus, Rhee was a unifying force for a group of Americans looking for a "Korea market," like the storied China market, and for a group of Korean landlord-entrepreneurs who, because of the widespread belief that they had collaborated with the Japanese, stayed behind the scenes and obtained money for Rhee, with American connivance that may have reached to the highest levels of the Occupation command.

The contributor's association was chaired by Kim Hong-yang, a wealthy landlord formerly from Hwanghae Province in north Korea; he was also among the individuals who advised General Arnold on rice collection procedures. The association also included among its fifty members: Kong Chin-han, chief of the planning section of the New Korea Company; Chŏn Yŏng-sun, one-time finance chief of the Korean Democratic Party, described by the American Counter-Intelligence Corps as a "narcotics magnate"; Ch'oe Ch'ang-hak, a mine owner who provided Kim Ku with a palatial residence; Min Kyu-sik, a former member of the Japanese Central Advisory Council; and Ku Cha-guk, secretary of the Korean Banker's Club.[138]

General Hodge later said of Rhee:

> He got into the influence, early in his stay here, of some of the wealthy people . . . a lot of them could probably be well charged with pro-Jap sympathies, because they made a lot of money under the Japanese.[139]

Even this, however, is something of an understatement; certainly it does not mention the American role in bringing Rhee back to Korea and providing the necessary permits for Rhee's bankroll from Occupation-controlled banks. And it only insinuates what was in fact crystal clear: Rhee provided, in return for their contributions, protection for a class of people who might well have been dispossessed for their collaboration, by either a communist or nationalist Korean regime. Although the Korean Democratic Party had similar arrangements with wealthy individuals, Rhee was the one who could provide patriotic legitimacy; soon he had the wealthy class, the KDP, and even the police under his wing.[140] All in all, Rhee's performance was worthy of, and rather similar to, Chiang Kai-shek's marriage of convenience with Shanghai bankers in 1927.

The free market and rice policy debacles, of which the above account is an integral part, demonstrate the close interrelation between political and economic policy during the Occupation. The Americans could not separate political actions from their economic consequences. A de facto political policy of support for the old order closed off reformist policies toward the economy. American opposition to political forces of change tended to politicize all decision making in other arenas. Hodge, in particular, was unwilling to make changes and reforms that would play into the hands of the Left. Even when the American command actively sought reform, by the end of 1945, it had to contend with the opposition and intransigence of Koreans in key bureaucratic positions. The inevitable result was that Occupation impulses toward land reform became lukewarm and transitional and reform proposals were drawn out from 1946 to 1948 with no resolution. This was the context in which an unnamed American colonel could comment facetiously, but with no small measure of truth:

> Our mission in Korea is to keep the absentee landlords from being chucked out unceremoniously. Korean masses want farm land divided up among those who work it. Our job is to force those laborers to pay rent. Chief Russian atrocity is having expropriated and divided up the large estates of the absentee landlords and given them to small fry.[141]

Conclusions

It is appropriate to conclude these two chapters on American policy making in the first months of the Occupation by considering Hodge's remarkably candid report on "Conditions in Korea," received in Tokyo on December 16:[142]

> After 3 months in occupation of south Korea, I have reached the following definite conclusions. These are considered a further crystallization of previous reports.
>
> A. The dual occupation of Korea with Russian north and US south . . . imposes an impossible condition upon our occupation missions of establishing sound economy and preparing Korea for future independence. In South Korea, the US [is] blamed for the partition and [there] is growing resentment against all Americans in the area including passive resistance. . . . Every day of drifting under this situation makes our position in Korea more untenable and decreases our waning popularity and our effectiveness to be of service. The word pro-American is being added to pro-Jap, national traitor, and Jap collaborator. The only advantage of Russian presence is to absorb a portion of the people's resentment against the

partition of Korea. Every Korean knows full well that under the dual occupation any talk of real freedom and independence is purely academic. . . . Every day of delay fosters further and permanent division of the people.

B. The Koreans want their independence more than any one thing and they want it now. . . . By occidental standards Koreans are not ready for independence, but it grows daily more apparent that their capacity for self-government will not greatly improve with time under current conditions.

C. The situation in the South Korea [sic] makes extremely fertile ground for establishment of Communism. In my opinion Koreans do not want Communism, but the unsettled conditions, the lack of clear policies . . . may easily push those in US zone to radical leftism, if not raw Communism. There is currently a flow of Manchurian and Chinese who are giving active assistance to Communistic elements already present. . . . The approximate international influences and our occupation policies of insuring all freedom and maintaining property rights among liberated oriental people favor Communistic activities. Under these policies conservative groups tend to obey laws and ordinances while the radicals do not. . . .

D. The Koreans are the most politically minded people I have ever seen. Every move, every word, every act is interpreted and evaluated politically. . . .

E. In the minds of all Koreans, "Trusteeship" hangs over them as a sword of Damocles. If it is imposed now or at any future time it is believed possible that the Korean people will actually and physically revolt.

F. The Russian methods of occupation north of the 38th degree are not understandable to Americans. There is evidence that they have constructed and maintain an effective field works system of defense against invasion just north of 38 degree. It is certain that they have constructed and constantly man with armed guards a line of road blocks. . . . There are also rumors south of 38 degree that US and Russia are preparing for war. . . . Koreans well know that the Russians have a force locally of about 4 to 1 to Americans and with the usual oriental slant are willing to do homage and are doing homage to the man with the largest weapon. On the part of the masses there is an increasing tendency to look to Russia for the future.

After recommending the abandonment of trusteeship and negotiations to remove Korea's division, Hodge ended the report as follows:

> Under present conditions with no corrective action forthcoming, I would go so far as to recommend we give serious consideration to an agreement with Russia that both the U.S. and Russia withdraw forces from Korea simultaneously and leave Korea to its own devices and *an inevitable internal upheaval for its self purification* (emphasis added).

This was a classic Cold War document, except for Hodge's unique last paragraph. It soon reached President Truman's desk and apparently had some impact on his thinking.[143] It echoed the difficulties and Hobson's choices that Americans were facing in many other parts of the world in the aftermath of the war, but in Korea the problems were more acute and American remedies less effective. The document also betrayed Hodge's ambivalent attitudes toward Koreans, alternately showing compassion and understanding for Korean needs and then engaging in racist characterizations. Finally, the report managed to detail most of the problems of the Occupation without saying a word about the remedies that Hodge and his advisors had already decided upon and begun to carry out.

Hodge essentially relied on the Russian bogey as an explanation and justification for his actions. The official history spent some 352 pages making a case for complete Russian intransigence: "the Russians possessed no will to cooperate" in Korea.[144] American-Soviet relations in Korea in the fall and winter of 1945-1946 were far more complex, however, and the objective reader will find two sides to the tale. Hodge cited Russian roadblocks along the thirty-eighth parallel, for example, but neglected to mention that he ordered roadblocks established below the line four days after he arrived in Korea (September 12) and directed that "positive action" be taken "to prevent infiltration across the border"; by October 15, some twenty road blocks were in place along the southern edge of the thirty-eighth parallel.[145] Hodge also neglected to report that on September 21 he had requested a larger American occupation force owing to "presence of Soviet Army in North Korea."[146] A reading of the record of various Russian-American disputes and alleged violations by each side in these months suggests a fairly equal distribution of hostility and compatibility, provocation and cooperation, trust and distrust.[147] Both sides received gravely distorted information from Koreans passing from one zone to the other, since most of them were excited with grievances of one sort or another. In spite of the Russian presence, however, Hodge's main problem was Koreans in the south who resisted American policies; and these Koreans were not controlled by the Russians or by communists in the north. Occupation G-2 and CIC reports from September through December 1945 say little about communist control or infiltration from the north. The official history stated, "General Hodge, though perfectly convinced in his own mind since early in the occupation, found it very difficult to establish a firm proof of extra-political forces pulling the lead strings on the southern Korean communists."[148] Later research has demonstrated that the southern communists were often at loggerheads with those in the north and were determined to act independently.[149]

Hodge was also the victim of his own prejudices about Koreans. In a cable of November 30, he expressed his view that "internal events show organization and direction beyond the estimated capabilities of local Communist leaders."[150] The belief that Koreans were "largely incapable of intelligent political action" was widespread among Americans;[151] any Koreans who were able to build organizations and mobilize support were therefore suspect. The attitudes of some of the highest ranking Americans were suffused with condescension toward Koreans.[152] Hodge himself made abusive remarks to his staff about Koreans.[153] Such prejudices were by no means characteristic of all Americans; and at the individual level, in spite of Occupation policies, it is probably fair to say that Koreans liked the Americans better than the Russians. Russian policies were popular, while Russians were not. The opposite was true of the Americans. We are reminded of Louis Hartz's remark that the American with his small-propertied, Lockean-liberal personality "is a man who may satisfy no one but he is also a man whom no one can thoroughly hate."[154]

During the last three months of 1945, established American policy toward Korea and toward the Russians came under virtual assault in Seoul. The United States had not abandoned the plans for multilateral arrangements that would guarantee American influence in Korean affairs while also providing for substantive participation by the Soviets and assuring the integrity of the Korean nation. The Soviet Union had not given up its earlier adherence to such policies and had not set up a separate regime in the north. Had the Occupation command abandoned its support for the KDP, for the police, for the incipient army, for the KPG, for Rhee; had it undone all this in subsequent months, we might look back on this period as a bad start, an anomaly, a series of mistakes. But the search for a separate force, with the "governing commission" planning as its centerpiece, continued apace through 1946. Thus, the south Korean state, which had been a colonial appendage to the Japanese sphere, came to assume national form.

There are aspects of this early period that still remain obscure. It is fairly clear that Syngman Rhee was spirited back to Seoul, against established policy, by Goodfellow, MacArthur, and Hodge. It is also reasonable to assume that Rhee had an influence on the separatist governing commission thinking, which resulted in the return of the Korean Provisional Government. Goodfellow's role is less clear. This man, who had been deputy director of the Office of Strategic Services (the forerunner of the Central Intelligence Agency) during the war, appeared in Seoul in November or December, arranged for the transfer of a large sum of money to Rhee, and went on to claim, as we will see in the next chapter, that he helped set up the first Korean government. He then returned to the United States in May 1946, amid allegations that he had secret deals with Rhee (he did) and that he advocated a separate southern administration (he did).

As 1945 ended, the Americans in the south blamed the Russians for their predicament, but they really had no one but themselves to blame. The Occupation could not enroll the forces of the old order on its side and proclaim neutrality, or avoid opposition from other Koreans, or gain cooperation from the Soviets. It could not pursue the policies detailed above and avoid the consequences. But neither could it "leave Korea to its own devices and an inevitable internal upheaval for its self purification." That option, which had its virtues in the light of the past thirty years of violence in Korea, was impossible in light of the decisions made in the last three months of 1945. The Occupation had made largely irrevocable commitments to its Korean charges, who would be entirely vulnerable without the Americans. So the Occupation command rushed ahead into 1946, unaware that greater crises awaited them.

Chapter Seven

INTERNATIONALIST POLICY AND NATIONALIST LOGIC: HARDENING AT THE CENTER IN 1946

If we do not include the left wing, we will not be able to achieve unification.

Kim Ku

There are a few reactionary elements that consider Russia as their fatherland, and that intend to divide our people and create confusion under the banner of the so-called KPR and eventually to have our country become one of the Soviet states. . . . Let us carry out the desperately needed amputation.

Syngman Rhee

From the time of the Japanese surrender until the beginning of 1946, American policy toward Korea had two contradictory manifestations: one was the formal commitment to multilateral trusteeship, or the internationalist path; and the other was the actual commitment to _de facto_ containment, or the nationalist path. Within south Korea, the critical decisions taken by the Occupation from September through December 1945 followed the latter path with remarkable consistency. The basic structures of a south Korean state had been established; and as each day passed, they became more solid and entrenched, and the costs of overturning them became more dire. Soon the American command came to take its Korean governmental apparatus for granted. MG policy making came to be concerned largely with working out the "arrangements of the top," that is, the composition and structure of executive organs that would command the bureaucracy. During 1946 much of this policy making assumed an improvised and reactive quality, as the Occupation sought to adjust south Korean arrangements to mollify critics within Korea and in Washington and Moscow. Yet Occupation policy never really diverged from the plan outlined in the governing commission proposal prepared by William Langdon in November 1945. The Americans in 1946 concentrated on often hasty and harried variations on this theme.

The year 1946 began, however, with a head-on clash between the nationalist and internationalist currents; only when that was resolved could the Occupation get on with its tasks. It is remarkable the degree to which the timing of major shifts in postwar American policy repeated themselves in far-off Korea. Just as the emergence of George Kennan in early 1946 signaled the decisive defeat of Roosevelt's policy for dealing with the Russians, so the undoing of the Moscow agreements of December 1945 dealt a decisive blow to the trusteeship alternative for Korea. A complex dialectic arrayed a frightened Korean elite, the Occupation command, and nationalists in Washington against the internationalist path and trusteeship, thus further isolating a liberal contingent that still found value in Rooseveltian policy.

This chapter will be concerned with the fruits of several elaborations on the governing commission proposal: the Representative Democratic Council of February; the Coalition Committee that emerged in the summer; the South Korean Interim Legislature of autumn 1946; and the inauguration of the South Korean Interim Government (SKIG) that came as the year ended. It will also consider various events that intruded on Occupation planning: Soviet-American joint agreements on Korea at Moscow and the subsequent Soviet-American Joint Commission that met in Seoul in early 1946; periodic rightist attempts to seize the initiative in the south; and the continuing strength of the Left in south Korea, which provided the essential background to understanding American behavior.

TUTELAGE AND INDEPENDENCE, TRAITORS AND PATRIOTS: THE TRUSTEESHIP IMBROGLIO

On December 16, 1945, the foreign ministers of the United States, Great Britain, and the Soviet Union convened in Moscow to discuss a variety of postwar problems that had remained unresolved in wartime negotiations, Korea being an important part of their agenda. The United States had proposed a multilateral trusteeship for Korea on several occasions during the war, but as we have seen, no meaningful negotiations or agreements were possible in the atmosphere of mutual distrust and recrimination that surrounded the trusteeship issue at Yalta and Potsdam. The three powers met in Moscow with the hope that their faltering relationships could be restored to the mutually advantageous basis of the wartime alliance.[1] The Moscow Conference ended on December 27 with apparent success. The *New York Times* heralded the results with a massive headline reading, "Big Three Re-Establish Unity in Wide Accord."[2] The Moscow accords included provisions for a four-power trusteeship for Korea of up to five years.

At Moscow, as during the war, the United States was the prime proponent of trusteeship for Korea. The record of wartime discussions indicated that the Soviets were more inclined toward quick independence for Korea than toward trusteeship. In November 1945 Ambassador Harriman reported that the Soviets were silent about trusteeship but had advocated Korean independence in several forums. He noted, "Soviet predominance [in Korea] is more likely to be realized through establishment of 'independent friendly' Korean regime than through any system of international tutelage." Harriman maintained that the trusteeship scheme was therefore important, because, "far from assuring Soviet paramountcy, a trusteeship would probably mean USSR having but one of three or four equal votes."[3] In January 1946 George Kennan stated:

> USSR has since San Francisco [United Nations Conference] made it plain that in general it did not go along with either American or British conception of trusteeship. With regard to Korea in particular USSR has indicated that it favored prompt independence for that former Jap colony.[4]

It seems fairly obvious that the Soviets thought their interests in Korea would be better served through an independent government than through a multilateral body that the Americans had the capacity to dominate. Thus the Soviet agreement on a trusteeship for Korea that was reached at Moscow must be seen as a *compromise* and as a return to the "spirit of Yalta."[5] The Soviets probably also thought that their agreement to a trusteeship in Korea would aid them in gaining American acquiescence to Russian plans for Eastern Europe.

The American draft proposal on trusteeship for Korea presented at Moscow called for the establishment of a joint administration of Korea by the Soviet and American military commands, which would handle such matters as trade, transportation, and currency. This transitional body would be superseded by a four-power (United States, USSR, China, and Great Britain) trusteeship, which would perform executive, legislative, and judicial functions and would administer Korea until the country was deemed ready for independence. The suggested tenure of trusteeship was five years, but there was provision for an additional five years if it proved necessary. The proposal said nothing about a Korean administrative body or interim government that might function under the trust powers, although it made some allowance for individual Korean administrators and consultants.[6]

The Soviets countered with their own draft proposal, which differed from the American one in providing for a provisional Korean government and for a Joint Commission (JC) drawn from the Soviet and American commands in Korea that would offer assistance in forming such a Korean government. The Soviet draft was adopted by the three powers, after minor amendments.[7] A careful reading of the American and Soviet proposals and then of the final draft of the agreement on Korea demonstrates that the explosive trusteeship issue was decisively muted in the final draft. The term does not appear until the third paragraph. Instead, the emphasis is largely on the development of a provisional Korean government. Only *after* that government was formed and *after* it had consulted with the Joint Commission would the four powers concerned jointly consider "the working out of an agreement concerning a four-power trusteeship of Korea for up to five years."[8] The text thus implied that a trusteeship might not be necessary.

The agreement improved on American wartime proposals in several ways: (1) it reduced the trusteeship tenure of forty or fifty years to a realistic "up to five years"; (2) phrases in paragraph one that were designed to appeal to Korean patriotic pride implied that considerations of independence and national dignity now overrode those of paternal tutelage; (3) whereas during the war the American plan had received no firm Soviet commitment, but only informal, verbal acceptance of trusteeship, now the agreement had the support of both Soviets and Americans; and (4) perhaps most important, the agreement showed clear recognition that the Soviets and the Americans were the two powers most concerned with Korea. The unrealistic wartime assumption that the British or Chiang Kai-shek's weak government had interests in Korea equal to the United States and the USSR now appeared in only vestigial form.

The result of the Moscow Conference was thus a compromise agreement that reversed the sequence of American wartime planning: now a Korean government would come before, not after, trusteeship. In truth, it was barely a trusteeship agreement at all, in the sense that it did not question Korean competency for self-government or suggest that Koreans necessarily needed tutelage. The agreement implied that Soviet-American cooperation would result in an early end to zonal occupation. It recognized that this was the only way Korean unification could be achieved. Everything depended on how the agreement was implemented and on how it was received in Korea. Careful Soviet-American coordination and strict adherence to the text itself were essential.[9]

Unfortunately, the accord on Korea foundered overnight, primarily because of American and Korean actions in the south. The American command in Korea was aware from mid-October if not earlier that a multilateral trusteeship for Korea was in the offing. But as we have seen, from that point on, Hodge, Benninghoff, Langdon, and others urged Washington to abandon or "by-pass" trusteeship. On October

20 John Carter Vincent had stated publicly that American policy contemplated a trusteeship for Korea. All elements of the political spectrum in south Korea expressed their opposition. They linked the plan to similar Japanese policies, some hinting darkly that certain Koreans were urging "a period of tutelage" under the Americans.[10] The Occupation command quite rightly communicated this opposition to Washington and urged that trusteeship be dropped. Without approval from Washington or consideration of Soviet or other Allied nations' interests, however, it encouraged Koreans to unite behind the Occupation so that trusteeship could be avoided; it also suggested that if some form of tutelage were imposed, the tutelage would be on American terms.

The SWNCC "Basic Initial Directive," received in Seoul in mid-October, told the Occupation:

> In all your activities you will bear in mind the policy of the United States in regard to Korea, which contemplates a progressive development from this initial interim period of civil affairs administration by the United States and the U.S.S.R., to a period of trusteeship under the United States, the United Kingdom, China, and the U.S.S.R, and finally to the eventual independence of Korea.[11]

On October 30, however, General Arnold was quoted as saying that Vincent's statement on trusteeship represented his idea alone, not American policy, and that Koreans could therefore ignore the statement.[12] Hodge said much the same thing in an important discussion with the KDP chief, Song Chin-u, on October 31. As we noted in chapter five, Hodge had worked closely with Song in such important decisions as the appointment of Cho Pyŏng-ok to head the KNP. He also used Song as a conduit for explaining American actions in Korea; Song and the KDP used their propaganda apparatus to transmit and embellish several Occupation decisions.[13] On November 1 Song said Hodge had told him the day before that "all this talk about trusteeship is the opinion of one man, the chief of the [State Department] Far East Office [Vincent] and he is in no position to control Korean politics." The document went on to quote Hodge as follows:

> If I see Koreans unite and exert efforts worthy of independence, I will recognize that independence right now. . . . With respect to the problem of the thirty-eighth parallel, if Koreans in the south follow my directions and unite as one body, we will see one national government and the division of Korea will be quickly resolved.[14]

Other evidence suggests that Song did not unfairly distort Hodge's remarks.[15] Moreover, the timing and substance of such statements seems clearly related to the governing commission planning, which was contingent on the abandonment of a multilateral trusteeship. Some time later, a Korean newspaper quoted Song Chin-u as saying that when Vincent, described as a "pro-Russian," issued his trusteeship statement, Hodge and other American authorities "advised us to accomplish the task of unification within a month, fearing the possibility of a trusteeship."[16]

The Moscow accords thus placed Hodge in an extremely difficult position. From mid-October, possibly earlier, he had opposed trusteeship; no doubt he thought it to be the work of muddle-headed State Department policy planners. He had tried to find cooperative groups of Koreans who would unite behind the essentially unilateral actions that he and his advisors had taken in the first three months of the Occupation. The KDP had proved most reliable in this regard and had expressed its wish for unilateral American tutelage rather than multilateral tutelage that would include the Soviets. Close Soviet-American administration of Korea, as provided for in the Moscow accords, might call into question virtually everything of importance that the Occupation had done since September.

Immediately after the publication of the Moscow decision in Seoul on December 29, Hodge called Song Chin-u in for a conference. Nothing is known about the substance of their talks, but Hodge later said that Song "went out and told his friends that he was ready to act sensibly and the next morning he was dead."[17] It seems that on the night of December 29-30 Song also met with Kim Ku; Song's biographers say that he tried to get Kim to avoid a head-on clash with the MG over trusteeship.[18] Kim apparently failed to convince Song to support an antitrusteeship movement and, perhaps, took it as proof that Song still advocated a period of tutelage under the Americans. At any rate, the meeting broke up at 4:00 A.M., and two hours later Song had been shot. Song's assassin, Han Hyŏn-u, later said that his motive had been Song's espousal of tutelage. Other evidence linked Han to Kim Ku.[19]

In the days immediately afer the assassination, however, it was widely believed that leftists had killed Song, since they had been the ones publicly charging certain Koreans with advocacy of American tutelage. Perhaps for this reason Hodge sent MacArthur a cable on December 30 citing "definite evidence that Leftist groups here are . . . spreading word that capitalistic United States alone responsible for all mention of trusteeship."[20] Hodge thereupon tried to turn the tables and picture the Americans as opponents of trusteeship and advocates of quick independence. Richard Robinson said that Hodge presently began to issue statements opposing trusteeship.[21] Yi Kang-guk reported that on December 29 Hodge instructed a group of Koreans to oppose trusteeship.[22] On December 30 Hodge transmitted Kim Ku's statement opposing trusteeship to MacArthur and urged that the United States distribute it to the heads of state of the other three powers mentioned in the Moscow accords.[23] Although a cable of December 30 also showed Hodge trying to point out to Koreans that the actual text of the Moscow agreement emphasized the setting up of a provisional government before trusteeship,[24] his other activities gave impetus to a rightist antitrusteeship movement (*pan-t'ak un-dong*)[25] that within days was blaming the Soviets alone for trusteeship. Leonard Hoag is correct in saying that "the American authorities . . . allowed the popular conviction in Korea to . . . develop, that the Soviet Union was the party to blame for the contemplated enforcement of trusteeship upon Korea."[26]

Hodge and others tried to convince Koreans that pro-Russians, "pinkos," or communist sympathizers in Washington—all names that nationalists on the scene in Korea used to describe internationalists —were the only Americans favoring trusteeship. This was possible because it was a time, after all, when American Ambassador to China Patrick Hurley's charges that procommunist types in the State Department were subverting Nationalist China had just surfaced, and when Truman's close advisor Admiral William Leahy had begun to worry that even Secretary of State Byrnes might not be "immune to the communistically-inclined advisors in his department."[27] The first report on the Moscow decision in the *Seoul Times* stated that the Americans had advocated Korean independence whereas the Soviets had urged a trusteeship.[28] The official history of the Occupation stated that both Americans and Koreans in the south thought that the Soviets were to blame for trusteeship; moreover, its account of Korean conflicts over the trusteeship issue suggested that the MG was against those who supported the Moscow decision and for those who opposed it.[29] Another factor that contributed to the appearance of American opposition to trusteeship was Secretary of State Byrnes's statement of December 30: "The Joint Soviet-American Commission, working with the Korean provisional democratic government, may find it possible to dispense with a trusteeship." This was an acceptable interpretation of the text of the Moscow agreement, but Koreans naturally seized on the last nine words.[30]

The first fruit of the antitrusteeship movement was a series of work stoppages and demonstrations led by Kim Ku, culminating in an attempted *coup d'état* in the south. On December 29 Kim called a nationwide strike, told MG Korean employees to take orders from him, urged all political parties to dissolve, and demanded immediate recognition of the KPG as the government of Korea. Large street demonstrations ensued in Seoul and in a few other cities. On December 31 Kim issued a series of proclamations that amounted to a direct attempt to take over the government in the south. The coup was easily repulsed, however, and on January 1 Hodge called Kim into his office and gave him "a going over" that became the talk of the Occupation; Hodge told Kim that he would "kill him if he double-crossed me" again. Kim responded by threatening to commit suicide on Hodge's carpet. Thereafter, "the *coup d'etat* fizzled." Kim Ku suffered "a serious loss of face" from which he and the KPG never really recovered.[31] There is no evidence, however, to indicate that the Occupation punished Kim for this attempted overthrow, which, however ineffectual, went much further in intent than any People's Republic activities had.

Kim Ku's abortive plot was primarily directed at securing immediate Korean independence rather than at opposing the Soviets. The initial opposition to trusteeship had developed independently of Left/Right affiliation, with people of such vastly differing political beliefs as Pak Hŏn-yŏng and Helen Kim jointly signing statements against the plan.[32] Kim Ku's first speech against trusteeship blamed not the Soviets, but "traitors and pro-Japanese" within Korea; he urged that the country be purged of such people and called for "progressive democracy."[33] From December 28 to January 1, Kim and other KPG leaders met with People's Republic leaders and sought to form a coalition against trusteeship, an effort that ended with Kim's abortive coup. Thus Kim Ku's activity was directed primarily at the Occupation, and especially at Koreans allied with it, such as Song Chin-u, who seemed to be advocating American tutelage at the expense of immediate independence. Another important factor in the KPG reaction to the Moscow decision was the agreement's specification of a provisional Korean government—not, that is, the Korean Provisional Government. In the aftermath of Kim's failed efforts, the antitrusteeship struggle passed to Syngman Rhee and the KDP,[34] and the movement became indistinguishable from an anticommunist, anti-Soviet affair.

For the Korean Democratic Party and its associates within the MG bureaucracy, the trusteeship imbroglio provided a crucial opportunity to define what the essential issue was to be in liberated Korea. If it was to be the nature of the social order under which Koreans would live, these leaders were rather compromised. They had little to offer beyond the perpetuation of their own interests. But if they could frame the issue as being control by the Soviets (through a trusteeship) versus "independence," they could hope to restore an aura of patriotism and some degree of legitimacy to their cause. They sought to achieve this through opposition to trusteeship. Through the end of 1945, the KDP had failed in its attempts to render its narrow interests as universal ones, to transcend the appearance and reality of its nature as the representative of minority concerns. But the trusteeship imbroglio provided the opportunity to present itself as acting in the broad national interest. This is a prime example of how threatened groups can succeed in enlarging the scope of political conflict and thus gain a more advantageous power base.[35] Syngman Rhee and the KDP thus accused the Soviets, their "puppets" in the south, and communist sympathizers in the State Department of being the only parties supporting a trusteeship for Korea.

The opening shot in this antitrusteeship campaign came on December 17, the day after the Moscow deliberations opened and ten days before the content of the decisions was known. Rhee gave a radio speech in which he enunciated themes that would later become critical to the anticommunist program in the south: he alleged that the Soviet Union wished to make a slave of Korea and Koreans; that Korean communists called Russia their motherland and wished to make Korea a part of the Soviet Union; and that the communists, Soviet and Korean, wanted to divide Korea. He continued, "If we do not now solve this problem through our own efforts, our country will be divided into two and we will not be able to avoid civil war."[36] Then on December 27 the KDP Propaganda Department published a statement linking the trusteeship proposals to the Yalta agreement on the Far East and blaming the Soviets alone for the idea; at the same time, Rhee added "people who sound like communists" in the State Department to the list of supporters of trusteeship.[37] A KDP publication of January 10, 1946 carried a lead article under the headline, "Soviets Advocate Trusteeship, U.S. Advocates Immediate Independence."[38]

In addition, a resolution that was passed at a meeting of Rhee's CCRRKI in early January stated that Truman, Byrnes, MacArthur, and Hodge "all oppose trusteeship and advocate independence for Korea" but that a faction in the State Department sympathized with communism and thus agreed with the Soviets on a trusteeship. This faction was the same one that had earlier refused diplomatic recognition of the KPG and that had been urging reforms on the Kuomintang in China. The resolution noted that the charges of communist leanings among certain State Department officials raised by the American Ambassador to China had provided "an opportunity that Koreans can utilize" to denounce trusteeship. American MG officials were on the podium when the resolution was adopted.[39]

Such provocative charges deeply confused Koreans who already had a natural opposition to trusteeship, and the Moscow accords on Korea became hopelessly distorted. The news of the agreement arrived in North Ch'ungch'ŏng Province in the form of a threat that the Russian Army would soon move into the region and enforce a five-year trusteeship under sole Russian control.[40] A full-blown anticommunist and anti-Soviet movement thus emerged, and the extreme Right was able for the first time to mobilize popular support for its policies.

Another essential element in rightist activities in January was the attempt to link the domestic Left in the south with the Soviets and thereby to picture leftists as servants of alien, anti-Korean conspiracies. Former collaborators with Japan and members of the extreme Right, we might suspect, perceived little future for themselves under a joint Soviet-American administration, as provided for in the Moscow agreement. A genuine coalition of Left and Right would undoubtedly be a prerequisite for Soviet-American collaboration, and the Left was still dominant in both north and south Korea in early 1946; it could overwhelm the Right with or without Soviet or American aid. The rightists thus saw the antitrusteeship movement as a means of driving a wedge between the United States and the USSR.

Two key events in January aided this effort. On January 3, 1946, leftist groups that had been expressing opposition to trusteeship abruptly switched their stand. They came out *not* in favor of trusteeship, as has so often been charged, but in favor of the *full text* of the Moscow agreement. The Americans, as well as Korean rightists at the time and South Korean historiography ever since, claimed that this switch was the result of orders from Moscow or P'yŏngyang. The official history of the Occupation made much of this, citing KCP leader Pak Hŏn-yŏng's statement to Hodge on January 1 in which he opposed trusteeship and contrasting it with his statements on January 3 and thereafter in support of the Moscow decision. According to this account, Pak's behavior signaled "the beginning of the end so far as effective cooperation with the Communists was concerned."[41]

But was there an order from Moscow or P'yŏngyang? Documentary evidence of such an order did not appear until April 1946, when on April 21 a document was taken from a Korean crossing the thirty-eighth parallel into the south, said to have been issued by the "North P'yŏngyang Provincial Committee of the Korean Communist Party." More important than the fact that there was no "North P'yŏngyang" province in north Korea was that the order informed south Korean

KCP branches that Korea's division could not be solved save through the Moscow agreement. It clearly set forth the position agreed upon by the Soviets and the Americans at Moscow and urged communists in the south to support it.[42]

What seems to have happened on the Left is more complicated. From December 28 through January 1, leaders of the People's Republic sought a coalition with Kim Ku and his KPG group to oppose trusteeship. During this period, the leftist newspapers inveighed against trusteeship, everyone at that time in the south thinking that the Moscow agreement was solely concerned with a protracted trusteeship. Newspapers stated that the KPG and the KPR would "fight hand-in-hand against trusteeship." Then on January 1 Hodge met with both Kim Ku and Pak Hŏn-yŏng, and possibly with others as well. The general saw his policies falling apart, with Kim Ku having mounted an attempted *coup d'état*, Song Chin-u dead, Rhee in temporary eclipse, and a possibility that the KPG and KPR would coalesce. Thus it is possible that Hodge not only dressed Kim Ku down for his fizzled coup but forbid him to work with the outlawed KPR. In any case, on January 2 the coalition talks ceased, and the next day the KPR organ published a resolution expressing support for the Moscow accords. In succeeding days, other newspapers on the Left came to support this position.[43]

Thus the Left's somewhat belated shift to support of the Moscow agreement probably occurred because of the failed coalition talks and the recognition that the agreement could work in the Left's interests —and because of the rightist initiatives in opposing trusteeship, their denunciations of Moscow and the Left, and the Right's support by American authorities. It is also likely that the Russians urged the KCP to support the agreement, both because it was, after all, agreed upon by both occupying powers at the highest level and because the Russians may also have feared the potency of a KPG-KPR coalition. They much preferred, we would presume, that the Americans continue to sponsor the extreme Right. Within days, rightist propaganda had worked its effect: the Left found it all but impossible to refute charges of collusion with the Russians, the Americans came out as champions of independence, and the Left suffered a temporary but distinct diminution of support in the south.[44]

The other important event that aided the rightist attempt to discredit the Left was a news conference with Korean and foreign journalists present, held by Pak Hŏn-yŏng, the KCP leader, on January 5. Richard Johnston, the correspondent in Korea for the *New York Times*, quoted Pak as advocating an extended Soviet trusteeship over Korea to be followed by the incorporation of Korea into the Soviet

Union. Thereupon, the KDP circulated a "Down with Pak" handbill publicizing Johnston's statement.[45] Other American correspondents present at the news conference claimed that Pak wanted nothing more than a Korea "run by Koreans for Koreans," and many Korean newsmen supported this interpretation.[46] Internal MG reports said Pak had advocated "immediate independence" and that his remarks had been "completely misrepresented."[47] But Hodge said he found Johnston's report most interesting and refused to require him to publish a retraction.[48]

Pak's reputation was severely damaged by this affair. He became known, even among leftists, as an inveterate pro-Soviet sympathizer.[49] More important, from early January on, Korean rightists never mentioned communists without calling them "country-selling Soviet stooges," "those who wish to make Korea a part of the Soviet Union," and so on. As Hodge later put it, "it became so that trusteeship, Russian control, and communism are all synonymous. They don't mention that wod [word] without rolling these connotations all into one."[50]

The Russians were well aware of rightist antitrusteeship activities in Korea. On January 23 Stalin called in Ambassador Harriman and said that "he was of the opinion that there had not been a favorable start in our relations in Korea." Harriman recalls:

> He read a telegram to me which he had received from Korea which reported that the US representatives there were advocating that the decision to set up a trusteeship be abrogated; that meetings were being held in public at which demands were being expressed to this effect, and that articles had been carried in the Korean press which stated that only the USSR and not the US had insisted on a trusteeship. General Lerch, Chief of Civil Administration, was named by him as being specifically implicated with the above.[51]

Two days later the Soviets published through Tass a detailed and accurate analysis of the actual sequence of negotiations leading up to the Moscow agreement on Korea, citing the longstanding American advocacy of trusteeship and the Soviet advocacy of an early provisional Korean government, which had been "utterly unprovided for in [the] American draft."[52] Harriman was forced to make a hurried trip to Seoul to remind Hodge that trusteeship had been "Roosevelt's baby" and that the Americans rather than the Soviets had pushed trusteeship in Moscow and that the Moscow agreement had to be honored.[53]

The complexities of the trusteeship imbroglio are not generally known. But this was an important episode in the developing Soviet-American conflict, not only in Korea but around the world. Solemn agreements had been signed in Moscow, with each side giving up something in the interests of compromise and conciliation. The Russians lined up Koreans in the north behind the agreement, at considerable cost to their image as a champion of immediate independence for postcolonial nations, and to the detriment of the nationalist-communist Korean coalition with which they had been working.[54] What were they to think when the American command supported rightist antitrusteeship forces in the south? American support for the Korean Right since the early days of the Occupation was probably something that the Soviets expected.[55] Moreover, the Soviets played a strong hand in Korea because of widespread support for native leftists and probably thought their interests could prevail through or in spite of the Moscow agreement. But such an overnight collapse of the agreement was something they could not have anticipated; they probably interpreted it as a double cross and a sign that cooperation with the Americans was possible only on American terms.

By late January the Moscow agreement on Korea was in serious jeopardy, but not only as a result of American and Korean actions in south Korea. Truman, too, was dissatisfied with the Moscow agreement and with Byrnes's performance in Moscow. Byrnes came to realize that in adhering to the spirit of compromise at Moscow, he had, in John Lewis Gaddis's words, "strayed from the prevailing mood in Washington"; thus he subsequently adopted "a firmer position in his dealings with the Russians."[56] Truman himself remarked in the aftermath of Moscow that he was "tired of babying the Soviets" and suggested that the United States create strong central governments in China and Korea, and in late February commented to Eben Ayers that "we were going to war with Russia or words to that effect. He said that the situation looks bad and said there are two fronts, one Korea." Five years later Truman remarked to his cabinet that "our present policy was initiated on December 30, 1945, when President on U.S.S. Williamsburg reversed the then Secretary of State Byrnes and decided on firm policy toward Soviet."[57]

The view thus developed that the Soviets not only had won unfortunate advantages at Moscow but had also disregarded the agreement on Korea, in Herbert Feis's words, "completely." In February came two critical events in the development of the Cold War: Kennan's famous "long telegram," which became the bible of containment advocates; and Stalin's so-called "cold war speech" of February 9.[58] Korean affairs thus added to the litany of charges against the Soviets, exercising a refractory effect on the development of the Cold War. Individuals like Kennan, Harriman, and Truman, knowing nothing of internal events in Korea, interpreted what they heard in the light of events in Eastern Europe. The Soviets, aware of the situation in Korea, no doubt saw American perfidy stretching from Truman to Hodge in the apparent betrayal of the Moscow agreement. Yet the truth was that the Korean element of the accords was betrayed by a group of frightened Korean rightists and American nationalists in Seoul, acting provocatively and independently, against a formal internationalist policy that they all rejected.

HODGE IN A COCKED HAT

General Hodge had stepped dangerously beyond the bounds of his authority in supporting Korean opposition to the Moscow agreement. Recognizing this, on January 28 he offered his resignation.[59] On February 2, however, having been convinced to stay on, he took the offensive and sent a blistering message to the State Department. When the dust had cleared in early February, the governing commission proposal remained alive, in the form of the Representative Democratic Council; little had changed in south Korea.

In his February 2 cable, Hodge referred to a State Department message he had received in Seoul on January 27 that had informed him that Soviet statements about the negotiations at Moscow were substantially correct. This news no doubt discomfited Hodge, for he had just ordered that the January 25 Tass press release be censored in south Korean newspapers.[60] Hodge asserted in his cable:

> [The January 27 message] contains and implies information that should have been passed to this headquarters by the State Department several weeks ago. . . . It is in itself complete evidence that the Department has paid little attention either to the information painstakingly sent in from those actually on the grounds [in Korea] as to the psychology of the Korean people or to the repeated urgent recommendations of the commander and State Department political advisors. The verification of the full truth of the Tass statement comes as real news to me, particularly in view of my urgent recommendations beginning in October and the recent State Department attitude and broadcasts which shy away from the trusteeship idea and hold out hope that possibly it may not be necessary. Just after the quelling of the revolt and riots brought about by the announcement of the trusteeship, our position here was the strongest since our arrival.

After saying that the Tass statement had made Koreans feel that "the United States has again 'sold them down the river,' this time to the Russians instead of the Japanese"; and that his "best guess now is that north and south will never be really united until the Russians are sure that the whole will be soundly communistic"; he continued:

> I do not know who have been the experts on Korea who have advised and guided the State Department in their disregard of my recommendations. It may be the educated Koreans in the United States. It certainly has not been anyone who has seen and really knows Korea since the war. I hope that it can be impressed upon the Department that here we are not dealing with wealthy U.S. educated Koreans, but with early [*sic*], poorly trained, and poorly educated Orientals strongly affected by 40 years of Jap control, who stubbornly and fanatically hold to what they like and dislike, who are definitely influenced by direct propaganda and with whom it is almost impossible to reason. We are opposed by a strongly organized, ruthless political machinery designed to appeal to the millions of this type.[61]

Hodge sent this communication via War Department channels and asked that it be transmitted to the State Department. Unaccountably, the transmittal was deferred until March 18. Shortly thereafter, Secretary of State Byrnes responded by saying that Hodge had, in fact, been kept informed of American plans for a trusteeship since mid-October 1945. The SWNCC "Basic Initial Directive" had expressed the essential American ideas about trusteeship, and a draft of the American trusteeship proposal presented in Moscow had been sent to Seoul before the Conference of Foreign Ministers opened. Byrnes also drew attention to Hodge's accusations of the Russians, noted that the American-Soviet Joint Commission had just opened up, with the American side under Hodge's direction, and said, "I should feel less concern as to the outcome if General Hodge were not so convinced of failure at the very outset of the discussions."[62]

Byrnes was correct in asserting that Hodge knew about the American proposals on trusteeship. When Hodge received the text of the Moscow agreement in late December he could have compared it with earlier American drafts and deduced that the Soviets would react violently to charges that they alone were responsible for trusteeship.[63] But all that was quite beside the point. The point was that Hodge and his advisors saw no hope of cooperation with the Soviets in Korea, through a joint trusteeship or on any other basis, and from the beginning of the Occupation, they had acted unilaterally to solidify a pro-American base in the south. As noted earlier, even the "Basic Initial Directive" that arrived in mid-October was impossible to implement because of Occupation actions taken in the month preceding. Moreover, Hodge enjoyed the support of State Department political advisors in Korea and emissaries from Washington like John J. Mc-Cloy. This was the background to his statement in the February 2 cable that his "urgent recommendations beginning in October" had been ignored in Washington. Hodge's remedy for Korea's problems, like Rhee's, was separatist and nationalist: as Hodge acknowledged some time later, he thought that in place of the Moscow agreement, the United States "might have worked toward a permanently separated South Korea."[64]

Such Occupation policy making did not proceed in a vacuum. It was pursued over the strenuous opposition of many south Koreans, and it contravened Soviet-American plans at the highest level. Thus the Occupation command was bound, sooner or later, to be charged with insubordination, double-dealing, or treachery, depending on who made the charges. Within the State Department, dissatisfaction with Hodge and his allies on the scene grew. Vincent told Acheson on January 28 that the Korea command might be better separated from MacArthur's, so that the State Department would have direct contact with Seoul; he related a conversation he had had with General Hull of the War Department who maintained that Hodge was "a good man, but in need of political direction." Vincent also suggested that the State Department's political advisors on the scene, Benninghoff and Langdon, were not "of the caliber that General Hull and I had in mind."[65] Edwin M. Martin, chief of the department's Division of Japanese and Korean Economic Affairs, later referred to "the view which we have about the limited outlook of the military mind operating on the scene."[66] The State Department's reaction was rather mild, however, considering what had happened in Korea since September; we would suspect that State officials did not realize how far things had gone.

There were other problems with the State Department's criticism of the Occupation command, however. Since 1943 its own planning for Korea had encompassed elements quite in consonance with Hodge's vision. Guaranteeing that Korea, or the southern part, be free of Soviet influence or control depended entirely on the raw materials at hand in southern Korea; and Rhee, the police, and the KDP were the only forces who could be trusted to oppose the Soviets. Also, it seems self-serving for Vincent to have accused Benninghoff and Langdon of being low caliber, or for Martin to raise the construct of a "military mind" operating in the Occupation. Benninghoff and Langdon had participated in Korean policy planning since 1943, and Benninghoff had chaired the SWNCC Subcommittee for the Far East in early August, 1945.[67] Furthermore, the basic nationalist and containment assumptions held by Hodge seem to have been shared by such critically important figures in postwar American foreign policy as John J. McCloy, Dean Rusk, George Kennan, Averell Harriman, and perhaps even Harry S Truman.[68] Was the problem therefore nationalist logic? Or was it the incompatibility between internationalist policy and the postwar world?

Hodge's allies responded to State Department criticism by composing an apologia that maintained that the Occupation had received no policy directives until the end of January 1946. This was a useful way of getting around the fact, noted in chapter four, that the policies of a military occupation are supposed to be set by political authorities, primarily the State Department. The official history of the Occupation stated that "no political directive in the true sense of the word had been received by the XXIV Corps" until late January.[69] The problem, of course, was not that no directives had been received, but that the directives Seoul received could not be implemented while preserving an anticommunist, pro-American orientation. SWNCC and State Department policies that opposed utilizing rightist Koreans, such as Rhee and the KPG, or that directed a thorough purge of the police, or that urged uniformity in administrative policies in south and north, all had the potential to play into the hands of the Left. The trusteeship fiasco, like the Vincent-McCloy colloquy cited in chapter six, thus highlighted contradictions in American planning at the highest levels.

Just as when McCloy weighed in on Hodge's side in November 1945, so in February 1946 Harriman joined the ranks of Hodge's supporters. Secretary of War Robert F. Patterson included Harriman's evaluation of Hodge in his April 10, 1946 response to Secretary of State Byrnes's query about Hodge's capabilities:

> Harriman indicated that, prior to his visit to Korea, he had felt that it would be well-nigh impossible to reach a satisfactory solution to the problem there, but that he was so favorably impressed by General Hodge's ability and diplomacy that he now believes that there is a possibility of reaching a solution in Korea which will be satisfactory to the United States.
>
> [Harriman said] I was very favorably impressed by General Hodge when I visited Korea in January.[70]

With this endorsement to back him, General Hodge got on with the business of creating an anticommunist bulwark in the south.

The trusteeship imbroglio eliminated the Kim Ku faction of the KPG from consideration for the role of figurehead for the governing commission planning. Hodge had given Kim and his supporters bodyguards, American vehicles, the use of traditional Korean Court facilities, and so on; and they had turned around and betrayed him. Within days of his arrival back in Korea, Kim had engineered the assassination of Hodge's trusted advisor, Song Chin-u, not to mention having mounted an abortive *coup d'état*. The salt for Hodge's stew had proved a bit strong. Hodge referred to this episode when he told General Wedemeyer in 1947 that an effort to get Koreans to work together had been "knocked into a cocked hat" in late December 1945.[71] On December 31 Hodge informed his staff that Kim Ku and the KPG were behind the antitrusteeship demonstrations and that "he couldn't possibly sell them to the four-power commission [American-Soviet Joint Commission] if they continued in their present vein."[72] Thus Hodge turned back to Syngman Rhee and his CCRRKI, and to KDP leaders who still remained outside the MG bureaucracy, and tried to sell them to the Joint Commission instead.

As the true meaning of the Moscow agreement began to sink in in south Korea, it became apparent that the essential task was to present a united front of south Korean political groups that the Americans could offer to the Joint Commission as a basis for the stipulated provisional Korean government. Hodge and Langdon saw this effort through the lenses of the governing commission proposal. The official history paraphrased a cable Hodge sent to MacArthur on March 18 as follows:

> The proposed American stand [at the JC] was that the Representative Council of South Korea should consult with the representatives of democratic parties and social organizations in North Korea, and, in agreement with them, submit to the Commission a list of leaders, both in and out of the Council and the northern representation, to form a consultative union whose duty it would be to prepare for the Commission a slate of candidates for the provisional government.
>
> It will be proposed that the first of [the JC committees] . . . work on administrative measures, namely, *the adaptation of the civil government of South Korea as the machinery of the provisional government* and the reintegration of the postal, transportation, power and telecommunications services, and the educational system, and other government agencies [in north and south Korea] (emphasis added).[73]

In other words, the people's committee structure in north and south Korea would be abandoned and certain north Korean leaders would be integrated into the executive arrangements, while what was essentially a slightly reworked Government-General would be extended throughout the peninsula. Hodge and Benninghoff had earlier referred to the Representative Democratic Council (RDC) as "the newly organized Korean government" and described it as "a coalition group of all important parties." They seemed to imply that the provisional Korean government, which was to be the product of the American-Soviet Joint Commission efforts, had been formed before the JC had even met.[74]

What was this Representative Democratic Council? M. Preston Goodfellow, Rhee, and Hodge were the architects of the RDC. Since his arrival in Seoul in late November, Goodfellow had sought to unify the KPG, the KDP, and other non-leftist political groups under Rhee's leadership. By January 28 he had succeeded in getting the KPG to dissolve and in obtaining Kim Ku's support for a coalition effort led by Rhee.[75] Of course, the KPG had already dissolved (or destroyed itself), and Kim Ku's severe loss of face meant that he had no choice but to play second fiddle to Rhee. Around this time, a profusion of conservative councils, meetings, assemblies, and "coalitions" appeared. These included the Preparatory Meeting for the Emergency National Council (*pisang kungmin hoeŭi chunbihoe*) of January 23, the Emergency National Council (ENC) of February 1, a new elaboration of Rhee's CCRRKI called the National Society for the Rapid Realization of Korean Independence (*Taehan tongnip ch'oksŏng kungmin-hoe*—NSRRKI) of February 8, and several offshoots of these assemblies, which claimed to represent students, women, and other groups throughout north and south Korea.[76] These various councils soon claimed the adherence of literally millions of Koreans.[77] All represented attempts to unify the Right in the south before the JC opened; all consisted of tenuously linked rightist factions existing in Seoul and a couple of other cities; and all demonstrated the poverty of rightist organizational capacities. When the ENC opened, it was announced as a broad coalition. But even the moderate Kim Kyu-sik was absent; and no leftists attended the opening meeting.[78] Those assembled elected Rhee and Kim Ku as the leaders of the ENC by a vote of 102 to 2.[79] Rhee dominated all these councils, in the sense that he rode herd on an extraordinary proliferation of factions. Rhee and the various councils constituted the ephemeral will-o'-the-wisp that Goodfellow sought to solidify into a united front.

In late January Hodge recognized that the Right was in disarray and urged Washington to seek a delay in the opening of the Joint Commission, which might "give the Koreans time to form some kind of united front regarding an interim govt."[80] Benninghoff also reported that efforts toward securing "national unity" had made "little concrete headway . . . due to the intransigeance [*sic*] of right wing elements."[81] By early February, however, the Occupation had succeeded in putting

7. Preparatory meeting for the founding of Korean National Defense Forces (the Constabulary), Chung'- ang Middle School, Seoul, 1945

8. Kim Il Sung (left) and Pak Hŏn-yŏng at a party meeting

9. Yŏ Un-hyŏng (left) and his brother Yŏ Un-hong, in 1946

the rightist councils together in the RDC. Official sources noted that the development of the RDC "took place rapidly, without advance publicity, and without the knowledge of the Russians. It was thought that the element of surprise would still further strengthen the hand of the American delegation [to the JC] politically."[82] Hodge and his advisors did not make the mistake again of pursuing policies without Washington's approval. Instead, they interpreted a "significant paragraph" in a document that they took to represent their first political directive "in the real sense of the word" and used it to justify the creation of the RDC. This directive was the SWNCC's "Political Policy for Korea" of January 28, and the operative paragraph read as follows:

> With a view to facilitating the creation and smooth functioning of a provisional Korean government, the United States Commander in Korea should, without delay, encourage the various Korean political factions to reach fundamental agreements on the political, economic and social policies to be applied by the new government, including essential democratic reforms.[83]

The directive also urged the Occupation to incorporate south Korean political parties according to the principle that "the larger and stronger parties and organizations should have representation proportionate to their political strength and popular support." It warned against using extremists of Right or Left, or Koreans who were "puppets of foreign powers." But proportional representation would have required a leftist majority in any southern political arrangement. Internal MG organs continued to report on a daily or weekly basis that the Left was overwhelmingly dominant in the provinces. American intelligence reported in February that the Korean Democratic Party existed as a political party in only thirteen counties and had no organization at lower levels; its constitutents were "capitalists, landlords, conservative nationalists, [the MG] bureaucracy, small portion of Catholics." The KPR was still "far ahead of any of the other political groups," with a constituency made up mostly of "laborers, farmers, and youths." The American G-2 report concluded as follows:

> Whether their strength is spontaneous or forced is a matter of conjecture; but the fact remains that the leftist group, mainly through the organizational force of the People's Republic, represents the majority of the people of South Korea.[84]

A leftist majority from the south would meet a leftist majority from the north in the Joint Commission proceedings. For that reason, perhaps, the Occupation had to ignore this part of the directive and seek a rightist majority in the RDC. But the SWNCC policy statement had given those actually on the scene in Korea "wide latitude" in carrying out the directive anyway.[85]

On February 14, the day the Representative Democratic Council held its first meeting, the *Kwanghwa-mun* route leading into Seoul's capitol building was lined with policemen at ten foot intervals, right up and into the room where the session was held.[86] The RDC consisted of twenty-eight political leaders; twenty-four were from rightist parties (KDP, NSRRKI, KPG, and An Chae-hong's tiny KMT), and four were "leftists." The latter four were Ch'oe Ik-han, Yŏ Un-hyŏng, Hwang Chin-nam, and Paek Sang-gyu. Only Paek, the Brown University graduate and landlord, showed up. KPR leaders were completely unrepresented. Pak Hŏn-yŏng reportedly asked, "What will the Russians think of this?"[87] Kim Kyu-sik gave a speech in which he said that Rhee and Kim Ku had selected all the members of the RDC. In his own speech, Rhee declared, "Hereafter, the [RD] Council will represent the Korean people in its dealings with General Hodge and the Military Government."[88] In subsequent sessions in February, the RDC passed resolutions declaring that "the RDC will consist of the ENC's Supreme Political Council" and that "the duties of [the RDC] are to establish a Democratic Provisional Government . . . [and to] negotiate with foreign nations."[89] Many observers noted the similarity between the top leadership of the ENC and the RDC.[90] But these leaders could not attain unity sufficient to do more than declare March 1 a holiday or change highway traffic from the left side of the road to the right.[91] Hodge was in his cocked hat again.

Leonard Bertsch put it well when he said that the RDC "was neither representative, nor democratic, nor did it ever counsel." Washington later had to agree that it was unrepresentative, having "no leftists of any kind."[92] Hodge and his advisors had marched down the primrose path again, but they had no other alternative than to continue backing the RDC. The MG provided the RDC with a motor pool and the use of Changdok Palace and paid each member 3,000 *wŏn* [$200] per month. Kim Sŏng-su apparently provided one million *wŏn* [$67,000] from his own pocket, and two million more came from the Korean Economic Contributor's Association.[93] Much of this money went into Rhee's pocket and into his bank accounts in the United States.[94]

Hodge overlooked such activity because he saw the RDC in the terms of the governing commission proposal, as the kernel of a Korean government whose one virtue was loyalty to American plans for Korea. He continued to use the RDC as an advisory body until the Interim Legislature was founded in November 1946.[95] He blamed the Left for the Council's unrepresentative nature, saying:

The National Emergency Congress [ENC] . . . drew representatives from all but regularly announced Communists, who, as always, refused to confer with anyone not under their control . . . the Emergency Congress . . . selected [RD] Council representing all major groups.

Hodge also interpreted Yŏ Un-hyŏng's refusal to attend the inaugural RDC meeting and his participation in the newly formed Democratic National Front (DNF) as evidence that the People's Party "has completely sold out to the Russian directed Communists" and that this provided "the first real fix on Lyuh [Yŏ] as a full fledged Communist." Hodge viewed leftist actions in the south in terms of communist activities in Yenan, Manchuria, and north Korea; he perceived in them "an all out effort now to gain full control of this entire area of the Orient through political penetration." For this reason, Hodge came to the following conclusion:

For the present I plan to keep up the prestige of the Korean Representative Democratic Council, make every effort to gain the full backing of the Korean people, and discredit the communists. This will probably get liberal and pink press of US on my neck, but [I] feel any other local action now would be fatal.[96]

The RDC was the first of several unsuccessful attempts by the Occupation during 1946 to create a coalition in the south that would separate moderate leftists from "extremists" in the KCP and KPR and thereby isolate the latter.[97] Leaders of the RDC wanted no coalition with leftists, however. From the first meeting on February 14, they acted impulsively to portray themselves as the government of Korea. Hodge gave them an inch, hoped they would be discreet, and watched them take a mile. The result was that they isolated themselves rather than the Left.

The Left responded by creating a coalition mentioned above, called the Democratic National Front (minjujuŭi minjok chŏnsŏn), a united front that extended from the KCP (and the old Changan faction) to the leftist faction of the KPG led by Kim Wŏn-bong. It included Yŏ's People's Party and the moderate leaders within it who emerged with the Kŏn'guk tongmaeng and the CPKI; Changan faction people like Ch'oe Ik-han and Chŏng Paek; KCP leaders Pak Hŏn-yŏng, Pak Mun-gyu, and many others; Koreans who had returned from Yenan or those linked with Yenan Koreans like Han Pin and Paek Nam-un; and leaders of Chŏnp'yŏng, Chŏnnong, and other KPR mass organizations.[98] The DNF was the direct successor of the KPR. At the center in Seoul, the DNF replaced the Seoul Central People's Committee, while in the provinces, DNF branches "were based on the people's committees."[99] The DNF thus had ready-made provincial organization, while the RDC and the factions that made it up hardly existed outside Seoul.

The opening session of the DNF was held on February 15-16 at the *Chongno* YMCA building. American CIC investigators who were present said some 480 people attended the meetings. Speakers included Pak Hŏn-yŏng, Hŏ Hŏn, Yi Kang-guk, Han Pin, Kim Wŏn-bong, Hong Nam-p'yo, and Yŏ Un-hyŏng. Yŏ received a thundering ovation. All speakers lauded the Soviets for turning over the administration in the north to the people's committees and said Korea could be unified quickly if the Americans would only do the same in the south.[100] DNF meetings were later held in a number of places in the provinces. In late April the second national conference of people's committee representatives was held in Seoul, and those present again called for the transfer of power to the people's committees.[101]

The Americans were correct in seeing the DNF as a response to the RDC and to the upcoming Joint Commission. But they were wrong to see it as being, in the words of one member of the Political Advisory Group to the JC, "directed by a competent group of Russian-trained Korean Communists."[102] None of the key DNF leaders in the south were trained or directed by the Russians. The organization was, in fact, a response not only to rightist initiatives in the south but also to the inauguration in north Korea on February 14 (the same day that the RDC first met) of the Interim People's Committee led by Kim Il Sung. Even a cursory review of DNF publications and programs would demonstrate its independence from the north; rather it served as an organizational base for leftists in the south who were in competition with as well as in consonance with events in the north.[103] The DNF, like the KPR and the people's committees in the south, was a creature of indigenous southern leftists. Neither Americans in Seoul nor those in Washington were perspicacious enough to grasp these distinctions and shape policies accordingly.

Developments in Korea in early 1946 coincided with and provided part of the basis for a general American reevaluation of relations with the Russians and the perceived threat of communism on a world scale.[104] Reports from Korea were judged from perspectives that had been distorted by developments in Eastern Europe, even though the internal balance of political and social forces was wholly different in the two regions. Thus Hodge's reductionist vision of the Korean political world now found favor in Washington. From early 1946 on, although differences continued between Seoul and Washington, American policy became uniform in its essentials. Initiative was in the hands of those on the scene, thus every new policy tack in 1946 had its origin with Hodge and his advisors.

FROM THE JOINT COMMISSION TO SKIG

General Hodge made the following assertion on March 11, ten days before the opening of the Joint Commission:

> First and foremost, it has been the object of the American forces to establish and perpetuate the freedom of speech, assembly, religion, and press in Korea. These freedoms are not mere words to be used to gain political favor.[105]

In the weeks before the opening of the Joint Commission on March 20, Washington and Seoul jelled on basic American polices toward Korea. Washington now accepted the status quo in the south; there were no more calls for a purge of collaborators, no more orders to seek complementarity in administering north and south, and little criticism of Hodge. Within the State Department, dissatisfaction with Occupation policies continued, but the intervention on the Occupation's side of McCloy, Harriman, Kennan, and others undercut the internationalists like Vincent. Thus, instead of challenging Hodge on the fundamentals, Vincent and his allies now jousted with the Occupation over the merits of individual Korean politicians, rightists and moderates, or differed in just how bluntly each was willing to admit that cooperation with the Soviets was impossible and that Korea was effectively divided, or at least was to be governed by separate Korean administrations. In essence, Washington fell in behind Seoul during this period but spruced up Hodge's unceremonious rhetoric with a measure of diplomatic sophistication. The internationalists had lost a good bit of their effectiveness[106] in bureaucratic struggles over policy, thus the element of State Department policy that stressed "effective control" of Korea or a part of it came to dominate both in Washington and Seoul.

This emerging congruence can be seen in various documents having to do with Korean policy in the first months of 1946.[107] But it is apparent in brief in a March 20 memorandum written by a State Department-appointed, but unnamed member of the American Political Advisory Group to the Joint Commission. At a time when policy statements publicly pledged American commitment to quick Korean independence, self-determination regardless of governmental form, and a willingness to cooperate with the Soviets so that the dual foreign occupation could be ended quickly, this document said that the goal of American policy was as follows:

> To bring about an independent, democratic, stable Korean Government capable of resisting Russian domination over a protracted period of time. In the American view, freedom from Russian domi-

nation is more important than complete independence. . . . Unless coerced by force, it is believed that Korea will, if left to itself, orient itself toward the United States rather than toward the Russians for the forseeable future.

The paper described the American "primary objective" as preventing Russian domination and the "secondary objective" as Korean independence, and then went on to say:

Since Korean independence is a secondary objective, it is not believed to be in the U.S. interest to form a Korean Government which could be granted complete independence within the next few years. Unless and until the U.N.O. [United Nations Organization] can give reasonable proof of its ability to prevent aggression, the United States, together with Russia, if necessary, must extend some form of territorial guarantee to Korea and exercise certain essential prerogatives in Korea's international relations. . . . Any method of forming a provisional government of Korea must, therefore, be based on the condition that some form of disguised control at least on the highest level shall continue to be exercised by the United States for some years.[108]

This analysis reverberates not only with the element of State Department planning stressing the Russian threat in Korea from 1943 on but also with the subsequent use of the United Nations to sanction the Rhee regime in 1948 and with the United Nations-sponsored intervention in the Korean War. In terms of the analysis presented above, the memorandum did three things: (1) in effect and by implication, it sanctioned the de facto policies followed by the Occupation since September; (2) in particular, it defined Soviet-American relations along the lines of the governing commission proposal—the Soviets would have to acquiesce in American plans for Korea, or else the plans would be carried out for south Korea alone; and (3) it defined the problem of the Left in south Korea much as the Occupation had—the indigenous Korean Left was not a spontaneous and widely supported revolutionary force, but an instrument of Soviet domination. This, then, was the standpoint from which the Americans hoped to negotiate with the Soviets on a provisional government and on joint procedures for a unified administration of Korea.

American-Soviet Negotiations

The Americans and the Soviets held a Joint Conference from January 16 to February 5 to discuss mutual agreements on limited economic and administrative matters, as stipulated in paragraph four of the Moscow agreement on Korea. This conference was important as a prelude to the Joint Commission primarily because it demonstrated how existing American policies in the south had affected Soviet-American relations. Although a few minor agreements on exchange of mail and the like between north and south were reached, the Conference deadlocked on the American inability to supply rice to the north. Colonel General Terenti Shtikov, representing the Soviet command in north Korea, cited a "catastrophic" food situation in three northern provinces and asked the Americans to supply surplus rice from the south in exchange for northern products, coal in particular. But, as noted in chapter six, the southern rice surplus had disappeared because of the institution of a "free market" policy. The Soviets offered 89 million yen in goods for exchange, while the Americans were able to offer goods worth only 10.35 million yen, and not the rice needed in the north. When the conference ended in deadlock, Arnold said that the Soviets "must accept full responsibility."[109] The Soviets may have suspected that the Americans or their Korean charges in the south were trying to undermine the regime in the north by refusing to alleviate rice shortages, although there is no evidence to support this suggestion. In any case, the State Department ignored the rice issue and decided to politicize the resulting Soviet refusal to supply coal to the south; it suggested to the Occupation on February 28 that "it might be advisable to . . . point out that we are importing coal from Japan in order to assist the Korean people in the south because of the fact that the Soviet authorities refuse to release Korean coal."[110]

The Joint Commission opened on March 20 at its permanent site, Seoul, with five members each from the American and Soviet commands, each side being assisted by a number of political and economic experts and advisors. Major General Arnold and Colonel General Shtikov led the respective delegations.[111] After six weeks of detailed discussion, the two sides could reach no significant understanding concerning which groups of Koreans should be consulted in pursuance of the Moscow agreement to form a provisional Korean government. At the American suggestion, the commission adjourned sine die on May 16.[112]

Throughout the proceedings, the Soviets argued that the Korean political groups that had vigorously denounced the Moscow agreement had no right to be consulted regarding its implementation. They accused such groups of seeking to frustrate solemn Allied agreements and being demonstrably anti-Soviet. The Soviets also insisted on a close, literal interpretation of the full text of the Moscow agreement, including the paragraph on trusteeship.[113] Why did they assume this new position? After the excitement of the trusteeship imbroglio in the south died down, it had become apparent that the Americans had always been the proponents of trusteeship. The Soviets knew that the Americans now had little choice but to continue supporting a Korean trusteeship. More important, the Soviets were aware that the Koreans on the Occupation-supported Representative Democratic Council were the prime movers in antitrusteeship, anti-Soviet demonstrations. The Soviets also knew something that even the State Department may not have known: the heretofore secret minutes of the first Joint Commission meetings show that the American side proposed to use the RDC as the sole consultative Korean body from the south. At the first session on March 20:

> The specific program outlined [by the American side] . . . appeared to startle the Soviet delegates by its candid, logical approach. The proposal to create a Korean advisory body, or consultative union, to aid in the selection of a provisional government and a tentative constitution, and to have such body be selected on a basis proportional to the populations of the two zones, was stated clearly and succinctly. It was made clear that in the selection of the personnel, the American intention was to use the Korean Representative Democratic Council of South Korea, and agencies of the northern zone, as the primary sources of advice.

The Soviets did not respond directly to this proposal at the first session, but read a prepared statement saying, "We must not consult those parties and groups which are opposed to the Moscow decisions." The American rapporteur, Glenn Newman, noted that "the Shtikov statement differed in basic approach from the American idea, in that it seemed to envisage actual conferring by the Commission with many individual Koreans directly, rather than through or with Korean assistance."[114]

At the second session of the Joint Commission on March 22, the Soviets defined their position on consulting solely with the RDC, by saying, "The Moscow decisions do not foresee any consultative body, but rather foresee discussion with democratic parties and organizations."[115] Newman commented as follows on this Soviet position:

> The fact that the Moscow decisions do not call for the creation of such a body is irrelevant. The Moscow decisions call for a result, leaving the means of achieving that result to the discretion of the commission.

Newman also peppered his minutes with breathless comments about the vast gulf separating self-governing peoples (Americans) from the totalitarians of the world (Soviets).[116] He, and other American participants on the JC, might better have attempted to understand the content of the Moscow decisions. The accords did not call for consultation with a single body in either the north or the south; had the Soviets proposed a single northern group, the Americans would have charged immediately that it only represented the communists. Yet the Americans proposed exclusive consultation with the RDC, recognized by all American officials, whether in Washington or in Seoul, to be an organ of the extreme right wing.

It appears that the American side pushed this idea until the tenth session, held on April 6, when it was decided that each side would simply prepare initial lists of groups that might be consulted. Still, the south was to have a two-thirds majority on the basis of its population, a position that the State Department knew would be unacceptable to the Soviets. Bertsch remarked that the Soviets seemed "incredulous" at the idea of proportional representation.[117] At the tenth session, the Joint Commission very nearly agreed on a formula for consulting Korean political groups; it was, in essence, the position that was finally agreed upon in the second Joint Commission of 1947: "All parties and organizations consulted must declare that they recognize the Moscow decision, and will support it as implemented by the Commission." Bertsch noted that the atmosphere was very good at this session.[118]

At the eleventh session, on April 8, however, the American side revised the position agreed upon at the previous session:

> The Joint Commission will consult with those parties and organizations which are truly democratic . . . and which declare that they will abide by the decisions *of the Joint Commission* in the fulfillment of paragraphs one and two of the Moscow Decision on Korea and the measures worked out by the Joint Commission with the participation of the Korean Provisional Democratic Government, when formed, as specified in paragraph three of the Moscow Decision on Korea, with a view to the reestablishment of Korea as an independent state (emphasis added).

The Soviets responded by saying, "The Soviets have already made concessions in having offered to consult those parties which were opposed, but which now declare their support [of the Moscow decision]."[119] At the thirteenth session, the Soviets stated that the formula worked out at the tenth session was the only reasonable basis for agreement. The two sides went back and forth over the consultation issue in the fifteenth and sixteenth sessions, and then the first Joint Commission was suspended.[120]

The American position at the eleventh session abrogated the trusteeship clause of the Moscow accords, something the Soviets remarked upon at the time. The Soviets knew that the Americans were in a bind, having agreed to the trusteeship provision in Moscow, but tied to Koreans in the south who would have no part of it. The American side was left in an untenable position, since no local negotiating body had any authority to revise Soviet-American accords agreed upon at the summit in Moscow. By opening the JC meetings with the RDC as their trump card, so to speak, the Americans enabled the Soviets to trump them with ease. The Americans were left with the Hobson's choice of repudiating the Koreans who had been most loyal to the Occupation, which would completely isolate these Koreans and leave only the leftist DNF and a handful of moderate parties to consult with the JC; or of opposing the Soviets and thus making joint Soviet-American action on the Korean question impossible.

The American side sought to reinterpret the Soviet-American dispute during the JC as a matter of differences over essential democratic freedoms. The Russian position, it was argued, denied Koreans their rights to be consulted freely and to speak their minds freely on issues such as trusteeship (and, by implication, communism). Hodge had first suggested this tack on February 12. Having interpreted the failures of the Joint Conference as a matter of American inability to publicize its case in the northern zone, he said:

> I accordingly propose to instruct American delegation to begin proceedings of Joint Commission with a strong demand for complete freedom of speech, press and movement within Korea of Koreans, on grounds that until that is accomplished Joint Commission will be unable freely to consult Korean parties.[121]

On February 28 Washington (SWNCC and JCS) approved Hodge's suggestion and urged that Hodge "make public a statement citing your attempts to encourage freedom of speech, press, and travel" should the Soviets prove to be "obstructionist" during the Joint Commission.[122] The threat of publication was used in seeking Soviet cooperation throughout the JC meetings.[123] The "free speech" issue thus became, in the American view, a means of testing the Russians.

Was free speech a real issue or one manufactured for the occasion? For many Americans working on or with the Joint Commission, it was a real issue. Some of them had just arrived in Korea and were largely unaware of the record of the Occupation's activities since September. Leonard Bertsch once described to me how one member of the American contingent labored for days to express the American commitment to essential democratic freedoms in a manner that the Soviets would understand. If only the proper words could be found, he believed, the deadlock could be broken.[124] But such Americans operated on the assumption that full democratic freedoms flourished in the American zone. In fact, however, they flourished only for Koreans who accepted Occupation arrangements. The Russians knew that their differences with the Americans were not over words, but over the most fundamental questions of political, economic, and social structure in Korea.

The Soviet delegation constantly drew attention to the Occupation's suppression of the people's committees and other leftist organizations throughout the south. Shtikov's opening statement on March 20 cited this history, and incidentally, caught and appealed to the atmosphere of liberation in Korea in a manner that the Americans never matched:

> The great armies of the United States of America and the Soviet Union, having crushed the Japanese imperialists, have forever eliminated Japanese domination in Korea and liberated the Korean people.
>
> Korea has entered a new state of her development—a stage of national rebirth and reestablishment of state independency.
>
> Gentlemen: The people of Korea with their ancient culture vividly expressed national self-consciousness, year after year suffering hardships and the humiliation of colonial slavery; this people deserves the best future possible. With their blood and innumerable sufferings, the Korean people have earned the right of independence and a free way of life.
>
> The Soviet people warmly support this right of the Korean people. The Soviet Union has always championed and will always champion their self-determination and [the] free existence of any nation without exception.
>
> The great aims of creating a democratic independent Korean state have brought to life wide political activity of the whole of the people of Korea.
>
> The Korean people have formed their democratic parties, public organizations, people's committees as an organ of democratic self-government.
>
> However, in the way of gradual democratization of the whole of the internal life of the Korean people, there stand serious difficulties, brought about by the furious resistance of reactionary and

anti-democratic groups and certain elements, whose object is to undermine the work of creating and firmly establishing a democratic system in Korea. . . .

The future provisional Korean democratic government must be created on a basis of wide unification of all the democratic parties and organizations, supporting the decision of the Moscow Conference of the Ministers of Foreign Affairs.

Only such a government will be able to abolish entirely the remnants of the former Japanese domination in the political and economic life of Korea, to launch a decisive battle with reactionary antidemocratic elements inside the country, to carry our [out] radical measures in the rehabilitation of economic life, to give political liberties to the Koreans and fight for the peace of the Far East.

Throughout the 1946 (and subsequent 1947) Joint Commission meetings, the Soviet delegation continued these themes, emphasizing in particular the widespread presence, in *both* zones, of people's committees and associated groups. Thus the central issue of the JC was that the Americans had a Korean government that they hoped to extend to the Soviet zone, and the Soviets had one that they hoped to extend to the American zone. The problem for the Americans was that the Soviet-supported form of government existed throughout the south as well. This is what made the people's committees the central, if often unspoken, issue of the liberation period.

In talking about this Soviet statement with Americans who served in the Occupation, I have found that they are barely aware of, or even cannot remember, the passages quoted above. But they all seem to remember the paragraph that came next:

The Soviet Union has a keen interest in Korea being a true democratic and independent country, friendly to the Soviet Union, so that in the future it will not become a base for attack on the Soviet Union.[125]

This statement was seized upon as proof of aggressive Soviet designs on Korea. Yet taken in the context of 1945/46 and the earlier history of Japanese aggression, it would not seem an unreasonable position for the Soviets to take. It might be unreasonable if Korea were not a strategic peninsula on the Soviet border.[126] But it seems that many Americans at the time had difficulty conceiving of any Russian national interests worthy of American respect.

Thus, for many Americans, the free speech issue seemed to be the quintessence of what distinguished Americans from Russians. They believed that the Soviets sought to dominate and communize Korea, while the Americans sought to protect Koreans who wished only to exercise their fundamental freedoms. But other Americans like Hodge, Arnold, Langdon, and Benninghoff had been in Korea since the fall of 1945. For them, we cannot but conclude, as Richard Robinson did, that the free speech issue was "a false issue manufactured for the occasion to cloud the real issues and discredit the Russians."[127]

Opposition to the Left During and After the Joint Commission

On February 23 the Occupation issued Ordinance no. 55, "Registration of Political Parties." Among its requirements were the following: "any group of three or more persons associated for political activity in any form" must register with the MG and provide a declaration of its purpose and "the name and designation of each person holding office or exercising any function or influence in the party"; each party must give the MG or the provincial governors the "exact address and description of any places used by the party" and "an accurate list of its members residing in each province"; each party must make its financial accounts and lists of contributors available for inspection; and provincial governors may dissolve any party for failing to adhere to registration procedures.[128]

On May 4 Ordinance no. 72 was issued, detailing punishable "offenses against the Military Government." These offenses included: "influencing or attempting to influence the official action or conduct, or contemplated official action or conduct, of the occupying forces or any member thereof . . . by the use of force, duress, threat, promise, or . . . boycott"; "willfully interfering with or misleading any member of the occupying forces or person acting under their authority, in the performance of his duties"; "communicating information which may be harmful to the security or property of the occupation forces"; and any unauthorized forms of communication "with any person outside of the occupied territory" (that is, in north Korea). They also included the following:

> Acts or conduct in support of, or participating in the formation of, any organization or movement dissolved or declared illegal by, or *contrary to the interests of*, the occupying forces.

> Publishing, importing or circulating printed, typed or written matter which is detrimental or *disrespectful* to the occupying forces.

> Organizing, promoting, publicizing, aiding or *attending* any public gathering, parade, or demonstration for which no permit has been granted.

Knowingly making *any false or misleading statement,* orally or in writing, to any member of or person acting under authority of, the occupying forces, in a matter of official concern; or in any manner defrauding, misleading or *refusing to give information* required by the Military Government (emphasis added).

Ordinance no. 72 listed eighty-two separate and distinct punishable offenses.[129]

The *Chosŏn inmin-bo* claimed that Ordinance no. 55 was "worse than the Japanese Peace Preservation Law," while the KDP stated that it was "natural for this ordinance to be published."[130] General Lerche told Korean newsmen on March 5 that the provisions of Ordinance no. 55 were "the usual provisions for regulating political parties in democratic countries and under circumstances such as obtain in Korea."[131] Official sources, however, reported that the prime reason for the ordinance was the Occupation's need for better information and intelligence on communist activities in the south before the Joint Commission opened.[132] The purpose of both ordinances was to provide a legal framework for the KNP to search out and arrest leftists and to dissolve their organizations. From the opening of the Joint Commission in March until the uprisings in September, the suppression of the Left went hand-in-hand with American policies aimed at creating Korean leadership that was at once responsible and loyal to the Occupation.

The impetuosity of the RDC had been a prime reason for American difficulties during the Joint Commission. While the American side was trying to argue the merits of consulting RDC leaders in spite of their opposition to trusteeship and to the Soviets, these leaders continued to provide the Russians with abundant reasons for rejecting their counsel. The palpable inadequacies of the RDC were thus an essential aspect of the eventual American suggestion to adjourn the JC.[133] The Occupation responded to the problems surrounding the RDC in two ways. First, it decided to attempt a move away from the extreme Right by forming a Coalition Committee and planning for an elected parliamentary body (see below). Second, it attributed the inability of the Right to form viable political organizations not to the Right's inherent weakness and lack of mass support, but to the continued presence of the Left. In March and April, this took the form of virtual hysteria over communist and Soviet intrigue; later on, it took the form of policy decisions aimed at the uprooting of the south Korean Left.

On March 2 a group of Occupation-employed Korean secret agents had reported back to Seoul from forays into the north "to secure military information."[134] These agents, probably northerners who fled south after the liberation, apparently convinced Hodge that a Russian invasion might be in the offing. He cited alleged large-scale Soviet army maneuvers in the north as proof that Korea might soon "be the battlefield for World War III."[135] Difficulties with the Soviets in Iran reinforced a general war scare, whether in Seoul or Washington; Truman himself feared that the trouble in Iran might "lead to war."[136] On April 20 Hodge responded by ordering the strengthening and reinforcement of roadblocks and preparation for the destruction of critical points along the thirty-eighth parallel. MG intelligence organs also tried vigorously to ferret out communists among Americans within the MG.[137] The hysteria of this period (which coincided with the JC meetings) was evident in remarks Hodge made to his staff on March 25. Hodge said that communist activities in Korea and elsewhere were all "the result of one great master plan":

> All the moderates and supposedly middle-of-the-road Koreans now could be proved to be radicals or communists. They were all handsomely paid to work to discredit the U.S. These had been their orders from August 15 on. They'd been working at it ever since. It was all clear now. All the pieces were fitting together perfectly.

Hodge then predicted "horrible trouble" unless the Americans "clean up our own skirts pretty soon."[138] On March 29 he again discussed the communist "master plan," and said, perhaps with a touch of defensiveness:

> I'm enough of an imperialist to want to preserve the standards of living we've achieved in the U.S. and I firmly believe that we have benefited the nations into which we have extended our influence. All nations with a high standard of living have been imperialist. Our imperialism hasn't been a bad imperialism.[139]

Hodge was truly in a pickle. The Russians would not cooperate. His handpicked Koreans would not cooperate, to say nothing of Koreans who opposed his policies. Then, on May 18, in the wake of the JC dissolution, a United Press International report appeared that, based on information apparently leaked from the State Department, blamed Hodge for the JC breakdown. It cited his support of Korean opposition to trusteeship, which had led the Soviets to believe the United States was trying to revise the Moscow agreements. Therefore, the report charged, the Joint Commission was sabotaged before it even opened.[140]

Opposition to the Left in the south had been the *facta non verba* of the Occupation since September, with the KNP bearing the burden of enforcement, but suppression was stepped up as the Joint Commission proceeded and was bolstered by the repressive ordinances cited above.[141] As the deadlock held in the Joint Commission, the Occupation determined to "clean up its skirts" by attempting to root out the leftist opposition in the south. By the end of March, however, the MG's G-2 section had concluded that the arrest of leftist leaders "could only serve as temporary setbacks at best"; and it would not be effective in eliminating their organizations. According to intelligence: "The only answer to their control was the establishment of a rival organization not merely in the cities and [provincial] capitals, but in every village and hamlet, which could capture popular support and publicize the rightist viewpoint." Intelligence thought that perhaps Rhee's NSRRKI might be able to "serve as the vehicle for a publicity and organization drive by the rightists [in the provinces]."[142] But, the implication was, leftist organization would have to be dismantled first.

By May 1946, according to official sources, "it was evident to American observers travelling throughout south Korea that an order apparently had been issued down through Korean police channels to arrest all leftist leaders."[143] MG Public Opinion Bureau internal reports noted that Ordinance no. 72 had "been used as a carte blanche by the police in many areas to launch a wholesale attack upon the Left."[144] Although the official history hedged on the responsibility for this activity,[145] Langdon reported on April 30 that "many . . . arrests of Leftists were made in the southern part of the American Zone for illegal assumption of government prerogatives, such as issuance of rice permits, as well as for other activities against established order and authority."[146]

After the JC adjourned, Rhee toured the provinces, hoping to stimulate NSRRKI organizing activity. Soon the NSRRKI was being described by the official history as "the first Rightist movement which enjoyed a successful organizing drive in the provinces." NSRRKI branches "had become successors to the People's Committees" in some regions. The history also noted, however, that "there was abundant evidence that high police officials were closely allied with Rhee and Kim Koo and [were] causing Leftist groups to be harassed severely throughout south Korea."[147]

KNP support for Rhee was apparently within the bounds of Occupation policies, but Rhee overstepped these bounds when he called for a separate southern government (*Nam Chosŏn tandok chŏngbu*) in a speech in Chongŭp.[148] This came too close on the heels of an anticommunist demonstration in Seoul on May 12 in which truckloads of rightist youths connected with Rhee rampaged through Seoul, vilifying the Soviets at their *Chŏngdong* consulate and wrecking the offices of the *Chosŏn inmin-bo, Chungang sinmun,* and *Chayu sin-*

mun.[149] The Occupation was forced to repudiate Rhee and his supporters publicly. Shortly thereafter, under circumstances that remain unclear, Goodfellow left Korea. It was reported that he had met with Rhee a number of times just before his departure, and he consulted with MacArthur in Tokyo on his way to the United States.[150] On May 25 *Stars and Stripes* quoted him as saying that the Koreans were ready for self-government and that such a government should be established separately in the south if the Soviets would not cooperate.[151]

After Goodfellow's departure, Hodge sought to moderate Rhee's behavior. As Hodge said in a letter to Goodfellow on June 23, 1946, "The old man has made a lot of unfortunate statements . . . he wants to set up separate government now and *drive* Russians out. . . . I've had a couple of stormy sessions with the old rascal trying to keep him on the beam. Reminds me of the Biblical all night wrestling with the Lord's angels"[152] (emphasis in original). The Occupation ordered that the leaders of the May 12 demonstrations be given short jail sentences and that the rightist *Taedong ilbo* be closed temporarily for supporting the demonstrators.

Almost simultaneously, Chang T'aek-sang announced that his police had "smashed" a counterfeiting ring in which sixteen Korean Communist Party officials and members were allegedly involved. Chang charged that some three million yen in counterfeit bills had been seized in the Chikasawa *(Chŏngp'an-sa)* building, which housed the *Haebang ilbo* presses and the KCP headquarters.[153] Warrants were issued for the arrests of top KCP leaders, Yi Kwan-su, Kwŏn O-jik, and Pak Nak-jong. Their trial became the scene of a violent riot on July 29.[154] Yi, Pak, and two others eventually received life imprisonment in this case.[155]

The KCP charged that the entire affair was a frame-up by the police and that the trial was run by KDP-associated judges. It asked for, but apparently never received, the evidence upon which the charges were made.[156] At the trial, the defendants claimed that they had been tortured; but lawyers for the defense were warned that they themselves could be tried if they made "malicious statements."[157] Although there were obvious irregularities in trying this case, there is no way of knowing which side told the truth. The Chikasawa Printing Company *had* run off some 100 million yen in Bank of Chōsen notes when it was under Japanese control from August 15 to September 8, 1945.[158] The existence of such a large pool of bank notes could mean either that the police used them for a frame-up, or that the KCP used them for its expenses.

Using the opportunity provided by the counterfeiting case, the MG "moved, and searches of various Left Wing headquarters were

10. Kim Tu-bong, circa 1947

11. Hŏ Hŏn, circa 1947

12. Kim Sŏng-su in the 1940s

conducted throughout South Korea."[159] A particular target was the Inch'ŏn KCP branch leader, Cho Pong-am. Cho's earlier apostasy had led to "embarrassing connections with the Japanese during the war." In mid-May, the MG sought to embarrass him again by releasing a private critique he had written of Pak Hŏn-yŏng; he was jailed on June 12, and upon his release on June 22, he again denounced Pak and quit the party.[160]

Arrests of leftists continued throughout the summer of 1946. On August 16 the *Chŏnp'yŏng* headquarters in Seoul was raided and its membership records, accounting books, and other files were seized.[161] In early September Hodge issued warrants for the arrests of Pak Hŏn-yŏng, Yi Kang-guk, and Yi Chu-ha of the KCP. They were each charged with "endangering the security of America troops." The three men went underground to evade arrest. On September 7 the Occupation closed the *Chosŏn inmin-bo*, the *Chungang sinmun*, and the *Hyŏndae ilbo*, all leftist newspapers charged with making "inflammatory statements." The statements included demands for the transfer of power to the people's committees and for the release of political prisoners. An August 23 statement, "We must protect ourselves against the American authorities. We cannot sit idly by and watch our brethren being killed or injured," was specifically cited as inflammatory.[162] Thus, by the end of September, most KCP leaders were in jail or being hunted.

As late as mid-July 1946, the MG's G-2 section was still hoping that the NSRRKI would make inroads on leftist strength in the provinces.[163] By early September, however, that hope had completely faded. The top leadership was so fragmented and factious that the NSRRKI could hardly be called an organization at all.[164] Only former collaborators and the KDP element in the NSRRKI were cohesive. At a convention held from September 7 to 9, Rhee's list of nominees for the NSRRKI Central Committee included some "notorious pro-Japanese collaborators," while fully two-thirds of the nominees were KDP members.[165] In spite of a concerted attack on the Left since March, the Right still had no viable political party organization in the provinces.

The Coalition Committee and the Interim Legislature

In the summer of 1946, the Occupation sponsored discussions among Korean political leaders that were aimed at a coalition of Left and Right in the south. Then in the fall, the Americans held elections for an interim legislature. Both of these moves seemed to augur new American policies in south Korea. The official history suggested that, at the behest of the State Department, the Occupation had decided to moderate its ties to the extreme Right and cultivate ties to moderate and comparatively progressive Koreans. It cited a State Department cable of February 28, 1946, which stated:

> While it is realized that at the present time it may be difficult, it is felt that every effort should be made to find leaders in our zone who are neither associated with the Kim Koo group nor the Soviet dominated groups, who will put forth a progressive program for Korea . . . which will stress the four freedoms and basic land and fiscal reforms which would appeal to the vast majority of Koreans, with the object of winning over to such a progressive program people who now believe that the communist program offers the best hope for them.

This directive had China in mind as well, citing Kuomintang support for Rhee and Kim Ku and urging that the Occupation either find "a group of progressive leaders" to replace them or "make a strong effort to force the Kim Koo group to adopt and put into effect a progressive program."[166]

The Occupation waited some months before opting for such a policy, however, and the decision was based less on State Department directives than on Hodge's disgust with the bungling and political antics of the Representative Democratic Council. The operative policy statement that led to the coalition effort and to the interim legislature was drafted by Langdon on May 24—after the dissolution of the JC and the rightist excesses that followed it. Langdon referred to a Russian "united front policy," which he thought the Soviets hoped to impose on Korea and which differed "only slightly" from Soviet policies in Yugoslavia, Bulgaria, and Rumania, and urged that the Soviets be informed firmly that the United States had no intention of leaving Korea as long as the threat of "Soviet domination" existed. He also suggested that the Occupation "take advantage of the Korean Communists' unpopularity" (a reference to criticism of the KCP in the wake of the counterfeiting disclosures) to develop its own united front policy—"the formation of a true coalition of all democratic parties." Langdon specifically linked this policy to the Koreanization effort that had been going on since the end of 1945:

> Consolidation of democratic elements can in our view be best accomplished by increasing the participation in Military Government [of Koreans] and preparing them to take over more responsibility. . . . Provided a satisfactory coalition of patriotic parties can be achieved, without Communist collaboration, General Hodge proposed to increase their participation in affairs considerably by cre-

ating a Korean Nonadministrative Cabinet and Legislative Body which, subject to his supreme authority, will enact regulations and laws for the period prior to the establishment of a Unified Provisional Government under the Moscow decision. . . . In this connection there are indications that Korean puppets in the north are finding their position more and more difficult and might possibly be induced to enter into private negotiations with a southern coalition to form a government slate which an American delegation might eventually put forward for consideration by the Commission should it reconvene.

This was the governing commission proposal again. Kim Ku was no longer suitable, however; "as a result of his own political ineptitude [he] has almost dropped out of [the] political scene." As for Rhee:

General Hodge does not necessarily feel that Rhee is essential or even desirable in a future provisional government, but so long as he is one of the few nationally known leaders among democratic elements, his cooperation now can hardly be dispensed with.[167]

In early June the State Department forwarded an important memorandum to the Occupation command, entitled "Policy for Korea," which sanctioned Langdon's policy, while adding different emphases. It urged that the RDC be superseded by an advisory legislative body chosen "through broad electoral processes" and that, through consultation with this body, economic and democratic reforms be enacted. The "discussion" section of the paper charged that the elderly émigré Koreans (like Rhee and Kim Ku) had "on the whole hampered rather than aided" American objectives and suggested they be discarded.[168] Well before this policy statement arrived, however, Hodge had begun the coalition effort.

Hodge authorized a young first lieutenant, Leonard Bertsch, to begin discussions with Korean political leaders, with the aim of forming a centrist coalition that would include moderates but isolate the extremes on both the Left and Right.[169] The coalition would be the magnet that, with the aid of progressive reforms, would bring the mass of Koreans to support American goals. Land reform, in particular, would create a class of agricultural smallholders who would be content with their status and form the basis of a new middle class, giving Korea the stable middle it so desperately needed.

This effort was one of the truly interesting "third force" programs attempted by the Americans in Asia since 1945. It foreshadowed similar programs in Vietnam and was pursued with much more sophistication and shrewdness than other Occupation policies. Bertsch insisted on absolute parity between Right and Left instead of trying to tip the scales with rightists. He centered most of his efforts on winning the commitments of Yŏ Un-hyŏng and Kim Kyu-sik. Bertsch's particular focus was on Yŏ because he saw Yŏ as "the authentic voice of the Korean peasantry," and because Yŏ was just sympathetic enough with Western liberalism to listen. Bertsch viewed Yŏ as the indispensable element of his plans; Koreans to the left of Yŏ, like Pak Hŏn-yŏng, were not included. For this very reason, Yŏ was under intense pressure from his left either to quit the coalition effort or to participate on leftist-dictated terms. Yŏ sought to play both ends against the middle.

Bertsch, for his part, sought to manipulate Yŏ into the American camp. He held a number of meetings with Yŏ in April, hoping to convince him to break with the DNF and the KCP; but Yŏ resisted. Thus in early May, Bertsch tried "to blast Lyuh out of the People's Party by getting his personal friends and advisors to initiate the exodus . . . [and] set up a new political group free from Communist domination." Yŏ Un-hong, the pliant and vacillating younger brother, along with some "second-stringers," agreed to leave the Peoples Party and set up the Social Democratic Party (*Sahoe minjudang*—SDP) on May 8. On May 9 Yŏ Un-hong alleged that the PP had been "disturbed and misled by the actions of the Communist group." The SDP platform had anti-Soviet code phrases such as "opposition to interference by any foreign countries which might desire strategic bases, harbors, or economic privileges in Korea." The SDP received its funds from the Occupation.[170]

Kim Kyu-sik was under the same sort of pressure from the Right. Apparently Syngman Rhee provided funds for the coalition effort and for the fledgling SDP, perhaps from his stash of money provided by the Korean Economic Contributor's Association. He and Goodfellow, as we have seen, had a policy of splitting communists from leftists and moderates; but Rhee was now anxious to avoid getting cut off himself.[171]

The gambit with Yŏ Un-hong and the SDP severely embarrassed the elder Yŏ but did not cause him to break with the DNF or the PP. Bertsch therefore determined that the communists must have been blackmailing Yŏ over some skeleton in his closet. A G-2 report of August 2 suggested that the skeleton might be a number of trips Yŏ had made to Japan during the war. So a delegation of American officers was sent to Japan to search government records and interrogate former Japanese officials in Korea. Yŏ came up clean as a hound's tooth.[172]

Bertsch made two errors in trying to pry Yŏ loose from his leftist friends. First, he completely overestimated the influence of Yŏ Un-hong, whose lack of integrity had long been a source of embarrassment to his brother. Second, he viewed Yŏ as somehow dominated or controlled by conspiratorial communists, when in fact Yŏ fought openly and intensely with Pak Hŏn-yŏng for leadership of the Left throughout 1946. Yŏ was willing to ally with the Americans as a means of besting Pak, but unwilling to cut his ties with the extensive organizational base of the DNF—especially not for the dubious value of running the SDP. Occupation historians thought that the SDP had the merit of splitting the People's Party and driving a wedge between Yŏ and Pak, thus making Yŏ's participation in the coalition effort possible.[173] But it is more likely that Yŏ pragmatically and somewhat opportunistically saw that (1) the American occupation was in Korea to stay, and (2) its resources might be turned to his favor in leftist leadership struggles.[174]

Until early June, Bertsch had met only on an informal basis with Yŏ Un-hyŏng and Kim Kyu-sik. Hodge and Langdon probably had not decided to give official backing to the coalition program before the last week in May. On June 14, however, Bertsch's discussions were enlarged with Yŏ bringing in Hŏ Hŏn and Kim bringing in Wŏn Se-hun. Hodge publicly endorsed the coalition effort on June 30.[175] Much comment on the coalition idea followed in the Korean press. Finally, on July 22, the Left-Right Coalition Committee (*Chwau hapjak wiwŏn-hoe*—CC) held its first meeting. Present from the Right were Kim Kyu-sik, Wŏn Se-hun, Ch'oe Tong-o, An Chae-hong, and Kim Pong-jun. Present from the Left were Yŏ Un-hyŏng, Hŏ Hŏn, Kim Wŏn-bong, Yi Kang-guk, and Chŏng No-sik.[176] Bertsch had chosen discriminatingly from leftist and rightist groups precisely those political leaders whose commitments to each side seemed mutable. The CC was to meet every Monday and Friday from 2:00 to 5:00 P.M. to work on a joint program that would unify Left and Right in the south. The chairmanship would alternate between Left and Right from meeting to meeting.[177]

Every political leader or group that had been left out of the coalition effort viewed it as a mortal threat, however; Pak Hŏn-yŏng, for instance, apparently returned from north Korea to Seoul on July 22 and strenuously objected to the coalition meetings within the councils of the DNF. According to American accounts, Pak called for the Left's refusal to participate in the CC but was overridden by a majority decision.[178] Pak then offered to support the coalition if it would adhere to five demands: (1) complete support for the Moscow decision, including efforts at unity with north Korean parties; (2) land reform without compensation to owners as well as labor and other democratic reforms; (3) exclusion of pro-Japanese, traitors, and fascists from political life and an end to political terrorism; (4) transfer of power in the south to the people's committees; and (5) opposition to a Korean advisory body or interim legislature under the MG.[179] The DNF passed and published these demands on July 25 as conditions for the Left's participation in the coalition meetings. Yŏ Un-hyŏng and Kim Wŏn-bong apparently dissented from this position within the DNF.[180] But they absented themselves from the CC meeting for July 29, probably to avoid an open split in leftist ranks.

The rightist delegation to the CC refused to agree to the Left's five demands, as could be expected, and responded with its own eight-point program on July 29. They supported the provisions of the Moscow agreement except for trusteeship and called for the establishment of democratic freedoms throughout Korea (a refererence to the American position at the JC) but left the question of land and other reforms, and the problems of defining and dealing with collaborators and traitors, to the future interim legislature.[181] No coalition meetings were held in August because of the absence of the leftist delegation.

Yŏ and Pak continued to struggle with each other for control of the Left. According to American accounts, Yŏ approached Occupation planners with the story that Pak had been ordered to oppose the coalition effort by the north Koreans and "hinted" that "it was essential to the success of the American program that Pak be dealt with drastically at this juncture, perhaps jailed by some juggling of the counterfeit trial due July 29."

> We asked why [Yŏ] himself did not expose Communist intention to sabotage unity. His answer was that large labor, farmer, and youth elements in southern Korea divide their allegiance between him and Pak, that if an open break between him and Pak came now it would harm the unity movement. He suggested that if Pak could be made to lose face at this moment Lyuh might be able to win a considerable portion of these elements over to his, and, therefore, our, side.[182]

Thus the Americans were led to believe that the way to aid the coalition effort was to arrest recalcitrant leftists. On August 7 and 8 the CIC raided the homes of Kim Se-yŏng and Yi Kang-guk (two men who had sided with Pak in DNF disputes), searching for information that would implicate them in subversion against the MG. Kim's family was detained for five days.[183] This and other raids on the Left mentioned above forced the split in DNF ranks into the open.

In mid-August Yŏ resigned his positions in the PP and the DNF and made one of his periodic withdrawals to the countryside. Shortly thereafter the PP voted to merge with the KCP to form a new "worker's party" (*nodongdang*), by a vote of 48 to 31 with 50-odd abstentions. By implication, this vote opposed leftist participation in the CC. The losing group walked out of the meetings and declared itself to be the true People's Party, still led by Yŏ Un-hyŏng. The Americans thought that "the effect of the split will probably be a smaller but cleansed People's Party."[184] Yŏ's supporters continued to be the old *Kŏn'guk tongmaeng* people like Chang Kŏn-sang, Yi Man-gyu, Yi Yŏ-sŏng, Yi Im-su, and Cho Han-yong.[185]

After the split in leftist ranks and after warrants were issued for the arrest of Pak Hŏn-yŏng and Yi Kang-guk, the CC was able to meet again. The rightist delegation remained the same, but Chang Kŏn-sang and Chang Kwŏn (the Seoul *ch'iandae* leader in August 1945) now replaced Hŏ Hŏn and Yi Kang-guk on the Left. Biweekly meetings resumed in September. On September 22 Yŏ reported that the KCP would support the coalition effort if Hodge would rescind the arrest warrants for Pak and Yi and allow the three suspended leftist newspapers to reopen; but Hodge refused.[186] On October 4 the CC published a seven-article declaration, which reflected a compromise between the five-point and eight-point platforms of Left and Right. The first and third articles were the significant ones, the first calling for a provisional government under the Moscow agreement to be formed through a "Left-Right coalition" in south *and* north Korea, and the other urging land reform with *conditional* compensation to the owners but with free distribution to tenants.[187] Unfortunately the coalition effort dissolved shortly after the program was published, in the wake of the autumn uprisings.

This coalition effort sharply defined the American parameters of acceptable political participation in south Korea. Pak Hŏn-yŏng and his supporters were written off from the start. Leftists like Yŏ and Hŏ Hŏn were acceptable if they proved cooperative. Hŏ did not, and he was ousted. Those to the right of these men were acceptable; their occasional attempts at *coup d'états* and the like were passed off as indiscretions.[188] Rhee railed against the coalition effort and set up his own "General Headquarters for Korean Unification" in August; but he was not hounded like Pak.

The KDP was totally opposed to the coalition idea; it called the participants "wobblers" and "opportunists"; it opposed the CC's compromise land reform proposal; and it later took credit for the CC demise.[189] Cho Pyŏng-ok, the KNP director, later acknowledged that he too sought to block the CC; liberated Korea, in his view, reduced only to "communism" versus "nationalism" and to moderates who always had *the potential* to succumb to the Left.[190] Hodge and other Americans eventually came to see things in the same way. Hodge told General Wedemeyer in 1947 that, in his opinion, a coalition government "would go to a communist government" quickly. Hodge said he had recommended "ceasing local dealings with the Russians and stamping out the Communists here [in south Korea]."[191] The American delegation to the Joint Commission disagreed slightly with Hodge, arguing in November that the moderate-Left element of the CC represented "the only known Leftist political group of sufficient reliability with which Commanding General could negotiate on political matters."[192] As long as Hodge's views dominated, any such political effort would be transitory. Bertsch pursued the coalition with intelligence and vigor, but he was ill-served by his superiors. Moreover, his view of the Korean political spectrum as a continuum in which the middle, if bolstered, could attract Left and Right was fallacious. The middle had no base, while the Left was rooted in strong organization and mass support, and the Right was anchored in real property and in the bureaucracy.

In short, as 1946 drew to a close, the rightist entrenchment in the bureaucracy was the basic and irremovable element of American plans, while everything to the Left was negotiable and contingent on proof of reliability, responsibility, loyalty—all words the Occupation used to characterize acceptance of American-imposed arrangements in the south. But, just as at the beginning in 1945, American standards of acceptability continued to do injustice to the actual distribution of popular support between Right and Left. They did not exclude all but the cooperative Left and thereby only a handful of individuals. Rather they excluded social forces represented by strong organization throughout the south. That is one reason why the first year of Occupation ended with unprecedented violence and destruction.

The dominance of the Right within the bureaucracy was also evident in the elections held for the interim legislature in October 1946. The South Korean Interim Legislative Assembly (SKILA) was the fourth attempt within a year to set up a figurehead body of Koreans that would be responsive to Hodge and still provide an aura of legitimacy to Occupation arrangements. Like the Advisory Council, the RDC, and the CC, it ended in failure.

After the dissolution of the Joint Commission in May, American policy planners in Washington and in the Occupation had seen democratic electoral processes as a means of sanctifying the politics of the south. If elections could be held, they reasoned, they would give meaning to the American position on fundamental freedoms taken at the Joint Commission and give the Occupation command an image of popular control then sadly lacking.[193] The Occupation saw elections as an adjunct to the Koreanization policy, as discussed above: "Consolidation of democratic elements can in our view be best accomplished by increasing the participation in Military Government [of Koreans] and preparing them to take over more responsibility as our occupation and Military Government forces are perforce reduced."[194] The "Policy for Korea" paper that arrived in early June also linked Koreanization and electoral processes, by urging the use of qualified Koreans "in as many posts of responsibility as possible" and by suggesting that the Occupation "establish through broad electoral processes an advisory legislative body which shall supersede the present Representative Democratic Council."[195] The first public word of such plans appeared in early July; and on August 24 Ordinance no. 118 authorized elections for an interim legislative assembly.[196]

It appeared to many Koreans that the plans for a legislature augured a separate southern government, since they came on the heels of the JC dissolution and Rhee's calls for a separate government. The Occupation fueled such suspicions by linking the SKILA elections to Koreanization. On September 11 General Lerche announced that the Koreans had made "remarkable progress in learning how to handle Korean affairs" and thus *all* MG departments would be turned over to Korean directors, with Americans functioning only in advisory capacities.[197] This was not the beginning of Koreanization, but the end of a process that had begun in the fall of 1945. Many Koreans knew that KDP leaders had advocated such a policy for months.[198]

Hodge envisioned the interim legislature as being a small body along the lines of the United States Senate, but with certain modifications: he would retain the right to appoint half of its ninety members; and he would have absolute veto power over its activities.[199] After successive failures, Hodge wanted to immerse Koreans in representative politics slowly, just letting them get their feet wet at first. The hope for "broad electoral processes" also became attenuated in practice. By late August, Langdon had determined that "because of high illiteracy and lack of any political training elections of a national scope, as we understand them, are not feasible."[200]

By the time the elections were held, the electoral process differed little from the Japanese system that had been used to select members of advisory councils. According to an American participant in the election planning, in many regions in the provinces, only taxpayers and landlords voted, as provided for in Japanese electoral laws still in effect.[201] There was no place where the Korean masses actually walked in and cast secret ballots. At the lowest level, village elders voted in place of their constituents and selected representatives to vote at the next highest level. Only at the county level were representatives from lower levels allowed to vote on actual candidates for the legislature, and only here was the secret ballot used. Legislative representatives were allotted on the basis of one for each 550,000 people, with representatives-at-large from Seoul and from each province. According to Robinson, the MG used these procedures to accord with their understanding of Korean tradition and to "assure a conservative delegation."[202]

The elections were held during the uprisings in October, however, and proceeded so quickly that many Koreans were unaware of them.[203] Kim Kyu-sik maintained that "in certain places even the electors were not notified" of the elections; and in other places, the *panjang*s and other officials collected the seals (*tojang*) of their constituents and "used them as [they] pleased." Kim said that in Kangwŏn Province "the whole affair was manipulated" by the NSRRKI, which forced the electors to vote for the candidates it sponsored. He charged that one of the NSRRKI men elected, Sŏ Sang-jun, had been a police inspector for the Japanese who "incarcerated many a Korean patriot." He also said that the KDP had nominated Sŏ Sang-il (also described as a collaborator) in North Kyŏngsang, in spite of his legal residency in Seoul.[204] The American Advisory Group to the JC told Hodge that "the legislature, if brought into being, would consist solely of members of the Right and would in fact be a replacement of the RDC."[205]

Under pressure from the Coalition Committee and from his American advisors, Hodge decided to nullify the Kangwŏn and Seoul elections. When elections were held again, however, rightists won again. In Seoul, all of the ten candidates standing for election were from the KDP or NSRRKI except for Yŏ Un-hyŏng. Yŏ lost. The final Seoul delegation consisted of Kim Sŏng-su, Kim To-yŏn, and Chang Tŏk-su, all early leaders of the KDP in September 1945.[206] Still the KDP was upset with Hodge. In early December, its leaders had warned him that if he held new elections, the KDP "would not be able to control legislative action." When Hodge proceeded with the new elections in Kangwŏn and Seoul, the KDP called this action "undemocratic."[207] Only Cheju Island elected leftists to the SKILA, and when the two men arrived in Seoul, they "promptly disappeared."[208]

Hodge had to recoup his legislative policies somehow, thus he appointed the remaining forty-five members of the SKILA from among moderate rightists and leftists. The Right still managed to slip in fourteen supporters, however. The political breakdown in the legislative assembly, as reported by Chang Tŏk-su, is indicated in Table 10.

TABLE 10

POLITICAL AFFILIATION OF SKILA MEMBERS, DECEMBER 1946

Political Party	Elected Members	Appointed Members	Total
Left and moderate	0	31	31
KDP	21	2	23
NSRRKI	13	3	16
KIP*	6	4	10
"Non-partisan but sympathetic to Right"	5	5	10
	45	45	90

SOURCE: Chang Tŏk-su provided this breakdown to McMahon (see "Antecedents, Character, and Outcome," p. 45).
* Korean Independence Party, an old KPG group led by Kim Ku.

The SKILA opened on December 12 but could not achieve a quorum owing to a KDP boycott in protest of Hodge's decision to hold new elections in Kangwŏn and Seoul. Kim Sŏng-su and Chang Tŏk-su also expressed to Hodge their worries about laws regarding collaborators and pro-Japanese and the nature of the land reform program that might be developed in the legislature.[209]

CONCLUSIONS: "A NOTE OF QUERULOUSNESS"

William Langdon provided an explanation for the SKILA election failures:

As the [State] Department may be aware, the administrative officials of military government, because of the antagonism and virtual boycott of military government by the Left from the very beginning, are predominantly rightist. Thus the administrative preparations for the elections have been largely in their hands; and because of their tendency toward partisanship on the one hand and the disorganization and studied absence of interest in the elections by most of the local leftists on the other hand, it is a foregone conclusion that an overwhelming majority of rightist members will be elected.[210]

The Left was blamed for refusing to participate in the Advisory Council with its ten to one ratio in favor of the Right, and for boycotting the RDC when the ratio was forty-five to four, and for showing lukewarm interest in a coalition effort accompanied by widespread attacks on leftist leaders, and for opposing rigged elections that would create a powerless legislature as an adjunct to the bureaucracy. Is this where the blame for the failures of the first year of Occupation lay?

The real problem was with "the administrative officials of military government" and the American policies that had selected them and dictated their use. A random sample of 115 high South Korean Interim Government (SKIG) officials in 1947 showed that 70 had held office under the Japanese; 23 had been owners, managers, or officials of public and private business firms during the colonial period. Of 10 police officers in the sample, 7 had been on the Japanese force, including 3 in north Korea and 1 in Manchukuo. Of 4 Justice Department officials, 3 had worked in the colonial police or justice apparatus. Of 9 county magistrates in the sample, 8 had been magistrates or other high county officials during Japanese rule. Only 11 of these officials had any record of exile, imprisonment, or the slightest hint of anti-Japanese activity in their backgrounds.[211] The consistent prominence of rightists and Koreans who had served the Japanese was not an accident, but the direct and inevitable result of American policies.

The policies themselves had a startling consistency, a consistency quite evident in a Langdon memorandum of August 23, 1946. He noted that "the law of diminishing returns had set in so far as our program is concerned." This was because "the general feeling of the small articulate element of the population is that the basic job of the US in Korea has been done." The Japanese had been sent home, "a police force had been created, the framework of the administrative and judicial systems has been put together again," and so on. Thus, for the articulate element, "a note of querulousness is asserting itself with respect to almost anything we undertake outside of straight basic administration." The Left had its grievances as well:

The abiding grudge of these elements is that the administration of people's committees they had established after the Japanese surrender was first not recognized and later outlawed as MG came from the "Conservative" elements that fared reasonably well under the Japanese. The Leftist elements feel that they have been cheated out of a social revolution, with MG merely perpetuating a traditional social order that had been maintained by the Japanese.

Langdon wondered if the State Department's idea that a reform administration in the south would undermine the Left had merit. Could the United States match the program in the north, described by Langdon as follows?

The Soviets now take pains to prevent abuses of the Korean people by their soldiery, the administration is outwardly 100% Korean, lands of Japanese and native landlords have been distributed free to tenant farmers and landless refugees, former Japanese factories are operated by committees of organized workers and officials instead of by industrialists under an operating mandate as in our zone, labor law has been passed, and the people are very much left to their own devices. These reforms have fallen heavily on the unfortunate conservative and propertied classes, many of whom have taken refuge in our zone, and even the peasantry and poor townspeople have not gotten over the earlier excesses and exactions of the Soviet soldiery, but large elements of the population now like their new deal, including a new class of officials and committee men with central and local executive and administrative powers.

In the south, Langdon saw no such positive developments, only "a policy of drift." On the first anniversary of the Liberation, "not a note of joy or optimism featured Seoul editorial comment"; one journal asked, "should we celebrate this day with joy or tears?"[212]

Langdon ended his paper with a recapitulation of the problems that the Americans faced in south Korea, one year after the Liberation:

Widening sectional and ideological cleavages in Korean society; diminishing popularity of the US among Koreans generally; apathy from the right; non-cooperation or opposition from the left; . . . entrenchment of Soviet influence and system in North Korea.[213]

And Washington's response to this remarkable statement? As if nothing had happened, as if an entire year of experience in Korea could be shrugged away, the State Department replied:

It seems to us that all evidence of the past year clearly indicates that the Koreans are not psychologically or technically now prepared to undertake self-government . . . it seems to us that a provisional government would at best have to function for some time under the very close supervision and guidance of the Joint Commission . . . we feel that no encouragement should be given to the Koreans to think that abandonment of trusteeship is or may be feasible.[214]

Thus, in Washington thinking about Korea continued to oscillate between internationalist hopes and Korean realities as perceived from afar. On the scene, nationalist logic had clearly won the day.

KOREANS AND AMERICANS
IN THE PROVINCES, 1945-1947

Chapter Eight

AN OVERVIEW
OF THE PEOPLE'S COMMITTEES
IN THE PROVINCES

> All social movements expand in jerks; the history of all contains
> abnormally, often fantastically rapid and easy mobilization of
> hitherto untouched masses. Almost always such expansion takes
> the form of contagion: a propagandist arrives in a locality, and
> within a short time the whole region is affected.
>
> _Eric Hobsbawm_

CONSIDER the following paradox. In 1945 and 1946 the entire Korean
peninsula was covered with "people's committees" (_inmin wiwŏn-
hoe_—PC), existing at province, city, county, and village levels. In the
north, they provided the popular basis upon which the regime was
built. In the south, they governed for varying periods of time in more
than half of all the counties. These people's committees are examples
of that rarest of Korean political forms, locally rooted and responsive
organization. They marked a period of rural participation unmatched
in Korean history before or since. Yet the phenomenon remains un-
studied in the literature. We can begin to appreciate how difficult it is
to apprehend a politics in which illiterate peasants are the majority.
Our goals must therefore be modest. The following three chapters will
do no more than present an interpretation of provincial politics from
1945 to 1947, based on only meager information. Perhaps at some later
point, when various archives may make available more information,
the story can be told in the full richness it deserves—a story of people
who, in Leon Trotsky's words, "vote with their feet"; who fling stones
to make a point; who express their humanity in a thousand protests.
We begin our account with the people's committees and end with a
peasant war, or rather, with many peasant wars—local wars scattered
throughout most provinces as 1946 came to an end; small wars that
prefigured major battles.

In the beginning of this study, we surveyed various processes of
change begun during the Japanese era that developed to a point but
were then interrupted in 1945, changes that had their greatest effect

not in their development, but in their interruption. The main elements in the process were the increasing concentration of landholdings (with a corresponding increase in numbers of tenants and peasant household dissolution), the entry of the market, the growth of industry, colonial mobilization policies, and the great population movement caused by these forces. As the diaspora later returned to Korea, and to native counties and towns, it detonated explosions all over the southern provinces. Returning Koreans found the structure of agrarian relationships to be much the same as it was when they left, but landlords had more than they did before. And more important, the remaining landlords were Koreans and were, for the most part, the nonentrepreneurial type, now tainted by associations with the ousted Japanese. After the heyday of liberation in August and September, these same landlords were protected by the revived Korean element of the colonial police force. The simple injustice of such arrangements particularly impressed peasants who, shall we say, did not consciously participate in their own mobilization. If the peasants, who had been drawn or pushed off the land into industry, had stayed away longer, they might have developed a consciousness appropriate to their new work. But because the process was interrupted, most of them did not. Their bodies had been mobilized, but not their minds. They were still locked into a peasant consciousness, but one that had been shown a different, if not necessarily better, world. Such peasants returned to the land with a distinct sense of grievance over their mobilization in service to Japanese interests and perhaps a surer sense of the iniquity of the basic arrangements of Korean agrarian structure. Worker-peasants became, in many cases, peasant-politicos.

The spontaneity and eclectic makeup of the people's committees make it possible to determine the relationships between levels of political participation in particular regions and environmental, or "ecological," variables such as land conditions, geographic location, population movement, and degree of modernity. Ecological studies of politics in peasant societies proliferated in the period of heavy American involvement in Indochina, as scholars sought to understand and explain the successes and failures of guerrilla insurgencies in China, Vietnam, the Philippines, and elsewhere.[1] But the information on Korea in the late 1940s is probably better than that available for China or Vietnam. The statistical base is unquestionably superior, since the Japanese carefully counted and surveyed the people they ruled. Even for Korea, however, maddening gaps in the data remain. We can get down to the county (*kun*) level in Korea, a division much smaller than the Chinese *hsien*, and yet we are still dealing with tens or hundreds of thousands of people and with areas of considerable internal variance. Even if we could relate politics to environment at the village level, we would find that Korean villages vary significantly in their structure (especially clan structure). Thus, in what follows, I have limited myself to pointing out certain apparent relationships between politics and environment; I make no pretense to mathematical precision.

The significant relationships that appear to have developed in Korea between rural politics and environmental factors are the following: the effects of population dislocation; rates of tenancy and landlordism; gross differences in geographic location; and the presence or absence of modern transportation and communication facilities. The one remaining factor that almost certainly had a significant influence on rural politics, but about which little data are available, is the level of commercialization of agriculture.[2] Commercialization proceeded most rapidly in the regions contiguous to the big rice exporting cities of Kunsan, Mokp'o, and Pusan; and it is in these regions that we also find relatively high rates of political activity. In the commercialized regions, political currents affected the agrarian classes in a complex fashion. Richer peasants, for example, might oppose land reform programs that would equalize holdings at a low, inefficient level. Commercialization had had a layered pattern during the colonial period as well, however, with landlords moving into marketing, speculating, and exporting, yet continuing to utilize "feudal" methods for extracting surpluses. Peasants in these circumstances generally remained unaware of the workings of the market, or the uses to which the extracted grain was put; they would be likely to favor a land redistribution program, regardless of the size of the plot they might receive. There is little information on this aspect of the agrarian situation, however, so further study must be left to later research.

Other considerations that are important in understanding the PCs are, for the most part, political: the length of the interregnum between Japanese and American rule; conflicting policies pursued by both the Americans and the local committees; diverse composition of the committees; and the existence of similar organizations in the later years of Japanese rule. As indicated elsewhere in this study, the prime factor in the eventual demise of the KPR and the people's committees was the presence of American and Korean power directed against both. Thus we acknowledge the primacy of autonomous political organization over environment.

As we saw in chapter three, local branches of the CPKI spread rapidly throughout Korea within days of the organization of the central body on August 15. By the end of August, there were said to be 145 local branches. But this figure was never broken down into organizational levels or geographic regions; it simply appears repeatedly in Korean sources. It should be used with reservations.[3] It is likely that the number of local branches was higher than 145 by the end of August, but, again, no reliable information exists to allow us to pinpoint their location and number.

It appears that all thirteen Korean provinces had provincial-level CPKI branches within a few days after liberation. Most major cities also had branches by the end of August. And throughout the three-month period after August 15, committees proliferated at all administrative levels down to the smallest villages. After the formation of the Korean People's Republic on September 6, there was a relatively easy transformation of the local CPKI organs into people's committees. Only in a few cases did the local branches refuse this designation and either retain the CPKI name or ally with other political groups such as the Korean Democratic Party or, in October, the fledgling People's Party. As in Seoul, the committees were supplemented at all levels by peasant unions (*nongmin chohap*), workers' unions (*nodong chohap*), peace-keeping groups (*ch'iandae* or *poandae*), and students', youths', and women's groups. This phenomenon should be seen as a political *movement*, not just a scattering of factions and parties. In nearly every region, the committees and the various mass organizations worked together; they often had common members, or even common offices. The movement touched nearly every nook and cranny of the peninsula. If the total numbers involved could be known, the movement would no doubt represent a degree of rural political organization and participation unmatched in Korea before or since.

Nearly all of the local committees with known organizational structure had cabinet or departmental structure similar to that of the central CPKI and KPR. Most committees had sections for organization, propaganda (*sŏnjŏn*), peace-keeping (*ch'ian* or *poan*), food provisions, and finances. Depending on the predominant needs of a local region, the committees might also include sections dealing with welfare relief, returning refugees, consumer affairs, labor relations, or, most often, tenant rent. Many local committees were surprisingly adept at raising revenue through voluntary and forced contributions from local Japanese and Korean individuals (usually wealthy ones). Many succeeded in obtaining affidavits from departing Japanese, giving the local committee title to or responsibility for the managing of local Japanese assets, from small homes to major factories. A representative example of county-level committee structure and platform follows:[4]

T'ongyŏng-kun People's Committee, South Kyŏngsang Province

Sin Sang-hun, Chairman
Hwang Tŏk-yun, Vice-Chairman
An Sŭng-gwan, Director, General Affairs
Ko Hak-su, Director, *ch'iandae*
Kim Chae-su, Director, Organization
Hwang Ha-su, Director, Propaganda
Kim Yong-sik, Director, Economics
Pak Yong-gŭn, Director, Transportation
Ch'oe Su-man, Director, Provisions

Platform

All Japanese property should revert to Koreans.

All land and all factories should belong to workers and farmers.

All men and women should have equal rights.

The rest of the platform corresponded to that of the national KPR.

It is harder to determine precisely who accomplished the organizational feat of dotting the peninsula with hundreds of local committees. In chapter three, we noted the major role played by students and released prisoners returning to their native homes. Many of these people were communists who developed a party cell structure in the provinces. But students, demobilized soldiers, local village elite, local landlords, and even former officials under the Japanese also organized committees. They all were part of the organizational explosion occurring in Korea after August 15.

How is such a phenomenon to be understood? How could it all happen so fast? Perhaps the initial phase of organization in the halcyon days following Japan's surrender corresponded to the spontaneous mobilization Eric Hobsbawm noted in the Italian and Spanish villages he studied, where quiescent peasants came overnight to wholehearted participation in politics. Hobsbawm evoked the mood well: "some piece of news would penetrate into the village," such as the news that "a Republic had been proclaimed":

An atmosphere of high exaltation greatly facilitates the spreading of [such] news. It provides teams of men who will spread the joyful tidings wherever they can . . . everyone becomes a propagandist . . . nothing is more contagious than success. By these means a movement can almost simultaneously mobilize masses over a wide area.[5]

Numerous analysts have pointed to the paradoxical phenomenon of plodding sameness, drudgery, and resignation in peasant societies interrupted by periodic outbursts of discontent, taking the form of banditry, *jacqueries*, rebellion, and under certain circumstances, revolution. Korea, like China, had had a long history of peasant rebellion. In the context of millennial release accompanying the end of Japanese rule, it is no surprise that Korea was thrown into a period of intense rural turmoil. But it was not simply the lifting of Japanese bonds that led to peasant radicalism. There seems little question that a sense of injustice and deprivation, particularly regarding land relationships, lay behind the activities of many PCs and *nongmin chohaps*.

The heady atmosphere of August 1945 and the existence of deeply felt peasant grievances help us to understand the rapid extension of the people's committees throughout the Korean peninsula. In county, town, and village, "classical" revolutions occurred, a classical revolution being defined as "taking power from the local officials, policemen and landlords when [peasants] saw the chance of doing so profitably."[6] The last phrase, "saw the chance of doing so profitably," aptly catches the calculation of interests and opposing forces that helped determine whether a PC was organized or not, and if organized, what its nature, strength, and tenure would be. Small-scale revolutions took place, but their natures varied from place to place and from time to time: the rapidity of change varied; the participation of different groups and classes varied. In most localities, entirely new police forces appeared, new committees took over administration, and most Japanese and many Korean landlords found their property threatened. In other places, the old order persisted alongside the new. And in a few places no new order appeared. The one predominant characteristic in all localities where change occurred was the indigenous aspect of the changes; change was not imposed from outside. If General Hodge and his advisors had been more discerning, they might have seen that south Korean peasants, like peasants everywhere, were just as distrustful of non-native "agitators" (including those from north Korea) as were the Americans themselves.

For weeks the CPKI, the KPR, and the PCs represented the first Korean government in nearly half a century. Particularly in the countryside, the PCs stole a march on their inactive Korean opponents that was really never made up. The committees and their affiliates appropriated the field of rural organization in a matter of weeks. Furthermore, their quickly rooted presence meant that later attempts to forge alternative organizations necessitated the prior elimination of the PCs. But even *communicating* the news in the fall of 1945 that the committees were not legitimate, that different groups of Koreans had gained power, that there was no Republic, proved difficult. News of the KPR and the PCs had spread through signal fires on the hills, drums in the mountains, couriers, and word-of-mouth. The method of communication had to be different in the second case. The news of the Republic and the committees had spread like wildfire. But the word that the committees were to be eliminated took months to filter down.

No conservative opponent of the KPR could light a signal fire in the hills and expect the results to be to his liking. In Seoul, how could opponents of the committees be sure that the telephone operator in Taegu was trustworthy? Maybe he was a PC man. What of the boatman in Mokp'o? Or the courier in Kangwŏn? Or, God help the Americans, the local English interpreters? We begin to see how difficult this movement was to overturn and understand how perspicacious General Hodge was in picturing Seoul as sitting atop a yawning abyss or in describing the Occupation as "walking on the edge of a volcano." The general's Midwestern forthrightness caught the situation perfectly. The people's committees had all the advantages that their opponents, particularly those in Seoul, lacked: popular support, knowledge of local conditions, control of popular forms of communication, programs to appeal to grievances, and—perhaps most important—the advantage of having been first. Moreover, the local committees in 1945 were not hampered by knowledge of what we know now, that their attempts at self-government would come to naught.

Nearly all existing literature on the politics of the liberation era mentions the presence of the people's committees, but nowhere can we find an attempt to portray the extent of the movement. Information on the committees is scarce in available Korean language materials. It is strange to find such scant information in communist and leftist sources on a movement that many have characterized as "communist"; the suggestion is that they themselves did not know the breadth of the movement. Leftists at the time (and since in North Korea) lauded the PCs as the true governing organs of the people, but rarely tried to define their extent or their location. Yi Kang-guk, the prominent leader in the KPR and its successor, the DNF, said that by December 1945 there were 13 province-level PCs, 31 city PCs, 220 county PCs, and 2,282 township PCs. This is an exaggerated total; Yi did little more than tote up the number of administrative units at each level.[7] The *Chosŏn inmin-bo* stated that the committees controlled all of the counties in South Chŏlla Province, 15 of 22 counties in South Kyŏngsang Province, "most" of the counties in North Kyŏngsang and South Ch'ungch'ŏng, and "part" of the provinces of North Ch'ungch'ŏng and Kangwŏn.[8] That estimate does not include all the provinces of southern Korea, but it is closer to the truth.

Figure 5[9] shows the locations of PCs which assumed governmental functions. This map, and the others in this and the succeeding chapter,

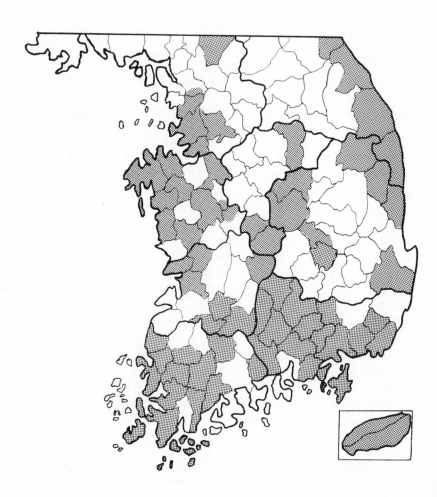

5. Known Assumption of Governmental Functions by People's Committees (indicated by shaded area)

are based on American information—specifically MG company operations reports, G-2 information, Counter-Intelligence Corps studies, and reports of the MG Department of Public Opinion.[10] If anything, the maps underestimate the extent of the committees, since a committee often did not come to the attention of the the Americans unless it posed a problem. If a PC voluntarily disbanded or reorganized itself as a political party upon the arrival of American forces, as some did, it would not appear on these maps. Further inaccuracies enter into the calculation with the use of American information, particularly that taken from MG company operations reports, because some Americans were less responsible than others in detailing the political situation in the localities they controlled. Certainly some MG companies doctored their reports to give superiors in Seoul an image of smooth functioning; others described the situation in their locality on a weekly basis, warts and all. Some of the operations reports talked of little but local politics. So there remain discrepancies in information. We should not surmise, however, that the Americans in the provinces lacked information or ignored the political situation and therefore discount their reports entirely. They had access to local police information, and the local police, in turn, were not uninterested in providing data on the PCs. The MG files still hold several police reports on the PCs in the original Korean.

Figure 5 indicates that roughly one-half of all south Korean counties were at one time governed by PCs. The committees, governing and nongoverning, very nearly spread into all of southern Korea at one time or another. The provinces, in order of PC strength, are: (1) South Kyŏngsang, (2) South Chŏlla/North Kyŏngsang, (3) North Chŏlla/South Ch'ungch'ŏng/Kyŏnggi, (4) Kangwŏn, and (5) North Ch'ungch'ŏng. In figure 5, North Kyŏngsang does not appear to have been a strong PC province, but it was, as we shall later see. Cheju Island, which was part of South Chŏlla Province until 1946 when it was given provincial status, represents a special case; PCs dominated the island throughout the three-year tenure of the American Military Government.

"Assumption of governmental functions" in figure 5 means that some report or record indicates PC control of a county government. Although there were great variations in the degree of control from county to county (some PCs controlled outlying townships [*myŏn*], or rice collections, or schools, but not the county government), those counties in figure 5 identified as having assumed governmental functions actually controlled the county government for some period of time. In counties where the PCs did not govern, it is difficult to know whether the committee simply represented a few individuals in a political faction or whether it had a degree of control just short of operating the county administration. As will be seen in chapter nine, the latter was true of several nongoverning PCs, especially in North Kyŏngsang. The following sections of this chapter will discuss some of the broad factors relating to the strength or weakness of the local PCs.

A problem this study faces is that there exists no index of committee strength, or of political participation in general, that can be easily reduced to mathematical terms and correlated with other variables such as population change, conditions of land tenancy, and so on. In most studies, the political index used is something like rates of voter participation in elections. But here we have to make do with indications that are considerably less quantifiable, recognizing that any relationships must of necessity be approximate. Our concern is with radical activity at the provincial and county level, as evidenced by the following: (1) information that a PC governed a county for a certain period of time; (2) the prior existence of radical activity in the 1930s, meaning in all cases the presence of Red Peasant Unions; and (3) reported rebellions during the period 1945-1946, which involved either resistance to American-imposed arrangements, or open and widespread rebellion during the autumn uprisings in 1946. I have developed a ranking system on a scale of one to twenty that gives counties a value of three for the prior existence of an RPU, six for a governing PC, eight for indications of rebellion, and ten for counties judged to be particularly rebellious. A county with a nongoverning PC, no RPU, and no rebellion would get a value of two. Cheju Island, a special case having an RPU, a PC that governed for three years, and a major insurgency beginning in 1948, was subjectively given the highest value of twenty. A county with an RPU, a governing PC, and high rebellion would get a value of nineteen, and so on down the scale (see Appendix D). The scaling is arbitrary and subjective in part, of course, but as the evidence was digested, it seemed to provide an appropriate means of ranking counties according to radical tendencies and of providing a value that could then be compared with various environmental factors.[11]

POPULATION CHANGE

As we saw in chapter two, pronounced population growth in and uprooting of peasant societies were central factors in loosing the peasants from their ties to tradition and "making them available" for social and political mobilization. The Korean peasants who were sent from their native homes to Japan, Manchuria, and northern Korea, from agrarian to industrial circumstances, returned to Korea no longer peasants and yet not quite workers. We have seen that, taking the nation as a whole, such extensive population shifts were probably responsible for stimulating political consciousness in Koreans of the liberation period. In this section, we will be concerned with provinces and counties as units of analysis.

The significant interprovincial migration caused by Japanese industrialization in northern Korea had its prime political impact in south Korean provinces, because after the liberation, most industrial workers in north Korea who were natives of the south returned home. The development of a working class in the latter years of Japanese rule was partly artificial, since many Koreans became workers against their will, either through actual conscription or through loss of land and status degradation. This artificiality meant that in 1945 Korea had an inflated or spurious working class. Many of the members did not wish to be wage laborers; after the liberation, they returned to their homes hoping to reclaim lost status, and no doubt bearing deep grievances. The same was true of the many Korean workers in Japan who, as we saw earlier, returned by the hundreds of thousands to Korea in the months before and after liberation.

Figures 2 and 3 in chapter two indicated that North and South Kyŏngsang provinces had extremely high population losses to north Korea in the last fifteen years of Japanese rule. Migrants from Korea to Japan also tended to come from the Kyŏngsangs; although figures on the birthplaces of these migrants are not available, the 1930 and 1940 county census figures clearly show this pattern. Of forty-one counties in both Kyŏngsangs, only fifteen gained population in absolute terms during the decade, and most of those were marginal gains, or gains of less than 1 percent. Only the urbanized counties like Tongnae (the city of Pusan was in Tongnae County) had high gains. This may be compared to South Ch'ungch'ŏng, where all counties gained population, or Kyŏnggi, where eighteen of twenty-one showed gains. If the likely natural increase of population during the years from 1930 to 1940 is taken into consideration, the losses in Kyŏngsang counties appear staggering. After liberation, much of the dispersed population returned, including a flood from Japan, where Koreans had been influenced by leftist ideology and the harsh discrimination against Koreans in Japan.[12]

How did such population change influence radical activity in the provinces? At the provincial level, the relationship is clear. The two most rebellious provinces, North and South Kyŏngsang, also ranked first and second in degree of population loss between 1930 and 1940 and degree of population gain between 1944 and 1946 (table 11).[13]

TABLE 11

SOUTH KOREAN POPULATION INCREASE BY PROVINCE, 1944 TO 1946

Province	1944	1946	Percent Increase
Kyŏnggi*	2,264,336	2,486,369	9.0%
Seoul city	826,118	1,141,766	38.2
N. Ch'ungch'ŏng	970,623	1,112,894	14.7
S. Ch'ungch'ŏng	1.647,044	1,909,405	15.9
N. Chŏlla	1,639,213	2,016,423	23.0
S. Chŏlla	2,486,188	2,944,842	18.4
N. Kyŏngsang	2,561,251	3,178,750	24.1
S. Kyŏngsang	2,318,146	3,185,832	37.4
Kangwŏn*	946,643	1,116,836	18.0
Cheju Island	219,548	276,143	25.8

SOURCE: USAMGIK, *Population of Korea*, p. 2.
* Includes only portion of province south of thirty-eighth parallel

Cheju Island, another center of rebellion, also suffered heavy losses in the 1930s and experienced a sharp gain of nearly 26 percent from 1944 to 1946. In provinces that grew by more than 20 percent between 1944 and 1946, North Chŏlla is the only one not to show significant radical activity. People's committees were strong there initially, but could not sustain their strength.

At the county level, the relationship is more complex. Population changes at first seem to explain nothing about radical counties in Kangwŏn, South Ch'ungch'ŏng, and South Chŏlla; large influxes in these counties show no relationship, or only a slight one, to radical activity. This can be explained, however, by the fact that counties that were remote or had mostly dry-field rather than paddy agriculture did not experience the *pattern* of population change depicted above. The mobilized Koreans came mostly from rice-paddy counties with surplus population. The pattern we are looking for should appear in those counties having 50 percent or more of the arable land in paddies and in provinces showing population loss during the 1930s. This would eliminate Kangwŏn, South Ch'ungch'ŏng, and South Chŏlla provinces. Within the remaining provinces, we would expect to find radical counties showing a loss or slight gain in absolute population from 1930 to 1940 and a significant influx from 1944 to 1946. If the lost population had dribbled back before liberation, it would presumably have had less of an impact.

Table 12 depicts the relationship between radicalism at the county level and a population pattern showing a loss or a gain of less than 3 percent between 1930 and 1940; a gain of more than 15 percent

TABLE 12

Population Change, Tenancy, and Radicalism

Estimate of Radicalism	Number	Percent of Total	Average Radical Value	Average Rate of Tenancy
I. Counties That Fit Population Pattern* (N = 41)				
High (range 11-20)	20	48.8%	16.5	61.2
Medium (range 6-10)	13	31.7	8.0	64.3
Low (range 0-5)	8	19.5	2.6	73.3
Total	41	100	11.1	64.5
II. Counties That Do Not Fit Population Pattern* (N = 89)				
High (range 11-20)	18	20.2%	15	64.8
Medium (range 6-10)	29	32.6	6.8	70.2
Low (range 0-5)	42	47.2	2.4	70.8
Total	89	100	6.3	69.4
III. Counties That Do Not Fit Population Pattern*, With 8 Anomalies† Disregarded (N = 81)				
High (range 11-20)	11	13.6%	13.1	68.1
Medium (range 6-10)	28	34.5	6.7	70.8
Low (range 0-5)	42	51.9	2.4	70.8
Total	81	100	5.3	70.4
IV. All Counties, Regardless of Population Pattern (N = 130)				
High (range 11-20)	38	29.2	15.8	62.8
Medium (range 6-10)	42	32.3	7.2	68.4
Low (range 0-5)	50	38.5	2.4	71.2
Total	130	100	7.8	67.9

Source: All information taken from Appendix D.

* Counties losing population or gaining at less than 3%, 1930-1940; gaining 15% or more, 1944-1946; 1944-1946 gain is at least 50% of total gain, 1930-1946; paddy area in county is at least 50% or more. Koyang and Tongnae not included because presence of Pusan and Seoul skews figures.

† Andong, Ch'ŏngsŏng, Hwasun, and Kwangsan because they are close to the above population pattern; and Kangnŭng, Samch'ŏk, Ponghwa, and Uljin because they are on the east coast and have unique population patterns.

between 1944 and 1946; and a gain between 1944 and 1946 that was more than 50 percent of the total county population gain from 1930 to 1946. Only counties having 50 percent or more of the arable land in paddy were included, since dry-field counties were less subject to the population shifts that we are interested in. Among all counties showing this pattern (N=41), the average radical value (drawn from Appendix D) is 11.1; among counties not showing this pattern, the average radical value is only 6.3. When counties are grouped according to high, medium, and low radical values, the relationships are even clearer between population and radicalism. Part III of table 12 shows that, once eight anomalous counties are thrown out, only eleven radical counties, having an average radical value of 13.6, are unaccounted for by our population pattern.

Here we are concerned with the relationship between population change and radical activity at the aggregate level. No one can tell without having been on the scene in numerous counties in 1945, just how individual Koreans returning to native provinces and counties reacted to the emergence of the people's committees. But at a broad level, population change seems to have been an important variable.

TRANSPORTATION AND COMMUNICATIONS ECOLOGY

We noted in chapter one that in 1945 Korea possessed a transportation and communications infrastructure second only to Japan among Asian countries. With the accompanying industrialization of the peninsula, Korea came to be poised between modernity and backwardness, with its internal facilities developed to a point quite beyond its own requirements, developed rather to serve Japanese interests. For radical activity in times of political unrest, such facilities can cut two ways. In the hands of insurgents, they make possible rapid communication; but in the hands of the forces of order, they can be potent retardants. Thus, we find the paradox in liberated south Korea of PCs being strong in both the most advanced and most backward regions.[14] But as the national police and other agencies of order regained control of this infrastructure, they put it to effective use. This was an indispensable element in their successful pacification of Korea and was among the prime reasons why, in the years from 1945 to 1950, southern Korea developed a rooted insurgency only in certain relatively isolated regions.

Available statistics are unsatisfactory indicators of levels of modernization in liberated Korea, particularly when the unit of analysis is the province or county. Statistical tables do not indicate the conditions of roads and highways, for example. But we do know that Kyŏnggi, the Kyŏngsangs, and North Chŏlla all had several important railroad junctions and relative ease of access to significant percentages of the province area by railroad. The Ch'ungch'ŏng provinces and Kangwŏn Province were less accessible, with no line running over the mountains from mid-peninsula and the eastern coastal line, meant to run from Wŏnsan in north Korea down to Pusan, incomplete and thus useless in 1945. And Cheju Island had no rail lines. PCs governed in regions with and without railroads; but it is fair to say that those regions in close proximity to railroads were easier to subdue, except for those along the rail line running west from Pusan to Chinju. Where there were no rail lines to bring police down from Seoul, such as Cheju, the coast of Kangwŏn, and the inner mountainous counties, the committees were harder to overturn.

North Chŏlla had more than twice as many road kilometers per square *ri* than did Kankwŏn. Kyŏnggi and South Kyŏngsang, representing the most industrialized provinces of south Korea, ranked slightly below North Chŏlla. Of course, no precise correlations with PC strength are possible here; but in broad terms, we note that the committees in North Chŏlla, a province well-laced with roads and railroads, were easily deposed, while those in Kangwŏn, a province of opposite characteristics, had good staying power.

TABLE 13

COMPOSITE RANKING OF PROVINCES ON INDICES OF MODERNIZATION AND
POPULATION DISLOCATIONS

Province	Road Kilometers Per Square *Ri**	Literacy†	Urban Growth‡	Industrial Work Force§	Population Increase‖	Unemployment#
. Kyŏngsang	2	1	1	2	1	1
J. Kyŏngsang	7	4	4	3	3	2
Kyŏnggi	2	2	7	1	9	6
. Chŏlla	4	9	2	4	5	4
J. Chŏlla	1	7	5	5	4	7
Cheju		8		9	2	3
. Ch'ungch'ŏng	5	6	3	6	7	8
N. Ch'ungch'ŏng	6	5	8	8	8	5
Kangwŏn	8	3	6	7	6	9

SOURCES: *Chosŏn kyŏngje nyŏnbo, 1948*, pp. I-12, I-203 (†, #); *Chosŏn t'onggye nyŏngam, 1943*, 52 (*); SKIG, *Industrial Labor Force and Wage Survey*, p. 19 (§); USAMGIK, raw census data, IV Corps Historical File (‡, ‖).

1943
Knowledge of pure Korean, 1947
1944 to 1946
Percentage of total industrial work force in each province, 1944
‖ 1944 to 1946
November 1946

Table 13 combines the above indices with other indices of modernization to show the most advanced and least advanced provinces. The table is necessarily but an approximation of reality, concerned as it is with modernization at the aggregate level. We do find the Kyŏngsang provinces again at the top of the listing, however, and the Ch'ungch'ŏngs and Kangwŏn at the bottom. We will also find in chapter nine that committee strength in the latter three provinces derived primarily from geographical remoteness, which in Korea implied general backwardness. Without belaboring the point, we can conclude by saying that modernization was, at the least, not detrimental to PC growth, but it may have been harmful to PC staying power; whereas general backwardness did not foster PC growth particularly, but once radicalism got started (for example, in the four coastal counties of Kangwŏn), backwardness made overturning the PCs more difficult.

LAND RELATIONSHIPS

We might expect that the growth of organizations acting in the name of the poor and downtrodden, such as the PCs and *nongmin chohap*, would develop in regions of marked poverty rather than in ones of comparative wealth. Few nations in 1945 could surpass Korea in inequitable land relationships. Certainly the deep grievances resulting from such conditions fueled the committees, made their appeals believable, and made committee and peasant union attacks on the rent system, rice collection practices, and landlordism appealing to peasants. The land question dominated political discourse in liberated Korea and was a prime factor in distributing groups and classes at the poles of the political spectrum, rather than along a continuum.

But it was not land relationships alone that were the cause of peasant radicalism. The objectively wretched living conditions of subservient tenants are often more easily perceived by intellectuals and radicals than by the peasants themselves. This is not to say that peasants do not feel exploited or that they do not have grievances, but that in ordinary times, they tend to express their grievances in ways that will not threaten their tenuous existence as tenants or marginal smallholders. In ordinary times, peasants are hamstrung by crosscutting ties and cleavages and by tradition. As suggested in chapter two, peasants only act as a class in the analytical sense—in other words, as a force for social change—when they become aware of their collective interests and perceive the chance for change. Moreover, we cannot talk of "the peasant" without breaking that down into several classes according to whether he owns his own land, works another's land as a tenant, works for wages, and so on.

There were significant differences in land conditions from province to province in 1945. Tables 14 and 15, drawn from different time periods and different sources, demonstrate the high rate of tenancy throughout Korea. But table 14 shows that only one north Korean province, Hwanghae, had a percentage in the pure tenant category higher than the average rate for all Korea. It is impossible to discount

TABLE 14

LANDOWNERSHIP BY PROVINCE, 1943

Province	Owner-Cultivators*	Part-Owners†	Tenants‡	Other§
Kyŏnggi	6.8%	11.8%	80.8%	1.3%
N. Ch'ungch'ŏng	11.6	15.0	72.0	1.4
S. Ch'ungch'ŏng	8.3	13.7	75.9	2.1
N. Chŏlla	5.1	10.1	81.1	3.6
S. Chŏlla	18.6	25.9	63.2	1.9
N. Kyŏngsang	20.4	19.4	59.9	0.4
S. Kyŏngsang	15.9	19.4	62.5	2.1
Kangwŏn	22.1	19.8	56.8	1.2
Hwanghae	16.2	12.1	71.4	0.4
N. P'yŏng'an	23.3	12.9	63.5	0.3
S. P'yŏng'an	24.0	17.0	58.3	0.8
N. Hamgyŏng	47.4	21.3	30.9	0.4
S. Hamgyŏng	32.7	21.6	43.7	2.0
All Korea	17.6	15.9	65.0	1.4

SOURCE: *Chosŏn t'onggye nyŏn'gam, 1943,* pp. 42-43.
* Those who own more than 90% of land worked; landlords excluded from figures
† Those who own 50-90% of land worked
‡ Full tenants and those who own 10-50% of land worked
§ Mostly hired farm laborers

TABLE 15

LANDOWNERSHIP BY PROVINCE, SOUTH KOREA, DECEMBER 1945

Province	Owner-Cultivators*	Part-Owners†	Part-Tenants‡	Tenants§
Kyŏnggi‖	7.3%	11.2%	14.5%	65.5%
N. Ch'ungch'ŏng	12.5	17.1	18.8	54.3
S. Ch'ungch'ŏng	8.2	13.9	17.9	58.2
N. Chŏlla	5.1	10.2	15.3	64.1
S. Chŏlla#	19.6	17.0	18.2	41.5
N. Kyŏngsang	18.3	21.8	22.4	35.2
S. Kyŏngsang	14.7	19.2	20.3	43.6
Kangwŏn‖	23.9	20.4	18.7	36.5
All south Korea	14.2	16.8	18.8	50.2

SOURCE: USAMGIK, Department of Agriculture, raw data, **XXIV** Corps Historical File.
* Those who own more than 90% of land worked; landlords excluded
† Those who own 50-90% of land worked
‡ Those who own 10-50% of land worked
§ Those who own less than 10% of land worked
‖ Area south of thirty-eighth parallel only
Includes Cheju Island

the role of Soviet and north Korean organization in the growth of the committees there, of course; but if north Korean provinces were higher rather than so much lower in rates of tenancy than south Korean provinces, the poverty thesis might hold up better in explaining the thoroughgoing social revolution that occurred in north Korea after August 15. This revolution, which had as its first major act a sweeping land reform, took place in regions where tenancy was much less of a problem that it was in most south Korean provinces.

North Chŏlla Province in south Korea had the highest rates of tenancy, exorbitant rents, and the highest concentration of landlords. The most productive rice bowl in Korea, it escaped the attention neither of the government, interested in revenue, nor of Japanese settlers, interested in profits. Fully 5.7 percent of the land area in North Chŏlla was owned or controlled by Japanese settlers, a figure twice as high as that for South Chŏlla, and six times higher than that for any other southern province.[15] Japanese and Korean landlords taxed tenants in North Chŏlla at the highest rates in Korea.[16] Kyŏnggi Province had the next highest rates of tenancy, although tenants and smallholders there tended to work larger plots of land than in North Chŏlla.[17] South Chŏlla, the Ch'ungch'ŏng provinces, and South Kyŏngsang all had conditions of landlordism and tenancy that distinguished them only in degree rather than in kind from North Chŏlla. Only Kangwŏn, North Kyŏngsang, and Cheju Island had significantly greater percentages of small freeholding peasant proprietors. Still, the rate of tenancy in Kangwŏn and North Kyŏngsang approached 60 percent.

Table 16 gives an approximate ranking of south Korean provinces along various indices of rural poverty. North Chŏlla and Kyŏnggi, which had the highest degrees of poverty, did not have strong people's committees, and those that existed were easily undone. This hardly suggests that provinces with higher degrees of rural exploitation had stronger committees. In fact, something like the opposite is closer to the mark. But is Samuel Huntington then correct in saying that poor people are too poor for politics? Is Edward Mitchell correct in saying that "there exists in the areas of unequal distribution a powerful landlord class exercising firm control over a conservative peasantry which has thoroughly rationalized the inevitability of the existing situation"?[18] Such judgments are far too simple.[19] Peasants in such circumstances cannot be labeled "conservative" or "radical"; we cannot know what their attitudes are apart from evidence of resistance. Acquiescence to landlord power demonstrates nothing more than acquiescence. It says nothing about the appeal of radical programs to peasants; it says nothing about whether the peasants view existing arrangements as legitimate or not. What *can* be said is that landlord authority in re-

TABLE 16

COMPOSITE RANKING OF PROVINCES ON INDICES OF RURAL POVERTY

Province	Tenants as Percentage of Farm Population*	Peasants Farming 1 Chŏngbo or Less†	High Rent	Landlords Owning 10 Chŏngbo or More‡
1. N. Chŏlla	1	1	2	1
2. Kyŏnggi	2	6	1	2
3. S. Ch'ungch'ŏng	3	2	8	3
4. N. Ch'ungch'ŏng	4	3	7	4
5. S. Kyŏngsang	5	4	4	6
6. S. Chŏlla	6	5	6	5
7. N. Kyŏngsang	7	7	3	8
8. Kangwŏn	8	8	5	7

SOURCES: *Chosŏn kyŏngje nyŏnbo, 1948,* pp. I-30-31; *Chosŏn t'onggye nyŏn'gam, 1943,* pp. 42-43; Lee, *Land Utilization,* p. 164; USAMGIK, Department of Agriculture, raw data, XXIV Corps Historical File.

* Full tenants and those owning less than 50% of land worked
† As a percentage of total farming population in province; one *chŏngbo* barely sustains a peasant household on an annual basis.
‡ As a percentage of total landlord population in province

gions of very high tenancy can constitute a simple but formidable structure of restraint, especially when buttressed by mobile national policing apparatuses. *Access* to the peasantry is much more difficult in polarized settings where the people cluster at the extremes of outright tenancy or extensive landlordism. In agrarian settings that are more differentiated—that have more "middle" peasants, for example—organizers and reform programs have a better chance of success. It seems, therefore, that this question of access, which is also a question of political power, is part of the reason why agrarian radicalism is more likely to appear in the less exploited regions.

In the Korean case, North Chŏlla and Kyŏnggi were also core areas of high land values, high productivity, and a profitable rice export trade through the ports of Inch'ŏn and Kunsan, and were the bases of the landlord-entrepreneurs. It would therefore seem that these factors, along with the strong structure of governmental and landlord control, counteracted the effects of returning population in North Chŏlla after 1945. It is also true, of course, that North Chŏlla counties, while generally high in rates of population return, did not approach the levels of the Kyŏngsang provinces. And Kyŏnggi had most of its population gains in the 1930s; it did not have a big influx after 1945.

The relationship between radicalism and rates of tenancy, therefore, is that radicalism is weak at the upper extremes, that is, the counties having the highest rates of tenancy. Table 12 illustrates this pattern, using tenancy rates, known or estimated, for 130 counties in southern Korea, and comparing those rates with radicalism. Part IV of table 12 demonstrates that radicalism is inversely related to tenancy; Part I shows that counties of high radicalism, subject to population shifting, have an average of twelve percent less tenancy than counties of low radicalism with the same population pattern. In regions of high tenancy and high land values the landed class is stronger, differentiates more quickly, is more adaptable and therefore is more able to deflect dissent.[20] In the regions of middling tenancy, the higher numbers of middle peasants and owner-cultivators, and the correspondingly lessened dominance of landlords, provide more space for either collective action or individual, family-oriented upward mobility. Middle peasants may either ally with poorer ones, or seek their fortunes in accumulating more land or wealth, hoping to become rich cultivators or landlords. This is what makes such peasants more dynamic, more yeasty in terms of economic and social change, and more responsive to peasant political movements; it is what makes the fate of the middle peasantry critical to the course of peasant revolutions.[21] The Korean situation also suggests that a peripheral peasantry with middling tenancy—counties along the upper east coast and Cheju Island —also possesses more freedom of action or space for political activity, since landlords are either absent, or have less formidable means of control.

GEOGRAPHICAL LOCATION

The geographical location of various people's committees is a very important factor to consider in assessing their strength. Proximity to major transportation and communication centers did not hinder the development of the PCs, as noted above, but it did hurt their staying power. Geographical remoteness, on the other hand, enhanced staying power. If we look again at figure 5, we note that in the generally inaccessible coastal counties in Kangwŏn and North Kyŏngsang PCs governed in all but one county. In the inner counties of central south Korea, like Mun'gyŏng and Yŏngdong, extending down toward the Sŏbaek range and Chiri Mountain, there was a cluster of strong PCs. And in the remote island counties of South Chŏlla and in the relatively remote northwestern counties of South Ch'ungch'ŏng, strong PCs developed. But Cheju Island presents the best example of the virtues of remoteness, for here, outside the interest and attention of the Americans, PCs flourished as nowhere else.

LENGTH OF INTERREGNUM

The length of the hiatus between Japanese and American rule was determined in part by geographical location and in part by American personnel requirements. In general, the more remote counties and provinces were the last ones occupied, which naturally made the tenure of the committees there longer. Certain provinces were also neglected, however, because of personnel inadequacies or shifts. Thus the length of the interregnum was greatest in the Chŏllas and Cheju Island and in the other aforementioned geographically remote counties. In certain counties, no interregnum ever occurred, as American teams simply came in and accepted the Japanese apparatus. In general, the longer the interregnum was, the stronger the PC would be. Time for entrenchment was crucial to establishing a strong committee. Time allowed organizers to change committee power into a process of revolution, as discussed in chapter two. New organizations and leaders had to have the time within which to do something for constituents and followers, to mobilize, educate, and provide various incentives for participation in the new order.

POLITICAL ANTECEDENTS AND INDICATORS

Numerous antecedents to the political movements of the liberation period could be sought in Korean history. Beginning with the *Tonghak* Rebellion of the late nineteenth century, we could do an analysis of the regions in Korea where the *Tonghak*, the *Ŭibyŏng* [Righteous Army] of 1907-1910, the March First Independence Movement of 1919 and other similar movements found their strength. But that task must await future research. There is a striking correspondence between counties showing strong contingents of the most immediate antecedents to the movements of the liberation period, the Red Peasant Unions (*Chŏksaek nongmin chohap*—RPU) of the 1930s, however, and those governed by PCs after liberation (see figure 6).[22] Of thirty-seven south Korean counties with reported RPUs, twenty-five had governing PCs in 1945/46. Only one county with an RPU had no reported PC; that is Namhae in South Kyŏngsang, a county about which no political information is available right after liberation, but which spawned a rebellion in 1946. In some cases, members of the RPUs reappeared in the PCs and *nongmin chohap* that emerged after August 15. Certainly this is an area that could bear further inquiry. This also suggests that the PCs and peasant unions did not simply materialize out of thin air.

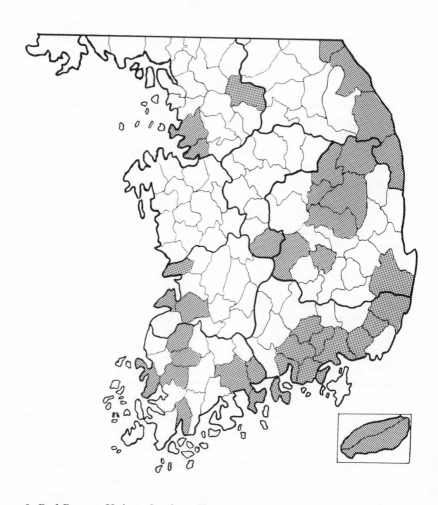

6. Red Peasant Unions, Southern Korea, 1930 to 1940
   (indicated by shaded area)
   SOURCE: Based on research presented in Yoo, "Korean Communist Movement
   and the Peasantry," pp. 129-130 (with permission).

Committee strength or weakness at the province level also bears some relationship to the provincial distribution of *nongmin chohap*. Table 17 gives official figures on the provincial strength of peasant unions in mid-1946 from the headquarters of *Chŏnnong*. It shows that, as one would expect, *nongmin chohap* strength paralleled PC strength in south Korea. South Kyŏngsang and South Chŏlla rank at the top

TABLE 17

CLAIMED PROVINCIAL STRENGTH OF PEASANT UNIONS, MID-1946

Province	City, County, Island Branches	*Myŏn* Branches	*Ri* Affiliates	Members
S. Chŏlla	14	110	3,019	369,414
N. Chŏlla	12	103	2,075	301,645
S. Kyŏngsang	15	182	1,877	459,759
N. Kyŏngsang	17	127	2,598	275,913
S. Ch'ungch'ŏng	12	97	1,890	212,563
N. Ch'ungch'ŏng	6	57	1,750	116,978
Kyŏnggi	15	134	3,329	193,549
Kangwŏn	21	176	1,857	175,852
Hwanghae	17	227	981	204,277
S. P'yŏng'an	14	140	1,640	173,545
N. P'yŏng'an	19	178	1,600	179,424
S. Hamgyŏng	15	135	1,979	450,746
N. Hamgyŏng	11	76	783	199,532

SOURCE: *Chosŏn haebang illyŏn-sa*, p. 167.

in terms of peasant union strength in mid-1946. *Chŏnnong* probably exaggerated the actual strength of these unions, yet North Ch'ungch'-ŏng appears with only 6 of 10 counties having unions, and with the fewest members of any province. Unfortunately, almost no information is available that would allow us to pinpoint provinces and counties where peasant unions were strong or weak, as we have done with the PCs. It has been indicated elsewhere, however, that leftist organizations in south Korea pictured their own strength with somewhat more fealty to reality than did rightist organizations.

AMERICAN OCCUPATION OF THE PROVINCES

The final factor we must consider before making a province-by-province analysis of the fate of the committees is the American occupation of the provinces. The Occupation may be divided into three phases. The first was a brief period in which observation teams of American officers arrived at key points such as Pusan (September 16) to show the flag and observe the situation. The second phase was a longer one of occupation by tactical troops. It lasted in some places until December 1945 (see figure 7). The final phase consisted of occupation by civil affairs teams (Military Government companies) with training and preparation specifically geared to running a full military government. Most of these teams were in place in the provinces by the end of 1945.

In the early weeks after the initial American entry on September 8, occupation of the provinces had the highest priority. General Hodge was most anxious to spread his troops throughout south Korea as rapidly as possible. Initially, he hoped to land the 40th Division, responsible for tactical occupation of the Kyŏngsang provinces, at Pusan to save time.[23] This could not be done, however, and the 40th arrived in Inch'ŏn on September 22 and went by rail to Pusan, arriving within a couple of days.[24]

The haste in occupying the provinces was caused by the same considerations that dictated the initial American "scramble" into Korea. Japanese officials remaining in the provinces, like those in Seoul, were most anxious to see American faces and sent numerous reports to Hodge in the early weeks of the Occupation expressing their fear of Koreans and grossly overestimating the degree of disorder.[25] The Japanese, their Korean charges, and conservative Koreans had a common interest in urging a rapid American assumption of power and in painting Korean activities directed against the old colonial order as communist-inspired. General Hodge, finding the remaining Japanese more palatable than presumed Korean communists, thus directed the Japanese Army to guard railroads, utilities, supplies, and jails pending the arrival in the provinces of American units.[26] Initial American observation teams dispatched to Pusan and other key points utilized Japanese Army detachments to preserve order; this resulted in a number of incidents in which combined American and Japanese units broke up Korean demonstrations of one sort or another. The official history of the Occupation commented, somewhat defensively: "To the obvious question of whom these installations [and cities] were being guarded against, the equally obvious answer was that they were being guarded against lawless elements among the Koreans."[27]

The mission of the tactical occupation forces was primarily to maintain law and order and if necessary to effect minor changes in local affairs.[28] The presence of tactical units was to be symbolic; they were not to implement direct military government. Responsibility for local policy was in the hands of the respective division commanders, which resulted in certain policy variations from province to province. Units of the 40th Division were in place in the Kyŏngsangs by the first week in October. The 96th Division was to have arrived at nearly the same time to occupy the southwestern provinces, but it was diverted to

7. Tactical Occupation of Southern Korea, Fall 1945

China "in view of the delicate situation in the Tientsin Area."[29] This "delicate situation" was of course the developing civil war in China; but what the decision-makers behind this transfer did not know was that a similarly delicate situation existed in the Chŏlla provinces of Korea. For the 96th, it meant a move from the frying pan into the fire.

This transfer enraged General Hodge; on September 21 he radioed MacArthur in Tokyo that Korea required "a strong armed force . . . particularly in view of [the] presence of agitators throughout the nation." Thus on September 23 MacArthur's headquarters substituted the 6th Division for the mobile 96th. This was not a happy switch, however. The 6th Division had seen 219 days of continuous combat on Luzon in 1945, a record for the southwest Pacific.[30] But Hodge wanted these men, exhausted or not. On September 30 he again asked MacArthur to move the 6th Division in quickly, saying, "southwest Korea is becoming a hotspot requiring early full control."[31] Units of the 6th began arriving at Inch'ŏn in mid-October, and its teams were in place in the Chŏllas by the end of the month. Tactical occupation was completed on November 10 when the 20th Infantry of the 6th Division arrived on Cheju Island.[32]

During the period from October to December 1945, these tactical units were relieved at different times and places by incoming military government companies. The MG teams found, to the dismay of some, that in many regions the tactical forces had found in power and sanctioned local people's committees, both for purposes of expediency and because alternative local governments were unavailable at the time. The tactical phase of occupation thus assumes considerable importance in our understanding of the tenure of the committees. Policy differences from region to region gave varying opportunities for PC entrenchment. Such policy differences were not resolved until MG companies were in place and a full military government had begun on January 14, 1946.

Chapter Nine

THE FATE OF THE COMMITTEES
IN THE PROVINCES

> To maintain and transmit a value system, human beings are
> punched, bullied, sent to jail, thrown into concentration camps,
> cajoled, bribed, made into heroes, encouraged to read news-
> papers, stood up against a wall and shot, and sometimes even
> taught sociology.
>
> _Barrington Moore, Jr._

F OR the next two chapters, we will consider the very anatomy of
American intervention in Korea, the countless incidents in which
the postwar order was defined for the Korean people—defined with
the appointment of a police chief or a county magistrate, with the
arrival of American tactical troops, with a blow on the head. The
fundamental cause of the eventual demise of the people's committees
was American power (or American-sanctioned Korean power) directed against them. The environmental conditions in which various
committees existed made overturning them easier in some places,
harder in others; but always there came a time when, through a menu
of methods, the PCs came to an end. Some ended just as they began.
Others ended with the first arrivals of American tactical troops in the
fall of 1945. Most managed to persist into early 1946, particularly if
tactical troops had tolerated their activities for a time. Some committees became so solidly entrenched that they were not eliminated until
the fall of 1946. In a few isolated regions of south Korea, the PCs and
their affiliated groups were influential throughout the three-year tenure of the MG. Indeed, in some remote towns of south Korea, wizened
old village leaders may still exist who emerged with the local committees in August 1945, no doubt with a wistful eye cast back on their
youth and that of their "new" country in 1945, when all things
seemed possible.

General Hodge and his advisors tended to see the committees, and
the KPR in Seoul, as inspired by communists and allied with the Russians in the north. The presence of communists and leftists in the
People's Republic, and the PR's recognition by the Russians, provided
justification enough in the American mind for suppressing the committees throughout the south. But Hodge also saw local control much

as the Japanese Governor-General had, and as Korean kings before the Japanese had—from the center outward, from the vantage point of Seoul. Hodge, as these others before him, saw Seoul without provincial control as an island amid chaos, or a brain without control over the nervous system. Given the traditional self-regulatory nature of the Korean village, it was not a foregone conclusion that stripping off the layers of central controls would loose the floodgates of chaos. Eliminating the machinery of the center might just as well have promoted the local autonomy, egalitarianism, and fraternity for which, at its best, the Korean village stands. But local autonomy and spontaneity, although a traditional ideal in Korea, is an ideal of visionaries,[1] not of those who must extract rice, conscript laborers, provide for the defense of the country, or prevent the development of political movements hostile to the center. The latter concerns informed the desire for centralism so characteristic of those who rule in Seoul. Traditionally, the center had to virtually compete with the periphery for resources and for the requisites of control. It was these concerns, along with a residual anticommunism, that led the Americans to revive the full array of centralism in south Korea; they and their Korean allies saw central control as their prime advantage in the political struggles of the liberation period.

American opposition to the local people's committees was part of the general de facto policy making that we discussed in chapters five and six. Particularly in November and December 1945—when military government teams had established headquarters in the countryside and had begun feeding reports back to Seoul, when the Americans in Seoul began to grasp the extent of the movement in the provinces—occupation planners came to recognize that any development of alternative political forms in the provinces would be possible only after elimination of the people's committees. We find the kernel of this idea in American intelligence reports in December.[2] The basic policy developing out of this recognition was to use the one reliable, centrally controlled organization, the national police, to break up the committees and their affiliates and create a vacuum into which, it was hoped, rightist and conservative organizations could move. American intelligence reports periodically voiced the hope that conservative parties would make inroads on committee strength.[3] Yet conservative leaders, particularly those in the Korean Democratic Party, often did not recognize the importance of a broad base of support. Why organize peasants? Peasants follow leadership like grass bending with the wind. These leaders concentrated their efforts instead on gaining positions of advantage in the bureaucracy and police, knowing much better than the Americans that this would be the key to power if the old arrangements prevailed in Korea. Thus, after the demise of most of the committees, we do not find alternative mass political organizations, but just a mass, and the periphery again at the mercy of the center. That is why we said in chapter eight that the people's committees stole a march on their conservative opponents that was really never made up.

It is interesting to consider this Korean experience in light of Samuel Huntington's thesis that Americans working in developing countries are good at economic development but poor at political development, poor at building viable political organization.[4] In Korea the Americans tried systematically to abolish the already-existing, viable, provincial political organization and then tried to provide conditions in which alternative rural political organization could flourish. But the Americans could not do for conservative Koreans what the Koreans could not do for themselves. Thus the problem was less some inherent inability to develop or stimulate viable organization on the part of the Americans than the parochial decision to support political groups who could not manage this task.

The foregoing analysis should set the stage for a consideration of the fate of the committees in the provinces. We must backtrack a bit, however, to the provincial situation in the fall of 1945 and the entrance of the Americans.

SOUTH CHŎLLA PROVINCE

South Chŏlla in 1945 was a relatively remote province, with no major cities and marked difficulties in communication and transportation. Several of its coastal counties were inaccessible except by relatively primitive road and boat transport systems. Even the counties surrounding the capital, Kwangju, suffered from an "almost complete lack of transportation"; some 420 kilometers of roads linked these counties to Kwangju, but they were in very poor condition.[5] Rates of tenancy in South Chŏlla were high by most standards but relatively low for south Korea; the province ranked sixth on our index of rural poverty (here, and throughout this chapter, refer to tables in chapter eight). Perhaps 60 percent of the peasants here could be classed as full- or part-tenants. South Chŏlla also had the largest percentage of tenants in any province working land operated by the Oriental Development Company (ODC). ODC tenants farmed 46 percent of all rice lands in the province when ODC land and other land worked by ODC tenants was included.[6]

In terms of our analysis in chapter two, we would predict the following to have been true for South Chŏlla: (1) traditional ties between lord and peasant would be eroded by the high degree of ODC ownership; (2) ethnicity would not affect class cleavages as markedly, since peasants dealt more with the Japanese ODC bureaucracy than with Korean landlords; (3) the lack of opportunities for upward mobility on the part of individual peasants or tenants (given the fairly uniform smallholding and the resultant homogenization of the peasantry) would direct their individual interests horizontally, toward solidarity, rather than vertically, toward individual mobility; and (4) the significant commercialization of the region, with considerable rice-export traffic through Mokp'o, combined with one of the few plantation patterns in Korea, as cotton production grew near Mokp'o, would also erode traditional agrarian relationships. We would therefore expect South Chŏlla peasants to have been more rebellious than those of some of the other provinces at the time of liberation.[7]

Population changes were not as great in South Chŏlla as elsewhere, however, so on this important index the province has only a middling character. Only five counties lost population during the 1930s, and the gain after liberation was only about 13 percent on the average.[8] Even in those radical counties like Naju that gained more than 20 percent from 1944 to 1946, the gain was only about half the total gain from 1930 to 1946. And Kurye, a county with a population loss in the 1930s and a gain of 19 percent from 1944 to 1946, was not radical at all. The Mokp'o region was the region most affected by population changes, with the city of Mokp'o gaining by more than 60 percent in the period between 1944 and 1946; this is reflected in its radicalism. But at the county level, population change does not seem to have made much difference in the radical and nonradical leanings of counties—an unsurprising result, since far fewer South Chŏlla peasants were transported out of the province during the 1930s. American reports do not mention serious population strains here, except in the port of Mokp'o. Thus with an erosion of agrarian relations, but without a large influx of returning worker-peasants, we would expect to find in South Chŏlla a pattern of peasant rebellion, undifferentiated and incapable of sustaining itself over time.

A prime factor in the early growth of the PCs in South Chŏlla was the long interregnum between Japanese and American rule. Because of the transfer of the 96th Division to China, tactical occupation forces did not arrive in Kwangju until October 8. The first MG company arrived on October 22. When the Americans arrived, they found that PCs controlled virtually the entire province (see figure 8). Organizers native to South Chŏlla had set up a CPKI branch on August 17 and secured the releases of 1,400 provincial political prisoners on August 18. Soon thereafter, *ch'iandae* units began functioning.[9] In

■ known people's committees
□ known assumption of governmental functions

8. South Chŏlla Province People's Committees

mid-October the Americans found Kwangju controlled by some 300 *ch'iandae* youths and students under the direction of Kim Sŏk, a man released from prison after serving eleven years for "subversive" activities against the Japanese.[10] An all-province "People's Representative's Congress" (*Chŏlla namdo inmin taep'yoja taehoe*) met several times during September and October.[11] Some 147 *ch'iandae* functionaries controlled Mokp'o, and various worker's committees had taken over several factories there.[12] PCs existed in all counties and, according to an American observer, controlled the government "in nearly every county."[13]

The composition of local committees varied greatly. In Posŏng and Yŏnggwang local landlords ran the PC. In Kangjin and Kohŭng the old Korean police and government officials remained in control, while PCs ran the outlying townships.[14] In the counties such as Naju, Hwasun, Posŏng, and Changhŭng that were later the responsibility of the 61st MG Company, elections were held shortly after August 15 to choose PC leaders. These elections proceeded from the bottom or village level on up to the county level. Committees on tenant rent, education, and relief were formed along with the PCs.[15] The 61st Company found later that in the committee elections former officials had generally been excluded on the criterion that anyone who had served the Japanese within the past ten years was ineligible. Yet in certain other counties, "pro-Japanese" dominated the PCs. Some committees included both tenants and wealthy landlords on the same leadership rosters. People whom the Americans labeled communist had "a sizeable membership and have shown considerable vigor in all the counties . . . their membership came [*sic*] chiefly from the poor tenant farmers." In Hwasun, miners from the local mines (third largest in south Korea) dominated the PC.[16] We can begin to see the complexities of the people's committees.

Why were communists not able to dominate all of the county PCs in South Chŏlla? How could traditional village and county leadership survive in a time of agrarian turmoil? How discredited was the old Korean order in 1945? It has been stated earlier that the prime test of political legitimacy in liberated Korea was a leader's perceived role under Japanese colonialism. If an individual was viewed as a collaborator or traitor, or if he had caused hardship for the local community in concert with the Japanese, it would be difficult for him to emerge dominant in organs like the PCs in 1945. The legacy of the systematic attempts to use traditional Korean leadership in pursuit of Japanese goals was the irreparable tearing of the fabric of consensus surrounding traditional authority. However, if local village elders, for example, had managed to avoid the taint of collaboration or were perceived to have acted in the interests of their constituents, they no doubt could play a central role in local committees. The novelist Richard Kim described the selection of his father (a nationalist) as a local committee leader in his book, *Lost Names*. The primary reason for choosing his father was that, unlike other prominent local men, he had refused to accept a Japanese name or to compromise himself in other ways.[17] Thus in Korea, as in countries such as Russia after the 1917 revolution, traditional local leadership might prevail even in uproarious times. Many people's committees, like many peasant soviets in Russia, thus "were nothing but the old village councils in revolutionary guise."[18]

The American response to this more or less full PC control of South Chŏlla paralleled the de facto policies followed in Seoul, although the long phase of tactical occupation here meant that the understaffed Americans had often worked through the committees, giving them time to get firmly established and, at the beginning, bestowing a stamp of approval on their authority. But after tactical occupation units were relieved, the Occupation pursued a general policy in all provinces of reviving the Japanese state apparatus and staffing it with former Korean colonial employees or conservative Koreans (particularly those associated with the KDP). In the provinces, however, even remaining Japanese nationals were retained long after they were removed in Seoul. Although General Hodge had been instructed by Washington on September 23 to eliminate all Japanese in the provincial administration, he decided to go "somewhat more slowly than Washington advised."[19] Moreover, as noted earlier, even when Japanese officials were removed, they still functioned as advisors: "The Americans were, in many instances, able to obtain from these Japanese officials a complete picture of the governmental structure."[20] Japanese officials and advisors as a general practice provided lists of recommended Korean personnel to fill administrative positions. The overall effect was to prolong direct Japanese influence in the provinces until late November.[21]

A former American official detailed the problems that PC control of South Chŏlla presented and the remedy decided upon:

Either the whole provincial government had to be turned over to the Republic or its control had to be broken. The conclusion finally reached was to use the Japanese framework of government and incumbent lesser officials as a basis, and to staff it with Korean key officials as rapidly as suitable leaders could be found.[22]

This is a succinct statement of the policy followed in South Chŏlla, and, indeed in all the provinces under American control. Rarely has a decision for counterrevolution been so frankly put.

American forces in South Chŏlla retained the Japanese provincial governor, Yaki Nobuo, until December 1945 and even suggested that he change his citizenship and remain indefinitely. Yaki declined, but secret lists of Koreans submitted by Yaki and the former Korean head of the provincial Finance Bureau, Im Mun-mu, determined the American selection of a Korean provincial governor to replace him. Im later became head of the Bureau of Home Affairs of South Chŏlla. Colonel D. R. Pepke, commander of the 20th Infantry of the 6th Division, wrote of Yaki in a letter of recommendation:

> It was largely through his efforts that the turning over of the government to the United States Army was accomplished with such speed and efficiency. His work not only enabled the Tactical Forces in their maintenance of law and order, but helped immeasurably in the work of the Military Government authorities in their efforts to establish the new system in this province.[23]

The Americans selected lesser officials in the provincial government in the following manner: "the senior Korean government employee in each office was temporarily appointed to replace his Japanese superior."[24] Additional appointments were made

> on the advice of CIC agents, recognized community leaders, the Catholic priest (who had spent the war in Korean prisons, and was loved and respected by Koreans and Americans alike), Japanese officials, and those Koreans already chosen for government service.[25]

In South Chŏlla, as in Seoul, we find the Americans making the curious assumption that appointments made on the above basis were not "political," while personnel selections of PC leaders, or appointments by those leaders of *ch'iandae* chiefs or township officials, *were* political. Kim Sŏk, the Kwangju *ch'iandae* leader, was replaced by Sŏ Min-ho (designated mayor), but this was a "non-political" personnel shift, since Kim Sŏk had allegedly been guilty of criminal activities. The nonpolitical Sŏ Min-ho shortly acquired a reputation as a strong anticommunist and leader of rightist youth groups.[26] Kim Sŏk was arrested on October 28 and soon thereafter convicted on charges of an alleged "assassination plot."

One observer, who was not actually opposed to Kim's removal, wrote that the United States tactical command ordered the judge to give Kim his sentence; he charged that the trial "was one of the greatest travesties on vaunted Anglo-Saxon justice that the writer had ever witnessed." He also suggested that advice from the former Japanese provincial governor, cited in the following quotation, swayed the Americans toward arresting Kim rather than working with him:

> If [the MG is] able to harmonize the present governmental agencies with the organization of the so-called "People's Republic," it may be regarded as a transitional and conciliatory measure. But such a course is impossible, I believe. . . . Therefore, in order to regain the public peace of the Province and maintain it in time to come, it is quite necessary for you [either] to approve all the demands of the People's Republic or decisively to refuse them and arrest all the radical elements. There is no other way.[27]

Thus, for Kim Sŏk, his release from prison on August 18 proved only to have been a heady furlough.

The arrest of Kim Sŏk highlighted the nature of the provincial police apparatus in South Chŏlla that the Americans revived and utilized. Information that led to Kim's arrest and conviction was supplied by the provincial secret police.[28] The provincial police force retained virtually all of the Korean police officers who had been on the Japanese force in South Chŏlla and made additional personnel appointments based on their recommendation and that of previous Japanese police officials.[29] According to Donald MacDonald:

> [This police force] continued for many months a watered-down version of the secret "thought police." . . . Their activities in the first months of occupation were actually responsible for much of the undue repression and persecution of left-wing groups—in some cases torture—which went on *without the knowledge* of Americans *struggling for impartiality* (emphasis added).[30]

McDonald may have been overly generous in asserting American innocence, however, for in mid-1946 American investigators reported:

> [In Kwangju there was] a special police corps composed of men who served under the Japanese in the same capacity. It is charged that they change county officers at will, work against all Leftists and enforce a law very similar to the Japanese Peace Maintenance Law. A special survey conducted of public opinion in Kwangju indicated an unnatural fear of the police on the part of the general public.[31]

Many Americans in Korea in these months firmly believed that their own intentions were nothing but the best and that they were striving against great odds to maintain an impartial and nonpolitical stance. But it is difficult to sustain this justification in light of the continued use of the provincial police as the prime tool in eliminating governing county people's committees. Surely some Americans, at some level, must have recognized the bias in using a cohesive force such as the provincial police against the politically unacceptable people's committees. In Seoul, as we have seen, the Occupation's recognition of the ally it had in the police dictated the revival and utilization of the national police. For the Korean victims of this provincial police force, many of whom found themselves once again incarcerated by the same system, perhaps even by the same police officials, as during the colonial period, the American use of this force must have appeared a monstrous injustice.

Other American tactics used in this province were also similar to those used in Seoul. When the Americans arrived, they found that the Kwangju PC was publishing the *Chŏllam sinbo* (South Chŏlla News); the tactical command shut it down, then reopened it under censorship until "responsible" journalists could be found. PC newspapers in Mokp'o were also shut down.[32]

Most of the county PCs in South Chŏlla were suppressed by the provincial police, sometimes with the help of American tactical forces. This happened in Yŏng'am, Changhŭng, Chindo, Wando, Haenam, Posŏng, and various other counties. In the Changhŭng case, for example, the PC and *ch'iandae* were disbanded in the third week of October, the leaders were arrested, and the police force was reorganized with the aid of the former Korean inspector on the Japanese police force in Changhŭng.[33] Forcible suppression did not occur everywhere in South Chŏlla, however. In two sets of counties, the Americans followed different policies and achieved different results. An understanding of these differing policies is important in assessing the staying power of local committees.

Throughout the provinces, it seems that, where committees were suppressed outright in the fall of 1945 or in early 1946, they rarely emerged again, unless the committees could recruit new members from the influx of Koreans returning from north Korean provinces or from abroad. But where the PCs were maintained or only partially reorganized, or where the committees did not seize entire counties but coexisted in strained opposition to other forces, unrest tended to occur later—sometimes much later.

Something less than full PC control prevailed in the Yŏsu/Sunch'ŏn/Kwangyang/Kurye region controlled by the 69th MG Company. Only Kwangyang was governed by a PC. In the other counties the composition of the PCs was so mixed and their structures so different that the Americans apparently did little to curb their activities. The 69th Company thought that the PCs were "strictly local organizations" and had "no direct chain of contact reaching up to a national level"; they saw no indication of policy "emanating from a strong central head-quarters":

> The People's Committee is a designation applied to some faction in every town. However its influence—and also its character—varies in each community. In one county, it represents the "roughnecks"; in another, it is perhaps the only political party and represents no radical expressions; in others, it may even possibly have the [former] county magistrate as its party leader.[34]

The 69th Company thought that the sphere of influence of the committees was confined to "their own immediate locality," thus, we suspect, they saw no reason to suppress them.[35] Of course, the local aspect was characteristic of most if not all county-level PCs. Peasant communities do not generally follow outside leadership. But American perceptions in 1945 are the important factors here. The 69th Company, not realizing the national character of the committees, gave them breathing space and time to establish themselves. It may also be that the PCs found additional recruits from among returning population, since all four counties were above the provincial average in rates of population change. The county police had to be reorganized in Yŏsu in May 1946, but in general, the 69th Company had little trouble from these four counties. It worked through the strong Kwangyang PC, was happy with the conservatism of Kurye and Sunch'ŏn, and did little to suppress the leftist opposition to the county government in Yŏsu. Thus the PCs, or their remnants, survived, and the region was widely described by conservative Koreans in 1946 and 1947 as being "Red." There may be a link between the laissez-faire policies of the 69th Company and the subsequent outbreak of the Yŏsu/Sunch'ŏn Rebellion in the fall of 1948, when rebels took over much of this area and proclaimed a "People's Republic."[36]

American forces followed an entirely different policy in another set of counties in South Chŏlla. PCs were solidly entrenched in three of the four counties of Chindo, Haenam, Wando, and Kangjin upon the arrival of the 45th MG Company on November 23, 1945. In each county tactical occupation forces had recognized the PCs and the *ch'iandae* as de facto administrations.[37] The committees controlled all governmental levels except for the Kangjin county seat (Kangjin townships were under PC control). Since August 15 the PCs had maintained law and order, operated local transport and communications facilities, and managed food stocks and schools.

A major reason for the strength of the committees in these counties was their remoteness. All of them are made up of islands (more than sixty of them in Wando) or island-peninsulas. Chindo and Wando are nowhere connected to the mainland. Transportation to these islands consisted of inefficient boat systems; and shallow bays, strong currents, and high and unpredictable tides complicated navigation. Remoteness not only encouraged committee growth, but led to pronounced localism: the committees in Wando and Chindo took orders from no one, including the Kwangju provincial committee.[38] Population change was not great in these four counties, topping the provincial average for the years from 1944 to 1946 only in Kangjin, while Wando and Chindo had very low rates (6.5 and 10.8 percent, respectively). The primary factor in PC strength was thus geographic remoteness and the resulting lengthy interregnum between Japanese and American rule.

The 45th MG Company was one of the few civil affairs teams that had had training geared specifically to running a military government in Korea. Most MG teams assigned to Korea had been trained for Japan and then diverted to Korea; but the 45th had received daily briefings on Korea during training.[39] The company was led by Lieutenant Colonel Frank E. Bartlett, who from the outset urged his men to "know the tenor of native public opinion . . . to be thoroughly acquainted with the local political situation, parties, leaders, and their programs." The 45th carefully watched Korean publications, and used police channels to assure the distribution of MG directives and publicity information.[40] Colonel Bartlett felt that MG companies should not only know the local situation, but act upon it to keep lower levels in step with national MG policy. What did the 45th Company do about the PCs in its region?

In Haenam "the People's Committee was without question the strongest and most active political group." It controlled the county at all levels and allowed former Korean officials from the colonial county administration to work under PC direction.[41] The Haenam PCs operated local bus services, the county laver industry, and twenty-one primary schools.[42] In early December the 45th Company officially appointed the Haenam PC chief as the county magistrate (hereafter designated *kunsu*). At the county level in Kangjin, the "Right wing" was in charge and the old officials were still around; thus this county presented "a much simpler problem." These officials were simply confirmed in office.[43] PC leadership in Chindo was termed "efficient" and "moderate"; here too the PC leader was appointed *kunsu* under the Americans. American forces did not even reach Wando until December 19. They found "political usurpers" in office but did nothing about them until early January 1946.[44]

At the beginning of 1946 the Americans arrived at a decision to effect a "reorganization" of these four counties. It is unclear at what level this decision was made, but it may have related to Colonel

Bartlett's known desire to be in step with national MG policies. The existing record says nothing about trouble from or lack of cooperation by the PCs.[45] It simply states that the PCs "usurped" governmental authority. There is also a suggestion that the lack of a chain of command in the PC structure from the county level down to the townships and villages would have made control at all levels difficult were the Americans to utilize the PC apparatus.

In all four counties, the Americans brought in special provincial police details from the reliable Kwangju force to supplant local PC and *ch'iandae* leaders. Nothing so aptly demonstrates the Americans' inability to develop alternative but still indigenous political leadership. Only outsiders from the province capital could accomplish the task. These police units arrested PC leaders and then provided alternative police forces sent in from Kwangju. When new men could be recruited from the county populations, they were dispatched to Kwangju for training. The provincial police were given use of MG communications and transportation facilities, and American troop escorts, if needed. Only the Kangjin county seat escaped reorganization. Here the old officials were still in place and "with little difficulty a good governmental situation rapidly developed." Some rioting occurred in the PC-controlled townships of Kangjin in February and April of 1946, however. Provincial police were dispatched, and numerous arrests were made for "assault."[46]

Reorganization was more difficult to achieve in the other three counties. Wando required several months of suppression. The 45th Company replaced Wando PCs through "the extension of police power . . . from the center outward to the outlying islands." Provincial police details arrested PC leaders and shipped them to Kwangju. They then reorganized the Wando county police force in late January. Shortly thereafter, the 45th Company reported that thirty-five men on the police force were from Kwangju. Wando's jails held twenty-seven prisoners. Rioting ensued in some peripheral townships, but by March 4 the situation was apparently under control, as a Kwangju-appointed *kunsu* arrived to take up his new duties.[47] Provincial police moved into Chindo in late January, and "political changes followed closely upon the heels of police action." Provincial policemen supplanted the county *ch'iandae*. A Kwangju-appointed *kunsu* arrived on February 12: "nine days later he made a clean sweep of the myŏns, appointing new chiefs in all instances."[48] In Haenam provincial police arrested nineteen PC leaders at the end of December. Around January 19 the PC police chief and thirty-eight of his men were replaced by thirty-eight special police from Kwangju. In February and March rioting occurred in Haenam, followed by more arrests. At the end of

March the county police force numbered eighty-five. The county jails held fifty prisoners, fourteen of them charged with "impersonating a police officer."[49] Similar reorganization occurred on Anch'ang Island, where on January 22 twenty-three Kwangju policemen arrived and arrested thirty-two PC leaders.[50]

Official sources offered the following justification for the suppression of the committees in these counties:

> It is to be noted that, everywhere, the general trend was to relieve left-wing groups from office. The reason was not fundamentally concerned with political beliefs but rather because such elements acted in the role of usurpers and in too many cases introduced inefficient or dishonest men into office. It was further evident that in such places where the power had been seized by local groups, the extension of control and the establishment of effective government was definitely dependent on the establishment of a loyal police force.[51]

The 45th Company itself offered no evidence that the PCs in these counties were all "left-wing," and as we have seen in several other counties in South Chŏlla, leftists often did not dominate local PCs. Moreover, the 45th Company found that the Chindo PC was moderate and efficient, not inefficient. And finally, the real inefficiencies attendant on the use of a wholly discredited police force in liberated Korea should be obvious by now. Yet there is a kernel of truth and candor in the above justification. The problem in Chindo, Wando, and Haenam was the same one that confronted Americans throughout south Korea —the extension of effective control. "Effective control," as noted in chapter four, was the problem that State Department planners somewhat ambivalently wrestled with in presurrender planning for Korea. As with the other de facto actions taken by the Americans, the suppression of the PCs in South Chŏlla effectively resolved previous ambiguities. It is in conditions of crisis that relationships of political power are revealed.[52] The crisis in South Chŏlla revealed that the old order, slightly modified, prevailed. By the end of February 1946, American intelligence sources reported that seventeen of twenty-one *kunsu*s in South Chŏlla were members of the Korean Democratic Party.[53]

The Americans and their Korean charges hoped to place the southwestern, coastal counties under the control of Mokp'o rather than the somewhat distant capital at Kwangju. But Mokp'o presented its own problems. During the colonial period, it was a key exporting point for rice, and commercialized agriculture, including extensive cotton fields, had developed in its environs. From 1944 through 1946, its population grew by 60 percent, as returnees converged on the port. The Mokp'o PC and *ch'iandae* controlled the city in January 1946; various *nodong chohap* managed factories in the city; the workers had the "impression" that they had "inherited the plants" from the Japanese.[54] On January 14, however, a branch of Rhee's NSRRKI held an antitrusteeship, anti-Soviet rally, and people described as hecklers and bullies broke it up. The next day some thirty Kwangju policemen arrived and took over the Mokp'o police department. The same day they raided the city PC headquarters and arrested thirty-three individuals, including the *ch'iandae* chief, Im Tae-ho; those arrested were charged with malfeasance, illegal census-taking, and illegal use of government vehicles.[55] Shortly thereafter, seventy additional Kwangju policemen arrived and staffed the new Mokp'o force. On February 11 the Americans demanded the resignation of all city employees; 5 of the 6 city department directors and some 124 lesser employees were not rehired; "this in effect eliminated all subversive political activity among personnel in the city office."[56] Finally, in May, the Occupation had changes to make in the factory system:

> The last of the major concerns operated by a worker's committee—a device uniformly adopted in all local concerns until modified by the Military Government—was brought under direct Military Government control and a manager appointed who established an employer-employee basis of operations.[57]

Such factory managers were recommended by the "Industrial Advisory Council," a five-man committee of "leading industrial members of the community."[58] At the county level in South Chŏlla, similar bodies were organized, called property committees, consisting of one American officer, the county magistrate, the county chief of police, and heads of county relief sections.[59] This was, of course, almost identical to the structure of such bodies under Japanese rule.

The Mokp'o *mise en scene* after liberation is fascinating, because the agrarian class structure in the region had differentiated rapidly in the last decade or so of Japanese rule. This region was a center for the landlord-entrepreneurs we discussed in chapter one; the export trade in rice provided opportunities for upward mobility and new forms of wealth; yet the peasants in the region had not been mobilized for factory work in northern Korea or abroad to the degree of, say, peasants in the Kyŏngsangs. The landed class in the Chŏllas was also more self-assertive and confident than that in the Kyŏngsang provinces. In any case, the committees were more easily overturned here than they were in the Kyŏngsangs. The process was more difficult in South

Chŏlla than in North Chŏlla, however; and South Chŏlla was consumed in the uprisings of late 1946, whereas North Chŏlla was relatively untouched.

As for the people of the southwestern counties (Wando, Chindo, and so on), they quickly learned that the new order after liberation was just a fleeting fancy. It is the very swiftness and finality of the demise of the PCs in this region that may account for the fact that, in succeeding years, no record of severe disorders appears, not even during the autumn uprisings of 1946. Lacking strong organization and protection, the peasants returned to their only refuge, the day-to-day drudgery of cultivating land in someone else's interest. Lacking a steady influx of returning population, the PCs could only recruit new members from the existing county residents, and the latter had noted which way the wind blew. The pattern here was thus a classic one of peasant rebellion.

NORTH CHŎLLA PROVINCE

North Chŏlla, as we have seen, had the highest rates of tenancy in south Korea, with an effective rate of 80 percent—certain counties (Iksan, Kimje, Chŏngŭp) approaching 95 percent—and with the number of self-cultivating smallholders almost equalling the number of landlord families. Counties such as Koch'ang and Sunch'ang were centers of immense landed wealth for two key leaders of the Korean Democratic Party, Kim Sŏng-su and Kim Pyŏng-no; indeed the mainstay of the KDP was often called the "Honam group," Honam being a designation for the Chŏlla provinces. North Chŏlla's alluvial valleys and fertile soil provided a significant percentage of all rice production in Korea.

Population changes were substantial in North Chŏlla during the later years of Japanese rule, although the average county growth rate from 1944 to 1946 of 16.2 percent was much lower than that in the Kyŏngsang provinces. The province was well-laced with roads, particularly in the Chŏnju and Kunsan regions, ranking first in Korea in this category; it was considerably less remote and was superior in transportation facilities to South Chŏlla. In the 1930s Red Peasant Unions penetrated only three counties—Okku, Puan, and Chŏngŭp.

People's committees existed in every county in North Chŏlla and governed county affairs in about half the counties (see figure 9). It is in this province that we first see a significant relationship between population change and radicalism. The three most radical rice-paddy counties—Namwŏn, Sunch'ang, and Okku—all had population losses in the 1930s and had gains of 20 percent or more between 1944 and

■ known people's committees
□ known assumption of governmental functions

9. North Chŏlla Province People's Committees

1946; these gains were in all cases more than 90 percent of the total gain between 1930 and 1946. The least radical counties—Ch'inan and Puan, for example—gained population in the 1930s and had gains between 1944 and 1946 that were less than half of the total gain from 1930 to 1946. The only anomaly is Changsu, which had a population pattern similar to Namwŏn but was not radical. Three other counties with governing PCs—Iksan, Kimje, and Muju—had high rates of change (above 20 percent) from 1944 to 1946, although only Muju lost population in the 1930s. Four of seven counties with nongoverning PCs had rates of population change that were below the county average, and only Chŏngŭp had a rate that was more than 1 percent above the average. The high growth rates and strong PCs in the Kunsan/Okku/Iksan region perhaps resulted from the influx of Koreans returning through the rice-exporting port of Kunsan. Muju not only had a high growth rate but was also a remote and primarily forested county. The strength of committees in Namwŏn and Sunch'ang was probably reinforced by the border and mountainous character of these counties. The initial strength of the PCs throughout North Chŏlla had much to do with the long interregnum resulting from the transfer of the 96th Division to China.

Information on committee strength in North Chŏlla is excellent. The MG files still hold a copy of a report prepared by the Korean province chief of police in November 1945, giving locations and strength in numbers of PCs, *nongmin chohap*, and PC-affiliated youth groups throughout the province.[60] The province-level PC at Chŏnju had a full cabinet and some 6,000 members, led by Pak Yong-hŭi and Ch'oe Hong-yŏl. The Kimje PC, like several others, had departments for home affairs, industry, peace-keeping, education, and propaganda. Most of the county PCs had between 30 and 100 members. Nearly all had youth group affiliates and most had *nongmin chohap* affiliates. In the Muju county seat, the seventeen sections (*pan*) of the town were represented by fifteen PCs. A long list of subcounty towns and villages with PCs is also given in this report. The KDP was reported to have had 2,500 members in North Chŏlla, but no locations of branches or breakdowns on numbers involved were given. The report named only five KDP leaders for the entire province. Later American reports attested to the early strength of certain county people's committees, like that in Kimje: "The People's Committee claims undisputed control of the activities of Kimje *kun*. There is much evidence to support this claim and little to refute it."[61]

The particularly strong PCs in North Chŏlla existed at opposite sides of the province: Namwŏn and Sunch'ang in the southeast, Muju in the northeast, and Kunsan/Okku/Iksan in the northwest. When the Americans arrived in Namwŏn in late October, they found the entire county under PC control, with units of the National Preparatory Army drilling in the streets. The Japanese had given the Namwŏn PC title to most of their property in the county. Here, and in neighboring counties of Sunch'ang and Imsil, the PCs were running training schools for committee leaders.[62] Although information is very limited on the Okku/Iksan region, a region of extensive commercialization, PCs were reported to be strong and in complete control.[63] In the three southwestern counties of Koch'ang, Chŏngŭp, and Puan, PCs existed, but they had not supplanted old Japanese and Korean officials except in the outlying *myŏns* of Puan. No *ch'iandae* had supplanted the former police. The Americans had little trouble in reemploying the old police and organizing new county governments with former officials as the nucleus. By January 1946 government affairs were functioning so smoothly in the southwestern counties that Americans served largely in supervisory capacities.[64] In the four northeastern counties of Muju, Wanju, Kŭmsan, and Chin'an, the transition to American rule was apparently orderly and without moment. There are no reports of difficulties from the strong Muju PC.[65] The pattern we find in North Chŏlla is of a comparatively easy transition from Japanese to American rule, with minor obstruction from the PCs only in Namwŏn, Sunch'ang, Kimje, and Iksan.

When the Americans entered North Chŏlla, no provincial government was functioning. Japanese officials had left and remaining Korean officials were absent or inactive. The Americans thus thought that the PCs controlled the entire province. They rehired the Korean provincial governor from the colonial administration and retained some Korean advisors who had earlier served the Japanese, such as Yun San-hŭi, one-time advisor to a Japanese provincial governor.[66] They employed as chief prosecutor in Chŏnju a Korean with the Japanese-Korean name of Emoto Taekyo who had been a prosecutor in Kunsan under the Japanese.[67] In general, "trained and experienced government officials were reappointed . . . [although] in some cases, men who had held government positions many years ago or had never worked for the Japanese were appointed." The provincial government "remained generally the same, both in its structure and the number of personnel employed."[68] Korean colonial officials were also allowed to select Korean appointees for province- and county-level advisory councils. All this occurred with seeming smoothness. By January 1946 North Chŏlla was termed a "model" for the rest of south Korea in the policy known as "Koreanization." The official American justification for what was in essence a revival and bolstering of the old order was as follows: "As a general rule, Military Government hesitated to give the People's Committee a position of importance in the government because of its ties with the Communists and possibly with a Russian fifth column."[69]

At the county level, however, Koreanization was not achieved without incident, although counties in North Chŏlla presented far fewer problems than those in South Chŏlla. The revived Korean elements of the Japanese police in North Chŏlla had so little authority that Americans had to accompany them on details throughout the province.[70] In Namwŏn only the provincial police had the strength to confront the local committee. This resulted in the Namwŏn Incident of November 1945. When the Americans arrived in Namwŏn in late October, the PC chief had produced an affidavit from the Japanese as justification for the widespread committee control of Japanese properties in the county. He was told that all such property had to be turned over to the MG for disposition. The PC refused to do this. Thus on November 15 the Chŏnju chief of police arrived in Namwŏn with a contingent of provincial policemen, ordered several PC leaders arrested, and departed for Chŏnju with them in tow. A short distance outside of town,

> his car was ambushed and about one hundred persons armed with clubs and other weapons demanded that he release his prisoners. When he refused they proceeded to beat him. That evening additional [American] troops were sent to Namwŏn. The following day sixteen of the mob were arrested. Early in the afternoon of the 17th a mob began to congregate in Namwŏn until between 700 to 1,000 people were milling around. From three directions they converged on the police station, which was guarded by tactical troops. The members of the mob were ordered to disband numerous times; finally they were given two minutes or they would be dispersed by force. When the two minutes were up the troops fired into the air and advanced with fixed bayonets. In the scuffle that followed two Koreans were killed, several injured, and one policeman stabbed to death.[71]

After fifty more arrests, Namwŏn quieted down.[72]

Similar actions had to be taken on a smaller scale in the other counties of North Chŏlla having strong PCs. Kimje was "reorganized" in December, with police seizing PC records and ordering the committee to move out of the public buildings it occupied. After the county seat was secure, the *myŏn*s and the lower levels were similarly reorganized. By December 26 a branch of Syngman Rhee's party was able to hold its first meeting in Kimje.[73] At about the same time, the records and bank accounts of the Iksan PC were seized. American sources reported that the Iksan PC "seems to have lost a lot of its power when its leaders were tried and found guilty of extortion."[74] Many people associated with these PCs literally lost the roofs over their heads, since the county police took charge of homes formerly owned by Japanese residents and distributed them among themselves, other officials, and individuals who claimed to have bought them from departing Japanese.[75] Rent collections were taken out of PC and *nongmin chohap* hands and returned to *kunsu* and police responsibility. The Kimje *kunsu* also had full control of Japanese residences and rice rationing once again.

In January 1946 the townships of Kimje were still unruly; so county police, sometimes with the assistance of tactical troops, raided *myŏn* PCs and arrested their leaders: "the raids were made primarily for records," but arrests were made if there was evidence of "past misdeeds." The Americans in Kimje reported that "we are doing a rather thriving transient business at the local Bastille."[76] In February they stated that the Kimje police chief and all his section heads were "veterans" of the Japanese force; the chief himself "had been in police work for many years." The only exception was one section head sent in from Chŏnju.[77] The county police force, which under Japan had numbered 100, now had 128 men; but the Americans claimed, "with the present situation an increase is urgently needed." They placed the new police manpower requirement at 232. Arrests were being made at the rate of forty per week; still the Americans were afraid that if they withdrew tactical troops the Kimje PC might return to power.[78] Puan presented less of a problem than Kimje, as the PCs operated only in the outlying townships. But even in Puan the Americans ousted six *myŏn* chiefs and arrested numerous "subversives."[79]

In Chŏngŭp county there was a fairly easy transition from Japanese to American-Korean rule, with Korean landed elements dominant under both. This was an overwhelmingly agrarian county, with more than 80 percent of all families engaged in agriculture in eleven of fifteen townships and very high rates of tenancy. A branch of Rhee's NSRRKI opened in Chŏngŭp no later than March 1946, with Pak Myŏng-gyu among its top leaders. Pak was a landlord who had been head of the Chŏngju Irrigation Association in 1940 and was later a member of the North Chŏlla Advisory Council under the Japanese. He headed the local *Tonga ilbo* office as well.[80] Thus, in this individual county, we can trace the predominance of the Honam landlord-entrepreneurs through the transition from Japanese to Korean rule. The same was true of the city of Iri.

Iri was more of a town than a city in 1945, its sole *raison d'être* deriving, as it still does, from its strategic location as a railroad junction.

Just after August 15 an Iri PC emerged, led by Im Chŏng-han.[81] American tactical forces arrived in Iri on October 19, however, and the 28th MG Company followed within a week. The Americans arrested leaders of the Iri PC on November 6, allegedly for extorting money and other property from local Japanese residents.[82] Shortly thereafter, three men from Seoul and two from Iri set up an Iri branch of the Korean Democratic Party. Unlike the situation in several other provinces, the KDP managed to establish several branches in North Chŏlla before the end of 1945. Men would arrive from Seoul, organize the key elite in a town or county into a KDP branch, and then depart again for Seoul. The Americans said that the KDP in North Chŏlla was "poorly organized . . . [and] represented the money interests."[83] But that is because when Americans look at a political party, they expect to find well-articulated organization, mass participation, patronage, and so on. Five men in Iri do not make a well-organized party in American eyes. Leaders of the KDP knew they had little mass appeal; but they also knew that a handful of individuals was preferable to and more potent than mass membership, if that handful included the local *kunsu*, police chief, New Korea Company operative, or others who occupied key points of access in the local bureaucracy. It is likely that the three men who came from Seoul to Iri were absentee landlords with a keen interest in local political and economic arrangements in North Chŏlla. The Americans in Iri reported that they expressed their extreme concern with MG rice purchasing and price control programs.[84]

At the end of 1945 the Iri Advisory Council was set up; of twelve members with an average age of fifty, there were two landlords, two landlord agents (*marŭm*), four businessmen, a doctor, a journalist, a Christian minister, and a "farmer."[85] A month later the Iri police department was functioning well without American help—and with few differences from its role under Japanese colonialism: the department issued all business, transport, and industry licenses; it recorded all public meetings of political organizations and "all speeches made by political speakers at political meetings"; it controlled all assemblies and demonstrations; it checked and investigated "all newspapers, magazines, radios, and movies for propaganda"; it controlled the handling and disposition of all former Japanese properties. Assistant Inspectors Chŏn Yong-man, Chŏn U-sŏn, and Pak Hyŏng-bak were all "old-time policemen," and newly-hired men were "under their charge and guidance."[86]

Even officials who took over counties after MG-sponsored reorganizations, officials deemed trustworthy, found themselves the objects of suspicion if they advocated changes or reforms in existing arrangements. Thus the American-appointed *kunsu* in Kimje, Ch'oe Chae-myŏn, who reportedly gave speeches that were "somewhat tinted with pink" and who was rumored to be a "communist" because he had relatives in the People's Party, had his movements and his activities carefully watched.[87] Such was the Manichaean political world of postwar North Chŏlla.

North Chŏlla in these months presented a classic example of how a landed elite may manage to perpetuate itself in a time of turmoil. Events never got much out of hand in Iri, Kimje, Namwŏn, or the rest of the province. In counties like Koch'ang, home of Kim Sŏng-su, the transition from Japanese to American (or better, Korean) rule was easy, and in fact, almost unnoticeable. No doubt the relatively extensive transportation network in North Chŏlla aided this transition. Unlike the situation in China and Vietnam, for example, a bureaucrat or national policeman or landlord could entrain from the capital and be in Iri within hours. Or the provincial chief of police could drive down quickly from Chŏnju to Namwŏn. This ease of access made a difference. But perhaps the most significant hindrances to the development of strong people's committees in North Chŏlla were the wealth and high land prices of the province's rich alluvial soil, the predominance of more entrepreneurial landlords, and the unparalleled extent of tenancy. The wealth of the province made it an area of intense concern both for landlords and for a central government needing revenue. In addition, some individual landlords like Kim Sŏng-su were widely known for their moderate activities on behalf of Koreans during the colonial period. These activities included sponsoring schools (such as North Chŏlla's *Kobu* school) that provided both a measure of upward mobility and an emphasis on Korean culture amid Japanese repression and the general lack of Korean opportunity of the colonial era. The extensive commercialization in response to the export trade in rice going through Kunsan also provided opportunities for richer peasants and landlords.

As for the majority of the population here, the tenants, it would appear that two factors account for their relative quiescence, both in the period after liberation and in the autumn of 1946, when uprisings touched only the counties of Namwŏn and Sunch'ang, this being little more than a spillover from South Chŏlla. First, such an extensive system of landlordism provided a variety of controls on tenants. Furthermore, many more landlords here were Koreans, so that traditional bonds were less disrupted. Colonially induced ethnic cleavages were less intense as well, since many Korean landlords in North Chŏlla were able to avoid the taint of unseemly closeness to the Japanese. Second, the presence of many Japanese landlords in North Chŏlla, as contrasted to the predominance of ODC-held land in South Chŏlla, meant that after liberation, as many of the individual Japanese fled home, they either sold their land at cheap prices to tenants or simply abandoned it. Although there are no useful data on this process, it was a widespread phenomenon. It meant that many tenants solved the collective problem of tenancy status through individual remedies— buying or occupying a parcel of land. The possibility of an individual solution through upward mobility thus undercut the solidarity of North Chŏlla's tenants. Collective solutions might have been more apparent to tenants who had been mobilized out of their native province during the 1930s; but most North Chŏlla counties had relatively low population change. Tenants who remained in their native places might have seen their fortunes take a dip, but they would not have experienced the catastrophe of losing land or rights to work land. Given the bountiful production of the region, also, there was less necessity to press tenants to the limit, and indeed, the data suggest that tenant rights were more secure here. Finally, the differentiation of the landed class into rice export enterprise and other endeavors would provide a more flexible mode of controlling tenants, relying more on remunerative and less on coercive measures.

SOUTH KYŎNGSANG PROVINCE

This province led all others in committee strength and radicalism. PCs existed in all counties except Namhae and governed county affairs at one time or another in all but five counties (see figure 10). South Kyŏngsang also had a higher rate of population change in the years from 1944 to 1946 than any other province and was perhaps the most modern region as defined by our admittedly sketchy ranking. It was a middling province in rates of tenancy, and those counties that *were* high in tenancy, such as Miryang and Kimhae, which had rates of about 80 percent,[88] were not particularly radical. RPUs existed in nearly all the counties west of Pusan during the 1930s. In the terms of the environmental factors discussed in chapter eight, South Kyŏngsang seemed ripe for committee growth in 1945.

In South Kyŏngsang we find particularly strong committees in those counties that experienced high population change. Fifteen of seventeen counties with governing PCs gained more than 20 percent from 1944 to 1946. Masan and Chinju, two cities with strong committees and marked rebellious tendencies, grew at the astonishing rates of 75 and 70 percent, respectively. Ŭiryŏng, one of the most radical counties, had the highest rate of population change in south Korea, 73 percent. Haman and Chinyang were not far behind, with rates of

■ known people's committees
□ known assumption of governmental functions

10. South Kyŏngsang Province People's Committees

between 40 and 50 percent. We thus find a belt of counties and smaller cities leading west from Pusan with firmly established PCs and rates of population change surpassing any region in Korea. Only four counties did not lose population, or gain at less than 3 percent, during the period between 1930 and 1940. Of these four, Tongnae should be disregarded, however, because the presence of Pusan skews the result. Namhae gained about 12 percent between 1930 and 1940 and had the lowest growth rate in the province from 1944 to 1946; it was also the least radical county. Sach'ŏn also gained about 10 percent in the 1930s, and although it had a high gain between 1944 and 1946, it was the next least radical county. Kimhae, the only anomaly, was a radical county that gained just over 2 percent in the 1930s but also had a large gain from 1944 to 1946 of almost 40 percent—not much of an anomaly, really. Thus, particularly at the extremes, the population pattern almost completely predicts radicalism here. Koreans displaced to Japan returned to South Kyŏngsang in great numbers; but there were also many who returned from northern Korea and Manchuria. We will find that although the Americans tried to root out the committees using much the same methods as they used in South Chŏlla, their efforts were frustrated by the deep disordering of the province that had taken place in the latter years of colonial rule and by the continuing influx of profoundly discouraged and resentful people available for mobilization by the PCs and related groups.

Certain intangible factors may have aided PC strength here as well. Both the Kyŏngsangs had a reputation for rebellious inclinations; more Kyŏngsang natives took part in the 1919 independence demonstrations than did those of any other region, for instance.[89] The region was also closest to Japan, making the colonial association more palpable. Pusan in South Kyŏngsang and Taegu in North Kyŏngsang were considered to be just like Japanese cities, at least by the Japanese. This was the area of most intense contact and change. The Kyŏngsangs also had something of a separatist tradition, reinforced by a notably distinct dialect. Several prominent leftists had their birthplaces in South Kyŏngsang, including Kim Tu-bong, the important leader of Koreans at Yenan, and Chang Kŏn-sang, Yŏ Un-hyŏng's close associate, both of whom came from Tongnae. Miryang was Kim Wŏn-bong's home, and when he toured the county in March 1946 he was reported to have had a strong personal following.[90]

The length of interregnum in South Kyŏngsang was considerably shorter than that in South Chŏlla. As stated earlier, an initial American observation team arrived in Pusan on September 16. They found the city in extreme disorder, with Japanese streaming through on their way back to Japan and Koreans returning in droves from Japan. Pusan presented a sorry picture—refugees camped all over, stores and banks shuttered, the city at a standstill except for the huge volume of human traffic. Machine-gun-toting Japanese soldiers guarded major traffic routes; it was essential for the mass Japanese exodus that this port be firmly controlled.[91]

Existing information is contradictory on the development of the Pusan PC. The Americans reported that "huge numbers" of Japanese soldiers controlled Pusan, but also that a Pusan *ch'iandae* with 3,000 members, a headquarters, and twelve substations "had assumed many police functions" in the city.[92] Perhaps *ch'iandae* units maintained order in parts of Pusan not under direct Japanese Army control. A province-level PC existed, led by Yun Il, but it apparently did not run the city government. Workers' committees had succeeded in taking over numerous factories, however. In several cases, they got plants functioning by choosing managers with needed skills after first accepting bids from applicants, a common practice among workers' committees throughout south Korea.[93]

The Americans in Pusan disbanded the city *ch'iandae* on September 28.[94] They then ordered the PC to reorganize into a political party and to drop its claims to being a government, which resulted on October 5 in a factional split among PC leaders, with some maintaining the KPR tie and others joining the fledgling People's Party (see chapter six).[95] Fortieth Division authorities prolonged the tenure of the Japanese mayor, Osamu Tomiyama, until October 6 and thereafter retained him and his Japanese and Korean underlings for weeks as advisors.[96] They made appointments to high provincial posts on the advice of the Japanese, Koreans in their employ, and other "prominent" Koreans.[97] Japanese provincial police officials were not dismissed until October 20 by which time 1,600 of an authorized provincial force of 2,900 Korean policemen were in place.[98]

In the weeks immediately following the Japanese surrender, the Japanese advised the Americans that Koreans in the Kyŏngsang provinces were an untrustworthy and volatile lot: "If the United States Military Government gives up political power to Koreans the administration of Korea will be communist. The idea of communism is deeply rooted in the Korean people."[99] There is in this statement a rather unsubtle linking of Korean political power or self-government with communism; in the minds of Japanese colonial officials, of course, the two were nearly synonymous. The unfortunate thing is that such arguments impressed the Americans. Thus, "many competent Japanese officials were temporarily retained, in some cases for several months, however much they were despised by the radical elements in Korea."[100]

As in the Chŏlla provinces, the Korean element of the Japanese police was reconstituted as the prime force for order. A number of high offices in the police, American investigators later determined, were assumed by Koreans who had been members of the *kōtō keisatsuka*, or "higher police section," a secret police organization during the colonial period. Activities of this secret police force before 1945 "ranged from spying on the Korean people and giving intelligence to their [sic] Japanese superiors . . . on anti-Japanese, anti-war, and anti-imperialist [that is, Imperial Japan] movements, to general supervision and control of all activities in the field of literature, speech, and assemblage."[101] Individuals in the provincial force who were once in this special colonial force included Ha Pan-nak, chief of accounts; Kang Nak-jung, Tongnae police chief; and Yi Tae-u, chief of the detective section of the provincial police apparatus.[102]

American forces spread into most counties in early October and found PCs governing in nearly every county. There seem to have been fewer instances of committee leadership by landlords or former officials in South Kyŏngsang than in South Chŏlla; in fact, no reports of such leadership are available. In Hamyang so-called "returned student soldiers" led by Chŏn Su-ha ran the county administration; these were individuals who had fled into nearby mountains in 1944 rather than serve in the Japanese Army. Upon their return to Hamyang, they took over the county seat and jailed former Korean police and government officials.[103] The PCs in Haman, T'ongyŏng, and Chinyang were reported to have had mostly peasant leadership,[104] and in Hadong the committee people put landlords in jail in October.[105] On Kŏje Island, with particularly strong committees, the leadership was youthful (as it was in so many other places): the PC head was Sŏng Nak-hyŏn, aged 26.[106]

Even in places like Ulsan where the local PC apparently did not control the county government, strong affiliated organizations existed. A document from the Ulsan *nongmin chohap* called for tenants to give no more than 30 percent of their crops as rent to landlords, for the Ulsan PC to manage and control all former Japanese farmlands, and for members of both organizations to be "conciliatory" with the MG. It also urged that members hide the fact that the PC and the *nongmin chohap* had many common members.[107] In Samch'ŏnp'o the old *kunsu* was kidnapped on October 15, although there is no report of a governing PC in that town.[108]

Unlike the situation in several other provinces, American tactical forces in South Kyŏngsang intervened continuously in PC affairs before the arrival of MG companies. American military strength was used time and again to depose PCs and install either the old county officials or new ones dispatched from Pusan. This harsh policy was matched by equally harsh and adventurous actions on the part of the committees. Unlike many of the governing PCs in other provinces, those in South Kyŏngsang refused to accept the overturning of their new order and continually met force with force. American and PC actions turned the province into a scene of riotous disorder lasting well into 1946.

To deal with the PCs at the county level, the 40th Division adopted a "standard operating procedure":

A tactical unit occupying a community was to expel the former head of the local government, if he was a Japanese, but retain him as an advisor if necessary. Other Japanese were to be replaced by Koreans as soon as possible. If the head of the government was a Korean, he was to be retained until a suitable replacement could be found. If a political party [that is, people's committee] had expelled the former officials and taken over the government, the officials put in by the party were to be arrested and suitable substitutes appointed. Former police officials were to be used, if they were available and suitable, and backed up if necessary by the [American] military.[109]

Former police officials were often not readily available, yet they were located and marched back to duty. Few former officials could function without the presence of American troops, however. The old police, in particular, often required Americans in their stations and boxes if they were to function at all.[110] As soon as the Americans withdrew, the PCs usually returned to power and sometimes jailed American-appointed officials. Then the Americans would have to return again. This process occurred in several counties, including Hadong, T'ongyŏng, Yangsan, Kosŏng, and Haman.[111] Martial law had to be declared in T'ongyŏng on October 12 after Koreans imprisoned 200 Japanese residents and ransacked the home of the new, American-appointed *kunsu*.[112] Imprisonment of American-appointed government and police officials occurred in Kosŏng and Hamyang. Tactical troops suppressed strikes in October in Masan, Chinju, Ulsan, Kimhae, and Hadong.[113] Thus, the general American policy in South Kyŏngsang became the removal of "the self-appointed *kun* and *myŏn* officials throughout the province. Those who had usurped office were deposed and some were jailed." By October 24 the Americans had attempted to depose fifteen county PCs.[114]

At the *myŏn* and lower levels, alignments were less clear and American policies more subtle. On November 22 the provincial military government promulgated an order to take the selection of *myŏn* officials out of PC hands and return it to representatives of family groups (elders), "in accordance with ancient Korean tradition."[115] The Americans and the conservative Koreans who advised them hoped that this would remove committee influence from the *myŏn*s and bolster the old order and the traditional social hierarchy in general. In December such elections were held—and the village elders elected PC people to about 50 percent of the *myŏn* posts.[116] How did this happen?

As this study has tried to demonstrate, the committees were not handpicked and organized by "radicals" or communists. They most often accurately depicted the complex of social forces dominant in a particular county or township. PC leadership ranged from local landlords to peasant proprietors, tenants, former Korean officials who served the Japanese, former leaders of peasant unions in the 1930s, to communists. When a communist emerged to lead a committee, it was probably because of his staunchness in the anti-Japanese struggle or because of the communist land reform program, which held such basic appeal to tenant farmers—not because of some devious "organizational weapon" or sinister technique that only communists, presumably, could master. Political organization, communist and noncommunist alike, succeeds or fails to the extent that it appeals to and mobilizes support from existing needs and grievances. It is clear that in Korea in 1945, long-suppressed economic and social grievances, and the aura of legitimacy conferred upon communism by the return of many communists from Japanese prisons to their native communities, enabled such men to dominate certain PCs. But there was also the chance that groups of village elders and local committees could be nearly conterminous in membership. There is no way of knowing how many township committees were originally chosen by village elders, but we would expect it to have been a substantial percentage.

At any rate, it is not strange that village elders might pick committee leaders in the South Kyŏngsang *myŏn* elections. But it is unfortunate that the Americans tended to see all PC leaders as radicals and communists. The overall effect, like a self-fulfilling prophecy, was to turn the committees rapidly leftward. At all levels, committees that more often than not were composed of coalitions of communists and noncommunists were forced to defend themselves or find themselves charged as common criminals. The unsurprising result was the emergence of people willing to sacrifice and to fight fire with fire. Given their experience of persecution and tempering under Japanese colonialism, the communists persisted in the struggle while less hardy individuals dropped by the wayside. The Americans, in a sense, ended up getting what they asked for. Moreover, we would not be overly cynical in suggesting that the Americans in the provinces, as in Seoul, may have preferred operating in a situation where political alignments were clearer or even placed in relief, where the grays of coalition turned to the blacks and whites of communist and anticommunist.

In spite of the relatively continuous American effort to depose the county committees in South Kyŏngsang in the fall of 1945, county PCs were still strong in the succeeding spring. In many counties, they were still collecting taxes, managing grain collections, and assembling vital statistics: "in short, [the PCs] had a large degree of control which amounted to a pseudo-government."[117] The inability of the MG to collect rice in many counties attested to continuing PC strength. Attempts to transfer collected rice out of Hadong, Kŏch'ang, and Hyŏpch'ŏn met bitter resistance from local peasants. They surrounded MG trucks and refused to let them leave.[118] The American reaction was as follows:

> It was not until 1 April 1946 that this threat to Military Government was removed. At this time, Military Government initiated a province-wide purge of Left Wing elements, arresting about three hundred persons. . . . [MG] relieved four kunsus and 160 police, as well as numerous minor officials. . . . After this purge of officials, more encouragement and cooperation was forthcoming from the people, who then recognized Military Government as the legal government.[119]

American authorities and their Korean employees made a clean sweep of Kŏch'ang, Ŭiryŏng, Hadong, and Hamyang in April. In Hadong the police chief, the *kunsu*, and all *myŏn* chiefs were fired. Most of them were arrested. During the night after the Hadong operation, the *kun* office and several other buildings were burned to the ground. American tactical troops came in and enforced a dawn-to-dusk curfew. The local residents were uncooperative, refusing to say who had burned the buildings.[120]

The people in many South Kyŏngsang counties remained confused as to their legal government for several months longer. In the fall of 1946 numerous counties erupted in bloody violence. Only after that was the province under relative control. Whereas in the southwestern counties of South Chŏlla, a thoroughgoing purge in early 1946 was apparently sufficient to root out the committees, in South Kyŏngsang it had to be done over and over again. The difference between these

two regions shows the impact of the severe population strains occurring in South Kyŏngsang throughout 1945 and 1946. Every boatload
of Koreans returning from Japan brought new recruits for the committees. These people had had their outlook broadened. They had scores
to settle in Korea. They adapted imperfectly to the political order
constructed by Americans. It is likely that the prime factor in the final
demise of the strong committees in this province was, as with other
governing PCs in south Korea, the lack of potent, locally controlled
armed force and the resultant inability of PC leaders to protect people
under their control from political opponents.

NORTH KYŎNGSANG PROVINCE

In many ways North Kyŏngsang should be considered as of a piece
with South Kyŏngsang. It too was occupied initially by tactical troops
of the 40th Division, following the same "standard operating procedure." All counties had people's committees (see figure 11). Information on the early months of Occupation in North Kyŏngsang is very
limited, however; it is likely that many more committees actually governed county affairs than is indicated in figure 11.

Among the various provinces, North Kyŏngsang had the second
highest population increase in the years 1944 to 1946. Fourteen of
twenty-two counties lost population in absolute terms in the 1930s,
and of the eight counties that gained, only two had more than marginal gains—Yŏngdŏk, which gained a little over 10 percent from
1930 to 1940 and had a small influx after liberation, indeed the smallest in the province; and Ponghwa, which shared the same population
pattern, having only a slightly smaller gain in the 1930s and a slightly
larger influx between 1944 and 1946. Yŏngdŏk was one of the least radical counties in North Kyŏngsang, which would fit our expectations;
but Ponghwa was quite radical. Ponghwa, however, was a mountainous, remote county, with less than 40 percent of the arable land in
paddy; its radicalism can be explained in much the same terms as that
of the coastal counties of Uljin, Kangnŭng, and Samch'ŏk in Kangwŏn
Province (see below). In the core counties surrounding Taegu—Ŭisŏng, Sŏnsan, Kunhwi, Talsŏng, Sŏngju, Koryŏng, Ch'ilgok, Yŏngch'-
ŏn, Kyŏngsan, and Ch'ŏngdo—we find strong if not necessarily governing committees and the base area for the uprisings in the fall of 1946.
All of these counties fit the pattern of population losses in the 1930s,
followed by sharp gains between 1944 and 1946. American reports
from the scene during 1945/46 also provided much qualitative evidence that returnees, particularly conscripted laborers, played major

known people's committees
known assumption of governmental functions

11. North Kyŏngsang Province People's Committees

roles in civil disorders; many reports spoke of reprisals against officials who had dispatched laborers abroad or to northern Korea.

In the peripheral counties, people's committees governed primarily because of geographic remoteness. If we look at figure 11, we can see that six of the eight counties with governing PCs were located in coastal and border regions of North Kyŏngsang. The result of this geographical location was a comparatively long interregnum between Japanese and American rule, which is probably why only these counties still show governing PCs when American political reports and information become available in early 1946.

In terms of roads and communication facilities, literacy rates, urbanization, and industrialization, North Kyŏngsang ranked below South Kyŏngsang but above most other provinces. This province had severe unemployment problems throughout 1946, but it was not a province of abject rural poverty when compared to other south Korean provinces. The proportion of the population classified as full tenants here, about 35 percent (57 percent when both full tenants and half-owners are included), placed it in the middling category. Furthermore, tenants and smallholders generally worked larger plots than in other provinces.

North Kyŏngsang presented a mixed picture, however. Remote counties like Mun'gyŏng and Ponghwa were extremely poor. In some months of 1946, starvation conditions prevailed; Mun'gyŏng's peasants were in the hills searching for roots and bark to eat, and peasants in Ponghwa staged food riots.[121] In May and June 1946 some 16,000 refugees swelled the Mun'gyŏng population and so strained the food supply that there was "no rice whatsoever."[122] Some 2,600 miners in Mun'gyŏng were out of work for most of 1945 and 1946. Yet Mun'gyŏng is an anomaly in North Kyŏngsang. At one time, it had a governing PC, led by Chŏn Pyŏng-yong. And as late as the end of February 1946, no conservative parties existed, only the PC, a PC-affiliated youth group, and nongmin and nodong chohaps.[123] Yet by May 1946 no disorders occurred in Mun'gyŏng when local PC leaders were arrested for "crimes" committed in the fall of 1945.[124] When the autumn uprisings swept through North Kyŏngsang in 1946, Mun'gyŏng was untouched. The early appearance and strength of the PC in Mun'gyŏng, and in other poor and remote counties like Yŏngyang, can be attributed to geographic location and a comparatively long interregnum. The apparently bloodless fall of the PCs in these counties perhaps demonstrates the inability of a population living on the brink of economic ruin to sustain strong political organization. These counties belong in the same category as Wando, Chindo, and Haenam in South Chŏlla.

The dominant pattern of county politics in North Kyŏngsang is revealed in the more central counties of Andong, Kunhwi, Ŭisŏng, Talsŏng, Yech'ŏn, Yŏngch'ŏn, and others. In this region a political complexion emerged like that of the Yŏsu/Sunch'ŏn region of South Chŏlla—one of strong but not necessarily governing PCs coexisting in tenuous opposition to other forces. In fact, this pattern was repeated in the provincial capital, Taegu, and in the North Kyŏngsang Constabulary detachment.[125] Many of the county PCs were the objects of only sporadic attempts at suppression, until the fall of 1946, which gave them time to build some support. No real crisis occurred in most of North Kyŏngsang until fourteen months after the liberation.

American policies followed in North Kyŏngsang differed little from those followed in South Kyŏngsang. But their implementation was made more difficult by the greater problems with transportation and communications and the political complexities of various counties. In North Kyŏngsang, strong PCs often existed side-by-side with conservative and right-wing parties having considerably more support than did those in South Kyŏngsang. Suppressing the committees was neither easy nor neat.

American tactical forces, acting under standard 40th Division procedures, at first retained Kim Tae-u, the provincial governor under the Japanese and a notorious collaborator:[126] "Kim proceeded to change large numbers of *kun* and other local officials, removing Japanese and appointing Koreans. The resulting chaos, together with his reputation for being pro-Japanese, made Kim's retention seem undesirable."[127] On October 11 Colonel Edwin A. Henn, a man with "an extensive academic background in political science," was substituted for Kim. Henn retained Kim as his advisor, however, and ordered "all political organizations in the province to register at his office, giving their names, purposes, officials, and financial status." He "forbade the distribution of political propaganda without permission from his office . . . [and] the seizing or harming of any private property." He also revealed that even political scientists can be ethnocentric: "almost any Korean who could make himself understood in English was employed."[128]

Henn and the Americans retained Japanese officials for a month (October 6 to November 6) in Taegu. Japanese police officials stayed on even longer as advisors, and "the next ranking Koreans were retained in office as understudies. . . . Several Koreans with former police experience were recalled from civilian life to re-enter police work in positions of high responsibility."[129] Police who had earlier been "driven away" from their duties were reinstated. Police morale remained low, however, because they were "despised by the people as collaborators." All police stations were "recaptured" by January 1946. The authorized strength of the provincial police force was then expanded from 2,200 to 3,100.[130] In North Kyŏngsang, South Kyŏngsang, and several other provinces, the Americans utilized as many as 50 percent more provincial policemen than had the Japanese during the colonial era. The augmentation of police power may be taken as yet one more index of the highly mobilized setting of postwar Korea and of the heightened requisites of control.

In early 1946 the Americans appointed Kim Pyŏng-gyu as the new Korean provincial governor (Henn was dismissed in late 1945); Kim had been a high-ranking official in the Government-General Home Affairs Ministry.[131] This and other actions, including similar appointments at lower levels, rather effectively brought the provincial administration under reliable control. Still, even in Taegu, an entrenched PC, led by Yi Sŏng-hun, Cho Chung-sik, and Kim Il-sik, remained a power in city politics in the first year after liberation. Conservative power in this provincial capital rested primarily in the provincial government and police. In March 1946 American sources reported that right-wing political parties in Taegu still had few members and were "largely inactive."[132] In the summer of 1946 right-wing and left-wing groups were brought into a local coalition effort that paralleled the activities of the Coalition Committee in Seoul. The provincial body was called the Taegu Community Council. This act had the effect of aligning Taegu politics with the politics of numerous North Kyŏngsang counties: a pattern of tenuous coexistence between Right and Left.

American tactical forces occupied all counties in North Kyŏngsang by middle to late October 1945. In Ponghwa, Ch'ilgok, and most of the counties in the eastern part of the province, tactical units did little more than supervise county PC administration.[133] Later attempts to depose these committees were unsuccessful below the county level, and PC officials continued to run the local townships. The 99th MG Company arrived in Taegu on October 29, and within days MG companies were in place throughout the province. Their policies were justified in the following manner: "Government and its activities and attitudes were modelled upon the experience in enemy countries and on the usual instructions and training of an army in a hostile country."[134] As we saw in chapter four, however, no official policy statement exists that declared Korea to be an enemy country in 1945. The application of the above policy in North Kyŏngsang meant, in effect, that Japanese and Korean colonial officials were the liberated and those Koreans associated with the committees were the enemy. At least we can agree with the official judgment that the distinction between an enemy and a liberated people "was not sharply drawn or felt" in the hostile environs of North Kyŏngsang.[135]

The MG companies brought in Taegu-appointed county officials to replace PC officials, with selection based on "the amount of experience each had received while working under the Japanese administration."[136] As in other provinces, these officials had to have American troops present to secure their precarious mandate. As in South Kyŏngsang, the continual infusion of returnees from Japan and elsewhere meant that when PC leaders were arrested, new blood was available to take their places. This was particularly true of the counties around Taegu where rates of population change were high. The PCs in these counties were able either to control lower levels of county government or to muster sufficient strength to maintain their organizations throughout the first year of liberation. A prime environmental factor in continuing PC strength was their early and persistent influence in the strategic points of Andong, Kŭmch'ŏn, Sangju, Yŏngju, and Yŏngyang. Andong was the terminal point of navigation on the Naktong River and a junction point for many railroads and highways. Kŭmch'ŏn, Sangju, Yŏngju, and Yŏngyang occupied the entrances to key mountain passes leading into the alluvial basin of central North Kyŏngsang.[137] But the presence of strong PCs in these counties meant that opposing forces were also desirous of controlling these strategic points. It is in these counties, among others, that we find the general North Kyŏngsang pattern of tentative coexistence between Right and Left.

In Andong, the county PC, led by Sŏ P'yŏn-no, was a potent factor in county politics but apparently never controlled the county seat. PCs and *nongmin chohap* controlled outlying villages and townships, however, and were capable of mobilizing as many as 5,000 people for demonstrations in the town of Andong.[138] But Andong also had branches of the KDP and NSRRKI, and the Right seemed to gain control of the county seat in early 1946. Because of the dominance of the rightists, Andong was one of the few counties to meet its rice collection quotas, for example.[139] In addition, the Andong police were reliable enough to be used continuously in putting down PC and leftist activities, not just in Andong but in the neighboring counties of Yech'ŏn and Yŏngju as well. They arrested sixty-three individuals in Kudam-dong, west of Andong, after a March First (Independence Day) demonstration,[140] and intervened in Yŏngju in late March after a performance by the well-known leftist comedian Sin Pul-ch'ul erupted in violence.[141] The Americans made several changes in Andong county officials during early 1946, seeking to ensure the county seat's reliability. In May, for example, they appointed Kang Il-sŏk as the new county police chief; Kang had been a *kunsu* and police officer under the Japanese in North Ch'ungch'ŏng.[142] Neighboring counties apparently had a similar political complexion, since there were frequent reports of relatively strong right-wing demonstrations in these months in Yŏngju and Yech'ŏn. In Yech'ŏn, Right and Left often engaged in soccer matches that invariably erupted in brawls.[143]

A similar pattern of coexistence between Right and Left, with neither completely dominant, prevailed in the coastal counties of Yŏngdŏk, Yŏng'il, and Kyŏngju. In the spring of 1946, PCs were reported to be strong in these counties, but with conservative groups making inroads. In Yŏngdŏk the PC was dominant, but a branch of the NSRRKI was being organized with the support of "the upper classes."[144] The same was true of the coastal city of P'ohang.[145] In Kyŏngju the PCs still controlled all but two townships, but the county police chief and magistrate were old Japanese employees who were "distrusted" by the people. In P'ohang nearly all top police officials were former colonial policemen; they informed some Americans who were put off by their methods that they found it impossible to run their stations without beating prisoners.[146] They and other police officials in North Kyŏngsang used rice collection and rationing procedures as a prime tool in coercing political opponents. Those who cooperated with the police received either lower collection quotas or more ration stamps.[147] General Hodge, as we noted in chapter five, could not have been more precise in his observation that the man with a gun and rice stamps controlled everything in Korea.

PC strength was also evident in Sŏnsan and Yŏngyang in March 1946 when committee leaders occupied many of the township administrative posts and organized local rice collections.[148] The PC in Sangju ran a school in an old *sŏdang* (traditional, private schools for teaching the Chinese classics) for which students were selected by each township committee. But at the end of March the school was closed and its books were sent to Seoul for inspection.[149] The chaotic aspects of the North Kyŏngsang pattern of coexisting rightist and leftist factions, and simultaneous non-PC *kunsu*s and PC *myŏn* chiefs, are illustrated in the following quotation, taken from an interview conducted by an American official with the Yŏngyang PC chief:

> Eighty per cent of the people belong to the People's Committee and believe in it. These people do not like the *kun* head, Mr. O, because he is narrow and considers only the people of the Democratic National Foundation Party.* This party represents only a few people.

* Perhaps a branch of the *kungmin taehoe* faction of the KDP.

The *kun* head dislikes the People's Committee because he is a former Japanese official and misunderstands it [misunderstands the PC]. He knows the people do not like him so he dislikes them. Six *myŏn* heads are not functioning because they are former Japanese officials and the people do not want them in office.[150]

Some of the above may be dismissed as exaggeration, yet the strength of this PC was considerable: it was able to raise 1.7 million *wŏn* to purchase rice for needy people in Yŏngyang.[151]

A Yŏngyang local history reveals a distinctive pattern in county magistrate appointments in the months after the Americans arrived in the provinces. Mr. O in the above quotation was O Kwang-jin, appointed as Yŏngyang *kunsu* on October 13, 1945. He had been section chief in the Home Affairs Department in Ŭisŏng County and magistrate in Kunhwi County before liberation. O was replaced in Yŏngyang in May 1946 by Shin Wŏn-jae, who had also been magistrate in Kunhwi (following Mr. O around the province, as it were). The magistrate in Yŏngyang at the time the Americans arrived was Yi Hwa-wŏn, who had been there since 1943; he was transferred to Yech'ŏn county when Mr. O came into Yŏngyang.[152] Thus, this small region, like most others, had a musical chairs pattern in which colonial officials, instead of being ousted, were simply transferred from place to place, much as the Japanese had done. The old "law of avoidance" worked in such cases to allow officials to avoid the consequences of their own rule in service to Japanese interests and to enable them to begin serving American interests.

The success of a locally powerful family in Yŏngyang in placing several relatives in key positions in provincial governments provides in microcosm a pattern repeated throughout southern Korea, whereby threatened elite were able to perpetuate their influence through the turmoil of liberation. Cho Jun-yŏng, a member of this wealthy, landed family in Yŏngyang, emerged in August 1945 to chair a local branch of a committee to welcome back the Korean Provisional Government. Shortly thereafter, he, like the committee, joined the Korean Democratic Party. After the Americans arrived in Yŏngyang, he was appointed chief of police in nearby Mun'gyŏng county. He went on to become police chief in Sangju and then in Taegu, the capital. In January 1950 he became provincial chief of police. His brother, Cho Hŏn-yŏng was an initiator of the Korean Democratic Party and later chief of the KDP provincial affairs department. He was elected to the National Assembly from Sŏnsan in 1948 and 1950. A third brother, Cho Kŭn-yŏng, was also a KDP leader in the province and had served on the provincial advisory council under the Japanese. A fourth man, Cho Yong-gi, who gave the same domicile in Yŏngyang as did the Cho brothers, became province chief of Rhee's NSRRKI and was a member of the central committee of Noch'ong, the rightist labor organization.[153] Thus, within one family, we find recapitulated the general pattern of affiliations and appointments followed from Seoul on down. Information is not sufficient to allow firm generalizations about county PCs in North Kyŏngsang. It does appear that the PCs with early strength in the more remote and impoverished counties were eventually deposed with relative ease. In the more central counties, with higher rates of population change and strained patterns of coexistence between Right and Left, many PCs remained potent until the fall of 1946. The complexities of county political alignments, particularly the absence of clear-cut PC dominance or subordination, made action against the PCs that much more difficult. The Americans and Korean county officials not affiliated with the PCs had to accommodate PC entrenchment by allowing committee leaders to run many townships. It is no accident that, fourteen months after the liberation, a major insurrection swept through North Kyŏngsang. The rooted presence of the PCs in this province provided the necessary organization, and severe population strains offered rootless and resentful individuals more than willing to take up the sword.

THE CH'UNGCH'ŎNG PROVINCES

North and South Ch'ungch'ŏng provinces constituted the most orderly and easily governed region in south Korea under the American Occupation. Only in the western and northwestern counties of South Ch'ungch'ŏng and in the southern counties of North Ch'ungch'ŏng do we find strong people's committees or difficulties in the transition from Japanese to American rule (see figures 12 and 13). Both provinces were primarily agricultural, although South Ch'ungch'ŏng also had a significant fishing industry and the eastern counties of North Ch'ungch'ŏng had several important mines. The northern province is the only landlocked province in south Korea and is studded with mountains that made transportation quite difficult. Both provinces were comparatively backward, although Taejŏn had become an urban center owing to its location on the major railroad lines; provincial rates of population change from 1944 to 1946 were well below the national average. The Ch'ungch'ŏngs both had higher degrees of tenancy than the Kyŏngsang provinces or South Chŏlla.

North Ch'ungch'ŏng is one of two provinces in south Korea for which rates of tenancy are available on a county-by-county basis.[154] Rates ranged from a low of 58 percent in Okch'ŏn to a high of 78 percent in Chinch'ŏn. Yŏngdong, by far the most radical county in this province, was in the middle at 67 percent; it also ranked second in the province in numbers of farms over twelve acres, whereas Chinch'ŏn had none of that size. That is, in Chinch'ŏn tenancy was extensive, but based in small farms; in Yŏngdong it was more intensive, based in larger farms. It is likely that land relationships in Chinch'ŏn had survived largely intact from precolonial times, with few Japanese landlords and many small Korean landlords. Chinch'ŏn, in fact, could symbolize most of North Ch'ungch'ŏng, a province long noted as a base for Korea's aristocracy, where tradition and social dominance were much less interrupted by Japanese rule than in other provinces. Like Yi Dynasty kings, Syngman Rhee soon came to get his own personal rice supply from an estate here. North Ch'ungch'ŏng also had by far the highest rate of volunteers for the Japanese military, including those willing to sign in blood their fealty to the emperor.[155] If we exclude the southernmost Yŏngdong, which bordered two other provinces and whose politics were closer to the Kyŏngsang provinces, we have remaining the most conservative counties in Korea.

The interregnum between Japanese and American rule was somewhat longer in South Ch'ungch'ŏng than in North Ch'ungch'ŏng because of the transfer of the 96th Division to China. Tactical occupation forces arrived there in the third week of October, two weeks after their arrival in the northern province.[156] MG companies were in place in both provinces by the beginning of November. American control was facilitated in both provinces by relative ease of communications. The Japanese had developed an excellent transportation system in South Ch'ungch'ŏng, with Taejŏn as the hub of railways, and good, usable roads leading out in all directions. Transportation was more difficult in North Ch'ungch'ŏng, but the key police communications lines were barely disrupted after August 15, and by December they had been reestablished in nine of ten counties.[157] This is quite at variance with other provinces.

All South Ch'ungch'ŏng counties had substantial population gains in the 1930s, thus population change, as we have discussed it, is irrelevant here. In North Ch'ungch'ŏng three counties gained population—Ch'ŏngwŏn, Ch'ungju, Ŭmsŏng—and none were radical. Of those counties that lost population in the 1940s, Yŏngdong had the highest gain (25 percent) from 1944 to 1946. Chinch'ŏn is the only anomaly here, showing a population loss in the 1930s and a gain of 23 percent between 1944 and 1946, but having no reported radicalism. The depth and longevity of tenancy here, mentioned above, may explain this lack of correspondence with our predictions.

Upon arrival, the Americans found people's committees in nearly all counties of South Ch'ungch'ŏng and in seven of ten counties in

known people's committees

known assumption of governmental functions

12. South Ch'ungch'ŏng Province People's Committees

■ known people's committees
☐ known assumption of governmental functions

13. North Ch'ungch'ŏng Province People's Committees

North Ch'ungch'ŏng. According to American sources, PCs in the southern province "had seized control of administrative and police functions throughout the province" (thus figure 13 may underestimate committee control).[158] PCs in North Ch'ungch'ŏng represented a "major problem," yet unlike most other provinces, former police officials were functioning effectively and even held colonial-era prisoners in local jails.[159]

A province-level PC in Taejŏn governed that city and controlled county PCs; a worker's committee under its direction published the only Taejŏn newspaper, the *Taejŏn ilbo*.[160] In both provinces, the strongest committees were in the remote counties—Sŏsan, Tangjin, Yesan, and Hongsŏng in South Ch'ungch'ŏng, and Yŏngdong in North Ch'ungch'ŏng. Yŏngdong provided an ideal setting for a people's committee, since it was in a border region, had a history of peasant union organization, a middling rate of tenancy, and a high population gain after liberation. It was the only county in the province to be touched by the autumn uprisings in 1946 and had a reputation throughout the liberation era as being a "Red" county.[161]

When the Americans arrived in North Ch'ungch'ŏng, the provincial government was at a standstill, but the Japanese-Korean police force still maintained order.[162] At the county level, however, former police had been disarmed in some places and it appeared that, to the extent that any county government existed, it was people's committee government.[163] The Americans found seventeen Korean provincial officials still in office, though, and reemployed them all. The Ch'ungju PC controlled the only newspaper in the province, the "Tong Shee" (*T'ongsin?*). But the Americans closed it down and authorized "a group of local citizens" to start another newspaper, the *Kungmin ilbo* (National Daily).[164] In December they sent KDP leader and National Labor Mediation Board member Kim To-yŏn into North Ch'ungch'ŏng to organize provincial advisory councils. Americans reported, upon occupying the province, that the "people would not talk to or look at any MG officials."[165] At the county level, however, the MG experienced few problems in governing. In the northern counties of Ch'ungju, Koesan, Chinch'ŏn, Ŭmsŏng, and Chech'ŏn, incoming Americans found that PCs were "active"[166] but that the former police were still "functioning well." The Americans tried to employ former *kunsu*s in these counties but found that they "were not supported by the people and wanted to resign."[167] They also encountered great difficulty in finding interpreters, since potential employees were afraid of being attacked if they worked for the MG. In the northern counties, the Americans reported, "the communist elements were possibly more active than less radical [groups] . . . [and] in general there was a wish by farmers to own all farm lands."[168] In the early months of 1946, leftists were reported to be quite strong in several *myŏn*s near Ch'ungju where a number of important mines existed, and police in the region operated "in fear of" the local committees.[169] Tactical troops had to be called out in Okch'ŏn in January 1946 when some 300 individuals associated with the county PC attacked a jail in Okch'ŏn, seeking the release of four imprisoned leaders.[170] In Yŏng-dong there were several attempts to depose the county PC, none of which was entirely successful.[171] But in general, the occupation of North Ch'ungch'ŏng was smooth; and when the uprisings occurred in the fall of 1946, the Americans described this province as "the strongest rightist province in south Korea."[172]

The smattering of existing information on North Ch'ungch'ŏng still demonstrates that the basically counterrevolutionary policy followed by the Americans was fully applied in this province. But it also indicates that some Americans experienced noticeable cognitive dissonance in using means that so greatly conflicted with American ideals. Rice collection practices in North Ch'ungch'ŏng, as in many other regions, often amounted to forced confiscation, for example; one report put it, "Rice raid in Ŭmsŏng: Raiding parties consisted of Korean police and Civil [*sic*] officials, with U.S. troops maintaining peace and order."[173] Many Americans found such practices abominable. One noted that Koreans saw the Korea Commodity Corporation as "a huge exploitative organization determined to take all and give nothing."[174] Another urged the MG in Seoul to abolish the police practice of torturing prisoners to obtain confessions, saying, "It is hard to conceive of such a practice flourishing within an agency of an American-staffed military government."[175]

South Ch'ungch'ŏng was somewhat more unruly than North Ch'ungch'ŏng, perhaps because of the longer interregnum between Japanese and American rule. The Occupation commander there, Lieutenant Colonel William Karp, brought the provincial PC at Taejŏn under control by "revitalizing the local police"; he retained forty Koreans formerly on the Japanese force, including the Taejŏn police chief.[176] Karp also employed former Korean colonial officials in the provincial administration, one of whom was later attacked, allegedly for surpassing his quota in conscripting Korean laborers during the war.[177] On November 1 the workers' committee managing the *Taejŏn ilbo* changed the newspaper's name to the *Inmin ilbo* (People's Daily); the next day Karp suspended it. It reopened on November 13 after Korean shareholders in the newspaper—that is, shareholders from the colonial era—recommended "suitable" Koreans to staff it.[178] Thus, as with the *Maeil sinbo* in Seoul, we find Americans in the provinces seizing and reorganizing key communications media in November 1945.

At the county level in South Ch'ungch'ŏng in the fall of 1945, official sources reported "rioting, disorder and resistance to Military Government."[179] When the Americans arrived in Yesan they found Ch'oe Yong-gil and 300 supporters running the county. PCs also controlled the police in Kongju, Puyŏ, Hongsŏng, Sŏsan, and Tangjin. In the four northwestern counties, serious disorders attended the inauguration of military government, but little information on them exists.[180] There were also reports of widespread arrests in these same counties in the spring of 1946.[181] In the other counties, the transition to American rule proceeded more smoothly. In Ch'ŏnan, for example, the Japanese police chief was still in charge of the county in mid-October.[182]

The premier position of the police as an agency of political power in preliberation and postliberation Korea was highlighted in a meeting of county PC operatives held in Taejŏn in January 1946, where the representatives complained that police persecution made their organizational efforts most difficult.[183] This was true throughout south Korea, but more so in provinces where the old police controls were only loosened rather than broken. Peasant populations will not respond to the appeals of organizers in such conditions, particularly when the peasants themselves bear the brunt of the repression. We again see how important it is for political organizers to be able to provide protection to peasants under their control.

The paucity of information on the Ch'ungch'ŏng provinces leaves frustrating gaps and ambiguities in the existing historical record. Even though the PCs were never terribly strong in North Ch'ungch'ŏng, for example, it is intriguing to learn that in the spring of 1946 the Americans had to institute a purge of provincial advisory councils; this resulted in "a sweeping shift" from Left to Right.[184] Yet the original advisory councils, organized by Kim To-yŏn, were based on the Japanese system of election by ward (ku) and township officials.[185] This suggests that, as in South Kyŏngsang, even traditional or colonial-style elections often resulted in a predominance of PC influence.

Major disorders occurred in the four northwestern counties of South Ch'ungch'ŏng and in Yŏngdong County in North Ch'ungch'ŏng during October and November 1946. It is likely that the strong PCs in these counties were not eliminated until sometime after these uprisings. But in general, the Ch'ungch'ŏngs did not provide a congenial setting for the growth of the committees. A relatively short interregnum and comparative ease of transportation and communication made the reimposition of central controls fairly simple. Most important, however, was the relative lack of population change here. The

Ch'ungch'ŏngs had far fewer people transported out of the region during colonial rule, and thus far fewer returnees after liberation. The result was an easy transition from Japanese to American-Korean rule.

KANGWŎN AND KYŎNGGI PROVINCES

Kangwŏn and Kyŏnggi provinces presented contrasting settings in nearly every respect. Kyŏnggi had well-developed communications, transportation, and industrial systems in 1945, while Kangwŏn was perhaps the least modern of Korean provinces. Good railroad and highway networks linked the counties of Kyŏnggi together, but Kangwŏn was virtually impassable from east to west because of the forbidding Taebaek mountain range. Communications in Kyŏnggi were easily accomplished by rail, road, or telephone, while contact with the coastal counties of Kangwŏn was made by courier.

Population changes were significant in Kangwŏn, but in an entirely different direction from other Korean provinces. All of its counties had gains during the 1930s, considerable gains in the coastal counties of Kangnŭng, Samch'ŏk, Uljin, and Yangyang. Kangnŭng and Samch'ŏk gained more than 40 percent, and Uljin and Yangyang gained more than 20 percent. Unlike the others Kangnŭng also had a significant gain of 37 percent from 1944 to 1946, meaning that county population nearly doubled between 1930 and 1946. This was a very radical county; it was also the only county in Kangwŏn that had more than 50 percent of the land in paddy. Its population change pattern does not correspond to that of any other county in the south, and the reasons for it are not clear. But there was certainly a gross population change, even if in a unique direction. Kyŏnggi had only three counties with absolute population loss in the 1930s, although several others had only marginal gains. The gain from 1944 to 1946 averaged about 9 percent, suggesting that this would be a generally conservative province within the general pattern prevailing in the south.

Tenancy rates among peasants farming the fertile paddies of Kyŏnggi were among the highest in all Korea—second only to North Chŏlla, in fact, while tenancy rates in Kangwŏn were the lowest in south Korea except for Cheju Island. Kyŏnggi counties were the least remote in our survey, while the coastal and inner mountainous counties of Kangwŏn were the most remote. Red Peasant Unions in the 1930s penetrated only three counties in Kyŏnggi but were strong in the coastal counties of Kangwŏn.

The environmental characters of these two provinces profoundly affected the growth of the their people's committees. The dominance of the CPKI and KPR in Seoul until the American arrival occasioned a rapid extension of PC control throughout Kyŏnggi. In all counties of known political complexion (there is no information on those counties in figure 14 having no committees), PCs existed or governed in the initial weeks after liberation (see figure 14). Yet the easy communications and the high rates of tenancy meant that Kyŏnggi, like North Chŏlla, saw its early committee strength dissipate in a matter of weeks. The presence of a strong, centralized, mobile police force in Seoul made deposing local committees that much easier. The opposite was true of Kangwŏn. Especially in the inaccessible coastal counties, strong committees emerged quickly and remained dominant well into 1946 (see figure 15).

The Americans experienced great difficulties in occupying the coastal counties of Kangwŏn. No railroads or usable highways ran over the mountains to the east coast, and upon American arrival, only one telephone link was in operation from Ch'unch'ŏn (the province capital) to the coast.[186] Kangwŏn required rice imports to feed the local population, but the Americans found food supplies low and no system operating to transfer rice into the province. Tactical occupation forces reached the coast in early October and MG companies followed within a month, but they did little more than sanction the rule of county committees.

The CPKI branch in Ch'unch'ŏn was run from the beginning by conservative Koreans who allied with the KDP rather than with the KPR in September.[187] This naturally affected the character of the county PCs surrounding Ch'unch'ŏn. Moreover, the Japanese did not relinquish control of this province capital before the Americans arrived. Ch'unch'ŏn was a major relay point for Japanese and Korean refugees and returnees from north Korea; in August and September the Japanese deputized some 500 army soldiers to control this human traffic.[188] The capital thus presented few problems to the incoming Americans. When MG companies arrived in late October, they removed from office the top five Korean employees in the provincial administration and reemployed the rest. They appointed non-PC people to run seven counties in Kangwŏn, but sanctioned PC *kunsus* in Kangnŭng, Samch'ŏk, and Uljin.[189] This anomalous situation lasted until the latter three leaders came out in favor of the Moscow accords in January 1946; they were then relieved and "the Rightist elements gained power" in the coastal county administrations.[190] The 48th MG Company in Ch'unch'ŏn seemed to run an effective administration in the counties around Ch'unch'ŏn; rice collections proceeded smoothly and no disorders were reported in 1945 and 1946.[191]

In spite of the removal of the three people's committee *kunsus* in the coastal counties, the PCs there remained strong in the spring of 1946. Public Opinion Department teams found in March 1946 that

Yŏngwŏl was also dominated by the Left, with its strength based in the mining population in the county, particularly in Yŏndŏng-ni. Kangnŭng was termed "the most powerful left wing *kun* in south Korea." Informants indicated that the entire county government, most of the police, and most of the MG interpreters, were "communists." The Left in Kangnŭng had "led the resistance movement. Consequently the Left wing has had extremely good leadership." This perhaps indicates that leaders of the Red Peasant Union in Kangnŭng in the 1930s also led the county PC after liberation. Similar conditions prevailed in Samch'ŏk, where the PC derived its strength from the workers in south Korea's largest coal mines (944,000 metric tons in 1944).[192] One public opinion team found, in fact, that PCs dominated the entire coast of Kangwŏn and North Kyŏngsang and predicted, "civil war will develop along the entire east coast as soon as MG leaves."[193] The situation along the coast had changed somewhat by July 1946 when another public opinion team found systematic suppression of the Left and numerous PC leaders held in miserable conditions in county jails.[194] Yet the American prophecy of civil war proved true: uprisings occurred in Kangnŭng and Samch'ŏk in the fall of 1946, eventually devolving into guerrilla fighting in the Taebaek range in 1947, and thereafter, involving local Koreans and Koreans coming down from the north.

There was never much question about who ran Kyŏnggi Province after the American entry in September. MG teams, numbers 1, 2, and 3, were in place by September 11. The Americans retained the Japanese provincial governor until October 2. He and the Korean head of the colonial labor conscription section of the Kyŏnggi Department of Home Affairs, Sin Yun, were asked to submit separate lists of qualified Koreans for appointment to the provincial administration. When the two lists were compared, "they were found to be almost identical," which somehow surprised the Americans.[195] Appointments were then made from these lists. Sin Yun became chief of the Kyŏnggi Department of Home Affairs in April 1946.[196] Other Japanese officials were officially relieved to appease protestors, but were then given the title "Councillor" and kept on in advisory capacities for a period of weeks.[197] At the provincial level, political affairs were well in hand after the appointments of Chang T'aek-sang as chief of Division A of the Korean National Police (responsible for Seoul and Kyŏnggi) and Ku Cha-ok as Korean provincial governor. Chang and Ku were both important early leaders of the Korean Democratic Party and took it upon themselves to assure that PC influence in Kyŏnggi was quickly extinguished.

At the county level in Kyŏnggi, MG teams found PCs running county affairs in P'och'ŏn, Sihŭng, Suwŏn, Yongin, and P'yŏngt'aek.[198]

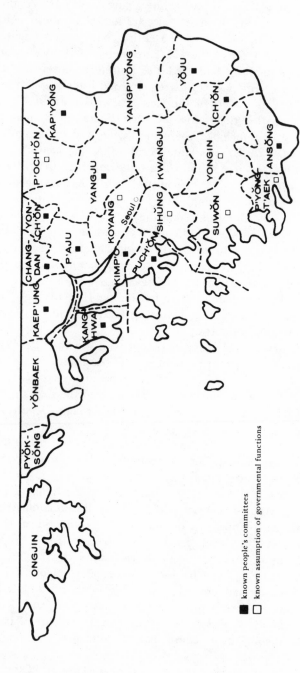

14. Kyŏnggi Province People's Committees

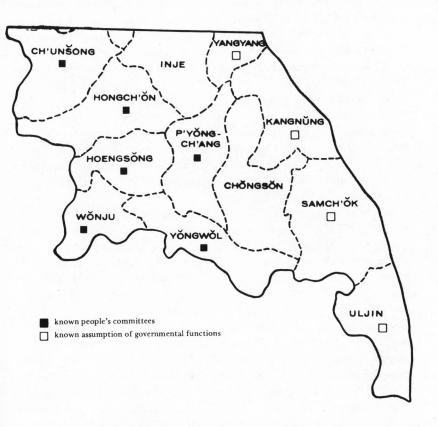

15. Kangwŏn Province People's Committees

In Suwŏn and most of the surrounding counties, the PCs had either taken over county government buildings or operated out of nearby addresses. Their representatives were in most *myŏn*-level offices.[199] Upon American arrival in eastern and northeastern counties of Kyŏnggi, the old county governments were generally not functioning, but there is no information on levels of committee control except for P'och'ŏn. It is likely that the PC had substantial strength in Yangp'-yŏng county, the native home of Yŏ Un-hyŏng. A popular court was set up in Yongin to deal with the past conduct of police and government officials.[200] PCs also had strength in Ich'ŏn, Yŏju, Ansŏng, and Kap'yŏng.[201] The Inch'ŏn committee was quite strong, with a basis in the local communist party branch and in the extensive labor unions in city industries.

By mid-1946 there were few reports of PC activity in Kyŏnggi. The P'och'ŏn PC, led by Pak Sŏng-bŏng, still controlled county police appointments in May, a practice which one American officer said violated the general policy of "keeping politics out of police affairs."[202] PC leaders also staffed the *myŏn* offices and schools of P'och'ŏn; but in June 1946, the provincial board of education had fired all teachers in the *myŏn*s.[203]

A public opinion team interviewed two committee leaders in the Kaesŏng/Paekch'ŏn region near the thirty-eighth parallel in February 1946. In both places, they found that the PC leaders were wealthy landowners. (Kaesŏng traditionally had a very high concentration of absentee and occupying landlords; the situation was no different in the 1940s.) The PC leader in Paekch'ŏn reported that his family owned an immense estate totaling some 480 acres; he also said he and his brother were both communists. When the Americans asked the obvious question, why should such men be communists, he responded: "Korea is very poor, and those who have much must share it with those who have little. . . . We need a very great change in our country." He said he had been sharing his rice with the needy in his area and noted, "people are starving in our neighborhood. The rice control laws should have been put into effect weeks and months ago."[204] This supports a point made earlier: when considered as a class, landlords had reason to oppose the Left and the committees; when considered as individuals, however, they could be found at either end of the political spectrum.

CHEJU ISLAND

Cheju presents an anomalous case in our consideration of the people's committees. Unlike most south Korean regions, the island had very low rates of tenancy; most of the islanders engaged in agriculture were freeholders. Other islanders raised horses and cattle in the sandy and infertile soils. Cheju's occupational structure was quite diversified; only 49 percent of the island population worked in agriculture, a proportion radically different from that of the rest of south Korea. No railroads existed on the island, and only one narrow road around the perimeter linked towns together (the road that now cuts through from Cheju City to Sŏgwip'o was impassable in the late 1940s). Travel to the island was possible only by airplane or by infrequent, slow steamers and ferries from Pusan and Mokp'o.

Owing to an indigenous cottage industry in shellfish and seaweed, run and populated by women divers, there was a significantly larger proportion of females to males in the population of the island. Here we also find the only major dialectical variation in the Korean language: islanders are not easily intelligible to mainlanders. The dialect, and the traditionally blue rather than white clothing worn by islanders, reinforced a separatism deriving from Cheju's geographical location and its history as a place of political exile.

Cheju had become closely integrated with Japan, especially with communities of Korean residents (mostly workers) in Japan, during the colonial period, as the population moved back and forth in large numbers. This close association and frequent contact with Japan radicalized many Cheju migrants. After liberation, the island experienced a pronounced influx of returning population; its rate of growth from 1944 to 1946 was 25 percent, this without a real city on the island. The geographic remoteness of the island resulted in the longest interregnum in south Korea between Japanese and American rule. Cheju also had a Red Peasant Union in the 1930s and a history of peasant rebellion in the nineteenth century. This provided an ideal milieu for the growth of the committees.

A branch of the CPKI was established in Cheju City on September 10, 1945. Soon thereafter, representatives of this branch met with Emory Woodall of the MG Justice Department (Woodall was part of the initial American observation team that arrived on Cheju in September) and presented three demands: (1) the Americans must not interfere with peace preservation and other work of the CPKI; (2) the Americans must immediately disarm and remove the Japanese Army and police; and (3) the Americans must transfer administrative power to CPKI organs at all levels throughout the island.[205] Woodall and the Americans did nothing more than accept the Japanese surrender on the island and then return to the mainland.[206] In the succeeding weeks, "organs of local sovereignty" (*chibang chugwan kigwan*), soon renamed people's committees, spread throughout the island. The committees had numerous affiliated organs: peace-keeping units (here called *poandae*), youth groups, *nongmin chohap*, factory managing committees (*kwalli wiwŏnhoe*), and consumer's unions (*sobi chohap*). The primary Korean language source on this movement stresses the spontaneity, local initiative, and unique form of these Cheju organizations.[207] Communist leadership was present on the island, but apparently did not dominate the committees. The various PCs and associated groups conducted study meetings and offered lectures, training in physical education, and entertainment throughout the island. They controlled many elementary and middle schools and published the only newspaper on the island, the *Cheju sinmun*.[208] Cheju presented a picture in 1945 and 1946 of nearly total PC control.

American tactical forces arrived on Cheju on October 22 but did nothing more than evacuate remaining Japanese troops and civilians. Real tactical occupation began when the 20th Infantry of the 6th Division arrived on November 10.[209] The 59th MG Company arrived shortly thereafter, but it was continually undermanned and did little real governing. The disinterest of the Americans did not please some Koreans: "the rightist groups complain that the police and MG do nothing to suppress the People's Committee."[210] Cheju was simply too remote to be of much concern to Americans with their hands full on the mainland.

A leftist source claims that the Americans and rightist Koreans suppressed PCs in Hallim, Ongp'o, Kosan, Taejŏng, Andŏk, Sŏgwip'o, and other towns. It also claims that island PCs had to go underground after the counterfeiting case broke in May 1946.[211] If so, suppression could not have been too severe or effective. There were several reports in 1946 indicating that Cheju PCs still dominated the island.[212] Americans stated that the committees were numerically very strong and were following moderate policies. In fact, these moderate policies were so attractive that rightists feared the PCs would become stronger yet.[213] In Independence Day demonstrations on March 1, 1946, PCs throughout Cheju were able to mobilize thousands of people.[214]

Very little information is available concerning American administrative policies and appointments on Cheju. The American-appointed island governor, Pak Chong-hun, was alleged to have been a collaborator with the Japanese.[215] In a strange coincidence, an interpreter accompanying an American public opinion team to Cheju recognized the newly appointed Cheju police chief, arriving with them, as a former secret police agent for the Japanese. When the interpreter queried the appointee, named Sin U-gyŏn, about his new position, Sin replied that he too "found it strange that he, a policeman under the Japanese, should now hold so important a position."[216]

Certain rightist organizations, such as the *Halla-dan,* were also present on Cheju. Thus we find a pattern here, as in North Kyŏngsang, of Right and Left coexisting for a long period of time, although leftists were unquestionably the dominant party. In the Interim Legislative Assembly elections in the fall of 1946, Cheju elected two leftists; but they promptly disappeared upon reaching Seoul.

The relatively diversified and differentiated occupational structure of Cheju Island may have aided the growth of the committees. We would assume that increasing differentiation among peasant populations would break their ties to tradition and to longstanding work patterns and make them available for new forms of activity, including political participation. Figures on the occupational breakdown of other Korean provinces and counties are for the most part unavailable. They do exist for fifteen counties in 1947, however (see table 18).

TABLE 18

OCCUPATIONAL DISTRIBUTION AND SCHOOL GRADUATES IN FIFTEEN COUNTIES
1947, MALES 15 YEARS AND OVER

County	Agriculture	Skilled/ Unskilled*	Students & Professionals†	Unemployed	School Graduates‡
Ŭmsŏng	78.7%	7.6%	3.8%	4.0%	21.1%
Ch'ungju	74.7	10.3	5.3	2.6	22.7
Hoengsong	72.5	13.1	3.7	6.7	12.1
Kangnŭng	54.9	24.1	7.0	5.3	25.6
Posŏng	67.3	16.2	4.9	4.3	19.0
Changsŏng	74.8	12.4	4.1	3.9	22.8
Chŏngŭp	70.6	10.6	4.3	5.8	21.9
Chin'an	83.5	10.0	2.8	0.1	16.8
Yongch'ŏn	71.2	15.3	3.6	5.1	17.4
Andong	71.0	11.2	4.9	6.4	21.7
Changwŏn	60.7	12.9	3.8	4.0	26.7
Ulsan	64.1	16.4	4.3	4.1	23.8
Kongju	74.3	8.6	6.0	4.5	22.8
Poryŏng	78.3	12.3	3.0	4.8	23.5
Puk Cheju	65.6	8.1	6.7	3.2	35.7

SOURCE: Derived from USAMGIK, raw census data, XXIV Corps Historical File.
* Fishing, mining, industry, commerce, transportation, service, and common labor
† Government workers, clerks, and higher professionals
‡ Primary school graduates or higher

It would appear that the counties were selected on a random basis, since there are two counties from each of south Korea's provinces except Kyŏnggi and one from Cheju. Of the fifteen counties included, one had no reported PC, eight had nongoverning PCs, and six had governing PCs. There seems to have been a significant relationship between PC strength and a more differentiated occupational distribution. They are ranked from one to fifteen below, assuming that a low percentage in agriculture and high percentages in skilled and unskilled occupations, students and professionals, and school graduates indicated relative degrees of occupational differentiation:

Rank	County
1	Kangnŭng*
2	Ulsan†
3	Ch'angwŏn*
4	Puk Cheju*
5	Posŏng*
6	Andong†
7	Kongju*
8	Chŏngŭp†
9	Ch'ungju†
10	Changsŏng†
11	Yŏngch'ŏn†
12	Hoengsŏng†
13	Poryŏng*
14	Ŭmsŏng‡
15	Chin'an†

Of counties with governing committees, only Poryŏng ranks low in occupational differentiation. Kangnŭng, called the most powerful left-wing county in south Korea, ranks first. Ulsan and Andong, without governing PCs, rank second and sixth; but both had strong PCs and affiliated mass organizations, and PCs ran the *myŏn*s in Andong. Ŭm-sŏng, without a reported PC, ranks fourteenth. A subjective ranking of these counties according to PC strength would very nearly parallel the ranking according to occupational differentiation.

CONCLUSIONS

If we were to describe the ideal milieu for the growth and longevity of a people's committee in liberated Korea, the criteria would include the following: (1) a pattern of population loss in the 1930s or early 1940s, followed by a sharp gain after liberation; (2) land conditions in which peasants were not primarily tenants but possessed some independence and leverage within an eroded or weak landlord structure of power; (3) a long interregnum between Japanese and American

* Counties with governing PCs.
† Counties with nongoverning PCs.
‡ Counties with no reported PCs.

rule; (4) either relative difficulty in communications and transportation, or possession of those facilities by the committee; (5) a history of peasant radicalism; (7) a relatively differentiated occupational structure; and (8) a political complexion where, over a substantial period of time, neither Right nor Left were completely dominant, or where a dominant Left followed moderate policies. Cheju Island possessed all of these attributes, and in greater degree than other regions. The result was that the committees became deeply entrenched, controlling the island until 1948, and were rooted out only through one of the most brutal, sustained, and intensive counterinsurgency campaigns in postwar Asia.[217] The Kyŏngsang provinces, and clusters of counties in South Chŏlla, South Ch'ungch'ŏng, and Kangwŏn, possessed similar attributes and commensurate committee strength. There is no question that, had the Americans been as inattentive there as they were in Cheju, the committees would have ruled unchallenged. In other counties, however, such attributes existed in lesser degree or not at all, and the committees either had a conservative cast or never got started.

Apart from regional or county-level differences, the experience in Korean provinces also suggests critical differences at different levels of administration. At the city and province level, there existed a "modern" politics in which strong leftist parties, labor unions, and experienced leaders confronted sophisticated opponents who had at their disposal the most advanced infrastructural facilities and well-developed bureaucratic organizations such as the national police. There was a rapid leftist mobilization at these levels after liberation, but an American-supported opposition in the bureaucracy mustered sufficient resources to restrain, if not to turn back, this tide. The Seoul people's committee, for example, was quickly transformed into little more than an opposition party.

At the county level, modern and traditional politics mingled in most complex fashion. In the Kyŏngsangs, the deep Japanese penetration, the population shifting, and the presence of significant industries and concentrations of workers in Pusan and Taegu led to a pattern of strong committees with good staying power. This culminated in 1946 in a near revolution in these provinces. In the Chŏllas, the committees were also initially quite strong at the county level; but leadership here mingled the old with the new, there was much less population change, fewer industrial workers, so there was not good staying power. Resistance tended to take the form of sporadic peasant rebellions. Elsewhere, at the county level, those regions that had felt less impact from the Japanese era also seem to have felt less impact from the committees, and conservative leadership perpetuated itself through a transition that was more or less difficult, depending on the county. It is certainly clear that a viable Korean leadership, opposed to the committees, emerged in these regions, and the likely explanation is that the lesser impact of colonialism in such places enabled the perpetuation of indigenous traditional leaders.

At the village level, Korean politics was almost entirely traditional. Although information is quite limited on this aspect, many presumed Left-Right conflicts were clan conflicts, many presumed leftist leaders were village elders in modern political guise, and peasants resisted in the tried and true fashion of traditional Korean rebellions. This aspect was clearer in 1947, when the opposition to the committees finally penetrated to the village level. There was a distinct pattern of opposition to the committees, or radicalism, moving through successively deeper levels of administration: Seoul was the problem in 1945; the provinces were a problem a bit later, as occupation forces reached the hinterlands; the counties were the focus of conflict during most of 1946; and 1947 was a year of village struggles.

Just as the opposition to the committees proceeded down through the reaches of the administration, effecting a centralization at each stage and giving a distinctly top-down cast to this effort, so the committees had a spontaneous, bottom-up quality that gave them a rootedness that the opposition never matched. This same spontaneity also proved to be one of the great weaknesses of the committee structure, however. After decades in which the Japanese, in effect, *opened* Korean counties and villages to market or administrative penetration, the Japanese demise led to a *closure* at each level. It was as if the committees were watertight compartments, content to govern the affairs of a given county but largely unconcerned with events elsewhere. The segmented, localized administration of the committees led to a cellular structure, but not to the cell-based, hierarchical Marxist-Leninist structure that the Americans kept looking for but not finding. These structural weaknesses made suppressing the committees easier, for each level could be dealt with apart from the others.

Standing above all of these complex considerations was the primary role of American power in defeating the committees. In spite of the mass popularity of the committee form, attested to time and again in American reports, the Americans consciously and systematically rooted out this movement because it could not be counted upon to serve American interests. The effect of these actions on rural political integration and participation can be felt to this day in South Korea.

Chapter Ten

THE AUTUMN HARVEST UPRISINGS

> Look, the people in the southern provinces are up with rifle and
> sword. . . . Now our young patriots have risen in an effort to
> protect our fatherland from the danger of re-colonization! It is
> [their] aim to clear this land of bad policemen who repress our
> true patriots, bad officials who extort excessive quotas of rice,
> and pro-Japanese traitors who are behind them.
>
> _Leaflet found in Paekch'ŏn_

I N THE autumn of 1946, peasant uprisings swept through the Kyŏngsang and Chŏlla provinces and other regions of people's committee
strength, as the people of southern Korea sought to reverse the effects
of a year of American Occupation. The uprisings were significant in
several respects. First, they brought into sharp focus the failures of
Military Government policies in political, economic, and social
realms; in this period, the Americans reaped the whirlwind of Korean
discontent over the experiences of the previous year. Second, the rebellions marked the effective end of the people's committees and the
mass organizations associated with them as strong political forces competing openly for hegemony in the provinces. Third, the suppression
of the uprisings and the demise of the committees represented a significant turning point in the fortunes of the Right, and particularly
in those of the Korean National Police. And last, the spread of the
uprisings manifested the effects of environmental factors on the politics of liberated Korea.

Nothing in the three years of the Occupation so shook Americans at
all levels as the autumn uprisings of 1946. At the top, they caused
outright panic. General Hodge immediately suspected that leaders in
P'yŏngyang or Moscow had ordered the uprisings and feared that they
heralded a military attack from the north.[1] Other American observers
inside and outside the MG recognized the indigenous origin of the
uprisings and saw in them "a full-fledged revolution."[2] But when the
uprisings had run their course, it became apparent that they represented neither war nor revolution. War would come later, and revolution was denied to peasants who lacked the organization necessary to
depose their masters. The autumn uprisings thus appear as a classic

instance of peasant rebellion, the most significant peasant rebellions in Korea since the *Tonghak* of the nineteenth century.

The sequence of unrest in the fall of 1946 began with a general strike by railroad workers in Pusan on September 23 and quickly spread throughout south Korea. Mass demonstrations in Taegu on October 2 touched off successive waves of disorder in the Kyŏngsang provinces, South Ch'ungch'ŏng, Kyŏnggi, Kangwŏn, and South Chŏlla lasting into December. As might be expected, the pattern of the uprisings as delineated in figure 16 closely resembles our earlier rendering of people's committee strength (see figure 5 in chapter eight). We find the uprisings centered in the Kyŏngsangs, and occurring (with a few exceptions) in those counties of South Chŏlla, South Ch'ungch'ŏng, and Kangwŏn having strong or governing PCs. The correspondence is most striking in the belt of counties leading west from Pusan. These counties, as we noted earlier, had Red Peasant Unions in the 1930s, governing PCs after liberation, and rates of population change that were among the highest in all Korea in the years from 1944 to 1946. In North Kyŏngsang the disorders were most severe in the counties surrounding Taegu; most of these counties had strong if not governing PCs and high population change rates. Thus the autumn uprisings represented a last, massive attempt by the people's committees and the groups associated with them to seize power in the provinces. They centered in the Kyŏngsang provinces because of the established presence of the committees there for the year following liberation and because both provinces harbored an uprooted and aggrieved peasant population. The uprisings were fomented not by outsiders, but by local committee leaders and their supporters driven by deep grievances and life-and-death interests.

THE GENERAL STRIKE

On September 23, 1946, some 8,000 railroad workers walked off their jobs in Pusan. Within hours, railroad work stoppages spread to Seoul, immobilizing rail transport throughout south Korea. Within a few days, work stoppages had spread to printers, electrical workers, telegraph office and postal employees, and other industries, until the proportions reached those of a general strike.[3] Masses of students joined the strikers; nearly all students at prestigious Kyŏnggi High School in Seoul refused to attend classes, for example.[4] Most newspapers across the political spectrum supported the goals of the strikes.[5] In Seoul alone, some 295 enterprises were struck, and some 30,000 workers and 16,000 students reportedly participated.[6] The total number of workers

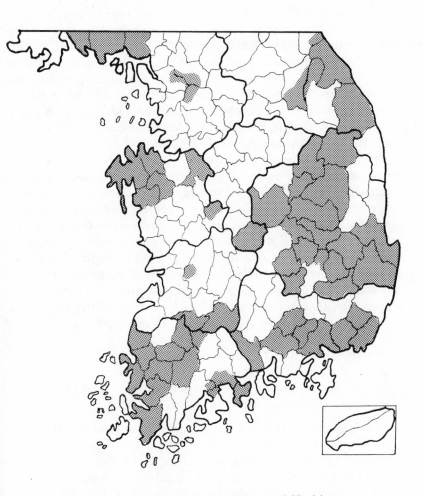

16. Overview of September-December 1946 Uprisings

involved throughout south Korea was estimated to have been 251,000, most of them mobilized under *Chŏnp'yŏng* auspices.[7]

Very little violence attended the first week of the strikes. Demonstrations were orderly.[8] The demands of the workers were largely reformist: they wanted increases in rice rations, higher wages, housing and rice for jobless workers and returnees to south Korea, better working conditions in factories, and freedom to organize workers.[9] Certain other demands, however, had revolutionary implications. The workers called for a "democratic labor law" like the one already passed in north Korea. They demanded the release of political prisoners and an end to "reactionary terror."[10] Most significant, they called for the transfer of power to the people's committees.[11] This demand was also included in a letter of September 30 from the chairman of *Chŏnp'-yŏng*, Hŏ Sŏng-t'aek, to General Hodge.[12]

The Military Government responded publicly to the strikes in the same manner it had responded to similar crises in the past: it accused communists in north Korea of stirring up the trouble and suggested that the strikes indicated Koreans were not yet ready to govern their own affairs. On September 24, the day after the strike began, the MG accused the North Korean Worker's Party of ordering its allies in south Korea to carry on "a struggle" on the first anniversary of the founding of the KPR (September 6, 1946).[13] Perhaps such an order *was* issued, but no mention of it appears in the MG histories, G-2 reports, or CIC reports. Moreover, as we shall presently see, intelligence analysts within the MG later came to think that Pak Hŏn-yŏng was behind the agitation.

General Hodge issued a characteristic statement in response to the strikes, indicating at once his own feeling that his experience as an American was applicable to the rest of the world and his paternal approach to Korean strivings:

> I have been a worker myself and have known the pinch of real poverty . . . no man can say that I do not know personally of the worker's life and his hardships. This is all the more reason that I regret to see the worker misled into blind alleys by those who make great promises of something for nothing . . . serious disturbances of this nature can only further confuse the Korean people and mislead the rest of the world into a belief that the Korean people are not ready to handle their own affairs.[14]

Korean workers were beyond the reach of these quaint homilies, however, and at the end of September, the strikes took a violent turn.

On September 30 severe disorders occurred at the Yongsan railroad yards in Seoul. It is, of course, not surprising that strike organizers had begun with the railroads. If the railroad network could be shut down for weeks or months, suppression of strikes and uprisings in the provinces would prove much more difficult. The Seoul CIC branch had reported earlier that Yongsan railroad workers were overwhelmingly leftist in sentiment and firmly supported *Chŏnp'yŏng*.[15] Several thousand strikers and strikebreakers took part in battles at the yards on September 30. The *Seoul Times* eyewitness account said that some 3,000 striking workers fought a like number of strikebreakers organized by management, with the latter backed by 3,000 police and youths from rightist organizations.[16] American Intelligence estimated the number of police to have been 2,100 and reported that around 1,400 strikers were arrested, which would suggest a much larger total number of strikers.[17] Mass arrests continued throughout the day, and strikebreakers "armed with sticks and clubs roamed downtown streets and industrial areas." They attacked the offices of the *Chayu sinmun*.[18] Similar clashes occurred at railroad yards in Inch'ŏn on October 2, followed by more mass arrests.[19] Arrested workers were allowed to return to their jobs if they pledged not to strike or to associate with *Chŏnp'yŏng*; workers who refused were summarily fired and denied rice rations.[20] This violent suppression of striking railroad workers succeeded in getting about 45 percent of south Korea's trains back in operation by October 3.[21] But by then, much more serious disorders had erupted in North Kyŏngsang.

In chapter nine, we noted a pattern of coexistence between Right and Left in North Kyŏngsang that persisted throughout the first year of liberation, especially in Taegu and numerous neighboring counties and in the North Kyŏngsang Constabulary regiment. In Taegu this pattern found expression in the Taegu Community Council, a body made up of twenty members evenly selected from the local leaders of the Korean Communist Party, the Korean Democratic Party, the Korean Independence Party, and the People's Party. The council met once a week beginning June 28, 1946. Provincial MG officers solicited its advice and used it as a sounding board for MG policies;[22] they found it particularly helpful in gaining compliance with grain collection policies.[23] This council was one of the few successful coalition efforts in postwar Korea, and it was opposed by the extremes of Right and Left for that very reason. It also played a key role in giving the Left in North Kyŏngsang a breath of life and a certain legitimacy. Like so many other hopeful initiatives in postwar south Korea, however, it ended amid bloody and violent conflict.

Strikes had taken place in about forty factories and enterprises in Taegu by the end of September. Some 3,000 workers took part.[24] The American command attempted to lay the blame for such strikes on outside agitators, but a south Korean source published many years later said that the Taegu strikes were led by Son Ki-yŏng of the Taegu branch of the KCP; Na Yun-ch'ul, the chief of the Taegu *poandae*; Yun Chang-hyŏk of the Taegu branch of *Chŏnp'yŏng*; Ch'oe Mun-sik of the Taegu branch of the People's Party; and Yi Mok, editor of the *Minsŏng ilbo* in Taegu.[25]

THE INSURRECTION

On October 1 between 200 and 300 demonstrators marched through Taegu in support of striking workers. Like the strikers, these demonstrators (who appeared to be mostly children of all ages)[26] demanded increased rice rations. Sometime that day, police killed one of the demonstrators.[27] On the morning of October 2, a crowd, variously estimated at 1,000 or 2,000, marched through Taegu bearing the body of the demonstrator who had been slain the day before.[28] According to a later account by an American prosecutor who tried court cases arising from the demonstration, the leader of the October 2 affair was Chae Mu-hak, a 31-year-old medical student who had been sent first to Japan and then to Manchukuo for forced labor during the war. In Manchukuo, reportedly, "he came under the influence of the Chinese Communists." He then returned to Taegu after the liberation.[29]

The demonstrators carried the body as far as the Taegu central police station where they gathered outside. Major John Plezia, who was within the station, ordered police to disperse the crowd. When they refused, he left the station, apparently hoping to find American reinforcements. The crowd surged into the station shortly thereafter, causing some twenty to thirty policemen to flee, throw away their uniforms, and go into hiding. The Americans thought that this "downright cowardice" on the part of the police indicated that some of them were communists.[30] Most of the American-employed Korean police in Taegu had formerly served the Japanese, however, and it was this history, not communist sympathies or cowardice, that convinced these policemen that retreat was the only option.

The policemen who escaped were fortunate. The mob in Taegu captured some fifty others; and by October 6 thirty-eight Taegu policemen had been murdered.[31] But they were not simply murdered— they were tortured to death, burned at the stake, skinned alive. And once dead, their homes and families became objects of attack. Rioters sacked the homes of Korean officials all over Taegu, including that of the provincial governor; they looted their belongings, beat their families, attempted to stamp out every trace of their existence. When the

Americans later found policemen's bodies with eyes gouged out, limbs hacked off, or with hundreds of spear wounds, they attributed it to Korean barbarity.[32] An official KNP history said that one could expect little else from "idiotic peasants" *(umae nongmin)*.[33] But the occurrence of such extremes of violence is an historical datum of considerable significance. This violence was not unleshed indiscriminately. It was directed at hated officials, many of whom had been responsible for similar brutalities against Koreans during the colonial era and the first year of liberation. In no instance were Americans the objects of such attacks. As in Hunan in 1927, the peasant's eyes were very discerning.[34] Racist or class prejudices cannot strip these acts of their historical content. It was the inchoate violence of the oppressed—political in the sense that it was directed at the agents of oppression, but apolitical in that no organization capable of channeling and utilizing the social force that Korean peasants represented existed in sufficient strength in North Kyŏngsang.

Only a few Americans in Korea understood the grievances that fueled the violence against the Korean police. General Hodge, not one of them, explained why he thought the police were objects of attack:

> The police stand for and enforce law and order and protect law-abiding people and their property. The police stand in the way of other disorders these agitators wish to stir up, so they work up a great hate campaign in an attempt to destroy and demoralize them.[35]

In other words, Hodge equated Korean police with those in his home town of Golconda, Illinois. He made, in effect, the usual distinction between the authoritative monopoly on coercion possessed by police in a legitimated political system and the unsanctioned violence of the lawless. But many Koreans viewed former colonial policemen as ipso facto illegitimate; their monopoly on the means of violence in postwar Korea was improper, inappropriate, and therefore, by that definition of legitimacy, unsanctionable.

Since the Taegu uprisings came on the heels of the general strike, the Americans and their Korean allies were already aroused and ready to move quickly. American tanks patrolled Taegu streets by noon on October 2. Roadblocks were set up all over the city. Koreans were forbidden to cluster in groups. At 7:00 P.M. martial law was declared and a dawn-to-dusk curfew imposed.[36] But the sparks from Taegu set off a major conflagration in the Kyŏngsang provinces. Hodge's image of south Korea as a smoldering volcano or tinderbox proved, to his chagrin, no doubt, to be all too true.

On October 3 a mob of an estimated 10,000 people overran the police station in Yŏngch'ŏn, killing the *kunsu* and kidnapping about forty county policemen. Many officials and police were murdered, and the police station and post office were burned to the ground.[37] American tactical troops restored order within a couple of days. Then remaining Yŏngch'ŏn policemen and their rightist allies sacked the homes of arrested rioters.[38]

The violence in Yŏngch'ŏn marked a move beyond mass attacks against police and officials—which could be explained simply as nationalist or patriotic outrage, given the officials' service to the Japanese—to attacks on the landed class. According to a leftist source, some twenty "reactionaries and evil landlords" were killed in the Yŏngch'ŏn area. A particular target were so-called "big landlords," defined as possessing or disposing of 10,000-15,000 *sŏk* (1 *sŏk* = 5.12 bushels) of grain. Peasants apparently entered and destroyed the palatial home of Yi In-sŏk, a local "big landlord" and the father of an important Korean Democratic Party activist, Yi Hwal. A Yŏngch'ŏn activist later related that local peasants bore deep grudges against the propertied because of unfair practices in summer grain collections and because of the resultant inflation and high cost of food. He also said that in the four months preceding October there had been around forty-five incidents of suppression directed at the Left and more than 140 arrests that left the local peasants leaderless when the uprisings began.[39]

The county police station in Ŭisŏng was in the hands of some 5,000 demonstrators from October 3 to 5, during which time sixteen police substations throughout the county were also attacked. The Ŭisŏng police chief reported that all the rioters in Ŭisŏng and nearby Kunhwi were local natives. He had spoken with nine representatives of the 5,000 demonstrators in Ŭisŏng and indicated that of the nine, five belonged to the local PC, two to the People's Party branch, one to the Ŭisŏng *nongmin chohap*, and one was an unaffiliated schoolteacher. Americans on the scene said that almost all political groups in Ŭisŏng and Kunhwi belonged to or were affiliated with the local PCs.[40]

In the town of Kumi, south of Kunhwi, a mob of 2,000 took over the police station on October 3. They jailed the police and wrecked fully eighty-six homes belonging to local police and government officials.[41] In the Kunhwi county seat, a crowd of 1,000 put the police chief and *kunsu* in jail and demanded that the county be turned over to the local people's committee. The next day, police sent in from Ch'ŏngju in North Ch'ungch'ŏng Province quelled the Kunhwi uprisings; they reported that the rioters were members of the Kunhwi

PC, the local People's Party affiliate, the local *nongmin chohap*, and PC-affiliated women's and youth groups.[42] On the same day, rioters attacked eight outlying police stations in the Kunhwi jurisdiction.[43]

In neighboring Waegwan some 2,000 rioters attacked the county police station on October 3. They mutilated and then killed the police chief and beat to death seven of his men. They took over the police station and its weapons. They then proceeded to wreck fifty homes belonging to local police, government officials, and wealthy families. Similar events took place in small towns in the vicinity.[44] The highway bridges between Waegwan and Kŭmch'ŏn were blown up on the same day.[45] Demonstrators then took over the Sŏnsan county police station and successfully beat off an attack by seventy-five provincial policemen dispatched from Taegu. An American commented that "the people were in charge when the police arrived and the people were in charge when the police left." In Naksŏng-dong, just south of Sŏnsan, a mob of 2,000 people armed with bamboo sticks, spears, farming implements, and clubs seized the summer grain collection stocks and distributed them to local residents.[46] In Sŏngju, south of Waegwan, around 350 people attacked police and government officials and members of "patriotic organizations" on October 3. The next day, a crowd of several thousand surrounded the police station in Sŏngju, locked up twenty-one police officers, and attempted to set the station afire. A provincial police brigade stopped them.[47] A week before the disorders here, two Sŏngju officials had been arrested for some infraction; they had declared to American investigators their opposition to the proposed SKILA and its implications of a separate southern government. They told the Americans, "we don't want our country to be a colony of the U.S.," and condemned the American collections of summer grains as being "more cruel than former Japanese type."[48]

Severe disorders also occurred from October 3 to 5 in the coastal counties of Kyŏngju and Yŏngil. About 700 young people marched through P'ohang on October 3 and presented a letter to a local MG official that said:

Build democracy on this crisis
We must save people who are starving and weeping
We refuse to be a nation of traitors[49]

The Americans declared martial law in P'ohang that night. Demonstrators burned the county seat and the homes of three *myŏn* chiefs in Kyŏngju on October 4. There, too, the Americans responded with a declaration of martial law.[50] American CIC agents seized documents written by the leaders of the Kyŏngju demonstrations and found that the leaders came from the Kyǒngju PC and from local *nongmin cho-hap* and DNF branches. The documents said, among other things, "we must use this opportunity to set our roots deeply," and urged people *not* to indulge in violence.[51] In general, political organizers in North Kyǒngsang probably did not incite peasants to violence. Anyone with experience in such affairs would know that unsparing violence would be politically useless and would bring with it equally unsparing repression. Indeed, leftist leaders later criticized the autumn uprisings on just such grounds. Political organizers in the Kyǒngsang provinces, like a young Mao Tse-tung in Hunan in 1927, probably stood by amazed by the force unleashed by cathartic peasant violence.[52]

Rioters described as "farmers" killed a county magistrate in An'gang in Yǒng'il county on December 3 and took over the local police station. In nearby Kigye a mob burned the government offices and homes of officials and attacked a missionary.[53] (This is the only known report of a direct attack on a non-Korean during the autumn uprisings.) Some 2,000 rioters armed with dynamite and grenades attacked the police station in Kuryongp'o on October 6 but were driven back by police and rightist groups.[54] By this time martial law had been declared throughout North Kyǒngsang.

The disorders in the northern counties of North Kyǒngsang conformed to the analysis of PC strength in these counties given in chapter nine. The Andong county seat, which had been controlled by the Right, experienced little more than a minor strike by railroad workers on September 25.[55] The only complaint came from a "prominent rightist," who said Andong policemen were assessing him and his wealthy friends for funds to rebuild destroyed homes and stations in outlying areas.[56] Apparently no disorders occurred in Mun'gyǒng, where the local PC had been eliminated in May of 1946. But in Yech'ǒn, with its stronger PC group, the Americans reported "wholesale destruction of property" and some ten dead in rioting on October 3. Order was not restored there until tactical troops arrived on October 5. Even after that, the police could do little more than barricade themselves in the Yech'ǒn station. There were no police in outlying *myǒn*s a week after the riots began. The same was true of Ponghwa and Yǒngju.[57] By October 19, however, control was back in the hands of remaining (or surviving) *kun*sus and police. The jails overflowed with prisoners: 213 in Yech'ǒn, 137 in Yǒngju, and so on.[58] Andong, Mun'gyǒng, Yech'ǒn, and Yǒngju were also described as places of unusually strong antileftist sentiment, because of the presence of refugees from the north Korean provinces of North and South P'yǒng'an, who had fled to the region after the people's committees assumed power in the north in the fall of 1945.[59]

The rioting spread into South Kyŏngsang Province on October 7, with the most severe violence occurring in Chinju and Masan, where strong PCs had been able to depose the American-appointed local governments on several occasions in 1945 and 1946 and where the extremely large influx of returning Koreans caused especially volatile milieus. On October 7 in Chinju, Korean police fired on a crowd of demonstrators, killing two. Later on the same day, American tactical forces fired on a crowd and killed four. Another 100 demonstrators were arrested. Three days later, a Chinju police box was overrun, and on October 14 a major confrontation erupted in which ten rioters were killed and eleven wounded.[60] A later analysis of captured rioters showed that they were peasants, wage laborers, small peddlers, and merchants. They called for the MG to stop collecting rice for the benefit of "privileged classes, bad landlords, and profiteers" and said the proper course was to "North Koreanize South Korea." Their pamphlets accused the Chinju police of being "the faithful dogs of Japan," asking the police, "Are you not from the Korean nation? Have you not the same blood and bone? Why do you fire on Koreans?" Most of the rioters belonged to the Chinju PC or PC-affiliated youth groups.[61]

American troops and Korean police fired on a crowd of 6,000 in Masan on October 7, inflicting "heavy casualties"—eight to fifteen dead, depending on the source, scores wounded, and some 150 arrests.[62] On the same day, police fired on a crowd in Namji-ri, near Ch'ang-wŏn, killing two. There were ten separate attacks on police in Ŭiryŏng in a four-day period in the second week in October. American tactical troops intervened there on several occasions. Some 500 demonstrators destroyed the town hall and the police station in the coastal town of Sŏsaeng-ni on October 14. Crowds attacked police in Yangsan and Tongnae around October 8 to 10. On October 11 American troops and Korean police fired on a crowd in Ungch'ŏn, near Chinhae, killing five people.[63]

In Hadong, another town of high population influx on the path west from Pusan, a number of attacks on police and other officials occurred in the days from October 8 to 11. In an attack on October 8, some 200 peasants carrying bamboo spears went after policemen, stabbing several; four of the peasants were killed. Most of the peasants were reported to be members of the local *nongmin chohap* and KPR-affiliated youth group. Later on fifteen members of the latter group were arrested; fourteen were found to be peasants, ranging in age from 18 to 35. The leader, Yi Pyŏng-gu, was a schoolteacher, aged 25, who had written in his diary that the purpose of the attacks was to get the "pro-Japanese and traitors." Handbills distributed by this group stated that "a spark of revolution has been struck in the whole of south Korea" symbolizing "the explosion of the angry oppressed class," and continued:

> It is not that we hate the police, but that we are ready to die for the independence of the fatherland.

* * *

> To the peasants: Let us build an independent country with our own hands. Transfer all power to the people. Distribute the land among the people equally. Let us oppose the collection of all grains.[64]

In Pusan, students in all of the city's schools were on strike from September 23 to October 8. On October 9 bloody battle broke out, resulting in twenty-four policemen and rioters killed. The mayor of Pusan was assaulted. American tactical troops were called in.[65]

In the third week of October, according to the Americans, the "communists" tried to "bring Taegu to Seoul," hoping to foment disorders there. As official sources noted, however, "Seoul was a Rightist city, with excellent communications, its police well organized, and aid from American troops readily available."[66] This is a succinct acknowledgment of the uses of modern communications in suppressing dissent. But the Americans were also reportedly aided by Yŏ Un-hyŏng, who gave advance warning that attacks were planned for October 22.[67] In any event, no significant disorders occurred in Seoul. But there was trouble in towns near Seoul.

In the small town of Kwangju to the east of Seoul, the police station was attacked and burned on October 20, and the prisoners inside were released. About 500 people attacked police in Susaeng-ni, north of Seoul, around the same time.[68] More widespread rioting occurred in the Kaesŏng region near the thirty-eighth parallel beginning October 20. The Kaesŏng police chief was murdered and several police boxes were taken over. American tactical troops intervened here and in the nearby towns of Yŏn'an, Paekch'ŏn, Ch'ŏngdan, and Yŏnbaek. Rioters murdered two policemen in Yŏnbaek on October 20 and apparently kidnapped four others. The KNP estimated that forty police and rioters were killed in the Kaesŏng region; the police made 3,782 arrests.[69]

In these towns, as in the Kyŏngsang provinces, the demonstrators consisted exclusively of local residents, most of them affiliated with people's committees, *nongmin chohap*, or PC-run youth groups. As elsewhere, the police were aided by the rightist youth groups. The American CIC reported that in the Paekch'ŏn uprisings the rioters were nearly all peasants and students associated with the Paekch'ŏn PC, *nongmin chohap* (led by Cho Tae-jun, a returnee to Paekch'ŏn from Manchuria), and *nodong chohap*. The police here were backed up by the local NSRRKI youth group.[70] Rioters in Inch'ŏn surrounded and dynamited a police station on October 26, killing two policemen and thirty-two members of the Inch'ŏn NSRRKI youth group who were inside.[71] Thus each of these local battles throughout south Korea in the fall of 1946 recapitulated the structure of division and polarization found in Seoul.

Disorders in South Ch'ungch'ŏng occurred for the most part in the four northwestern counties having strong and governing PCs in 1945/46. A mob of an estimated 300 in Tŏksan (Yesan-kun) murdered a police sergeant and his daughter on October 13. Four days later, some 1,000 people attacked the police in nearby Haptok. American tactical forces rescued the police in the nick of time. The next day, several police boxes in Hongsŏng were attacked, and Hongsŏng police fired into a crowd, killing 4. Similar disturbances occurred at about the same time throughout the counties of Sŏsan, Yesan, and Tangjin. Disorders also took place in Ch'ŏnan, another county with a governing PC after liberation.[72] The 41st MG Company, responsible for the four northwestern counties, reported at the end of November that they still had 350 court cases waiting to be tried: "these cases are of a political nature."[73]

There is little doubt that the rioting in South Ch'ungch'ŏng was of a political nature. Several leaflets passed out by demonstrators in Hongsŏng said things like, "Return the Korean government to the People's Committee!" "All forms of government [should be] returned to the People's Committee." These leaflets urged the abolishment of the SKILA and the Military Government; they called for labor and land laws like those in north Korea; they criticized MG rice collection policies and its alliance with the KDP.[74] The leader of the demonstrations in Haptok was Yi Su-ha, chairman of the local *nongmin chohap*. The class background of rioters, as in North and South Kyŏngsang, seems to have been primarily working or peasant class. Of thirty-one demonstrators in Taejŏn, six were peasants, seven were workers, nine were unemployed, three were doctors (probably herb doctors or doctors of Chinese medicine rather than M.D.s), two were businessmen, and four were classed as "miscellaneous." They ranged in age from twenty-five to sixty-three, but most were in their late twenties and early thirties.[75] American investigators noted that the police in Taejŏn worked closely with rightist parties; the police gave the latter armbands for identification and commandeered trucks for combined police-rightist operations.[76]

North Ch'ungch'ŏng largely escaped the autumn uprisings. Disturbances occurred only in remote Yŏngdong, led by the strong people's committee in that county.[77] The Americans thought uprisings were prevented in the province by the cooperation and quick action of police and rightist groups working with them and concluded that North Ch'ungch'ŏng was the "strongest rightist province in South Korea."[78]

At the end of October, the uprisings spread into South Chŏlla Province. In the archival materials of the American Military Government is a comprehensive, thirty-nine-page report on the rebellion here.[79] There were more than fifty separate incidents reported during the first two weeks of November, most of them involving mobs of peasants attacking police boxes, armed with clubs, spears, rocks, scythes, hoes, knives, and rice-cutting hooks. Most of the entries read as follows: "mob composed of People's Committee types attacked police box; police fired into mob, killing six"; "1000 attacked police station . . . cops fired 100 rounds into mob killing (unknown)"; "police fired on mob of 3000, killing 5"; "police fired into mob of 60 . . . tactical troops called out; captured 6 bamboo spears and 2 sabres"; "600-800 marched on police; police killed 4." As we read down the list of these individual peasant wars, we eventually arrive at the end; but in fact there is no end, only an abyss that the reader stares into, containing the bodies of countless South Chŏlla peasants.

The South Chŏlla insurrection began on October 30 when miners in Hwasun started to march on Kwangju. Hwasun had presented constant problems to the Americans throughout 1945 and 1946. A strong people's committee there drew support from several thousand miners in the area. Production in 1946 in the Hwasun mines, third largest in southern Korea, dropped to less than half the total average output recorded for the years from 1939 to 1943.[80] Thus many miners were out of work, and Americans on the scene continually reported that the people were hungry and restless and that the entire county was one of unspeakable poverty. A widely reported demonstration had occurred on the first anniversary of liberation when the miners sought to march on Kwangju, the province capital.[81] On October 31 some 3,000 miners, led by the head of the Hwasun *nodong chohap*, made a second attempt to march on Kwangju. American CIC agents and tactical troops managed to turn them back without violence. The Americans reported that the crowd included some 300 women, most with small children, who were crying and complaining that they were starving.[82] The next few days were punctuated with minor incidents and arrests. Then on November 4:

> Colonel Peake, with twelve U.S. soldiers, four CIC agents, ten Korean police, and several military government personnel, left Kwangju for Hwasun to apprehend the leaders of the [October 31]

mining strike in Hwasun. Returning to Kwangju with five prisoners, they encountered a road block of three carts, and a mob of 1,000 to 2,000 miners who retreated. However, rescue of the prisoners was attempted in the next town. Some members of the mob threw a log through the window of one of the jeeps, causing it to go into a ditch. The second jeep rammed the first and also overturned. Both vehicles were abandoned, and the occupants returned to Hwasun in the remaining vehicles of the convoy. The convoy was stoned and fired upon, and was forced to run through a crowd which suffered 33 injuries and three killed. Two American soldiers were injured.[83]

After this, the local Constabulary detachment took over the mines, and the Hwasun police were given reinforcements. Shortly the police reported, "we're definitely in control of the situation . . . [with] prisoners in our cells." Yet on November 6 another raid had to be conducted on Hwasun, resulting in fifty arrests.[84]

On the same day that the Hwasun miners began their march, switchboard and telephone operators in the port city of Mokp'o went on strike, cutting off all communication. American tactical troops were called out to disperse several thousand workers and students who marched on police stations there on October 31 and November 1, "many rioters were injured" when the troops drove a truck through the crowd of demonstrators. Police fired on a mob of 600 in Imsŏng, just north of Mokp'o, on October 31.[85] Drumming in the mountains near Naju on October 31 summoned thousands of peasants for demonstrations the next morning. (The drumming was not the least of what made many Americans feel that South Chŏlla was Indian country.) At least three groups of more than 1,000 each converged on Naju from different directions. They were met by a platoon of the 20th Infantry, 250 policemen, and 80 Constabulary soldiers. Two C-47s buzzed the crowds, which led angry peasants to climb a high hill to throw rocks at them. The mobs attacked five police boxes and the police fired numerous volleys into the crowds of attackers, killing ten peasants at one point and three in a subsequent volley.[86] Police also fired into a crowd numbered at more than 1,000 in Hamp'yŏng on November 1 and killed an unknown number. Two days later, seven rioters were killed in Muan.[87] Peasants in P'ungnyang (near Yŏsu) killed one policeman by sticking bamboo spears in his rectum and cut off the lips of another before killing him. On November 11 coordinated attacks on police boxes in the Haenam area by peasants wielding the implements of their mode of production resulted in the following: 54 peasants killed, 61 wounded, 357 arrested; 10 police killed,

33 wounded, 11 missing; 24 police stations and boxes destroyed by fire; 28 "rightists" killed. The forces of order captured only twenty-four rifles from the thousands of rebels.[88] Numerous minor disorders and attacks on police occurred throughout the province, except in the remote southwestern counties. For example, in Chilsŏng-ni on November 3, 380 peasants overran a New Korea Company warehouse, burning all records. From November 1 to 3, police fired on crowds of peasants in Yŏnsanp'o, Yŏnggwang, Kwansun, and Kwangsan, killing a total of sixteen.[89] Countless other incidents and deaths appear in the archival records, and no doubt many went unrecorded.

In the first two weeks of November, in South Chŏlla, a total of forty-seven cities, towns, and villages, and two-thirds of all counties, were touched by the uprisings. Five of the incidents involved 500 to 1,000 people; eight involved 1,000 to 5,000; one had more than 5,000. The Americans estimated that 65,000 people took part, although the actual recorded number of participants was 23,760.[90] American sources noted:

> Mobs destroyed all official records that they could get their hands on, and this is particularly true of rice and grain collection records. In fact in some cases the sole purpose of attacks on police stations and city halls seems to have been to secure and destroy these records. This also applied to rice collection records of the New Korea Company.[91]

Organizers of the insurrections played upon two basic grievances of South Chŏlla peasants: they used (1) the "opposition of the average farmer to the food collection policies of MG," and (2) "the almost universal hate which the average Korean, both city dweller and farmer, has for the police force":

> This hatred is deeper in Chŏlla-South Province than in the other provinces because the leftist "People's Committee" was in actual control of the government here for a longer period of time after the Jap surrender than in any other province.[92]

The Americans thought that outside Communist agitators and the "superb" organization of the people's committees were responsible for the spread of the disorders: "the Communists controlled approximately 75% of the population" during the uprisings. Yet the Americans in South Chŏlla also wondered why the demonstrators did not strike simultaneously throughout southern Korea, instead of one province after another: "Whether this error on the part of the Communists was due to a lack of trained agitators or to a faulty over-all plan is not known."[93] Most likely, however, there was no overall plan and there were few organizers, let alone "outside agitators." The uprisings seem to have traveled in waves, beginning in the Taegu area, spreading southward, then westward into South Chŏlla. Organization sufficient to direct tens of thousands of peasants throughout Korea did not exist. The committee and peasant union organization existed in and drew strength from the localities; its structure was cellular, not hierarchical. Thus one rebellion touched off another in contiguous areas as word spread by informal and popular means of communication. The sequence may be likened to a self-contained system of billiard balls striking each other successively. The evidence suggests that South Chŏlla peasants rose up not because of communist agitation, but because of deep grievances arising from land conditions and relations, grain collection inequities, and the local interlocking of landlord, government official, and policeman.

This conclusion is supported in one of the few extant leftist accounts of the uprisings.[94] The ostensible organizers of the rebellions, most of whom were probably members of the Korean Communist Party, wrote extensively about the towering crimes of the United States: it wants to turn Korea into its colony; its policies derive from the interests of Wall Street financiers; it hopes to make Korea a military base for future aggression. When the account turned to the recollections of local participants in the uprisings, however, the emphasis was exclusively on local problems, such as the authority of colonial police, brutal grain collection policies, hoarding of grain by landlords and rich peasants, and the systematic suppression of the local people's committee structure. In other words, the account suggests petty extremism on the part of the communists (who admit their leadership failure during the autumn crisis) and real and understandable grievances on the part of local activists.

As rebels retreated into the border region between South and North Chŏlla in mid-November, minor disorders began occurring in Namwŏn and Sunch'ang, two counties of PC strength in North Chŏlla.[95] Otherwise, North Chŏlla was largely untouched by the autumn uprisings—precisely what we would expect, given the early demise of the committees there and the strength of the landlords. Only Chŏnju, the province capital, experienced real trouble. On November 12 some 417 prisoners escaped from the Chŏnju jail. Internal documents referred to them as having been incarcerated for "political crimes."[96] Then in mid-December local leftist youth groups received permission for a peaceful march through the capital. The Chŏnju police erected barricades, however, that were used to trap the demonstrators (and some uninvolved bystanders); then they ordered the crowd to disperse:

Because they were trapped in the middle of a city block, the crowd could not find an exit. The police began firing into the air. The mob milled around. The jittery policemen lowered their fire into the crowd and followed this with a horseback charge into the screaming people. Clubs and rifle butts flew. When the street was clear, twenty persons lay dead—including men, women, and children. This incident was reported by CIC to American authorities. No action was taken to discipline the police concerned.[97]

As one might expect, violence in Kangwŏn Province occurred primarily in the remote coastal counties having strong people's committees. An attack on local police occurred in the port town of Chumunjin, north of Kangnŭng, reported by American investigators to be, like Kangnŭng, "95% leftist." On October 29 police in Mukho, aided by 200 rightists, were able to beat back an attack by local peasants. American CIC investigators also reported "general unrest" throughout Samch'ŏk and Kangnŭng counties in the first week of November. There were numerous reports from this region of attacks on the homes of policemen and rich landlords. Policemen and their rightist allies reciprocated by wrecking and looting the homes of arrested rioters.[98] Americans on the scene in Samch'ŏk said the primary cause of unrest was the inability of leftists to get work in the local mines. Rightist youths patrolled the mines wearing old Japanese uniforms. Local officials also denied leftists ration cards for rice.[99]

After most of the uprisings had subsided, the *Pi'p'an sinmun* (Critical News) stated that the autumn uprisings were the most significant in Korea since the *Tonghak* rebellion.[100] That judgment is not far from the mark. Certainly the uprisings of 1946 resembled the *Tonghak* in some ways. Participants in the autumn uprisings borrowed their techniques from the *Tonghak*, and from peasant rebels everywhere. They wielded the implements of their work, like scythes, hooks, and hammers. Lacking firepower, they rushed at the police en masse, often when the police had paused to reload their rifles.[101] They were able to summon huge crowds overnight by primitive communication methods: signal fires on hillsides, drums in the mountains, couriers, and word-of-mouth. Furthermore, Korean peasants chose their targets with discriminating awareness of the agencies of their oppression: policemen, magistrates, landlords and their agents. When a local office was seized, records of rice and grain collections were the first objects destroyed.

METHODS OF SUPPRESSION

The manner in which the autumn uprisings were suppressed highlighted several aspects of politics in postwar south Korea. First, the make-up of the suppression forces placed in relief the fundamental political alignments of the liberation era. Second, the success of the suppression demonstrated the advantages of controlling south Korea's comparatively well-developed communication and transportation facilities. Third, the necessity for constant use of American soldiers, weaponry, and machinery such as tanks in suppressing the uprisings illustrated the relative weakness of the native Korean forces of order. The Korean National Police, in spite of its well-articulated organization and its monopoly on most of the resources of control in south Korea, could not have prevailed without American help. Had Americans not been on the scene in the fall of 1946, Korea would have been thrown into civil war then instead of four years later.

The close association of the police with rightist organizations, particularly with rightist youth groups, was clear for all to see during the three months of strikes and uprisings in the fall of 1946. Official American sources, which generally denied that the police were anything but nonpartisan, lauded several rightist organizations for their help. The official history cited the NSRRKI and its youth group, *Taehan tongnip choksŏng ch'ŏng ch'ŏngnyŏn tongmaeng*, in particular, for their aid, saying that these groups exposed "the crimes being committed by the Communists" and called attention to "the good work of police authorities who arrest 'only the offenders in order to protect your property.' " The history also reported that in the Kaesŏng region "the use of volunteer police, made up of young men's groups, to reinforce police in all affected areas, proved quite effective."[102] Furthermore, at a time when Korean newspapers across the political spectrum were pointing out the very real grievances fueling the strikes and uprisings, a handbill signed by the Yŏngju NSRRKI branch and a local "patriotic" youth group claimed that the uprisings were carried out by "communists, that is to say, those who oppose [Korean] independence." It lauded the police for their "great sacrifices" and urged the "ignorant peasants" to get back to work.[103] American reports from the provinces constantly called attention to the alliance between the police and rightist groups. An official Korean police history also noted the aid of "patriotic, right wing" groups in putting down the riots.[104]

In the aftermath of the riots, there appeared numerous reports of police soliciting funds from wealthy local citizens to replace the losses of individual policemen and to help rebuild police homes and stations. At the Korean-American Conference in November 1946, a man from Sangju in North Kyŏngsang reported that the police had beaten his wealthy father and demanded a 500,000 *wŏn* payment for restitution of losses. This man's father was a particular target because he had made earlier contributions to the Sangju people's committee. Once the funds were obtained, the police reportedly used much of it for revelry with *kisaeng* girls.[105]

The Military Government relied primarily on the KNP in suppressing the peasant uprisings. They first sent in the provincial police; then, to the extent necessary, they called on the Seoul police or American tactical forces. In the critical days from October 2 to 5, the Americans in Taegu dispatched provincial police in the following disposition: Sŏngju—100; Sŏnsan—69; Yŏngch'ŏn—50; Kyŏngju—75; Kunhwi—100; Kŭmch'ŏn—150; Waegwan—100; Talsŏng—70.[106] In South Chŏlla the Americans reported that the disorders were brought under control by the rapid mobilization of provincial police backed up by tactical troops.[107] In North Kyŏngsang, however, the situation was beyond the control of available provincial police and tactical forces. Thus, as we saw above, police were sent in from the quiescent North Ch'ungch'ŏng Province. When those forces proved insufficient, several hundred police and auxiliary forces entrained from Seoul. On October 5 a train arrived in Taegu, carrying 411 policemen from "Division A" in Seoul.[108] Apparently another train arrived the next day, carrying about 80 "strike-breakers" led by high officials in the Transportation Department and the Seoul police.[109] Railroad transportation and the highly developed police communications network were key factors in the successful suppression of the North Kyŏngsang uprisings.

The police, as might be expected, reacted to the violence directed against them with excesses that shocked many Americans. The official history of the Occupation conceded that "during the course of the disturbances there were numerous instances of extreme police brutality." It quoted an eyewitness account by an American CIC agent:

> On October 9 I saw a Provincial Police detective strike a Korean across the shoulders with a club 30 inches long and approximately one and a half inches in diameter, two or more times. I disarmed him but had not [*sic*] authority to administer any disciplinary action. Another example, an agent from my office saw a policeman from the 19th District Police Station strike a Korean girl across the shoulders with a piece of steel tube. . . . My agent disarmed the policeman but had no authority to beat the living daylights out of him. The girl was supposed to have pointed out a house where the policeman lived during the mob violence.[110]

Another American who witnessed the police torturing arrested Koreans "walked over to the Korean Lieutenant, grasped a stick out of his hand and told him, 'I had told you before never to do a thing like that—we are Americans and you Koreans are Korean, but decent people don't do things like that.' "[111]

Cho Pyŏng-ok, director of the KNP, asked his American superiors on October 20 for a free hand in arresting leaders of the KCP, *Chŏnp'-yŏng, Chŏnnong*, and the people's committees, "in advance of their actual criminal activities." He offered the following defense: "There is an old law still existing which gives legal ground for making such precautionary arrests. I refer to the administrative and executive ordinance, issued July, 1912, by the Japanese Governor-General."[112] Some Americans thought that this and other recommendations by Cho were in essentially the same vein as "the old Japanese 'Thought Control.' "[113] Yet leaders of the above-named groups were arrested on a wholesale basis after the strikes and uprisings began. *Chŏnp'yŏng*, as we will see, was nearly ruined as a viable labor union because of mass arrests of its leaders in September and October. At least one knowledgeable American on the scene charged complicity between the top levels of the American command and the KNP in wrecking this union.[114] The director of the MG Department of Transportation also acknowledged that American methods used in suppressing the uprisings and strikes differed little from "Korean" methods:

> We went into that situation just like we would go into battle. We were out to break that thing up and we didn't have time to worry too much if a few innocent people got hurt. We set up concentration camps outside of town and held strikers there when the jails got too full. It was war. We recognized it as war. And that is the way we fought it.[115]

CAUSES OF THE STRIKES AND UPRISINGS

No single cause can be isolated to explain events as complex as those that occurred in south Korea in the fall of 1946, nor can the months from September to December be abstracted from the experience of the first year of Occupation. In fact, the autumn uprisings were really the climax of events occurring throughout the preceding year.

The official history of the Occupation arrived at an easy and self-serving explanation for the rebellions:

> Boiled down, all evidence points to the fact that, but for Communist instigation and direction, the bloody events of 2 October would not have occurred, nor would the serious disturbances which followed. In short, the riots were Communist-inspired, and in no sense spontaneous.[116]

The uprisings were "directly fostered from North Korea," through orders to Pak Hŏ-yŏng and through infiltrators from the north.[117] What is the evidence for these assertions?

The order from the north that was revealed by the MG on September 24, and which we mentioned earlier, does not appear in the evidence for the above allegations. There is no mention of it. Most of the evidence for the above conclusions was drawn from information provided by the Korean National Police and from articles in rightist newspapers such as the *Taedong Press*.[118] Cho Pyŏng-ok told the Americans:

> It has been an open secret that the Commies have been planning, since last May, to stage a nation-wide opposition to the Military Government . . . this plan was mapped out by leaders of the Communist Party, and was and is carried out by mobilizing its organizations of national and local level and the nucleus of organizations of other sister institutions.[119]

The police provided the Americans with charts designed to show communist control of all organizations on the Left, and the Americans accepted such information as definitive. They apparently did not question the possible motives of the KNP in defining all opposition to the police as communist-inspired. Although there is no doubt that south Korean communists *sought* to control other leftist organizations, there is considerable evidence to show that they could not even manage to discipline the factions within the party in Seoul. How could they then exercise authoritative control over groups of the noncommunist Left in the provinces? Communists in south Korea simply did not have the capacity to push buttons and give orders from Seoul that would cause peasants in North Kyŏngsang to attack police and destroy grain collection records. Something deeper motivated peasants in the autumn uprisings.

An American intelligence report in early October alleged that some 10,000 individuals had "infiltrated" south Korea from the north over a period of several months preceding the uprisings.[120] I have seen no evidence in archival materials on these uprisings that infiltrators from north Korea were arrested during the disorders, however. Richard Robinson supports this finding: "among the thousands of arrests made during the strike, not one individual was found who was other than a bona fide resident of South Korea."[121]

Yŏ Un-hyŏng, who visited north Korea from September 23 to October 1, 1946, reportedly informed the MG on his return that the strikes in south Korea were the work of Pak Hŏn-yŏng. Yŏ said, according to American accounts, that Kim Il Sung and Kim Tu-bong did not support the strikes and suggested that Pak was in league with Mu Chŏng (then out of favor in the north). Thus, presumably, the strikes were aimed at aggrandizing Pak's and Mu Chŏng's power at the expense of other communist leaders. Apparently Yŏ also charged that Pak, unlike Kim Il Sung, was an inveterate pro-Soviet and desired a Korean government linked closely to the Soviet Union. The latter, Yŏ said, was something that neither he nor Kim Il Sung desired.[122] Shortly after Yŏ's return to the south, the Americans found a document accusing Pak of ordering the strikes on September 9 to exploit the mounting economic crisis and to ruin the efforts of the Coalition Committee. The allegation was contained in a document from a September 19 meeting of an anti-Pak communist faction, however, which would cast doubt on the authenticity of the charge.[123]

The problem here is one that confronts every analyst of Korean politics: Korean leaders always seem to couch complex events in terms of factional struggles. Throughout the summer and fall of 1946, Yŏ and Pak were struggling with each other for control of the Left in Seoul, as we saw in chapter seven. Thus Yŏ had reason to blacken Pak's name with the Military Government. It is also known that leaders in north Korea like Kim Il Sung and Kim Tu-bong feared Pak's influence among Korean communists. A subtle factor here too is the pro-Soviet reputation Pak had acquired as a result of the distortions of his remarks concerning the USSR at the news conference on January 5, 1946. But it is a simple fact that no individual could have single-handedly "caused" the conflagration in the fall of 1946.

In fact, Yŏ himself did not think the uprisings were the work of one man, as is shown by his letter to Hodge of November 29, 1946: "You will agree with me, dear General, that things are not going well. . . . The widespread unrest all over southern Korea is an indication of deep dissatisfaction." He agreed that "agitators" may have taken advantage of the situation but insisted:

> The cause of dissatisfaction is much more deep-rooted. The embers are there, it was only fanned to a conflagration. In the last few days I have been in the country. . . . There is almost no authority. It is a case of everyone for himself.

Yŏ laid much of the blame for the trouble on "tyranny and abuse of authority" by the police. He urged that Hodge give Kim Kyu-sik full authority to rectify the situation and vowed, "I will give him my full and unqualified support."[124]

The involvement of north Korea in the uprisings, it would seem, was achieved less through direct instigation than through the "demonstration effect." Their implementation of thoroughgoing land reform and labor reform laws seemed to answer the grievances of peasants in south Korea. We find demonstrators in south Korea calling for land and labor laws such as those in north Korea and for "political organs like the people's committees," not because they were being ordered to do so by leaders in the north, but because the reforms in north Korea struck responsive chords in the south.[125]

If we try to classify the organizers of the strikes and uprisings (who may or may not have been the cause of them) according to political association, we find over and over the involvement of local people's committees, *nongmin chohap, nodong chohap,* and other PC-affiliated organizations. The autumn uprisings, far from being pathological anomalies or the work of scheming individuals, were the predictable and logical culmination of more than a year of unheeded Korean demands for meaningful reforms, labor unions, peasant unions, and self-governing organs of power. Official American accounts barely mention this experience and its effects, but virtually all internal reports from the field specified the key role of these native, local organizations in the uprisings. Stewart Meacham strongly emphasized the frustrations met by *Chŏnp'yŏng* in the months preceding the strikes. After detailing numerous instances of flagrant opposition to and abuse of *Chŏnp'yŏng* organizers in factories and enterprises throughout south Korea, he noted that "in no instance was it claimed that Chung Pyong [*sic*] had been doing anything more than attempting to get wage conditions improved or some other working conditions bettered." But, he continued, "this period of mounting attack against Chung Pyong met with significant American approval and cooperation." Meacham therefore concluded that *Chŏnp'yŏng* called the September strikes because "the war of attrition that the factory managers, police and Americans were carrying on against the organization had reached a point where its very life was at stake."[126] Labor unions, peasant unions, and people's committees throughout south Korea had undergone similar "wars of attrition" in the year preceding the autumn uprisings.

Official Korean sources openly acknowledge the role played by local people's committees and labor and peasant unions in mobilizing people for the uprisings.[127] But official American sources do not. Korean opponents of these groups never felt compelled to differentiate local "communists" from Moscow- or P'yŏngyang-dominated communists. But Americans had more difficulty in justifying suppression of communists or leftists who could not be linked to outside agitators. The Korean governor of North Kyŏngsang could write with equanimity that there were in his province some 3,000 native leftist leaders, "strong men, ingenious, courageous, and ready to die."[128] Americans could not stomach suppressing such people unless they could perceive a tie to the Soviets.

It is reasonable to conclude that the systematic suppression of the committees, peasant and workers' unions, and associated groups during the first year of Occupation laid the seeds of the autumn uprisings and gave them the desperate quality of a last-ditch stand. But this would not explain the timing of the strikes and uprisings. South Korea erupted when it did, not because certain anniversaries came due or because of concerted agitation, but because of the agricultural cycle. Autumn is harvest time in Korea.

As we noted in chapter two, Korea's economy essentially functioned on a rice standard rather than a gold or other monetary standard. We also noted that the MG institution of a free-market policy caused the bumper rice harvest in the fall of 1945 to evaporate virtually overnight, owing to the profiteering, speculation, hoarding, and increased rates of consumption of a population unaccustomed to the psychology of exchange on the open market. But the full effects of the disastrous MG rice policies were not felt until the rice harvest came due in the fall of 1946. By that time, the MG had completely reverted to the Japanese system of collections based on the triumvirate of policeman, magistrate, and landlord. Had the Americans simply continued the Japanese system, they might have had fewer economic problems. But by inaugurating a free market—which not only allowed landlords to profit but also provided opportunities for people's committees and *nongmin chohap* to control rice collections in regions where they were strong—and then attempting to return to the old extractive mechanisms, the Americans wreaked havoc on rice prices, the extractive capability of the central government, and the very willingness of peasants to sow and harvest crops. By the fall of 1946, south Korea's agricultural producers, and the economy itself, were at the end of their tether. As rice goes, so goes the Korean economy.

Open-market wholesale prices in Seoul began a steep rise in August 1946 and did not peak until February 1947, by which time the already-inflated prices of August had nearly trebled (see figure 17). The exceedingly sharp rise from October to December 1946 no doubt represents both a cause and an effect of the strikes and uprisings. The price of rice rocketed to its highest point, 14,000 *wŏn* a bushel, just prior to the 1946 harvest.[129] Although grain prices had fallen somewhat from their autumn peaks by February 1947, table 19 gives an indication of the severe increases in the prices of important grains in the preceding year (the increases were greatest in the last quarter of 1946):[130]

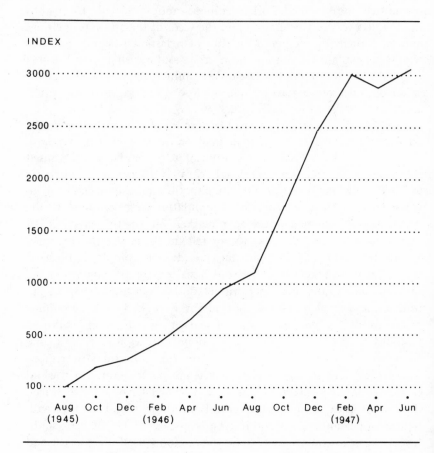

17. Index of Open Market Wholesale Prices, Seoul, August 1945 to June 1947 (August 1945 equals 100)

Source: United States Delegation to Joint Commission, "Report on the Occupation Area of South Korea Since Termination of Hostilities," (Seoul: USAMGIK, 1947).

TABLE 19

PRICE INCREASES IN AGRICULTURAL PRODUCTS
FEBRUARY 1946 TO FEBRUARY 1947
(IN *wŏn* PER *sŏk*)

Product	February 1946	February 1947
Rice	1,348	10,146
Barley	810	5,000
Wheat	1,390	6,785
Millet	1,410	7,310
Soy beans	1,060	7,805

The chaotic rice economy naturally led to increases in inflation and unemployment. In the period between September 1945 and June 1946, the amount of *wŏn* in circulation rose by about one billion, to a total of 9.4 billion. But by December 1946, *wŏn* circulation had nearly doubled the June figure and stood at 18 billion.[131] Increases in wages did not even begin to keep up with inflation. If prices and wages in August 1945 are given an index of 100, by December 1946 the price index stood at 1,459, while the wage index was only 411.[132] Even those with jobs could not make ends meet: "the wage picture in Korea is desperate. Living costs have risen enormously."[133]

There were more than one million Koreans in the labor force who could not find jobs in December 1946 (see table 20). This figure is

TABLE 20

UNEMPLOYMENT BY PROVINCE, NOVEMBER 1946

Province	War-related* Unemployment (A)	(A) as Percentage of Province Population†	Unemployment (B)	(A) and (B) as Percentage of Province Population†
Kyŏnggi	6,883	0.3%	8,050	0.6%
N. Ch'ungch'ŏng	24,209	2.2	15,745	3.6
S. Ch'ungch'ŏng	19,993	1.0	23,723	2.3
N. Chŏlla	37,045	1.8	28,719	3.3
S. Chŏlla	70,283	2.4	36,694	3.6
N. Kyŏngsang	152,239	4.7	197,638	11.0
S. Kyŏngsang	284,578	8.9	111,303	12.4
Kangwŏn	4,609	0.4	17,766	2.0
Cheju Island	20,591	7.5	2,422	8.3
Total	637,203	3.3	464,520	5.7

SOURCE: *Chosŏn kyŏngje nyŏnbo*, 1948, p. I-203; and USAMGIK, *Population of Korea*, p. 2.

* Primarily returnees from Japan and Manchuria
† Percentage of total provincial population, not of labor force

based on Department of Labor information. Hodge's labor advisor, Stewart Meacham, thought that if anything the figures underestimated the level of unemployment.[134] Most striking is the situation in the Kyŏngsang provinces. Of all unemployed Koreans, 68 percent were located in these two provinces. And 58 percent of the total unemployed in the Kyŏngsang provinces were returnees. Thus, according to these figures, these two provinces had 436,817 returnees looking for work, or about 6.9 percent of the *total* population of both provinces. The plight of these returnees was so dire that in the six weeks before the outbreak of strikes in September 1946, some 15,000 of them had actually tried to return to Japan in search of food and jobs.[135] Korean officials in the Kyŏngsangs later attributed the severity of the autumn uprisings there to the status of the returnees and the resulting population strains.[136] Thus the Kyŏngsang provinces again show a significant relation between population uprooting and resulting economic dislocation on the one hand, and high rates of political participation on the other.

Rice collection practices were perhaps as important in stimulating peasant participation in the autumn uprisings as was the economic chaos caused by MG rice policies. In liberated Korea, as we have seen, disputes over the control and allocation of resources, particularly land and its products, distributed Koreans at the poles of the political spectrum—aligned them in a classic zero-sum situation in which the stakes were great and the chances for avoiding conflict minimal. The land reform carried out in north Korea in the spring of 1946 coincided with the American revival of the colonial apparatus for rice collection in south Korea and deepened the south's already severe polarization. Moreover, the responsibility for extraction of rice was returned to the experienced hands of the national police, a group that was despised because of their service to the Japanese. Returning the extraction of rice to their hands was like pouring salt on a festering wound. Nothing else can explain why Korean police were the objects of such elemental violence during the autumn harvest of 1946.

The summer grain collection in 1946 had been a violent affair, with only half of the national quota collected. Opposition to the collection had included some landlords, who desired a return to the free-market program of late 1945. American agricultural officials later cited "the brutal methods" employed by police in the summer grain collections as "basic factors" in the autumn explosion. And the rationing program, described as follows, did not help:

> The general pattern of rationing is uniform throughout South Korea. Local city officials, usually the mayor, appoint private indi-

viduals to operate ration stores. . . . In practice, political considerations are often responsible for appointments.[137]

During the September strikes, before the uprisings occurred, American CIC investigators warned that rice collection practices were stimulating support for the strikers: "the people are in complete sympathy with the railroad strikers as a result of the rice situation."[138] The collections, as we have seen, were often made forcibly and were nearly always based on political considerations. Peasants who were suspected of leftist political activity were given high collection quotas and allowed smaller rations. When peasants could not meet the quotas established by local police and government officials, the police would make up the difference by confiscating cattle and other farm property. Beatings were administered to recalcitrant peasants as a routine practice.[139] Furthermore, extensive corruption existed at all levels of the collection process. American investigators often found large stocks of rice in the homes of policemen during the autumn uprisings.[140] Speculators in the Kyŏngsang provinces and elsewhere bought rice from police and other local officials and shipped it into black markets in major cities and even in Japan.[141] In early November, American CIC investigators in Taegu found stores of looted rice in the warehouses of a rightist youth group.[142] In the aftermath of the uprisings, the Americans interviewed nineteen "prominent" Koreans in Taegu, seeking the causes of the uprisings. Nearly all of them cited peasant grievances over grain collections, particularly the corruption and the arbitrary and cruel methods of the police. Even a high police official in North Kyŏngsang told the Americans that the police were "too harsh in enforcing grain collections."[143] Hatred of the police was so intense that hospitals in North Kyŏngsang refused to treat wounded policemen. American troops had to take over the provincial hospital in Taegu on October 2.[144]

CONCLUSIONS

The costs of the autumn uprisings were staggering. More than 200 policemen were killed. The total number of officials, rioters, and civilians who died is not known (families of dead rioters, for example, feared to report their losses because of the threat of reprisals), but it may have topped 1,000. Property damage was extensive. Much of the rice crop was lost. The total number of arrests is not known, but it may have approached 30,000 or more in the three-month period. Apparently 7,000 to 8,000 people were arrested in North Kyŏngsang alone.[145] *Chŏnp'yŏng* claimed that 11,624 of its workers were arrested in October.[146] As we noted earlier, more than 3,000 people were arrested in the Kaesŏng region and another 2,000 were arrested in one day at the Yongsan railroad yards. At least 4,000 were arrested in South Chŏlla.

When the dust had cleared by the end of 1946, it was apparent that the forces of the Left had been the biggest losers. The successful suppression of the uprisings marked a turning point in the strength and viability of the Korean National Police. The forces of order in the south now dealt with a deeply intimidated peasant population. The autumn uprisings sharpened the efficiency of the bureaucracy in dealing with disorder, while demonstrating to the peasants the frailty of their marginal existence. Opposition to the forces of order had resulted in death, destruction, the loss of a year's crop or vital ration cards.

The autumn uprisings brought into focus the discontinuous and even fractured structure of postwar Korea. We find a remarkable pattern of peasant rebellion overlaid with groping organizational immaturity. Like the many Koreans who were suspended somewhere between worker and peasant mentality, provincial organizations were more than peasant bands but not quite modern political structures. In the Kyŏngsang provinces a potent mixture of urban labor strikes and rural peasant rebellion gave the insurrection considerable force, but as it spread to South Chŏlla the pattern became peasant rebellion. In time of crisis, the people's committees and peasant unions failed to link up with each other across provincial boundaries and instead took on a cellular organization much like archaic peasant rebellions. Thus, instead of the structured, communist-led revolution that many Americans kept looking for and not finding, they got a spreading mosaic of unsystematic, empirical, spontaneous peasant wars. Taken one at a time, they were the products of a thousand local frustrations. Taken as a whole, they amounted to a lusty shriek of dissent over the arrangements of liberated Korea. But precisely because they were local and spontaneous, they could be suppressed by the overdeveloped apparatus of control bequeathed by the Japanese. With railroad, road, and communications facilities largely in American and rightist Korean hands, and with a national police network that could be mobilized on a countrywide basis to deal with what were, after all, regional uprisings, the denouement was all but determined.

Korean leftist leaders sought to direct and channel the astonishing human force loosed in the autumn of 1946. Whatever may be said of their role in inciting the violent outbursts of the peasantry, it is clear that they failed to harness raw peasant power into organized politics. There were few sanctuaries in southern Korea to which they could withdraw. There were no central highlands, as in Vietnam, a region never integrated under the central control of the regime in the capital. There was no Yenan base area, as in China, competing with an alter-regime that itself lacked integrated control of the nation. And there was little time to strengthen the essential process of enrolling peasants into organizations that could, over time, provide benefits, positions, and the essential element of defense against enemies. On the one hand, the south Korean leftists and communists continued to reflect the failings of leaders with little experience in organizing masses of people; they therefore simply organized themselves. That is, they spun off one faction after another and concentrated too much of their effort in Seoul. On the other hand, they faced a bureaucratic apparatus trained in the control of peasant populations, one that had at its disposal superior communication, transportation, and other material resources and that was capable of withering repression. That this apparatus had to have recourse to United States Army support on so many occasions during the autumn of 1946 perhaps attests as much to the success as to the failure of communist and leftist organizers.

The greatest loss to the Korean peasants in the aftermath of the uprisings was the effective demise of the local organs that had defended their interests. The death knell of most people's committees and peasant unions rang throughout southern Korea. The leaders of most of the important organizations of the Left on the national and local levels wound up dead, in jail, hunted, or underground. Thousands of their supporters either quit politics or were deeply radicalized. The authentic claims of the Democratic National Front to be an all-embracing coalition of the Left were shattered, which resulted in a dire loss of mass support and the emergence of a more extreme and less inclusive organization, the South Korean Worker's Party. For the peasants, simple rationality, if nothing else, dictated a return to quiescent cultivation.

Chapter Eleven

THE NORTH WIND

The south Korean reactionaries once clamoured for the abolition of the 38th parallel . . . but now they dare not utter a single
word about its abolition. It seems that they are now very much
afraid of the north wind, far from sending the south wind toward us.

Kim Il Sung, April 1946

I N THE first year after liberation, the northern half of Korea accomplished what most Koreans and many Western observers thought
would be the inevitable result of the end of Japanese rule—a thoroughgoing revolution. Within nine months of the liberation, landlordism had disappeared, the land had been redistributed, major
industries had been nationalized, radical reforms had eliminated the
worst abuses of the colonial factory system and had established formal
equality for women. Within a year of the liberation, a powerful mass
party, enrolling hundreds of thousands of Koreans, and a rudimentary
army provided the organization and coherence that Korean politics
had so long lacked. By the end of 1946, north Korea, like the south,
had delineated the contours of the separate state that formally emerged
there in September 1948. Furthermore, most of the unique features
that have come to be associated with North Korean communism had
emerged during this period: a heavy dose of nationalism, stress on
the critical role of the leader, an inclusive united front policy, and
the ideological mix of socialism and self-reliance that has become the
peculiar vehicle for communism in Korean national form. All this was
done quickly, efficiently, not to say ruthlessly, but comparatively speaking, with a minimum of bloodshed. In other words, north Korea went
through the "normal" process that we might expect from the residual
effects of Japanese colonial rule.

Colonial development had transformed the relationship between
northern and southern Korea. Historically, the south had been the
region of landed wealth and aristocratic dominance; agricultural production covered the peninsula, and the richest, most productive lands
were in the south. The north, except for certain areas in Hwanghae
and South P'yŏng'an provinces, had large regions of dry- rather than
paddy-field production and upland penury that led in many places to

slash-and-burn cultivation. Wild regions in the upper peninsula were never fully integrated into the traditional Korean state. Regional prejudices, in typical fashion, came to overlay these material distinctions —but these were by no means so strong as to invite a rationale for national division.

By 1945, however, north and south faced each other in the context of a recent, rapid reversal of the traditional relationship. The north had moved out of backwardness into modern industrial relations, giving a dynamic basis to the society in a new mode of production; even the wild border regions yielded something new—an anti-Japanese guerrilla leadership. The north became the repository, therefore, of what was young, dynamic, and progressive. The south retained an exalted status and a traditional legitimacy as the home of Korea's rulers, but Japanese rule had deeply eroded that structure of status and authority and had bequeathed to the north the essential basis for a reversal of the old relationship.

The recent emergence of industry in the north also required and stimulated the emergence of a modern Korean state on a new basis. For any leadership, northern industrialization and its growth under public rather than private auspices would have suggested the need for a strong center. Managerial and planning needs, the integrated grid of transportation and communications associated with industry, the requirements for steady supply of labor and materials, all spell extended functions for the state. For a radical anticolonial leadership, however, a strong state could also prove useful in reorienting a skewed infrastructure toward national rather than colonial needs and in insulating Korea from the dislocations of open involvement in the world market. Polanyi wrote:

> If the organized states of Europe could protect themselves against the backwash of international free trade, the politically unorganized colonial peoples could not. The revolt against imperialism was mainly an attempt on the part of exotic peoples to achieve the political status necessary to shelter themselves from the social dislocations caused by European trade policies. The protection that the white man could easily secure for himself, through the sovereign status of his communities was out of reach of the colored man as long as he lacked the prerequisite, political government.[1]

The radical tonic for Korea's plight, therefore, would be social revolution at home and a withdrawal and insulation from a world economy dominated by advanced industrial states. The sundering of the colonial sphere left a tightly organized, highly nationalistic polity in the north that quickly began to restructure and reform colonial distortions in agriculture, industry, and society. By the end of 1946, one of the first examples of revolutionary nationalism in a postcolonial "Third World" setting was in place.

To say that even today few Western observers would agree with all, or any, of the above is only to begin to appreciate the gulf in understanding that separates the existing Western historiography from the reality of postwar north Korea. The reasons for these differences of opinion are many, among them: (1) because the Soviet Red Army occupied north Korea, so that this Korean revolution went on under the protective umbrella of Joseph Stalin, many Stalinist abuses of socialism have been assumed to characterize north Korea during this period as well; (2) the existing historiography in the West has been and remains subject to the distortions of the Cold War and the special pleading of South Korea, so that the literature tends to be classically biased; (3) North Korea itself has failed to deal honestly and thoroughly with its own history during the period so that most of its histories are of marginal use; (4) the Korean revolution occurred in the earliest days of the Cold War, presenting a hard image of Third World revolution to Westerners, especially Americans, who hoped to fashion a liberal-democratic path to postcolonial development; and (5) none of the Korean revolutionaries had experience in or ties with the West, as had those in the Vietnamese or Chinese revolutions. For all these reasons it is necessary to begin again at the beginning and to attempt to abandon received wisdom to get at the reality.

The Soviet Occupation

We have outlined in earlier chapters the general contours of Soviet presurrender policies for the Korean peninsula. At his meetings with Roosevelt at Teheran and Yalta, and in discussions with Harry Hopkins in May 1945, Stalin left the Americans with the impression that he had agreed to a four-power trusteeship over Korea. He carefully avoided committing such agreements to paper, however, and the actual written record shows for the most part a Soviet emphasis on Korean independence. At Potsdam in July, Molotov asked specifically for a thorough discussion of a Korean trusteeship, calling it an unprecedented and unusual arrangement; no substantive discussions occurred, however, and the matter had to be put off to the Moscow Foreign Minister's meeting at the end of 1945.

Military discussions at Potsdam touched on likely Soviet operations in Korea and, in effect, left the Japanese forces in Manchuria and Korea, and the losses likely to be incurred in defeating them, to the massive Soviet land armies. The American atomic bombings of Hiroshima and Nagasaki and the quick successes of the Soviet army in Manchurian battles forced an abrupt Japanese surrender and left a vacuum on the Korean peninsula that the Soviets were best poised to fill. George Lensen describes the Soviet move into Korea:

> Soviet planning and preparations for the campaign [in Korea and Manchuria] were elaborate and the offensive . . . was mounted on a large scale, with over 1½ million men, 5½ thousand tanks and self-propelled guns.[2]

On August 10 units of the Soviet 25th army attacked the north Korean cities of Ŭnggi and Najin, meeting only light Japanese resistance. After the August 15 Japanese surrender, the Russians entered the major port city of Wŏnsan on August 21. Three days later they marched into Hamhŭng and P'yŏngyang.[3] Although various Korean groups aided the Soviet entry with attacks against the Japanese, and although Koreans were in the 25th army detachments, there is no mention of participation by Kim Il Sung and his guerrilla followers in either Soviet or North Korean accounts.[4]

Through their quick and extensive engagement of Japanese forces, the Soviets won military and political advantage: militarily, they were in a position to march down the peninsula to Pusan; politically, they won favor among the Korean population because, as General Hodge later put it, the Koreans "saw the Russians come in here and fight," whereas the Americans were unable to reach Korea until early September, and did not fight on Korean soil.[5] Yet in retrospect, Korean communists in the north must have wondered why the Soviets did not exploit their military advantage to unify the peninsula and present the Americans with a *fait accompli*. The reasons for Soviet moderation were two: (1) a desire not to needlessly offend the United States, when half the peninsula would in any case guarantee Soviet security; (2) the rapidity of the Japanese collapse must have upset the Soviet calculation on the ending of the Pacific War. In early August, before Hiroshima, the Russians probably expected to have to advance a long and costly campaign for Manchuria and Korea; yet by mid-August it was clear that they could have half of the peninsula at little cost. Kim Il Sung and other Korean guerrillas probably rued the rapid Japanese collapse, however, which denied them the opportunity to participate directly in the final liberation of their homeland.

The rapid end to the war also left Soviet policies toward Korea relatively unformed and thus reactive to American policies in the south. There is little indication that the Soviets thought much about Korea before the war ended; and in 1945/46 they had to cope with awesome human and material destruction at home. This period of "domesticism,"[6] and the general emphasis of Soviet foreign policy on Eastern Europe, meant that Korea took a back seat. The Soviets apparently had neither the resources nor the will to create full satellite states in Manchuria or Korea; thus they quit Manchuria in 1946 and allowed a degree of autonomy in north Korea greater than that allowed in several Eastern European states. Their basic goal was to assure that Korea would not again provide a launching board for attacks on Manchuria or the Soviet Far East. Within the bounds of that outer limit, Koreans were able to carve out a degree of autonomy that was particularly significant in the first year of liberation.[7]

Soviet expansionism in 1945 was accomplished by a huge military machine; it was lateral, agglomerative, incremental expansion-in-width. As Franz Schurmann, Hannah Arendt, and others have suggested, such expansion depends on military force, having no internal economic dynamic like that of capitalist empires. It thus may be more repressive, but when stretched to the limit it is also weak. The Soviets in Manchuria and Korea were stretched across the Urals into the frontier hinterlands of the Russian land mass, unsustained by the Soviet industrial and agricultural base. This is the fundamental reason why, in my view, the Soviets perforce had limited aims in China and Korea.

The lack of Soviet preparation upon entering Korea was manifest in contradictory policies followed during the first days and weeks after their entry into Korea. Japanese activities added to the disorder of the initial Soviet occupation. Unlike the Japanese welcome for the Americans in the south, Japanese authorities in the north extended virtually no cooperation to the Soviets. In fact, they destroyed factories, mines, banks, official records, and the like.[8]

The Soviets seem either to have had no uniform policy for governing northern Korea or to have tailored their policies to suit conditions in different provinces and localities. Upon their arrival in Wŏnsan on August 21, the Soviets ousted the Japanese administration, took over government facilities, and authorized Kang Ki-dŏk, the chief of the Wŏnsan people's committee, to take charge of peace preservation in the city. In the town of Yangyang, just north of the thirty-eighth parallel, entering Red Army troops were met by representatives of a local Red Peasant Union, part of the underground peasant movement of the early 1930s, and also by members of local workers' and fishermen's unions and the local people's committee. The leader of the PC urged the elimination of all Japanese and Japanese influence through "lightning-flash action." The leading Soviet officer stated that he wished to follow the Korean people's views but that he had no instructions on what to do about the Japanese, or Japanese property. He said he would inform his superiors that it was "the people's will" that they remove Japanese influence immediately; he also left administration in the hands of the people's committee.[9] A report of August 30 said that upon entering Hamhŭng on August 24, however, the commanding Soviet officer and the provincial governor of South Hamgyŏng Province issued a statement saying the following:

> Until the political course for Korea is determined, the Soviet Army will administer [the province] through the existing government and military apparatus [Japanese]. . . . Those who harm or destroy public peace will be severely punished or given the death sentence.[10]

A later report said that as soon as the Soviets found that a Hamhŭng PC existed, however, they kicked the Japanese out and turned over administration to the committee.[11] On August 25 the Soviet command in P'yŏngyang authorized the local branch of the CPKI to take over the administrative powers of the Government-General and immediately nationalized major Japanese property.[12]

In late September, a leftist newspaper in the south printed a proclamation from the political office of the Red Army entitled, "General Policy for the Establishment of People's Power":

> What we must do is establish a completely independent country embracing all strata of the population who are not [part of] the Japanese enemy. The Soviets will to the end advocate among the four powers the setting up of workers' and peasants' sovereignty.
>
> The land question: since this has become the most important question, the land must be newly apportioned among the population. With respect to indigenous [Korean] landlords, all land above that tilled by the landlord himself should be confiscated and the government should of course redistribute it to the peasants. Whether or not this is actually achieved will depend entirely on how great our efforts are.
>
> With respect to factories now belonging to the Japanese, we will completely expel Japanese elements and the factories will be managed by the workers and technicians. If the Japanese are needed in technical areas, we will put them to work temporarily but we must train Korean technicians very rapidly. Medium and small enterprises owned by Koreans will be allowed to operate freely under the superintendence of the people's committees. There must be a great expansion in facilities producing everyday necessities; this must be done urgently.
>
> There will be no agricultural products sent to Japan this year, and harvests belonging to Japanese will all be requisitioned by the people's committees. In addition there will be provision for those

things needed for emergency use and that needed for the Soviet Army. . . . With respect to peasants' taxes, this is something to be resolved by the executive department of the tax committee, but it will certainly be far less than in the past.

Evil, pro-Japanese elements will be thoroughly swept out; a strict purge of all impure elements within and without [the pro-Japanese] camp is needed.[13]

The remainder of the statement urged the opening of cultural, health, and educational facilities to peasants and workers, dealt with currency problems, and placed the northern banks under the control of the people's committees. It also urged that in dealing with the Japanese a distinction be made between propertyless Japanese, who were to be treated decently, and the rest of the colonizers.

The above statement appeared after the Soviets had recognized the northern people's committee structure and reflects demands made by the committees throughout the peninsula. It seems clear that the Soviets planned to establish some sort of socialist regime in the north. They brought with them into Korea an undetermined number of Koreans who had lived out part or all of the colonial period in the Soviet Union, some of whom were Soviet Communist Party members.[14] The spread of the people's committees, however, provided a convenient and popular local basis for the establishment of the northern regime, and one that had the additional advantage of being at least as widespread in the south. Therefore, although the Soviets clearly followed contradictory policies in various cities and regions of north Korea, by mid-September they were working through provincial PCs and had begun the restructuring of colonial legacies. Such policies were immensely popular among the mass of Koreans in the north.

There is another aspect to the initial Soviet occupation, however, which severely tarnishes their record. The Soviet troops who entered Korea committed depredations against the Japanese and Koreans, including rape and looting, on what appears to have been a wide scale and which went quite beyond taking revenge against the enemy and its Korean allies. As a result of the terrible destruction wrought upon an entire generation of Soviet youth by the European war, the Soviets had been forced to recruit soldiers, young peasant men and women, just for the campaigns against the Japanese. The new recruits came into Korea lacking even uniforms and shoes in some cases and lived off the Korean land with no provisions for themselves, took what they needed without paying for it, and, like Soviet soldiers in Eastern Europe and especially Germany, were allowed to accumulate personal booty and ship it home.[15] According to Han Kŭn-jo, who served as mayor of P'yŏngyang under the Soviet occupation for the first few weeks, the Russians requisitioned two-thirds of the food supply set aside by the people's committees. Han also stated, however, that many Koreans participated in the looting of Japanese colonials and Korean "capitalists," suggesting a class rather than racial basis to the depredations.[16] The accounts of rape and pillage were inflated in the south by fleeing Japanese, who were in no position to cast blame, since they had done their best to destroy colonial industries, mines, and the economy itself (through printing reams of money to try to buy their way out of the north). But there remains no doubt that the behavior of Soviet occupation forces was largely uncontrolled in the early weeks and cast a pall upon the Soviet effort in the north.

By January 1946 the Soviets had brought in military police who placed strict controls on their troops; MPs were to shoot on sight any Russian caught raping a Korean.[17] A German Benedictine priest, Father Hopple, who lived in north Korea from 1945 to 1949, related that early Soviet occupation contingents seemed as miserable as refugees from China, poorly clothed and hungry. They "gave themselves to rapine and pillage on an extensive scale." The situation quieted down after the MPs came in, however, and from then on "the deportment of Soviet officials . . . was always correct," and the troops were under strict control. The Soviets continued to requisition supplies, but they issued redeemable receipts for everything.[18]

It is also widely believed that the Soviets carted off many north Korean factories, as they did with colonially developed industry in Manchuria. But in fact, there is no evidence that they made more than a few removals. The Pauley Commission, which documented Soviet removal of industry in Manchuria, concluded that no substantial removals occurred in Korea.[19] American intelligence thought for some months that the Soviets were making significant removals but decided in June 1946 that earlier reports may have been based on destruction done by the retreating Japanese and noted that Soviet technicians were in fact doing their best to restore damaged industries and that production by mid-1946 was above 1945 levels. A Korean electrical engineer who came south in September 1946 reported that the Soviets were making "conscious efforts" to leave north Korean industry intact.[20] It may be that the disfavor the Soviets earned in Korea through the behavior of individuals in the troops led them to pursue different policies on industrial removals in Manchuria and Korea; or perhaps the difference may be accounted for simply by Soviet plans to stay longer in Korea than in Manchuria.

It has become commonplace in Western writings on the period to emphasize Soviet depredations in the north (without noting the relative absence of such behavior by early 1946),[21] and to speak freely of Russian racism toward Koreans. It might be instructive to put this experience in perspective, however, by asking, were the Americans any better?

American soldiers too committed various depredations in the south, although there is nothing to suggest that this occurred on the scale of Soviet behavior in the north. There were continual reports of rapes throughout the three-year American Occupation, however, and in 1945 Keijo Imperial University (soon renamed Seoul National University) had some of its buildings requisitioned as a billet for American soldiers, resulting in much looting and destruction of libraries and laboratories.[22] There is also considerable evidence to suggest that Americans confiscated money from refugees coming across the thirty-eighth parallel, enough evidence to suggest that it was a common practice.[23] It cannot be said that such activity was a common feature of the American Occupation. Racism against Koreans, however, was ubiquitous.

As we have seen in earlier chapters, racism against Koreans was exhibited by the highest levels of the American command. There is also a most useful study of American-Korean and Russian-Korean relations by an anthropologist, David Olmsted, who was stationed along the thirty-eighth parallel for six months in early 1946.[24] According to his observations of the many Americans rotated periodically into duty at his observation post, only a handful ever took "the slightest interest in the affairs of Koreans." Those Americans who had any interest in Koreans he put at about 5 percent of the total; he estimated the Russian figure, from his many discussions with Russian officers and soldiers at a corresponding observation post in the north, at 15 percent. The Russians also had Korean officers who on occasion commanded Russian soldiers—something not lost on the local population; the Americans, in contrast, had two Korean houseboys, whose "status as servants was never in doubt." Olmsted saw no evidence that the Russians employed Koreans as servants. Racism against Koreans was widespread among Americans; for example, the number of Americans who did not use the pejorative "gook" to refer to Koreans could be "counted on the fingers of both hands." In his many conversations with Russians, Olmsted found that "at no time did any attitudes of this sort come to light," although the Russians occasionally disparaged Korean food and religion. The result was that, in his observation at least, Russian-Korean relations generally seemed to be cordial, whereas Korean villagers were "sullen, surly and aloof" toward Americans.

Politics From the Bottom Up

The spread of local participatory politics that we have examined in the south had its analogue across the thirty-eighth parallel. Virtually every southern leftist political grouping or organization had its expression in the north as well in the months after liberation. The difference was that the Soviet occupation provided a womb in which this politics could be nurtured and it offered no support to rightist politics; thus it stimulated a rapid mobilization across north Korea. The Soviets, like the Americans, had physical limits, which made it impossible to occupy or administer the north below the highest levels in the period from August to December 1945. Thus people's committees, peasant unions, labor unions, and other organizations were formed everywhere, and their political complexion, although oriented to the Left, varied greatly. In general, each northern province had its own people's committee structure, with its own policies and composition; thus a pronounced regionalism developed, which persisted through the first year after liberation. Uniformity began to be imposed from the top in 1946, but this process did not have its full effect until 1947 at the earliest.

Korean politics began in the north much as it had in the south, with the organization at liberation of provincial branches of the Committee for the Preparation of Korean Independence (CPKI). In P'yŏngyang, Cho Man-sik led the South P'yŏng'an Province CPKI branch. Cho was a moderate nationalist, a Christian educator who had graduated from the law course of Meiji University in 1913, had taught at a number of Korean colleges and universities, and had participated in the 1919 March First Movement. Thereafter, he was active in gradualist nationalist activities with, among others, Kim Sŏng-su and Song Chin-u.[25] We can delineate his politics precisely, in fact, by saying that he was akin to Song Chin-u and Kim Sŏng-su, except that he had managed to keep his nationalist credentials intact during the latter stages of Japanese rule. He was not a populist like Yŏ Un-hyŏng, but like Yŏ, he was willing to work with leftists and communists in the interests of Korean unification. His vice-chairman was O Yun-sŏn, an obscure figure who apparently was also a Christian moderate nationalist. In South Hamgyŏng Province the CPKI branch was formed by what official South Korean sources term "political prisoners," that is, people who emerged from Japanese jails on August 16. Among its leaders were Song Sŏng-gwan, Kim Chae-gyu, and Pak Kyŏng-dŏk;[26] Kim had led a well-known peasant union incident on the early 1930s in Tanch'ŏn. Other provincial CPKI branches were also established in the days from August 15 to 17.

On August 22 the Soviets arranged a merger of the South P'yŏng'an CPKI and the P'yŏngyang city CPKI branch, taking sixteen members from each.[27] South Korean sources claim that sixteen communists were simply added to Cho's CPKI to form the new body.[28] Although this cannot be verified, it is certainly true that the addition of members of the P'yŏngyang CPKI had a radicalizing effect on Cho's group, since most of them were released Japanese prisoners. The new organization was called the People's Political Committee (*inmin chŏngch'i wiwŏnhoe*), a designation not used in the south. Cho Man-sik remained chairman, with O Yun-sŏn and Hyŏn Chun-hyŏk as vice-chairmen.[29] Hyŏn had been a student leader of leftist demonstrations against the Japanese in the early 1930s, emerging from jail in 1945. He helped organize the communist party in the north in the month after liberation; but as Scalapino and Lee rightly note, his politics were simply leftist, comparable to someone like Hŏ Hŏn or Yi Kang-guk in the south.[30] The interior department of this committee was headed by Yi Chu-yŏn, a communist, while Kim Ik-jin, a nationalist, was responsible for peace preservation and Han Chae-dŏk, a lawyer and also a nationalist, became mayor of P'yŏngyang.[31] At the end of August, people's committees emerged throughout north Korea, often with a similar balance between nationalists and communists. It appears that the Soviets, or leftist Koreans, stepped in to assure at least parity for the Left, thus rearranging the CPKI branches at the top.

It is unlikely that the Soviets were able to dominate or manipulate the provincial committees. American intelligence stated in December 1945 that the Soviets did not set up a military government, having no civil affairs personnel with them; nor did they establish a central government, but instead "recognized People's Committees as governing bodies from the provincial level to the ward or township level." The Soviets were "said to have been very careful in pointing out that Northern Korea was not Russian territory," and one American reported a conversation with a Soviet official who remarked, "We like the English and the Americans, they look like us. . . . We don't like the Koreans. We will stay until a suitable stable government has been set up, then we will go." American intelligence suggested that no central government emerged because the Soviets thought the north would soon return to the control of a central administration in Seoul.[32]

It is unlikely that communists and leftists just released from jail would tolerate nationalist dominance in the committees, especially when the region was under Red Army occupation. What remains surprising is that throughout 1945 these committees continued to recognize Seoul as the political center and to retain the moderate nationalists. Cho Man-sik's committee immediately recognized the Korean People's Republic and placed itself under its authority after September 6.

When the KPR was not recognized in Seoul, the northerners established a Five Provinces Administrative Bureau (*Puk Chosŏn o-do haengjŏngguk*); but it did not claim to be a central body. It was in fact based mostly on the South P'yŏng'an Province People's Political Committee, with the same chairman, Cho Man-sik, and vice chairmen.[33] This bureau remained the only central grouping in the north above the people's committee structure until February 1946, but it did not constitute a real political center at all. Under its aegis, real power was exercised on a regional basis by the provincial people's committees. An informant from north Korea told American intelligence in January 1946 that the center was "weak and poorly organized" and that it had to depend almost entirely on the provincial people's committees for administration.[34] This came to an end only in the aftermath of the trusteeship imbroglio and the apparent inability or unwillingness in the south to implement the Moscow decisions. There is simply no evidence to support the assertion that the Soviets or their allies planned for a separate regime in the north before February 1946.

For most north Korean citizens, their concerns in the first months after liberation were with life and politics at the local levels. Below the provincial people's committees, they were largely free to improvise county, township, and village politics along the people's committee, peasant union, and worker's union lines. Although information is severely limited on this aspect of northern politics, subsequent policies adopted at the center to remedy "defects" in the localities pointed to the same spontaneous, amorphous, and popular qualities that we noted in the provinces of the south. In this period, Koreans took their destinies in their own hands and fashioned a politics that reflected the complex of social forces in each locality. As we saw earlier in the town of Yangyang, Red Peasant Union members from the 1930s emerged from the woodwork to greet incoming Soviet forces, having already established a local people's committee. A proclamation from a PC in South Hamgyŏng Province perhaps catches the flavor of local politics: it gave all men and women over 18 the right to vote and to be elected to office; it maintained, "the sovereignty of the Korean nation resides in all the people themselves"; it said that all factories, mines, farms, transportation facilities, utilities, and so on, belonging to the Japanese or to pro-Japanese Koreans would be confiscated and appropriated by the state and would be managed by worker committees. In general, the proclamation urged Koreans to take Korean affairs into their own hands and exert all efforts on behalf of themselves instead of a colonial master.[35]

From October 8 to 10, 1945, representatives of local PCs met in P'yŏngyang to attempt to work out a uniform structure for all the committees. They determined the following: there were to be nineteen members at the provincial PC level, fifteen to seventeen on city committees, thirteen to fifteen on county (*kun*) committees, and seven to nine at the neighborhood (*tong*) level. In the villages, the committee head was to be elected by the whole population, not chosen by village elders (as had been the case among many PCs). Village electors would in turn choose district committees, and electors from the districts would choose county committees, who would in turn elect provincial committees. City PCs were to be elected by the whole urban population.[36] Like most bureaucratic organizations, the committees quickly proliferated offices and members such that by April 1946 the typical structure looked like this:[37]

Provincial PCs	45-47 members, 315-423 staff
County PCs	15-17 members, 25 staff
City PCs	25-27 members
Township PCs	7-9 members, 5 staff sections

The degree to which policy percolated up from the localities rather than trickling down from the top during the six months after liberation is revealed in the pages of various local newspapers. The People's Daily (*Inmin ilbo*), published in South Hamgyŏng Province during the period, proclaimed in its September 6, 1945 issue, "sovereignty is in the hands of the people." Issues on each of the next four days proclaimed new educational programs, plans for reorganizing the province government administration, and warnings to the population to continue paying taxes as usual and to preserve Japanese property in the interests of Koreans. The same process, with differences in emphasis, was detailed in the daily issues of a myriad of northern newspapers: *Chayu Hwanghae* (Free Hwangwae), *P'yŏngbuk sinbo* (North P'yŏng'an News), *P'yŏngyang minbo* (P'yŏngyang People's Report), and others. All carried extensive articles on new policies in education, health, justice, forestry, and so on.[38] Provincial peace maintenance groups (*poandae*) were given "ten commandments" in their dealings with Koreans, guidelines analogous to the famous "eight points for attention" of the Chinese People's Liberation Army: be kind with the people, lead-a disciplined social life, pay for what you need.[39] American intelligence reported that the northern PCs were the effective local governing agencies and the *poandae* the only police; the *poandae* aided PCs in collecting rice and taxes and in examining people in transit from one place to another. The unanimous view of Koreans coming south who talked to intelligence officials was that "the Russians themselves do not mix in local administration."[40]

In mid-October rents paid by tenants were readjusted according to the KPR's "3/7" system, whereby the landlord received 30 percent and the tenant 70 percent of the crop in kind.[41] It is likely that the wealthier landlords had earlier been subject to attack and ouster; certainly collaborators were weeded out quickly, often violently, and there is some indication that people's courts were used to oust colonial county magistrates and township chiefs.[42] The presence of Korean landlords, colonial officials, and police was, of course, much thinner in the north than in the south where the overgrown bureaucratic center existed, and the higher-ranking colonial accomplices fled south quickly at liberation. This may explain in part why the postliberation revolution in the north could be accomplished quickly and with little apparent bloodshed.

The scholarly literature on North Korea has paid little attention to this early period after liberation in the north and has explicitly or implicitly denied that any revolution took place or that, if it did, it was imposed from without. Chong-sik Lee argued that "an alien system" was imposed upon the north by the Soviets, "transplanted outright and made to grow," and that the numbers of actual communists in the north were miniscule, and their overall influence "minute."[43] Such a judgment is impossible to reach unless one concentrates upon only the handful of leaders at the top and declares them, for one reason or another, to be alien to Korea, a matter we will get to shortly. Taking the society as a whole, however, it is undeniable that the people's committees provided a broad forum for participation at all levels and were populated by leaders who derived a raw legitimacy from their resistance to the Japanese. A sampling of the PC leadership demonstrates this. We have seen that in the P'yŏngyang PC, at the center, resisters who had fought the Japanese in the early 1930s and who had spent an average of perhaps a decade in colonial prisons emerged into the light on August 15 and immediately assumed positions of authority. Some of them, like Pak Chŏng-ae (a woman), remained in the highest ranks of the northern leadership thereafter. The head of the Hwanghae Province PC, Kim Tok-yŏng, had also done time for political crimes at several points before 1945. The head of the education department of the Kangwŏn Province PC, Yi Ki-yŏng, was a famous writer of proletarian literature whom the Japanese had arrested and whose works had been banned. The early chief of the Hongwŏn PC, later to become chief of the industrial department of the South Hamgyŏng PC, was Yi Pong-su, a native of Hongwŏn who had majored in economics at Meiji University, was active in the March First Movement, edited the financial page of the *Tonga ilbo*, and had done "numerous stretches in prison."[44]

It is fair to say that, from the standpoint of the majority of Koreans, the Soviets followed policies (or allowed Koreans to do so) that were a stark contrast to those pursued by the Americans in the early months of Occupation. Whether by design or simply because the people's committees were convenient, the Soviets gave Koreans their head and retreated to the background, to what George McCune aptly called a position of "inauspicious but firm authority."[45] It goes without saying that Soviets were concerned with the top command in P'yŏngyang, as we will see. But elsewhere, they left real authority in the hands of Koreans. American intelligence noted these policies in December 1945, thought they indicated "a limited occupation," and reported the "lack of any move to establish a central government."[46]

Thus in north Korea in the months after liberation, an entirely new elite emerged from the colonial abyss, which was drawn, as an official American source grudgingly acknowledged, "almost exclusively from the ranks of workers and peasants."[47] The colonial hierarchy was turned on its head; in American democratic argot, the bastards were thrown out. Of course, from the standpoint of Americans in the south, new bastards were thrown in.

Politics From the Top Down

We have seen in earlier chapters that the people's committee structure tended to take on a cellular organization in which lines of authority and disciplined hierarchy remained undeveloped. Each committee at each level was intent on running its own affairs and had little concern for those committees above or below. This is precisely what is to be expected in a fundamentally peasant society. Six months after liberation, however, northern authorities began to reverse the flow of politics; the spontaneous organization moving up from the bottom was met by an articulated and disciplined politics coming down from the top. The essence of this assertion of central authority was to give vertical coherence to the horizontal and cellular structure of the people's committees, to make them responsive to the desires of the center as well as to the pressures of the localities.

What we may inelegantly call "top-downism" has been a characteristic of Soviet socialism from the beginning, more especially a characteristic of Stalinism. The Soviet revolution proceeded from the center or the cities outward; in China it was the reverse. Therefore the Soviet revolution did not have the rich development of peasant politics that we find in China. Instead, the peasantry was at best a vehicle and at worst a victim of the Soviet revolution. As Teodor Shanin notes, Stalin himself saw agrarian revolution as a species of bourgeois revisionism: "The peasantry had to have achieved its aims under the leadership of the urban proletariat; the land had been *given* by the

Soviet state and not taken by spontaneous action" (emphasis in in original).[48]

The north Korean leadership had experience with both the Chinese and Soviet revolutions and confronted a situation in liberated Korea in which all the inchoate spontaneity of peasants in revolt seemed to well up before their very eyes. This leadership, and its policies, therefore came to embody a combination of central and peripheral impulses and an ideology that mixed Stalinist top-downism with Maoist mass line politics. Quintessential Stalinist slogans such as "cadres decide everything" were blazoned alongside quintessential Maoist slogans such as "from the masses, to the masses."[49] Mao himself once remarked on this matter:

> [Stalin] did not undertake the class struggle from the bottom to the top, but introduced peaceful land reform in Eastern Europe and North Korea, without struggling against the landowners and rightists, only proceeding from the top to the bottom and struggling against the capitalists. We proceed from the top to the bottom, but we also add the class struggle from the bottom to the top.[50]

Mao was only half right, Stalin did not dominate events in north Korea as he did in Eastern Europe, thus there emerged a unique brand of socialism that melded Stalinism and Maoism, or, more accurately, molded a Korean socialism in the space between. A key agency of this melding was Kim Il Sung, who had himself been attached to both Soviet and Chinese communism before 1945.

The Rise to Power of Kim Il Sung

It is most remarkable that the two Korean leaders who emerged on top during the liberation period, Syngman Rhee and Kim Il Sung, should have returned from exile to their native land in such similar fashions. At the end of September 1945, neither had appeared in Korea, although both were known through legend surrounding their names. (Whether either was known to the average Korean, by name or legend, is quite another matter.) In mid-October both men were given fulsome introductions to their compatriots by the respective foreign commands, and by February 1946 Kim, as chairman of the North Korean Interim People's Committee, and Rhee, as head of the Representative Democratic Council, seemed to be the designated leaders of the northern and southern halves of Korea.

Kim, like Rhee, became the focus of further mythmaking and hagiography by his supporters, a phenomenon that continues today as a major industry in North Korea and that has spawned its opposite in

South Korea, where the truth about Kim's past is obscured behind a smokescreen of opposing propaganda. It remains difficult to separate fact from fancy in the career of this controversial individual. It might be useful in describing Kim to begin with the mythology. In the north, especially in recent years, Kim and his guerrilla allies are given credit for the liberation of Korea in 1945, with little or no reference to Soviet aid. Furthermore, Kim is said to have become the leader of the Korean communist movement by the mid-1930s if not earlier, introducing ideology and organization into the ranks of an immature, factious, and scattered group of intellectual and petty-bourgeois types claiming to be communist leaders. In the late 1930s Kim reportedly dealt telling blow after blow to Japanese imperialism, until approximately the time of Pearl Harbor. For the next three years until the liberation, the northern literature betrays a deafening silence about Kim's whereabouts.[51]

In the south, and to some extent in scholarly American literature, the line on Kim's past runs from denying outright that he played any role in the anti-Japanese struggle, to charging that he impersonated the real, legendary Kim Il Sung, to labeling him variously a Soviet-Korean, Chinese-Korean, or an alien to Korean communism. The dominant interpretation, however, identifies Kim as a distinctly minor anti-Japanese guerrilla with a tiny band of followers who struck a blow here and there against the Japanese, but whose eminence is to be explained almost entirely by his being hand-picked by the Soviets as their man in the north. How Kim came to the attention of the Soviets is a question never explained well or documented these accounts, but they seem to suggest it had to do with his rumored service in the Soviet Army, including action at Stalingrad, or training by the Soviets in the vicinity of Khabarovsk during his dark period, 1942-1945.

Behind these assertions lie a raft of unstated assumptions, however. Some are based on the assumption that there was a real, legendary Kim Il Sung who would have made a good leader of liberated Korea.[52] Others assume that a Korean who fought on the Soviet side in World War II is distinctly suspect (whereas one who fought on the Japanese side is not? Remember that the vast majority of Koreans who did take up arms in the war fought either for Japan or the Soviets). Still others maintain that there was a coherent communist movement to which one could be alien—and that a leader of the mainstream would have been more acceptable to conservative Koreans. Finally, some argue that Kim's effort against the Japanese, although obviously small in absolute numbers of participants, was also *relatively* small in relation to what other Koreans were doing against the Japanese.

But all of these assumptions are fallacious. As stated in chapter one, there was no legendary Kim Il Sung; and if there had been, he would have been no more willing to work with collaborators than other anti-Japanese fighters. There is no proof that Kim fought in the Soviet Army, either; and if he had, and had been decorated at Stalingrad as the story goes, this would have enhanced rather than detracted from his reputation in the eyes of most Koreans in 1945. Moreover, after 1931 there was no coherent central leadership to the communist movement. Had Pak Hŏn-yŏng, the leader with a rough sort of seniority by virtue of his scattered activities going back to the early 1920s, emerged on top in the north at Kim's expense, we can imagine that the literature would have much to say. Finally, and most embarrassing to the South, there was no other nationalist or communist force fighting against Japan after 1931 that can be proved to have been larger or more active than Kim's. The Kwangbok Army in Chungking numbered about 600 in 1945, but was made up mostly of students, intellectuals, and politicians with only rudimentary military training or potency. Its leadership existed at the sufferance of the Nationalist regime and did not really begin to think about contributing to the war effort in the China theatre until early 1944. Koreans allied with Yenan did more fighting against the Japanese, but as a fighting force they numbered perhaps no more than 300 and were apparently not well integrated into the Eighth Route Army or the base area leadership structure.[53] Thousands of other Koreans, leaders and followers, struggled valiantly against the Japanese only to find their place in history go unnoted in contemporary North Korea. But the fact remains that Kim Il Sung's record was formidable compared to that of other Koreans in 1945; and he had the Japanese police records to document it. In addition, he had an armed contingent of several hundred guerrillas under his control. All of the other Korean exile leaders, with the exception of Mu Chŏng and the Yenan-aligned leadership, returned to Korea either individually or with at most a coterie of close supporters, few of them armed. This was Kim Il Sung's most important advantage.

The literature on Kim thus remains largely subjective, quite reminiscent of similar literature about, say, Castro, Tito, or Ho Chi Minh.[54] Perhaps we can now move from mythology to what is known about Kim in the period of liberation. In recent years, the North Koreans and their advocates have claimed that Kim Il Sung and his forces engaged the Japanese at Ch'ŏngjin in early August in conjunction with the Soviet attack against the Japanese Kwantung Army.[55] There were, according to some sources, Koreans who participated in amphibious landings in northern Korea. Such a claim for Kim Il Sung was never made in the north before the 1960s, however. In an official chronology of the period after liberation, published in 1948, Kim's name does not appear until early October 1945, and an official history in 1961 mentions no military activity by him in connection with the Soviet rout of the Japanese in August.[56]

In materials published in the months just after liberation, there is, to my knowledge, but one statement that locates Kim within the borders of Korea in August, and it gives no indication of his whereabouts or activities. A book published in mid-1946 stated that Kim first appeared in north Korea on August 22.[57] Another source, published in early 1946, said that Kim appeared in Haeju, just north of the thirty-eighth parallel, on September 16; apparently he hoped to contact political leaders in the south and had dispatched lieutenants to Seoul to survey the situation.[58] But no real verification of his whereabouts during the period from August to September exists; it is only in early October that newspapers and other sources begin to speak of his presence in P'yŏngyang.

The best evidence that I have been able to locate suggests that Kim got no further than Khabarovsk, just across the Manchurian border, during the period from 1941 to 1945; did not fight at Stalingrad; was not an officer in the Soviet Army; but did have contact with and training by the Soviets. American intelligence developed information in 1947 that Kim and his guerrilla allies retreated to the Khabarovosk area after the intense Japanese counterinsurgency campaigns in Manchuria discussed in chapter one and stayed there until the liberation:[59]

> Faced with the threat of extinction [by the Japanese], a few hundred under the leadership of KIM, Il Sung, long time Communist, made their way North and into the Soviet Maritime Province. After verifying their political and military backgrounds, the Soviets established these people in a training camp at YASHKI Station, in the general area of KHABAROVSK. Here and later at BARABASH, near the junction of the USSR-Korean and Manchurian frontiers these Koreans were trained in espionage, radio communications, sabotage and general military subjects. From 1941-45 these people were utilized by the Soviets as agents in MANCHURIA. In the spring of 1945, in addition to normal political training, they were briefed on KOREA and Korean politics.

Yashki cannot be identified on Soviet maps, but Barabash is a village on the Sino-Russian border about fifty kilometers north of the Russo-Korean border. This important information squares with a Japanese police report cited in chapter one that places Kim in the same region in 1944 and states that he hoped to aid the American Air Force in attacks then beginning in Manchuria.

This sort of Soviet involvement in Kim's exploits seems to be little different than American OSS training of Ho Chi Minh's guerrillas in the same period in Vietnam. Kim's Soviet period was also considerably shorter than the period he spent fighting with Chinese Communist guerrillas in the 1930s, during which he reputedly joined the Chinese Communist Party. This report on Kim argues that he landed at Wŏnsan on September 25, and there is other evidence to support this.[60]

Kim's public emergence in the north came only after the initial period of contradictory and unformed policy and may have been as much his doing as that of the Soviets. He was in a position to confront and face down Korean opponents, on the following bases: (1) his anti-Japanese record was known to all the parties concerned with Korean liberation, as we saw in chapter one; (2) he had never been captured by the Japanese police and subjected to their methods of interrogation, and therefore, unlike most other Korean communists, there was no possibility of his apostasy or of his having turned in or named his comrades; (3) he had an armed force under his own control; and (4) more than most Korean leaders, he was vigorous and even charismatic, and melded communism and nationalism in an appealing combination.

On October 14 some 70,000 people turned out for a ceremony to welcome "General Kim Il Sung" back to Korea.[61] Cho Man-sik introduced him. The top brass of the Soviet command lined up behind him as he spoke on the podium, an endorsement identical to General Hodge's welcome for Syngman Rhee on October 20. Kim was 33 years old at the time and, judging from the photographs, looked even younger; his age quickly became an issue in both north and south. Some sources embellish this issue considerably,[62] but it was obviously difficult to argue that this Kim Il Sung was the peer of the older generation of Koreans who had resisted the Japanese throughout the colonial period. In fact, he represented a new generation, one that had contempt for the failures of their fathers; so generational splits were added to the many others separating north and south.

The first biography of Kim to appear was highly laudatory, speaking of his exploits and those of his family members and of his myriad outstanding qualities; here we mark the opening shot in the personality cult that continues to play upon North Korea. Yet even this article noted Kim's youth and argued weakly that "his greatest accomplishments are yet to come."[63] In south Korea the organ of the Chang'an KCP faction ran an article on Kim on October 27, referring to him as "our great revolutionary and national leader," likening him to Tito, but also stating that "no one in our country has seen him" and that his rise had been "comet-like."[64] The rightist *Independence News* listed Kim as one of the four leaders of the Korean Provisional Government, while the *Liberation Daily*, under Pak Hŏn-yŏng's control, wrote a welcome to Kim Il Sung, "young hero of Korea."[65] By mid-November south Korean leftist groups were regularly including Kim in the listings of leaders to whom they wished long life.[66]

American intelligence sources in the south seemed unaware of Kim until late December 1945. At the beginning of November, the Americans thought Mu Chŏng was heading the northern branch of the KCP and was thus the Russian designate for leader.[67] But a report in early January, carrying information as of late December, said the following about Kim: "He is conceded by all circles to have vast popular prestige, being credited with having killed a thoroughly satisfactory number of Japanese troops." The report went on to say that Kim was not previously regarded as a communist and suggested that the Soviets were putting him out front "to gain a wider popular following at the cost of some party orthodoxy."[68] A declassified American study, based on intelligence reports, supported this view. It said that after his introduction in the north "Kim became immediately popular" and attributed this to his sponsorship by Cho Man-sik:

> [Kim] cultivated Cho Man-sik, an able Korean Nationalist and the most respected non-Communist leader in North Korea, telling him privately that he, Kim, was a fervent nationalist and did not believe in some of the Communist plans for Korea. Taken in, Cho introduced Kim at a liberation celebration in Pyongyang on 3 October, 1945 . . . describing him as an ardent Korean patriot and nationalist. Cho's reputation assured Kim of an enthusiastic reception from the general public, which did not stop to think that the real Kim Il Sung must have been a much older man.[69]

The general thrust of this statement is probably correct, in that Kim Il Sung was not only more nationalistic than many other communist leaders but was perceived to be so by noncommunist Korean leaders. As we have seen, Yŏ Un-hyŏng held this opinion of Kim; and Kim Kyu-sik later said of him, "There is perhaps a ray of hope in Kim Il Sung . . . he was a good guerrilla leader and had some popularity among young men."[70]

Kim achieved no formal leadership role in the north in the weeks after his introduction. But on December 17 he replaced Kim Yong-bŏm as head of the northern branch of the KCP, which still recognized Pak Hŏn-yŏng and Seoul as the party's leader and center. Kim's own armed guards reportedly surrounded the meeting, an indication of the value of this force to his fortunes.[71] Kim still had no position in the Five Provinces Administrative Bureau, however, and Cho Man-sik remained the top leader in the north, assisted by a mix of northern nationalists and communists. This situation held true until the trusteeship crisis at the beginning of January.[72] Until this time, neither the Russians nor the top Korean leaders had made moves toward the establishment of a separate northern administration. The bureaucracy was functioning on a provincial pattern, the top level being the provincial capital people's committee administration; this was quite in keeping with the temporary status of the division of the peninsula.[73] The police force consisted of those peace preservation units that had emerged with the people's committees. There were no reported or recorded moves toward the creation of a separate northern military apparatus. Political bodies, whether the committees or various parties, continued to recognize Seoul as the center of the country.

In the aftermath of the trusteeship crisis, however, this decentralized pattern ended. Beginning in February, the rudiments of a separate northern administration emerged, and soon thereafter, fundamental societal reforms were pushed through and northern military bodies appeared. The nationalist-communist coalition also broke down over trusteeship, as the moderate nationalists steadily lost power. It remains true, however, that the early and preemptive action toward the creation of separate regimes occurred in the south, during the last three months of 1945. It was only in the aftermath of the results of southern policies that the north began to follow suit. We could argue, of course, that a separate northern regime was inevitable. But the sequence remains undeniable: the south moved first.

Centralization In the North

The opening shot in the subsequent centralization process in the north occurred on December 17, 1945, when Kim Il Sung became head of the northern branch of the Korean Communist Party, in the circumstances described above. Although this event does not mark a decision to establish a separate northern administration but rather the emergence of a strong party center, still the northern KCP (hereafter designated NKCP) was the basic organ of the subsequent centralization.

Kim's speech on December 17 detailed both the agenda for creating a center and the numerous failings in communist organization in the preceding five months.[74] In so doing, it made obvious the general lack of a cohesive central organization in the north. Kim only claimed 4,350 members for the NKCP, a figure that would increase one hundredfold within a year; and even these members had not yet received "uniform membership cards." Furthermore, he said:

> Party organizations have yet to be created in a large number of factories, enterprises, and farm villages. . . . Procedures for admission to the Party have not been established. . . . A certain Kim, secretary of the Yangdok County Party Committee, for instance, was a police sergeant at the police station in that county during Japanese imperialist rule. . . . The ranks of our Communist Party are infested with pro-Japanese elements.

He went on to note that there were too many peasants and intellectuals in the party and that regular reporting procedures had not been established; he then quoted Lenin as follows:

> The Communist Party will be able to perform its duty only if it is organized in the most centralized manner, if iron discipline bordering on military discipline prevails in it, and if its Party centre is a powerful and authoritative organ.

Kim then characteristically mixed his Leninism with a bit of Maoism, urging party members to "go among the masses," "go to the factories and talk to the workers, listen to their demands," adding:

> If we do not continually strengthen our ties with the masses, teach them, and, in addition, learn from them, the Communist Party . . . will not be able to become a truly mass party, competent to lead the entire working people.

The December 17 meeting was important not just to the subsequent emergence of a separate center in the north but to the development of Korean communism as we know it today. Three themes ran through this event and Kim's speech that the North Koreans have yet to depart from: leader, organization, and the mass line. One wonders what the listeners thought of this brash young man, presuming not simply to chair the party but to chart its course and detail so many organizational failures. Ever since in the north, it has been this same leader who plays multiple roles of guidance, exhortation, and criticism, and physically displays his role by appearing all over the country giving "on-the-spot guidance." The ubiquitous Kim has always stressed the importance of both core organization and going to the masses. Unlike the Chinese (or Mao), Kim used phrases like "cadres decide everything," "organization decides everything," phrases associated with Stalinism and with top-down mobilization of the masses.[75] Like Mao, Kim used many mass line phrases ("from the masses, to the masses").

The December 17 meeting also signaled the emergence of a new and separate center for the KCP. Although the northerners continued to pay lip service to the authority of the central organization in Seoul led by Pak Hŏn-yŏng, from this point on, two centers existed, and the northern one was much more powerful.[76] This development caused much controversy among old-line communists throughout Korea, and nationwide leftist organizations such as the *Chŏnp'yŏng* labor union were forced to watch as their southern and northern operations inevitably diverged.

There is much evidence to suggest that Kim's urgings on December 17 hardly remedied the severe organizational defects of the northern party. A secret document signed by Kim Il Sung in March 1946 complained of illiteracy, inefficiency, and a general lack of training at all levels of the party. He was also concerned that members did not make enough use of the party newspaper (*Chongno*) in their work and urged them to organize small study groups everywhere to discuss each issue of the paper. Local reports forwarded to the party center, he said, should "recognize and report as vividly as possible the people's real lives and problems at hand," avoiding exaggeration and false reporting. Party correspondents should "serve the people" and be "progressives," no doubt an indication that many were not.[77] The next month, a central committee directive urged an increase in membership from the working class and the establishment of more party schools and said that in organizational work "each locality must develop a struggle according to the local situation." Another such directive in the same period asked that membership lists be forwarded to the center, gave instructions for cell organization, stressed the importance of establishing relationships with local workers' and peasants' unions, and asked for feedback reports on any anticommunist disturbances among students and teachers.[78]

Thus it seems that the spontaneous origin of the people's committees and worker and peasant unions that we witnessed in the south had its corollary in the north and presented quite a problem even for committed communist organizers. The communists under Kim's direction responded with, first, emphasis on cultivating a core (*haeksim*) of dedicated followers and, second, expansion of the core in ever-widening concentric circles until it had under its domination the amorphous product of liberated Korea's politics.

In February the North Korean Interim People's Committee (NKIPC) emerged in response to two matters: the organizational failures of the Korean People's Republic in Seoul and the consequent necessity to provide leadership for the PCs in the north; and the emergence of separate administration in the south. In retrospect the North Koreans have come to link the development of the NKIPC with the failure, and even treachery, of the KPR leaders themselves, saying that no KPR government could be established "simply by a declaration issued by a handful of people" with "no mass basis whatsoever." They also argue that "a central state organ" was needed "which could lead the local people's committees in a unified way."[79] The justification was put a bit differently at the time:

> [After August 15] the People's Committee of the People's Republic was created to take charge of central political power. However, in Korea south of the 38-degree line, the committee could not sufficiently develop central political power because of special conditions under the military administration of the U.S. Army. Therefore, it is a fact that organic connections between political powers in south and north Korea could not be maintained.[80]

The interim committee was deemed necessary because there was "no central organization that maintains liaison with the various provinces and controls them, giving rise to various [difficulties]." The NKIPC was also meant to serve as "a model for the future Korean Provisional Government" as provided for under the Moscow accords.[81] Kim Il Sung's report on the formation of the NKIPC said it would function "until such time as the united Korean government is established." It also mentioned the need to counteract "administrative organizations in local districts [which] have become powerful."[82] The NKIPC provided an alternative to the Representative Democratic Council then being organized as the southern model for the upcoming Joint Commission talks, indeed being proposed as the prime body to be consulted. The NKIPC would meet the same need.

It is important to remember the timing of these events. The NKIPC appeared only *after* the first meetings of the American-Soviet Joint Conference in January, and only *after* the manifest undoing of the Moscow agreements in the south. In the north, in contrast to actions taken by the Americans in the south, the Soviets had obtained, by whatever means and at the expense of Cho Man-sik's leadership, Korean agreement to the Moscow decisions. Rallies in the north held to discuss the accords made no mention of the term "trusteeship," using instead a term translated as "guardianship" and arguing that the Soviets had sought to shorten its duration, in contrast to the Americans —which was of course true.[83] Kim Tu-bong also wrote an article explaining the Soviet position on what transpired at Moscow in great detail, basing his account on the Tass January 25 dispatch discussed in chapter seven.[84] After extensive public affairs work among Koreans who were naturally anxious about the Moscow accords, the Soviets and the northern leadership realized that the American Occupation was not following suit; instead it was proffering the Representative

Democratic Council as the southern consultative body, a council made up mostly of antitrusteeship rightists.[85]

Kim Il Sung was named chairman of the NKIPC, his first major administrative post in the north. Still, however, most of his trusted followers from his guerrilla days, such as Kim Ch'aek and Kim Il, were not among the members; the majority came from the old domestic factions and the Yenan group. His role and new-found eminence still met substantial opposition from all these groups.[86]

In the aftermath of the establishment of the NKIPC, American intelligence, which in early December found no moves toward a separate administration in the north, concluded "it is quite apparent that Russia is committed to Sovietization of northern Korea."[87] These events were pursued as much at Korean as at Soviet initiative, however, although they certainly had Soviet support. The Koreans had to find a means of integrating their politics, if they were to create a viable base of power. The ancient regime had foundered, in part through the weakness of its politics; and especially for the younger generation of leaders, the thought that the liberation regime would not defend itself or provide Korea with cohesive organization was an anathema. The people's committee structure, for its part, was unique in its spontaneity and breadth, but it embodied weaknesses in its horizontal and layered structure. In the south, it could not withstand the strong opposition of a centrally and hierarchically organized system. An assertion from the center was essential if the northern regime were to last. Another way of putting this is to say that in north Korea a strong state asserted itself against society, seeking to transform it. The opposite was true in the south, where a strong central bureaucracy was used to preserve and perpetuate social dominance. In both cases, the center put an end to the diverse and creative politics that had emerged with the liberation. The center in the north also put an effective end to conservative and Christian political organization, although it continued to allow religious freedom. The one religio-political organization not routed out was the *Ch'ŏndogyo*, which persisted because of its strong base among peasants.

The general task of establishing a center and rooting it in the countryside was not an easy one. As Glenn Paige has rightly pointed out, the Koreans had not had extensive experience with organizing masses of people in base areas, as had the Chinese. Furthermore, they did not take over and utilize the existing administration, as did the Bolsheviks in Russia. They had to create an administration.[88] Soviet personnel in north Korea could provide guidance, but this had to be mainly a Korean operation. In the words of a newspaper account published at the time of the establishment of the NKIPC, Korea could not establish either a "bourgeois democracy" or a "proletarian democracy" like that in the Soviet Union; this had to be a revolution deriving from Korea's particular characteristics, done by Koreans—a *Chosŏn chach'e hyŏng-myŏng*, in the Korean.[89]

The first task was to rectify the administration of the people's committees. North Korean sources, at the time and since, no matter how much they glorify the role of Kim Il Sung, still recognize the prior existence of the committees, describing their role as "organ[s] of state power established by the people themselves on their own initiative."[90] Thus the north did not have to start entirely from scratch, but could build on the committee structure. According to the special edition of *Chongno* published to explain the NKIPC, a key purpose of the central organ would be to "improve the leadership of democratic rural administrative organs."[91] Two weeks later, *Chongno* reported that staff members of people's committees at the city and county level in South P'yŏngan Province were given ninety hours of training during the period February 11-25: sixty-three hours of study on organization work, twenty-one on public leadership, six on current topics. Thirty more hours were spent in debate, criticism and self-criticism sessions, and discussions of how practically to implement their training. Similar to Chinese communist practice, merit awards were given for "free and unhesitant participation in discussion."[92] Such training sessions ensued for leaders of all PCs at the county and higher levels. These leaders journeyed to provincial capitals and to P'yŏngyang for training, education, and political guidance. This process also provided the center with numerous opportunities to weed out undesirable elements from the committees, another purpose of the rectification.

Similar though less intense rectification occurred among the workers' and peasants' unions. Major industrial enterprises that had been controlled by workers' committees, often employing the previous Korean and Japanese personnel under committee control, were put under central direction. A newspaper in Wŏnsan reported that the chief of the Commerce and Industry Bureau explained that: "The enemy-owned factories have been in the custody of the People's Committee and have been managed by the custodians who were appointed by the Committee." Such factories were now being centralized under "certain powerful managing agencies," however.[93] These measures applied to heavy industrial enterprises such as steel, ship-building, and chemicals and were meant to gain economies of scale and efficiency in capital utilization as well as to assert central control.[94] Members of the workers' and peasants' unions, many of whom were illiterate, entered short-term and night schools that taught them reading, writing, and arithmetic with a heavy admixture of politics.[95] By May 1946 the northern branch of *Chŏnp'yŏng,* claiming at the time a membership of half a million, became independent of the Seoul central organization. The northern branch of *Chŏnnong,* however, had become independent of the south at the end of January, "because of the special situation in north Korea,"[96] a reference perhaps to the upcoming land reform program in the north. The variant timing in the separation of these national organizations may also have had to do with the strength of the working class and the weakness of the peasantry in the north. The north, of course, had a true industrial proletariat, whereas the south did not, being instead the location of the majority of Korea's peasant-tenants. It must have taken longer to impose central controls on worker organizations in the north.

Developments in the police and military represent another important aspect of the centralization of early 1946. Peace-keeping forces emerged in the north with the demise of the Japanese regime on the same regional pattern existing in other organizations. They went under the names *ch'iandae* or *poandae* (as in the south), "Red Guards," "People's Guards," and so on. Koreans who had served in the Japanese police force were allowed to continue only in isolated localities; for the most part they were swept out.

The new local police were mostly poor peasants; according to an official American source, such people "filled up the ranks of the ordinary police."[97] Peace preservation groups also took on the color of local politics. Thus, it appears, People's Guard organizations in North Hamgyŏng were guided by Koreans who had returned from Manchuria, including Ch'oe Yong-gŏn, whereas in South P'yŏng'an Province, the so-called Red Guards were under the direction of Hyŏn Chun-hyŏk, Kim Chang-il, and Chang Si-u, among others.[98]

The Soviets, like the Americans, had to confront the problem of numerous unofficial peace-keeping and quasi-military organizations exercising power in the localities. From the standpoint of the center, the more the situation persisted, the more would centrifugal forces weaken central authority and intensify regional power. Therefore, General Chistiakov reportedly issued an order on October 12 disbanding all armed organizations in north Korea and authorized the provincial people's committees to organize peace protection units under their control.[99] Provincial police bureaus were established in October. Then in November Ch'oe Yong-gŭn called conferences of high *poandae* officials to address various problems in police administration: a lack of uniform procedure from province to province, the continued existence of numerous unsanctioned peace-keeping groups, the need to form a national peace-keeping corps. And in December Ch'oe headed a Department of Public Safety under the aegis of the Five

Provinces Administrative Bureau.[100] Given the later prominence of Ch'oe in the northern leadership, and a report that Kim Il Sung and his allies helped supervise provincial police bureaus beginning in November,[101] it would appear that early involvement in or control of the *poandae* may have been an essential advantage in their subsequent rise to power.

As late as mid-February 1946, however, American intelligence continued to report that decentralization remained such a problem in northern police affairs that *poandae* units continued to fight each other over jurisdiction disputes, and even to jail members of opposing units.[102] But a central Justice Bureau appeared with the NKIPC in February, headed by Ch'oe Yong-dal (leader of the southern CPKI *ch'iandae* in August 1945),[103] and a central school for police officials opened in P'yŏngyang during the same period. Thereafter, American intelligence reports depict a centralization process for the police analogous to that for other agencies in the north. In late March *poandae* leaders from the provinces were being sent to P'yŏngyang for two-month training courses, leading American intelligence to remark that the "formerly loose-knit semi-volunteer organization . . . [was] apparently being tightened and disciplined."[104] Province, city, and county people's committees recommended candidates for schooling, a prerequisite being at least a middle school education. In nine weeks the candidates got 384 hours of lessons in politics, police affairs, and basic reading and writing. A police directive of mid-April, sent to the Chŏrwŏn people's committee, stated that *poandae* staff dispatched for training in P'yŏngyang should be "sound in politics, thoughts, and morals" and should "have in their hearts the best interests . . . of the people." The object of education was first to "purify and strengthen" the *pondae* by building its revolutionary consciousness; the rest of the curriculum was mundane: current affairs, police policy, practical police work, "political common sense," Korean and world history, and study of the "new democracy." Teaching methods stressed student participation; students discussed all problems thoroughly and then led more discussions, "so that they will have complete understanding and full development of ideas."[105] The teaching methods and the reference to the "new democracy" may bespeak the presence of many Koreans returned from Chinese communist base areas in the *poandae* administration, a presence that American intelligence often remarked upon.[106]

By late April the center had succeeded in organizing proper lines of authority within the national *poandae* structure; police power had flowed upward to the center, but some power remained in the regions as well. The total police allocation for the north at this time was

15,600, with provincial allocations varying between 2,300 and 2,600 (except for North P'yŏng'an, which had 3,900, and Kangwŏn, which had 1,560). The center provided the appropriate numbers, but the provincial PCs appointed and allocated police within each province.[107] The result was a popular and locally rooted police force that presented a complete contrast with that of the Japanese era. Even a hostile official American source recognized this achievement: "The new policeman [many were women] gained his experience on the job. He was expected to maintain his roots among the masses, gaining the respect and cooperation of the people."[108] A township police chief later interrogated as a POW during the Korean War was found to be "honest, well-informed . . . proud," with a "most vigorous belief" in "the complete reorientation of the police force from its Japanese traditions." Interrogations by torture and force were legally forbidden; although "used on occasion," such methods were generally replaced by emphasis on extended questioning and reeducation. Thus the northern police "avoided the stigma of association with the symbol of Japanese tyranny—confessions induced by torture."[109]

It was also in early- to mid-1946 that evidence of rudimentary military organization in the north appeared. A precise recapitulation of this development is impossible, in part because of poor and conflicting sources, but also because during the first two years of liberation in the north, peace preservation groups merged police and military functions, making distinctions between the two difficult. In retrospect North Korean and American official sources have located the origins of the northern military in events of November and December 1945—that is, parallel to similar American activities in the south. Baik Bong identifies the first political-military school to appear in the north as the P'yŏngyang Institute, founded in November 1945. Thereafter, the northerners established an officers' training school in July 1946; and in August 1946 training centers for regular national security forces emerged as "the first basic units for a regular army."[110] An unpublished American history of the northern military supports this interpretation in its essentials, stating that a "P'yŏngyang Military Academy" headed by Kim Ch'aek, Kim Il Sung's close ally, opened in October 1945 to train *poandae* officers. It says the first class from this academy graduated in the spring of 1946 and the second in August or September 1946. The first class of graduates apparently took up duties in railroad security forces, and the second went into the ranks of the *poandae*.[111] American intelligence sources in the south thought in early 1946 that this academy opened in late December 1945 and that it offered a four-month course in military and police training to about 500 students. They cited evidence in late April 1946 that *poandae* units growing out of this academy and its trainees had detachments of 100-200 in places like Sŏnch'ŏn and Sinŭiju, a strong presence in South P'yŏng'an Province, but weak development in other provinces, and a total reported size of 10,000. Also finding reports of a small air force and coast guard in the north, American intelligence concluded that "the parallel with South Korea is now complete," thereby acknowledging even on their own terms a northern recapitulation of the previous military development in the south.[112]

Scalapino and Lee suggest that this "military academy" was in fact a small operation existing only in South P'yŏng'an Province and under the control of the province people's committee *poandae* bureau. They find no moves toward the creation of a northern military before the end of 1946, although they do argue that *poandae* and railroad security police "were the basis for" the subsequent North Korean People's Army.[113] Dae-sook Suh's account says nothing about the creation of a northern military in any form during this period.[114]

The declassified American history of the northern military maintains that "the actual beginning of the North Korean Army" was in September 1946, when Korean enlisted men from China arrived in the north. An intelligence report in 1947 agreed, arguing that although "the decision to form a 'National Korean Army' was made in the spring of 1946," its implementation was delayed until September.[115]

It is possible to reconstruct what must have actually happened when it is remembered that before liberation there were two armed Korean anti-Japanese forces—those under Kim Il Sung, and those in North China associated with Yenan, under Mu Chŏng, Kim Tu-bong, and others. The north Korean military originated from a merger of these two forces. From November 1945 on, Kim Il Sung's forces established themselves in the northern *poandae*, with Kim Ch'aek commanding the small *poandae* military academy in South P'yŏng'an and Ch'oe Yong-gŏn heading the public security bureau under the Five Provinces Bureau and the subsequent NKIPC. It is this development that Baik Bong of course chooses to emphasize, since his aim is to glorify Kim and denigrate the contributions of Yenan-aligned Koreans who were purged after the Korean War. But what about the Yenan-aligned Korean forces?

Korean forces fighting with the Eighth Route Army, going under the name Korean Volunteer Army (KVA), and numbering perhaps 300 before liberation, headed home after August 15, picking up recruits as they moved through Manchuria. In late September or late October (depending on the source), they materialized in the Sino-Korean border town of Antung, numbering by this time between 2,000 and 2,500. According to one account, the commanders of the detachments were very young (like Kim Il Sung himself); one, Kim Kang, was 26 years old, with much of his young life spent in the Eighth Route Army; another, Kim Ho, was a 36-year-old graduate of the famous Whampoa Academy in China.[116] Both South Korean and American accounts state that this force was stopped by Soviet security forces at the border. Those who wished to come into north Korea were disarmed, and the majority of the footsoldiers were returned to Manchuria.[117]

These sources make much of these events, arguing that the Soviets and Kim Il Sung were afraid to let armed Yenan-aligned units enter the north, lest they rival Kim's power. This is not an unreasonable assumption, except that it is impossible to argue that the Yenan-aligned Koreans failed to win power and position subsequently in the north; as we will see, Kim Tu-bong and others quickly joined the top ranks of the northern leadership. Furthermore, what would the Americans have thought had the Soviets allowed more than 2,000 soldiers to enter the north and encamp above the thirty-eighth parallel in the fall of 1945? The disarming of those who did enter was entirely in keeping with Soviet-American agreements on Korea.

The significance of this action is much broader than its presumed effect on high north Korean politics. The Soviets reportedly told the armed detachments of the KVA to return to Manchuria to fight with the Chinese Eighth Route Army,[118] where they spent the next several years growing in size and gaining extensive experience. By 1949 when the Chinese civil war ended, tens of thousands of crack Korean troops were available to form the main shock units of the Korean People's Army. This important development, to be treated at length in the second volume of this study, means that the northern army had two mothers—Kim's partisan force, and that of the Yenan-aligned Koreans. One grew after liberation within the north, through the *poandae* and railroad security ranks, while the other grew to maturity in the Chinese civil war. Thus, from the fall of 1945, it can be said that the north had an army, but it existed in China; until 1948 there existed in north Korea proper only lightly armed security forces. These latter, too, were made up of both Kim's forces and parts of the Yenan-aligned group, as we know from American intelligence reports, which found that small detachments of *poandae* in Sŏnch'ŏn, Sinŭiju, and elsewhere in late spring 1946 consisted mostly of KVA veterans.[119] Instead of being disarmed, then, the KVA forces were armed, expanded, and tempered in China. We would suspect that this shrewd strategy had the complete support of Kim Il Sung and the Yenan-aligned leaders, Mu Chŏng and Kim Tu-bong.

Thus we can say that both the Soviets and the Americans supported the creation of Korean military forces beginning in the fall of 1945, but that Soviet policy was strictly correct within the borders of the north. They and their Korean allies used Manchuria as a convenient training ground. The American Occupation command was forced to create a southern military force within the confines of south Korea, both for internal security reasons and because their intelligence apparatus made them aware of the existence of the KVA both in north Korea and Manchuria. Like MacArthur during the Korean War, however, they had trouble recognizing the boundary between Korea and China as one they were bound to respect. It must also be emphasized, finally, that both Kim's forces and the KVA were spawned not by the Soviets, but by the Korean resistance to the Japanese in China and Manchuria. The Soviets may have fostered its development, but this was a Korean army.

Social Revolution

Shortly after the formation of the NKIPC, and as the Americans and Soviets came together at the Joint Commission meetings, the north pushed through fundamental reforms that restructured northern society and, more than any other action in 1946, served to separate the north from the south. After these reforms, unification of the peninsula could only occur in two ways: through a similar revolution in the south, or through a war that would be fought both for unification and for the domination of classes—that is, unification would occur through revolution or counterrevolution. From early 1946 on, in Korean eyes, the conflict between north and south was a conflict of classes, around which were arrayed the other existing conflicts of politics, nationalism, region, and generation.

In his speech of February 8, which inaugurated the NKIPC, Kim Il Sung spoke of the need for a thoroughgoing renovation of the "feudal" land situation in the north. In March the northerners attacked the problem at its roots, at the bottom of Korean society, in the villages. In so doing, they broke the power of a landed class of centuries' duration. They accomplished this by organizing those with the least to lose, making poor peasants and agricultural laborers the shock forces in some 11,500 rural committees organized under people's committee aegis to push the reform through. Much like Chinese Communist practice, poor peasants were relied on, middle peasants were cultivated, rich peasants were isolated, and landlord control was broken.[120] The organization of the land reform committees and the work of the reform itself was accompanied by a nationwide mass campaign, in which about 1,000 urban workers took the lead in going to the countryside amid an intense hoopla of posters, handbills, and loudspeaker broadcasts that penetrated to the smallest villages, thereby mobilizing millions of people and spreading the authority of the NKIPC far and wide.[121] At the end of the process, the central committee had a loyal village leadership that had been both tested and rewarded. In this manner Kim Il Sung and his allies "drove the flagpole to the ground," penetrating the countryside to the lowest level.

At the township level the reform committees (called *nongch'ŏn wiwŏnhoe*) were made up of five to nine members, nearly all poor peasants who were tenants or possessed tiny parcels of land. With the help of the local people's committees and workers and cadres sent down from above, they recorded all property of the landlords, protected it, and held it for redistribution. Problems that proved insoluble at the local levels were referred to the people's committees at the next highest level.[122]

Like later Chinese land reforms, "anti-traitor" meetings were held, and reform enforcement regulations said that all peasants must participate in compiling lists of individuals who would have their land confiscated, "in order to expose the pro-Japanese." Absentee landlords had their land confiscated for redistribution, unless they had also engaged in the anti-Japanese resistance. If landlords had already voluntarily given up their land, they were allowed to keep their homes and stay in their communities. For richer peasants who worked their own land, the emphasis was placed on whether the land had been used "parasitically," determined on the basis of the amount of land rented out to tenants. Thus if an individual owned seven *chŏngbo*, worked four *chŏngbo* and rented out the remainder, only the three rented *chŏngbo* would be confiscated. On the other hand, if all seven were rented, all would be taken for redistribution. A peasant who worked all seven would keep all his land, even though this exceeded the stipulated five *chŏngbo* limit. Redistribution to tenants was based on a point system in which males from 18 to 60 would get one point, females from 18 to 50 one point, youths 15-17, .7 points, and children .5 points. The village reform committees then reapportioned land on the basis of total points for each family and differences in the quality of the land being provided to them.[123]

A total of 4,751 landlord households had their land taken, although most of them were allowed either to keep 5 *chŏngbo* or to move to different districts where they received small plots of land, if they were willing to till the land themselves without using tenants. Land was also confiscated from previous Japanese holdings and various public institutions and churches and was then distributed as follows:[124]

Category	No. of Households	Amount of Land Received
Landless peasants	407,307	583,304 chŏngbo
Smallholding peasants	255,993	336,039 chŏngbo
Agricultural laborers	5,540	14,855 chŏngbo
Landlords moved to other counties	3,911	9,622 chŏngbo

This north Korean land reform was achieved in less violent manner than that in China and North Vietnam. Official American sources commented that: "From all accounts, the former village leaders were eliminated as a political force without resort to bloodshed, but extreme care was taken to preclude their return to power." Former landlords were given small amounts of land, moved to different districts, and then kept under "strict surveillance."[125] American intelligence reports at the time noted the lack of violence, and quoted a refugee schoolteacher as saying, "If a rich man works himself, he is allowed to keep some land. However, he must move to another district. Those rich men who do not work themselves are relieved of their properties."[126]

The relative ease of the reform process is owed to several unique factors in the north Korean situation. First, a large number of Korean landlords had already fled south, and, of course, Japanese landowners were long gone. Second, only a couple of northern provinces (Hwanghae and South P'yŏng'an) had extremes of tenancy such as existed throughout the south; northern peasants were more often smallholders already, most working dry fields rather than paddies, and had a frugal, hardy reputation. Thus class conflict was less intense. These are just the sort of peasants who would benefit from a redistribution that puts a bit more land in their hands, some new tools or draft animals, and a strong incentive to produce. Third, the north Koreans did not begin immediately with mutual aid teams and then collectivization, as the Chinese did, but allowed the land to remain in private (although nontransferable) status. They made no moves toward collectivization until 1950. Thus the reform had a distinct "land to the tillers" flavor, making it very popular among poor peasants and lessening the degree of opposition among all agrarian classes. Last, the existence of a porous thirty-eighth parallel and a greater degree of landlordism in the south offered two advantages to the north. They could allow landlords to flee south, knowing that they could deal with them at a later point and knowing also that they would intensify the polarization of southern politics, thus weakening the moderate leftists whom the northerners feared. And they could work a "demonstration effect" on the south, showing the way toward the thorough reforms demanded by the majority of Koreans throughout the peninsula. With the influx of northern landlords and the threat implied to southern ones by the reform, there was less chance that land reform on a moderate rather than a revolutionary basis would occur in the south and win peasants away from the Left. All in all, the reform was a master stroke, since no one could claim that a bloodbath had eliminated landlordism, the hardworking northern peasants got what they and their ancestors had longed for, and the ball was placed in the southern court with a distinct thud. It was in this context, in his comments on the results of the land reform, that Kim Il Sung remarked that the southern reactionaries "are now very much afraid of the north wind."

The land reform had two other unique characteristics. First, it was widely trumpeted as a model for the rest of Asia. Kim claimed that it would "greatly inspire the oppressed peoples of the East in their liberation struggle against imperialism and the domestic feudal forces."[127] This sort of modeling behavior then became quite the order of the day for the Koreans; in somewhat solipsistic fashion, they began to think that all eyes were upon them as they blazed a trail for the rest of Asia. Second, the reform was followed by ubiquitous posters saying "thank you, Kim Il Sung" for the land—as if the benevolent leader had presented each parcel to each peasant.[128] Mao later criticized this sort of practice, arguing that it worked against the task of raising peasant consciousness and getting peasants to struggle for their own rewards.[129]

It is true that Kim's top-downism was not good Maoism, but then the Chinese followed very moderate land reform policies when they were locked in struggle with the Nationalists and the Japanese during the Yenan period. Moreover, it would have been provocative for the north to have embarked on the village class struggle procedures subsequently used in North China[130] at a time when they confronted the American Occupation and the opposition of well-organized Koreans in the south. Kim referred many times to the necessity to implement the "mass line" during the reform period, however,[131] and as we have seen, the class basis of the reform committees was similar to that in China. In short, the land reform, like other north Korean policies, mingled Maoist and Soviet practices together with some unique Korean ones.

American sources noted that the reform left the new regime with a "vast reservoir of popular goodwill." A refugee during the period said that the "intelligentsia and the rich" had come south but that the poor were "pleased with conditions"; the "overwhelming majority" of workers and peasants supported Kim Il Sung and the NKIPC leadership, although most disliked the Russians.[132] Furthermore, the land reform was quickly followed by a labor law that did away with the worst excesses in factories. Promulgated in June 1946, it provided for an eight-hour workday, social security insurance, better work conditions (or more pay for difficult or hazardous work), and equal pay for equal work, irrespective of sex. The next month a law on the equality of women appeared, a real milestone given the Korean context. It did away with concubinage, prostitution, female infanticide, and numerous other practices that exploited women (and that continued in south Korea). Although the letter of these reforms did not become practice overnight, in the aftermath, there were few reports of the sort of abuses of workers and women that had been their lot for millennia.

Major industries and enterprises, most of them previously owned by the Japanese, were nationalized, while middle and small entrepreneurs were given permits by province and county PCs and encouraged to remain active, invest, and produce.[133] In this manner, and with the help of remaining Japanese technicians and Soviet experts, the economy and especially the major industries were put back in order and registered increases in output by the end of 1946.

A dry narrative done three decades after the fact strips from these events both the exhilaration of those who participated in and benefited from them and the anguish and terror of those who were the objects of this revolution. The observer can find in the record of the Korean situation in the late 1940s, north and south, evidence of unspeakable brutality and atrocity on both sides. This makes Korea no different from China during the same era, or Iran, Nicaragua, or southern Africa during our era. But such situations have no place for a detached philosophy that renounces all violence directed toward political ends. What human being cannot but detest, in the abstract, violence against other humans? But it is just as human to respond in kind to the severe conflict that divided Koreans from day one after the Japanese demise. In liberated Korea neither side gave quarter; in means there was little distinction. But in ends and goals there was a large measure of difference, and it is among these that the choice had to be made. The quizzical American, staring blankly at the situation with an amnesiac unawareness of the violence of American politics going back to the Civil War and the Revolution, even unable to comprehend how others would view a liberating army that brought in racially segregated troop contingents, found it easy to condemn the communists, north and south. The hard-bitten Russian, who learned about violence and politics the hard way under Stalin's terror, or in locked struggle with Hitlerite fascism, found the Korean situation familiar and acted accordingly. Add this to a Korean milieu that had experienced decades of Japanese brutality and that was classically revolutionary in the late 1940s, and one wonders why the opposing sides stayed their hands as much as they did.

UNITED FRONT POLICIES

In mid-summer 1946, after the social reforms had been enunciated, the north Koreans embarked upon a political course of action aimed at uniting those on the Left and cultivating wavering elements in the middle. The policy had two complementary goals: bringing together disparate factions in the north; and presenting an image of unity and strength to the south that would make a pointed contrast to the coalition effort then being pursued under American auspices. The summer of 1946 was a good time for seeking coalition. The north brought in a bumper summer harvest, making it possible to spread a bit of wealth to workers and peasants.[134] The earth's bounty appeared as if to mark the first year after liberation, and to sweeten the prospects for unity.

Unity was also important for Kim Il Sung. He may have attained the chairmanship of the NKIPC in February, but his position remained insecure. He faced determined opposition from older leftist and communist leaders, especially those of the potent Yenan-aligned group. Thus, as Dae-sook Suh put it, "from February to July, Kim Il Sung worked tirelessly to unite" the NKCP and the Yenan-aligned group, which had reorganized itself into a political party, the *Sinmindang*, or New Democratic Party (NPP).[135] The object was reached at the end of July, when a three-day conference was held to discuss and explain the circumstances in which merger would occur. Both Kim Il Sung and Kim Tu-bong, the NPP leader, saw a class basis for the merger of the two parties: the NKCP had a majority of peasants and workers, whereas the NPP included many intellectual and petty-bourgeois elements; combining the two would thus combine all those classes included in the definition of the "people" in the north. The NPP apparently had about 120,000 members at the time, the NKCP some 300,000.[136] A month later, another three-day conference, beginning on August 29, ratified the united front policy and created the North Korean Worker's Party (NKWP), the party that, with the later addition of the South Korean Worker's Party, has ruled in North Korea ever since. Kim Tu-bong became chairman of the NKWP, while Kim Il Sung shared a vice-chairmanship with Chu Yong-ha.

The speeches given by Kim Il Sung and Kim Tu-bong at the August meeting offer an interesting contrast.[137] Kim Il Sung spoke almost entirely about Korea and its needs. He related the formation of the NKWP to the history of Korea's independence movement and to the needs of democratic development, of building a new country, a new life: "the new Korea will be a people's Korea, built by the people themselves." The north's program, he said, was one of "complete independence" (*wanjŏn tongnip*) and "true democratization" for all of Korea; the NKWP would work with "patriots" in the south toward a "unified and completely independent country." He referred to the Japanese not as imperialists but as *waenom*, a racial pejorative; southern rightists were not capitalists or landlords in this speech, but "reactionaries," "country-sellers," "pro-Japanese," who go about "putting patriots in prison while every day *kisaeng* houses increase in number." In other words, the entire thrust of the speech was to trumpet the specifically Korean virtues of nationalism, patriotism, resistance to the Japanese, and reform of outmoded "feudal" practices. Kim's words were almost bereft of Marxism-Leninism or reference to the presence of the Soviets.

Kim also referred to a number of themes that have since been commonplace in the north. The Korean revolution would show the way for other countries of the East; NKWP cadres must "go deep among the masses," this was the key to everything: "our party is always to be found among the masses and never leaves the masses"; all efforts should be devoted to strong, rocklike unity among all organizations.

Kim Tu-bong's speech was quite a contrast. He made many references to the "new Soviet camp," a group of nations liberated by the Soviet army from fascism who were now building a new life. He remarked on "democratic reforms" being implemented in Bulgaria, Czechoslovakia, Rumania, and Yugoslavia. He said that since October 1917 there had been but two forces in the world, socialism and capitalism, and the two were in "basic opposition"; the struggle between the two had been developing on a broad scale since the end of the war. All of these conditions were essential, he thought, in enabling Korea's own development.

Kim Tu-bong's words were more eloquent and more informed with Marxist-Leninist theory than were Kim Il Sung's. He spent much effort pointing out how various classes and Korea's current stage in the world revolution could be "scientifically" distinguished and digressed on theory before coming to his central points. Apropos of the current merger, he quoted Stalin on making sure one can distinguish proper tactics for the future when one makes alliances in the present. It was Kim Il Sung, however, who found his words punctuated with applause from the assembled delegates at a much greater frequency than did Kim Tu-bong.

It is entirely possible, of course, that Kim Il Sung was given the most popular lines on this particular day. But it is more likely that the speeches reflected real differences between the two leaders. Kim Il Sung has always been what we might call a "Korea-firster." His ideology was revolutionary nationalist rather than Marxist-Leninist; Marxism-Leninism might be important, but it could come later. The approach in Kim's speeches was designed to appeal not to Marxist intellectuals, but to Korea's masses in the era of national liberation. This may have been poor theory from the standpoint of some Korean communists, but it was effective and popular practice.

Later Pak Il-u provided the assembly with statistics on its membership.[138] In so doing, he left a full picture of the background of NKWP leadership:

Age of 801 People in Attendance

Between 20 and 30	299	28%
Between 31 and 40	417	52%
Between 41 and 50	129	17%
Over age 50	26	3%

Class Background

Workers	183	23%
Peasants	157	20%
Samuwŏn*	385	48%
Others	76	9%

Education

Elementary	228	29%
Middle	359	45%
College	214	26%

Pre-1945 Occupation

Revolutionary (chigop hyŏngmyŏngga)	112	13%
Worker	142	19%
Peasant	120	15%
Samuwŏn*	296	37%
Other	131	16%

Anti-Japanese Activities

"Those who actively participated in the anti-Japanese struggle"	373	46%
Those who were arrested	291	36%
Those who served 1-5 year prison terms	149	18%
Those who served 6-10 year prison terms	71	7%
Those who served 10-year plus† prison terms	26	3%
Total number of delegates imprisoned	263	
Total number of years in prison meted out	1,087	
Total number of those imprisoned, in the underground, in armed struggle, or in revolutionary work abroad	427	53%

* Pak defined these as clerks, bureaucrats, technicians, scholars, and doctors of philosophy.

† One delegate had served 18 years, that is precisely half the colonial period.

Pak Il-u also related that only sixty-two, or 7 percent, of the delegates had been members of either the NKCP or the NPP before August 15, 1945, which must have been the total present from among Yenan-aligned Koreans and Kim Il Sung's followers, since neither party officially existed at that time.

A year later, the NKWP claimed nearly 400,000 members. This figure is very high for vanguard parties and represents another aspect of the north's united front policies at the time: almost anyone could join the NKWP. Kim Il Sung said at the founding meeting that "even if a person does not understand Marxism-Leninism but actively fights for democracy" this person could become a member; through his "love of country" he would demonstrate his "progressive" nature.[139] Thereafter, the idea of a "mass party" was proclaimed as yet another Korean contribution to world revolution.[140] The NKWP has had the highest percentage of population on its rolls of any communist party in the world. As Scalapino and Lee have rightly emphasized, this has to do with the north Korean commitment to mass mobilization, to organizing everyone who can be organized.[141] The NKWP was one more addition, albeit the most important one, to the "organization society" that emerged in the north after liberation.

The formation of the NKWP brought together three strong-willed leaders—Kim Il Sung, Kim Tu-bong, and Mu Chŏng—and also aligned northern and southern leftist politics, in that the South Korean Worker's Party, led by Pak Hŏn-yŏng, appeared shortly after in the south. These four men subsequently formed the top segment in the leadership of the northern regime, and it is possible to say something about their relationship in the fall of 1946.

Kim Tu-bong was a classically educated activist and noted scholar of the Korean language who was born in 1888 in South Kyŏngsang Province. He remained abroad, mostly in China, from 1919 to 1945; active in the Korean Provisional Government in Shanghai, he subsequently became a teacher in a Shanghai school. In 1942 he traveled to Yenan, where he became a teacher in a Yenan political school (possibly *K'ang-Jih Tahsüeh*) and a top leader of the Korean Independence Alliance. He reportedly returned to Korea in 1945 by foot.[142] He was a somewhat frail, learned man, intellectual in fact and in appearance, and not known for military leadership in the pre-1945 period. There is little to indicate much friction between him and Kim Il Sung; he probably held Kim in contempt intellectually, but he lent his presence as a grey eminence to the NKWP and remained in the top leadership in the north until the war.

Mu Chŏng was the only leader in the north who could rival Kim Il Sung in anti-Japanese prowess and the only one with a clear and close link to the Chinese Communist leadership. He was born in North

Hamgyŏng Province, probably in 1905, and went to China in 1922. He apparently began his military career under the warlord Yen Hsi-shan, quickly developing an expertise in artillery warfare. He was an artillery lieutenant during the Northern Expedition and joined the Chinese Communist Party in 1927. Thereafter, he reportedly became chief of artillery in the Red Army commanded by Mao Tse-tung and Chu Teh. Mu Chŏng was the only Korean to survive the Long March, among thirty who began it in Kiangsi Province; he was wounded several times during this legendary démarche. After his arrival in Yenan he commanded the Korean Volunteer Army and fought with the Eighth Route Army as an artillery commander. He was reported to be close to Chu Teh.[143]

Mu Chŏng made a big splash upon his return to Korea. Some Koreans thought he was the "vice-commander" of the Eighth Route Army, and American intelligence termed him "the Chinese Communist . . . choice to assume leadership" in Korea.[144] One writer deemed Mu Chŏng along with Kim Il Sung and Ch'oe Yong-gŏn, to be "the greatest of the anti-Japanese fighters" in 1945.[145] He held no political position in the northern leadership in the fall of 1946, however, and was reported by Yŏ Un-hyŏng to be out of favor; he apparently had the relatively minor military position of deputy chief for artillery in the *poandae*.[146] American intelligence sources stated that he was "intelligent, able, informed," but too outspoken: "his temper is fierce, hot and course [*sic*]—he curses freely when angry." He inspired devoted allegiance among his troops.[147]

It seems unlikely that the Chinese leadership had either the time or the inclination to sponsor leaders in Korea, but it is likely that the Soviets and Kim Il Sung feared Mu Chŏng's Chinese connection. He seems to have been corraled and cloistered in training the northern military, with Kim Tu-bong and others providing political leadership for the Yenan-linked Koreans.

Pak Hŏn-yŏng had his hands full in the south during this period and ended up being confronted by a warrant for his arrest in the fall of 1946; he also had to accommodate Kim Il Sung's and Kim Tu-bong's emergence on top in the north. There is no doubt that Pak, the titular leader of Korean communism, found Kim Il Sung's new-found eminence repugnant. At a news conference in late March, when asked if he would support Kim, he responded woodenly that Kim had support in both north and south and that "therefore when he is elected president of the Korean government the northern Koreans will support him and we will also support him in the south."[148] In his speech at the NKWP inauguration, Kim Il Sung pointedly singled out Yŏ Un-hyŏng as being responsible for the unity movement in the south and left Pak unmentioned.[149] This was also the period when

Yŏ wanted the Americans to arrest Pak to aid in the coalition effort. At another point, however, Kim praised Pak, defending him against criticism by Arthur Bunce.[150] Although the existing literature dwells overly long on the Pak/Kim conflict, and often reads things into it through the lenses of hindsight, the conflict was real. Paradoxically, the Soviets might well have preferred Pak to Kim had circumstances permitted, since Pak was much better versed in Marxism-Leninism, possessed the imprimatur of decades in the communist movement, and was much more of a proletarian internationalist than was Kim Il Sung.

THE NORTH WIND BLOWS SOUTH

Part of the reason for the rapidity of change in the north in the first year after liberation was its intended "demonstration effect" on the south. The image of efficient, throughgoing renovation of colonial legacies made, and was meant to make, a dissonant contrast to the stagnation and violence in the south. The north wind was carried south by a steady flow of refugees who had a further disordering effect and constituted a north Korean Trojan horse in the southern milieu.

Beginning in the fall of 1945, southern newspapers carried frequent reports on changes in the north. The moderate as well as leftist press lauded the various reform measures and generally tended to discount the reports of atrocities and depradations carried in the rightist press. The *Kŭnyŏk chubo* provides a representative example in its contrast of northern with southern policies:

> The Soviet Army's policies are different from American Army policies. Immediately after entering north Korea the Soviets disarmed the Japanese army, stripped off the Japanese people's fine clothes . . . gave Japanese-owned houses to homeless Koreans, gave their assets to the Korean people, and put political and economic authority completely in the hands of the Korean people.[151]

Whatever the *sub rosa* role of the Soviet command in the north may have been, the Soviets and the north Koreans convinced Koreans in the south that the people's committees were the effective governing agencies. For example, On Ak-jung wrote that no matter where one traveled in the north, one saw the signboard of the people's committees, a "new form" of government "established by the people with their own hands"; this was government "by the people, for the people."[152] Even in rightist sources, the north was described simply as being under the rule of the people's committees.

The north Korean land reform in March 1946 had a particularly strong impact on the south. For days after its announcements, southern newspapers ran banner headlines about it, with highly laudatory editorials calling for similar reforms in the south and almost no criticism.[153] Thereafter, many peasant demonstrations in the southern provinces were punctuated by demands for land reform like that in the north. Perusal of the southern press during this period reveals the degree to which southerners thought that Korean dynamism was emanating from the north.

South Korea received a steady, massive stream of refugees from the north during the first year. Although the American Occupation usually called these people refugees from communism and Soviet rule, the procession was more complex than that. According to a study of the problem by the USAMGIK Office of Foreign Affairs,[154] the largest number of refugees flooded into south Korea during the fall and winter of 1945/46 and was composed mostly of Korean peasants returning from Manchuria and north Korea to homes in the south. In the spring of 1945 the land reform and other measures stimulated a flow of refugees from the higher classes; for the next several months the influx consisted mostly of well-educated types—landowners, merchants, doctors, lawyers, engineers, teachers, and government officials. After a peak in the spring of 1946, the flow tapered off and again had a more mixed class composition. There was a seasonal flow as well; bad agricultural or food conditions in the north prompted higher rates in certain months.

The flow of refugees was therefore stimulated by both natural and political causes: part of it involved Koreans returning to native homes in the south, the region from which most of the mobilized Korean diaspora came; another part represented dispossessed and aggrieved classes. As the upper classes moved south, there was a corresponding movement northward. Although the numbers coming from the south were comparatively few, hundreds of thousands of Koreans left Japan for the north.[155] Thus, to some extent, Korean classes realigned on a north-south basis.

North Korea encouraged the movement southward because of the disordering effects it would have on the south; there are three aspects to this. First, the returning diaspora would strain southern food supplies and relief facilities and would locate an aggrieved and dispossessed *lower* class in the south; as we have seen, this uprooted population figured in much of the provincial disorder. Second, by allowing landlords to flee southward, the north also located an aggrieved and dispossessed *upper* class in the south, while avoiding the thorny problems of dealing with a hostile, uprooted landed class in the north after the reform. The entrance of these northern elements, including former police and bureaucrats from the colonial period, had a polarizing effect on the south; it squeezed out moderate possibilities and left the Americans with a choice between communism and reaction. The north certainly welcomed this effect as well. At a minimum, the porous border enabled them to postpone the eventual reckoning that their radical reforms promised. Last, the southward flow enabled the north to implant their agents among the refugee mass, a cause for constant concern among Occupation officials and the southern police.

Conclusions

By the end of 1946 the Soviets and their Korean allies could reflect on the first year of liberation with considerable satisfaction. The Soviets had pursued a highly cost-effective strategy in creating a regime that was responsive both to their minimum demand—a friendly border state—and to the desires of the mass of Koreans in the liberation era. Their policy of retreating to the background and giving the Koreans their head enabled them to staff their occupation cheaply and unobtrusively, quite in contrast to the American Occupation.[156] The Soviets contented themselves with reordering the arrangements at the top, leaving the provinces mostly to the people's committees and the *poandae*; the Americans had to mount surgical operations at both top and bottom, time and time again.

For the Korean leadership in the north, the first year gave them virtually all their demands save one. The top leadership constituted a coalition of the Left, including Kim Il Sung and his allies; Kim Tu-bong, Mu Chŏng, and the Yenan-aligned forces; an undetermined number of Koreans returned from the Soviet Union; and a substantial number of Korean leftists and communists who had remained within Korea during the colonial period. This leadership was overlaid upon the popular basis of the people's committees and was allowed to carry through fundamental reforms demanded by the majority of Koreans. By the end of the year, this leadership also had effective police and military arms, with a substantial contingent gaining fighting experience in the Chinese civil war. The one thing they did not get was an end to foreign occupation. As long as Soviet forces remained in the north, Kim Il Sung and his allies could not be free of the suspicion that they had been installed and backed up by foreign power and existed only at its sufferance. For Koreans who rued a history of foreign subservience, and for a nation that had been forced for so long to work out its destiny among competing imperialisms, an authentic revolutionary regime would have to establish its independence and clearly move away from the embrace of the Soviet bear. The early atrocities of Red Army troops in the north and the continuing evidence of, if not atrocities, at least preemptive and domineering treatment of Koreans by the Soviets, simply added to the northern leadership's problems.[157]

If one is to strike a balance on the first year after liberation in the north, however, it must be on the positive side. An American study based on extensive interviewing of northern POWs and refugees during the Korean War found that the informants believed that northern officials and police "were less brutal than in previous governments . . . the officials gave the impression of being hardworking, efficient, and honest." A tailor from Hamhŭng said that "laborers and ignorant people came to power," while others found the extent of change "shocking":

> Farm laborers, divorced women, and party members strode about the streets running the towns . . . uneducated people, servants during the Japanese rule, and prisoners let out at the liberation became the new leaders.

A manager of a company in Wŏnsan said:

> [The leaders of the city] were farmers and laborers. They went about enthusiastically learning the Korean alphabet and Chinese characters and in no time they got communism deeply instilled in their minds. It was amazing that these people turned from being ignorant to intelligent.

A south Korean educator who had lived in the north argued that "the best thing the Communists did . . . was to make it possible for the children of lower class families to go to school." There was general agreement among the informants that the lot of laborers was vastly improved, and "for the first time laborers had a chance to rise to the upper ranks in politics." The same was true for women: "it was the custom to appoint at least one woman to every People's Committee."[158] Thus by the end of 1946 the north wielded a formidable challenge to the continuing stagnation and violence in the south; with each passing day the north wind seemed to blow more insistently.

Chapter Twelve

CONCLUSIONS: LIBERATION DENIED

> Koreans shared with other peoples in Asia and Europe released
> from Japanese or German control a joyous anticipation of a new
> age, a new destiny. We were suddenly free of a hated alien rule.
> . . . To be released from these hardships, to see Koreans walk
> proud and tall again, to have the jail doors swing open and our
> patriots come out into the sun, to speak our own language, to
> plan and hope for a new Korea . . . these were the ecstatic aspi-
> rations of our freedom on August 15, 1945. But Korea was not
> freed from foreign control . . . and liberation was an illusion
> sanctified into a myth.
>
> _Chong Kyong-mo_

> When the empty space in which potentialities might have been
> realized is bared, we become aware of our losses.
>
> _Henry Kariel_

As 1946 came to an end, the two Koreas that still exist three decades
later had taken form. The first year after liberation was truly the
crucible from which sprang the political and social forces that continue to play upon the Korean peninsula. With this consolidation
a deux in north and south, however, came the end of the fertile and
creative initiatives occasioned by the liberation, a cauterization of
diverse forces, and the effective termination of the opportunity to
create a truly independent country that, as Koreans at the time and
since have noted, was both the gift and the challenge of liberation. To
release Korea from Japanese monopoly only to lock it in a Soviet-
American duopoly was to make a mockery of liberation and an halluci-
nation of the unified republic that seemed to be emerging in August
1945.

In the fervid atmosphere of the war's end, this "people's" regime had
established itself throughout the peninsula. Led for the most part by
heroes of the resistance to Japan, it possessed a raw appropriateness,
or legitimacy, based on the records of its leaders and on its indigenous
origins. August 1945 provided the perfect setting, a release from four
decades of colonial domination and, many hoped, from centuries of
inegalitarian land distribution. The People's Republic struck first and
struck deepest. It was a time when, in Marx's words, "the conditions
themselves cry out: Hic Rhodus, hic salta! Hier ist die Rose, hier

tanze!"[1] The Korean leap to Rhodes was caught in midair, however, with the entries of the American and Soviet troops. Although the regime of liberation provided the popular basis for the northern state, the Soviet presence and the ambition of Kim Il Sung skewed the result. The regional cast of the committees made the imposition of central authority easy, child's play for experienced revolutionaries. With the accompanying land, labor, and social reforms, the mass of Koreans still got much, if not all, of what liberation promised. But in the south, a different imposition from the center was accomplished, one that dashed the expectations of August 1945 and even raised the possibility of a turn backward.

In the last three months of 1945 the American Occupation and its Korean allies built or reinforced bureaucratic, police, and military structures as, so it seemed, their only alternative to the regime of liberation. Because it was an alternative, however, and because it had to supplant an existing structure and lacked the legitimacy of the first regime, the imposition of central controls turned southern politics into a raucous affair of dissent and rebellion. The southern administration took on the reactive and negative cast that marked its birth and offered little to the Koreans that was better than the previous colonial regime, save that it was, for the most part, Korean. Even in this the result was dubious, since most of the Korean officials and organizations appropriate for constructing an alternative political edifice in the south were linked to the hated Japanese era. Americans seeking noncommunist allies met anxious Koreans hoping to perpetuate class and bureaucratic privilege through a most difficult transition. The resulting mix pleased no one, except the threatened Koreans. Nothing demonstrated this dissatisfaction more than the activities of the KPG-aligned nationalist leaders who returned in late 1945, whose participation in plans laid by General Hodge, Syngman Rhee, Korean Democratic Party leaders, and others, was half-hearted at best and subversive to the entire effort at worst. Their refusal to acquiesce to the southern arrangements is the most eloquent comment on Occupation policies during this period.

The conceptions held by Americans on the scene and by conservative or Japan-associated Koreans merged on the question of the role of the state. Both saw in the ubiquitous colonial apparatus a critical resource for controlling political struggles. The Americans sought a state that would possess means of coercion sufficient to maintain stability, law and order, and prevent an orientation of southern Korea away from American interests—or to put it another way, toward perceived Soviet interests. The Koreans sought to utilize the state in traditional fashion, to preserve social and economic privilege and to

foster aristocratic prerogative and landed wealth. Collaborators in colonial rule sought to prevent the purgative that liberation seemed
to promise. Neither the Americans nor the Koreans could legitimate
such pragmatic and self-serving policies, however, thus they both
sought to introduce Korean nationalists into the government, who
could, by their participation, provide a stamp of approval. In this
the Occupation and its Korean allies ran headlong into conflicts going
back to the 1920s, conflicts that involved the exiled anti-Japanese
resistance and the elite who had remained in colonial Korea. The
landlord-entrepreneurs and moderate, gradualist nationalists possessed, by the 1940s, many of the skills necessary to manage a conservative, postcolonial Korea. But even their partial and muted resistance disappeared in the late 1930s when Japan pushed its war
effort; thus their response to liberation was halting and anxious. These
elements, who constituted the backbone of the Korean Democratic
Party, were tainted to the degree that nationalists like Kim Ku would
not work with them, at least not openly, and would have risked com-
promising themselves and tarnishing the record of their own resistance if they did. Even Syngman Rhee found it necessary to maintain
his distance from the KDP. As for leftists and communists, the absence
of nationalist color in these new bourgeois elements that emerged
during the colonial era simply made it easier to disregard them or
deny them a role in postcolonial government. As in so many other
aspects of the Korean colony, Japanese midwifery had produced if
not a stillborn child, at least a schizophrenic one. Korean landlord-
entrepreneurs did not cut their tie to the land, preferring the safety
of landed wealth to the much newer risks of entrepreneurial endeavor;
nor could they stand alone on their own, so instead they retreated
to the safer and surer method of populating or controlling the state
bureaucracy.

Thus it was that the nationalists were the prime losers of the first
period after liberation. They returned from exile to find conservatives
and collaborators entrenched in Seoul with American support and
communists and resisters, with an equal or better claim to the imprimatur of the anti-Japanese movement, ensconced in P'yŏngyang
with Soviet support. The first acts of the Kim Ku faction bespoke the
frustration of the nationalists: they assassinated Song Chin-u, chief
of the KDP, and attempted the futile *coup d'état* attempt in the wake
of the Moscow announcement. The nationalists played out the fate
of a movement that lacked ideology and organization, content as it
had been to resist—more often to subsist—in the land of the infidels,
awaiting the day when it would return triumphantly to Korea and
claim its mantle. Their program was simple: they sought restoration

(*kwangbok*) of a Korean state, which had the prime virtue of being Korean. The rest was opaque; it would work itself out. But in liberated Korea, the race went to the agile and the quick, and the nationalists lacked both qualities. Syngman Rhee, a patriot who worked best alone, had both in abundance.

Rhee's manipulation of southern politics must be judged a marvel. In the past his presence had been noted within the nationalist movement and in the Korean Provisional Government; but all along he had really been involved with but one movement, and that was the Syngman Rhee movement. Although a failure as a conductor, he did marvelous solos. In early 1945 he was an obscure exile politician, pounding Washington's pavements and the corridors of Foggy Bottom, passing himself off as "Minister Plenipotentiary" of a failed exile regime, one that subsisted at the sufferance of the Chinese Nationalists, one that had booted Rhee in 1925. By late 1945 he came and went from the Chosŏn Hotel, billet for the highest American officers, disposed of millions of dollars of contributions, chose allies from a congeries of politicians-in-waiting who needed him more than he needed them, manipulated a host of factional groupings in his interest, and parlayed his peculiar blend of assets before a troubled occupation. This last was the true index of his success. Rhee, far better than any other Korean leader, could take the measure of Americans. They needed his political skills, his mastery of the right wing, and his prestige as a patriot who had devoted his life to the goal of Korean independence. He could provide two things no other Korean could: patriotism and a sure bulwark against communism. He needed the Americans as well, also for two things: to provide the conditions in which he could emerge on top in the south and to guarantee the south against communism. After that, he preferred to be left alone and resented any interference. He was a master at grabbing the tail and wagging the dog. Whether we speak of the manner in which he was returned to Korea, or his influence over rightist politics, or his likely role in the planning for a separate southern administration, his was a virtuoso performance.

Another aspect of Rhee's virtuosity was his patience. Having assessed the outer limits of American political tolerance and knowing that this tolerance grew thin and vacillating as it reached the left side of the political spectrum, he could wait out Leonard Bertsch's studied attempt throughout the summer and fall of 1946 to bring Left and Right together in the middle. The middle could not hold, of course; but within the Occupation and the State Department, neither could the American liberal, anti-Rhee elements. Such people, whether in Korea or elsewhere, ran the risk throughout the postwar period of being accused of playing into the hands of the communists. As they moved left, they moved from firm to weak ground, while their American and Korean opponents remained solidly rooted, their motives not in question. The former thought accommodation with the Left was preferable to cutting it off; the latter thought the opposite.

Rhee's patience was also evident in the trusteeship imbroglio. During this episode, Rhee remained silent, while most of the other important political forces suffered. Kim Ku mustered his supporters for an assault on the Occupation only to end up pleading and threatening suicide before Hodge a few days later. The Korean Democratic Party lost its leader to the Kim Ku forces. The Left saw its popular support erode—in the north, where the Soviets lined up Koreans to the detriment of a communist-nationalist coalition; and in the south, where the Left's switch to support of the Moscow Accords made many Koreans believe it to be the servitor of alien influence. Finally, the trusteeship crisis dashed Hodge's de facto policy making to the ground; to pick up the pieces, he turned again to Rhee and the Korean Democratic Party. Yet by that time, the Right had found an issue in a stance against the Soviets and had become shrill and vituperous in its anti-Soviet attacks, making it that much more difficult for Hodge and his allies to present them, in the guise of the Representative Democratic Council, as the southern consultative body in the United States-Soviet Joint Commission proceedings. This situation illustrates the political pattern of the first year in microcosm—one of internationalist or liberal policies, whether those urged in Washington or in Seoul, foundering upon the irremovable obstacle of rightist obstructionism. Rhee and his allies had little that was positive to contribute to the Occupation, but they had an abundance of negative ploys that constituted virtual veto power in the south.

This pattern continued even after the autumn uprisings, which were the most palpable demonstration of the American failure. In the aftermath of the terrible violence in the provinces, there occurred in nearly every arena of south Korean political life the consolidation or rise to power of the forces of rightist autocracy. The Korean National Police, in spite of severe loss of life among its membership, had confronted and bested a frontal challenge to its authority. This, according to official sources, "constituted a turning point in the history of the police."[2] In other arenas, the Right also predominated: in the bureaucracy, the Interim Legislative Assembly, the media. The widespread arrests of labor union, peasant union, and people's committee activists provided a vacuum into which alternative organizations could move. Rightists were able to turn to a mass politics from above, organizing youths, workers, and urban unemployed on a wide scale. For the first time, rightist organizers moved outside the bureaucratic apparatus and Seoul's parties and factions, and sought to organize masses of people to compete with the Left in the streets. Youth groups proliferated in succeeding months, as a classic counterrevolutionary pattern emerged of ties and alliances between respected patrons and the shock forces of the street. The prime result of the autumn violence was thus consolidation on the Right and the emergence of a mass politics willing to do battle with the Left for Korean allegiances. This phenomenon, to be dealt with further in the second volume of this study, proved very important to the fortunes of the conservatives. It also sharply polarized Korean politics and skewed the civil conflict toward ever more violent means. The unsystematic, frustrated, ineffectual terrorism of nationalists like Kim Ku was now replaced by potent, preemptive politics flourishing in the grievances of dispossessed and threatened classes.

In spite of these developments, only incipient as 1946 drew to a close, the Right remained a brittle and defensive holding effort that continued to require American sustenance. It still lacked much popular support and effective legitimation. In the year after liberation, the Right had failed to frame a convincing and forward-looking ideology,[3] and its key organizational weapon remained the national police. The Left, on the other hand, had demonstrated in the first year that its powers of organization were far superior to those of its opponents, especially in the early months of liberation, when leftist organizing proceeded almost in the absence of rightist initiatives, let alone in conflict with any viable alternative politics. In spite of American opposition to the Left, this was still true six months later in most of south Korea, and a year later in some provinces. In the end, however, the People's Republic and its allied organizations were not strong enough to survive a full foreign occupation, except in isolated regions like Cheju Island, where leaders had the time necessary to forge strong links with the population before the Americans arrived and where beneficial environmental conditions provided recruits who were less susceptible to the old forms of control of agrarian Korea; elsewhere, initial mobilization by the people's committees had proceeded at a rapid pace but faltered when confronted by strong opposing forces. Had there been no foreign occupation in 1945, the People's Republic and its committees would have won control of the peninsula in a matter of months.

F. G. Bailey remarked that peasants plan "for the round of time" on the assumption that "with minor variations and barring accidents next year will be this year over again."[4] The year after liberation was, uniquely, set apart from this "round of time." A whole complex of unprecedented circumstances suggested that this year, for Korea's peasants, might be wholly different from what went before. Thousands of peasants therefore gave themselves over to varieties of political participation, on the assumption that the time for real change was at hand. People whose conception of politics involved little more than their own interests or those of their villages against a predatory state that took all and gave little or nothing experienced a politics in which provinces, counties, towns, and villages organized themselves, largely without reference to higher authority or to central administration in the capital. The structure of the committees and peasant unions was distinctly segmented and local, responsive to regions rather than to the center. It was an intermediary political form, something absent during the highly centralized colonial period and largely lacking in the North and South Korea of today.

This remarkable structure did not last much past the first year, however; in fact, its effective end came with the autumn bloodletting in 1946. Most of Korea's peasants retreated to plying the tools of their trade in raising rice instead of cutting down policemen. A year of liberation thus served not to liberate the peasantry, but to warn them of the consequences of unacceptable forms of political participation in years to come. The organizations of the Left and the peasants themselves were no match for the close-knit, cohesive national police. That is, they had a high consciousness of injustice leading to raw class struggle, but a weak politics. The result was disastrous for thousands of peasants, who no doubt closed out the first year hoping that the next one would be anything but that year over again.

Why should this be the case? Why could the provincial organizations not sustain themselves for a longer period? The living conditions of Korean peasants, especially those in the southernmost Chŏlla and Kyŏngsang provinces, resembled those of peasants in south China, particularly in the Canton Delta, and peasants in South Vietnam, particularly in the Mekong Delta. All these regions were penetrated by world market forces and the export trade in rice, which led to rapid commercialization, high rates of tenancy and peasant dissolution, high taxes and rents, and so on. But such regions also generated high surpluses and revenues, making them intensely interesting to the state and to the landed class. The structure of landed power in these regions thus is both stronger, given the attention and the possibilities for revenue and profit, and more dynamic, given the rapid changes accompanying the rise of the market. It is a more formidable power structure than that of the premodern era. In southern Korea the situation was very mixed, however, with certain landlords emerging as entrepreneurs and others sitting back and reaping surpluses. In North

Chŏlla, the richest rice-producing province in Korea and the home of newly emergent landlord-entrepreneurs, the people's committees got going early but did not last; peasants there did not revolt in the fall of 1946. It was in the more middling provinces and remote areas, where grievances arising out of tenancy arrangements and the dislocations of the Japanese era were strong, but where the resources of the state and the structure of landed power were weaker, that the committees tended to flourish. But why were the strong committees unable to sustain themselves in the middling and marginal areas?

When compared to China and Vietnam in 1945, Korea had unique characteristics that both promoted and retarded the process of revolution. Korea had changed more rapidly in preceding decades than had the other two nations, the Japanese accomplishing a deeper penetration by modern facilities such as the world market or the railroad. These forces, and other Japanese policies, combined to produce tremendous Korean population mobility and uprooting. Thus when the colonial "co-prosperity sphere" abruptly shattered or was carved up, its greatest effect was in Korea where its presence had been the most longstanding. The colonial state came undone at that critical point when Korea's landed classes, peasants and landlords, had begun but by no means completed the cutting of their ties to the land. Lord and peasant remained in an ambiguous status, poised between two worlds, such that the abrupt lifting of Japanese controls offered the potential of either pushing forward with the new or recapturing the old. Both landlord-entrepreneurs and worker-peasants sought the latter more than the former, giving rise to intense rural conflict. Korea in the first year of liberation thus speaks volumes of testimony to Barrington Moore's acute observation that it might as well be dying classes, those "over whom the wave of progress is about to roll,"[5] who provide the motive force of revolutions—as much or more than those emerging classes whom the revolution will benefit. Within a single generation, Korean peasants experienced a startling "wave of progress," forcing them out of their old routines, and then a sudden receding of that wave, raising the possibility of return to the old routines. Korea's landed class did not change at nearly the rate the peasantry did and thus did not achieve the resiliency and adaptability that comes with escape from old patterns. Not making a transition to commerce or industry and facing peasant revolution, its response to liberation and the events that followed was so brittle and unyielding that all hope of class reconciliation and moderate outcomes disappeared.

Korea had an encrustation of landed and aristocratic privilege of longer standing than that in China or Vietnam. Concern for class and its prerogatives was imbedded in the hereditary principle defining aristocratic position, in the Korean language itself, with its multiple forms of address that varied according to station, and in the everyday interaction of the classes, where extremes of deference and hierarchy were the rule. Also unlike either the China or the Vietnam of the 1940s, Korea had a formidable state apparatus, the residue of colonial rule. The strong state manifested itself in the Korean countryside in the form of a national police, an agency unknown in China or Vietnam, which, although drastically weakened at the Japanese demise, could be revived as the one cohesive instrument of conservative Korean power. The spectacle in the fall of 1946 of hundreds of peasants hurling rocks at handfuls of policemen armed with carbines makes the point. Moreover, the insidious colonial practice of pitting Koreans against Koreans through this force persisted after 1945; yet it became even more confusing to Koreans, since American liberators rather than Japanese colonists were giving the orders.

Although the police were well organized as an entity in themselves, they also had the colonial infrastructure at their disposal, whether we speak of the internal, self-contained police communications, access to road and rail transportation, or control of the country's nerve center at Seoul. What we have called Korea's overdevelopment in the interests of the metropole, when combined with the peninsular geography, meant that there were few regions comparable to the central highlands in Vietnam or the Yenan and other base areas in north China that were peripheral to the purview of the state, unintegrated into the national unit. Such areas existed in northernmost Korea, which is precisely where Kim Il Sung and his guerrillas were to be found in the late 1930s. In southern Korea, however, there was just the upper part of the east coast, the mountainous but underpopulated central rib, and Cheju Island. No forest or jungle sanctuaries, like those in Vietnam, provided guerrilla redoubts along the borders. In such circumstances, peasants cannot be protected against their antagonists. The confrontation of peasant and state in Korea thus can be likened more to, say, the Spanish experience, with the national police playing the role of the Guardia Civil, than to the recent history of insurgency in Vietnam and China.

In the north, Soviet occupation provided the necessary protection, a womb within which a socialist state could incubate until it was strong enough to stand alone. The revolution came swiftly and, comparatively speaking, bloodlessly; overnight, fundamental reforms of land relations, working conditions, and social relations were accomplished. By the end of the first year after liberation, the marked regionalization of politics that the people's committees spawned was arrested, as a strong center emerged under the aegis of Kim Il Sung and Kim Tu-bong.

Compared to the Americans in the south, the Soviet task was conspicuously easier. It was a simple matter of reinforcing leftist control of the bureaucracy, replacing unreliable or untrustworthy Koreans in the arrangements of the top, training and educating lower-level people's committee leaders, and then giving Koreans their heads. This the Soviets did, ruthlessly, efficiently, quickly, and with a minimum of revolutionary violence. Even so, as noted earlier, there is no evidence that the Soviets moved as quickly as did the Americans to set up separate executive, police, judicial, and military organs.

In their essentials American and Soviet goals in Korea were remarkably similar: to bolster and support sets of leaders and a social order that would preserve a continuing orientation toward the metropolitan power. Within that range, the possibilities could include more or less independence and self-determination, depending on the Korean leadership and organization at hand and their relative strengths. Each power had distinct outer limits on its policies: the Soviets would not stimulate reaction, and the Americans would not stimulate revolution. And neither power was ever willing to make concessions toward Korean independence and reunification if such concessions would dilute their ability to control the outcome or to prevent domination by the opposing power.

The Koreans in the north would have had a comparatively easy task, if their goal had been to rule only half of the peninsula under the Soviet umbrella. But this was not their goal. They sought unification and revolution in the south and competed with southern leftists and communists for leadership. Thus many of their activities in the first year after liberation were accomplished with an eye to the situation in the south and the demonstration effect of northern policies. This included loosing a flood of population southward across the thirty-eighth parallel, to disorder the south and effect a Trojan horse condition. Of those crossing the parallel, some were northern agents; but most were dissatisfied and resentful peasants returning from Manchuria or from northern industry to their homes in the south, or the dispossessed and their families. The effect of this massive influx was to roil southern waters—whether we speak of returning peasants or the flow of aggrieved, dispossessed privileged elements—and to polarize and radicalize southern politics.

The Soviet-sheltered regime in the north, however, was not without problems. The northern leadership was tainted by the circumstances of its birth under Soviet auspices. Although its nationalist credentials were superior to those of the American-supported Koreans, it could never escape the suggestion that without a Soviet entry a different leadership would have emerged—especially since the Korean resistance was so rich in available leaders. Furthermore, the deplorable behavior of Soviet troops in the initial weeks and months of occupation reflected badly on Koreans whom the Soviets protected. The northern dilemma was therefore how to unify and revolutionize Korea while at the same time breaking the Soviet grip and shedding its influence.

Thus 1947 dawned with the north looking expectantly southward, the south looking warily northward, the Soviets sitting contentedly on the major fruits of their minor struggle, and the Americans seeking to retrieve honor, prestige, and a stable south from the edge of an abyss. This volume can be concluded with some last reflections on American policies toward Korea.

From its beginnings in 1943, American policy was afflicted with contradictions, within and without. President Roosevelt thought Korea would fit his plans for postwar, multilateral trusteeships nicely, but State Department and military experts thought actual occupation might be necessary to secure American interests in Korea; Korean nationalists protested even the suggestion of a delay in declaring their homeland independent. In August 1945 these contradictions were not resolved but were instead made manifest in the de facto partition of Korea into Soviet and American spheres, while maintaining trusteeship as the goal of American policy. By the time the Americans finally laid a trusteeship proposal on the table before the Soviets in December 1945, however, the Occupation had done so much policy making of its own that the Moscow agreements could not be implemented. The momentum to force events and define positions was in the hands of those on the scene in Seoul, which left those in Washington far behind and out of touch. State Department policy in 1945 and 1946 often had a considered and thoughtful aspect to it, but it was usually months behind the course of events in Korea.

The liberal internationalism of Roosevelt and of certain State Department officials concerned with Korea, such as John Carter Vincent, foundered upon its inability to guarantee the interests either of the United States or of the Koreans whom the United States supported. The internationalist focus on restoring the world economy, reinvigorating the advanced capitalist nations, encouraging the free flow of trade, and liberalizing the domestic structure of countries under American influence was opposed at home and abroad. American anticommunists seized on the apparent acquiescence of Roosevelt and others to Soviet gains in Eastern Europe as yet more evidence of FDR's perfidy stretching back to the New Deal and urged instead a forceful resistance or even a rolling back of communist gains. Within Korea, conservative anticommunists thought that any sort of coalition with the Left, or multilateral arrangement involving the Soviets, would mean sacrificing their interests; they too urged resistance and rollback policies. Essentially, the question for postwar American policy was how to respond to the vigor and strength of communism; between internationalists like Vincent and nationalists like Hodge, this was often a question of means rather than ends. Thus both internationalists and rollback advocates could find a good compromise position in the containment policy. It was a low-risk strategy, which left open the possibility either of accommodating communism in a new global order or pushing it back. Containment was the point at which Korean and American opponents of internationalist policy and its supporters could meet. It is where they did meet, although for one like Syngman Rhee this was only a temporary compromise, a postponement of his preferred strategy, rollback.

The containment policy achieved a fundamental accommodation of disparate views—nationalists versus internationalists, liberals versus conservatives, realists versus rollback advocates—and brought together individuals such as Hodge and Vincent, placing common ground between them. This accommodation dates from early 1946, the critical period in the development of the Cold War; it was also, in the Korean case, the time when Washington fell in behind Seoul. The very serious policy differences between the State Department planners in Washington and those on the scene in Korea that marked the first months of occupation could be bridged because Americans differed not in their opposition to revolution in Korea, but on the question of how to deal with it.

In Korea the containment compromise was forced early, however, through activist, preemptive, even insubordinate actions of Americans in the Occupation. The *endiguement* mentality of Hodge and others sought to make the south a bulwark against communism in the north and revolution at home. The problem was that in the first year of occupation the ostensible bulwark was a frail and leaky edifice, necessitating constant plugging of holes and fissures and effecting a deep politicization of the entire American effort. Hodge made do with whatever was available, but his actions struck those in Washington as unseemly and even subversive at times. Hodge manned the ramparts, however, and was forced to act; he did not have the time for reasoned contemplation or the chance to escape responsibility. He did what he thought necessary to implement a fundamental policy shared at all levels of the American government, which maintained that control of

Korea or a part of it was essential to Pacific security and that this took precedence over the desires of Koreans. Hodge emerges not as insubordinate or blameful, but as a paradigmatic figure in the early development of the Cold War.

There is, in fact, a remarkable correspondence in the persons of John R. Hodge and Harry S Truman. Both were born within a few hundred miles of each other in the rural midwest, to similar class backgrounds. Both were thrust into their positions unexpectedly, without the usual sorts of preparation. Both were tough, blunt, no-nonsense individuals, capable of cutting through fogs of rhetoric to the essential point, and then acting. Both were honest to the core. Neither lost much love on petty tyrants like Chiang Kai-shek or Syngman Rhee, yet both ended up tied to them. Both practiced a courageous but ill-considered "decisiveness." Both thought the proper way to deal with the Russians was to "talk turkey" to them. Both had little trace of Rooseveltian internationalism, and were in fact classic nationalist and containment figures.

There were of course differences between the two. Truman was broader in outlook and more experienced politically as well as more liberal. Still, the correspondence is there, just as there was a distinct correspondence between the spectrum and limits of American politics at home and of American policies in Korea. All but a tiny handful of Americans in the Occupation could be divided between anti-Rhee (or anti-right-wing) liberals and pro-Rhee conservatives; the cleavage lines were much like those between Democrats and Republicans at home. The revolutionary content of certain SWNCC surrender policies for Korea, calling for thorough land reform, a purge of collaborators, support for labor organizing and reform, and so on, ran up against the inability of such policies to guarantee American interests or those of their Korean supporters; within weeks, or at least months, the advocates of such policies were silenced or rendered irrelevant to the process of the occupation. The revolutionary hypothesis that Korea needed a big change, or in Hodge's words should "be left to its own devices and an inevitable upheaval for its own self purification," had almost no supporters among Americans involved with Korea. Policy differences instead resolved to what mix of means might best prevent the rise of communism.

Such differences can be traced in several colloquys and memorandums that sought to explain or justify the widespread sense that the first year of occupation was rather a failure. General Hodge and Stewart Meacham, labor advisor to the commander, had a most interesting dialogue over the latter's *Labor Report*, which has been cited several times herein. Several commentaries and rejoinders were circulated by both men within the top levels of the Occupation in 1947 and 1948.[6] Meacham had, of course, advocated American support of the *Chŏn-p'yŏng* labor union and its demands for labor reform, arguing that there was no alternative to it except rightist company unions. Hodge, however, responded that Meacham's "idealistic humanitarian approach" was inappropriate to the conditions in Korea, where the United States faced "Communism in the raw" and where *Chŏnp'yŏng* had been "the most potent Communist tool." The People's Republic, which Meacham said should have been recognized by the Americans, was called by Hodge, "the southern branch of the same Communist People's Committee government that was established in North Korea by the Russians" and was directed in the south by the Soviet Consulate in Seoul. Yŏ Un-hyŏng was not the liberal that Meacham thought him to be, but "a well-indoctrinated Comintern Communist." The "1946 Revolution" (or autumn uprisings) had little to do with police repression or other issues, but was an attempt at communist revolution, as evidenced by the "primary demand" of the rioters: the reestablishment of the people's committees. Hodge thought that in truth the Koreans "had too much freedom" under the MG.

Meacham responded by saying, "It is interesting to note that the General does not deny that reaction is in the saddle in South Korea. Nor does he claim that any democratic reforms have been established that are likely to endure after we leave Korea." He then urged once again a thorough land reform, police reforms, removal of "extreme rightists" from the government, fair election procedures, all of which, if delayed, would leave the mass of Koreans no choice but communism.

Hodge's own typically unvarnished views on the first year of occupation are also available in a memorandum of his conversations with General Wedemeyer in 1947.[7] He argued that the Russians had sent trained and directed communist organizers into the south to set up people's committees and other bodies throughout the peninsula, using leaders who, because of resistance efforts against the Japanese, "became known as patriots and had considerable popularity." The Americans countered this effort by bringing in "some of the old, exiled patriots" like Rhee and Kim Ku. Unfortunately, he remarked, "these people have embarrassed our efforts more than anyone else. It is a case of those who might benefit most by American success, refusing to help us in our fight to bring democracy." Hodge suggested that such men were hoping for the final failure of Soviet-American negotiations so that they could set up "a unilateral extreme Rightists government." But the United States could not break with these men: "we will have to consider them in any future here . . . they are the bulwark against communism."

Hodge told Wedemeyer, "In my opinion, if we are going to stay over here, we are going to have to tackle the job in a big way . . . build up this area as an oasis of real democracy and sound economy." The only alternative was a face-saving withdrawal. He cited "a build-up for a civil war" in north Korea, backed by the Russians, and thought the United States would respond to such a war. He said that he and MacArthur "have a plan" to meet such a contingency; indeed in the fall of 1946, "we had the boys alerted in Japan when the revolution started. . . . They were alerted and I think they had some units actually assembled to move."

Hodge was a continual source of such candid and provocative statements, making him a sure guide to the essential nature of the Occupation. Such honesty also got him in trouble, however; many in the State Department, at the time and since, blamed something they called "the military mind" for policies that all took to be disastrous.

In 1949 the State Department compiled a study of the American liberation of Korea, which is a definitive brief for the liberal internationalist viewpoint held by many in the State Department.[8] The author argued that the Americans probably should have recognized the People's Republic, since it had established itself throughout the peninsula and since communists came to dominate it only *after* the Occupation opposed it. However, he charged, "army circles almost at once [thought] that the 'Republic' was Communist-dominated and controlled" and therefore turned to rightist groups. This, the author said, is now history: "Nevertheless, it has set the pattern for political power development in South Korea and has contributed to the difficulties involved in unification of the country." After also blaming the military for misinterpretations of trusteeship, the author went on to argue that the better path would have been the internationalist one:

> It is arguable (with hindsight) . . . that without the presence of a Soviet Army, and under a four power "trusteeship," where there would always have been three votes to one, the result might have been as in France and Italy. Such a calculated risk does not appear from the record at any time to have entered the thinking of either Washington or its representatives in Seoul.

The writer, of course, errs in suggesting that such internationalist devices were unknown in Washington; they were the whole point behind trusteeship planning beginning in 1943. More important is the suggestion that the United States might have recognized the KPR and then moved to a multilateral arrangement to unify Korea, and that this was not done because the military was "in the saddle" and understood neither the virtues of the KPR nor those of trusteeship. This argument, which I have heard many times from participants in the Occupation who were critical of American policies, suggests that better policy, fewer mistakes, and fewer military minds in important positions would have made all the difference in Korea.

This would be a cogent argument if Korea were the only place in the postwar world where allegedly mistaken policy held sway, the only place where Americans supported anyone calling himself an anticommunist. But instead it was the early exemplar of policies later followed in places as diverse as Iran, Guatemala, and Vietnam. There can be no postulation of a putative "military mind," either; this would be possible only if State Department advisors like Langdon and Benninghoff had dissented seriously from Hodge's policies. They did not. Most important, at several critical junctures in the first year, Hodge received the support of such distinguished diplomats as John J. McCloy, George Kennan, and Averell Harriman. And the internationalists did not have a more viable policy for Korea. The trusteeship policy had one great virtue: it did envision the reunification of Korea, and was the only American policy ever to take cognizance of this most fundamental of Korean demands. Otherwise such tutelary policies took little more account than did Hodge's of the realities of Korea and the desires of its people as Japanese rule came to an end. Korea was *not* France or Italy but had an entirely different history and social structure. Furthermore the suggestion that the United States might have recognized the KPR raises the question, and what then? How far down the path toward land reform, ousting collaborators, and mass mobilization would the Americans have gone? This question answers itself.

American leaders, on all sides of the issues we have discussed, were not ill-intentioned, nor were they conspirators, nor were they would-be exploiters. They were not evil men or hypocrites. They believed sincerely in what they sought to do in Korea. They were, however, historically shaped by the experience of their own country and therefore had little to offer a very different country, Korea. If they had been evil, the problem would be much simpler. That they were not expresses just how formidable were the problems of, in Louis Hartz's words, a born-free country in an unfree world.

In witnessing the consequences of occupation policy in the first year, whether in the military government or the State Department, Americans look into a mirror. The policies reflect American assumptions about people in countries like Korea, assumptions so basic as to be largely unacknowledged, so central and universal as to need no statement: that American views on society and the good life are those of all peoples; that Americans had the right to remake Korea in their own image; that American motives are beyond question. American good intentions, good will, and blithe spirits, exemplified by the gum-chewing G.I. with a candy bar always at the ready, were recognized and liked by the Koreans. But American policies, in their conception and their consequence, took no heed of Korean needs and demands for a full restructuring of colonial legacies; the best of intentions were no substitute. This was not a matter of ignorance and mistakes, but was the essence of the American failure in Korea. The first year after liberation thus provided a crucible for Americans as well as Koreans, in which a new imperium worked out the logic of its own interests.

ROSTER OF THE CENTRAL PEOPLE'S COMMITTEE
OF THE KOREAN PEOPLE'S REPUBLIC, SEPTEMBER 6, 1945

e	Age	Education	Political Experience	Imprisoned by Japanese?	Political Affiliation after Liberation
,man Rhee	70	Ph.D., U.S.	Exile/KPG		Right (NSRRKI)
Jn-hyŏng	60	Study in China	Exile/KPG; underground in Korea	Yes	Left (PP, DNF)
Hŏn	60	Meiji U. lawyer	3/1 Movement; _Shinganhoe_	Yes	Left (DNF)
Kyu-sik	64	M.A., U.S.	Exile/KPG		Right (KPG)
wan-su	41	Japan	Domestic communist	Yes	Left (KPC)
Ku	69	Classical	Exile/KPG	Yes	Right (KPG)
Sŏng-su	56	Waseda U.	Domestic nationalist		Right (KDP)
Wŏn-bong	51	Whampoa (China)	_Ŭiyŏldan_; exile/KPG		Left (DNF)
ong-sŏl					
g Nam-p'yo	57	Classical	3/1 Movement; domestic communist	Yes	Left (KCP)
Pyŏng-no	58	Meiji U. lawyer	_Shinganhoe_		Right (KDP)
Ik-hŭi	55	Waseda U.	Exile/KPG		Right (KPG)
Chae-hong	50	Waseda U.	Domestic nationalist	Yes	Right (KMT)
hu-sam					Left (KCP)
Man-sik	63	Meiji U.	3/1 Movement; domestic nationalist	Yes	Right (Chosŏn Minjudang)
Ki-jŏn					Left (DNF)
e Ik-han	50	Waseda U.	3/1 Movement; domestic communist	Yes	Left (KCP)
e Yong-dal	44	Keijo U.	Domestic communist	Yes	Left (KCP)
ang-guk	41	Keijo U.	Domestic communist	Yes	Left (KCP)

Name	Age	Education	Political Experience	Imprisoned by Japanese?	Political Affiliation after Liberat
Kim Yong-am					Left (DNF)
Kang Chin	41	China	Domestic communist	Yes	Left (KCP)
Yi Chu-ha	40	Grammar School (Korea)	Domestic communist	Yes	Left (KCP)
Ha P'il-wŏn	47	Waseda U.	Domestic communist	Yes	Left (KCP)
Kim Kye-rim					
Pak Nak-jong	47	Waseda U.	Domestic communist	Yes	Left (KCP)
Kim T'ae-jun					Left (KCP)
Yi Man-gyu		M.D./Korea	*Kŏnmaeng*		Left (PP)
Yi Yŏ-sŏng	46	Waseda U.	Domestic communist	Yes	Left (PP)
Kim Il Sung	33	Middle school (Manchuria)	Exile guerrilla; CCP China		Left (NKWl
Chŏng Paek	49	Meiji U.	Domestic communist	Yes	Left (KCP)
Kim Hyŏng-sŏn	40	Grammar school (Korea)	Domestic communist; CCP China	Yes	Left (KCP)
Yi Yŏn-yun	48	Moscow	3/1 Movement; domestic communist	Yes	Left (KCP?)
Kim Chŏm-gwŏn					Left (KCP)
Han Myŏng-ch'an			Domestic communist	Yes	Left (Kangwŏ PC leader)
Yu Ch'uk-un					Left (NKWP)
Yi Sŭng-hwa					Left (KCP)
Kang Ki-dŏk			Domestic Left; *Shinganhoe*		
Cho Tu-wŏn					
Yi Ki-sŏk	49			Yes	Left (PP)
Kim Ch'ŏl-su	54	Classical	Domestic/ Irkutsk communist	Yes	Left (KCP)
Kim Sang-hyŏk					Left (DNF)
Chŏng T'ae-sik					Left (DNF)
Chŏng Chong-gŭn					
Cho Tong-ho	51	China	Exile & domestic communist		Left (KCP)

e	Age	Education	Political Experience	Imprisoned by Japanese?	Political Affiliation after Liberation
hung-sŏk					Left (DNF)
Mun-gyu	40	Keijo U.	Domestic communist	Yes	Left (KCP)
Kwang-hŭi					Left (KCP)
Se-yong	42	Moscow/ Seoul Medical	Kŏnmaeng	Yes	Left (PP)
g Pyŏng-du					
ın-gŭn	45	Waseda U.	Domestic communist	Yes	Left (NKWP)
Chŏng	40	8th Route Army	CCP/Yenan guerrilla		Left (NKWP)
ıg Ki-uk					
ıg Chin-t'ae					
ın-gŭm	47	Waseda U.	Domestic communist	Yes	Left (KCP)
ıng-hun					
sors:					
-ch'ang	79	Classical	Signer of 3/1 Declaration	Yes	Right (NSRRKI)
n Tong-jin	84	Classical	3/1 Declaration	Yes	
Ch'ang-suk	66	Classical	Domestic nationalist	Yes	
ıg Un-yŏng			Ch'ŏndogyo		
-yŏng	77	Classical	Exile/KPG		Right (KPG)
g Myŏng-hŭi	56	Classical	3/1 Movement; early socialist	Yes	Left
Hang-gyu					
Sang-un					
ıg To-bin					
Yong-gi			Exile nationalist (Hawaii)		
Kwan-sik	58	Christian minister			
ŏng	57	China	Domestic communist	Yes	Left (KCP)

ırces: *Han'guk inmyŏng tae sajŏn,* 1967; Kim Chong-bŏm and Kim Tong-un, *Haebang hu ŭi Chosŏn chinsang,* pp. 169-218; Kim-O-song, *Chidoja kunsang;* Scalapino and Lee, *nunism in Korea,* v. I; Dae-sook Suh, *Korean Communist Movement;* USAMGIK, G-2 sec- "G-2 Biographies," XXIV Corps Historical File; USAMGIK, G-2 section, "Biographies of ı Korean Leaders"; and Yi Man-gyu, *Yŏ Un-hyŏng t'ujaeng-sa,* pp. 260-261.

To the People of Korea

The armed forces of the United States will soon arrive in Korea for the purpose of receiving the surrender of the Japanese forces, enforcing the terms of surrender, and insuring the orderly administration and rehabilitation of the country. These missions will be carried out with a firm hand, but with a hand that will be guided by a nation whose long heritage of democracy has fostered a kindly feeling for peoples less fortunate. How well and how rapidly these tasks are carried out will depend upon the Koreans themselves. Hasty and ill-advised acts on the part of its residents will only result in unnecessary loss of life, desolation of your beautiful country and delay in its rehabilitation. Present conditions may not be as you would like them. For the future of Korea, however, remain calm. Do not let your country be torn asunder by internal strife. Apply your energies to peaceful pursuits aimed at building up your country for the future. Full compliance with these instructions will hasten the rehabilitation of Korea and speed the day when the Koreans may once again enjoy life under a more democratic rule.

John R. Hodge
Commanding General
U.S. Army Forces in Korea
(2 September 1945)

To: Kim Kyu Shik   Cabinet Members of
    Kim Koo   Korean Provisional Government
    Shin Ik Hee   at Chungking, China
From: Wun Sai Hoon
    Cho Byung Ok   14 September 1945

Your Excellencies:

I write now with historic excitement. We congratulate you on the victory of our race and offer thanks for your efforts.

We write you about conditions after the surrender of Japan, for your information.

Since the Japanese surrender the people have been in ectacy [*sic*], but, there has come a political confusion. It is the most important problem to concentrate the powers and movements of the people on foundation of New Korea, and to organize an able government to meet the expectations of the people.

Political confusion above mentioned is due to two reasons. The one is the difference of policies between U.S. and Russia, on carrying out the Cairo Declaration. The other is Japanese power still remains here, for example, Japanese Government tried to organize such pro-Japanese Government through Lyo [that is, Yŏ Un-hyŏng] as comparable to those of China and Philippines. Lyo has organized so-called Korean Foundation Committee, and founded so-called Korean People's Republic, deceiving the people. Since Russian Army occupied North Korea, they have been agitating the masses to Communism.

After U.S. Army occupied Seoul, we, nationalists, organized Democrat Party [KDP] and made known our platform and schedule. And now we are prepared for People's General Meeting. If Russian Army is evacuated from North Korea, we may be supported by whole nation.

But the situation is serious now. Therefore, you, Korean Provisional Government should come back here rapidly to meet the expectation of the people.

Please write us on articles as follows:

1. The date you are to come to Seoul.
2. How we should meet you.
3. How we can make known your return to the people.

SOURCE: American G-2 translation from the original Korean; in XXIV Corps Historical File.

POLITICAL, POPULATION, AND AGRARIAN DATA
BY COUNTY, ALL SOUTH KOREA

County	Population Change 1930-1940 Percent	1930-1946 Percent	1944-1946 Percent	Tenancy Rate* Percent	Percent Land in Paddy†	Ra V
South Chŏlla						
Kwangsan	−2.3	+21	+14	72	60-70	
Tamyang	−3.5	+24	+20	72	60-70	
Koksŏng	−7.5	+20	+14	72	60-70	
Kurye	−6.2	+19	+19	80	70-80	
Kwangyang	+4.0	+31	+22	80	70-80	
Yŏsu	+25	+59	+16	60	40-50	
Sunch'ŏn	+7.4	+41	+22	80	70-80	
Kohŭng	+22.5	+43	+13	68	50-60	
Posŏng	+4.0	+36	+22	80	70-80	
Hwasun	−1.9	+14	+10	68	50-60	
Changhŭng	+10.3	+36	+19	80	70-80	
Kangjin	+10.1	+45	+19	80	70-80	
Haenam	+23.1	+51	+14	68	50-60	
Yŏng'am	+8.3	+42	+20	72	60-70	
Muan	+2.2	+29	+15	68	50-60	
Naju	+5.4	+41	+22	72	60-70	
Hamp'yŏng	+9.7	+44	+17	68	50-60	
Yŏnggwang	+9.6	+30	+.7	na	na	
Changsŏng	+2.5	+27	+17	72	60-70	
Wando	+20	+37	+10	72	60-70	
Chindo	+5.7	+26	+15	60	40-50	
North Chŏlla						
Wanju	−14.6	+34	+18	90+	60-70	
Chin'an	−3.7	+5	+16	70	40−	
Kŭmsan	+1.2	+23	+15	75	40-50	
Muju	−7.4	+23	+26	75	40-50	
Changsu	−6.9	+23	+23	80	60-70	
Imsil	−5.5	+15	−19	78	50-60	
Namwŏn	−2.0	+23	+23	83	70-80	
Sunch'ang	+.5	+22	+20	80	60-70	
Koch'ang	+8.2	+34	+13	78	50-60	

County	Population Change 1930-1940 Percent	1930-1946 Percent	1944-1946 Percent	Tenancy Rate* Percent	Percent Land in Paddy†	Radical Value‡
∢n	+5.0	+47	+22	80	60-70	2
∩je	+6.8	+49	+27	90	70-80	6
ku	−10.9	+17	+22	85	80-90	9
∢n	+5.9	+54	+26	90	70-80	6
ŏngŭp	+4.0	+46	+27	90	60-70	5
∢ Kyŏngsang						
∢nyang	−11.6	+28	+39	65	80-90	17
yŏng	−8.5	+63	+73	61	60-70	17
man	−0.3	+59	+49	61	60-70	19
∢angnyŏng	−2.8	+45	+37	59	50-60	6
∢yang	−3.8	+43	+33	63	70-80	2
∩gsan	−4.4	+28	+32	63	70-80	17
∢an	+0.5	+37	+31	63	70-80	5
ngnae§	−10.9	−32	+26	63	70-80	14
∩hae	+4.2	+61	+39	65	80-90	14
∢angwŏn	−3.4	+43	+37	63	70-80	19
∩ngyŏng	+13.2	+34	+17	61	60-70	9
∢ŏng	+1.2	+39	+33	61	60-70	9
h'ŏn	+10.4	+75	+42	61	60-70	5
∩hae	+12.3	+31	+24	61	60-70	3
dong	−5.5	+36	+31	65	80-90	16
∢ch'ŏng	−7.8	+33	+36	61	60-70	6
myang	−2.7	+29	+20	61	60-70	6
ch'ang	−6.4	+32	+28	61	60-70	6
ŏpch'ŏn	−11.0	+35	+36	61	60-70	6
∢ Kyŏngsang						
∢sŏng	−34.7	−12	+21	60	60-70	15
nhwi	−8.5	+19	+25	57	50-60	10
∢ŏng	−3.9	+31	+30	57	50-60	15
dong	−4.1	+27	+18	54	40−	13
∢ŏngsong	−19.8	+4	+19	54	40−	12
∩gyang	−12.2	+0.2	+9	54	40−	6
∩gdŏk	+10.1	+20	+7	57	50-60	6
∩g'il	+1.5	+34	+19	57	50-60	10
ŏngju	−2.5	+24	+16	60	60-70	19
∩gch'ŏn	−6.1	+30	+26	60	50-60	12
ŏngsan	−0.5	+49	+31	60	50-60	12
∢ŏngdo	−9.0	+23	+32	60	60-70	10
∢yŏng	−7.9	+28	+38	60	60-70	10
∩gju	−5.9	+27	+26	60	60-70	10
∢ilgok	+1.8	+36	+30	60	60-70	16

County	Population Change 1930-1940 Percent	1930-1946 Percent	1944-1946 Percent	Tenancy Rate* Percent	Percent Land in Paddyt	R. V.
Kŭmch'ŏn	−2.0	+30	+25	60	60-70	
Sŏnsan	+2.7	+31	+21	60	60-70	
Sangju	+2.6	+30	+25	60	60-70	
Mun'gyŏng	−1.5	+36	+25	56	40-50	
Yech'ŏn	+4.0	+31	+23	57	50-60	
Yŏngju	+3.9	+41	+18	57	50-60	
Ponghwa	+8.9	+28	+7	54	40—	
North Ch'ungch'ŏng						
Ch'ŏngwŏn	+9.6	+32	+13	70	50-60	
Poŭn	−14.7	+9	+18	65	40-50	
Okch'ŏn	−4.1	+12	+13	58	40-50	
Yŏngdong	−2.3	+31	+25	67	50-60	
Chinch'ŏn	−4.9	+35	+23	78	50-60	
Koesan	−5.4	+19	+16	62	40-50	
Ŭmsŏng	+8.5	+31	+15	72	50-60	
Ch'ungju	+8.6	+29	+11	76	40-50	
Chech'ŏn	−0.1	+27	+10	68	40—	
Tanyang	−17.7	+16	+7	66	40—	
South Ch'ungch'ŏng						
Yŏn'gi	+7.0	+34	+17	74	60-70	
Taedŏk	−15.7	+4	+12	68	40-50	
Kongju	+3.9	+30	+16	74	60-70	
Nonsan	+4.4	+43	+24	76	70-80	
Puyŏ	+7.6	+34	+16	76	70-80	
Poryŏng	+8.4	+31	+13	74	60-70	
Ch'ŏngyang	+15.5	+27	+8	74	60-70	
Hongsŏng	+13.1	+40	+13	72	50-60	
Yesan	+14.0	+35	+13	72	50-60	
Sŏsan	+10.4	+33	+10	72	50-60	
Tangjin	+11.7	+41	+15	74	60-70	
Asan	+13.8	+45	+17	74	60-70	
Ch'ŏnan	+23.3	+52	+15	72	50-60	
Sŏch'ŏn	+12.6	+43	+15	76	50-60	
Kyŏnggi						
Koyang§	−39.2	−19.6	+21	85	60-70	
Kwangju	+8.0	+23	+6	80	na	
Yangju	+13.4	+46	+15	81	50-60	
P'och'ŏn	+8.9	−7	−23	73	40-50	
Kap'yŏng	+10.6	+61	+5	61	40-50	
Yangp'yŏng	+6.2	+11	+8	73	50-60	
Yŏju	+7.1	+25	+7	77	60-70	
Ich'ŏn	+12.6	+40	+11	80	60-70	

County	Population Change 1930-1940 Percent	1930-1946 Percent	1944-1946 Percent	Tenancy Rate* Percent	Percent Land in Paddy†	Radical Value‡
ıgin	+1.7	+17	+8	80	60-70	6
sŏng	+9.6	+34	+12	81	60-70	2
ŏngt'aek	+9.1	+26	+6	79	60-70	9
vŏn	+9.1	+33	+9	75	60-70	9
ŭng	−1.4	+21	+7	78	60-70	6
:h'ŏn	−16.9	+8	+9	78	50-60	2
np'o	+14.8	+31	+5	80	70-80	2
ıghwa	+16.3	+33	+9	63	70-80	2
ju	+10.6	+61	+33	81	60-70	2
ıngdan	−4.0	−39	−40	80	50-60	2
:p'ung	+1.1	−5	−13	85	50-60	2
ıbaek	+33	+60	+5	81	na	0
gjin	+34	+81	+22	60	na	0

ıngdan, Pyŏksŏng: portions south of 38th parallel not counted in 1946 census

County						
vŏn						
unsŏng	+19.8	+42	+4	55	40—	2
ıgnŭng	+41.4	+93	+40	63	50-60	19
ıch'ŏk	+44.4	+88	+8	55	40—	19
in	+19.0	+37	+14	55	40—	9
ıngsŏn	−6.9	+5	+9	55	40—	0
ŏngch'ang	+9.6	+21	+1	55	40—	2
ıgwŏl	+14.3	+36	+2	55	40—	2
ıju	+6.8	+41	+23	55	40—	2
:ngsŏng	+6.5	+31	+11	55	40—	2
ıgch'ŏn	+13.2	+88	+52	55	40—	2

:, Yangyang: portions south of 38th parallel not counted in 1946 census

County						
Island	+0.5	+34	+26	35	na	20

.ces: All population data drawn from official Japanese censuses of 1930, 1940, and 1944; om USAMGIK census in 1946.

unty figures arrived at by using known provincial tenancy parameters and known differ-
in tenancy depending on percentage of arable land in paddy and dry fields; rates for
gi and N. Ch'ungch'ŏng counties are actual ones given in *Chosŏn kyŏngje nyŏnbo 1948*,
cial section, pp. 56-57, 76-77.

sed on information in Koo, *Study of Regional Characteristics of Korean Agriculture*, as-
; that paddy percentages did not vary greatly from 1945 to early 1960s.

lue arrived at by giving 2 units for a non-governing people's committee, 3 for a Red Peas-
ıion in 1930s, 6 for a governing people's committee, 8 for evidence of rebellion in the au-
uprisings in 1946, and 10 for counties judged particularly rebellious. Cheju Island, a
 case having an RPU, a governing PC for three years, and a major insurgency beginning
3, was given the highest value of 20 for its two counties (data for the island are aggre-
for both counties).

ınties eliminated from comparisons of population and radicalism because presence of
cities makes population data useless.

NOTES TO PREFACE

1. Harry S Truman, *Years of Trial and Hope* (New York: Signet Books, 1956), p. 379; two pages later Truman states that the Russians "were obviously testing us" in Korea. Secretary of State Dean Acheson's view on the genesis of the war is similar, although less bluntly stated. See *Present at the Creation: My Years in the State Department* (New York: Signet Books, 1969), pp. 527-528.

2. David Rees, *Korea: The Limited War* (New York: St. Martin's Press, 1964), p. 19; Adam Ulam, *The Rivals: America and Russia since World War II* (New York: Viking Press, 1971), p. 166.

3. Glenn Paige, *The Korean Decision* (New York: The Free Press, 1968); see p. 66.

4. I. F. Stone, *The Hidden History of the Korean War* (New York: Monthly Review Press, 1952, 1970). On p. 44, Stone writes:

> Could it be that for so minor a prize as South Korea the Russians were prepared to pay so high a price? Was the war Stalin's blunder? Or was it MacArthur's plan? Did the attack begin from the North? Or could it be that . . . the Northern attack was deliberately provoked by minor forays from the South? . . . The hypothesis that invasion was encouraged politically by silence, invited militarily by defensive formations, and finally set off by some minor lunges across the border when all was ready would explain a great deal.

5. Robert R. Simmons has made an important advance in arguing for the civil and nationalist character of the war; in *The Strained Alliance: Peking, P'yŏngyang, Moscow, and the Politics of the Korean Civil War* (New York: The Free Press, 1975), pp. 102-110, he traces the northern decision to attack to factional conflicts within the leadership. Robert A. Scalapino and Chong-sik Lee, in *Communism in Korea* I (Berkeley: University of California Press, 1972), pp. 394-398, seem to argue that the USSR aided and abetted the attack but that a tiny handful of North Korean leaders hatched the actual plan for and timing of the initial assaults in the early weeks of June, keeping it secret from nonmilitary officials, including cabinet members. The authors also note that "many aspects of the decision to invade are still shrouded in mystery." Joyce Kolko and Gabriel Kolko are among the very few who understand the civil genesis of this war, going back several years, although they too tend to focus their narrative on the weeks and months preceding June 1950. See *The Limits of Power: The World and U.S. Foreign Policy, 1945-1954* (New York: Harper & Row, 1972), pp. 565-599.

6. I use the terms Right and Left throughout the text, for a number of reasons. First, Koreans at the time and the Korean literature since use them. Second, the American Occupation came to describe the Korean political spectrum in like manner. Third, there are no better terms that will provide a convenient shorthand to describe political conflict. Finally, the reader will not be unduly

misled if he pays attention to the substance of political programs of each side as the narrative proceeds.

NOTES TO CHAPTER ONE

Class and State

1. There is, of course, no need to conjure such views. See the representative examples cited in Andrew J. Grajdanzev, *Modern Korea* (New York: Institute of Pacific Relations, 1944), ch. 3. Of particular note is George Kennan's (a relative of the prominent postwar strategist George Kennan) "Korea: A Degenerate State," *Outlook* (October 7, 1905). Kennan writes:

   The first impression that the Korean people make upon an impartial and unprejudiced newcomer is strongly and decidedly unfavorable. In the fantastic and unbecoming dress of the Ming Dynasty, which they all wear, they look so much like clowns in a circus. . . . [the laborers] do not compare at all favorably with the neat, alert, industrious laborers of Japan. Generally speaking, the whole Korean population seems to be lacking in dignity, intelligence, and force. . . . They are the rotten product of a decayed Oriental civilization (quoted in Grajdanzev, p. 35).

2. Perry Anderson, *Lineages of the Absolutist State* (London: New Left Books, 1974), pp. 412-420; and John W. Hall, "Feudalism in Japan—A Reassessment," in John W. Hall and Marius B. Jansen, *Studies in the Institutional History of Early Modern Japan* (Princeton: Princeton University Press, 1968), pp. 15-51.

3. See, among others, Thomas C. Smith, *The Agrarian Origins of Modern Japan* (Stanford: Stanford University Press, 1959); Barrington Moore, Jr., *Social Origins of Dictatorship and Democracy: Lord and Peasant in the Making of the Modern World* (Boston: Beacon Press, 1966), pp. 228-254; and Anderson, *Lineages*, p. 415. To say that Japan's response was "quick" does not necessarily imply that it was successful. Estimations of success depend on a time frame. Koreans did not find the price they paid for such success acceptable; Americans, Chinese, and others did not appreciate the costs in the 1930s and 1940s; and Japanese peasants perhaps never wished to pay the price that Meiji exacted from them. On this point, see Moore, *Social Origins*, p. 271; and John Dower, "E. H. Norman, Japan, and the Uses of History," in E. H. Norman, *Origins of the Modern Japanese State*, ed. John Dower (New York: Pantheon Books, 1975), pp. 3-101.

4. Jon Halliday, *A Political History of Japanese Capitalism* (New York: Pantheon Books, 1975), p. 22; and Frances V. Moulder, *Japan, China, and the Modern World-Economy* (New York: Cambridge University Press, 1977), pp. 96-97, and *passim*. Moulder, in my view, places inordinate weight on degrees of incorporation into the world system as an explanation for the divergent paths taken by China and Japan after the intrusion of the West. E. H. Norman first used the term "breathing space" to capture Japan's opportunity in the decades after Meiji (see *Origins of the Modern Japanese State*, p. 153). On the world system in general, as it is conceived in this chapter, see Immanuel Wallerstein, *The Modern World-System: Capitalist Agriculture and the Origins of the European World Economy in the Sixteenth Century* (New York:

Academic Press, 1974); and Daniel Chirot, *Social Change in the Twentieth Century* (New York: Harcourt Brace Jovanovich, 1977), esp. chs. 3 and 4.

5. See Wallerstein, *The Modern World-System*, pp. 73-74.

6. Movement abroad was no more than a suggestion until the 1890s, although one that was the focus of intense debate after Meiji. The standard work on Korea as it figured in these debates is Hilary Conroy, *The Japanese Seizure of Korea, 1868-1910* (Philadelphia: University of Pennsylvania Press, 1960); Conroy deemphasizes economic motivation in Japan's eventual annexation of Korea. For a cogent alternative view, see Wonmo Dong, "Japanese Colonial Policy and Practice in Korea, 1905-1945: A Study in Assimilation" (Ph.D. dissertation, Georgetown University, 1965), esp. ch. 2.

7. Various scholars have recently debated whether Japan's modernization came "from above," with a strong role for the state, or "from below." See Thomas C. Smith, "Pre-Modern Economic Growth: Japan and the West," *Past and Présent*, no. 60 (August 1973), pp. 127-160. This article somewhat revises Smith's views as stated in *Political Change and Industrial Development in Japan: Government Enterprise, 1868-1880* (Stanford: Stanford University Press, 1955), esp. p. 102. See also Hugh Patrick, "Japan, 1868-1914," in Rondo Cameron, ed., *Banking in the Early Stages of Industrialization* (New York: Oxford University Press, 1967), esp. pp. 241-242, 249, 288; Kozo Yamamura, *A Study of Samurai Income and Entrepreneurship* (Cambridge: Harvard University Press, 1974), pp. 137-162; and Yamamura's somewhat revised position, placing emphasis on the Meiji state's military expenditures as a technological foundation for industrialization, in "Success Illgotten? The Role of Meiji Militarism in Japan's Technological Progress," *Journal of Economic History* 2, no. 1 (March 1977), 113-136. I am indebted to Kenneth Pyle for some of these sources.

8. See Alexander Gerschenkron, *Economic Backwardness in Historical Perspective* (Cambridge: Harvard University Press, 1962), ch. 1, esp. p. 14. David Landes argues that the Gerschenkron thesis is apt for Japan, in "Japan and Europe: Contrasts in Industrialization," in William W. Lockwood, ed., *The State and Economic Enterprise in Japan* (Princeton: Princeton University Press, 1965), pp. 93-182. See also Smith, *Industrial Development*, esp. p. 102; Norman, *Origins of the Modern Japanese State*; and Halliday, *Japanese Capitalism*, pp. 22-61.

9. Landes, "Japan and Europe," p. 182. The Prussian influence on Japanese leaders and their conception of the state was decisive. Halliday quotes Itō Hirobumi as saying, in reference to the Prussian scholars Lorenz von Stein and Rudolph von Gneist, "By studying under two famous scholars, Gneist and Stein, I have been able to reach a general understanding of the structure of the state. . . . I can die a happy man" (*Japanese Capitalism*, p. 37). Halliday places emphasis on the Japanese state as an organizer of latent surplus in the economy, a reorganizer of the internal "political and economic (class) situation," and a mediator with the outside world (pp. 22-23, 47, 56-57).

10. Norman, *Origins of the Modern Japanese State*, pp. 457, 461. On the Meiji bureaucracy, see also Kenneth B. Pyle, "Advantages of Followership: German Economics and Japanese Bureaucrats, 1890-1925," *Journal of Japanese Studies* 1, no. 1 (Autumn 1974): 127-164, esp. 162-164. Halliday refers to the bureaucracy as "the greatest achievement of Japanese capitalism," along with, of course, the economy itself (*Japanese Capitalism*, p. 39).

11. Norman, *Origins of the Modern Japanese State*, pp. 251-256.

12. See Wallerstein, *The Modern World-System*; and Chirot, *Social Change in the Twentieth Century*.

13. Wallerstein, *The Modern World-System*, pp. 47, 72-74, 89.

14. Chirot, *Social Change in the Twentieth Century*, pp. 9-10.

15. This term is used often in Japanese scholarship; see also Michael Hechter, *Internal Colonialism: The Celtic Fringe in British National Development, 1536-1966* (Berkeley: University of California Press, 1975), pp. 30-34.

16. Halliday, *Japanese Capitalism*, p. 102.

17. Thus the best comparison with Japan's colonial enterprise might be England's internal colonization of the British Isles; cf. Hechter, *Internal Colonialism*.

18. This would certainly be true of the African colonies; perhaps the closest comparable case to Korea is the French in Vietnam, if not in all of Indochina. For the remarkable similarities between the situations in Vietnam and Korea, see Ngo Vinh Long, *Before the Revolution: The Vietnamese Peasants Under the French* (Cambridge: The MIT Press, 1973); David G. Marr, *Vietnamese Anticolonialism* (Berkeley: University of California Press, 1971); John T. McAlister, Jr., *Vietnam: The Origins of Revolution* (New York: Doubleday Anchor Books, 1971); Robert Sansom, *The Economics of Insurgency in the Mekong Delta of Vietnam* (Cambridge: The MIT Press, 1970); and Christine Pelzer White, "The Vietnamese Revolutionary Alliance: Intellectuals, Workers, and Peasants," in John Wilson Lewis, ed., *Peasant Rebellion and Communist Revolution in Asia* (Stanford: Stanford University Press, 1974), pp. 77-98.

19. See Alexander Eckstein, *China's Economic Development* (Ann Arbor: University of Michigan Press, 1975), pp. 63, 102-103; and Wallerstein, *Modern World-System*, pp. 45-47.

20. James B. Palais, "Stability in Yi Dynasty Korea: Equilibrium Systems and Marginal Adjustment," *Occasional Papers on Korea*, no. 3 (Seattle: University of Washington, 1975); and Palais, *Politics and Policy in Traditional Korea* (Cambridge: Harvard University Press, 1976).

21. Gregory Henderson, *Korea: The Politics of the Vortex* (Cambridge: Harvard University Press, 1968).

22. Palais, *Politics and Policy*, p. 2.

23. On elite continuity after the 1894 *Kabo* reforms see Kenneth Quinones, "The Impact of the Kabo Reforms upon Political Role Allocation in Late Yi Korea, 1884-1902," *Occasional Papers on Korea*, no. 4 (Seattle: University of Washington, 1975).

24. Palais, *Politics and Policy*, p. 58.

25. See for example Cho Ki-jun, *Han'guk kiŏpga-sa* [History of Korean Entrepreneurs] (Seoul: Pag'yŏng-sa, 1973), pp. 19, 45-47; also Kim Yong-mo, *Han-mal ŭi chibae-ch'ŭng* [The Ruling Stratum at the End of the Yi Dynasty] (Seoul: Han'guk munhwa yŏn'gu-so, 1972), pp. 119-132; for the comparison with China see Eckstein, *China's Economic Development*, pp. 102, 103.

26. Clifford Geertz, *Agricultural Involution: The Process of Ecological Change in Indonesia* (Berkeley: University of California Press, 1966).

27. Moore, *Social Origins*, pp. 213.

28. Henderson, *Vortex*, ch. 4. The term is exaggerated to the extent that it depicts Japanese colonialism as harsher than the European variety.

29. Ibid., p. 77; see also Grajdanzev, *Modern Korea*, pp. 43-44.

30. Henderson, *Vortex*, p. 72. The Japanese call the policy applied to Korea, 1910-1919, *budanteki tojisaku* or "military control."

31. The March First Movement (*samil undong*) is best analyzed in Frank Bald-

win, "The March 1 Movement: Korean Challenge and Japanese Response" (Ph.D. dissertation, Columbia University, 1969).

32. Smith, *Industrial Development*, p. 102.

33. Karl Moskowitz, paraphrasing Tōgō, in "The Creation of the Oriental Development Company," *Occasional Papers on Korea*, no. 2 (Seattle: University of Washington, 1975). On the strength of the colonial state, see also William W. Lockwood, *The Economic Development of Japan: Growth and Structural Change*, 2d ed. (Princeton: Princeton University Press, 1968), pp. 515-519.

34. See McAlister, *Vietnam*, pp. 47, 74; and Grajdanzev, *Modern Korea*, pp. 75-79. I am indebted to Perry Anderson for suggesting this comparison.

35. On the importance of potent bureaucratic apparatuses in facilitating or retarding revolution, see in particular Harry Eckstein, "On the Etiology of Internal War," *History and Theory*, vol. 4, no. 2 (1964).

36. Heinrich Heine, quoted in Wolfgang Schivelbusch, "Railroad Space and Railroad Time," *New German Critique*, no. 14 (Spring 1978), p. 34.

37. Eric J. Hobsbawm, *Industry and Empire* (London: Penguin Books, 1969), p. 110. See also Schievelbush, "Railroad Space and Railroad Time."

38. Gordon Wright, *Rural Revolution in France: The Peasantry in the Twentieth Century* (Stanford: Stanford University Press, 1964), p. 11.

39. George McCune, *Korea Today* (Cambridge: Harvard University Press, 1950), p. 52, quotes the Director of the Government-General Bureau of Railways as stating in 1936:
> "With the advent of Manchoukuo as the turning point, there has taken place . . . an almost phenomenal economic development, naturally followed by the spectacular growth of general transportation means. Thus the mighty trio of Government railway lines, private lines and motorcar routes, coupled with the Japan sea routes . . . has elevated the peninsula to a position more valuable as a land-bridge connecting Japan with the continents of Asia and Europe."

40. Eckstein, *China's Economic Development*, p. 119. See also Herbert P. Bix, "Japanese Imperialism and the Manchurian Economy, 1900-1931," *China Quarterly*, no. 51 (July-September 1972), p. 431; and Edwin P. Reubens, "Opportunities, Governments, and Economic Development in Manchuria, 1860-1940," in Hugh G. J. Aitken, ed., *The State and Economic Growth* (New York: Social Science Research Council, 1959), pp. 158-159.

41. See data in Irving I. Kramer, *Japan in Manchuria* (Tokyo: Foreign Affairs Association of Japan, 1954), pp. 10-11. For railway data on the 1930s in general, see South Manchuria Railway Company, *Sixth Report on Progress in Manchuria, to 1939* (Dairen, 1939), pp. 110-112.

42. F. C. Jones, *Manchuria Since 1931* (New York: Oxford University Press, 1949), p. 103. See also Kungtu C. Sun, *The Economic Development of Manchuria in the First Half of the Twentieth Century* (Cambridge: Harvard University East Asian Center Monographs, 1969), p. 64. Manchuria, and to a lesser extent Korea, were prime areas of what might be called railway imperialism. Count Witte, the tsarist finance minister, had visions of Russian penetration of Manchuria "through the agency of railroads and banks"; the Chinese Eastern Railway was one manifestation of this (Jones, *Manchuria*, p. 100). The American J. R. Morse built Korea's first railway under concession from the Korean Government in 1896 and later had substantial concessions to exploit Korean gold mines. Before setting up the SMRC, the Japanese entertained a proposal by the American railway magnate, E. H.

Harriman, to agree upon "an economic and impartial administration," a multilateral and "Open Door" means, of running the Manchurian rail system. (See Japan Times, *Economic Development of Korea and Manchuria* [Tokyo: Japan Times Publishing Co., 1923], p. 166; and Jones, *Manchuria*, p. 103.) Later on the Japanese viewed Harriman's proposal as a way to put the railway system "under American influence or control," using "Open Door" rhetoric to "shield her intentions." Had Harriman succeeded, they thought, the history of East Asia would have taken an "altogether different course." (See *The Manchoukuo Yearbook 1942* [Hsinking, Manchuria: Manchoukuo Yearbook Co., 1942], p. 596.)

43. Jones, *Manchuria*, p. 116; Sun, *The Economic Development of Manchuria*, p. 79. The SMRC also developed such industries as electricity, chemicals, steel, airplanes, and automobiles in Manchuria. In spite of these extraordinarily far-flung activities, E. B. Schumpeter found it even more unusual that such activities "had all been planned from the founding of the new state" in Manchuria (E. B. Schumpeter, ed., *The Industrialization of Japan and Manchukuo, 1930-1940* [New York: Macmillan Co., 1940], p. 400).

44. Japan Times, *Economic Development*, p. 250.

45. Jones, *Manchuria*, p. 118; and SMRC, *Sixth Report*, p. 112.

46. The SMRC used this term in its *Sixth Report*, p. 115.

47. V. T. Zaichikov, *Geography of Korea*, trans. Albert Parry (New York: Institute of Pacific Relations, 1952), pp. 82-83.

48. Ibid., p. 83.

49. R. H. Tawney, *Land and Labor in China* (1932; reprint ed., Boston: Beacon Paperback, 1966), p. 85; and State Statistical Bureau, *China: Ten Great Years* [Wei ta ti shih nien] (Peking: Foreign Languages Press, 1960), p. 144. See also Philip W. Vetterling and James J. Wagy, "China: The Transportation Sector, 1950-1971," in *People's Republic of China: An Economic Assessment* (Washington, D.C.: Joint Economic Committee, Congress of the United States, 1972), pp. 151-156, 161.

50. Vetterling and Wagy, "Transportation Sector," p. 161; Zaichikov, *Geography of Korea*, pp. 82-83.

51. Moore, *Social Origins*, pp. 458-483. See also Etienne Balazs, *Chinese Civilization and Bureaucracy* (New Haven: Yale University Press, 1964), pp. 30 and 32. The eminent Koreanist Shikata Hiroshi is quoted in Bae Yong-kwang, "The Role of Entrepreneurs in the Modernization Process of Korea," *International Conference on the Problems of Modernization in Asia* (Seoul: Asiatic Research Center, 1965), pp. 756-757, as follows:

> "At the time of the opening of Korea, there was no accumulated capital, nor any class which possessed an enterprising spirit, nor enough machines or the techniques to match large scale production. . . . There were only farmers producing rice and barley, handicraftsmen who produced at a leisurely pace, merchants handling luxuries and surplus products, and government officials who enjoyed every right and absorbed [every] surplus."

52. Moore, paraphrasing Marx, in *Social Origins*, p. 437.

53. See for example Kang Man-gil, *Chosŏn hugi sangŏp chabon ŭi paltal* [The Development of Commercial Capital in the Late Yi] (Seoul: Koryŏ taehakkyo ch'ulp'an-bu, 1973). For an analogous North Korean view see Chŏn Sŏk-dam, Hŏ Chŏng-ho, and Hong Hŭi-yu, *Chosŏn esŏ chabon chuŭi chok kwangye ŭi palsaeng* [The Growth of Capitalist Relationships in Korea] (P'yŏngyang, 1970).

54. Martina Deuchler, *Confucian Gentlemen and Barbarian Envoys: The Opening of Korea, 1875-1885* (Seattle: University of Washington Press, 1977), p. 224.
55. Ibid., pp. 4, 69.
56. Daniel Juhn, "Nationalism and Korean Businessmen under Japanese Colonial Rule," *Korea Journal* 17, no. 1 (January 1977): 4.
57. Cho, *Han'guk kiŏpga-sa*, pp. 87-107, 114.
58. Ibid., pp. 19-21.
59. Hoon K. Lee [Yi Hun-gu], *Land Utilization and Rural Economy in Korea* (Shanghai: Kelly & Walsh, 1936), p. 33. See also Grajdanzev, *Modern Korea*, p. 69.
60. Lee, *Land Utilization*, pp. 31-32.
61. Ibid., p. 195.
62. Ibid., p. 195.
63. Juhn, "Nationalism and Korean Businessmen," pp. 6-7.
64. Industrialization in Korea and Manchuria coincided with a deepening, heavy industrialization in Japan proper in the 1930s and a corresponding heightened role for the state. Until 1930 light industries such as textiles, pottery, paper, and food predominated in Japan; a desire to lessen dependence on the outside world and to underpin militarist expansion marked the move to heavy industry. The state, the banks, and the *zaibatsu* were heavily involved. (See Schumpeter, ed., *Industrialization of Japan and Manchukuo*, pp. 272, 596, 602-607, 744; and Halliday, *Japanese Capitalism*, pp. 57-58.)
65. Lockwood's term, in *Economic Development*, p. 515.
66. The Bank of Chōsen functioned as a central and a commercial bank, combining activities usually kept separate. It had a paid-up capital of 25 million yen in 1939, compared to 45 million for the Bank of Japan; its activities extended far beyond Korea, with branches throughout Manchuria after 1931. It funded industrial development in northern Korea and Manchuria and served as fiscal agent for the Kwantung Army. (See ibid., pp. 515-517; and Schumpeter, ed., *Industrialization of Japan and Manchukuo*, p. 843.) Lockwood remarked that this and other special banks were "freely employed as instruments of imperialism" throughout the colonial realm (p. 517). Although the biggest *zaibatsu* were active in Korea, newer and smaller ones such as Nissan and Noguchi found opportunity in northern Korea and Manchuria, owing to the Kwantung Army's hostility to the older houses. Nissan interests under Aikawa Yoshisuke played a dominant role in Manchurian heavy industry, while Noguchi interests "nearly monopolized" fertilizer, mining, synthetic fuel, and electric power industries in Korea. (See Schumpeter, pp. 374-375.)
67. Grajdanzev, *Modern Korea*, pp. 152-153, 204, 206, 300-303. See also Juhn, "Nationalism and Korean Businessmen," p. 8; and Jerome B. Cohen, *Japan's Economy in War and Reconstruction* (Minneapolis: University of Minnesota Press, 1949), pp. 35-36.
68. Letter of April 6, 1977, from Edwin Gragert of Columbia University, who is currently conducting research in land registration records from the colonial period. In certain villages, Koreans were providing more and bigger mortgages than were local Japanese. Information on thousands of Koreans and Japanese engaged in commerce, money-lending, etc. is available in *Chōsen shōkō taikan* [Commerce and Industry in Korea] (Seoul, 1929).
69. Cho, *Han'guk kiŏpga-sa*, pp. 25-26; see also Juhn, "Nationalism and Korean Businessmen," p. 7.

70. Cho, *Han'guk kiŏpga-sa*, p. 151; Kim Yong-mo also discusses landlords-cum-entrepreneurs in *Hanmal ŭi chibae-ch'ŭng*, pp. 132-136.

71. Cho, *Han'guk kiŏpga-sa*, pp. 159-160, 257-260; see also Juhn, "Nationalism and Korean Businessmen," p. 9.

72. Cho, *Han'guk kiŏpga-sa*, pp. 159-163.

73. Ibid., pp. 151-152.

74. Ibid., pp. 169-170.

75. Ibid., pp. 139-140, 222-223, 360-369.

76. Juhn argues that there really was no national bourgeoisie in colonial Korea, and that Kim Sŏng-su and others like him were exceptions that proved the rule ("Nationalism and Korean Businessmen," pp. 8-9).

77. See, for example, Albert Hirschman's study of certain seventeenth- and eighteenth-century European thinkers, *The Passions and the Interests: Political Arguments for Capitalism before Its Triumph* (Princeton: Princeton University Press, 1977).

78. Gerschenkron, *Economic Backwardness*, p. 24.

79. See Maurice Meisner's comments on "internal foreigners" in his "Leninism and Maoism: Some Populist Perspectives on Marxism-Leninism in China," *China Quarterly* (January-March 1971). On Korean biases against capitalism, see, for example, Sohn Pow-key et al., *The History of Korea* (Seoul: Korean National Commission for UNESCO, 1970), part VI, chs. 1 and 4. Conservatives like Cho Pyŏng-ok describe capitalism as an alien intrusion that disrupted the traditional self-sufficiency of the Korean economy (*Na ŭi hoegorok* [My Recollections], [Seoul: Min'gyo-sa, 1959], pp. 2-5). The former South Korean President, Pak Chŏng-hŭi, said capitalism was "forcefully imposed by Japanese imperialism" on Korea (*Our Nation's Path* [Seoul, 1960], p. 113).

80. Hongkee Karl, "A Critical Evaluation of Modern Social Trends in Korea" (Ph.D. dissertation, University of Chicago, 1934), p. 77. This bald Marxist rhetoric was typical of Korean intellectuals during the pre-Korean War period.

81. *International Conference on the Problems of Modernization in Asia*, proceedings (Seoul: Asiatic Research Center, 1965); relevant pages for the citations in the text are: pp. 125-126, 753, 757-763, 766-767.

82. We are reminded of Gerald Brenan's observation that the Spaniards "do not naturally distinguish between the money transactions that are practiced by every European business man and simple stealing. In these matters they have a mediaeval conscience more delicate than ours, which tells them that all sudden or unjustified gain, unless of course it comes as the will of Allah in the form of a lottery price, is a crime" (see Gerald Brenan, *The Spanish Labyrinth* [Cambridge: Cambridge University Press, 1943], p. 125).

83. Even then, capitalist virtue was conceived in service to the nation and its economic growth, rather than in private pursuits, much as the Japanese after Meiji dignified businessmen as "warriors" serving the state. On this point, see Halliday, *Japanese Capitalism*, p. 110.

84. *Chōsen tōkei nempō* [Korean statistical yearbook], 1909, cited in Sang Chul Suh, *Growth and Structural Changes in the Korean Economy, 1910-1945* (Cambridge, Mass.: Council on East Asian Studies, distributed by Harvard University Press, 1978), p. 34.

85. Eckstein, *China's Economic Development*, p. 161.

86. I-te Chen, "Japanese Colonialism in Korea and Formosa: A Comparison of its Effects upon the Development of Nationalism" (Ph.D. dissertation, University of Pennsylvania, 1968), pp. 220-223.

87. Russian worker-peasants in the early twentieth century provide a fascinating comparison with the Korean situation. See Leopold Haimson, "The Problem of Social Stability in Urban Russia, 1905-1917," *Slavic Review* 13, no. 4 (December 1964): 619-642; Theodore Von Laue, "Russian Labor between Field and Factory, 1892-1903," *California Slavic Studies* 3 (1964), pp. 33-65; and Reginald E. Zelnik, "The Peasant and the Factory," in Wayne S. Vucinich, ed., *The Peasant in Nineteenth-Century Russia* (Stanford: Stanford University Press, 1968), pp. 158-190.

88. See Hugh Borton, *Japan Since 1931: Its Political and Social Developments* (New York: Institute of Pacific Relations, 1940), pp. 111-117.

89. *Ch'in-Il p'a kunsang* [The Pro-Japanese Groups] (Seoul: Samsaeng munhwa-sa, 1948), p. 161; and *Chōsen nenkan 1945* [Korea yearbook 1945] (Keijo, Keijo nippo-sha, 1945), p. 33. See also Takashi Hatada, *A History of Korea*, trans. and ed. Warren Smith and Benjamin Hazard (Santa Barbara, California: American Bibliographical Center, 1969), p. 125.

90. *Ch'in-Il p'a kunsang*, p. 161. In Manchuria the Japanese formed "labor societies" made up of "capitulated bandits," Chinese and Korean, and put them to work in mines (see SMRC, *Sixth Report*, p. 21).

91. See *Chosŏn kyŏngje nyŏnbo 1948* [Annual Economic Review of Korea, English title] (Seoul: Chosŏn unhaeng chosa-bu, 1948), p. 111-114.

92. *Chōsen nenkan 1945*, pp. 315-317.

93. Sohn Pow-key et al., *History of Korea*, p. 324. For a critical account of wartime mobilization, thought purification, etc. in Japan itself during the war, see Ienaga Saburo, *The Pacific War: World War II and the Japanese, 1931-1945*, trans. Frank Baldwin (New York: Pantheon Books, 1978), pp. 97-128. On pp. 158-159, Ienaga also refers to a little-known aspect of the Korean mobilization:

    Korean women were also mobilized by the thousands and shipped off to the battlefronts as "comfort girls" for Japanese troops. Called Chōsenpi (*pi* was soldiers' slang for "comfort girl"), they were a sexual outlet for the soldiers. The women were brought right to the front lines for fornication between combat opreations, and apparently many were killed in the fighting.

94. Edward Willett Wagner, *The Korean Minority in Japan, 1904-1950* (Vancouver: University of British Columbia, 1951), pp. 22, 37-38.

95. Cohen, *Japan's Economy*, p. 51.

96. Huang Sung-mo, "The Role of Industrial Laborers in the Modernization of Korea," in *International Conference on the Problems of Modernization in Asia*, p. 773.

97. Cohen, *Japan's Economy*, p. 283.

98. Ibid., pp. 271, 310-325, 386.

99. Ibid., pp. 307-317.

100. See USAMGIK, 97th MG Group, "Unit History," in RG no. 407, entry no. 427, "World War II Operations Reports."

101. See Mary E. Wilkie, "Colonials, Marginals, and Immigrants: Contributions to a Theory of Ethnic Stratification," *Comparative Studies in Society and History* 19, no. 1 (January 1977): 67-96; Richard Morrock, "Heritage of Strife: The Effects of Colonial 'Divide and Rule' Strategy upon Colonized Peoples," *Science and Society* 37, no. 2 (1973): 129-151; and Immanuel Wallerstein, "The Colonial Era in Africa: Changes in the Social Structure," in Peter Duignan and L. H. Gann, eds., *The History and Politics of Colonialism,*

1914-1960 (London: Cambridge University Press, 1970), pp. 399-421. Hechter finds a "cultural division of labor" in colonies, "a system of stratification where objective cultural distinctions are super imposed upon class lines" (in- *Internal Colonialism*, p. 30).

102. Wallerstein, "The Colonial Era," p. 410; Wilkie, "Colonials, Marginals, and Immigrants," pp. 80-81. Eugene Knez, in "Sam Jong Dong: A South Korean Village" (Ph.D. dissertation, Syracuse University, 1959), pp. 46-48, writes as follows about a Korean village elder and former district chief who was the local representative of the Japanese National Cooperative League in 1942:

> He, as a village leader, had to bow to pictures of the Japanese emperor at school or any public meetings. He had to supply men for labor in Japan, the South Pacific, or elsewhere in Korea to work in factories, mines, and similar projects.

Furthermore, about fifty villagers per month were conscripted to participate in local projects of various sorts. During the period from 1942 to 1945, fifteen villagers went to Japan, most as coal miners; *all* of them returned to the village thereafter. The village leader retired at the time of liberation, citing "gastric difficulties."

103. Chen, "Japanese Colonialism," pp. 242-243. Japanese workers in the Hŭng-nam factory complex were provided with brick homes, steam heat, flush toilets, and the like, while Koreans lived in cramped, barracklike, quarters, with common toilets (see Ienaga, *Pacific War*, pp. 157-158).

104. Cohen, *Japan's Economy*, p. 33. In Manchuria, colonial policies set three peoples against each other, leading to severe outbreaks of Chinese-Korean fighting. Even postwar Chinese accounts referred to Koreans as "instruments for penetration" of Manchuria. (See Mo Shen, *Japan in Manchuria: An Analytical Study of Treaties and Documents* [Manila, 1960], pp. 269-282.) The imperial ideologue Ishiwara Kanji is quoted in Ienaga's *Pacific War*, p. 12, as having articulated in 1930 the following racial division of labor for the Japanese sphere:

> "The four races of Japan, China, Korea and Manchuria will share a common prosperity through a division of responsibilities: Japanese, political leadership and large industry; Chinese, labor and small industry; Koreans, rice; and Manchus, animal husbandry."

Ienaga remarks that Ishiwara's ideas were "no personal idiosyncrasy."

105. Dae-sook Suh, *The Korean Communist Movement, 1918-1948* (Princeton: Princeton University Press, 1967), p. 132.

106. See, for example, Marr, *Vietnamese Anticolonialism*.

107. On Korean nationalism in general, see Chong-sik Lee, *The Politics of Korean Nationalism* (Berkeley: University of California Press, 1963). The disgust that revolutionary Koreans felt for the moderate nationalists is evident in *Song of Ariran: A Korean Communist in the Chinese Revolution*, rev. ed. (San Francisco: Ramparts Press, [1941] 1974), pp. 74-78, 91-92, 114. This remarkable and valuable account was compiled by Nym Wales in Yenan in 1937-38, on the basis of interviews with Kim San (the pseudonym of Chang Chi-rak), a Korean with two decades of experience in China, including the famous but abortive Canton Commune. See also the eloquent and prescient essay by Kim Kyu-sik in Dae-sook Suh, *Documents of Korean Communism, 1918-1948* (Princeton: Princeton University Press, 1970), pp. 91-105. It is clear from these accounts and others that the moderates hoped for American intervention to liberate Korea and thus cultivated American missionaries; often

the moderates were termed the "American group." As Kim San put it, "These were all 'gentlemen.' Most of them spoke good English. They actually expected to get Korean independence by being able to speak persuasive English!" (in *Song of Ariran*, p. 114). Kim Kyu-sik's essay is an excellent example of a general trend in the early 1920s, as Korean independence fighters gave up on the United States and turned to the Soviet Union—less some notable exceptions, like Syngman Rhee, who was perhaps the most prominent of the "American group."

108. Suh, *Korean Communist Movement*, p. 132; Lee, *Politics of Korean Nationalism*, p. 4.

109. Interested readers should consult Suh, *Documents of Korean Communism*; also Robert Scalapino and Chong-sik Lee, *Communism in Korea* 1 (Berkeley: University of California Press, 1972), chs. 1-3. On Vietnam, see especially McAlister, *Vietnam*; Long, *Before the Revolution*; and White, "The Vietnamese Revolutionary Alliance."

110. The note of realism that crept into the haggling and personal power struggles of Korean communism in 1930 or so may be found in Suh, *Documents of Korean Communism*, pp. 156-167. On the Red Peasant Unions of the 1930s, see Yoo Sae Hee, "The Korean Communist Movement and the Peasantry under Japanese Rule" (Ph.D. dissertation, Columbia University, 1974). See also the accounts in Scalapino and Lee, *Communism in Korea* 1, 155-170, 195-202.

111. The formal inauguration was on March 1, 1932, the same day that the Korean resistance began in 1919.

112. *Manchoukuo Yearbook 1942*, pp. 186-189; Tunghwa Provincial Government, "Report on the Result of Reconstruction Operations (1938)." *Senbu geppō* (Pacification monthly report), vol. 4, no. 4 (April 1939), in Chong-sik Lee, *Counterinsurgency in Manchuria: The Japanese Experience, 1931-1940* (Santa Monica, Calif.: The RAND Corporation, January 1967), pp. 271-306.

113. Lee, *Counterinsurgency in Manchuria*, pp. 9-50.

114. Ienaga, *Pacific War*, pp. 89-96.

115. The term meant Eastern border district and included the prefectures of Hangjen, Chian, Kuantien, Tunghwa, Linchiang, and Ch'angpai.

116. Itagaki Teiji, "Pacification Activities in the Communist Bandit Area, Personal Reflections," *Senbu geppō*, vol. 4, no. 4 (April 1939), in Lee, *Counterinsurgency in Manchuria*, p. 239.

117. *Manchoukuo Yearbook 1942*, pp. 189-190; Schumpeter, ed., *Industrialization of Japan and Manchukuo*, pp. 319, 396.

118. *Manchoukuo Yearbook 1942*, p. 486; Hayano Masao, "Propaganda and Pacification Activities in Tungbientao," *Senbu geppō*, vol. 4, no. 4 (April 1939), in Lee, *Counterinsurgency in Manchuria*, pp. 243-244. The mean mid-winter temperature in this region is about minus 20 degrees centigrade, according to Zaichikov, *Geography of Korea*, p. 96.

119. Kirin Province Police Department, "Plan for the Special Security and Purification Operation in Huatien Prefecture," *Senbu geppō*, vol. 3, no. 7 (July 1938), in Lee, *Counterinsurgency in Manchuria*, pp. 259-260; also *Manchoukuo Yearbook 1942*, p. 190.

120. Hayano, "Propaganda and Pacification Activities," in Lee, *Counterinsurgency in Manchuria*, p. 245.

121. *Manchoukuo Yearbook 1942*, pp. 745-746.

122. Lee, *Counterinsurgency in Manchuria*, p. 14, quoting official documents. The

Concordia associations sought "the creation of a moral world through racial concord" (see *Manchoukuo Yearbook 1942*, p. 759).

123. Suh, *Korean Communist Movement*, pp. 256-293; Scalapino and Lee, *Communism in Korea* 1: 202-230. These are the best accounts of Kim's pre-1945 exploits; Scalapino and Lee lay to rest the mythology about one, two, many Kim Il-sŏngs of legendary fame. Suh's study is a landmark work, resting on extremely diligent research. One of its major conclusions, that Kim Il Sung was "totally alien" (p. 253) to a putative "mainstream" Korean communist movement, I find difficult to sustain. On this point, see Jon Halliday, "The Korean Communist Movement," *Bulletin of Concerned Asian Scholars* 2, no. 4 (Fall 1970): 98-107.

124. "Report on The Result of Reconstruction Operations (1938)," in Lee, *Counterinsurgency in Manchuria*, pp. 281-287. The report said, "It seems that Kim Il-sŏng is under the command of Yang Ching-yu, but the two are equal in actual strength. It is very likely that Kim will succeed to Yang's post in the event of the latter's disappearance" (p. 285).

125. Ibid., pp. 281-282, 285-289.

126. Suh, *Korean Communist Movement*, p. 211. For a moving account of Japanese interrogation techniques, often highly sophisticated, and the suspicions among comrades fostered by incarceration, see Nym Wales and Kim San, *Song of Ariran*, pp. 247-267.

127. "Kin Nichi-sei no katsudō jōkyō" (General Conditions of the Activities of Kim Il-sŏng), *Tokkō gaiji geppō* (November 1944), pp. 76-78; quoted in Scalapino and Lee, *Communism in Korea*, p. 227; see also Suh, *Korean Communist Movement*, p. 292. The United States Air Force began bombing runs in Manchuria in July 1944.

128. Scalapino and Lee, *Communism in Korea*, p. 220n.

129. Suh, *Korean Communist Movement*, p. 292.

130. V. Rappaport, "Guerrilla Movement in the Northern Korean Regions," *Tikhii Okean* [Pacific Ocean] (April-June 1937), translation in RG 353, Records of the State-War-Navy Coordinating Committee and the State-Army-Navy Coordinating Committee, "SWNCC 101," 1945, box no. 21. Suh, *Korean Communist Movement*, cites this article in a footnote, but does not refer to its contents. I have found no other evidence in the presurrender files of the United States State Department of American knowledge of Kim Il Sung. George McCune, however, was actively involved in presurrender planning and was the only Korean expert in the Japan Affairs Division. State Department and United States Central Intelligence Agency personnel files in the period 1945-1950 are not available to researchers at this writing; they might show whether the information on Kim was used after he assumed leadership in North Korea.

    Tikhii Okean was published from 1934 through 1938 by the Pacific Section of the Institute of World Economics and Politics in Moscow. It was, according to Thomas T. Hammond, "the last of the Soviet scholarly journals on the Far East until after World War II." (See Hammond, ed., *Soviet Foreign Relations and World Communism* [Princeton: Princeton University Press, 1965], p. 751.)

131. See Suh, *Korean Communist Movement*, p. 284n.

132. Se-jin Kim, *The Politics of Military Revolution in Korea* (Chapel Hill, N.C.: University of North Carolina Press, 1971), pp. 49-50.

133. Suh, *Korean Communist Movement*, p. 287n, cites an article on the two Kims in the *Osaka Asahi Shimbun*, July 2, 1937.
134. Kim, *Politics of Military Revolution*, p. 50.

NOTES TO CHAPTER TWO

Lord and Peasant

1. Edward Willett Wagner, *The Literati Purges: Political Conflict in Early Yi Korea* (Cambridge: Harvard University East Asian Research Center, 1974), pp. 2, 6.
2. Susan S. Shin, "Some Aspects of Landlord-Tenant Relations in Yi Dynasty Korea," *Occasional Papers on Korea*, no. 3 (Seattle: University of Washington, 1975), p. 50; see also James Palais, *Politics and Policy in Traditional Korea* (Cambridge: Harvard University Press, 1976), p. 58; and Shin Yong-ha, "Landlordism in the Late Yi Dynasty I," *Korea Journal* 18, no. 6 (June 1978): 25-32.
3. Shin, "Landlord-Tenant Relations," pp. 57-59, 73-74.
4. Ibid., pp. 68-74; Shin, "Landlordism," pp. 27-30.
5. Palais, *Politics and Policy*, p. 67.
6. Palais, in *Politics and Policy*, p. 69, cites writings by the early nineteenth-century scholar Yi Kyu-gyŏng and by late nineteenth-century officials Hŏ Pu and Kim Yun-sik, as follows:

    > In comparing contemporary Korean society with China of the Han and T'ang they acknowledged the even greater power of private property and the yangban social elite in Korean society. They concluded that the yangban were too solidly entrenched to be eliminated and that egalitarian redistribution was out of the question.

    This is a most important finding.
7. Pak Ki-hyuk and Seung Yun Lee, *Three Clan Villages in Korea* (Seoul: Yonsei University Press, 1963), pp. 34-35, 69-70.
8. Kim Yŏng-sŏp. *Chosŏn hugi nong'op-sa yŏn'gu: nongch'ŏn kyŏngje sahoe pyŏndong* [Studies in the Agrarian History of the Late Yi Dynasty: The Peasant Economy and Social Change] (Seoul: Ilcho-gak, 1971); and Kim Yŏng-sŏp, "Yang'an ŭi yŏn'gu: Chosŏn hugi ŭi nonga kyŏngje" [A Study of the Land Registers: The Economy of Peasant Households in the Late Yi Dynasty], pts. 1 and 2, *Sahak yŏn'gu* (Seoul: May and November 1960). I am indebted to James Palais for many discussions on Kim's work.
9. See Thomas C. Smith, *The Agrarian Origins of Modern Japan* (Stanford: Stanford University Press, 1959); and Barrington Moore, Jr., *Social Origins of Dictatorship and Democracy: Lord and Peasant in the Making of the Modern World* (Boston: Beacon Press, 1966), pp. 10-11, 269-271.
10. See Martina Deuchler, *Confucian Gentlemen and Barbarian Envoys: The Opening of Korea, 1875-1885* (Seattle: University of Washington Press, 1977), pp. 67, 84.
11. Palais, *Politics and Policy*, p. 58.
12. Gregory Henderson speaks of the "final elimination" of the "leadership class" of the Yi Dynasty as Japan annexed Korea; in *Korea: The Politics of the Vortex* (Cambridge: Harvard University Press, 1968), p. 77. On this point, see my review of Henderson, "Is Korea a Mass Society?" *Occasional Papers*

on Korea, no. 1 (Seattle: University of Washington, 1973). On the persistence of landholding patterns into the colonial period, see Shin, "Landlord-Tenant Relations," p. 74.

13. Kim Yong-mo, a noted student of the Korean class structure during the transition to colonialism, argues that some 74 percent of Korean landlords were *yangbans* during the early colonial period. (See "Social Background and Mobility of the Landlords under Japanese Imperialism in Korea," *Journal of Social Sciences and Humanities,* no. 31 [Seoul: Korea Research Center, June 1971], pp. 87, 91-93). See also Kim Yong-mo, *Hanmal ŭi chibae-ch'ŭng* (Seoul: Han'guk munhwa yŏn'gu-so, 1972), pp. 124-137; and Pak Ki-hyuk et al., *A Study of Land Tenure System in Korea* (Seoul: Korea Land Economics Research Center, 1966), p. 44.

14. Gunnar Myrdal, *Asian Drama: An Inquiry into the Poverty of Nations* 2 (New York: Pantheon Books, 1968): 1,033. The Japanese also had the experience of post-Meiji surveys within Japan to go on (see E. H. Norman, *Origins of the Modern Japanese State,* ed. John Dower [New York: Pantheon Books, 1975], pp. 243-259).

15. Hoon K. Lee, *Land Utilization and Rural Economy in Korea* (Shanghai: Kelly & Walsh, 1936), pp. 102-105, 137. See also *Annual Report on the Administration of Tyosen* [sic] *1937-1938* (Keijo: Government-General, 1938), pp. 37-38, 54-55.

16. On these practices during the Yi Dynasty, see Palais, *Politics and Policy,* pp. 12-14.

17. Myrdal, *Asian Drama,* p. 1,035. For a comparative case in Africa, see Elizabeth Colson, "The Impact of the Colonial Period on the Definition of Land Rights," in Victor Turner, ed., *Colonialism in Africa* 3 (London: Cambridge University Press, 1971): 193-215.

18. Edwin H. Gragert, "Some Reflections on the Land Survey of 1910-1918 and its Treatment in Korean Historiography" (paper, Columbia University Faculty Seminar on Korea, December 1973), pp. 8-9.

19. Ibid., p. 16.

20. In *Manchuria Since 1931* (New York: Oxford University Press, 1949), p. 171, F. C. Jones writes that in Manchuria "the Japanese did not attempt to touch the structure of rural society." Regarding Korean land relations, Sang Chul Suh writes that Japanese policies "did not change the old system, but had the effect of legalizing it" (*Growth and Structural Changes in the Korean Economy, 1910-1945* [Cambridge, Mass.: Council on East Asian Studies, distributed by Harvard University Press, 1978], p. 81).

21. Myrdal, *Asian Drama,* pp. 1,037-1,039.

22. Lee, *Land Utilization,* p. 159.

23. Myrdal, *Asian Drama,* p. 1,034.

24. Lee, *Land Utilization,* p. 159; and James Dale Van Buskirk, *Korea: Land of the Dawn* (New York: Missionary Education Movement, 1931), p. 70. "Part-owners" were almost always peasants whose own small plots were insufficient to feed their families, necessitating rental of additional land.

25. See, for example, In Chŏng-sik, *Chosŏn ŭi t'oji munje* [Korea's Land Question] (Seoul: Ch'ŏngsu-sa, 1946), p. 105; and Wolf Ladejinsky, *Chosen's Agriculture and Its Problems* (Washington, D.C.: U.S. Department of Agriculture, 1940), p. 111. Ladejinsky also thought that Korea's tenancy situation had "few counterparts in the world." See also Sidney Klein, *Land Tenure Reform in East Asia after World War II* (New York: Bookman Associates,

1958), pp. 85-88; and various tables in the appendices to Kobayakawa Kurō, ed., *Chōsen nōgyo hattatsu-shi* I [History of the Development of Korean Agriculture] (Keijo: Chōsen nōkai, 1944).

26. Pak, *Study of Land Tenure*, p. 66; see Myrdal, *Asian Drama*, p. 1,039, on the signal importance of population growth in giving landlords "increasing opportunity for oppression." Lee made the same point in *Land Utilization*, p. 167.

27. Lee, *Land Utilization*, p. 165; Ladejinsky, *Chosen's Agriculture*, p. 31.

28. Gragert, "Reflections on the Land Survey," p. 16; see also Kobayakawa, *Chōsen nōgyo* 1, tables 3 and 9 in appendices.

29. Lee, *Land Utilization*, pp. 163, 167; Pak, *Study of Land Tenure*, pp. 60-61; In Chŏng-sik, *t'oji munje*, pp. 63-64; Pak, *Three Clan-Villages*, p. 53.

30. Conditions in China before the 1949 revolution varied widely, and statistics are often unreliable. R. H. Tawney's study, *Land and Labor in China* (1932; reprint ed., Boston: Beacon Paperback, 1966), pp. 37, 63, would suggest, however, that the extremes of tenancy and high rent in China corresponded to the norm in Korea.

31. Lee, *Land Utilization*, pp. 233-251.

32. Ibid., p. 165; Pak, *Study of Land Tenure*, p. 47; In Chŏng-sik, *t'oji munje*, pp. 63-64.

33. *Chosŏn ilbo*, March 27, 1932, quoted in Lee, *Land Utilization*, p. 171.

34. *Annual Report, 1937-1938*, p. 218.

35. On the sharp increases in *hwajŏn* farming, especially during and after the depression, see Kobayakawa, *Chōsen nōgyo* 1, table 3 in appendices. The numbers of pure fire-field farming households increased from 38,000 to 60,000 between 1930 and 1932. On fire-field farming as a form of peasant flight, and therefore peasant protest, see Jerome Blum, *The End of the Old Order in Rural Europe* (Princeton: Princeton University Press, 1978), pp. 351-352.

36. The quotation is taken from Lee, *Land Utilization*. See also Takashi Hatada, *A History of Korea*, trans. and ed. Warren Smith and Benjamin Hazard (Santa Barbara, Calif.: American Bibliographical Center, 1969), pp. 126-127; Ladejinsky, *Chosen's Agriculture*, p. 97; and Pak, *Study of Land Tenure*, p. 47.

37. Lee, *Land Utilization*, p. 171; Andrew J. Grajdanzev, *Modern Korea* (New York: Institute of Pacific Relations, 1944), ch. 10.

38. See, for example, Cho Jae-hong, "Post-1945 Land Reforms and Their Consequences in South Korea" (Ph.D. dissertation, Indiana University, 1964), p. 20 and passim. In *My Forty Year Fight for Korea* (Seoul: Chungang University, International Culture Research Center, 1951), p. 22, Louise Yim (Im Yŏng-sin), a South Korean landlord and politician, said that on her estate in the 1930s, "The people were peaceful, kind, and gentle. Their only ambition was to make next year as good as this year. They were content with what they had." A Korean informant and relative of Kim Sŏng-su told me in our conversation of March 1973 that Kim's large number of tenants were happy and lived harmoniously under, in his words, "feudalism."

39. Based on data in Kobayakawa, *Chōsen nōgyo* 1: 62-63; the figures are for Korean and Japanese landlords in 1933, and "absenteeism" is defined as residence outside the county in which the land is held.

40. In Chŏng-sik, *t'oji munje*, p. 134.

41. Moore, *Social Origins*, p. 471; see also Barrington Moore, Jr., *Reflections on the Causes of Human Misery and upon Certain Proposals to Eliminate Them*

(Boston: Beacon Press, 1970), pp. 53-55; and Myrdal, *Asian Drama*, p. 1,039. Jeffrey Race has elaborated on reciprocal exchange relations between lord and peasant in his important article, "Toward an Exchange Theory of Revolution," in John W. Lewis, ed., *Peasant Rebellion and Communist Revolution in Asia* (Stanford: Stanford University Press, 1974), pp. 196-197.

42. Jeffrey M. Paige, *Agrarian Revolution* (New York: Free Press, 1975), pp. 304-305.

43. Ladejinsky, *Chosen's Agriculture*, p. 114; see also Klein, *Land Tenure Reform*, pp. 17-18. Nowhere in the literature is the case made that Korean landlords were enterprising types.

44. United States Army Military Government in Korea, Department of Agriculture, *Present Agriculture Position of South Korea* (Seoul, 1947), p. 3.

45. Suh, *Growth and Structural Changes*, pp. 84-85, 96.

46. Myrdal, *Asian Drama*, p. 1,039. Lee made essentially the same point about Korean landlords in *Land Utilization*, p. 167.

47. See Robert Sansom, *Economics of Insurgency in the Mekong Delta of Vietnam* (Cambridge: The MIT Press, 1970), pp. 18-46; Paige, *Agrarian Revolution*, pp. 19-23, 304-306, 318; and Samuel L. Popkin, *The Rational Peasant* (Berkeley: University of California Press, 1979), ch. 4.

48. Karl Polanyi, *The Great Transformation* (Boston: Beacon Press, 1967), p. 71.

49. Myrdal, *Asian Drama*, p. 1,031.

50. See Robert Redfield's well-known distinction between farmers and peasants in *Peasant Society and Culture* (1956; reprint ed., Chicago: University of Chicago Press, 1960), pp. 18-19. On Korea, see Lee, *Land Utilization*, p. 97.

51. Teodor Shanin, "A Russian Peasant Household at the Turn of the Century," in Shanin, ed., *Peasants and Peasant Societies* (Baltimore: Penguin Books, 1971), p. 30. See a similar definition of peasants as "rural cultivators whose surpluses are transferred to a dominant group of rulers," in Eric Wolf, *Peasants* (Englewood Cliffs, N.J.: Prentice-Hall, Inc., 1966), pp. 3-4.

52. Tawney, *Land and Labor*, p. 77.

53. George M. Foster, "Peasant Society and the Image of Limited Good," *American Anthropologist*, no. 67 (April 1965), pp. 293-315.

54. The relevant works are Moore, *Social Origins*; Eric Wolf, *Peasant Wars of the Twentieth Century* (New York: Harper & Row, 1969); and Paige, *Agrarian Revolution*. See also Andrew Pearse, "Metropolis and Peasant: The Expansion of the Urban-Industrial Complex and the Changing Rural Structure," in Shanin, ed., *Peasants and Peasant Societies*, pp. 69-80. On the coming of the market in Japan, see Smith, *Agrarian Origins of Modern Japan*.

55. Karl Marx, *Pre-Capitalist Economic Formations*, introduction by Eric J. Hobsbawn (New York: International Publishers, 1965), pp. 67, 105, 106, 110-111, and Hobsbawn's introduction, pp. 30-46. See also relevant passages in Karl Marx, *Capital* I, pt. VII, "The So-called Primitive Accumulation" (New York: International Publishers, 1967). See also Maurice Dobb, *Studies in the Development of Capitalism* (New York: International Publishers, 1947, 1963), ch. 5; and Blum, *Rural Europe*, pp. 438-441.

56. Polanyi, *Great Transformation*, p. 3. I am indebted to James Kurth for several stimulating discussions on Polanyi's work.

57. Ibid., pp. 40-47, 62-76.

58. Ibid., pp. 159-160, 178-180.

59. Marx, *Capital* I: 716.

60. Moore, *Social Origins*, esp. pp. 419-432.

61. On the importance of irrigated rice production and the export market in Vietnam, see Sansom, *The Economics of Insurgency in the Mekong Delta*, pp. 18-52; Paige, *Agrarian Revolution*, pp. 62, 278-282. See also the important article by Arthur L. Stinchcombe, "Agricultural Enterprise and Rural Class Relations," *American Journal of Sociology*, no. 67 (September 1961), pp. 165-176.

62. Jerome B. Cohen, *Japan's Economy in War and Reconstruction* (Minneapolis: University of Minnesota Press, 1949), p. 369; Grajdanzev, *Modern Korea*, p. 93; and Lee, *Land Utilization*, pp. 134, 161.

63. Tobata Seiichi and Toshitaro Morinaga, eds., *Beikoku keizai no kenkyu* [Studies on the Rice Economy] (Tokyo, 1939), p. 379. I am indebted to Michael Donnelly for this source.

64. Cohen, *Japan's Economy*, p. 369.

65. Suh, *Growth and Structural Change*, pp. 88, 95.

66. Jeffrey Paige's work, *Agrarian Revolution*, helped me clarify my thoughts in this section (see pp. 21-25, 42-45, 57-59).

67. Hobsbawm, introduction to Marx, *Pre-Capitalist Economic Formations*, p. 46.

68. On this point, see Popkin, *Rational Peasant*, pp. 33-34, 73-82.

69. Lee, *Land Utilization*, pp. 257-261.

70. Suh, *Growth and Structural Changes*, pp. 79-81.

71. Glenn Trewartha and Wilbur Zelinsky, "Population Distribution and Change in Korea, 1925-1949," *The Geographical Review* 45, no. 1 (January 1955): 14. See also Hong Kyung-hi, "Han'guk ŭi toshihwa" [Korean Urbanization], pts. 1 and 2, *Kyŏngbuk University Theses* 6-7 (Seoul, 1962): 287-325, 355-381. I am indebted to Joseph Nowakowski for providing me with this source.

72. Irene B. Taeuber estimated that in 1940, 9 percent of all Koreans still in Korea were living in a province other than that in which they were born. In the age group 20 to 34, the proportion was 13 percent (see *The Population of Japan* [Princeton, Princeton University Press, 1958], p. 188).

73. *Chosŏn kyŏngje nyŏn'gam, 1948*, pp. III, 19-20; *Chosŏn t'onggye nyŏn'gam, 1943*, pp. 2, 16-22; Suh, *Growth and Structural Changes*, p. 135.

74. Suh, *Growth and Structural Changes*, p. 187; see also Hong, "Han'guk ŭi toshihwa," pp. 300-314.

75. Hatada, *History of Korea*, p. 114; see also Lee, *Land Utilization*, p. 273.

76. Edward Willett Wagner, *The Korean Minority in Japan, 1904-1950* (Vancouver: University of British Columbia, 1951), pp. 9-10; also Suh, *Growth and Structural Changes*, p. 93.

77. Taeuber, *Population of Japan*, p. 187. Jones, in *Manchuria*, pp. 69-71, writes that most Korean immigrants to Manchuria were rice farmers; the remainder included shopkeepers, "coolies," petty traders, servants, brothel owners, and the like. The Korean population grew from 800,000 in 1931 to 2 million by 1945. See also SMRC, *Sixth Report*, pp. 130-135. The Japanese population in Manchuria never was larger than 1 million.

78. Taeuber, *Population of Japan*, pp. 187, 193, 197.

79. The figures are taken from Trewartha and Zelinsky, "Population Distribution." See also Hong, "Han'guk ŭi toshihwa," pp. 292-294, 298.

80. Trewartha and Zelinsky, "Population Distribution," pp. 19-20; see also Irene B. Taeuber, "The Population Potential of Postwar Korea," *Far Eastern Quarterly* 5, no. 3 (May 1946): 304.

81. Hong, "Han'guk ŭi toshihwa," p. 289; see also Myrdal, *Asian Drama*, pp. 1,104-1,107; E. J. Berg, "Backward-Sloping Labor Supply Functions in Dual

Economies—the African Case," in Immanuel Wallerstein, ed., *Social Change: The Colonial Situation* (New York: John Wiley & Sons, 1966), pp. 114-136, esp. pp. 116-118; and E. P. Skinner, "Labour Migration and its Relationship to Socio-cultural Change in Mossi Society," in Wallerstein, ed., *Social Change*, pp. 137-157, esp. pp. 140-141. Of particular importance, as Skinner notes, is the young age of most colonial migrants (16-30 age group). This was as true of Korea as of Africa.

82. Wagner, *Korean Minority*, pp. 12, 27. See Wagner's table on the occupational distribution of Koreans in Japan in 1936 and 1941, p. 94; see also the figures in Hong, "Han'guk ŭi toshihwa," p. 369.

83. Wagner, *Korean Minority*, pp. 43, 96; and Hong, "Han'guk ŭi toshihwa," p. 369.

84. For a useful recent article on labor migration, see Alejandro Portes, "Migration and Underdevelopment," *Politics and Society* 8, no. 1 (1978): 1-48.

85. Official American repatriation figures indicated that 85 to 90 percent of Koreans returning from Japan were residents of south Korean provinces and that most were unskilled, manual laborers in Japan (see Wagner, *Korean Minority*, pp. 10-11).

86. Wolf, *Peasant Wars*, p. 292.

87. Wagner, *Korean Minority*, p. 15; Trewartha and Zelinsky, "Population Distribution," p. 25.

88. The Americans found that returnees from Japan tended to be "leftist" in orientation while early waves of refugees from north Korea (that is, after official repatriation was set up at the end of October 1945) represented "largely the dispossessed classes" and participated in political organizations of a "rightest tinge." (See United States Army Military Government in Korea, "Report on the Occupation of South Korea" [Seoul: Administrative Services Division, September 1947], pp. 6-8).

89. Karl Deutsch, "Social Mobilization and Political Development," *American Political Science Review* 55, no. 3 (September 1961): 493-514.

90. Samuel Huntington, *Political Order in Changing Societies* (New Haven: Yale University Press, 1968), pp. 33-37, 47-50, 53-57. See also Charles Tilly, "Does Modernization Breed Revolution?" *Comparative Politics* 5, no. 3 (April 1973): 429-447.

91. Huntington, *Political Order*, p. 57.

92. Ralf Dahrendorf, *Class and Class Conflict in Industrial Society* (Stanford: Stanford University Press, 1959), ch. 1; Peter C. Lloyd, *Classes, Crises, and Coups: Themes in the Sociology of Developing Countries* (London: MacGibbon and Kee, 1971), pp. 14-17; and Rudolfo Stavenhagen, *Social Classes in Agrarian Societies* (New York: Anchor Press/Doubleday, 1975), pp. 25-32.

93. Dahrendorf, *Class and Class Conflict*, p. 25; see also Isaac C. Balbus, "The Concept of Interest in Pluralist and Marxian Analysis," *Politics and Society* 1, no. 2 (February 1971): 151-177.

94. Balbus, "The Concept of Interest," p. 153.

95. Robert Michels, *Political Parties* (1915; reprint ed., New York: Dover Publications, 1959), p. 236 (emphases in original).

96. Karl Marx, *The Eighteenth Brumaire of Louis Bonaparte* (1852; reprint ed., New York: International Publishers, 1963), p. 124.

97. Teodor Shanin, "The Peasantry as a Political Factor," in Shanin, ed., *Peasants and Peasant Societies*, p. 253.

98. Marx, *Capital* I: 764n.

99. Paige, *Agrarian Revolution*, pp. 1-71.
100. Ibid., pp. 58-66.
101. William Hinton, *Fanshen: A Documentary of Revolution in a Chinese Village* (New York: Vintage Books, 1966), pp. 606-609; for another classic account of the process of the Chinese revolution in the countryside, see Jack Belden, *China Shakes the World* (1949; reprint ed., New York: Monthly Review Press, 1970).

NOTES TO CHAPTER THREE

Revolution and Reaction

1. See Gregory Henderson, *Korea: The Politics of the Vortex* (Cambridge: Harvard University Press, 1968), p. 114.
2. The first is Arno J. Mayer's definition in *Dynamics of Counterrevolution in Europe, 1870-1956: An Analytic Framework* (New York: Harper Torchbooks, 1971), p. 47; the second is H. Franz Schurmann's in *Ideology and Organization in Communist China* (Berkeley: University of California Press, 1968), p. xxxvi. Schurmann, of course, borrowed from Alexis de Tocqueville, as he acknowledged.
3. Quoted in United States Armed Forces in Korea, "History of the U.S. Armed Forces in Korea," Manuscript in Office of the Chief of Military History, Washington, D.C. (Seoul and Tokyo, 1947, 1948), vol. 1, ch. 3, p. 2. Harold Larsen, USAFIK chief historian, directed this study. It consists of more than 3,000 pages in three volumes. Various USAFIK historians were involved in writing the history; their accounts are all based on unpublished, official records. It is a most valuable source. (Hereafter designated "HUSAFIK.") Ienaga Saburo quotes an unidentified Japanese "man in the street" as follows: "To be lorded over by the Chinese and Koreans is such a disgrace that it might be better to kill ourselves and the children and get it over with" (*The Pacific War: World War II and the Japanese, 1931-1945*, trans. Frank Baldwin [New York: Pantheon Books, 1978], p. 269, n. 53).
4. See Jean-Paul Sartre, Preface, in Franz Fanon, *The Wretched of the Earth* (New York: Grove Press, 1966), p. 20.
5. "HUSAFIK," vol. 1, ch. 3, p. 4 (quoting conversations with Japanese).
6. Figure is from "HUSAFIK," vol. 3, ch. 5, p. 138.
7. See Kim Chun-yŏn, *Tongnip nosŏn* [The Path of Independence] (Seoul: Hŭnghan chaedan, 1947), p. 2. For other accounts of the approach to Song Chin-u, see Louise Yim, *My Forty-Year Fight for Korea* (Seoul: Chungang University, International Culture Research Center, 1951), pp. 227-228; Ko Ha sŏnsaeng chŏn'gi p'yŏnch'an wiwŏn-hoe, *Ko Ha Song Chin-u sŏnsaeng chŏn* [Collection on Ko Ha, Song Chin-u] (Seoul: Tonga ilbo ch'ulp'an-guk, 1964), pp. 295-299; Han'guk minjudang sŏnjŏn-bu, *Han'guk minjudang t'ŭkbo* [Special Report of the Korean Democratic Party], no. 3 (December 19, 1945); Kim Chun-yŏn, ed., *Han'guk minjudang so-sa* [A Short History of the Korean Democratic Party] (Seoul: Han'guk minjudang sŏnjŏn-bu, 1948), p. 1.
   Song Chin-u was a major figure in Korean politics until his assassination in December, 1945. Born into a landlord family in 1890 that had been affluent for several generations, Song was educated in law at Meiji University in Tokyo. After his imprisonment during the 1919 independence demonstrations,

he became chief of the prestigious Korean-language newspaper *Tonga ilbo* [East Asia Daily]. When the Japanese closed it in 1940, Song reorganized the company as the Tongbon-sa, dealing in real estate and other matters until 1945. Song was a close associate of Kim Sŏng-su and the grouping of "landlord-entrepreneurs" discussed in chapter one. During the war the Japanese placed great pressures on Song to collaborate; his biographers claim that he resisted by staying at home, feigning illness, and playing dominoes (*Ko Ha Song Chin-u*, pp. 289-292). Other sources, however, cite charges that Song had been, in George McCune's words, "a notorious collaborator." See McCune, "Occupation Politics in Korea," *Far Eastern Survey* 15, no. 3 (February 13, 1946): 35. Andrew Roth, a journalist, claimed that Song had been a spy for the Japanese police (see "Cross-Fire in Korea," *Nation*, vol. 162, no. 8 [February 23, 1946]). I have not been able to document these charges.

8. See Yim, *Forty-Year Fight for Korea*, p. 228; and Kim, *Tongnip nosŏn*, p. 5.

9. *Ko Ha Song Chin-u*, p. 297.

10. Kim, *Tongnip nosŏn*, pp. 2-3.

11. Yi Man-gyu, *Yŏ Un-hyŏng t'ujaeng-sa* [History of Yŏ Un-hyŏng's Struggle] (Seoul: Ch'ongmun-gak, 1946), p. 188; also Minjujuŭi minjok chŏnsŏn, *Chosŏn haebang illyŏn-sa* [History of the First Year of Korean Liberation] (Seoul: Munu insŏ'gwan, 1946), p. 79. The latter work is also known as *Chosŏn haebang nyŏnbo* [Yearbook of Korean Liberation] and is most valuable. (Hereafter designated *Haebang illyŏn-sa*.)

12. Yi, *Yŏ Un-hyŏng*, p. 188; Kim, *Tongnip nosŏn*, p. 4.

13. Yi, *Yŏ Un-hyŏng*, p. 188; also Chae-Mi Hanjok yŏnhap wiwŏn-hoe, *Haebang Chosŏn* [Liberated Korea] (Hawaii: Chae-Mi Hanjok yŏnhap wiwŏn-hoe, 1948), p. 2. Yŏ's demands for "training" (*hullyŏn*) of students, workers, and peasants really meant "mobilization."

14. November 5, 1945 interview with Oda, cited in "HUSAFIK," vol. 1, ch. 3, p. 6. Yŏ Un-hyŏng had a remarkable career as an Asian revolutionary. He was born in 1885 in Yangp'yŏng-gun, Kyŏnggi Province, into a family of poor *yangban* status. Ancestors had been part of the *Sŏron* faction in Yi Dynasty politics, and an uncle had been a *Tonghak* leader. When he was fourteen years old, he entered the famous Paejae School, a missionary-run institution that helped introduce Western learning in Korea. Yŏ traveled to China in 1914, and then played an important role in attempts to gain Korean independence in 1919 and in the founding of the Korean Provisional Government in Shanghai. In 1921 he, Kim Kyu-sik, and some thirty other Koreans attended the Congress of the Toilers of the Far East in Moscow, where Yŏ met Lenin and Trotsky. After his return to China, he served as a propagandist during the Northern Expedition, and claimed to have met Sun Yat-sen and Mao Tse-tung. He is said to have avoided Chiang Kai-shek's terror in Shanghai in 1927 by posing as a Westerner.

In 1929 Japanese agents captured Yŏ in Shanghai and returned him to Korea, where he served a three-year prison term in Taejŏn. Upon his release he assumed the editorship of the *Chung'ang ilbo* (Central Daily) in Seoul. Like other prominent Koreans, Yŏ was pressured from 1938 on to collaborate with the Japanese in their war effort. He resisted, telling the Japanese at one point that he had fought them to the death and there was nothing left but to kill him. Yŏ's younger brother, Yŏ Un-hong, succumbed to the Japanese; there is no evidence that the elder Yŏ ever gave in.

Yŏ's views were a mixture of socialism, Christianity, and Wilsonian democracy. Although he always was willing to work with communists and embraced Marxism as a "good idea," he never joined the Korean Communist Party and stated that he never could believe wholeheartedly in the materialist view of history. If anything, he was an Asian populist; he often contrasted the simple generosity and unrewarded toil of Korea's peasants with "the so-called intelligentsia, the intellectual stratum that knows ideographs, which for 500 years has paralyzed the spirit of our people."

He was a great orator with a charismatic presence; his robust good looks and easy charm later drew many Americans to him. An Occupation historian, Albert Keep, once said of Yŏ, "What an amazing Korean he was . . . grey fedora, grey tweed overcoat, grey flannel trousers, well-taylored tweed coat, blue shirt with clean collar and neatly tied foreinhand looking for all the world as tho' he were off for a date at the Greenwich Country Club."

Biographical information is drawn from Yi, *Yŏ Un-hyŏng*, pp. 2-29, 71-89, 141-167; Kim O-sŏng, ed., *Chijoda kunsang* [The Leaders] (Seoul; Taesŏng ch'ulp'an-sa, 1946), I: 1-14; Yŏ Un-hong, *Mongyang: Yŏ Un-hyŏng* (Mongyang was Yŏ's penname) (Seoul: Ch'ongha-gak, 1967); and *Yŏ Un-hyŏng sŏnsaeng e taehan p'an'gyŏl-so* [The Judicial Record of Mr. Yŏ Un-hyŏng] (Seoul: Kunsŏdang sŏjŏm, 1946), which translates Japanese interrogation transcripts after Yŏ's arrests. Albert Keep's reminiscence is in United States Armed Forces in Korea, "XXIV Corps Journal," November 11, 1945 entry; in RG 332, XXIV Corps Historical File. A detailed American investigation of Yŏ's background turned up no evidence of collaboration with the Japanese (see chapter seven). Yŏ was known to Americans as Lyuh Woon Hyung.

15. Yi, *Yŏ Un-hyŏng*, p. 189. These leaders included Yi Kap-su, Yi Yŏ-sŏng, Kim Se-yŏng, Yi Kang-guk, Pak Mun-gyu, and Yi Sang-baek.

16. Ibid., pp. 185, 190.

17. Literally, "serving the great," a term historically used for Korea's tributary relationship to China, but carrying in 1945 the pejorative connotation of a groveling sycophancy toward foreign powers and an unprincipled willingness to sacrifice Korean interests to curry favor with foreign power.

18. Yi, *Yŏ Un-hyŏng*, pp. 186-189.

19. Ibid., p. 187. For a pamphlet emphasizing the CPKI's stand for independence and self-determination and its opposition to *sadae*, see Wŏlch'u Sanin [pseudonymous ed.] *Chosŏn tongp'o ege koham* [To the Korean Brethren] (Seoul: Cho'gwang-sa, September 1945), pp. 6-9.

20. Yi, *Yŏ Un-hyŏng*, p. 208.

21. Ibid., pp. 191-192. For An's speech, see *Chosŏn tongp'o ege koham*, p. 31. An Chae-hong was a graduate of Waseda University in Tokyo, a YMCA activist, and a nationalist twice imprisoned for anti-Japanese activities (Robert A. Scalapino and Chong-sik Lee, *Communism in Korea* [Berkeley: University of California Press, 1972], I: 235). Rightists later castigated An for his "foolishness" and his "mistakes" in working with the CPKI (Ko Yŏng-hwan, *Kŭmil ŭi chonggaekdŭl* [Today's politicians] [Seoul: Tonga ilbo-sa, 1949], pp. 40-41). An became the Chief Civil Administrator of the South Korean Interim Government (SKIG) in 1947 and later went (whether voluntarily or involuntarily is unknown) to North Korea.

22. *Maeil sinbo*, August 16, 1945. A full run of this valuable newspaper is available at the Korean Research Center in Seoul.

23. Prisoners who remained in Japanese jails for political crimes until August 15 were widely viewed as "the true patriots" (see Kim Chong-bŏm and Kim

476 — Notes to Chapter Three

Tong-un, *Haebang chŏn-hu ŭi Chosŏn chinsang* [The True Situation of Korea Before and After Liberation] [Seoul: Chosŏn chŏnggyŏng yŏn'gu-sa, 1945], p. 85).

24. The American G-2 (intelligence) section later put the total number of prisoners released in Seoul at 10,000 (see United States Army Military Government in Korea, "G-2 Periodic Report," no. 4, September 12-13, 1945); on those released in Taegu, see "G-2 Periodic Report," no. 37, October 15-16, 1945. (G-2 reports used in this study may be found in record group no. 319 "G," National Records Center.) The figure on those released on August 15 and 16 is put at 11,000 in Taehan min'guk kukpang-bu p'yŏnch'an wiwŏnhoe, *Han'guk chŏnjaeng-sa* [History of the Korean War], 1, "Haebang kwa kŏn'gun" [Liberation and Establishment of the Army] (Seoul: Taehan min'-guk kukpang-bu, 1967): 46. On the importance of released prisoners in setting up CPKI branches and, later, people's committees, see *Haebang illyŏn-sa*, p. 80. *Han'guk minjudang t'ŭkbo* referred derogatorily to these people as "thought criminals" (no. 3, December 19, 1945), but that is hardly the way most Koreans viewed them. In a sense, we can say that while the early years of the nationalist and communist movements reflected the influence of Japanese-educated intellectuals, from about 1930 to 1945, Korean revolutionaries were getting their education behind bars.

25. "HUSAFIK," vol. 3, ch. 4, p. 6.

26. See this figure in *Haebang illyŏn-sa*, p. 81; this figure is often cited in Korean materials, but I do not know its origin.

27. Gerald Brenan, *The Spanish Labyrinth* (Cambridge: Cambridge University Press, 1943), pp. 173-174.

28. In Japan as well, "a rash of Korean organizations sprang up spontaneously" after August 15 and soon established links with the KPR in Korea. See Edward Willett Wagner's account of this "truly remarkable organizing effort" in *The Korean Minority in Japan, 1904-1950* (Vancouver: University of British Columbia, 1951), pp. 50-56.

29. Yi, *Yŏ Un-hyŏng*, p. 194. Chang Kwŏn was an associate of Yŏ's, while Ch'oe Yong-dal was a communist who had been imprisoned after labor organizing in Wŏnsan with Yi Kang-guk in 1937. Ch'oe soon went to north Korea and became chief of the Justice Department in the North Korean Interim People's Committee (early 1946). See also Kim *Chidoja kunsang*, pp. 177-186.

30. Han T'ae-su, *Han'guk chŏngdang-sa* [A History of Korean Political Parties] (Seoul: Sin t'aeyang-sa, 1961), p. 30. Han's account of the period draws heavily on Yi, *Yŏ Un-hyŏng*. The Korean words in the text mean student's corps, youth corps, self-defense corps, and worker's corps, respectively.

31. Ibid., p. 28.

32. Yi, *Yŏ Un-hyŏng*, pp. 194-195.

33. See *Haebang nyusŭ* [Liberation News] (Seoul: t'ongsin-sa, 1945), entry of September 1, 1945.

34. Richard Kim, *Lost Names* (Seoul: Sisayongo Publishing Co., 1970), pp. 171-183.

35. Sudo kwan'gu kyŏngch'al ch'ong, *Haebang ihu sudo kyŏngch'al paltal-sa* [History of the Development of the Metropolitan Police After Liberation] (Seoul: Sudo kwan'gu kyŏngch'al ch'ong, 1947), p. 94.

36. "HUSAFIK," vol. 1, ch. 3, p. 32.

37. *New York Times*, September 12, 1945. A Korean source stated that "all this did not come about by chance . . . but because the patriotic brethren who

had suffered under murderous and tyrannical oppression since the March First Movement in 1919 offered their services sincerely in the work of building the nation" *(Haebang Chosŏn,* p. 4).

38. *Sudo kyŏngch'al paltal-sa,* pp. 99-104.

39. Collaborators were marched through the streets with their heads shaved after the liberation in France, many were beaten, and so on. See Robert Brasillach's comments on the situation there in "The Liberation as Seen from an Attic," in Germaine Bree and George Bernauer, eds., *Defeat and Beyond* (New York: Pantheon Books, 1970), esp. pp. 360-361.

40. *Han'guk chŏnjaeng-sa* I: 252. On the NPA, see also *Haebang illyŏn-sa,* pp. 230-240; and *Maeil sinbo,* September 17, 1945.

41. *Han'guk chŏnjaeng-sa* I: 253.

42. Ibid., p. 252. By the middle of December 1945, leaders of the NPA estimated the total number of "standing" soldiers to be 17,000, and that of the "reserve" to be 70,000 (see *Chayu sinmun* [Free News], December 18, 1945; quoted in Kuksa p'yŏnch'an wiwŏnhoe, *Taehan min'guk-sa, charyo* [History of the Republic of Korea, Materials] [Seoul: Taehan min'guk mun'gyo-bu, 1970], I: 601-602 [hereafter designated *THMGS*]).

43. *Chohap* means "association" or "cooperative," as well as "union"; here the use of the term union does not necessarily connote the organization and direction we find in modern labor unions.

44. See the examples of such activity in 98th Military Government (MG) Group, "Unit History"; in XXIV Corps Historical File.

45. Stewart Meacham, *Korean Labor Report,* (Seoul: United States Armed Forces in Korea, 1947), p. 10. Meacham was "Labor Advisor" to the Commanding General. I am indebted to Gregory Henderson for bringing this valuable report to my attention, and to K. P. Yang for making it available to me. See also *Haebang illyŏn-sa,* p. 159.

46. *Chŏn'guk nodongja sinmun* (National Worker's News), April 19, 1946.

47. Ibid., November 1, 1945. This strike is mentioned in many newspapers from the period. The factory was founded by Kim Sŏng-su (see chapter one) and managed in 1945 by Kim Yŏn-su; both later became stalwarts of the Korean Democratic Party. The factory was one of three in Seoul in 1945 employing more than 1,000 people—about 1,300 people total.

48. At first some of them were called *nongmin wiwŏnhoe* (peasant committee) or *nongmin tongmaeng* (peasant league). See *Haebang illyŏn-sa,* p. 166; see also a provincial breakdown of peasant union strength in chapter nine of this book.

49. *Haebang illyŏn-sa,* p. 157; also In Chŏng-sik, *Chosŏn nongch'ŏn munje sajŏn* [Dictionary of Korean Agriculture] (Seoul: Sinhak-sa, 1948), p. 213.

50. *Haebang illyŏn-sa,* p. 165.

51. *Chŏn'guk nodongja sinmun,* November 1, 1945 and April 19, 1946. Interestingly, a document from the peasant organizing effort in the 1930s virtually urged spontaneity and voluntarism, saying: "The local committee shall not act as a centralized organ; each member shall act independently and instinctively to bring about maximum effectiveness" (see Dae-Suk Suh, *Documents of Korean Communism, 1918-1948* [Princeton: Princeton University Press, 1970], p. 180). This is a distinctly un-Leninist suggestion.

52. The term "communist" can mean a number of things to Koreans. It can mean a member of a communist party; it can mean a person with socialist or Marxist beliefs; or it can mean anyone who works on behalf of the poor or

opposes those in power (in postwar south Korea). I have tried to restrict my usage to the first meaning.

53. The following account is based on Yi, *Yŏ Un-hyŏng*, pp. 167-186; and on Han, *Han'guk chŏngdang-sa*, pp. 19-39. Readers interested in a full account of CPKI and KPR factional alignments and conflicts may consult my dissertation, "The Politics of Liberation: Korea, 1945-1947" (Columbia University, 1975), pp. 114-148; available from University Microfilms, Ann Arbor, Michigan.

54. Kim, *Chidoja kunsang*, pp. 179-180; Yi, *Yŏ Un-hyŏng*, p. 176.

55. Kim and Kim, *Haebang chŏn-hu*, pp. 58, 66. See the August 16 proclamation of the *Changan* KCP in *Kŭnyŏk chubo* [Korea Weekly], November 3, 1945. See also Chang Pok-sŏng, *Chosŏn kongsan-dang p'ajŏng-sa* [History of the Factional Struggles of the KCP] (Seoul: Taeryuk ch'ulp'an-sa, 1949), pp. 50-51. For biographies of Ch'oe Ik-han, Chŏng Paek, and Hong Nam-p'yo, see Kim and Kim, *Haebang chŏn-hu*, pp. 182-183, 197-198, and 202-203.

Hong Nam-p'yo's life was typical of Korean revolutionaries. He was born into a poor family in Yangju, Kyŏnggi Province, and was taught the classics by his father. His father committed suicide in protest of the Annexation. Hong was imprisoned for three years in the early 1920s, joined the KCP in 1925, and then went to Shanghai where he worked with the Chinese Communist Party. He was arrested again and brought back to Korea where he served an eight-year prison term. He farmed in Yangju in 1943-1945, then joined the KPR and the subsequent Democratic National Front (February 1946). Later he was prominent in the North Korean leadership. (Kim, *Chidoja kunsang*, pp. 123-132; Kim and Kim, *Haebang chŏn-hu*, pp. 207-208.)

56. *Haebang illyŏn-sa*, pp. 80, 82; also *Haebang nyusŭ*, August 22 entry.

57. See the listing in Cumings, "Politics of Liberation," pp. 118-119.

58. See the running debates in the *Changan* newspaper, *Chŏnsŏn* [Battle Front], nos. 1-4, October 1945.

59. South Korean historiography, in particular, tries to explain this period by reference to later events or the subsequent activities of the individuals involved; but one cannot assume, for example, that because a man decided to go to North Korea in 1948 he was *ipso facto* a communist in 1945 or somehow linked to leaders in north Korea.

60. Yŏ Un-hyŏng stated that he could hardly refuse communist participation in the CPKI, since communists had paid their dues against Japan (Yi, *Yŏ Un-hyŏng*, p. 230.)

61. Kim Pyŏng-no was a well-known lawyer and nationalist activist who had defended Korean communists arrested by the Japanese. Paek Kwan-su was a Waseda University graduate who had been active in the 1919 independence demonstrations in Tokyo; he later worked with Kim Sŏng-su and Song Chin-u on the *Tonga ilbo*. Both men joined the Korean Democratic Party in September 1945. See Kim and Kim, *Haebang chŏn-hu*, pp. 205, 210-211.

62. Kim, *Tongnip nosŏn*, p. 7; *Haebang illyŏn-sa*, p. 82.

63. *Haebang illyŏn-sa*, pp. 79-80; Ko Ha Song Chin-u, p. 305; also Han, *Han'guk chŏngdang-sa*, p. 33.

64. Interviews with Japanese officials and citations from an intercepted Japanese Army letter, in "HUSAFIK," vol. 1, ch. 3, pp. 12-17, 29.

65. Yi, *Yŏ Un-hyŏng*, p. 213.

66. *Haebang illyŏn-sa*, p. 87. It was also charged that the Japanese had urged rightists to aid in reigning in the CPKI (p. 84).

67. Ibid., p. 82.
68. This sense is very clear in ibid., p. 87.
69. *Haebang Chosŏn,* p. 5.
70. "HUSAFIK," vol. 1, ch. 3, pp. 18-20. Shortly after August 15, Japanese began streaming through Pusan back to Japan; the Koan Maru and the Tojuku Maru, two ferries plying the Pusan-Shimonoseki route, and numerous private vessels, were commandeered for the massive human traffic that reached 6,000 per day in September. Nearly one-fourth of all Japanese in Korea (approximately 160,000) had returned in this way by the end of September when the Americans began placing controls on repatriation. (There were some 435,000 Japanese in south Korea and 225,000 in north Korea on August 15.) Since many Japanese were loaded with colonial booty they naturally attracted thieves; a lively piracy flourished in the Japan Sea for several months, reviving memories of the ancient *Wakō* marauders. See "HUSAFIK," vol. 1, ch. 3, p. 24; also ch. 8, pp. 1-2, 58-61.
71. "HUSAFIK," vol. 1, ch. 3, p. 22.
72. This proclamation is available in *Haebang illyŏn-sa,* pp. 83-84; *Haebang Chosŏn,* pp. 4-9; and *Haebang nyusŭ,* August 28 entry.
73. See, for example, the proclamation of the KPG-related Korean Independence Party apparently received in Korea on August 28, calling for (among many other things) the elimination of "country-selling criminals" and of "feudal, fascist, and all antidemocratic influences," in *THMGS* I: 31.
74. Hŏ first won fame for his defense of arrested Korean nationalists in the wake of the March First Movement in 1919. He was later President of Posŏng College. He participated in the *Shin'ganhoe* and was imprisoned after the 1929 Kwangju student uprising. He was arrested twice more during the 1930s. See Kim and Kim, *Haebang chŏn-hu,* p. 183; also Kim, *Chidoja kunsang,* pp. 41-49. Han T'ae-su lauded Hŏ as a man of unswerving commitment to principle, in *Han'guk chŏngdang-sa,* p. 38. Hŏ was a top North Korean leader in 1948.
75. Pak had been an ardent communist organizer since 1919, active in the Tuesday Association and chairman of the KCP youth arm in 1925. He was imprisoned on two occasions in Sinŭiju, the second time for six years after 1933 when he reentered Korea from Shanghai to try to reconstruct the KCP. In 1939, upon his release, he achieved some success in tying together existing communists within Korea in the so-called "Communist Group" (*k'om kŭrup*). In 1941 he went underground for the duration of the war, working as a laborer in a South Chŏlla Province brick factory. (Kim, *Chidoja kunsang,* pp. 15-27; Dae-sook Suh, *The Korean Communist Movement, 1918-1948* (Princeton: Princeton University Press, 1967), pp. 71-72, 191-193; Chang, *Kongsandang p'ajŏng-sa,* pp. 52-53.) On August 15 Pak left Kwangju for Seoul, saying, "I go to begin my future" (*Chosŏn inmin-bo* [Korean People's Report], February 18, 1946).
76. Yi had been a leader of communist factions opposing Pak and the Tuesday Association in the 1920s.
77. The puerile factional infighting of the *Changan* and *Chaegŏn* groups may be followed in *Chŏnsŏn,* no. 3, October 27, 1945; and in the *Chaegŏn* KCP organ, *Haebang ilbo* [Liberation Daily], nos. 1, 2, and 5, September 19, October 12, and October 18, 1945. I am indebted to Chong-sik Lee for providing me with a detailed English translation of the *Haebang ilbo* from September through December, 1945. This paper is rare and I was unable to obtain original copies

in Seoul. It will be obvious, however, that I do not take these factional struggles as seriously as do Scalapino and Lee, in *Communism in Korea* I: 244-245, 250-256, and passim. (All references to *Haebang ilbo* are to Lee's translation.)

78. *Chŏnsŏn*, no. 4, October 31, 1945.
79. Kim and Kim, *Haebang chŏn-hu*, p. 66.
80. Hostile sources say only 300 or so attended; friendly sources place the total at upwards of 1,000.
81. *Chosŏn inmin-bo*, September 8, 1945. This newspaper became the organ of the KPR.
82. *Chwaik sakŏn sillok* [Record of Left Wing Incidents] (Seoul: Tae'gŏmch'al-ch'ong, susa-guk, 1964), I: 29. This official source based its account on a study written a good bit after the fact by a bitter anticommunist, Pak Il-wŏn, entitled *Nam-nodang ch'ong pip'an* [General critique of the South Korean Worker's Party] (Seoul: 1948).
83. Yi, *Yŏ Un-hyŏng*, p. 260.
84. The "Kim Il-sŏng" on the September 6 roster had a different middle character (一) in his name than that of the North Korean leader (日). It is likely that they refer to the same man, however. The *Haebang illyŏn-sa*, written by men who were Kim's rivals, reprinted the roster using the (日) character. The *Pyongyang Times* recently averred that

at first [the people] called him, Il Sung, meaning 'one star,' to express their ardent wish that he become a lodestar. . . . But they were not satisfied with that. . . . It was their ardent desire that he would become the Sun, rather than one star. The leader's name was changed into the characters Il Sung, meaning, "becoming the sun" (August 17, 1974).

85. See Yi Kang-guk, *Minjujuŭi ŭi Chosŏn kŏnsŏl* [The Construction of Democratic Korea] (Seoul: Chosŏn inminbo-sa husŏng-bu, 1946), which bears only faint traces of Marxist or communist thought. See Scalapino and Lee's interesting comments on Hyŏn Chun-hyŏk, *Communism in Korea* I: 320-321.
86. See the communist *Nodongja sinmun*, no. 5, September 22, 1945, which demanded pie-in-the-sky social reforms such as the following: no work on Sundays with pay; state-run housing and free kitchens for the unemployed without charge; and so on. See a similar document in Suh, *Documents of Korean Communism*, p. 182.
87. See Kim Kyu-sik's elegant essay, "The Asiatic Revolutionary Movement and Imperialism", in Suh, *Documents of Korean Communism*, pp. 91-105. For a recent biography of Kim, see Yi Chŏng-sik (Chong-sik Lee), *Kim Kyu-sik ŭi saengae* [The Career of Kim Kyu-sik] (Seoul: Sin'gu munhwa-sa, 1974).
88. See, for example, Paek Nam-un's stimulating book, *Chosŏn minjok ŭi chillo* [The Path of the Korean Nation] (Seoul: Sin'gŏn-sa, 1946), which begins with a discourse on Korean uniqueness. See also Yi, *Minjujuŭi ŭi Chosŏn kŏnsŏl*. Yi and Paek were both prominent in North Korea after 1948; Paek is still recognized as one of Korea's leading economic historians and chaired the Academy of Sciences in North Korea. For another interesting attempt at synthesizing Korean uniqueness with Marxist internationalism see Yi Chae-hun, *Minjok ŭisik kwa kyegŭp ŭisik* [National Consciousness and Class Consciousness] (Seoul: Tongyang kongsa ch'ulp'an-sa, 1946). I have argued the point in the text in my "Kim's Korean Communism," *Problems of Communism* 23, no. 2 (March-April 1974): 27-41.
89. Han, *Han'guk chŏngdang-sa*, p. 44.
90. *Han'guk chŏnjaeng-sa* I: 57-58, for example.

91. See *Chosŏn inmin-bo*, September 8, 1945; also a document written in 1920 by Pak Chin-sun, in Suh, *Documents of Korean Communism*, p. 56.

92. The Korean text is in *Haebang illyŏn-sa*, pp. 87-89. For an English translation (from which the quote in the text is taken), see Kyung Cho Chung, *Korea Tomorrow* (New York: Macmillan Co., 1956), pp. 304-306.

93. Chung, *Korea Tomorrow*.

94. Yi, *Yŏ Un-hyŏng*, p. 260.

95. This theme ran through much of the writing of the liberation period. Richard Kim quoted his father in condemnation of the generation of Koreans who were so "ineffective and disorganized" that they failed to liberate Korea (Kim, *Lost Names*, pp. 184-185).

96. Yi, *Minjujuŭi ŭi Chosŏn kŏnsŏl*, pp. 3-4.

97. Yŏ Un-hyŏng, "Kŏn'guk kwa chŏngch'i munhwa nosŏn," [Independence and Our Path in Politics and Culture]; in *Chungsŏng* [Voice of the Masses] (Pusan: February 1946), pp. 12-13.

98. Kim and Kim, *Haebang chŏn-hu*, p. 53; see also *Haebang illyŏn-sa*, p. 85.

99. *Hyŏngmyŏng sinmun* [Revolution News], October 4, 1945.

100. *Haebang illyŏn-sa*, p. 81.

101. *Haebang Chosŏn*, p. 6.

102. *Haebang ilbo*, no. 1, September 19, 1945.

103. Robert Michels, *Political Parties* (1915, reprinted ed.; New York: Dover Publications, 1959), p. 242.

104. *Haebang Chosŏn*, p. 7; on conservatives in provincial branches, see chapter nine. Kim O-sŏng in *Chidoja kunsang* called such men "yangsimjŏk chabon'ga-dŭl" or "capitalists with a conscience," a phrase that proved popular and is still used in North Korea.

105. Kim, ed., *Han'guk minjudang so-sa*, p. 8; *Han'guk minjudang t'ŭkbo*, no. 3, December 19, 1945; Han, *Han'guk chŏngdang-sa*, p. 60.

106. Kim, ed., *Han'guk minjudang so-sa*, p. 8; Han, *Han'guk chŏngdang-sa*, p. 60.

107. Han, *Han'guk chŏngdang-sa*, p. 59.

108. Kim, ed., *Han'guk minjudang so-sa*, p. 16; *Han'guk minjudang t'ŭkbo*, no. 3, December 19, 1945.

109. Kim, ed., *Han'guk minjudang so-sa*, p. 12. An Chae-hong's party was not included because of his "mistakes" in working with the CPKI (see n. 21 *supra*). An remained an important individual leader, but his party never amounted to anything.

110. See this identical phrase in *Han'guk minjudang t'ŭkbo*, no. 3, December 19, 1945; and in Kim, ed., *Han'guk minjudang so-sa*, p. 16.

111. Kim and Kim, *Haebang chŏn-hu*, pp. 66-67; Han, *Han'guk chŏngdang-sa*, p. 13.

112. Han, *Han'guk chŏngdang-sa*, p. 13. Kim Sam-gyu, a onetime member of the KDP, acknowledged the landlord and collaborationist element in the party (see his *Minjok ŭi yŏmyŏng* [Dawn of the Nation] [n.p., 1949], pp. 181-182).

113. "HUSAFIK," vol. 2, ch. 2, p 127; see also United States Army Military Government in Korea, "Report on the Occupation of South Korea," (Seoul: Administrative Services Division, September 1947), p. 53; also "XXIV Corps Journal," September 16 entry.

114. See one of Kim's 1943 speeches quoted in Paul Timothy Chang, "Political Effect of World War II on Korea: With Special Reference to the Policies of the United States" (Ph.D. dissertation, Notre Dame University, 1952), p. 85n. Chang identified four big financiers behind the KDP: Kim Sŏng-su, Min

Kyu-sik, Pak Hŭng-sik, and Han Sang-yong (p. 147). See also *Ch'in-Il p'a kunsang* [The Pro-Japanese Groups] (Keijo: Samsaeng munhwa-sa, 1948), pp. 15, 31. Kim Kyu-sik and others charged in a memorandum of November 4, 1946 that Kim Sŏng-su was a leader of mobilization organizations during the war ("SKILA Materials," XXIV Corps Historical File). Han Yung Chul wrote that the Central Advisory Council's personnel "were recruited from the most reactionary groups who were either elderly persons formerly connected with the old regime in Korea, or men closely connected in business affairs with the Japanese. . . ." (See "Traditionalism and the Struggle for Political Modernization in Contemporary Korea: With Special Reference to the Development of Political Parties" [Ph.D. dissertation, New York University, 1966], p. 63.)

115. Yi, *Yŏ Un-hyŏng*, p. 206.

116. The *Haebang ilbo*, no. 24, December 8, 1945, quoted Yŏ Un-hyŏng as follows: These [pro-Japanese] elements are attempting to cover up their past wrongs and are now joined up in the struggle for national reconstruction pretending to be patriots. This is a very unpleasant fact and a sad thing for the individuals involved. They are consciously recommitting their crimes of the past. Therefore, the judgment of the people must be very severe.

117. See *Ch'in-Il p'a kunsang*, pp. 6, 15, 50-52. Chang was a Columbia University Ph.D. Yi, Cynn, Ch'oe In, and Ch'oe Nam-sŏn were famous nationalist leaders who succumbed to the Japanese in the late 1930s.

118. *Seoul Times*, March 18, 1946; see also the memorandum of the Coalition Committee, November 4, 1946, XXIV Corps Historical File.

119. Leonard Bertsch, memorandum to Gen. Brown, November 26, 1946, in "SKILA Materials," XXIV Corps Historical File.

120. *Ch'in-Il p'a kunsang*, pp. 6-7, passim.

121. Ibid., pp. 6-7, 64-65.

122. I have used a list of some six hundred KDP "initiators" (*palgi-in*) available in *THMGS* I: 62-63, and have compared those listed with biographical information on more than six hundred Koreans prominent under the Japanese in the 1940s in *Chōsen nenkan 1945* [Korea Yearbook 1945] (Seoul: Keijo nipposha, 1945), pp. 354-426; with Koreans listed in *Ch'in-Il p'a kunsang*; with biographical information in *Han'guk inmyŏng tae sajŏn* [Dictionary of Korean Biography] (Seoul: Sin'gu munwha-sa, 1967); and with American G-2 biographies of Koreans in record group no. 319 "G." Many Koreans associated with the KDP had adopted Japanese names (given in *Chōsen nenkan*).

123. Kim and Kim, *Haebang chŏn-hu*, pp. 70-74. The "bodyguards" (*kyŏngho*) included people like Yi Ch'ŏl-sŭng, who later became a well-known leader of rightist youth groups.

124. Kim, ed., *Han'guk minjudang so-sa*, published in 1948, begins with eight pages of calumny against the KPR, which makes one wonder if the book was mistitled.

125. Available in Yi Hyŏk, ed., *Aeguk ppira chŏnjip* [Collection of Patriotic Handbills] (Seoul: Cho'guk munhwa-sa, 1946), I: 46-50.

126. See Kim, ed., *Han'guk minjudang so-sa*, p. 2; also *Han'guk minjudang t'ŭkbo*, no. 3, December 19, 1945; also Ko, *Kŭmil ŭi chŏnggaekdŭl*, p. 40.

127. *Han'guk minjudang t'ŭkbo*, no. 3, December 19, 1945; also no. 4, January 10, 1946. Yi, in *Yŏ Un-hyŏng*, p. 252, quoted Song Chin-u's statement to Yŏ Un-hyŏng in which Song said that Yŏ should not worry about the charges that

the CPKI got money from the Japanese, it's no big thing; Yŏ replied, "maybe not for you, but it is for me."

128. Cho Pyŏng-ok, *Na ŭi hoegorok* [My Recollections] (Seoul: Min'gyo-sa, 1959), p. 145.

129. Kim, ed., *Han'guk minjudang so-sa*, p. 14; see also Yi, ed., *Aeguk ppira chŏnjip* I: 93.

130. Quoted in Mayer, *Counterrevolution*, p. 82.

131. Kim, ed., *Han'guk minjudang so-sa*, pp. 90-91.

132. Han, *Han'guk chŏngdang-sa*, p. 13.

133. Kim, *Tongnip nosŏn*, pp. 7, 13.

134. *Ko Ha Song Chin-u*, pp. 318-19.

135. "HUSAFIK," vol. 2, ch. 1, p. 6. See also C. Clyde Mitchell, *Korea: Second Failure in Asia* (Washington, D.C.: Public Affairs Institute, 1951), p. 15. Han T'ae-su, in *Han'guk chŏngdang-sa*, p. 44, implied that the KDP's notion that no Korean government could be set up before the American entry was so much *sadaejuŭi*.

136. Cho, *Na ŭi hoegorok*, pp. 145-146.

137. An article in the *Haebang ilbo*, no. 1, September 19, 1945, asked, do the opponents of the KPR "think that a government is something that someone else make[s] for us? There is no greater mistake than to think that the Soviet Union, the United States, China and Great Britain would build a government for us."

138. C. Wright Mills, *The Sociological Imagination* (New York: Oxford University Press, 1959), pp. 40-44.

139. See James B. Palais, "Political Participation in Traditional Korea," *Journal of Korean Studies*, no. 1 (1979). See also Vipin Chandra, "The Independence Club and Korea's First Proposal for a National Legislative Assembly," *Occasional Papers on Korea*, no. 4 (Seattle: University of Washington, 1975). Virtually everything Palais and Chandra say about Korean politicians at the end of the Yi Dynasty can be transferred to the elder generation of the 1940s.

140. Eric J. Hobsbawm, *Industry and Empire* (London: Penguin Books, 1969), p. 18 (italics in original).

NOTES TO CHAPTER FOUR

Crucible of Policy

1. H. Franz Shurmann, *The Logic of World Power: An Inquiry into the Origins, Currents and Contradictions of World Politics* (New York: Pantheon Books, 1974), pt. I. This is a study full of seminal insights. Schurmann argues that "modern capitalism generates interests of both a national and an international character, producing two different capitalist world views. . . . The world view of the internationalists is of the primacy of a world market system ultimately covering the entire planet. The world view of the nationalists is of different national economies competing for scarce wealth, in which priority must of course go to one's own national economy. The internationalist view sees the sacrifice of national economy as essential for the generation of greater wealth, whereas the nationalist view sees national sovereignty as the indispensable prerequisite for the acquisition of wealth" (p. 187). For an interesting analysis of the conflict between internationalism and nationalism

(or "parochialism") in the 1970s, see Mary Kaldor, *The Disintegrating West* (New York: Hill and Wang, 1978).

2. Shurmann, *Logic of World Power*, p. 188. Perhaps the best example of the internationalist vision—one world economy shaped or dominated by the United States—is the "Grand Area" idea, articulated by the Council on Foreign Relations in the early stages of World War II. On this, see Laurence H. Shoup and William Minter, *Imperial Brain Trust: The Council on Foreign Relations and United States Foreign Policy* (New York: Monthly Review Press, 1977), pp. 135-148.

3. This diplomacy is nowhere better evidenced than in the following colloquoy between John J. McCloy and Henry Stimson:

    McCLOY: I've been taking the position that we ought to have our cake and eat it too; that we ought to be free to operate under this regional arrangement in South America, at the same time intervene promptly in Europe.

    STIMSON: I think so, decidedly. . . . I think it's not asking too much to have our little region over here which never has bothered anybody.

    (Quoted in Gabriel Kolko, *The Politics of War: The World and United States Foreign Policy, 1943-1945* [New York: Random House, 1968], pp. 470-471.)

4. Willard Range, *Franklin Delano Roosevelt's World Order* (Athens, Ga.: University of Georgia Press, 1959), p. 49. See also Schurmann, *Logic of World Power*, pp. 3-26.

5. Schurmann often succumbs to this error in *Logic of World Power*.

6. Louis Hartz, *The Liberal Tradition in America* (New York: Harcourt, Brace & World, 1955), pp. 13, 59.

7. See Karl Polanyi, *The Great Transformation* (New York: Beacon Press, 1967), p. 212. For an incisive essay emphasizing the nonterritorial nature of American imperialism, see Gareth Stedman Jones, "The History of U.S. Imperialism," in Robin Blackburn, ed., *Ideology in Social Science* (New York: Vintage Books, 1973), pp. 207-237.

8. For further reading, see Gordon Levin, Jr., *Woodrow Wilson and World Politics* (London: Oxford University Press, 1968); William Appleman Williams, *The Tragedy of American Diplomacy*, 2d rev. ed. (New York: Dell Publishing, 1972); Lloyd Gardner, *Economic Aspects of New Deal Diplomacy* (1964, reprint ed.; Boston: Beacon Press, 1971), esp. ch. 9; George Louis Beer, *African Questions at the Paris Peace Conference* (New York: Macmillan Co., 1923). (I am indebted to Dorothy Borg for suggesting this last work.)

9. Levin, *Woodrow Wilson*, pp. 24-26. Peter Duignan and L. H. Gann note that radicals like W.E.B. Dubois supported trusteeships at the end of World War I. (see "Introduction," *Colonialism in Africa, 1870-1960* 2, *The History and Politics of Colonialism, 1914-1960* [New York: Cambridge University Press, 1970], 12).

10. Anthony Eden, *Memoirs: The Reckoning* (Boston: Houghton Mifflin Co., 1965), p. 438. FDR apparently suggested to Molotov in mid-1942 that trusteeships should be set up for colonies once the war ended, but there is no record of Molotov's response (see Robert Dallek, *Franklin D. Roosevelt and American Foreign Policy, 1932-1945* [New York: Oxford University Press, 1979], p. 342).

11. See Cordell Hull, *Memoirs* (New York: Macmillan Co., 1948), 2: 1,596; also Eden, *Reckoning*, p. 595. The differences over trusteeship represented "the

most important conflict" of the March 1943 meetings, according to William Hardy McNeill, in *America, Britain, and Russia: Their Cooperation and Conflict, 1941-1946* (1953; reprint ed., New York: Johnson Reprint Corp., 1970), p. 319.

12. Hull, *Memoirs* 2: 1,237.

13. McNeill wrote, "the American plan to transfer responsibility for the tutelage of dependent peoples from individual nations to international trustees was even more directly a challenge to the traditional power and interests of Great Britain [than were proposals to remove trade barriers]" (see *America, Britain, and Russia*, p. 334).

14. Eden, *Reckoning*, p. 595.

15. For a concurring view, see United States Department of Defense, *United States-Vietnam Relations 1945-1967* (Washington, D.C., 1971), 1: A-2. (Hereafter designated *Pentagon Papers*.)

16. RG 49, Notter File, Box 31, T-169 and T-169a, December 1942, and T-169b, April 15, 1943; quoted in William George Morris, "The Korean Trusteeship, 1941-1947: The United States, Russia, and the Cold War" (Ph.D. dissertation, University of Texas, 1974), pp. 71-72.

17. Text in United States, Department of State, *Foreign Relations of the United States* (1945) (Washington, D.C., 1969), 6: 1,098. (Hereafter designated *FRUS*.)

18. *Star Exponent* (Los Angeles: Korea Society of Soldier's and Sailor's Relatives and Friends), 1, no. 2 (April 24, 1943): 4.

19. Japanese Premier Hara Kei, in announcing Japan's "cultural policy" toward Korea in the aftermath of the 1919 March First Movement, used a phrase that also was translated as "in due course": "It is the ultimate purpose of the Japanese Government in due course to treat Korea as in all respects on the same footing with Japan proper" (quoted in Hugh Heung-woo Cynn, *The Rebirth of Korea* [New York: Abingdon Press, 1920], p. 169). Among other exile publications, see *Korea Economic Digest* (New York: Economic Society, 1944-1945); *Voice of Korea* (Washington, D.C.: Korean Affairs Institute, 1943-1945); Changsoon Kim, ed., *The Culture of Korea* (n.p.: Korean-American Culture Association, 1945), p. ix and passim; *FRUS* (1943), 3: 1,090-1,096; and *Star Exponent* 1, no. 2: 4.

20. Herbert Feis, *Churchill, Roosevelt, Stalin: The War They Waged and the Peace They Sought* (Princeton: Princeton University Press, 1957), p. 253; James Peck, "America and the Chinese Revolution, 1942-1946: An Interpretation," in Ernest May and James C. Thomson, Jr., eds., *American-East Asian Relations: A Survey* (Cambridge: Harvard University Press, 1972), pp. 344-345.

21. Robert E. Sherwood, *Roosevelt and Hopkins: An Intimate History* (1948; reprint ed., New York: Harper & Bros., 1950), p. 773; Edward R. Stettinius, Jr., *Roosevelt and the Russians: The Yalta Conference*, ed. Walter Johnson (New York: Doubleday & Co., 1949), p. 71.

22. Peck, "America and the Chinese Revolution," pp. 344-345.

23. Ibid., p. 346.

24. *FRUS*, Diplomatic Papers, *The Conferences of Cairo and Teheran, 1943*, (Washington, D.C.: Department of State, 1961), pp. 257, 334.

25. Ibid., pp. 325, 389.

26. According to James MacGregor Burns, at Cairo Roosevelt also "offered China the leading role in the postwar military occupation of Japan—a role Chiang declined—and extensive reparations [from Japan]" (see *Roosevelt: The Soldier*

of Freedom, 1940-1945 [New York: Harcourt Brace Jovanovich, 1970], p. 404).
Gardner says FDR asked Chiang if China wanted to assume "suzerainty over
Indo-China after the war" (*Economic Aspects*, p. 188).

27. Walter LaFeber, "Roosevelt, Churchill, and Indochina: 1942-1945," *American
Historical Review* 80, no. 5 (December 1975): 1,280.

28. Feis, *Churchill, Roosevelt, Stalin*, p. 252; Hugh Borton, "American Pre-
Surrender Planning for Postwar Japan," *Occasional Papers of the East Asian
Institute* (New York: Columbia University, 1967), p. 12; also conversation
with Hugh Borton, April 1973. James Matray documents the considerable
attention paid to trusteeship plans by State Department officials prior to the
Cairo Conference, but there remains no proof that FDR consulted with them
or saw the plans. Cairo was mostly his show. (See Matray, "The Reluctant
Crusade: American Foreign Policy in Korea, 1941-1950" [Ph.D. dissertation,
University of Virginia, 1977], pp. 54-55.)

29. *Conferences of Cairo and Teheran*, pp. 399-400. It is often said that Koreans
misunderstood "in due course" and mistranslated it. It is true that sometimes
the proviso was simply omitted from translations of the Cairo Declaration.
See, for example, *Haebang nyusŭ* [Liberation News] (Seoul: t'ongsin-sa, 1945),
pp. 6-7. But when it was translated, it was *sangdanghan sigi e*, "at an appropriate time," which could not have been closer to the American intent. (See
Chae-Mi Hanjok yŏnhap wiwŏnhoe, *Haebang Chosŏn* [Liberated Korea]
[Hawaii: Chae-Mi Hanjok yŏnhap wiwŏnhoe, 1948], p. 15.) Ernest May in his
recent book, *Lessons of the Past* (New York: Oxford University Press, 1973),
pp. 53-54, perpetuates the myth that the phrase could not be translated into
Korean. The problem with "in due course," in fact, was that Koreans understood its meaning too well.

30. Eden, *Reckoning*, p. 433.

31. Quoted in Stettinius, *Roosevelt and the Russians*, p. 237.

32. See Burns, *Soldier of Freedom*, pp. 378-379; Range, *Roosevelt's World Order*,
p. 109; and Samuel Rosenman, ed., *Public Papers and Addresses of Franklin D.
Roosevelt, 1942* (New York: Harpers, 1942), pp. 473-476. In a radio address
in 1942, FDR stated, "I like to think that the history of the Philippine Islands
in the last forty-four years provides in a very real sense a pattern for the
future . . . a pattern of global civilization which recognizes no limitations
of religion, or of creed, or of race" (quoted in Burns, *Soldier of Freedom*,
p. 378). On Woodrow Wilson's similar view of the Philippine experience,
see Williams, *Tragedy of American Diplomacy*, p. 69.

FDR also made an analogy with good business practice: "There seems no
reason why the principle of trusteeship in private affairs should not be extended to the international field. Trusteeship is based on the principle of
unselfish service. For a time at least there are many minor children among
the peoples of the world who need trustees in their relations with other
nations and peoples" (quoted in John Lewis Gaddis, *The United States and
the Origins of the Cold War, 1941-1947* [New York: Columbia University
Press, 1972], p. 24).

33. Sherwood, *Roosevelt and Hopkins*, p. 777.

34. *Conferences of Cairo and Teheran*, p. 485.

35. Ibid., p. 869.

36. Ibid., pp. 869n, 566.

37. FRUS, Diplomatic Papers, *The Conferences of Malta and Yalta, 1945* (Washington, D.C.: Department of State, 1955), p. 770.

38. See Walter Millis, ed., *The Forrestal Diaries* (New York: Viking Press, 1951), p. 46. Stalin's remarks as quoted by Harriman do not appear in the minutes of this meeting taken by Charles Bohlen *(Conferences of Malta and Yalta,* p. 770.)

39. Quoted in Stettinius, *Roosevelt and the Russians,* p. 236. See substantiating account, *Conferences of Malta and Yalta,* 6th plenary session, p. 844.

40. Eden, *Reckoning,* p. 595.

41. *Conferences of Malta and Yalta,* p. 485; Stettinius, *Roosevelt and the Russians,* pp. 237-238.

42. Stettinius's statement of April 3, 1945, quoted in *Pentagon Papers* 1: A-2, A-20. More than a year earlier, John J. McCloy and Gen. George C. Marshall told the French ambassador to the United States, according to the ambassador's account, that they "expressed sympathy for France and the restoration of the empire" (quoted in Christopher Thorne, *Allies of a Kind: The United States, Britain, and the War Against Japan, 1941-1945* [New York: Oxford University Press, 1978], p. 464). On the waning American commitment to independence for colonies in general, see Thorne, pp. 339-351, 455-469.

43. See the memorandum, "Arrangements for Trusteeship"; in *FRUS* (1945), 1: 136. On American deliberations regarding trusteeship before and during the United Nations Conference, see also *FRUS* (1945), 1: 211-214, 290, 311-321, 350, 792-799. The minutes of the May 18 meetings of the American delegation show how far the Americans had retreated from an anticolonial trusteeship concept: "China and the Soviet Union wished to introduce the word 'independence' as an objective of the trusteeship system. We, on the other hand, with the French and the British, favored the phrase, 'progressive development toward self-government'" *(FRUS* [1945], 1: 792-793). See also McNeill, *America, Britain, and Russia,* pp. 596-597; and Gardner, *Economic Aspects,* pp. 192-193.

    Christopher Thorne, *Allies of a Kind,* pp. 598-600, 632, finds that by the time of the San Francisco Conference John Foster Dulles was describing trusteeship as merely "a legal device"; independence for colonies was not the goal; the Far Eastern Office of the State Department had come to agree with the European section that the United States should not oppose the restoration of Indochina to the French (although the Far Eastern Office thought the French should from now on be "more liberal"); and the Office of Strategic Services argued in a memorandum of April 2, 1945:

    > "The United States should realize its interest in the maintenance of the British, French, and Dutch colonial empires. We should encourage liberalization of the colonial regimes in order the better to maintain them and to check Soviet influence in the stimulation of colonial revolt. We have at present no interest in weakening or liquidating these empires *or in championing schemes of international trusteeship* which may provoke unrest and result in colonial disintegration and may at the same time alienate from us the European states whose help we need to balance the Soviet power" (emphasis added).

    Roosevelt's point, of course, was that trusteeships were the better and more realistic means of liberalizing the colonies and checking Soviet influence. Postwar history has surely proved the OSS argument wrong, if it has not necessarily proved Roosevelt right. All three empires in South and Southeast Asia were gone or disintegrating by 1950.

44. See, for example, Bernard Fall, quoted in *Pentagon Papers* 1: A-1.

45. Willard Range, in *Roosevelt's World Order*, p. 103, has written, "the humanitarian, paternalistic, missionary spirit of the imperialism of the liberals of the Progressive Era kept their imperialism from being sordid; and that spirit Roosevelt had in abundance."

46. Memorandum of conversation, March 24, 1945; in *FRUS* (1945), 1: 121-124.

47. Ibid., pp. 211-214, 290.

48. Minutes of the eleventh meeting of the American delegation to the United Nations Conference, April 17, 1945; in ibid., pp. 315-320.

49. LaFeber, "Roosevelt, Churchill, and Indochina," pp. 1,277, 1,288-1,295.

50. Schurmann, *Logic of World Power*, p. 77. On Truman's inexperience, see in particular Martin Sherwin, *A World Destroyed: The Atomic Bomb and the Grand Alliance* (New York: Knopf, 1975), pp. 220-228; see also Daniel Yergin, *Shattered Peace: The Origins of the Cold War and the National Security State* (Boston: Houghton Mifflin Co., 1978), pp. 69-86.

51. Memorandum to Acting Secretary of State Joseph C. Grew, May 15, 1945; in United States, State Department, Foreign Relations of the United States, *The Conference of Berlin, 1945* 1 (Washington, D.C., 1960): 14. (Hereafter designated *Potsdam Papers*.)

52. Transcript of Hopkins-Stalin talks; in ibid., p. 47.

53. See Ambassador Harriman's memorandum; in ibid., p. 234.

54. "Briefing Book Paper"; in ibid., pp. 928-929.

55. Ibid., pp. 188, 201.

56. *FRUS* (1945), 8: 914. See also Max Beloff, *Soviet Policy in the Far East, 1944-1951* (London: Oxford University Press, 1953), pp. 155-156.

57. See the British and American minutes of this meeting, in *Potsdam Papers* 2: 252-256, 264-266.

58. Memorandum of January 23, 1945, in *Conferences of Malta and Yalta*, pp. 78-91.

59. See Lloyd Gardner, *Architects of Illusion* (Chicago: Quadrangle Books, 1970), p. 35; see also Schurmann, *Logic of World Power*, pp. 76-83.

60. RG 59, Notter File, "Japan: Korea: Problems of International Trusteeship," November 30, 1943; quoted in Morris, "Korean Trusteeship," p. 75.

61. RG 59, Notter File, "Possible Soviet Attitudes toward Far East Questions," October 2, 1943; quoted in Morris, "Korean Trusteeship," p. 81.

62. "Korea: Occupation and Military Government: Composition of Forces," March 29, 1944; in *FRUS* (1944), 5: 1,224-1,228.

63. Ibid., pp. 1,226, 1,228.

64. Ibid., memorandum of May 4, 1944, pp. 1,239-1,242.

65. Briefing book paper, *Conferences of Malta and Yalta*, pp. 358-361. It is curious that Great Britain should be assumed to have "a real interest" in Korea, while the Soviet Union, whose borders touch Korea, would have such an interest only if it entered the war against Japan. It is especially curious when we consider the British view on Korea in 1945 as rendered by L. H. Fould of the London Far Eastern Department: "Korea . . . is not worth the bones of a single British grenadier" (quoted in Thorne, *Allies of a Kind*, p. 660).

66. Ibid., p. 359. The thinking and phraseology here is quite similar to an important State Department paper on Japan, "Japan: Occupation and Military Government" (*Potsdam Papers* 1: 933-935), in considering Soviet interests and the necessity for American dominance in postwar occupation arrangements.

67. *Potsdam Papers* 1: 313.

68. The Chinese case made the American political interest in trusteeship more

obvious than did the Korean case. In 1947 Gen. Wedemeyer suggested a five-power trusteeship or guardianship as a remedy for the possibility that Manchuria would become "a Soviet satellite"; "should one of the [five] nations refuse to participate in Manchurian Guardianship, China might then request the General Assembly of the United Nations to establish a Trusteeship, under the provisions of the Charter." Albert C. Wedemeyer, "Report to the President: Korea, September 1947" (Washington, D.C.: United States Government Printing Office, 1951), pp. 2-3.

69. LeFeber, "Roosevelt, Churchill, and Indochina," p. 1,278. See also Yergin, *Shattered Peace*, p. 57.

70. *FRUS* (1945), 5: 556-580. Also to be included among alternative views would be various papers prepared by George McCune, the only Korea expert in the State Department. On these, see Morris, "Korean Trusteeship," pp. 95-96.

71. Joint Chiefs of Staff memorandum, June 18, 1945; in *Potsdam Papers* 1: 905. See also Briefing book paper, *Potsdam Papers* 1: 924-926; also Herbert Feis, *The Atomic Bomb and the End of World War II* (Princeton: Princeton University Press, 1966), p. 8. On the American military view that Soviet entry against Japan was entirely necessary, see Feis, *Atomic Bomb*, pp. 465-466. See also Kolko, *Politics of War*, pp. 204-208, 344, 365, 535, 554-556, 560-567.

72. *Potsdam Papers* 2: 351-352.

73. Ibid., 1: 347.

74. Record of conversation with MacArthur, February 1945; in United States Department of Defense, *The Entry of the Soviet Union into the War Against Japan: Military Plans, 1941-1945* (Washington, D.C., 1955), pp. 51-52.

75. *Potsdam Papers* 1: 905.

76. Minutes of July 24, 1945 Tripartite Military Meeting; in ibid., 2: 345.

77. See the remarks of Gen. Marshall and Adm. King at a White House conference, June 18, 1945; in *Potsdam Papers* 1: 903-910.

78. See Yergin, *Shattered Peace*, pp. 101-102, 115-116. See also Mark Paul, "Diplomacy Delayed: The Atomic Bomb and the Division of Korea, 1945," in Bruce Cumings, ed., *Korean-American Relations, 1945-1953*, forthcoming; Matray, "Reluctant Crusade," ch. 5; and Thorne, *Allies of a Kind*, pp. 500, 529-550.

79. J. Lawton Collins, *War in Peacetime: The History and Lessons of Korea* (Boston: Houghton Mifflin Co., 1969), pp. 25-26n.

80. See Rusk's letter of July 12, 1950; in *FRUS* (1945), 6: 1,039. Over the years there have been many attempts to blame the military for a decision that all take to be disastrous. John Gunther, in *The Riddle of MacArthur* (New York: Harper & Bros., 1950), p. 178, reported the following story by Lewis Haskins, later the executive secretary of the American Friends Service Committee:

> Just before the surrender of Japan several one-star generals hurried into an office in the Pentagon with the statement, "We've got to divide Korea. Where can we divide it?" A colonel with experience in the Far East protested to his superiors, "You can't do that, Korea is a social and economic unit. There is no place to divide it." The generals insisted . . . "We have got to divide Korea and it has to be done by four o'clock this afternoon."

See also Arthur L. Grey, "The Thirty-eighth Parallel," *Foreign Affairs* 29, no. 3 (April 1951): 485, 487; and Soon Sung Cho, *Korea in World Politics, 1940-1950* (Berkeley: University of California Press, 1967), pp. 56-58. A recent official study attempts to locate the decision in the Operations Division of the War Department and implies that it was based on earlier planning for Korea done by the American military during the Potsdam Conference. This interpretation is strained and contradictory, however, and does not take into consideration Rusk's personal account. (See James F. Schnabel, *Policy and Direction: The First Year* [Washington, D.C.: Office of the Chief of Military History, 1972], pp. 7-9.)

81. Schnabel, *Policy and Direction*, p. 11.

82. The proposal to divide Korea at the thirty-eighth parallel was included in General Order No. 1, transmitted to the Allies on August 15. Stalin's response to it made no mention of Korea. (See *Stalin's Correspondence with Churchill, Attlee, Roosevelt, and Truman, 1941-1945* [New York: E. P. Dutton & Co., 1958] [originally published in Moscow by the USSR Ministry of Foreign Affairs], pp. 261-266.)

83. Schurmann, *Logic of World Power*, p. 566.

84. Cho, *Korea in World Politics*, pp. 47-50, offers an excellent account of various attempts to divide Korea dating back to 1592.

85. For instance, Stalin said on September 2, 1945, that "the turning of the tables on Japan in Manchuria was something for which the older generation had waited for the entire forty years since the Russo-Japanese War" (quoted in Beloff, *Soviet Policy*, p. 246).

86. Morris, "Korean Trusteeship," p. 118.

87. Kolko, *Politics of War*, p. 140.

88. Han-mu Kang. "The United States Military Government in Korea, 1945-1948: An Analysis and Evaluation of Its Policy" (Ph.D. dissertation, University of Cincinnati, 1970), pp. 1-2; Schnabel, *Policy and Direction*, pp. 7-8. See also Leonard C. Hoag, "American Military Government in Korea: War Policy and the First Year of Occupation, 1941-1946" (draft manuscript prepared under the auspices of the Office of the Chief of Military History, Department of the Army, Washington, D.C., 1970), pp. 69-78.

89. USAFIK, "HUSAFIK," Manuscript in the Office of the Chief of Military History, Washington, D.C. (Tokyo and Seoul: 1947, 1948), vol. 1, ch. 1, pp. 5, 18. Schnabel, in *Policy and Direction*, seems at one point to misconstrue these contingency plans as presaging the division of Korea at the thirty-eighth parallel (pp. 7-8) but then acknowledges that the actual partition came at the SWNCC meeting of August 10-11 and was made without reference to Operation Baker (p. 9).

90. Barbara W. Tuchman, *Stilwell and the American Experience in China, 1911-1945* (New York: Macmillan Co., 1971), p. 663.

91. Existing sources are contradictory on the actual date. USAFIK, "XXIV Corps Journal," XXIV Corps Historical File, says August 15; "HUSAFIK," vol. 1, ch. 1, p. 10, says August 12; Tuchman, *Stilwell*, p. 665, indicates that it was after August 14.

92. Tuchman, *Stilwell*, p. 665; "XXIV Corps Journal," March 11, 1946 entry. Tuchman suggests that MacArthur may have intervened with Washington in Chiang's favor. She also quotes Stilwell's reaction: "So they cut my throat once more—in deference to Chiang Kai-shek" (p. 665).

93. The official date of Hodge's appointment was August 18, 1945. ("HUSAFIK," vol. 1, ch. 1, p. 25.)

94. Ibid., pp. 12-13. See also XXIV Corps historian Albert Keep's comments on Hodge in "XXIV Corps Journal," February 11, 1946.

95. See Roy E. Appleman et al., *Okinawa: The Last Battle*, U.S. Army in World War II, (Washington, D.C.: United States Department of the Army, Historical Division, 1948), p. 26.

96. "HUSAFIK," vol. 1, ch. 1, p. 12.

97. See Hodge's obituary in the *New York Times*, November 13, 1963.

98. "HUSAFIK," vol. 1, ch. 1, p. 16.

99. Kang, "United States Military government in Korea," p. 27; Gregory Henderson in *Korea: The Politics of the Vortex* (Cambridge: Harvard University Press, 1968), p. 123, writes, "General Hodge was very possibly the first man in history selected to wield executive powers over a nation of nearly twenty million on the basis of shipping time." Stilwell might have objected that other considerations dictated Hodge's selection.

100. Memorandum of August 10, 1945; in *FRUS* (1945), 8: 967.

101. Ibid., p. 149.

102. Schnabel, *Policy and Direction*, p. 11. Gen. Lincoln was chief of the Strategy and Policy Group in the Operations Division of the War Department. His suggestion came as the Americans awaited Stalin's reply to General Order No. 1.

103. The 96th Division of the Tenth Army was diverted from Korea to Tientsin in late September ("HUSAFIK," vol. 1, ch. 6, p. 29). Many XXIV Corps officers originally expected to be sent to Japan.

104. "XXIV Corps Journal," August 14, 1945 entry: General Merrill "explained—for the ears of the staff only—that the occupation of Korea was still being discussed on a high political plane, and that there was a possibility that the Americans might not occupy Korea after all." See also "HUSAFIK," vol. 1, ch. 1, p. 2.

105. "XXIV Corps Journal," August 12 and August 27, 1945 entries; "HUSAFIK," vol. 1, ch. 1, pp. 34-36.

106. Memorandum of Hodge's discussions with Gen. Albert Wedemeyer, August 27, 1947; in XXIV Corps Historical File. Hodge also called the move to Korea a "scramble" in his August 27, 1945 cable to MacArthur's Headquarters (in XXIV Corps Historical File).

107. "HUSAFIK," vol. 1, ch. 1, p. 34.

108. Quoted in ibid., p. 34.

109. Cable, Joint Chiefs of Staff to MacArthur, August 24, 1945; in RG 218, JCS, 383.21 Korea (3-19-45) 1942-1945, box no. 638.

110. Morris, "Korean Trusteeship," pp. 114-115, quoting minutes of Far East committee meetings from July 31 to August 22, 1945.

111. "XXIV Corps Journal," August 25, 1945 entry.

112. "HUSAFIK," vol. 1, ch. 1, p. 59.

113. Ibid., p. 60.

114. Kolko erred in saying that "when the Americans arrived in Seoul and Inchon, deep in the American sector, they found the Russians in possession" (*Politics of War*, p. 603). Seoul is not really "deep" in south Korea, either, being about thirty-five miles south of the thirty-eighth parallel.

115. Henderson, *Vortex*, p. 121. See also Kang, "United States Military Government in Korea," pp. 3-4.

116. Ernst Fraenkel, *Military Occupation and the Rule of Law: Occupation Government in the Rhineland, 1918-1923* (New York: Oxford University Press, 1944), pp. 183-184. The Carnegie Endowment commissioned this study, in hopes that its lessons could be applied to the postwar occupation of Germany.

Fraenkel, however, ended up in the USAMGIK Department of Justice (see chapter five).

117. Ibid., p. x. There was much debate during the war about whether or not to extirpate fascist institutions after occupation. Although the issue was resolved in the occupation of Sicily through the temporary and "non-political" use of fascist officials in 1943, by the end of the war the consensus was that occupation forces would be used "as an instrument for the complete reorientation of political and social life" in defeated Axis countries. See Harry L. Coles and Albert K. Weinberg, *Civil Affairs: Soldiers Become Governors* (Washington, D.C.: Office of the Chief of Military History, 1964), pp. 144-146; also Frederick M. Watkins, "Military Occupation Policy of the Axis Powers," and Merle Fainsod, "The Development of American Military Government Policy During World War II," both in Carl J. Friedrich et al., *American Experiences in Military Government in World War II* (New York: Rinehart & Co., 1948).

118. "XXIV Corps Journal," August 14, 1945 entry. Dean Acheson, as American representative to the United Nations Relief and Rehabilitation Agency (UNRRA), urged in a memorandum of May 18, 1945, that although Korea was "technically enemy territory," it should be designated as "a liberated area" eligible for UNRRA aid, because of the Cairo Declaration pledge. The UNRRA approved the designation in August 1945. (See *FRUS* [1945], 2: 979-981, 1,003.)

119. The official "HUSAFIK" paraphrased MacArthur's "Operations Order No. 4" (which I have not seen) as follows: "The Korean were to be treated as liberated people, in spite of the obvious fact that they were enemy nationals." The second clause appears to be a construction of "HUSAFIK" historians. (See "HUSAFIK," vol. 1, ch. 1, pp. 63-64.) For conflicting interpretations on whether Koreans were enemies or friends, see also Hoag, "American Military Government," pp. 103-104.

120. Kang, "United States Military Government in Korea," quoting Hodge's directive of September 4, pp. 34-35.

121. USAMGIK, "History of the United States Army Military Government in Korea, Period of September 1945 to 30 June 1946" (Seoul. Office of Administrative Services, Statistical Research Division, 1946), 3: 139. (Hereafter designated "HMGK.")

122. Quoted in "HUSAFIK," vol. 1, ch. 1, p. 51-52. The message was sent to the Japanese government in Tokyo, which gave it to MacArthur, who in turn dispatched it forthwith to Hodge on Okinawa.

123. Ibid., p. 52. MacArthur's covering memo, without the Japanese message itself, is available in RG 5, SCAP, Japanese Surrender File no. 2, MacArthur Archives.

124. "HUSAFIK," vol. 1, ch. 1, p. 58.

125. Ibid., radio messages quoted in pp. 58-59, 70-71.

126. Ibid., p. 71.

127. *New York Times*, September 23, 1945.

128. Philip H. Taylor, "Administration and Operation of Military Government in Korea," in Friedrich et al., *American Experiences*, p. 355; and Arthur D. Bouterse, Philip H. Taylor, and Arthur A. Maass, "American Military Government Experience in Japan," in Friedrich, pp. 320-321. See also "HUSAFIK," vol. 3, ch. 1, pp. 28-30; and Kazuo Kawai, *Japan's American Interlude* (Chicago: University of Chicago Press, 1960), p. 20.

129. Compiled by the Joint Intelligence Study Publishing Board in April 1945, in

two long volumes classified "confidential," it is available in Modern Military Branch, United States National Archives. That the XXIV Corps had this study with them is verified in "HUSAFIK," vol. 1, ch. 1, p. 20.

130. Readers interested in other information that the XXIV Corps had with it on Okinawa may consult my dissertation, "Politics of Liberation," pp. 226-233.

131. "HUSAFIK," vol. 1, ch. 1, p. 64.

132. Schurmann, *Logic of World Power*, pp. 3-56.

133. In *Shattered Peace*, p. 83, Yergin quotes Truman as saying, with reference to his famous first meeting with Molotov on April 23, 1945, that the United States could not get 100 percent of what it wanted, but that "we should be able to get 85 percent."

NOTES TO CHAPTER FIVE

Forging a New Order

1. Franz Neumann, *The Democratic and the Authoritarian State* (Glencoe Ill.: Free Press, 1957) p. 236.

2. See E. E. Schattsneider's statement: "All forms of political organization have a bias in favor of the exploitation of some kinds of conflict and the suppression of others because organization is the mobilization of bias. Some issues are organized into politics while others are organized out" (in *The Semi Sovereign People* [New York, 1960], p. 71).

3. Politics in the provinces depicted more clearly than did Seoul the strength and import of revolutionary forces in Korea. For reasons of structure, this aspect is left to Part III of this study; but the reader might wish to consult those chapters, since they provide essential background to American policy at the center.

4. H. Franz Schurmann, *The Logic of World Power: An Inquiry into the Origins, Currents and Contradictions of World Politics* (New York: Pantheon Books, 1974), p. 97.

5. USAFIK, "HUSAFIK" Manuscript in the Office of the Chief of Military History, Washington, D.C. (Tokyo and Seoul, 1947, 1948), vol. 3, ch. 2, p. 10.

6. USAMGIK, "HMGK" (Seoul: Office of Administrative Services, Statistical Research Division, 1946), 1: 1. E. Grant Meade described a policy briefing in October 1945 at MacArthur's Tokyo headquarters for civil affairs officers departing for Korea in which the impression was given that United States policy in Korea was "to form a bulwark against communism" (see *American Military Government in Korea* [New York: King's Crown Press, Columbia University, 1951], p. 52).

7. See the account in "HUSAFIK," vol. 1, ch. 1, pp. 72-75. The convoy was part of the United States Navy 7th Amphibious Fleet under the command ship *Catoctin*—the same ship that took Roosevelt to Yalta.

8. An American advance party consisting of eight officers and ten enlisted men had landed at Kimpo Airport on September 4 to establish liaison with the Japanese. Twenty-one officers who had been forced to return to Okinawa because of bad weather on September 4 were able to reach Seoul on September 6. Maj. Gen. Toshimaro Sugai quartered the advance party at the Chosŏn Hotel. Several sources assert that the Americans refused audiences to a number of prominent Koreans. Richard Robinson described a party that the

Americans threw for ranking Japanese military and government officials that turned into "a glorious drunken brawl with the Japanese, which lasted for several days" (see Richard Robinson, "Betrayal of a Nation," 1947 [private copy at Massachusetts Institute of Technology], p. 15). (I am indebted to Dr. Robinson for allowing me to read his manuscript and for sharing with me his personal recollections of the period. He worked in the MG Department of Public Information and served as an historian for the War Department. "Betrayal of a Nation" is part of a larger manuscript that he was forced to burn before he was allowed to leave Korea.) For a partial confirmation of Robinson's account of the advance party's activities, see "HUSAFIK," vol. 1, ch. 4, p. 5.

9. "HUSAFIK," vol. 1, ch. 4, p. 6. *Maeil sinbo*, September 12, 1945, said the Japanese shot and killed labor union leader Kwŏn P'yŏng-gŭn and *poandae* activist Yi Sŏk-u.

10. *New York Times*, September 12, 1945.

11. See, for example, Andrew Roth, "Korea's Heritage," *Nation* 162, no. 5 (February 2, 1946): 122.

12. Robinson, "Betrayal of a Nation," p. 16. See also William Langdon's comments; in State Department, *FRUS* (1945), 6: 1,135.

13. "HUSAFIK," vol. 1, ch. 4, p. 7.

14. Based on accounts in ibid., pp. 7-9; and "XXIV Corps Journal," in XXIV Corps Historical File, September 9, 1945 entry.

15. *Seoul Times*, September 10, 1945; and "HUSAFIK," vol. 1, ch. 4, p. 15. Koreans had heard such paternalism *ad nauseum* from the Japanese. In 1920 Premier Hara Kei told Koreans essentially what Hodge did, that the success or lack of it of Japanese policies toward Korea "must necessarily depend upon the efforts of Koreans themselves toward their own upliftment." The Japanese, of course, would sit in judgment of Koreans and determine when they were ready for a greater share in government. (See Hara's statement quoted in Hugh Heung-woo Cynn, *The Rebirth of Korea* [New York: Abingdon Press, 1920], pp. 166-169.) See also Hodge's "To the People of Korea," in Appendix B.

16. *Seoul Times*, September 10, 1945.

17. "HUSAFIK," vol. 1, ch. 4, p. 17.

18. See A. Wigfall Green, *The Epic of Korea* (Washington, D.C.: Public Affairs Press, 1950), pp. 15, 33, 100.

19. *New York Times*, September 11, 1945. The *Times* asked editorially, "Are we to be 'soft' with the colonial riffraff of Japan and hard with the people we have come to set free?"

20. *FRUS* (1945), 6: 1,045. Truman released a statement on September 18, 1945, saying, "Such Japanese as may be temporarily retained are being utilized as servants of the Korean people and of our occupying forces only because they are deemed essential by reason of their technical qualifications." The statement also pledged "the elimination of all vestiges of Japanese control over Korean economic and political life," but said that that goal would require "time and patience" (*FRUS* [1945], 6: 1,048). See also "HUSAFIK," vol. 1, ch. 4, p. 18.

21. "HUSAFIK," vol. 1, ch. 4, p. 18.

22. Arnold was a West Point graduate who had been an All-American center on the academy football team. His experience during the war had included

command positions in the Leyte and Okinawa campaigns. He was known as an artillery expert ("HUSAFIK," vol. 3, ch. 1, p. 24).

23. "HUSAFIK," vol. 1, ch. 4, p. 19. The official title, USAMGIK (United States Army Military Government in Korea) was adopted on January 14, 1946. The Americans had originally titled it USAMGOK (Government of Korea); but that was changed, according to official sources, because it "ended in three letters which sounded like 'gook'" ("HUSAFIK," vol. 3, ch. 2, p. 25).

24. Seoul Times, September 14, 1945.

25. USAFIK, XXIV Corps Historical File, Military Government team no. 3, daily journal, September 11 and September 13, 1945 entries.

26. "HUSAFIK," vol. 1, ch. 4, p. 36; also ch. 7, p. 17; and vol. 3, ch. 2, p. 13. Apparently only a few of the original 350 memorandums remain in the MG archival materials.

27. See the accounts in Chosŏn inmin-bo (Korean People's Report), September 8, 1945; and in the Seoul Times, September 12, 1945. Another source, Haebang nyusŭ, August 26 entry, said that the CPKI had selected the three men on August 26 to serve as a welcoming committee for the Americans. The three men said nothing about the formation of the KPR and may have been unaware of it.

28. Yi Man-gyu, Yŏ Un-hyŏng t'ujaeng-sa [History of Yŏ Un-hyŏng's Struggle] (Seoul: Ch'ongmun-gak, 1946), pp. 237-238.

29. These included Kim Sŏng-su, Chang Tŏk-su, Ku Cha-ok, Hong Sun-yŏp, Yi Wŏn-ch'ŏl, Pak Yong-hŭi, Kim Ch'ang-su, and Cho Man-sik (Cho was listed in the KDP September 8 roster [see chapter three] but may not have given permission for the use of his name; in early September, he was still leading the north Korean branch of the CPKI). The remaining three were An Chae-hong, who had broken with the CPKI on September 1; Yi Im-su, a physician; and "Ch'oe Tong." (See the list in G-2 "Periodic Report," no. 1, September 8-9, 1945, in XXIV Corps Historical File.)

30. Yŏ Un-hong was charged with being a pro-Japanese in Ch'in-Ilp'a kunsang [The Pro-Japanese Groups] (Seoul: Samsaeng munhwa-sa, 1948), pp. 6, 25; Leonard Bertsch, who came to know Yŏ well, concurred (interview, May 19, 1973). That Yŏ and the other two men have gone beyond their CPKI mandate (that is, if they had one) is suggested by the fact that on August 26 Yi Kang-guk was also selected to be on the CPKI welcoming committee (Haebang nyusŭ, August 26 entry).

31. The second list of fourteen men included Yun Ch'i-ho, Pak Chong-yang, Kim Myŏng-jun, Han Sang-yong, and Yi Chin-ho, all of whom had received peerages from the Japanese; also Hugh Heung-woo Cynn (Shin Hŭng-u) and Rev. "J. S. Ryang," both leading Korean Christians and collaborators with Japan; industrialists like Kim Yŏn-su, owner of the Kyŏngsŏng Textile Company, and Pak Hŭng-sik, owner of the Hwashin Department Store and other enterprises; Ŏm Chang-sŏp, a high official in the Government-General Bureau of Education; and Cho Pyŏng-sang, Shin Yong-in, Kim Tae-un, and Yi Ki-yong. (See the list in G-2 "Periodic Report," no. 1, September 8-9, 1945, in XXIV Corps Historical File.)

32. "HUSAFIK," vol. 2, ch. 1, p. 2.

33. G-2 Periodic Report, no. 1, September 8-9, 1945.

34. Seoul Times, September 12, 1945. Andrew Roth said Hodge had told American reporters that "a Phi Beta Kappa graduate of Brown University took off

in a small boat, met us in the harbor, and told me he wanted to be Minister of Finance [in the Korean government]" (see "Cross-Fire in Korea," *Nation* 162, no. 8, [February 23, 1946], p. 220). This would be Paek Sang-gyu, a wealthy landlord, banker, and graduate of Brown who flirted with the CPKI, and the Left in general, in 1945 and 1946. He had the habit of approaching Americans and saying, "Hi! Brown '05" (conversation with Prof. Edward Wagner, Harvard University, April 1974).

35. Ernst Fraenkel, *Military Occupation and the Rule of Law: Occupation Government in the Rhineland, 1918-1923* (New York: Oxford University Press, 1944), pp. 33-34; Harry L. Coles and Albert K. Weinberg, *Civil Affairs: Soldiers Become Governors* (Washington, D.C.: Office of the Chief of Military History, 1964), p. 145. Such admonitions were emphasized in the military government manuals that the XXIV Corps carried with it to Korea.

36. G-2 "Periodic Report," no. 2, September 10-11, 1945.

37. G-2 "Periodic Report," nos. 3, 4, 6, 10, 12, September 10-21, 1945.

38. Louise Yim, *My Forty-Year Fight for Korea* (Seoul: Chungang University, International Culture Research Center, 1951), p. 242; Pak Induk, *September Monkey* (New York: Harper & Bros., 1954), p. 211. Ms. Pak, a staunch anti-communist who took a speechmaking tour through the United States at the behest of the MG, offered the following as an example of unreasonable "Communist" demands:

> In agricultural countries or areas where farm land is held in large estates, they promise to break up and distribute the holdings among the small people, but in industrial countries or communities they concentrate on the injustices and hardships experienced by the workers and thus create a state of agitation and unrest, holding out the promise that the workers shall have an equal share of production (p. 250).

39. "XXIV Corps Journal," September 10 entry; and "HUSAFIK," vol. 1, ch. 3, pp. 5-7.

40. Kim Chun-yŏn, ed., *Han'guk minjudang so-sa* [A Short History of the Korean Democratic Party] (Seoul: Han'guk minjudang sŏnjŏn-bu, 1948), pp. 16-18. Note that the KDP did not charge the leader of the north Korean branch of the CPKI, Cho Man-sik, with pro-Japanese leanings.

41. Yŏ Un-hyŏng, Hŏ Hŏn, and An Chae-hong all served terms of varying lengths in Japanese prisons. To my knowledge, there was never a shred of hard evidence to suggest that any of them were anything but die-hard resistors of Japanese rule in Korea. Among those KDP leaders mentioned as American informants in the text, however, the following had charges of collaboration raised against them in American and Korean sources: Kim Sŏng-su, Chang Tŏk-su, Sŏ Sang-il, Kim To-yŏn, Im Yŏng-sin, and Pak In-dŏk. See G-2, "Biographies"; in XXIV Corps Historical File; and *Ch'in-Ilp'a kunsang*, pp. 6, 15, 31, 50-53, 139. See also biographical information in chapter three.

James Palais described Yi Dynasty factional feuds: "The self-righteous moralism that was so characteristic of the Confucianists also tended to reinforce and perpetuate animosity engendered by contests for political power and disputes over substantive issues. One's opponent's wrong-doings were frequently castigated as morally heinous acts which had to be punished even after death." He also noted that vicious *ad hominem* attacks should not obscure the very real issues of political power at stake. (See *Politics and Policy in Traditional Korea* [Cambridge: Harvard University Press, 1976], p. 46.)

42. Yŏ implied that Hodge refused to see *him*, but Yi Man-gyu said it was Yŏ

who, revulsed by all the fawning on the Americans, refused to see Hodge until October 5 (see *Voice of Korea*, no. 90, September 16, 1947; and Yi, *Yŏ Un-hyŏng*, p. 239).

43. These quotes are taken from Yŏ's last letter before his assassination, written on July 18, 1947, and published in *Voice of Korea*, no. 90, September 16, 1947.

44. G-2 "Periodic Report," no. 3, September 11-12, 1945.

45. G-2 "Periodic Report," no. 10, September 18-19, 1945.

46. In the early weeks of the Occupation, Korean newspapers were full of contempt for the rank opportunism and power-seeking of KDP leaders and others. The *Seoul Times* on September 16 castigated the "sycophants" and "opportunists" who were "swarming" around MG headquarters. Without naming names, it said that Koreans who had studied in the United States and those who had known "how to insinuate themselves into the favor of the Japanese" were active; one now saw "on the same stage a same play." Another non-leftist source condemned the *sadaejuŭi* of a clique of capitalists and landlords who had fattened under Japanese rule while others starved and who now were cozying up to the MG. (See Pae Sŏng-nyŏng, *I hondong ŭl ottok'e susŭp halga* [How Will We Deal with This Chaos] [Seoul: Chŏn'guk chŏngch'i undongja huwŏn-hoe, 1945], pp. 10-12.) See also Chae-Mi Hanjok yŏnhap wiwŏn-hoe, *Haebang Chosŏn* [Liberated Korea] (Hawaii: Chae-Mi Hanjok yŏnhap wiwŏn-hoe, 1948), p. 10; and a leftist newspaper, *Munhwa chŏnsŏn* [Cultural Front], November 15, 1945.

47. It would be something of an understatement to say that this is not how the early days of the Occupation are depicted in several other accounts. Compare, for example, E.A.J. Johnson, a high official in the MG, who said, "Confused by the complex spectrum of Korean cliques and parties, we found it difficult to know which factions to favor, which to ignore. . . ." (*American Imperialism in The Image of Peer Gynt* [Minneapolis: University of Minnesota Press, 1971], p. 180.) The fact is, however, that Left and Right were like two scorpions in a bottle, and the Americans nourished one at the expense of the other.

48. Benninghoff to Secretary of State, September 15, 1945; in *FRUS* (1945), 6: 1,049-1,053.

49. Ibid., p. 1,051. Careful readers will note that Benninghoff transformed the demand of "all" Korean groups for Japanese property into a demand of "communists."

50. Herbert Feis, *The Atomic Bomb and the End of World War II* (Princeton: Princeton University Press, 1966), p. 166n.

51. Benninghoff to Secretary of State, September 15, 1945; in *FRUS* (1945), 6: 1,053.

52. Benninghoff to Secretary of State, September 29, 1945; in *FRUS* (1945), 6: 1,061-1,065.

53. Ibid., pp. 1,061, 1,063.

54. Ibid., pp. 1,063-1,064.

55. Ibid., pp. 1,064-1,065.

56. "HUSAFIK," vol. 2, ch. 1, pp. 3, 6-7. On September 13 the KDP propaganda department issued a statement saying that in discussions with Americans the KDP had learned that the United States would not recognize the People's Republic and that the United States would constitute the only government in south Korea (see Republic of Korea, Kuksa p'yŏnch'an wiwŏn-hoe, *THMGS* I [Seoul, 1970]: 97). This was the first of many statements issued by

the KDP that seemed to have American authorization, although none was formally given.

57. *Seoul Times*, September 27, 1945.

58. Benninghoff to the Acting Political Advisor in Japan (George Atcheson), October 9, 1945; in *FRUS* (1945), 6: 1,069.

59. *Seoul Times*, October 10, 1945.

60. Yi, *Yŏ Un-hyŏng*, pp. 240-241.

61. Ibid., pp. 241-242; *Seoul Times*, October 5, 1945.

62. "HUSAFIK," vol. 2, ch. 1, p. 8. Yi Yong-sŏl was a doctor, Kim Yong-sun was a businessman, O Yŏng-su was a banker, Kang Pyŏng-sun was a lawyer, and Yun Ki-ik was a mine owner (see *Chayu sinmun* [Free News], October 7, 1945; in *THMGS* I: 191-192).

63. Benninghoff to Atcheson, October 9, 1945; in *FRUS* (1945), 6: 1,069.

64. See the membership of the Central Advisory Council upon its dissolution, in USAMGIK *Official Gazette*, removal order no. 29, November 3, 1945. On Kim Sŏng-su and his Honam group, see chapter one.

65. G-2 "Periodic Report," no. 14, September 22-23, 1945.

66. Supreme Command, Allied Powers, *Summation of Non-Military Activities in Japan and Korea* (Tokyo, November 1945), p. 181. (Hereafter designated SCAP *Summation*.)

67. Arnold also said, among other things, "If the men who are arrogating to themselves such high-sounding titles are merely play-acting on a puppet stage with entertainment of questionable amusement value, they must immediately pull down the curtain on the puppet show. If some 'peace preservation' groups have sincerely but childishly acted to aid law and order, they will now disband and return to proper work." ("XXIV Corps Journal," October 10, 1945 entry; *Seoul Times*, October 10, 1945.) See also various news articles in *THMGS* I: 227-235.

68. Benninghoff to Atcheson, October 9, 1945; in *FRUS* (1945), 6: 1,069.

69. "XXIV Corps Journal," October 11, 1945 entry. Korean newsmen at a press conference on October 11 said that Yŏ Un-hyŏng was "a very much respected citizen" and that "this open attack will offend all Koreans." On a show of hands, *all* newsmen present refused to support Arnold's statement. Col. Glenn Newman replied to them that the KPR was not representative of Koreans; instead the Korean people "want order and food now" (thereby paraphrasing Napoleon III's famous statement that "France demands tranquility").

70. Ibid., October 12 entry.

71. "HUSAFIK," vol. 2, ch. 1, p. 10; see original copy attached to G-2 "Weekly Report," no. 7, October 21-28, 1945. Yi Yong-sŏl's speech was dated June 25, 1943; Paek Nak-chun's, June 25, 1943; Ku Cha-ok's, June 7, 1944; and Chang Tŏk-su reportedly called the Americans "vampires" in a speech carried in the *Maeil sinbo* four days after Pearl Harbor (December 11, 1941). The pamphlet also cited a speech by Yang Chu-sam, an advisor to the MG, in which he allegedly stated that "Americans are the enemies of humanity," *Maeil sinbo*, August 6, 1944. See also the KPR's October 5 pamphlet, "A Message to U.S. Citizens," which said, "Our people beg you to recognize the underlying reality of the Corean [*sic*] situation," where "there is no so-called middle class," only poor Koreans who suffered under Japan and "wealthy persons and men of political and upper social positions" who are "naturally pro-Japanese and

often naturalized Japanese" (in "XXIV Corps Journal," October 12, 1945 entry).

72. *New York Times*, October 30, 1945.

73. See the account in *Maeil sinbo*, October 13, 1945.

74. Benninghoff to Atcheson, October 10, 1945; in *FRUS* (1945), 6: 1,070-1,071. Most newspapers, not just those supporting the KPR, had compared American occupation policies unfavorably with those of the Soviets.

75. Cho Pyŏng-ok, *Na ŭi hoegorok* [My Recollections] (Seoul: Min'gyo-sa, 1959), p. 146.

76. *Haebang ilbo*, no. 5, October 18, 1945. Here and in other issues, the KCP depicted a basically decent United States being duped and misled by its Korean advisors. In another issue, the KCP said that "a certain party" had been telling the Americans that KPR leaders were extremists; it commented that if they were indeed extremists, "some of the leaders of the certain political party would have evaporated from this earth" (no. 15, November 25, 1945).

77. See USAMGIK Official Gazette, appointment no. 22, October 20, 1945.

78. "XXIV Corps Journal," October 20 entry; and Cho, *Na ŭi hoegorok*, pp. 147-148. Green, in *Epic of Korea*, p. 72, claimed that Hodge secreted Rhee behind a screen and then "histrionically" presented him to the crowd on October 20. On the circumstances of Rhee's return see chapter seven.

79. Langdon to the Secretary of State, November 26, 1945; in *FRUS* (1945), 6: 1,135. "HUSAFIK," vol. 3, ch. 2, p. 16, stated that "anybody who had been able to enjoy the privileges of higher education under the Japanese regime was suspect" in the eyes of other Koreans.

80. Langdon put his finger on an important aspect of the American-Korean relationship. C. Clyde Mitchell, later a high officer in the Occupation, wrote that Americans "found that they could work best with Koreans who were 'talented,' intelligent, educated in the arts and graces, and therefore from upperclass Korean society." (See Mitchell, *Korea: Second Failure in Asia* [Washington, D.C.: Public Affairs Institute, 1951], p. 15). Langdon simply erred in assuming that such ties were ever cut. They persist to this day; it is my experience that the highest calling for a Korean in American eyes is an ability to speak English and handle constructs that please Americans.

81. Although Korea did not have a feudal past, and the 1940s represented an era and not an epoch, the pattern of the south Korean state in the late 1940s resembles that described in Perry Anderson's analysis of the Absolutist period in Europe, as the old order effected "a *displacement* of politico-legal coercion upwards toward a centralized, militarized summit"; the essence of the Absolutist state was "a *redeployed and recharged apparatus of feudal domination*." Although this state acted fundamentally to protect aristocratic property and privilege, it "could *simultaneously* ensure the basic interests of the nascent mercantile and manufacturing classes" (emphasis in original). (See Anderson, *Lineages of the Absolutist State* [London: New Left Books, 1974], pp. 18-19, 40.)

82. "HUSAFIK," vol. 3, ch. 5, pp. 7-8.

83. See in particular the extremely detailed report of MG team no. 3 (Seoul), September 11-November 30, 1945, which is a daily journal of American activities in Seoul (in United States Army, RG 407, "World War II Operations Reports," entry no. 427).

84. Benninghoff to Secretary of State, September 15, 1945; in *FRUS* (1945), 6: 1,049; MG team no. 3, daily journal, entries for September.

85. MG team no. 3, daily journal, September 15, October 8, 1945 entries.

86. Lee Won-sul, "The Impact of United States Occupation Policy on the Socio-Political Structure of South Korea, 1945-1948" (Ph.D. dissertation, Western Reserve University, 1961), p. 2.

87. "HUSAFIK," vol. 3, ch. 5, p. 27; and ch. 2, pp. 17-19.

88. See the discussion in chapter one; and Barrington Moore, Jr., *Social Origins of Dictatorship and Democracy: Lord and Peasant in the Making of the Modern World* (Boston: Beacon Press, 1966), ch. 5.

89. Ralf Dahrendorf, *Class and Class Conflict in Industrial Society* (Stanford: Stanford University Press, 1959), p. 300.

90. See Wonmo Dong, "Japanese Colonial Policy and Practice in Korea, 1905-1945: A Study in Assimilation" (Ph.D. dissertation, Georgetown University, 1965), pp. 355-363. Among junior *(hannin* rank) officials, about one-third were Koreans.

91. This list is derived from a comparison of appointment lists in USAMGIK *Official Gazette* and a list of KDP "initiators" in *THMGS* I: 62-63. Most of these appointments were made in October and November 1945.

92. G-2 "Weekly Report," no. 24, February 17-24, 1946.

93. USAMGIK *Official Gazette*, appointment no. 101, July 11, 1946.

94. Yi Hun-gu was "Hoon K. Lee," author of *Land Utilization and Rural Economy in Korea*; he later directed the MG Department of Agriculture and Forestry.

95. *Seoul Times*, October 27, 1945. See also *Maeil sinbo*, October 27, 1945. For biographical information on Chang U-sik, see *Chōsen nenkan 1945* [Korea Yearbook 1945] (Seoul: Keijo nippo-sha, 1945), p. 393. Ch'oe Wŏn-t'aek, chief of the Seoul People's Committee, was arrested on November 2, 1945, for calling Yi Pŏm-sŭng a collaborator (MG team no. 3, daily journal, November 3, 1945 entry).

96. *Chōsen nenkan 1945*, p. 380.

97. See chapter nine.

98. *Chōsen nenkan 1945*, p. 368.

99. Eric Wolf, *Peasant Wars of the Twentieth Century* (New York: Harper & Row, 1969), p. 287.

100. Han T'ae-su, *Han'guk chŏngdang-sa* [A History of Korean Political Parties] (Seoul: Sin t'aeyang-sa, 1961), p. 13.

101. "HMGK" 1: 29-30. This study said that only "communists" criticized American appointments; also that "one merit" of the Japanese system was that it allowed centralized, countrywide controls of bureaucratic appointments (pp. 30-31).

102. Ibid., p. 30.

103. Cho, *Na ŭi hoegorok*, p. 149. Compare E.A.J. Johnson's bland apologetics: "*Before we knew what had happened*, we found that arch-conservatives were in control of all important positions in both the Police and the Justice departments" (emphasis added) (*American Imperialism*, p. 167).

104. Cho, *Na ŭi hoegorok*, pp. 150-151. See also Ko Ha sŏnsaeng chŏn'gi p'yŏn-ch'an wiwŏn-hoe, *Ko Ha Song Chin-u* [collection on Ko Ha, Song Chin-u] (Seoul: Tonga ilbo ch'ulp'an-guk, 1964), p. 324. Cho Pyŏng-ok was from a *yangban* and landowning family in Ch'ŏn'an, South Ch'ungch'ŏng Province, representing the twenty-fourth generation of the Hanyang Cho clan. He was

tutored in the classics and then studied under Kim Kyu-sik in the Paejae School. He graduated from high school in Kingston, Pa., received a B.A. from Columbia University in 1922, and claimed a Ph.D. from Columbia in 1925 (the Columbia Alumni Office shows no record of it). A nationalist and YMCA activist after his return to Korea, he was imprisoned for his role in the *Shin'ganhoe.* He managed the Poin Mining Company from 1937 to 1945. (Based on Cho, *Na ŭi hoegorok,* pp. 1, 23-43, 92-94, 108, 133-134; and USAMGIK, "Who's Who in the South Korean Interim Government" [Seoul, 1947].) Cho died during his campaign for the presidency of South Korea in 1960.

105. "XXIV Corps Journal," October 13, 1945 entry. Mr. "Chung" may have been Chŏn Yong-sun, one-time financial chief of the KDP and an organizer of the *No Ch'ong* company union in mid-1946, who was reportedly known as "the opium seller" for his speculation in drugs (see Counter-Intelligence Corps report, Seoul, September 25, 1946).

106. Interview with Leonard Bertsch, May 19, 1973.

107. National War College, *Korea: Problems of U.S. Army in Occupation, 1945-1947* (Washington, D.C.: Department of the Army, 1948), p. 4. "HUSAFIK," vol. 3, ch. 5, p. 43, placed the date of effective Koreanization in the Justice Department at February, 1946.

108. "HUSAFIK," vol. 3, ch. 5, pp. 73, 77; see also p. 17. For an excellent discussion of the system of justice during the colonial period, see Dong, "Japanese Colonial Policy," pp. 139-147.

109. "HUSAFIK," vol. 3, ch. 5, p. 30.

110. Ibid., pp. 29, 150.

111. Interview with Major George A. Anderson, executive officer of Bureau of Justice, March 25, 1946; in packet of information on "Justice," XXIV Corps Historical File. Dr. Kim is credited for his aid in getting policemen back to work ("HUSAFIK," vol. 3, ch. 5, p. 29).

112. *Haebang Chosŏn,* p. 11; Minjujuŭi minjok chŏnsŏn, *Chosŏn haebang illyŏn-sa* [History of the First Year of Korean Liberation] (Seoul: Munu insŏ'gwan, 1946), p. 122.

113. See Ordinance no. 11, October 9, 1945, in USAMGIK *Official Gazette,* for example.

114. Quoted in "HUSAFIK," vol. 3, ch. 5, p. 36.

115. See chapter ten.

116. "HUSAFIK," vol. 3, ch. 5, p. 61.

117. USAMGIK, Department of Justice, *Selected Legal Opinions of the Department of Justice* (Seoul, 1948).

118. For example, a Korean newspaper editorial in early 1946 that said that Koreans were worse off in south Korea than were Koreans in north Korea or under the Japanese regime was deemed "inimical" to the MG under provisions of Ordinance no. 19, section IV, October 30, 1945. See Opinion no. 95, March 21, 1946, in ibid.

119. Green, *Epic of Korea,* pp. 56, 100-101. On the lack of *habeus corpus,* see also *Selected Legal Opinions,* pp. 4-5.

120. Interview with Maj. George A. Anderson, March 25, 1946, in packet of information on "Justice," XXIV Corps Historical File. Emery Woodall was a lawyer with broad experience, who had lived in China for some time before the war and who had been a civil affairs officer in the China-India-Burma theatre ("HUSAFIK," vol. 2, ch. 2, p. 32).

121. See *Selected Legal Opinions*. Fraenkel and Pergler wrote many of them.
122. The volume in the *Taehan kyŏngch'al chŏn-sa* that deals with the liberation period is entitled, *Spearhead of the Nation*, or *Minjok ŭi sŏnbong*. See also Arno J. Mayer, *Dynamics of Counterrevolution in Europe, 1870-1956: An Analytic Framework* (New York: Harper Torchbooks, 1971), pp. 59-85.
124. *SCAP Summation*, no. 1, September-October 1945, p. 175.
125. "Basic Initial Directive to the Commander in Chief, U.S. Army Forces, Pacific, for the Administration of Civil Affairs in Those Areas of Korea Occupied by U.S. Forces," (SWNCC no. 176/8); in *FRUS* (1945), 6: 1,073-1,091. The original draft of this document was completed at the end of August, and after successive revisions it was sent to MacArthur on October 17. See the successive drafts in RG 353, SWNCC-SANACC, SWNCC no. 176/17, box no. 29.
126. "HUSAFIK," vol. 3, ch. 4, pt. 1, p. 1.
127. Ibid., pp. 2-4, 15.
128. "XXIV Corps Journal," September 13, 1945. Shick also said, however, that the police were then giving him better information than was the XXIV Corps G-2 section.
129. 97th MG Company, "Unit History." See also minutes of the Korean-American Conference, November 7, 1946, in XXIV Corps Historical File. Chang was another of the "landlord-entrepreneurs." The scion of one of Korea's oldest and wealthiest families, he was born in Ch'ilgok near Taegu and graduated from the University of Edinburgh in England. Although his father, a high Korean official in the early years of the colony, had been assassinated by a Korean nationalist, Chang himself was an early nationalist leader and a representative of the KPG at Versailles in 1919. After his return to Korea, he was active in moderate, reformist nationalism. In the 1940s he was managing director of the Bank of Taegu.

It should be noted that some Americans in the Occupation came to resent him more than any other high official. Harold Larsen, XXIV Corps chief historian, described him as "a crass, bastardly character with the face of Nero and the manners of Goering"; Department of State biographies referred to him as "the most reviled official in the interim government," and quoted an American advisor as saying Chang was "cruel, ruthless, and a potential 'strong man' in Korea." Chang became the first foreign minister of the Republic of Korea in 1948. (See State Department, "Biographic Reports on the Cabinet of the Korean Republic" [Washington, D.C.: Office of Intelligence and Research, 1948], in RG 94, USAMGIK; Harold Larsen's report of conversation with Leonard Bertsch, December 5, 1946, in XXIV Corps Historical File; and a packet of raw information in ibid., box no. 21. See also Sudo kwan'gu kyŏngch'al ch'ong, *Haebang ihu sudo kyŏngch'al paltal-sa* [History of the Development of the Metropolitan Police after Liberation] (Seoul: Sudo kwan'gu kyŏngch'al ch'ong, 1947), p. 129.
130. 97th MG Company, "Unit History."
131. Cho, *Na ŭi hoegorok*, pp. 154-155.
132. "HUSAFIK," vol. 3, ch. 4, pt. 1, pp. 11-12. As late as December 1947, the Americans continued to back such a police force and resist meaningful reforms of it, so as not to weaken "the one most strongly cohesive force in Korean political life" (see *Activities of the South Korean Interim Government*, no. 27, December 1947, p. 167).
133. "HUSAFIK," vol. 2, ch. 4, pt. 2, p. 43.

134. Kazuo Kawai, *Japan's American Interlude* (Chicago: University of Chicago Press, 1960), p. 108.
135. Mark Gayn, *Japan Diary* (New York: William Sloane Associates, 1948), p. 391. Col. Maglin was a professional policeman from New York City.
136. Donald S. McDonald, "Field Experience in Military Government: Cholla Namdo Province, 1945-1946," in Carl J. Friedrich et al., *American Experiences in Military Government in World War II* (New York: Rinehart & Co., 1948), p. 375. McDonald overestimates the American role in the centralization of the police. It was more a matter of reviving the Japanese system.
137. HUSAFIK, vol. 3, ch. 4, pt. 1, p. 19-20.
138. *Sudo kyŏngch'al*, p. 117.
139. During the colonial period, the foreign affairs section had responsibility for suppressing the activities of anti-Japanese Korean revolutionaries who infiltrated Korea from Manchuria.
140. All quotes in the text from "HUSAFIK," vol. 3, ch. 4, pt. 1, pp. 12, 23, 49-50.
141. Gayn, *Japan Diary*, p. 391.
142. This would be so, assuming that about two-thirds of the colonial force was in south Korea. John T. McAlister, Jr. noted the same process of augmentation of the forces of order over colonial requirements in post-colonial Vietnam, in *Vietnam: The Origins of Revolution* (Garden City, N.Y.: Doubleday Anchor Books, 1971), p. 106.
143. "HUSAFIK," vol. 3, ch. 4, pt. 1, pp. 29, 42.
144. Minutes of Col. Maglin's talk to the Korean-American Conference, November 5 and November 27, 1946; in XXIV Corps Historical File.
145. Minutes of the Korean-American Conference, November 20 and 25, 1946; in XXIV Corps Historical File. Ch'oe Nŭng-jin was a remarkable character. He was a *ch'iandae* leader in August 1945 who tried to work within the KNP to reform it. After he was ousted, he had the surpassing temerity to run against Syngman Rhee in the May 10, 1948 National Assembly elections. A running account of the harassment to which his candidacy was subjected is available in the *Seoul Times*, March-May 1948. Ch'oe was executed by firing squad in 1952 for alleged collaboration with North Korea during the Korean War. On his constant battles with Cho Pyŏng-ok in the KNP, see "HUSAFIK," vol. 3, ch. 4, pt. 1, p. 22.
146. "Who's Who in the South Korean Interim Government."
147. See Gregory Henderson, *Korea: The Politics of the Vortex* (Cambridge: Harvard University Press, 1968), p. 421n; also *sudo kyŏngch'al*, p. 88. No Tŏk-sul was termed "the tiger of the Japanese police," in Ko Wŏn-byŏn, ed., *Panminja choejang-gi* [Record of the Crimes of the Traitors] (Seoul: Paeg'yŏp munhwa-sa, 1949), pp. 98-100. This was after his "disappearance" following the discovery of the body of a prisoner he had tortured to death, once the ice on the Han River thawed. He later reappeared as a Liberal party activist under the Rhee government in the mid-1950s (Henderson, *Vortex*).
148. *Sudo kyŏngch'al*, pp. 88-90.
149. For Ch'oe's appointment, see USAMGIK *Official Gazette*, appointment no. 66, January 11, 1946. For biographical information, see *Chōsen nenkan*, p. 363.
150. For Underwood's lecture, see *Minju Kyŏngch'al* [The Democratic Policeman] (Seoul: Kyŏngch'al kyoyuk-kuk), no. 2, August 1947, pp. 21-22. Underwood was from a famous missionary family in Korea. On American advisors to the KNP, see "HUSAFIK," vol. 2, ch. 4, pt. 2, p. 42.
151. "HUSAFIK," vol. 3, ch. 4, pt. 1, p. 24.

152. Statement by Col. Erickson in October 1947, quoted in "HUSAFIK," vol. 2, ch. 4, pt. 2, p. 44.
153. John C. Caldwell said that "many of the American police advisors . . . were themselves convinced through race prejudice, ignorance, and lack of education in national differences that the 'gooks' only understood force" (see Caldwell, *The Korea Story* [Chicago: Henry Regnery Co., 1952], p. 8).
154. "XXIV Corps Journal," September 14, 1945 entry.
155. Henderson, *Vortex*, esp. pp. 196-197.
156. Hodge's letter of March 18, 1952, quoted in Robert K. Sawyer, *Military Advisors in Korea: KMAG in Peace and War*, ed. Walter G. Hermes (Washington, D.C.: Office of the Chief of Military History, 1962), p. 21.
157. Republic of Korea, Kukpang-bu p'yŏnch'an wiwŏn-hoe, *Han'guk chŏnjaeng-sa* [History of the Korean War], vol. 1, *Haebang kwa kŏn'gun* [Liberation and the Establishment of the Army] (Seoul: Kukpang-bu, 1967), p. 264. A rather complete history of the development of the South Korean Army is in this volume.
158. Sawyer, *KMAG in Peace and War*, p. 10n.
159. Ibid., pp. 9-11.
160. *Han'guk chŏnjaeng-sa* 1: 256.
161. Sawyer, *KMAG in Peace and War*, p. 10n.
162. See G-2 "Periodic Report," April 5, 1946; and "HUSAFIK," vol. 2, ch. 4, p. 39.
163. United States, Far East Command, "History of the North Korean Army" (Tokyo: G-2 Section, 1952), original classification, "top secret," manuscript in Office of the Chief of Military History, p. 6. This study terms Korean veterans of the Chinese Eighth Route Army the "core" of the subsequent North Korean People's Army and notes that they were not allowed into north Korea until the late spring of 1946 (pp. 6-7).
164. "HUSAFIK," vol. 2, ch. 4, p. 41.
165. Joint Chiefs of Staff to MacArthur, January 9, 1946; in *FRUS* (1945), 6: 1,157. The decision was made in SWNCC, December 18, 1945 and then forwarded to the Joint Chiefs of Staff. SWNCC stated that the United States "should not act unilaterally . . . in establishing 'Korean National Defense Forces,' since U.S. armed forces occupy only half of Korea and present U.S. policy envisages eventual multipartite trusteeship over Korea." (See SWNCC no. 232/1, in RG 353, SWNCC-SANACC, box no. 40.)
166. Sawyer, *KMAG in Peace and War*, pp. 20-21. The Constabulary continued to be seen as "the basis of a military force" or "national army" after the Department of Internal Security was set up (see USAMGIK, Office of Administration, *Manual of Military Government Organization and Function* [Seoul: n.d.], p. 57).
167. "HUSAFIK," vol. 3, ch. 2, p. 70. This study does not say whether "Alpha" and "Bamboo" were for all of Korea or just south Korea.
168. Sawyer, *KMAG in Peace and War*, p. 14.
169. *Han'guk chŏnjaeng-sa* 1: p. 256.
170. "XXIV Corps Journal," November 12, 1945 entry.
171. MacArthur to the Joint Chiefs of Staff, quoting Hodge's report, December 16, 1945; in *FRUS* (1945), 6: 1,147.
172. *Han'guk chŏnjaeng-sa* 1: 260-261, quoting an undated memorandum from Cho to Hodge.
173. Cho, *Na ŭi hoegorok*, p. 157.
174. *Han'guk chŏnjaeng-sa* 1: 248-249. Yi Ŭng-jun had been a colonel in the Japa-

nese Army and later became an advisor to the MG. He was the first ROKA chief of staff in 1948 and minister of communications in the Rhee regime in 1955. (See Kim Se-jin, *The Politics of Military Revolution in Korea* [Chapel Hill: University of North Carolina Press, 1971], p. 44; also *Han'guk chŏnjaeng-sa* 1: 259, 265, 268.)

Wŏn Yong-dŏk had been a lieutenant colonel in the Japanese Kwantung Army. He helped recruit officers for the MG English Language School, was the first Korean commander of the Constabulary, and later became a lieutenant general in the ROKA. He distinguished himself by his slavish loyalty to Rhee during the 1952 martial law episode. (See Kim, *Military Revolution in Korea*, p. 73; and *Han'guk chŏnjaeng-sa* 1: 258, 269.)

175. *Han'guk chŏnjaeng-sa* 1: p. 249.

176. The term "Constabulary" was used from January 1946 on, although the official designation did not come until June 1946.

177. Ibid., pp. 257-258, 262.

178. Ibid., p. 252. Kim Wŏn-bong was one of the best-known Korean anti-Japanese revolutionaries in China. He returned to Korea with the leftist faction of the KPG in early December and later joined with KPR leaders in the Democratic National Front. He became prominent in North Korea after 1948.

Yi Ch'ŏng ch'ŏn was an anti-Japanese guerrilla leader in the 1920s and later became one of the most prominent Koreans in the Chinese Nationalist Army. He led the KPG-aligned Kwangbok Army. Upon his return to Korea in 1946, he achieved prominence as the leader of the rightist Taedong Youth Corps (*Taedong ch'ŏngnyŏn-dan*).

Mu Chŏng was another famous Korean anti-Japanese revolutionary whose family name is variously given as Ch'oe or Kim. For more on Mu Chŏng, see chapter eleven.

179. *Han'guk chŏnjaeng-sa* 1: 253; *Sudo kyŏngch'al*, p. 94. The G-2 "Weekly Report," no. 21, January 27-February 3, 1946, said the development of the Constabulary in January was complemented by concerted action against the NPA *and* the KPG-aligned Kwangbok Army; "numerous arrests and convictions" were made. I have found no other verification that Kwangbok people were arrested. A subsequent American intelligence report put the total strength of the NPA in 1945-1946 at 60,000. (See G-2 "Weekly Report," no. 93, June 15-22, 1947.)

180. *Han'guk chŏnjaeng-sa* 1: 258. Classes were originally held in the capitol building, then moved to a Methodist school near Seoul's West Gate (Green, *Epic of Korea*, p. 62). Americans sometimes referred to the *Kwangbok Kun* as the "Shine Again Army."

181. Kim, *Military Revolution in Korea*, pp. 48, 52-53.

182. *Han'guk chŏnjaeng-sa* 1: 247, 254.

183. Chong-sik Lee, *The Politics of Korean Nationalism* (Berkeley: University of California Press, 1963), p. 223.

184. Clarence N. Weems, Jr., "Korea and the Provisional Government," September 28, 1945; in XXIV Corps Historical File. Weems based this memorandum on interviews with some sixty Kwangbok Army and KPG members in Chungking, August 1945.

185. See the late Chang Chun-ha's observations in "My Life with Magazines," in Marshall Pihl, ed., *Listening to Korea* (New York: Praeger Publishers, 1973), pp. 64-67. A SWNCC study in May 1945 estimated the number of Kwangbok soldiers to be around 100, compared with "several thousand" Korean guer-

rillas in the northern China base areas and Manchuria. It also stated that the Office of Strategic Services had to date trained only *nine* Koreans for work behind Japanese lines. (See SWNCC no. 115, RG 53, SWNCC-SANACC, box no. 22, "Utilization of Koreans in the War Effort," May 31, 1945.)

186. Weems, "Korea and the Provisional Government."

187. On Koreans in the Chinese Eighth Route Army, see the extensive information in "History of the North Korean Army," passim.

188. "HUSAFIK," vol. 2, ch. 4, pp 37-38. A KPG leader, Ŏm Hang-sŏp stated on November 24, 1945 that the Kwangbok Army was "about 10,000 strong" (see *Chayu sinmun*, November 25, 1945; in *THMGS* I: 462-465).

189. Quoted in *Han'guk chŏnjaeng-sa* 1: 307. The mission to Shanghai was apparently prompted by Gen. Albert Wedemeyer's suggestion to Hodge that he request Yi's participation in the Constabulary. Yi Pŏm-sŏk was one of the best-known Korean anti-Japanese fighters. He was born in Seoul in 1900. His father was a provincial governor prior to the Japanese Annexation. Yi went to China in 1915 and graduated from the Yunnan Military Academy Cavalry School in 1919. He then trained troops to fight the Japanese in Manchuria from 1923 to 1929. In 1933 he visited Germany to study military tactics and later, in 1938, rose through the ranks of the Chinese Nationalist Army officer corps to become a Company Commander at the Hankow Central Military Academy Training Center. He was, like Yi Ch'ŏng-ch'ŏn, a prominent leader of the Kwangbok Army. He studied the Hitler *Jugend* while in Germany as well and later was associated with the KMT's Blue Shirts. The American OSS returned him to Korea by airplane in August 1945, then inexplicably took him back to Shanghai. In spite of his reservations about the Constabulary, he apparently did become an advisor to it upon his return to Korea in the spring of 1946, but he resigned about five months later, because the Constabulary was too "pinkish." He then organized the Korean National Youth. (Based on Department of State, "Biographic Reports on the Cabinet of the Korean Republic"; also Kim Chong-bŏm and Kim Tong-un, *Haebang chŏn-hu ŭi Chosŏn chinsang* [The True Situation of Korea Before and After Liberation] Seoul: Chosŏn chŏnggyŏng yon'gu-sa, 1945], p. 211; also Yi Pŏm-sŏk, *Han'guk ŭi punno* [Korea's Indignation], trans. from the Chinese by Kim Kwang-ju, 2d ed. [Seoul: Kwangch'ang-gak, 1945], p. 80.) On the KMT Blue Shirts, see Lloyd Eastman, "Fascism in Kuomingtang China," *China Quarterly*, no. 49 (January-March 1972), pp. 1-31.

190. *Han'guk chŏnjaeng-sa* 1: 258, 279.

191. Irma Materi, *Irma and the Hermit* (New York: W. W. Norton and Co., 1949), p. 89. Irma's husband was Joseph Materi, head of the Constabulary Officer's Training School and an advisor to the KNP.

192. *Han'guk chŏnjaeng-sa* 1: 265. See also Kim, *Military Revolution in Korea*, p. 43. Song Ho-sŏng of the Kwangbok Army was made commander of the Constabulary briefly in 1946 to placate protests, but the Americans later found him lacking in qualifications for the position and replaced him (Materi, *Irma and the Hermit*, p. 90).

193. Kim, *Military Revolution in Korea*, pp. 41, 48. In Kim's tables (pp. 46-47 and 61-63) and in those in the *Han'guk chŏnjaeng-sa* (1: 277-278) may be traced the extraordinary influence of Korean officers from the Japanese military in the Constabulary and the subsequent ROKA.

194. Cho, *Na ŭi hoegorok*, p. 157.

195. *Han'guk chŏnjaeng-sa* 1: 258-259, 265, 268; and Kim, *Military Revolution in Korea*, p. 44.

196. Materi, *Irma and the Hermit*, pp. 72-74.
197. *Han'guk chŏnjaeng-sa* 1: 258, 269.
198. Ibid., pp. 260, 267, 268.
199. Compiled from ibid. and from Kim, *Military Revolution in Korea*. Pak Chŏng-hŭi and Kim Tong-ha were members of the second class, graduating in the fall of 1946. The third member of the triumvirate that made the military coup in 1961, Kim Chŏng-p'il, came out of the eighth class, in 1949.
200. Kawai, *Japan's American Interlude*, p. 92.
201. As in the KNP, "Koreanization" came almost immediately in the Constabulary. American supervision was limited and Koreans largely ran the show (Sawyer, *KMAG in Peace and War*, p. 25).
202. *Han'guk chŏnjaeng-sa* 1: 282, citing a meeting held in late November 1945. Yi had been a captain in the Japanese Army and commanded the ROKA Second Division in June, 1950. He and others were designated "Acting" commanders of Constabulary regiments because of the prevailing sentiment that they were collaborators (p. 269).
203. Ibid., p. 255.
204. Sawyer, *KMAG in Peace and War*, p. 25; see *Han'guk chŏnjaeng-sa* 1: 293, for similar evidence.
205. *Han'guk chŏnjaeng-sa* 1: 287. Many recruits objected to Japanese-style training.
206. Ibid., pp. 287, 292-293.
207. Sawyer, *KMAG in Peace and War*, pp. 25-26, 40.
208. Counter-Intelligence Corps report, Seoul, October 14, 1946. See also ibid., p. 26.
209. The Constabulary had one regiment in each province; by April 1946 seven regiments had been established with a total of 2,000 men. By the end of 1947, Constabulary strength was at 20,000 (Sawyer, *KMAG in Peace and War*, pp. 16-17, 29).
210. *Han'guk chŏnjaeng-sa* 1: 292, 294. In early 1946 the North Kyŏngsang regiment was shaken up, with a Kwantung Army officer, Ch'oe Nam-gŭn, appointed the new commander and charged with implementing "thought guidance" and spiritual education in the ranks. But he turned out to be a "leftist" as well, and leftist influence continued strong in this regiment (p. 295).
211. Sawyer, *KMAG in Peace and War*, p. 26.
212. *Han'guk chŏnjaeng-sa* 1: 259.
213. Ibid., pp. 265-266, 290. Severe "thought problems" were found in Constabulary ranks in June 1946, including handbills among the recruits that read, "Long Live the KPR." Leftists within the Constabulary caused "fear and trembling" among leading Korean officers. As in the KNP, rightists did not like American requests to be nonpartisan and impartial—how could they be impartial if impartiality led to a left-wing government (pp. 279, 290, 308)?

NOTES TO CHAPTER SIX

Toward a Separate Southern Government

1. George Atcheson to the Secretary of State, October 15, 1945; in United States, State Department, *FRUS* (Washington, D.C., 1945), 6: 1,091-1,092. Hodge had just spent two days in Tokyo conferring with MacArthur. It would seem from

a reading of various documents and unpublished sources that Hodge, with MacArthur's concurrence, played the key role in decision making within the Occupation, even when other names, such as those of Hodge's State Department advisors, appear on documents. Hodge might well have paraphrased Justice Jeremiah Johnson's famous utterance to read, "Do generals make policy? 'Course they do. Made some m'self."

2. Ibid., p. 1,092.

3. Dae-sook Suh, *The Korean Communist Movement, 1918-1948* (Princeton: Princeton University Press, 1970), p. 18. See also Chong-sik Lee, *The Politics of Korean Nationalism* (Berkeley: University of California Press, 1963), p. 136.

4. See Ralph Keating Benesch, "Kim Ku: A Study of a Nationalist" (M.A. thesis, University of Washington, 1964), pp. 56-57. Kim Ku was born in Haeju in 1875. He failed the civil service exams in 1890 and then in 1892 became a minor leader of the *Tonghak* rebels. In 1896 he killed a Japanese in Anak in revenge for the assassination of Queen Min, which led to an apocryphal story that he had strangled Queen Min's killer with his bare hands. He was tortured by the Japanese in 1909 and given a fifteen-year jail sentence for alleged involvement in An Myŏng-gŭn's attempt on the Japanese resident-general's life. He joined the KPG in Shanghai in 1919 and was its leader after 1926, when it had "a few score" members and hangers-on in Shanghai. Kim achieved wide notoriety for engineering the terrorist attack on April 29, 1932, in which Kawabata Teiji, chairman of the Japanese Residents Association, and General Shirakawa Yoshinori, died; and in which Shigemitsu Mamoru, Japanese minister plenipotentiary to China, lost his leg (causing him to limp aboard the U.S.S. *Missouri* to offer the Japanese surrender in Tokyo Bay in 1945). After that, Kim Ku's star rose with Chiang Kai-shek. After his return to Korea, he was widely known as "The Assassin," but it was he who was assassinated, in 1949 by An Tu-hŭi at Syngman Rhee's orders.

5. The Kuomintang's condescending attitude toward the KPG was well known to State Department officials in China. Ambassador Clarence E. Gauss said that in 1944 the KMT "curtly" instructed KPG leaders not to include any leftists in the organization and required them to adhere to the San Min Chu I (Three People's Principles) of the KMT. John S. Service reported that KPG leaders were dismayed that the KMT dealt with them through a committee whose members were the same as another committee for "border peoples" (i.e., barbarians). (See Gauss's letter of June 29, 1944, and Service's dispatch of June 7, 1944, in United States, State Department, RG 59, decimal file, 895.01/6-2944, 895.01/6-744). Although the KPG claimed to have been recognized by the French, a cable of March 30, 1945 in the State Department files from the French Foreign Ministry denied AP and UPI reports that the French had recognized the KPG in any way (895.01/3-3045).

For a full and excellent account of Rhee, the KPG, and the State Department during the war, see William George Morris, "The Korean Trusteeship, 1941-1947: The United States, Russia, and the Cold War" (Ph.D. dissertation, University of Texas, 1974) ch. 1.

6. Gauss to Secretary of State, dispatch with memorandum of conversation, May 19, 1944; in RG 59, decimal file, 895.01/338; quoted in Morris, "Korean Trusteeship," p. 32. See also George Atcheson's discussion with Cho So-ang in Chungking in February 1945, where Cho suggested—at that late date—that the United States support the KPG in organizing a Korean Army in China (Atche-

son to Secretary of State, dispatch with memorandum of conversation, March 3, 1945; in 895.01/3-345).

7. Rhee used this title in letters to the State Department. On his ouster from the KPG, see Lee, *Politics of Korean Nationalism*, p. 133; also Gregory Henderson, *Korea: The Politics of the Vortex* (Cambridge: Harvard University Press, 1968), p. 86. A short history of the KPG published just after liberation by followers of Kim Ku contained a very short biography of Rhee, placing him after Kim Ku, Kim Kyu-sik, and Kim Wŏn-bong in order of precedence (see *Taehan tongnip undong kwa imsi chŏngbu t'ujaeng-sa* [History of the Korean Independence Movement and the Struggle of the Korean Provisional Government] [Seoul: Kyerim-sa, 1946]).

8. See memorandum of conversation; in RG 59, decimal file, 895.01/9-3042, September 30, 1942.

9. Rhee to State Department, June 5, 1944; quoted in *FRUS* (1945), 6: 1,023n; also Rhee to State Department, July 21, 1945; quoted on p. 1,031.

10. Rhee to State Department, July 25, 1945; quoted in *FRUS* (1945), 6: 1,034-1,035. See also Robert T. Oliver, *Syngman Rhee: The Man Behind the Myth* (Cornwall, N.Y.: The Cornwall Press, 1955), pp. 184, 194. (Lublin refers to the Polish Committee of National Liberation then supported by the Soviets.) Oliver blamed Alger Hiss and Owen Lattimore for the State Department's unwillingness to recognize the KPG.

11. Oliver, *Syngman Rhee*, p. 182. Hornbeck, in fact, was much more impressed with Korean guerrillas in Manchuria. According to Matray, "Although these Korean exiles demonstrated an affection for Communist ideology, Hornbeck admired their willingness to fight for freedom without American assistance" (see James Matray, "The Reluctant Crusade: American Foreign Policy in Korea, 1941-1950" [Ph.D. dissertation, University of Virginia, 1977], p. 35).

12. See memorandums of February 5 and May 15, 1945; in *FRUS* (1945), 6: 1,023, 1,030.

13. Ibid., p. 561. The State Department had the concurrence of the Joint Chiefs of Staff and the director of the Office of Strategic Services in such judgments. The JCS decided as early as 1942 that no exile government commanded the allegiance of Koreans at home (see various memorandums, August 1942; in Joint Chiefs of Staff, RG 218, Geographic File, 1945-1947, 383.21 Korea, box no. 638). On the OSS view, see memorandum, William J. Donovan to JCS, July 29, 1944; in box no. 639.

14. "Basic Initial Directive"; in *FRUS* (1945), 6: 1,081.

15. Ibid., pp. 1,075, 1,081.

16. John Carter Vincent to Col. Russel L. Vittrup, War Department, November 7, 1945; in *FRUS* (1945), 6: 1,113-1,114.

17. McCloy to Under Secretary of State Dean Acheson, November 13, 1945; in *FRUS* (1945), 6: 1,122-1,124. McCloy's recommendations were based on his observations during a trip to Korea in early November. When proposing that Hodge be allowed to use "as many exiled Koreans as he can," McCloy must have meant noncommunist exiles.

18. William Langdon to the Secretary of State, November 20, 1945; in *FRUS* (1945), 6: 1,130-1,133. Langdon was a State Department advisor to Hodge who had replaced Benninghoff during the latter's return to Washington in November for consultations.

19. Col. Bonesteel, memorandum of conversation written for Gen. Lincoln, De-

cember 4, 1945; in War Department, RG 165, Army Staff, Plans and Operations division, ABC decimal file, box no. 31, section 17-A. A copy of Langdon's cable attached to this memorandum has the title, "Langdon Plan offered as substitute for trusteeship."

20. See the top secret telegram to Hodge, dated November 29, 1945, signed by Secretary of State Byrnes, and initialed by Vincent, Borton, Benninghoff, and others; in State Department, RG 59, decimal file 740.0019/Control (Korea), box no. 3827. See also Langdon's cable to the Secretary of State, December 12, 1945; in RG 59, decimal file 895.01/12-1445. A subsequent cable to Hodge for Langdon from Under Secretary of State Dean Acheson stated that Langdon's telegrams were receiving consideration and had been repeated to Moscow for the information of the Secretary of State, who was then preparing for the upcoming Foreign Minister's Conference (895.01/12-1945, December 19, 1945).

21. Clarence Weems, Jr., "Korea and the Provisional Government," XXIV Corps Historical File. Weems was with the OSS in Chungking.

22. Weems was correct about Yŏ Un-hyŏng, who had recommended to Hodge that KPG leaders be allowed to return to Korea *as individuals* (Yi Man-gyu, *Yŏ Un-hyŏng t'ujaeng-sa* [History of Yŏ Un-hyŏng's Struggle] [Seoul: Ch'ongmun-gak, 1946], p. 248), and who had probably been instrumental in placing KPG leaders on the September 6 KPR leadership roster. Weems's report is one of the few to mention Yun Ch'i-ho, one of the most famous Korean nationalists and a leading modernizer at the end of the Yi Dynasty, who much later accepted a peerage from the Japanese, and who died in 1945.

23. "HUSAFIK," manuscript in the Office of the Chief of Military History, Washington, D.C. (Tokyo and Seoul, 1947, 1948), vol. 2, ch. 1, p. 33.

24. See memorandum of September 24, 1945; in State Department, RG 59, decimal files, 895.01/9-2445.

25. R. Harris Smith, *OSS: The Secret History of America's First Central Intelligence Agency* (Berkeley: University of California Press, 1972), p. 3.

26. Ibid., p. 26. In May 1945, a SWNCC study stated that "nothing further has been heard of this scheme" (see SWNCC no. 115, "Utilization of Koreans in the War Effort," RG 353, SWNCC-SANACC). For various discussions between 1942 and 1945 on using Koreans in the war effort, all of which came to naught, see RG 165, P & O, ABC file, box no. 385 (3-4-42).

27. See Dolbear's letter of March 5, 1945; in RG 59, decimal file, 895.01/3-545. The lure of Korean gold was probably behind Dolbear's accepting this post. Americans had opened Korean gold mines under concession from the old Korean government, beginning in 1896. The American-owned Oriental Consolidated Mining Company held the largest gold mines in northern Korea until 1939, when they were sold to Japanese interests. Gold accounted for well over half the minerals produced in Korea and was the most important mineral export in the 1930s.

28. See memorandums of August 28, 1945 and September 13, 1945; in RG 59, decimal file, 895.01/8-2845 and 9-1395.

29. Henderson, *Vortex*, p. 128.

30. Cable in the papers of M. Preston Goodfellow, The Hoover Institution Archives, accession no. 69085-8.37, box no. 1. (Hereafter designated Goodfellow Papers.) On October 13 the War Department sent a cable to MacArthur, saying "[Rhee] cannot pose as approved representative of any political faction. . . . State Department fears, however, that approval of his return . . . may

indicate to Koreans that US supports Rhee and his faction" (see radio message, J. E. Hull to MacArthur, October 13, 1945; in RG 165, P & O, ABC decimal file, box no. 31, section 17-A).

31. "XXIV Corps Journal," November 2, 1945, XXIV Corps Historical File. Hodge apparently told his staff nothing about his trip to Tokyo. This was the first of several meetings between Hodge and MacArthur, and MacArthur and Rhee (assuming they met), for which no record exists. Robert H. Alexander, librarian at the MacArthur Archives in Norfolk, Virginia, wrote me as follows: "we have no minutes of meetings between MacArthur and Hodge or Rhee . . . [and] I strongly suspect that no such minutes exist" (February 14, 1974). This would hold true for meetings up to the outbreak of the Korean War.

32. Rhee sent this letter to Robert Oliver, another of his American supporters (see Robert T. Oliver, *Syngman Rhee and American Involvement in Korea, 1942-1960* [Seoul: Panmun Book Co., 1978], pp. 19-20). See also *Maeil sinbo* [Daily News], October 18, 1945, where Rhee is quoted as saying he met Hodge in Tokyo. In 1949 the State Department searched its records to determine how Rhee got back to Korea. The department's research division found no indication that established policy that would have prevented Rhee's returning in anything but an individual capacity had been modified. It stated that during late 1945 "most decisions appeared to have been made on a day-to-day operating basis in the field by the MG Command." (See Warren S. Hunsberger, "U.S. Involvement in the Return of Syngman Rhee to Korea," September 2, 1949, State Department, RG 59, decimal file, 895.00/8-1949.) It appears from this that the State Department never quite knew how it all happened.

33. See H. Franz Schurmann, *The Logic of World Power: An Inquiry into the Origins, Currents and Contradictions of World Power* (New York: Pantheon Books, 1974).

34. Based on Koh Kwang-il, "In Quest of National Unity and Power: Political Ideas and Practices of Syngman Rhee" (Ph.D. dissertation, Rutgers University, 1962), pp. 6-9.

35. Richard Allen, *Korea's Syngman Rhee* (Rutland, Vt.: Charles E. Tuttle Co., 1960), pp. 32, 41, 44. It is often stated that the Japanese imprisoned and tortured Rhee, but whatever torture he underwent during his imprisonment was at the hands of Koreans, in Korean prisons.

36. Lee, *Politics of Korean Nationalism*, p. 133.

37. Koh, "In Quest of National Unity and Power," p. 25.

38. Rhee was part of the so-called "American group" in the KPG (see chapter one).

39. See Evelyn McCune, "Introduction," *The Arts of Korea* (Rutland, Vt.: Charles E. Tuttle Co., 1962), p. 24.

40. Quoted in USAMGIK, G-2 "Periodic Report," no. 62, November 9-10, 1945. For the KPR's fulsome welcome for Rhee, see *Maeil sinbo*, October 18, 1945.

41. *Haebang ilbo* [Liberation Daily], no. 6, October 25, 1945. Communist and leftist publications continued to refer to Rhee as "Yi Paksa" (Dr. Rhee) long after he denounced the Left.

42. See the slogan in Chae-Mi Hanjok yŏnyap wiwŏn-hoe, *Haebang Chosŏn* [Liberated Korea] (Hawaii: Chae-Mi Hanjok yŏnyap wiwŏn-hoe, 1948), p. 13; also Yi Kang-guk, *Minjujuǔi ǔi Chosŏn kŏnsŏl* [The Construction of Democratic Korea] (Seoul: Chosŏn inminbo-sa husŏng-bu, 1946), p. 61. The *Tongsin ilbo* [New East Daily] referred to this as *pibimbapsik* unity, or unity in the style

of a Korean dish in which disparate ingredients are mixed together (November 29, 1945). See also articles in *Maeil sinbo*, October 25, 1945; and *Chayu sinmun* [Free News], October 24, 1945; both in Republic of Korea, Kuksa p'yŏnch'an wiwŏn-hoe, *THMGS* I [History of the Republic of Korea] (Seoul, 1970): 290-294.

43. "HUSAFIK," vol. 2, ch. 1, p. 34.

44. *Haebang Chosŏn*, pp. 13-14; Minjujuŭi minjok chŏnsŏn, *Chosŏn* haebang *illyŏn-sa* [History of the First Year of Korean Liberation] (Seoul: Munu insŏ'-gwan, 1946), p. 110. The latter work said that Rhee's "willy-nilly unity" appeared to traitors and pro-Japanese Koreans as "good tidings from heaven."

45. Kim Chong-bŏm and Kim Tong-un, *Haebang chŏn-hu ŭi Chosŏn chinsang* [The True Situation of Korea Before and After Liberation] (Seoul: Chosŏn chŏngyŏng yon'gu-sa, 1945), pp. 147-150.

46. Yi, *Yŏ Un-hyŏng*, p. 251. This was in late October, before leftists exited from the CCRRKI.

47. Han T'ae-su, *Han'guk chŏngdang-sa* [A History of Korean Political Parties] (Seoul: Sin t'aeyang-sa, 1961), p. 14. Stewart Meacham said that the KDP was "a small clique of frightened men who . . . found in Rhee a protector from the democratic storm that came close to engulfing them at the time of Liberation" (*Korean Labor Report* [Seoul: USAFIK, 1947], pp. 34-35). Later on the American Central Intelligence Agency said, "They [the KDP] dare not overthrow him [Rhee] but must maintain an uneasy coalition with him since they need his political prestige. At the same time, since he requires their money and ability, he cannot ignore their demands"; in United States, CIA, "Prospects for the Survival of the Republic of Korea," no. ORE 44-48, October 28, 1948, original classification "secret."

48. See the transcript of this address in Kim and Kim, *Haebang chŏn-hu*, pp. 151-155. Americans described Rhee's speeches over JDOK in December as "tirades" against the KPR and the Russians ("HUSAFIK," vol. 2, ch. 1, pp. 56-57).

49. "HUSAFIK," vol. 2, ch. 4, p. 39. The USAFIK historians commented mildly regarding Rhee's antics in November 1945, "it would appear that he had not been overly discreet in utilizing the non-partisan trust which General Hodge had placed in him" (ch. 1, p. 34).

50. See the memorandum of discussion of May 20, 1945, between Dr. Chu Heinming, chief of the Russian Department of the Chinese Ministry of Information, and DeWitt C. Poole of the OSS; in *FRUS* (1945), 7: 873. See also K. C. Wu's remarks, quoted in cable, Chungking to Department of State, September 25, 1945; in RG 59, decimal file, 895.01/9-2545. The United States Counter-Intelligence Corps also got a report saying that Chiang Kai-shek had provided as much as 10 million yen (equivalent) to Kim Ku upon his return (see Counter-Intelligence Corps report, Seoul, July 3, 1946; in XXIV Corps Historical File). The atmosphere in Chungking was much more favorable to the KPG after Patrick Hurley replaced Gauss as American ambassador (see Hurley's cable urging the return of the KPG to Seoul, August 31, 1945; in *FRUS* [1945], 6: 1,042).

51. "XXIV Corps Journal," November 2, 1945 entry.

52. Ibid., November 12, 1945 entry.

53. "HUSAFIK," vol. 2, ch. 1, p. 36.

54. Kim and Kim, *Haebang chŏn-hu*, p. 165; *Haebang Chosŏn*, p. 14. See also various articles in *THMGS* I: 448-452.

55. See the *New York Times*, November 27 and December 4, 1945. The USAMGIK

G-2 section cited rumors that the Occupation would appoint prominent Koreans to a cabinet that would take over the bureaucracy ("Weekly Report," no. 12, November 25-December 2, 1945). The G-2 section was apparently unaware of the Langdon proposal. In its January 15, 1946 report, it noted the "regal air" surrounding the KPG leaders, asked if the Russians might not think that the United States was prepared "to trot the Provisional Government out at the proper time" for recognition as the government of Korea, and said, "it is believed we have no such idea."

56. Han, *Han'guk chŏngdang-sa*, pp. 13-14; the writers of *Haebang Chosŏn* thought the same thing (p. 14). Their guesses were essentially correct.

57. Richard Robinson, "Betrayal of a Nation," Manuscript at Massachusetts Institute of Technology, pp. 66-67. Robinson said Kim had "a bevy of concubines" and "a flotilla of paid gunmen" in his entourage (pp. 67n, 120). The Occupation set up the KPG headquarters in Tŏksu Palace, and Ch'oe Ch'anghak, a wealthy landlord and mine owner, provided Kim Ku with the use of the *Sŏkjo sin'gak*, a palatial residence on the Tŏksu palace grounds. (See Justin Sloane, memorandum to Clyde Sargent, February 6, 1948; in USAFIK, USFIK 11071 file, box no. 62/96; also *Tŏksu sinmun*, November 24, 1974. [I am indebted to Eugene Chai of Columbia University for the latter reference.])

58. "HUSAFIK," vol. 2, ch. 2, p. 51; and ch. 1, p. 38. See also an article on one of these councils of state in *Tonga ilbo* [East Asia Daily], December 7, 1945; in *THMGS* I: 538-539. Ŏm Hang-sŏp, a spokesman for the KPG, said on November 24 that the KPG leaders may have come back as individuals as far as the Americans were concerned, but that the Korean people recognize it as their government (*Chayu sinmun*, November 25, 1945; in *THMGS* I: 462-465). Song Chin-u, the KDP leader, said the KPG must be treated as if it were the government and stated that the KDP would take orders from KPG leaders (*Chungang sinmun*, November 6, 1945; in *THMGS* I: 371).

59. Hodge, record of conversation with visiting United States congressmen, October 4, 1947; in USFIK 11071 file, box no. 62/96.

60. Han, *Han'guk chŏngdang-sa*, p. 67; *Han'guk chŏnjaeng-sa* 1: 67; and G-2 "Weekly Report," no. 15, December 16-23, 1945.

61. This statement was in Sin's personal portfolio, seized in a raid on his home by CIC investigators, August 28, 1946 ("*HUSAFIK*," vol. 2, ch. 2, pp. 136-137).

62. From two reports made after tours of the provinces; quoted in "HUSAFIK," vol. 2, ch. 1, p. 11; see also USAMGIK, "Political Trends," no. 11, December 8, 1945. One of the reports was submitted by Horace Underwood.

63. Quoted in Leonard C. Hoag, "American Military Government in Korea: War Policy and the First Year of Occupation, 1941-1946" (Draft manuscript prepared under the auspices of the Office of the Chief of Military History, Department of the Army, 1970), p. 312.

64. "XXIV Corps Journal," October 13, 1945.

65. "HUSAFIK," vol. 2, ch. 1, p. 26. See also the last issue of *Maeil sinbo*, November 11, 1945, which has an extensive account of the closure; in *THMGS* I: 391.

66. USAMGIK, "HMGK" (Seoul: Office of Administrative Services, Statistical Research Division, 1946), 1: 193-197; G-2 "Weekly Report," no. 11, November 18-25, 1945. The *Maeil sinbo*, which I have consulted, was "radical" only in the sense that it supported the CPKI and the KPR; otherwise its issues from August-November 1945 were exceedingly mild.

67. "HMGK" 1: 198; "XXIV Corps Journal," November 16, 1945 entry. On the closure of the *Tonga ilbo* in 1940, see Ko Ha sŏnsaeng chŏn'gi pyŏnch'an wiwŏn-hoe, *Ko Ha Song Chin-u sŏnsaeng chŏn* [Collection on Ko Ha, Song Chin-u] (Seoul: Tonga ilbo ch'ulp'an-guk, 1964), p. 279. In July 1946 Charles Thayer, an American delegate to the United States-Soviet Joint Commission, "stated that the printing presses are now distributed in a favorable proportion among the Korean political parties" (memorandum of conversation, July 16, 1946; in *FRUS* [1946], 8: 716). This was after the closure of the *Haebang ilbo* in May 1946. In September 1946 the MG saw the necessity of closing the principal remaining leftist newspapers (see chapter seven).

68. Chosŏn inmindang, *Inmindang ŭi nosŏn* [The Program of the People's Party] (Seoul: Sin munhwa yŏn'gu-so ch'ulp'an-bu, 1946), p. 2. This publication said that the PP was "the new name for the *kŏnmaeng*" (p. 13). On the PP—its membership, platforms, and so on—see also Kim and Kim, *Haebang chŏn-hu*, pp. 46-51.

69. "HUSAFIK," vol. 2, ch. 1, p. 13.

70. *Chwaik sakŏn sillok* [Record of the Left-wing Incidents] (Seoul: Tae'gŏmch'al-ch'ong, susa-guk, 1964), 1: 40; *Haebang illyŏn-sa*, p. 91. American intelligence reported that in South Ch'ungch'ŏng Province two delegates from each county people's committee met in Taejŏn on November 4-5 and selected provincial delegates for the national meeting (G-2 "Weekly Report," no. 11, November 18-25, 1945). KPR leaders said that this procedure was followed throughout south Korea. An undetermined number of delegates from people's committees in north Korea were also present at the national meeting. In the following discussion of this meeting, I have also relied upon original minutes in Korean written by unnamed secretaries; in United States, Far East Command, RG 242, Captured Enemy Documents, SA2006, item 13/65. (Hereafter designated PC meeting minutes.)

71. See Yi, *Minjujuŭi ŭi Chosŏn kŏnsŏl*, pp. 46-58; various proceedings and resolutions of the meeting are given on pp. 41-48. See also *Haebang ilbo*, no. 15, November 25, 1945. An eyewitness American account of the meeting is available in G-2 "Weekly Report," no. 11, November 18-25, 1945. See also PC meeting minutes.

72. Although KPR leaders credited the KPG leaders for their untiring efforts in Korea's behalf while in exile, the KPG was, they thought, but one of several important exile groups and could not claim the loyalties of the home Korean population; in Yi, *Minjujuŭi ŭi Chosŏn kŏnsŏl*, p. 47.

73. G-2 "Weekly Report," no. 11, November 18-25, 1945. See also *Chayu sinmun*, December 1, 1945.

74. *Chosŏn inmin-bo* [Korean People's Report], November 23, 1945.

75. *Haebang ilbo*, no. 15, November 25, 1945; see also Yi, *Minjujuŭi ŭi Chosŏn kŏnsŏl*, pp. 7-8; and *Haebang illyŏn-sa*, p. 90. One Korean later quoted both Thomas Jefferson's 1797 statement on the necessity for self-determination of all peoples regardless of the form of government they choose and the Atlantic Charter, and then asked rhetorically, "if Truman's democracy was the same brand as that of Jefferson and Roosevelt" (see On Ak-jung, ed., *Puk Chosŏn kihaeng* [North Korean Journey] (Seoul: Chosŏn chungang ilbo ch'ulp'an-sa, 1948], p. 20).

76. *Haebang ilbo*, no. 16, November 27, 1945; also PC meeting minutes.

77. *Haebang ilbo*, no. 16, November 27, 1945.

78. Hodge to MacArthur, November 25, 1945; in *FRUS* (1945), 6: 1,133-1,134, quoted in entirety.
79. Ibid., p. 1,134.
80. "HUSAFIK," vol. 2, ch. 1, p. 9. The KDP had, of course, called for the dissolution of the KPR since September. On December 6 the KDP called for the transfer of governmental power to the KPG and for the disbanding of the People's Republic. (See *Tonga ilbo*, December 7, 1945; in *THMGS* I: 535.) On the same day that Hodge declared the KPR to be unlawful, it was reported that the KPG began using Tŏksu Palace as its "temporary government office" (see *Chayu sinmun*, December 12, 1945; in *THMGS* I: 578).
81. See the *Chŏnp'yŏng* newspaper, *Chŏn'guk nodongja sinmun* [National Worker's News], no. 1, November 1, 1945. This was one of the few newspapers that consistently reported provincial organizing activities. See also Meacham, *Labor Report*, no. 22; and an article by Harold Zepelin, an officer in the Occupation, in *Korean Independence*, May 17, 1946. According to USAMGIK, "Opinion Trends," no. 6, November 9, 1945, some 505 people representing 217,000 workers in all Korean provinces (north and south) were present at the November 5-6 meeting.

  Hŏ Sŏng-t'aek was born into a peasant family in Sŏngjin county, the home of several Korean revolutionaries. At the age of sixteen, he joined the anti-Japanese movement. From 1931 to 1933, he hid in a forest near Sŏngjin to escape the Japanese, fleeing to the USSR in 1934. Upon his return to Korea in 1937, however, he was imprisoned, where he remained until August 15, 1945. American sources described him as "widely admired for his personal underground history" and depicted him as follows: "youthful, handsome, energetic . . . strongly built figure dressed in white-bloused trousers, blue vest, black overcoat . . . indistinguishable from the rest of Seoul's working populace." (See the information in memorandum from Jacobs to Secretary of State, June 1, 1948; in RG 59 decimal file, 895.00/6-148.)
82. *Chŏn'guk nodongja sinmun*, no. 1, November 1, 1945; also no. 15, April 19, 1946. See also *Haebang illyŏn-sa*, pp. 159-165; and USAMGIK "Political Trends," no. 5, November 5, 1945.
83. Meacham, *Labor Report*, pp. 10, 22.
84. See *Haebang illyŏn-sa*, p. 163.
85. "Labor Section Policy," unsigned memorandum, Bureau of Mining and Industry, November 16, 1945; in XXIV Corps Historical File. See also Meacham, *Labor Report*, passim.
86. "HUSAFIK," vol. 3, ch. 4, pt. 1, pp. 52-53.
87. George McCune, *Korea Today* (Cambridge: Harvard University Press, 1950), p. 164; *Chŏn'guk nodongja sinmun*, no. 1, November 1, 1945.
88. See opinion no. 306, May 6, 1946, in USAMGIK, Department of Justice, *Selected Legal Opinions of the Department of Justice* (Seoul, 1948).
89. Meacham, *Labor Report*, p. 11.
90. Ibid., p. 11.
91. *Selected Legal Opinions*, pp. 10-11.
92. "HMGK" 3: 24-25.
93. McCune, *Korea Today*, p. 100. Leonard Hoag remarked that "Koreans had strong reasons for preventing the property from coming under the control of Military Government. In many cases, large personal fortunes depended on keeping property like large warehouses out of official custodial hands." Thus

much property was never vested in the MG. Hoag noted that the chaotic property situation continued until 1948: "Military Government justified its inaction [in this respect] on grounds that ultimate decision should be made by a Korean government" (Hoag, "American Military Government in Korea," pp. 254-256).

94. Ambassador Edwin W. Pauley to President Truman, June 22, 1946; in *FRUS* (1946), 8: 706-709. Truman was much impressed with Pauley's letter. See his response, July 16, 1946; in *FRUS* (1946), 8: 713-714; and in Harry S Truman, *Years of Trial and Hope* (1956; reprint ed., New York: Signet Books, 1965), p. 366.

95. G-2 "Weekly Report," no. 22, February 3-10, 1946; Meacham, *Labor Report*, p. 22.

96. In Chŏng-sik, *Chosŏn nongch'ŏn munje sajŏn* [Dictionary of Korean Agriculture] (Seoul: Sinhak-sa, 1948, p. 208. Kim and Kim, *Haebang chŏn-hu*, p. 165, said that 600 representatives were present. See *Haebang illyŏn-sa*, pp. 165-168, for additional information and for a breakdown of *Chŏnnong* provincial strength.

97. See *Haebang illyŏn-sa*, pp. 183-184. Cho Pyŏng-ok, in *Na ŭi hoegorok* [My Recollections] (Seoul: Min'gyo-sa, 1959), p. 155, said this youth league had 300,000-plus members. KPR leaders formed the Korean Women's General League on December 22-23, 1945, which called for the "complete liberation" of women in all aspects of Korean life, equality of men and women, and an end to "feudal" practices of arranged marriage, sale of females, concubinage, and prostitution (see *Haebang illyŏn-sa*, pp. 178-182).

98. "HUSAFIK," vol. 3, ch. 4, pt. 1, p. 50.

99. "HUSAFIK," vol. 3, ch. 6, pp. 25-26. See also South Korean Interim Government, National Food Administration, "Food Report for South Korea as of March 1948," in "History of the National Food Administration"; in XXIV Corps Historical File.

100. USAMGIK, *Official Gazette*, Ordinance no. 9, October 5, 1945. The Americans asked Kim Sŏng-su in October 1945 for his recommendations on Ordinance no. 9. He said that the one-third/two-thirds split should be "a temporary measure for the 1945 crop only" (see the memorandum; in XXIV Corps Historical File).

101. *Official Gazette*, General Notice no. 1, October 5, 1945.

102. *Official Gazette*, General Notice no. 2, October 20, 1945.

103. *Official Gazette*, Ordinance no. 19, October 30, 1945.

104. See "HUSAFIK," vol. 3, ch. 2, p. 35; and C. Clyde Mitchell, *Korea: Second Failure in Asia* (Washington, D.C.: Public Affairs Institute, 1951), p. 17.

105. Pak Ki-hyuk et al., *A Study of Land Tenure System in Korea* (Seoul: Korea Land Economics Research Center, 1966), pp. 89-90.

106. G-2 "Weekly Report," no. 29, March 24-31, 1946.

107. See Gunnar Myrdal's excellent discussion on the difficulties of stimulating entrepreneurial activity in economies under the sway of landlordism, *Asian Drama: An Inquiry into the Poverty of Nations* (New York: Pantheon Books, 1968), 2: 1,064, 1,380.

108. "HUSAFIK," vol. 3, ch. 6, p. 5.

109. Robinson, "Betrayal of a Nation," pp. 77, 151. See also G-2 "Weekly Report," no. 22, February 3-10, 1946, which cited evidence of "large-scale" smuggling to Japan.

110. "HUSAFIK," vol. 3, ch. 3, pp. 39-40.

111. Ibid., p. 31.
112. 97th MG Company, "Unit History."
113. One *hap* equalled 150 grams, or 525 calories; the Japanese ration in 1939 (when rationing began) was 2.1 to 2.3 *hap*. (See "Food Report for South Korea as of March 1948," in XXIV Corps Historical File; this report is an excellent source on the effects of the free market policy.)
114. "HUSAFIK," vol. 3, ch. 6, pp. 6, 18. By November 1946 the United States had sent 4.2 million bushels of wheat, 15,000 tons of corn, 8,000 tons of flour, and other cereal items to Korea (p. 60). Thus an economic dependency on American grains was created in the south that has yet to be overcome.
115. Ibid., ch. 4, pt. 1, p. 51. See also In Chŏng-sik, *Chosŏn nong'ŏp kyŏngjeron* [On the Korean Agricultural Economy] (Seoul: Pangmun ch'ulp'an-sa, 1949), pp. 78, 95-99, in which the similarities in Japanese and American rice collection systems are detailed.
116. "HUSAFIK," vol. 3, ch. 2, p. 73.
117. Ibid., pp. 73-74.
118. 67th MG Company, report of February 15, 1946.
119. "HUSAFIK," vol. 3, ch. 6, pp. 29-30.
120. "HUSAFIK," vol. 3, ch. 2, p. 77.
121. USAMGIK, Office of Administration, *Manual of Military Government Organization and Function* (Seoul, n.d.), p. 77.
122. C. Clyde Mitchell, *Final Report and History of the New Korea Company* (Seoul: National Land Administration, 1948), pp. 20, 62.
123. Ibid., pp. 9, 16.
124. The average farm size of NKC households was 0.85 *chŏngbo*. Although 1 *chŏngbo* was generally considered to be the minimum size necessary to sustain one peasant household for one year, NKC peasants who did not raise enough to feed their family still had to turn over one-third of their crop as rent to the NKC and then apply for ration coupons (ibid., pp. 11, 19-20).
125. "HUSAFIK," vol. 3, ch. 5, p. 41.
126. Robinson, "Betrayal of a Nation," p. 149.
127. "HUSAFIK," vol. 3, ch. 4, pt. 1, pp. 43, 50-51, 54.
128. Ibid., p. 54. See also Richard Robinson's "Report on a Trip Through the Provinces," August 1946; in XXIV Corps Historical File.
129. Minutes of the Korean-American Conference, November 15, 1946; in XXIV Corps Historical File.
130. 67th MG Company, May 15, 1946; 68th MG Company, March 11, 1946.
131. Conversation between Hodge and General Wedemeyer, August 27, 1947; in XXIV Corps Historical File.
132. "HUSAFIK," vol. 3, ch. 6, pp. 32-33.
133. Public Information Department, report of December 13, 1945; in XXIV Corps Historical File. This organization was the *Taehan kyŏngje poguk-hoe*, meaning something like "the Korean society for the economic support of the nation."
134. Public Information Department, report of December 19, 1945; in XXIV Corps Historical File.
135. See Counter-Intelligence Corps report of July 3, 1946; in "Rightist Plots and Miscellaneous Politics, 1946-1947," XXIV Corps Historical File. This report also states that at the December 8 meeting a "wealthy landowner" from North Kyŏngsang proposed that a "notorious collaborator," "Yi, Chung Whe," be approved for membership in the contributor's association. Syngman Rhee,

who was present, refused, and the man making the proposal was shot by unknown thugs later that night. According to this report, Rhee got 12 million yen, and Kim Ku 1 million, from the total.

136. The circumstances of Goodfellow's appointment are fascinating. On November 5 Jay Jerome Williams, a longtime associate of Rhee's, wrote to President Truman suggesting Goodfellow "for a tour of duty in Korea." Truman then sent a note to Secretary of State Byrnes on November 7, saying, "It might be a good plan for me to send Colonel Goodfellow on a mission of this sort." John Vincent then stated on November 11 that Goodfellow and Williams had been, with Rhee, "outspokenly critical of the [State] department." On November 13, Byrnes wrote to Truman that there was "no objection" to Goodfellow's appointment, but that it would be "inadvisable" to designate him "your personal representative." Thus Goodfellow arrived in Korea much as Rhee did, after an end run around internationalist opposition within the State Department. (See the various notes and letters on this matter in RG 59, decimal file, 740.0019/Control (Korea), attached to doc. no. 740.0019/11-745, in box no. 3827.) Rhee, of course, did his part on the other end by making representations to Hodge and MacArthur on Goodfellow's behalf (see his letter of November 8, 1945 to Goodfellow, in Goodfellow Papers).

137. See Rhee's letters to Goodfellow of June 27, 1946 and August 5, 1946, in Goodfellow Papers. In the latter correspondence, Rhee also said, "You have my standing invitation and can come at once as my personal advisor which will mean an advisor to the Korean government when it is set up."

138. See Counter-Intelligence Corps report of July 3, 1946; and Public Information Department report of December 13, 1945; in XXIV Corps Historical File. *Haebang ilbo*, no. 24, December 8, 1945, gave the same names in a list of Rhee's financial backers, while *Tongsin ilbo*, January 9, 1946, referred to the fifty members of the contributor's association as "big landlords," or *tae chiju*.

139. See Hodge's monologue to a delegation of visiting congressmen, February 12, 1947; in USFIK 11071 file, box no. 62/96.

140. United States intelligence intercepted letters sent by KDP headquarters stating that those who funded the KDP included Pak Hŭng-sik (see chapter one), who gave 2 million yen, and Kim Ki-su, a "wealthy landowner" who gave 5 million yen (G-2 "Periodic Report," no. 113, January 1-2, 1946). Chang T'aek-sang, an early KDP leader and subsequently chief of the Seoul "Division A" police, reportedly provided living expenses to Rhee on occasion during the late 1940s (Sungjoo Han, *The Failure of Democracy in South Korea* [Berkeley: University of California Press, 1974], p. 20).

141. Quoted in "XXIV Corps Journal," October 27, 1945 entry.

142. *FRUS* (1945), 5: 1,144-1,148. MacArthur added the following comment to Hodge's cable: "The situation demands positive action as nothing could be worse than to allow it to drift to an ultimate crisis" (see Hoag, "American Military Government in Korea," p. 334).

143. Truman quoted Hodge's report at length in *Years of Trial and Hope*, pp. 361-362.

144. "HUSAFIK," vol. 2, ch. 4, "American-Soviet Relations: The First Year," p. 15.

145. Ibid., pp. 19-21.

146. Ibid., p. 26.

147. Ibid., ch. 4.

148. Ibid., ch. 1, p. 23. "Extra-political" here seems to mean "Soviet."

149. See, for example, Suh, *Korean Communist Movement*, ch. 10.

150. Quoted "HUSAFIK," vol. 2, ch. 1, p. 24.
151. Ibid., vol. 1, ch. 4, p. 42.
152. Ibid., vol. 3, ch. 2, p. 25. For a discourse on "gooks" by an American who held high position in the Justice Department, see A. Wigfall Green, *The Epic of Korea* (Washington, D.C.: Public Affairs Press, 1950), pp. 7-8.
153. Hodge told his staff the following on October 3, 1945:

    > Running [that is, commanding] Japs is the minor problem. The Koreans bleat loudly about being robbed and beaten by Japs but there is little evidence of this. . . . [Hodge] doesn't know a more 'muddle-headed' bunch of individuals. In looking back at their history one sees that the Koreans have raped, pillaged, and murdered at any opportunity. They love to beat up people.

    ("XXIV Corps Journal," October 3 entry). Several similar statements can be dredged up. To Hodge's credit, however, he came to have more respect and liking for Koreans than most high officials in the Occupation, according to Leonard Bertsch (interview, May 19, 1973).
154. Louis Hartz, *The Liberal Tradition in America* (New York: Harcourt, Brace & World, 1955), p. 116.

NOTES TO CHAPTER SEVEN

International Policy, Nationalist Logic

1. This was particularly so since the London Foreign Minister's Conference in September 1945 had gone poorly (see John Lewis Gaddis, *The United States and the Origins of the Cold War* [New York: Columbia University Press, 1972], pp. 263-268).
2. *New York Times*, December 28, 1945.
3. Cable to the Secretary of State, November 12, 1945; in State Department, *FRUS* (1945), 6: 1,121-1,122. Although in this memorandum Harriman assumed that the British would naturally go along with American policy, the British remained in the dark about policy toward Korea as late as September 1945. According to a memorandum written by George H. Lincoln dated September 9, the British had still not been informed about FDR's discussions with Stalin at Yalta about a Korean trusteeship or the subsequent discussions between Hopkins and Stalin in May 1945. Lincoln suggested that "it would be a good idea to take steps now to inform the British" (see United States, War Department, RG 165, ABD decimal file, box no. 31, section 17-A.)
4. Cable to Secretary of State, January 25, 1946; in *FRUS* (1946), 8: 619.
5. For Clemens's sense of Yalta as "an encounter in which [the Allies] prized agreement by traditional negotiation as preferable to unilateral action which might undermine international stability," see Diane Shaver Clemens, *Yalta* (New York: Oxford University Press, 1970), p. 288. Gaddis's account of the Moscow Conference indicated substantial compromise by the Russians regarding American control of Japan and American proposals for international control of atomic energy; the United States responded by agreeing, in effect, not to challenge Soviet control in Rumania and Bulgaria (see Gaddis, *United States and the Origins of the Cold War*, pp. 281-283). On the spirit of compromise at Moscow, see also James F. Byrnes, *Speaking Frankly* (New York: Harper & Bros., 1947), ch. 6; and Daniel Yergin, *Shattered Peace: The Origins*

of the Cold War and the National Security State (Boston: Houghton Mifflin Co., 1978), p. 148, 161-162.

6. See *FRUS* (1945), 2: 641. The State Department had completed a draft trusteeship agreement for Korea by November 8, 1945, which ran to thirteen pages and thirty-eight separate articles. Under its provisions, Korea would be placed under a four-power trusteeship as per Article 77 of the United Nations Charter, as a territory detached from an enemy state; the purpose would be "to enable the Korean people as soon as possible to accept the responsibilities of independence and . . . become a member of the United Nations." The administering authority, comprised of a high commissioner and an executive council (the latter having one representative from each of the four powers), would exercise executive, legislative, and judicial authority, with the advice of a cabinet or advisory committee of Koreans. Article 19 of the draft provided "increasingly to the fullest extent possible for the participation in administrative, judicial, and other official positions of suitable Korean personnel" and vowed "progressively [to] transfer responsibility to them"; trusteeship would terminate on March 1, 1951, unless the powers concerned agreed to an earlier end. (March 1 was chosen because of the March 1, 1919 independence movement in Korea—an ironic touch, since the proposal put off Korean independence for five years.) An attached protocol provided for, among other things, the termination of military government throughout Korea "upon the assumption of office by the High Commissioner" and the withdrawal of Allied armed forces one month later. (See "Draft Trusteeship Agreement for Korea," November 8, 1945. I am indebted to John Kotch for getting this document declassified and for providing me with a copy.)

There is no indication that this draft proposal was submitted at the Moscow Conference. At the first session on December 16, after Byrnes and Molotov both had noted that no Soviet-American agreement on a trusteeship for Korea existed (Molotov accurately described the Roosevelt-Stalin talks at Yalta regarding the issue as only "an exchange of views"), Byrnes said that the American delegation "would prepare a paper" on Korea for the next meeting. Accordingly, on December 17, the United States submitted a memorandum entitled "Unified Administration for Korea," the provisions of which are given in my text. It also stated, "our ideas on the provisions of a trusteeship have not taken definite form." (See *FRUS* [1945], 2: 620-621, 641-643.)

7. The Soviet draft was submitted on December 20 and accepted with what Byrnes called "a few slight changes," which provided more explicitly for Chinese and British participation. Byrnes described the latter two powers as having "a very large interest in the development of an independent Korea." Byrnes stated clearly on December 22 the quid pro quo that the Americans wanted for accepting the Soviet draft on Korea: "We had just accepted the Soviet proposals on Korea and he [Byrnes] hoped very much that Mr. Molotov would give some help in finding a solution to our difficulties in regard to Bulgaria and Rumania." (See *FRUS* [1945], 2: 699-700, 716, 721, 728; for the final text of the agreement, see pp. 820-821.) Note Ernest May's erroneous statement regarding the Korea provisions of the Moscow Accords: "With some changes in language, the Russians accepted Byrnes' terms" (*Lessons of the Past* [New York: Oxford University Press, 1973], p. 55).

8. *FRUS* (1945), 6: 1,151.

9. In June 1946 the State Department still urged, "it is imperative that the

United States strictly observe the Moscow Agreement" (see "Policy for Korea," June 6, 1946; in *FRUS* [1946], 6: 697).

10. See *Chŏn'guk nodongja sinmun* [National Worker's News], November 1, 1945; *Chŏnsŏn* [Battle Front], no. 3, October 27, 1945; *Tongnip sinmun* [Independence News], October 31, 1945; *Chayu sinmun* [Free News], October 27, 1945; and *Maeil sinbo* [Daily News], October 26, 1945; all in Republic of Korea, Kuksa p'yŏnch'an wiwŏn-hoe, *THMGS* I [History of the Republic of Korea] (Seoul, 1970): 308-309. *Haebang ilbo* [Liberation Daily], (no. 7, October 31, 1945), linked Vincent's statement to American policy in the Philippines, saying, "The U.S. government has promised independence even to the Philippines which is several thousand years behind Korea in terms of civilization." Syngman Rhee denounced trusteeship on November 7 and stated that MacArthur also opposed the idea (see Kim Chong-bŏm and Kim Tong-un, *Haebang chŏn-hu ŭi Chosŏn chinsang* [The True Situation of Korea Before and After Liberation] (Seoul: Chosŏn chŏngyŏng yŏn'gu-sa, 1945), p. 153.

Note also that Benninghoff's October 10 report, cited in chapter five, had quoted KDP leaders in support of American tutelage. From the beginning, the KDP saw tutelage as a means of defeating the KPR and was the only group willing to acknowledge publicly that Korean independence could not be immediate (see the September 8 "Down with the KPR" handbill, in Kim Chun-yŏn, ed., *Han'guk minjudang so-sa* [A Short History of the Korean Democratic Party] [Seoul: Han'guk minjudang sŏnjŏn-bu, 1948], p. 9).

11. *FRUS* (1945), 6: 1,074.

12. *Maeil sinbo*, October 31, 1945.

13. See, for example, the MG's October 27 statement that it was the only government south of the thirty-eighth parallel, and Hodge's December 12 declaration that KPR activities were unlawful, which were published in Seoul by the KDP Propaganda Department (in Yi Hyŏk, ed., *Aeguk ppira chŏnjip* [Collection of Patriotic Handbills] [Seoul: Cho'guk munhwa-sa, 1946], pp. 32, 33-37).

14. "Chosŏn chisik kyegŭp ege koham," [To the Intellectual Class], November 1, 1945; in ibid., pp. 56-58. According to this document, Hodge urged Song to transmit the substance of their talks to Korea's intellectuals.

15. USAMGIK, "HMGK" (Seoul: Office of Administrative Services, Statistical Research Division, 1946), 1: 217; written in the summer of 1946, this study specifically blamed Vincent for the trusteeship planning.

16. *Minjung ilbo*, December 30, 1945.

17. Memorandum of Hodge conversation with General Albert C. Wedemeyer, August 27, 1947; in XXIV Corps Historical File. The *Chungang sinmun* [Central Daily] reported their meeting of December 29 in its December 31 issue.

18. Ko Ha sonsaeng chon'gi p'yonch'an wiwŏn-hoe, *Ko ha Song Chin-u sŏnsaeng chon* [Collection on Ko Ha, Song Chin-u] (Seoul: Tonga ilbo ch'ulp'an-guk, 1964), pp. 337-338. For an account of the assassination, see *Tonga ilbo* [East Asia Daily], December 31, 1945; in *THMGS* I: 713-714.

19. Han T'ae-su, *Han'guk chŏngdang-sa* [A History of Korean Political Parties] (Seoul: Sin t'aeyang-sa, 1961), p. 69. The *Seoul Times* said that Song's assassin left behind a note saying that he killed Song because of Song's support for trusteeship (January 1, 1946). On Kim Ku's responsibility for the assassination, see information provided to the MG by Chang T'aek-sang and Wŏn

Se-hun, in memorandums of their conversations with Leonard Bertsch, August 16, 1946 and July 17, 1946; in USAFIK, XXIV Corps Historical File; "HUSA-FIK," manuscript in the Office of the Chief of Military History, Washington, D.C. (Tokyo and Seoul, 1947, 1948), vol. 2, ch. 2, p. 58; and Richard Robinson, "Betrayal of a Nation," Manuscript, Massachusetts Institute of Technology, p. 72. The MG apprehended Song's murderer in April 1946 when he returned to the south after inciting antitrusteeship demonstrations in north Korea (USAMGIK, G-2 "Weekly Report," no. 33, April 21-28, 1946).

20. *FRUS* (1945), 6: 1,153n.

21. Robinson, "Betrayal of a Nation," p. 26. Robinson said Hodge did this "unknowingly" because he knew nothing about the agreement on Korea "until well after" the Moscow Conference. When I pointed out to Dr. Robinson that drafts of the American proposal to be presented at Moscow had been sent to Hodge before December 28, Robinson stated that his own understanding was based on remarks that Hodge had made to his own staff. If Hodge did know of the trusteeship proposal, Robinson said, he must have lied to his own staff. (Conversation with Richard Robinson, March 27, 1974.) The rapporteur of a December 31 staff meeting said, "I got the impression that Gen. Hodge had come to the conclusion that he would oppose 'trusteeship' under any conditions" (see USAFIK, XXIV Corps Historical File, "XXIV Corps Journal," December 31 entry).

22. Yi Kang-guk, *Minjujuǔi ǔi Chosǒn kǒnsǒl* [The Construction of Democratic Korea] (Seoul: Chosǒn inminbo-sa husǒng-bu, 1946), p. 103.

23. *FRUS* (1945), 6: 1,154.

24. Ibid., p. 1,153.

25. Trusteeship was translated as *sint'ak tongch'i*, "trust rule," an acceptable rendering, but one with unfortunate connotations owing to similar Japanese usages. In south Korea *sint'ak tongch'i* was used as a tag for the whole Moscow agreement on Korea, which, as we have noted, was barely a trusteeship agreement at all. MG historians averred that Koreans could not understand the trusteeship concept, because of "the poverty of the Korean language in abstract words" ("HUSAFIK," vol. 1, ch. 4, p. 36).

26. Leonard C. Hoag, "American Military Government in Korea: War Policy and the First Year of Occupation, 1941-1946" (Draft manuscript prepared under the auspices of the Office of the Chief of Military History, 1970), p. 352. Hoag also quoted a *Stars and Stripes* article of December 27 as saying that the United States had urged immediate independence for Korea, whereas the Soviets had advocated trusteeship.

27. See Leahy's comments of November 1945, quoted in Yergin, *Shattered Peace*, p. 155.

28. *Seoul Times*, December 27, 1945.

29. "HUSAFIK," vol. 2, ch. 4, p. 77; and vol. 2, ch. 1, p. 21.

30. *Department of State Bulletin*, December 30, 1945, p. 1,036. Byrnes's statement was widely broadcast in south Korea. He later acknowledged that his statement was made in response to opposition to trusteeship within south Korea (see Byrnes, *Speaking Frankly*, p. 222).

31. Based on Hoag, "American Military Government in Korea," p. 291; and on accounts in "HUSAFIK," vol. 2, ch. 2, pp. 53-60; and vol. 3, ch. 4, pp. 48-49; and "XXIV Corps Journal," January 2, 1946 entry. Cho Pyǒng-ok later claimed that he mediated the January 1 encounter between Hodge and Kim Ku and that out of this meeting came the idea for the subsequent South Korean

Interim Government. There is no other evidence to support this interesting assertion. (See Cho, *Na ŭi hoegorok* [My Recollections] [Seoul: Min'gyo-sa, 1959], pp. 166-167.)

32. See, for example, *Tonga ilbo*, January 1, 1946; in *THMGS* I: 719-720.

33. *Tonga ilbo*, December 27, 1945; in *THMGS* I: 671-674.

34. Rhee was strangely silent in the days immediately following the publication of the Moscow agreement (A. Wigfall Green, *The Epic of Korea* [Washington, D.C.: Public Affairs Press, 1950], p. 52). This is probably because in 1919 he led a group of Koreans who petitioned President Wilson for Korea to be "guided by a mandatory until such time as the League of Nations shall decide that it is 'fit for self-government'" (Chong-sik Lee, *The Politics of Korean Nationalism* [Berkeley: University of California Press, 1963], p. 103). KPG leaders later attacked Rhee for this action. A north Korean newspaper brought it up again in early 1946, claiming that Rhee had urged the United States to colonize Korea in 1919 and that other Koreans had nearly killed him for this (*P'yŏngbuk sinbo* [North P'yŏng'an report], February 5, 1946). Among Koreans, it had long been known that the so-called "American group" of moderate nationalists had hoped first for some sort of mandatory or tutelage under the United States in 1919 and subsequently had settled for tutelage under the Japanese. Bishop Herbert Welch, a Methodist missionary in Korea, said the following in the aftermath of the March First Movement:

> Many [Koreans], including some of the most intelligent and far-seeing, are persuaded that there is no hope of speedy independence, and that they must settle down for a long period to build up the Korean people, in physical conditions, in knowledge, in morality, and in the ability to handle government concerns.

(Quoted in Alleyne Ireland, *The New Korea* [New York: E. P. Dutton, 1926], p. 69.

35. See E. E. Schattschneider's discussion in *The Semi Sovereign People* (New York, 1960), p. 36-43. Hodge later said that trusteeship gave the Right an issue: "They hung on that when they found that they had nothing else to talk about except that they don't want trusteeship" (Hodge, monologue to visiting Congressmen, October 4, 1947; in USAFIK, USFIK 11071 file, box 62/96).

36. See the transcript of this broadcast in *THMGS* I: 611-613. Kim Ku condemned Rhee's broadcast, saying instead that "right and left must join hands" in the interests of Korean unification (see *Seoul sinmun* [Seoul News], December 21, 1945; in *THMGS* I: 637).

37. See the KDP's leaflet in *THMGS* I: 678-679; and Rhee's radio broadcast of December 26, in *Tonga ilbo*, December 28, 1945; pp. 668-670.

38. *Han'guk minjudang t'ŭkbo* [Korean Democratic Party Special Report], no. 4, January 10, 1946.

39. See the text in Yi, ed., *Aeguk ppira chŏnjip* 1: 80-84. Rhee and his supporters charged repeatedly that Korean and (Nationalist) Chinese interests had been sold out by communist sympathizers in the State Department (see Robert T. Oliver, *Syngman Rhee: The Man Behind the Myth* [Cornwall, N.Y.: Cornwall Press, 1955], pp. 178, 184, 194). Rhee's small "Korea lobby" took its cues from the China lobby. An essential part of the latter's campaign against internationalists in the State Department (and against FDR) was that China's interests had been "sold down the river" at Yalta (see Ross Koen, *The China Lobby in American Politics* [New York: Macmillan Co., 1960], pp. 64-69).

Rhee campaigned against the Yalta accords beginning in the summer of 1945, charging that Roosevelt and Stalin had divided Korea during their talks. Many Koreans continue to believe this tale today.

40. 67th MG Company (Ch'ungju), report of January 15, 1946.

41. "HUSAFIK," vol. 2, ch. 1, pp. 24-26.

42. See ibid.; also ch. 4, pp. 78-80. These accounts are based on a G-2 report of April 21, 1946. The document in question was dated January 3, 1946.

43. See various issues of the *Chosŏn inmin-bo* [Korean People's Report], December 31, January 2, January 3; and of *Chayu sinmun*, January 1-2, January 5.

44. "HMGK" 3:52, said that the loss in the Left's strength in the south was "attributed to the linking of all communist sympathizers with the trusteeship proposals agreed upon at the Moscow Conference." Leftists acknowledged that this was the case (see Yi, *Minjujuŭi ŭi Chosŏn kŏnsŏl*, p. 113).

45. *Seoul Times*, January 19, 1946. See also *Han'guk minjudang t'ŭkbo*, no. 5, February 10, 1946, which said, "Down with Pak Hŏn-yŏng who hopes to make Korea part of the Soviet orbit," and called Pak a "country-selling criminal" (*maegukjŏk*).

46. See the *Seoul Times*, January 18, 1946, quoting Robert Cornwall (*Pacific Stars and Stripes* correspondent) and other newsmen.

47. G-2 "Weekly Report," no. 19, January 13-20, 1946; also "XXIV Corps Journal," January 6, 1946 entry.

48. "XXIV Corps Journal," January 6 entry. Johnston was one of the few American correspondents whom Hodge liked.

49. See Kim O-sŏng, ed., *Chidoja kunsang* [The leaders] (Seoul: Taesŏng ch'ulp'an-sa, 1946), p. 20. Many Americans came to see Pak as an archconspirator. His diminutive stature and dark complexion apparently reinforced this image; "HUSAFIK," vol. 2, ch. 1, p. 20, referred to him as "swarthy, crafty." Edward Bellamy in his *Fabian Essays* wrote that the average American "conceived of a socialist, when he considered him at all, as a mysterious type of desperado, reputed to infest the dark places . . . and engaged with his fellows in a conspiracy as monstrous as it was futile, against civilization and all that it implied" (quoted in Louis Hartz, *The Liberal Tradition in America* [New York: Harcourt, Brace & World, 1955], p. 246).

50. Memorandum of Hodge's conversation with General Wedemeyer, August 27, 1947; in XXIV Corps Historical File. A moderate rightist like Kim Sam-gyu would be a good example of one who rolled all the connotations together (see his *Minjok ŭi yŏmyŏng* [Dawn of the Nation] [n.p., 1949], pp. 9-11, 179). Louise Yim wrote simply that "only the Communist Party favored the subservience of Korean sovereignty to the great powers" (*My Forty-Year Fight for Korea* [Seoul: Chungang University, International Culture Research Center, 1951], p. 253).

51. Harriman cable of January 25, 1946; in *FRUS* (1946), 8: 622.

52. See the text of the Tass communiqué of January 25 in ibid., pp. 617-619. Kennan's comments in response to the communiqué show no comprehension of the actual situation in Korea (pp. 620-621).

53. "XXIV Corps Journal," February 6, 1946 entry. Harriman quoted Stalin as having said during their meeting, "The Soviet Government does not need a trusteeship [in Korea] any more than the United States . . . if both countries consider it desirable, the trusteeship can be abolished" (see W. Averell Harriman and Elie Abel, *Special Envoy to Churchill and Stalin, 1941-1946* [New York: Random House, 1975], p. 533). Just how far the Americans had come

from their advocacy of full trusteeship for Korea at Moscow was apparent in the remarks of John Carter Vincent during a radio discussion over NBC on January 19, 1946. When asked to summarize the Moscow agreement on Korea, Vincent left out any mention of trusteeship, prompting the moderator to ask, "But, Mr. Vincent, what about the question of trusteeship for Korea?" Vincent then described trusteeship as "a possible interim measure." The commentator responded, "I remember Sumner Welles said this was the most significant thing about the Moscow Agreement—it establishes for the first time the basis for an international trusteeship." Vincent went on to cite Byrnes' statement that trusteeship might be dispensed with, again describing it as "only a *procedure*, which may or may not be necessary." Asked to summarize the American position on Korea, Vincent stated, "We have only one objective in Korea—to bring about self-government and independence at the earliest possible moment" (transcript in *Voice of Korea* 3, no. 52, January 28, 1946). Alger Hiss had stated in November 1945 that the State Department's draft on Korean trusteeship would "be the first of several trusteeship agreements and should be a model for them" (quoted in James Matray, "The Reluctant Crusade: American Foreign Policy in Korea, 1941-1950," [Ph.D. dissertation, University of Virginia, 1977], p. 147).

54. Cho Man-sik, a nationalist, had led the north Korean branch of the CPKI and the subsequent North Korea Five Provinces Administrative Bureau until December 1945. Cho was relieved of his duties and confined to a hotel in P'yŏngyang thereafter, apparently for refusing to support the Moscow decision. (See Dae-sook Suh, *The Korean Communist Movement, 1918-1948* [Princeton: Princeton University Press, 1967], pp. 315-316, 319.)

55. Stalin remarked in the spring of 1945, "Whoever occupies a territory also imposes on it his own social system" (quoted in Walter LaFeber, *America, Russia, and the Cold War, 1945-1966* [New York: John Wiley & Sons, 1967], p. 15).

56. Gaddis, *United States and the Origins of the Cold War*, p. 283.

57. See Eben A. Ayers Papers, Truman Library, diary entry of February 25, 1946; and Yergin, *Shattered Peace*, p. 161. Truman's remarks on December 22, 1950 are quoted in Papers of Matthew J. Connelly, box 1.

58. Herbert Feis, *Contest Over Japan* (New York: W. W. Norton, 1967), p. 97; and LaFeber, *America, Russia, and the Cold War*, p. 30.

59. "HUSAFIK," vol. 2, ch. 1, p. 31.

60. Ibid., ch. 2, p. 53; Robinson, "Betrayal of a Nation," p. 30. On January 18 the State Department also sent Hodge the contents of a State Department public broadcast, saying, "Korean section of (Moscow) communique drafted by Soviets, with minor changes by U.S.," and expressing the hope that the trusteeship provision could be avoided. Thus, at least publically, the State Department was attempting to hide its responsibility for trusteeship. (See cable, "State to CINCAFPAC, info to CG USAFIK," January 18, 1946; in RG 43, Joint Commission, box 9.)

61. *FRUS* (1946), 8: 628-630.

62. Byrnes to the Secretary of War, April 1, 1946; in ibid., pp. 654-656. Byrnes's letter apparently was not transmitted to Hodge.

63. Furthermore, Benninghoff had been recalled to Washington for consultation in November and was back in Seoul by November 28 at the latest, with a "policy manual" in his hands. Various cables about trusteeship and the Moscow talks were sent to Seoul in late November and early December; and

on November 8 Langdon had sent a cable to Washington, saying, "we have noted with satisfaction instructions sent to Embassy Moscow and trust we shall be kept currently informed of progress of negotiations" (see various cables in RG 59, decimal file, 740.0019/Control (Korea); and nos. 740.0019/11-345, 11-845, 11-2845, and 1-2546; all in box no. 3827).

64. Hodge, monologue to visiting congressmen, October 4, 1947; in USFIK 11071 file, box 62/96.

65. Vincent to Acheson, January 28, 1946; in State Department, RG 59, decimal file, 740.0019/1-2846.

66. Martin to George McCune, undated; in State Department, RG 59, decimal file, 740.0019/3-1646.

67. See minutes of the 30th meeting of the Subcommittee for the Far East, August 1, 1945; in State Department, RG 353, file folder no. 334, SWNCC-SANACC, box no. 86. Benninghoff was acting chairman at this time; other subcommittee members included George Blakeslee, Hugh Borton, John Hilldring, and Edwin Martin.

68. A short time before Kennan penned his famous "long telegram," he sent a cable to the Secretary of State saying, "There can be little doubt that USSR wishes to assure earliest and most complete exclusion of other powers from all connections with Korean affairs." He went on to say that such people as Syngman Rhee and Kim Ku, "impractical and poorly organized though they may be," still constituted "a pro-American opposition to existing Soviet-sponsored 'democratic' parties and social organizations and to concept of Soviet domination of future provisional government." (See Kennan to Secretary of State, January 25, 1946; in *FRUS* (1946), 8: 619-620.)

69. "HUSAFIK," vol. 2, ch. 2, p. 91.

70. See RG 353, SWNCC-SANACC, box no. 76. See no. 62 *supra* for Byrnes's query. During his visit to Tokyo and Seoul, Harriman took a hard line toward the Russians, thus reinforcing what MacArthur and Hodge already believed. Harriman told MacArthur that the Russians sought "political domination" throughout Korea, just as they did in Eastern Europe. He maintained that they also wanted "industrial domination," so as to "support the development of Siberia." In Seoul Harriman "cautioned General Hodge against trying to form a Korean government in the south that would claim authority over the country as a whole," an obvious reference to the governing commission proposal and the return of the KPG. He told Hodge on February 3, in regard to dealing with the Soviets, that "little ground could be gained by being considerate or attempting to establish good will by generous gestures"; Hodge should be "friendly and fair" toward the Russians, "but lay it on the line when we have to." Harriman also recommended that Charles Thayer, an expert on the Soviet Union, be appointed as an advisor to Hodge, a recommendation later accepted in Washington. (See Harriman and Abel, *Special Envoy*, pp. 542-543.)

71. Memorandum of Hodge's conversation with General Wedemeyer, August 27, 1947; in XXIV Corps Historical File. About the same time, Hodge said, "It looked as though we might have a little success through the emigre group late in 1945, but the announcement of the Moscow decision split everything wide open." Hodge, monologue to visiting congressmen, October 4, 1947; in USFIK 11071 file, box no. 62/96.

72. "XXIV Corps Journal," December 31, 1945 entry.

73. "HUSAFIK," vol. 2, ch. 4, pp. 148-149, 149-150.

74. See Benninghoff's cable to the Secretary of State, quoting Hodge, February 9, 1946; in *FRUS* (1946), 8: 630-632. Hodge said that the RDC included all groups "other than Soviet (who have refused to cooperate) controlled Communist" (p. 631). Note also that the original RDC plan, like the governing commission proposal, included certain north Korean leaders. This was dropped as being "impractical" ("HUSAFIK," vol. 2, ch. 2, p. 79).

75. Benninghoff to the Secretary of State, January 28, 1946; in *FRUS* (1946), 8: 627. An unsigned, undated memorandum stated that "R.D.C. created by Goodfellow. Not well known what R.D.C. would be. R.D.C. [members] named by RHEE and KIMM Kiusic. R.D.C. to control M.G. agencies—education, agriculture and one other (Gen. Hodge did not concur)" (see "SKILA Materials," XXIV Corps Historical File). Autobiographical notes by Goodfellow referred to the RDC, saying that he "set up the first temporary government" in Korea in early 1946 (Goodfellow Papers, box no. 1).

76. See "HUSAFIK," vol. 2, ch. 2, pp. 61-63; G-2 "Weekly Report," no. 19, January 13-20, 1946; and no. 21, January 27-February 3, 1946; also Han, *Han'guk chŏngdang-sa*, pp. 70-71.

77. The NSRRKI claimed 512,852 members; NSRRKI Patriotic Women's Society (*Aeguk puin-hoe*) claimed 3,305,170 members in April 1946; Kim Ku's "Anti-Trusteeship [Pro-] Independence Struggle Committee" (*Pan't'ak tongnip wiwŏn-hoe*) claimed the grand total of 12,652,718—probably Kim's mistaken estimate of the total population of south Korea. (See USAMGIK, Department of Public Opinion, "Memorandum: Political Parties," 1948.)

78. "HUSAFIK," vol. 2, ch. 2, p. 62.

79. G-2 "Weekly Report," no. 21, January 27-February 3, 1946. G-2 observers noted how "markedly different" the ENC was from KPR gatherings; the participants were "close-shaven, well-clad, and of an intelligent, dignified appearance" at the ENC; very few were under thirty years of age.

80. MacArthur to the Joint Chiefs of Staff, quoting Hodge, January 22, 1946; in *FRUS* (1946), 8: 613.

81. Benninghoff to the Secretary of State, January 23, 1946; in *FRUS* (1946), 8: 616.

82. "HUSAFIK," vol. 2, ch. 4, p. 146. This study noted on the same page that the RDC was a "Rightist organ."

83. Ibid., ch. 2, p. 91; see also *FRUS* (1946), 8: 623-627. The revisions that this SWNCC document went through are most revealing. In the first version, dated January 24, the document stated that "The *Joint Commission* [i.e., not the American command] should select a group of *representative democratic* Korean leaders for the purpose of consultation with the Joint Commission" and that "special efforts should be made to find and select a definite majority of strong competent leaders who are not rightist or pronouncedly leftist but represent center and left of center parties." Navy and War Department members of SWNCC objected to the phrase beginning "rightist or . . ." and urged that it be replaced by the phrase, "leaders who are not extremists of either right or left." Assistant Secretary of War Howard C. Peterson thought this change necessary so that the United States would not be "liable to charges of pro-communism." A subsequent discussion paper of January 28, embodying the revisions, then stated the point as follows: the group of Korean leaders selected should be representative of Koreans *and* "acceptable to both the United States and the U.S.S.R." It continued, "It is felt that no group dominated by totalitarian leftists, such as the Communists, or by

rightist elements, representative of *capitalistic and land-lord interests*, would be representative of the Korean people as a whole. . . . These two provisions would be best met by a group in which center and left of center parties had a definite majority." This revision also recognized that proportional representation of Korean leaders in north and south, with one-third for the north and two-thirds for the south on the basis of the respective populations (a policy suggested in earlier revisions), would meet with "strong objections" from the Soviets. Yet this same unworkable formula has been the basis of American and South Korean unification policies ever since. See the various revisions in State Department, RG 53, SWNCC-SANACC, SWNCC no. 176/15, January 24, 1946; and SWNCC nos. 176/18-176/28, January 1946, in box no. 29 (emphasis added in all quotations).

84. See G-2 "Weekly Reports," nos. 23 and 24, February 10-17 and February 17-24, 1946. Justin Sloane, an officer in the Occupation, wrote that the Right "neglected to engage in any extensive organization activities and left the entire field wide open"; in "The Communist Effort in South Korea, 1945-1948" (M.A. thesis, Northwestern University, 1949), p. 45.

85. *FRUS* (1946), 8: 625.

86. "XXIV Corps Journal," February 14, 1946 entry. The RDC was translated into Korean either as *Nam-Chosŏn kungmin taep'yo minju ŭiwŏn* or as *Taehan kungmin taep'yo minju ŭiwŏn*, depending upon whether the translator wished to limit the RDC's function to south Korea (*Nam-Chosŏn*) or not.

87. "HUSAFIK," vol. 2, ch. 2, pp. 78-79. The membership broke down as follows: *KDP*—Kim Chun-yŏn, Paek Nam-hun, Paek Kwan-su, Wŏn Se-hun, Kim To-yŏn, Kim Pop-in; *NSSRKI*—Syngman Rhee, Kim Yo-sik, Hwang Hyŏn-suk, Kim Sun; *KPG*—Kim Ku, Kim Kyu-sik, Kim Pong-jin, Cho Wan-gu, Kim Chang-sŏk, Cho So-ang; *KMT*—An Chae-hong, Yi Yi-sik, Ham Tae-yang, Pak Yong-hŭi. Four men who leaned to the Right but were classified as "neutrals" were O Se-ch'ang, Kwŏn Tong-jin, Chŏng In-bo, and Chang Myŏn. Yŏ Un-hyŏng apparently wanted to participate in the RDC and wrote an eloquent address for its opening meeting; but on February 13, Ŏm Hang-sŏp of the KDP purposely and publicly insulted Yŏ, saying he had begged to be part of the RDC. Thus Yŏ, Hwang Chin-nam, and Ch'oe Ik-han did not show up. ("HUSAFIK," vol. 2, ch. 1, p. 29.)

88. "XXIV Corps Journal," February 14, 1946 entry; see also ibid., ch. 2, pp. 80-81.

89. G-2 "Weekly Report," no. 24, February 17-24, 1946. These resolutions were published as official MG releases. See also *Tonga ilbo*, February 26, 1946.

90. G-2 "Weekly Report," no. 23, February 10-17, 1946; see also Han, *Han'guk chŏngdang-sa*, p. 71. On March 19 Langdon reported that some KPR followers had tried to depict the RDC as "merely a projection of Emergency National Assembly of original Kim Koo Provisional Government"; in *FRUS*, (1946), 8: 648.

91. "HUSAFIK," vol. 2, ch. 2, p. 81. The change of traffic became the butt of many jokes.

92. Interview, May 19, 1973; also *FRUS* (1946), 8: 698. Hodge later said that the "extreme right" took the RDC over after the Occupation left personnel selection up to Koreans (Hodge monologue to visiting congressmen, October 4, 1947; USFIK 11071 file, box 62/96).

93. "HUSAFIK," vol. 2, ch. 2, p. 85. A memorandum from Yi Myo-muk to Hodge dated May 23, 1947, indicated that the RDC was still using Changdok Palace

at that time (memorandum in "Miscellaneous File, Korea," accession no. TS Korea U58, Hoover Institution).

94. Interview with Leonard Bertsch, May 19, 1973. Bertsch said that American missionaries in Seoul had changed Rhee's *wŏn* into dollars for him. When Lerche found out about these transactions, he wanted to have Rhee arrested for embezzlement, but he was overruled. Bertsch also stated that Rhee had extorted money from wealthy Koreans by threatening to expose their backgrounds under Japanese rule.

95. Memorandum of Hodge's conversation with General Wedemeyer, August 27, 1947; in XXIV Corps Historical File.

96. MacArthur to the Secretary of State, enclosing Hodge's cable of February 24, 1946; in *FRUS* (1946), 8: 640-642. Hodge told his staff on March 8 that the PP's unwillingness to participate in the RDC showed that it was "entirely a Communist organization and that [it] too just like the People's Republic and the Communists took [its] orders from Moscow." Therefore, Hodge thought, the RDC "was truly representative of Korea except for the small very small minority which are the Communists" ("XXIV Corps Journal," March 8, 1946 entry).

97. "HUSAFIK," vol. 2, ch. 1, p. 29; also ch. 2, p. 77. Goodfellow said, regarding the communists in south Korea, "My approach would be to constantly discredit them, separate them from the non-communist organizations so they stand naked and alone." Letter of August 2, 1946 to Syngman Rhee; in Goodfellow Papers, box no. 1.

98. See the extensive DNF membership lists in Minjujuŭi minjok chŏnsŏn, *Chosŏn Haebang illyŏn-sa* [History of the First Year of Korean Liberation] (Seoul: Munu insŏ'gwan, 1946), pp. 129-130 and 135-136. The DNF platform and programs were similar to those of the KPR (pp. 96-105).

99. Ibid., pp. 91-92; *Chosŏn inmin-bo*, February 13, 1946; *Chwaik sakŏn sillok* 1: 71-73; and "HUSAFIK," vol. 2, ch. 2, p. 40.

100. See a CIC eyewitness account in G-2 "Weekly Report," no. 23, February 10-17, 1946.

101. G-2 "Weekly Report," no. 24, February 17-24, 1946; and *Haebang illyŏn-sa*, p. 92.

102. Sloane, "Communist Effort in South Korea," p. 1.

103. On the competition between southern and northern communists and leftists, see esp. Suh, *Korean Communist Movement*, ch. 10. The North Korean Interim People's Committee, inaugurated in February, represented the first central political organ to be imposed on the northern PC structure. Until that time, the provincial PC apparatuses had been largely autonomous. As late as August 1947, the DNF in south Korea was still autonomous of north Korean control. A police raid on August 11 netted a number of South Korean Worker's Party (SKWP) documents; a statement of *Chŏnp'yŏng* receipts; a poem lamenting Yŏ Un-hyŏng's assassination; Pak Hŏn-yŏng's pamphlet, "The Tonghak Peasant Rebellion and its Lessons"; materials on the recent and future work of the DNF; and so on—but not a single indication that north Koreans were pulling DNF strings (see memorandum on documents confiscated in August 11, 1947 police raid on the DNF; in XXIV Corps Historical File).

104. See in particular Gaddis, *United States and the Origins of the Cold War*, ch. 9, "Getting Tough with Russia: The Reorientation of American Policy, 1946," esp. p. 284; and Yergin, *Shattered Peace*, ch. 7.

105. "HUSAFIK," vol. 2, ch. 4, p. 156.

106. The term "effectiveness" is used here in the sense Morton H. Halperin uses it in his *Bureaucratic Politics and Foreign Policy* (Washington: The Brookings Institution, 1974). See esp. pp. 90-91 on bureaucratic effectiveness and how to lose/keep it.

107. A State Department message to MacArthur dated February 28 linked Soviet actions in Korea with those in Eastern Europe. Byrnes's cable of April 5 reversed his earlier criticism of Hodge and Occupation activities in Korea, and demonstrated how the State Department had fallen in behind those actually "on the grounds" in Korea, as Hodge has put it (see *FRUS* [1946], 8: 619-620, 645, 657-658).

108. "U.S. Document no. 3, Joint Commission Files," quoted in "HUSAFIK," vol. 2, ch. 4, pp. 154-155. The "HUSAFIK" noted that "to the Korean public, the situation was described somewhat differently"; several paragraphs followed that expressed American commitment to early independence, self-determination of all peoples, and so on (pp. 155-157). The author of this document was probably Charles Thayer, who had been sent to Seoul to serve as a political advisor to Hodge and the Joint Commission. He had been a part of the Riga contingent watching the USSR in the 1930s and a member of General Mark Clark's staff in Austria (see cable, MacArthur to Hodge, January 31, 1946; in RG 43, Joint Commission file, box no. 9).

109. See the account in "HUSAFIK," vol. 2, ch. 4, pp. 100-115; also Benninghoff's report of February 15, 1946; in *FRUS* (1946), 8: 633-636. Hodge thought the Soviet delegation looked "highly suspicious" (p. 102).

110. *FRUS* (1946), 8: 645.

111. See Benninghoff's report in ibid., p. 637. The American delegation consisted of Arnold, Langdon, Thayer, Col. Robert H. Booth (former Executive Assistant to Lerche), and Col. Frank H. Britton from SCAP headquarters. The Soviet delegation consisted of Shtikov, Minister-Plenipotentiary Semeon C. Tsarapkin, Political Advisor Gerasim M. Balasanov, Col. Tikhon I. Korkulenko, and Maj. Gen. G. N. Lebedoff. (See "HUSAFIK", vol. 2, ch. 4, pp. 158, 159.) The Soviet delegation was more highpowered than the American one; Tsarapkin was the head of the American section of the Soviet Foreign Office.

112. Hodge to the Secretary of State, undated but received May 9; in *FRUS* (1946), 8: 665-667.

113. "HUSAFIK," vol. 2, ch. 4, pp. 168-172. The Soviets later claimed that the American delegation did not show a "readiness" to fulfill the intent of the agreement and "many times even declared that it did not quite understand the Moscow decision on Korea" (quoted in *FRUS* [1946] 8: 757). The Soviet position on Korea was similar to that regarding Poland, where "Molotov insisted that only Polish leaders who supported the Yalta decisions should be consulted about reorganizing the [Polish] Provisional Government" (see Martin F. Herz, *Beginnings of the Cold War*, [Bloomington: Indiana University Press, 1966], p. 86). This was part of the consistent Soviet policy that concessions won at the conference tables should not be lost in their implementation and that small nations or groups within small nations should not be allowed to disrupt Allied agreements (see Clemens, *Yalta*, pp. 129-131, 268-269, 290).

114. "Joint Commission Reports," originally "top secret"; in USFIK 11071 file, box 64/96. These daily summaries of the JC proceedings were prepared by Col. Glenn Newman and Leonard Bertsch. See copies of these minutes also in RG 43, Joint Commission file, box no. 3.

115. Ibid., Newman's minutes of the second session.

116. Ibid.
117. Ibid., Bertsch's minutes of the tenth session.
118. Ibid.
119. Ibid., Bertsch's minutes of the eleventh session.
120. Ibid., Bertsch's minutes of the thirteenth, fifteenth and sixteenth sessions.
121. Hodge to MacArthur, February 12, 1946, quoted in *FRUS* (1946), 8: 632.
122. Ibid., p. 644.
123. See cables in ibid., pp. 660-661. Byrnes firmly approved of the American position at the JC (pp. 657-658).
124. Interview with Bertsch, May 19, 1973.
125. Quoted in *FRUS* (1946), 8: 652-653.
126. In his talks with Stalin in May 1945, Harry Hopkins "said merely, and said it twice, that [the U.S.] . . . wished to see friendly countries all along the Soviet borders" (Herbert Feis, *Between War and Peace, The Potsdam Conference* [Princeton: Princeton University Press, 1960], p. 98).
127. Robinson, "Betrayal of a Nation," p. 312. The Russians later charged that the Americans excluded Chŏnp'yŏng, Chŏnnong, and other mass organizations from their list of south Korean political parties and social organizations with which the JC would consult, while including all parties that opposed the Moscow decision (see the Russian letter of October 26, 1946, quoted in ibid., pp. 757-759).
128. See the text in SCAP *Summation*, no. 5, February 1946; and in USAMGIK, *Official Gazette*, February 23, 1946.
129. USAMGIK, *Official Gazette*, May 4, 1946.
130. *Chosŏn inmin-bo* February 27, 1946; KDP spokesman quoted in *Seoul sinmun*, February 27, 1946.
131. Quoted in the *Seoul Times*, March 6, 1946. In fact, of course, both ordinances violated American first amendment freedoms.
132. "HUSAFIK," vol. 2, ch. 1, p. 32.
133. At the JC the Russians had insisted on consulting "only with central organizations representative of the people," another reason for excluding the RDC. In mid-March rightists had held a "series of secret conferences looking towards formation of a single party of the right," but continuing factional rivalry prevented agreement. Also, Rhee was forced to take a leave of absence from the RDC around the same time that newspapers published allegations that he had promised mining concessions to certain Americans should he become president of Korea (Langdon to the Secretary of State, April 10, 1946; in *FRUS* [1946], 8: 658-659).
134. "HUSAFIK," vol. 2, ch. 4, p. 31.
135. Ibid., pp. 28-29.
136. Yergin, *Shattered Peace*, p. 188.
137. "HUSAFIK," vol. 2, ch. 4, pp. 31, 312-314. Edgar Snow had visited south Korea in January 1946 as a correspondent for the *Saturday Evening Post*; contact with him was taken as evidence of communist leanings on the part of several Americans in the MG.
138. "XXIV Corps Journal," March 25 entry. In June 1946 a Korean reported that A. I. Shabshin of the Soviet Consulate in Seoul had told him at a cocktail party that he, Shabshin, was "the controlling leader of all Communists in south Korea and that Mr. Pak (Hŏn-yŏng) was his henchman." Mr. Shabshin may still be laughing about that one, but the Occupation apparently believed the story ("HUSAFIK," vol. 2, ch. 1, p. 27).
139. "XXIV Corps Journal," March 29 entry.

140. *Seoul Times*, May 18, 1946; "HUSAFIK," vol. 2, ch. 4, pp. 220-221.
141. George McCune noted the congruence between the opening of the JC and heightened attacks on the Left, in his *Korea Today* (Cambridge: Harvard University Press, 1950), p. 72.
142. G-2 "Weekly Report," no. 29, March 24-31, 1946.
143. "HUSAFIK," vol. 2, ch. 2, p. 67.
144. Public Opinion Bureau, raw reports, July 30, 1946; in XXIV Corps Historical File.
145. It left open the question of whether the KNP or the American command was responsible ("HUSAFIK," vol. 2, ch. 2, p. 67; and ch. 4, p. 344). But the KNP was, in a nominal sense at least, an agency of the MG.
146. Langdon to the Secretary of State, April 30, 1946; in *FRUS* (1946), 8: 662-663.
147. "HUSAFIK," vol. 2, ch. 2, pp. 65, 67.
148. Ibid., p. 69. See also *Haebang illyŏn-sa*, p. 115, which charged that Rhee had called for a "northern expedition" (*puk-bŏl*) to unify Korea after a separate southern government was established.
149. See account in the *Seoul Times*, May 14, 1946; also "HUSAFIK," vol. 2, ch. 2, p. 65.
150. The *Seoul Times*, May 25, 1946.
151. *Pacific Stars and Stripes*, May 25, 1946. See also *FRUS* (1946), 8: 689.
152. Goodfellow Papers, box no. 1. It is clear from reading through numerous letters and memorandums in Goodfellow's private papers that he supported Rhee's call for a separate government in south Korea. In a meeting of November 18, 1946, the Korean Commission in Washington, of which Goodfellow was a member, resolved to seek State Department recognition of a separate southern government. Another member, John Staggers, stated, "Forget about the Russians. Get the government recognized then we will take care of the northern situation" ("Excerpts from Conference at Korean Commission," Goodfellow Papers, box no. 1).

     After his return to the United States, Goodfellow acted as a publicist for Rhee's cause, for which he was handsomely compensated. On June 28, 1946, Rhee wrote in his own hand to Goodfellow: "Louise Yim will be going to the States soon I hope. She will arrange to use her money there. She will deposit a certain amount for you. . . . According to our understanding, you will have sufficient amount per year." Later on in the letter, Rhee specified a "total sum" that would be "equal to $40,000 or $50,000 a year" (Goodfellow Papers, box no. 2).

     In a letter to Hodge of June 21, 1946, however, Goodfellow denied the allegations then current in Korea that he and Rhee had financial ties, saying, "From letters I received I understand Dr. Rhee was deliberately misquoted by the Commies. That is their game and understandable. Some day *the Concentration Camps will be filled* with disloyal men and women who in their fanaticism are more dangerous than our late bundists" (emphasis added) (Goodfellow Papers, box no. 1).
153. *Seoul Times*, May 17, 1946. The discovery of the counterfeiting operation actually occurred on May 3, but it was not announced until the JC dissolved. The police closed the KCP's *Haebang ilbo* after this incident.
154. A demonstration in support of the defendants had apparently been organized for July 29 at a meeting of *Chŏnp'yŏng* held at Seoul Stadium on July 28. A crowd of 3,000 paraded outside the court building on the 29th. After a clash with police in which a middle school student was killed, the crowd

destroyed a police car and then surged into the courtroom itself. The demonstrators charged that the KDP was stage-managing the trial. On July 31 Chang T'aek-sang was quoted as saying he had personally ordered police to fire on the crowd and that "there is no reason to investigate the policeman" who killed the student. On August 22 seven alleged leaders of the demonstrations, including Seoul National University professor Sin Chin-gyu, were given prison terms of two to five years. (See the *Seoul Times*, July 31 and August 22, 1946; also CIC Seoul report of July 30, 1946, in XXIV Corps Historical File.)

155. *Seoul Times*, November 29, 1946; and *FRUS* (1946), 8: 779.

156. See the account in *Haebang illyŏn-sa*, pp. 242-251. American intelligence reports stated that no direct evidence linked the KCP to the case. The evidence consisted of notes printed in the same building that housed KCP headquarters, but "very little of the spurious currency was recovered" (see G-2 "Weekly Report," no. 100, August 3-10, 1947).

157. *Seoul Times*, August 22, 1946. See also *FRUS* (1946), 8: 782. Hŏ Hŏn petitioned to defend the accused. He had become famous in Korea for his defense of the 1919 independence demonstrators (p. 737).

158. See G-2 "Weekly Report," no. 36, May 12-19, 1946; also *Haebang ilbo*, no. 1, September 19, 1945. The 100 million figure is in the latter.

159. "HUSAFIK," vol. 2, ch. 4, p. 345. It also cited a CIC directive of June 29 authorizing "quiet" raids on KCP county offices; the CIC had been quite active in raiding leftist groups before this date, however (p. 339).

160. The use of Cho Pong-am to discredit the KCP was obviously the result of a policy decision within the MG. American CIC investigators had seized a personal letter of his to Pak Hŏn-yŏng in a raid in March. In early May the CIC apparently leaked the letter to the *Tonga ilbo*, which ran it in several installments from May 9-11. On May 14 Cho claimed that the wording of the letter had been altered, although he admitted writing it. It was highly critical of Pak's leadership and was used at the time, and subsequently, to discredit Korean communism. (See Robert A. Scalapino and Chong-sik Lee, *Communism in Korea* [Berkeley: University of California Press, 1972], 1: 290-291.) Cho apparently stayed with the KCP until June, when he was incarcerated and then dropped his "bombshell" on the day after his release (see accounts in G-2 "Weekly Report," no. 36, May 12-19, 1946; and no. 42, June 23-30, 1946; also Cho's biography in State Department, "Biographic Reports on the Cabinet of the Korean Republic" [Washington, D.C.: Office of Intelligence, 1948]). Cho was the first Minister of Agriculture in the Rhee regime and was executed by firing squad for alleged sympathy with North Korea in 1959.

161. G-2 "Weekly Report," no. 49, August 11-18, 1946. The records seized indicated that *Chŏnp'yŏng*'s total membership in all of south Korea stood at 1.9 million; that it was closely tied to people's committees and peasant unions in the provinces; that in February 1946 it had received 170,000 *wŏn* from its sister organization in north Korea, but that the relationship between the northern and southern bodies was informal. An American Labor Advisory Mission filed a report in June 1946, stating that *Chŏnp'yŏng* and its workers' committees were spontaneous in origin, "left wing" but not "party line." It added, "we have found no record of any bona fide labor union which is not affiliated with Chong Pyong . . . it is the only union federation." The report also criticized the wretched working conditions of Korean laborers, women and

children included. (See "Labor Problems and Policies in Korea," June 18, 1946; in USFIK 11071 file, box 62/96.)

162. See "HUSAFIK," vol. 2, ch. 2, pp. 119, 349-351; and the *Seoul Times*, September 7, 1946, and September 9, 1946. The August 23 statement quoted in the text was a reference to disorders in Hwasun (see chapter nine).

163. G-2 "Weekly Report," no. 44, July 7-14, 1946.

164. See the long report on the NSRRKI in G-2 "Weekly Report," no. 56, September 29-October 6, 1946.

165. Ibid.

166. See "HUSAFIK," vol. 2, ch. 2, pp. 91-92; and ch. 4, p. 147; also *FRUS* (1946), 9: 654-656.

167. Langdon to the Secretary of State, May 24, 1946; in *FRUS* (1946), 9: 685-689.

168. Ibid., p. 692-699.

169. The following section is based on an interview with Bertsch, May 19, 1973, and on "HUSAFIK," vol. 2, ch. 2, pp. 41-44, 96-108. Bertsch was a Harvard-trained lawyer from Akron, Ohio, who became, in his words, "the highest ranking first lieutenant in the world." He arrived in Korea in early 1946. He was not sent there on any special mission, as so many thought, but had simply "cleaned out a San Francisco bookstore" of everything possibly relating to Korea and read it all on his voyage over. He quickly became the most knowledgeable American in the Occupation on Korean politics and personalities and moved up to become political advisor to Arnold (and Hodge). Bertsch soon came to know personally most of the major Korean political leaders on the Left and the Right.

He was not "peremptorily shipped home in the summer of 1947," as Gregory Henderson put it, "without thanks or a chance to say goodbye" (*Korea: The Politics of the Vortex* [Cambridge: Harvard University Press, 1968], p. 419n), but remained with the Occupation until 1948. Until he passed away recently, he maintained nearly total recall of Korean personalities and the political situation in the late 1940s. I am deeply indebted to Mrs. Bertsch and her late husband for their warm hospitality and candor in sharing their experiences in Korea with me.

170. "HUSAFIK," vol. 2, ch. 2, p. 99. A common theme at the time was that the Soviets desired a warm-water port in Korea.

171. An unsigned memorandum dated July 31, 1946, in the Goodfellow Papers stated that Syngman Rhee financed Yŏ Un-hong's SDP, at the request of some MG officers. Kim Kyu-sik later stated that he "had been persuaded into the coalition movement by Syngman Rhee, Kim Koo, and Lt. Bertsch" (Maj. Gen. A. E. Brown, "Chronological Summary of Political Events in Korea," entry for November 22, 1946, in XXIV Corps Historical File). The American CIA later stated that although Kim nominally headed the Right side of the Coalition Committee, actually it was "under the influence of Rhee Syngman and Kim Koo" (Central Intelligence Agency, "Korea," SR 2, prepared in the summer of 1947). In his letter to Goodfellow of June 27, 1946, Rhee said:

> The General [Hodge] knows well enough that if I do not support Kimm [Kyu-sik], he cannot maintain his position. So I agreed to support Kimm if he succeeds in setting up a coalition government and when that government is recognized by the Powers, we will then hold a national election. There will be no doubt about my being the choice of the people. As a matter of fact, all our people, both North and South, are willing to die for me. They want me to give them the order and they will all rise up in open fight against the Soviet Occupation in the North.

This letter is unsigned, but it is obviously from Rhee. Also in the text is the statement, "This is all absolutely confidential. You should be clever in handling this information to give no hint that it was from me" (Goodfellow Papers, box no. 1).

172. "HUSAFIK," vol. 2, ch. 2, pp. 100-101. Yi Man-gyu's *Yŏ Un-hyŏng t'ujaeng-sa* [History of Yŏ Un-hyŏng's Struggles], published in May 1946, had candidly discussed Yŏ's trips to Japan.

173. "HUSAFIK," vol. 2, ch. 2, p. 103. Yŏ participated because, according to his biographer, he felt a "personal mission" to get Left and Right to work together (see Yi, *Yŏ Un-hyŏng*, p. 205).

174. Yŏ was a politician, and thus an opportunist almost by definition. Yet Korea could have used more such opportunism in the late 1940s, when shrewd politics so often gave way to shrill moral condemnation. Yŏ wanted a broadly based, unified government in Korea and recognized that compromise toward that goal was necessary, and that practical needs for unity transcended pettifogging passions. After the liberation, he became a tireless advocate of a Left-Right coalition; and for his efforts, he was beaten in August 1945, almost lynched in October 1946, saw his home partially destroyed by a grenade in March 1947, and was finally shot dead on July 19, 1947. In the end, Yŏ was a man for many seasons, but not for the season of liberated Korea and the Manichaean political world that eventually destroyed him.

175. "HUSAFIK," vol. 2, ch. 2, p. 108. A Korean text of Hodge's June 30 endorsement is in Chŏng Si-u, ed., *Tongnip kwa chwa-u hapjak* [Independence and Left-Right Coalition] (Seoul: Sammi-sa, 1946), pp. 31-32.

176. "HUSAFIK," vol. 2, ch. 2, p. 110.

177. Ibid., pp. 111-113. The meetings were held first at Bertsch's home, and later at Tŏksu Palace.

178. G-2 "Periodic Report," July 26, 1946; "HUSAFIK," vol. 2, ch. 2, p. 114. Pak apparently hoped to create a southern worker's party to correspond to the North Korean Worker's Party (NKWP), a coalition of the KCP and the Yenan-oriented New Democratic Party led by Kim Tu-bong then being formed in the north. But Pak was not successful until after the autumn uprisings and the intensified polarization that followed in its wake. His defeat within DNF councils would suggest that the DNF was not a creature of the KCP in the summer of 1946.

179. See "HUSAFIK," vol. 2, ch. 2, pp. 114-115; also Chŏng, *Chwa-u hapjak*, p. 46. These demands reflected a widely held feeling that the interim legislature augured a separate southern government.

180. See *FRUS* (1946), 8: 722-723; and the *Seoul Times*, July 29, 1946.

181. For Korean and English texts of the eight-point program, see Chŏng, *Chwa-u hapjak*, p. 47; *Seoul Times*, July 30, 1946.

182. *FRUS* (1946), 8: 722-723. In a cable of August 9, Hodge also stated that Yŏ had urged him to jail Pak ("HUSAFIK," vol. 2, ch. 2, p. 43).

183. "HUSAFIK," vol. 2, ch. 4, pp. 341-342; *Seoul Times*, August 13, 1946.

184. *FRUS* (1946), 8: 730-731; and "HUSAFIK," vol. 2, ch, 2, pp. 43-44.

185. *Seoul Times*, August 30, 1946.

186. "HUSAFIK," vol. 2, ch. 2, pp. 118, 122; *Seoul Times*, October 8, 1946. Pak Kŏn-ung, an anti-Pak Hŏn-yŏng leftist who had returned from Manchuria in early 1946, also participated on the leftist delegation from time to time.

187. "HUSAFIK," vol. 2, ch. 2, p. 125; Chŏng, *Chwa-u hapjak*, pp. 55-56. The first article probably reflected Langdon's earlier hopes for an MG-managed coalition that would include certain north Koreans. The compromise land reform

proposal was opposed by Right and Left; the rightists thought it would bank-rupt the future Korean government and prevent landlords from becoming capitalist entrepreneurs, and the leftists thought it was "unprincipled" and rewarded landlords who had fattened under the Japanese.

188. See, for example, the detailed account of an alleged attempt at a *coup d'état* by Sin Ik-hŭi, then closely associated with Kim Ku, timed to coincide with the anniversary of the 1910 Annexation (August 29, 1946); in "HUSAFIK," vol. 2, ch. 2, pp. 128-141.

189. Kim, ed., *Han'guk minjudang so-sa*, pp. 34-37. The coalition effort did suc-ceed in causing a public split in KDP ranks. Some fifty-five members quit the KDP, saying that its leaders "insist on maintaining landownership which will do no good for a liberation of the people" (quoted in *Seoul Times*, Oc-tober 22, 1946). "HUSAFIK," vol. 2, ch. 2, p. 127, said that the KDP "led the opposition" to the CC. For a KDP critique of the CC's and other land reform programs, see Hong Sŏng-ha's article in *Minju kyŏngch'al* [The Demo-cratic Policeman], no. 2 (August 1947), pp. 25-29.

190. Cho, *Na ŭi hoegorok*, pp. 186-187.

191. Memorandum of Hodge's conversation with General Wedemeyer, August 1947; in XXIV Corps Historical File.

192. Memorandum, American delegation to the JC to Hodge, November 22, 1946; in "SKILA materials," XXIV Corps Historical File.

193. See memorandum on meeting of secretaries of State, War, and Navy depart-ments, May 22, 1946; in *FRUS* (1946), 8: 681-682; and Langdon to the Secre-tary of State, June 3, 1946; p. 690. See also Byrnes's statement that an earlier Langdon cable had been "helpful here [Washington] in present thinking paralleling yours" (May 29, 1946; quoted on p. 685n).

194. Langdon to Secretary of State, May 24, 1946, in ibid., p. 686. This is the cable to which Byrnes referred (see previous note).

195. "Policy for Korea," June 6, 1946, in ibid., p. 694.

196. See the *Seoul Times*, July 2 and July 10, 1946, for statements by Lerche and Hodge on the projected interim legislature. See also Ordinance no. 118, in USAMGIK, *Official Gazette*, August 24, 1946.

197. *Seoul Times*, September 13, 1946.

198. On August 15, 1946, the KDP called publicly for the Americans to turn over the MG completely to Koreans (see *Chosŏn yŏn'gam 1948* [Korea Yearbook 1948] [Seoul: Chosŏn t'ongsin-sa, 1962], p. 162). Langdon reported on July 28 that "public reaction to suggestion [of interim legislature] generally was apathetic, such support as was given coming from certain Rightist groups who apparently saw in proposal at least a temporary opportunity to domi-nate political scene south of 38th Parallel by probably preponderant repre-sentation in Assembly" (in *FRUS* [1946], 8: 720).

199. Interview with Leonard Bertsch, May 19, 1973. See also *FRUS* (1946), 8: 762.

200. *FRUS* (1946), 8: 731.

201. John E. McMahon, "Antecedents, Character, and Outcome of the Korean Elections of 1948" (M.A. thesis, Berkeley, University of California, 1954), pp. 42-43.

202. Robinson, "Betrayal of a Nation," pp. 174-176. See also Kim Kyu-sik's mem-orandum of November 4, 1946 to Hodge; in "SKILA materials," enclosure no. 15, XXIV Corps Historical File.

203. Robinson, "Betrayal of a Nation," p. 176. Langdon said that only the Left "took exception to the short notice given for the elections" (November 3, 1946; in *FRUS* [1946], 8: 762).

204. Kim's memorandum to Hodge, November 4, 1946; in "SKILA materials," XXIV Corps Historical File. Sŏ Sang-il later drew up a constitution for SKILA that according to Charles Pergler of the MG Justice Department, would have been "tantamount to a recognition of an independent Korean state . . . [and] an unilateral abrogation of the Moscow declaration" (see "SKILA materials," enclosure no. 24, XXIV Corps Historical File). The 63rd MG Company reported on October 27 that club-wielding rightist youths guarded election meetings in North Kyŏngsang. For similar evidence, see Mark Gayn's account in *Japan Diary* (New York: William Sloane Associates, 1948).

205. Memorandum to Hodge, November 22, 1946; in "SKILA materials," enclosure no. 19, XXIV Corps Historical File.

206. *Seoul Times*, October 30 and 31, 1946.

207. See memorandum of December 10, 1946 conversation between Hodge and Kim Sŏng-su and Chang Tŏk-su; in "SKILA materials," enclosure no. 23, XXIV Corps Historical File; and Kim, ed., *Han'guk minjudang so-sa*, p. 35.

208. Memorandum of Hodge conversation with General Wedemeyer, August 27, 1947; in XXIV Historical File.

209. Memorandum of December 10, 1946 conversation between Hodge and Kim Sŏng-su and Chang Tŏk-su. KDP fears proved baseless. SKILA spent most of 1947 trying to define collaboration. When the legislators finally finished a detailed bill, the KNP served an ultimatum to Hodge; they said that they would "oppose the administration of law" throughout south Korea if Hodge did not veto it. Hodge vetoed it. (Robinson, "Betrayal of a Nation," p. 146.)

210. Langdon to the Secretary of State, November 3, 1946; in *FRUS* (1946), 8: 763. In a letter of January 28, 1947 to Goodfellow, Hodge said:

> The elected members [of the SKILA] were a disappointment, not because they are Rightists which I generally expected, but because they are all, except two, of one block representing the pro-Japs, wealthy land owners, and conniving politicians. . . . Although it did not get into the press, the Rightist groups, including police [KNP], carried out some rather strong-arm methods in elections at some points.

(See Goodfellow Papers, box no. 1.)

211. USAMGIK, "Who's Who in the South Korean Interim Government," vols. 1-2, compiled in 1947, XXIV Corps Historical File. These volumes include officials whose names begin with A through I, and thus constitute a random sample. Subsequent volumes were never completed.

212. Prisons in southern Korea that had emptied a year earlier were now bursting at the seams. Prisons in Seoul, Taejŏn, Taegu, Pusan, and Masan, with a total capacity of 8,700, held 8,850 prisoners as of August 15, 1946 (see raw information in box no. 21, XXIV Corps Historical File).

213. Langdon to the Secretary of State, August 23, 1946; in *FRUS* (1946), 8: 726-729.

214. Acting Secretary Clayton to Seoul POLAD, September 13, 1946 (responding to Langdon, ibid.); in RG 59, decimal file, 740.0019/Control (Korea); and no. 740.0019/9-1346.

NOTES TO CHAPTER EIGHT

People's Committees in the Provinces

1. See the following: Roy Hofheinz, "The Ecology of Chinese Communist Success," in A. Doak Barnett, ed., *Chinese Communist Politics in Action* (Seattle:

University of Washington Press, 1969), pp. 3-77; Robert McColl, "The Oyüwan Soviet Area, 1927-1932," *Journal of Asian Studies* (November 1967); McColl, "A Political Geography of Revolution: China, Vietnam, and Thailand," *Journal of Conflict Resolution* (June 1967); Edward J. Mitchell, "Inequality and Insurgency: A Statistical Study of South Vietnam," *World Politics* (April 1968); Mitchell, "Some Econometrics of the Huk Rebellion," *American Political Science Review* 63, no. 4 (December 1969); and Donald Zagoria, "Asian Tenancy Systems," *American Political Science Review* (December 1969).

2. A major study of South Korean agriculture argued that in the *mid-1960s* commercialization was still sufficiently underdeveloped such that a categorization of Korean regions according to rates of commercialization was infeasible. The author argued that subsistence farming continued to be the predominant form, with perhaps two-thirds of Korean farmers remaining in the "submarginal farming" category, producing for value in use rather than for value in exchange. Commercialization, the author thought, had occurred primarily in the "suburban" areas. (See Jae Suh Koo, *A Study of the Regional Characteristics of Korean Agriculture* [Seoul: Korea University, 1967], pp. 58-65, 135-136, 332-333.) This argument is suspect, however, since the same author produces statistics indicating that Korean rice yields per hectare in the period 1954-1963 were not far behind Japan's, and ahead of Taiwan's (p. 100).

3. Minjujuŭi minjok chŏnsŏn, *Chosŏn haebang illyŏn-sa* [History of the First Year of Korean Liberation] (Seoul: Munu insŏ'gwan, 1946), p. 81; Yi Man-gyu, *Yŏ Un-hyŏng t'ujaeng-sa* [History of Yo Un-hyong's Struggle] (Seoul: Ch'ongmun-gak, 1946), p. 210. The figure 145 (CPKI branches by the end of August 1945) appears in many other Korean and English language accounts.

4. USAMGIK, G-2 "Periodic Report," no. 63, November 10-11, 1945.

5. Eric J. Hobsbawm, *Primitive Rebels* (1959; reprint ed., New York: W. W. Norton, 1965), pp. 86-88, 106; see also Gerald Brenan, *The Spanish Labyrinth* (Cambridge: Cambridge University Press, 1943), ch. 8.

6. Hobsbawm, *Primitive Rebels*, p. 87.

7. Yi Kang-guk, *Minjujuŭi ŭi Chosŏn kŏnsŏl* [The Construction of Democratic Korea] (Seoul: Chosŏn inminbo-sa husŏng-bu, 1946), p. 4.

8. Article by Kim Kye-rim, in *Chosŏn inmin-bo*, February 11, 1946.

9. All maps in this chapter were constructed from the following sources: provincial maps contained in the 1930 Japanese census; a map developed by the XXIV Corps 69th Engineering Topographical Company in 1946; available in RG 53, Joint Commission file, box 12; and Kim Sang-jin, ed., *Tobyŏl haengjŏng yodo* [Administrative Maps, by Province] (Seoul: Taehan annaesa, 1947), vol. 2.

10. The Public Information Department prepared a map entitled "Political Organization, Fall 1945," showing a total of 130 county people's committees. There is no indication, however, of which PCs exercised governmental functions. The map also shows only eight provincial KCP branches. It was prepared in March 1946 and is available in Richard Robinson, "Betrayal of a Nation," Manuscript, Massachusetts Institute of Technology.

11. As studies of peasant politics go, my indices of PC strength are as good or better than those of other studies. Jeffrey M. Paige, *Agrarian Revolution* (New York: The Free Press, 1975), relied mostly on Western newspaper accounts of peasant radicalism, a source that if used in the Korean case would result in no knowledge at all of provincial developments. Edward J. Mitchell was able to isolate "critical" barrios in his study of Huk control in the

Philippines, thereby allowing precise correlation with certain other variables such as tenancy rates, population growth, and so on. Still, Mitchell's "critical" designation was based on Philippine Constabulary data, which was certainly subject to error, and his superficially neat correlations suffer accordingly. (See Mitchell, "Some Econometrics of the Huk Rebellion," p. 1,164.)

12. Glenn Trewartha and Wilbur Zelinsky, "Population Distribution and Change in Korea, 1925-1949," *The Geographic Review* 45, nq. 1 (January 1955), p. 25; Edward W. Wagner, *The Korean Minority in Japan, 1904-1950* (Vancouver: University of British Columbia, 1951), p. 15.

13. Provincial and county population figures are taken from the Korean population in the colonial censuses of 1930, 1940, and 1944, and from the Occupation census in 1946 (USAMGIK, *Population of Korea by Geographic Divisions and Sex* [Seoul, 1946]). I am indebted to Ted Kloth for providing me with copies of the 1940 and 1944 censuses. Although the 1944 census may have underestimated the number of males in Korea because of the introduction of conscription and resulting hiding of males, this bias would affect all counties. The growth from 1944 to 1946 mostly involved returning migrants (Trewartha and Zelinsky, "Population Distribution," p. 24).

14. Mark Selden rejected the idea that rural modernization in China helped to explain the rise of peasant movements and communism, in particular, there; he implied that the more developed a region, the easier the suppression of insurgency (see *The Yenan Way in Revolutionary China* [Cambridge: Harvard University Press, 1971], p. 36). Harry Eckstein, however, noted that the key question is not so much the existence of modern communications facilities, as the uses to which they are put ("On the Etiology of Internal War," *History and Theory*, vol. 4, no. 2 [1965]).

15. Hoon K. Lee, *Land Utilization and Rural Economy in Korea* (Shanghai: Kelly & Walsh, 1936), pp. 106-107, 288.

16. Ibid., p. 164.

17. In Chŏng-sik, *Chosŏn ŭi t'oji munje* [Korea's Land Question] (Seoul: Ch'ŏngsu-sa, 1946), p. 69 (using Government-General figures).

18. Samuel Huntington, *Political Order in Changing Societies* (New Haven: Yale University Press, 1968), p. 52; Mitchell, "Inequality and Insurgency," p. 437.

19. According to Jeffrey Paige, such judgments are *wrong* in the Vietnam case (see *Agrarian Revolution*, pp. 326-329).

20. See the discussion in chapter two; see also G. William Skinner, "Regional Systems in Late Imperial China," paper prepared for the Second Annual Meeting of the Social Science History Association, October 1977, where a similar pattern is discerned for tenancy and rebellion in China. (I am indebted to Elizabeth Perry for bringing this paper to my attention.)

21. See the discussion in Hamza Alavi, "Peasants and Revolution: Russia, China, India," *Socialist Register* (New York: Monthly Review Press, 1965); Stephen E. Cohen, *Bukharin and the Bolshevik Revolution* (New York: Vintage Books, 1973), pp. 189-201; and Eric Wolf, *Peasant Wars of the Twentieth Century* (New York: Harper & Row, 1969), pp. 289-294.

22. Yoo, Sae Hee, "The Korean Communist Movement and the Peasantry Under Japanese Rule" (Ph.D. dissertation, Columbia University, 1974).

23. "HUSAFIK," Manuscript in the Office of the Chief of Military History, Washington, D.C. (Tokyo and Seoul, 1947, 1948), vol. 1, ch. 6, p. 8.

24. Ibid., p. 30.

25. Ibid., ch. 7, p. 30.

26. Ibid., p. 47.
27. Ibid., pp. 38, 47. Information on these incidents is lacking.
28. Ibid., ch. 6, p. 43.
29. Ibid., pp. 6, 29.
30. Ibid., pp. 30-32.
31. Ibid., p. 36.
32. Ibid., p. 42.

NOTES TO CHAPTER NINE

Fate of Committees in the Provinces

1. One of these visionaries was An Yŏng-sŏp, whose recommended cure for Korea's "spiritual illness" of some 500 years was not Western medicine, but a return to the countryside and its tonics: "those who go down to the villages will be Korea's leaders . . . and the true patriots; the day when this begins will be the day when Korea becomes independent" (see his delightful book, *Chŏson minjok ŭi sal'kil* [The Livelihood of the Korean Nation] [Seoul: Chŏson-ŏ yŏn'gu-hoe, 1946], eps. pp. 50-56). On village spontaneity and egalitarianism, see also Vincent Brandt, *A Korean Village between Farm and Sea* (Cambridge: Harvard University Press, 1971), pp. 17-25, 68-77.
2. See USAMGIK, G-2 "Weekly Reports," no. 12, November 25-December 2, 1945, which cited approvingly a Korean document saying that recognizing the KPG would be a means of disbanding the KPR; and no. 13, December 2-9, 1945, which quoted KDP leaders as saying that disbandment of the KPR would have to come *before* other parties could win over its supporters.
3. This feeling was strongest regarding the NSRRKI in the summer of 1946 (see chapter seven).
4. Samuel Huntington, *Political Order in Changing Societies* (New Haven: Yale University Press, 1968), pp. 5-8.
5. "HUSAFIK," Manuscript in Office of the Chief of Military History, Washington, D.C. (Tokyo and Seoul, 1947, 1948), vol. 1, ch. 6, p. 32.
6. C. Clyde Mitchell, *Final Report and History of the New Korea Company* (Seoul: National Land Administration, 1948), pp. 6, 23.
7. South Chŏlla also had a traditional rebelliousness; as late as 1923, the Japanese reported that although the innovation of plantation agriculture had been quite successful in North Chŏlla, in South Chŏlla "Japanese capitalists . . . could not venture into the interior" of the province because of "the activity of insurgents" (see Japan Times, *Economic Development of Korea and Manchuria* [Tokyo: Japan Times Publishing Co., 1923], p. 71). See also E. Grant Meade, *American Military Government in Korea* (New York: King's Crown Press, Columbia University, 1951), p. 34.
8. All population statistics in this chapter are drawn from the 1930, 1940, and 1944 colonial censuses and from the USAMGIK, *Population of Korea by Geographic Divisions and Sex* (Seoul, 1946).
9. Kwangju-bu ch'ongmu-gwa kongbo-gye, *Haebang chŏn-hu hoego* [Reflections Before and After Liberation] (Kwangju: Kwangju-bu, 1946), p. 5. Initially the CPKI provincial head was Ch'oe Hŭng-jong, an activist in the March First Movement and, later, the YMCA. After the demise of the CPKI, Ch'oe became an advisor to the Military Government (see *Chŏlla namdo-ji*, p. 829).
10. "HUSAFIK," vol. 3, ch. 3, p. 45.

11. *Haebang chŏn-hu hoego*, p. 9.
12. 55th MG Company, "Unit History." Im Tae-ho led the Mokp'o *ch'iandae.*
13. Donald S. McDonald, "Field Experiences in Military Government," in Carl Friedrich, Jr. et al., *American Experiences in Military Government in World War II* (New York: Rinehart & Co., 1948), p. 369.
14. USAMGIK, Opinion Trends, no. 9, May 1, 1946. Two local histories state that county *poandae* and *ch'iandae* groups in Kohŭng took over policing functions in outlying townships and "illegally" put people in jail; but the county clearly had a conservative complexion from the beginning. The CPKI branch was led by conservatives like Pak P'al-bong, who later ran for the National Assembly as a member of Syngman Rhee's party and also served as an MG court official, and Sin Chi-u, who later became chief of police in Kohŭng and served as county magistrate in Haenam. Kohŭng was also the home of Sŏ Min-ho, first mayor of Kwangju after liberation and a Rhee ally. Local histories refer to Left-Right conflicts in the county as a whole, however. The conflicts apparently ended when the Americans aided local police in retaking police stations and boxes throughout the county in April 1946. (See *Kohŭng kun-sa* [History of Kohŭng County] [Kwangju: Chŏllam taehakkyo ch'ulp'an-bu, 1969], pp. 47-50, 365; and *Kohŭng kun hyangt'o-sa* [A Local History of Kohŭng County] [Kohŭng: Kohŭng-kun hyangt'o-sa p'yŏnch'an wiwŏnhoe, 1971], pp. 12, 140-141, 388, 395.)
15. 61st MG Company, "Unit History." Readers should refer to Meade's full account of PC activity in this region, and other regions of South Chŏlla. It is particularly good on the complexities of political alignments in various counties. Regardless of whether Left or Right controlled a given county, Meade notes that popular sympathies were almost always with the Left (*Military Government*, 151-189).
16. 61st MG Company, "Unit History."
17. Richard Kim, *Lost Names* (Seoul: Sisayongo Publishing Co., 1970), pp. 161, 182-183.
18. Eric Wolf, *Peasant Wars of the Twentieth Century* (New York: Harper & Row, 1969), p. 89.
19. "HUSAFIK," vol. 3, ch. 3, pp. 5-6.
20. Ibid., p. 6.
21. Ibid., p. 7.
22. McDonald, "Field Experiences in Military Government," p. 368.
23. Letter from Professor Chae-Jin Lee, February 6, 1974, quoting letter from Pepke in Yaki's diary. Im Mun-mu's appointment is noted in USAMGIK, *Official Gazette* (Seoul: 1945-1946), appointment no. 66.
24. McDonald, "Field Experiences in Military Government," p. 367.
25. Ibid., p. 372.
26. Gregory Henderson, *Korea: The Politics of the Vortex* (Cambridge: Harvard University Press, 1968), p. 140. Sŏ's son, Sŏ Kwang-sun, was named provincial chief of detectives in the KNP. Later on, Sŏ Min-ho was described as a wealthy backer of Syngman Rhee. (See the report of Donald S. McDonald, enclosure in U.S. Ambassador to Korea, John Muccio to Secretary of State, September 23, 1948, RG 59, decimal file, 895.00/9-2348.)
27. Meade, *Military Government*, p. 134; see also "HUSAFIK," vol. 3, ch. 3, p. 27.
28. "HUSAFIK," vol. 3, ch. 3, p. 27.
29. USAMGIK, "HMGK" (Seoul: Office of Administrative Services, Statistical Research Division, 1946), 3: 257.
30. McDonald, "Field Experiences in Military Government," p. 372.

31. USAMGIK, "Opinion Trends," no. 9, May 1, 1946.
32. Meade, *Military Government*, pp. 105, 171.
33. "HMGK" 3:257, 285: also G-2 "Periodic Report," no. 152, February 12-13, 1946, which described the wholesale replacement of *ch'iandae* by police brought in from Kwangju in the Naju county seat and in Yŏngsanp'o, a port near Naju.
34. 69th MG Company, "Unit History for 1945." The first county magistrate after liberation in Sunch'ŏn was Kim Yang-su, a member of the Korean Democratic Party. A local history stated that *ch'iandae* took over all police facilities in August 1945 and that provincial police then reclaimed the facilities at a later point. (See Chŏng Han-jo, *Samsan isu* [Three Mountains, Two Rivers] [Seoul, 1965], pp. 74-76, 82.) Meade wrote that most of the township heads were also KDP members and that conservative elements dominated the county throughout the first year of Occupation (*Military Government*, p. 183).
35. 69th MG Company, "Unit History for 1945."
36. An *inmin konghwa'guk* (people's republic) was set up in the Yŏsu/Sunch'ŏn region, which lasted for about a week (see Ko Yŏng-hwan, *Kŭmil ŭi chonggaekdŭl* [Today's Politicians] [Seoul: Tonga ilbo-sa, 1949] pp. 177, 180. See also part II of this study, on the Yŏsu/Sunch'ŏn uprising).
37. 45th MG Company, "Unit History"; and Meade, *Military Government*, pp. 175-178.
38. Meade, *Military Government*, pp. 99, 177-178. See also V. T. Zaichikov, *Geography of Korea*, trans. Albert Parry (New York: Institute of Pacific Relations, 1952), p. 135.
39. 45th MG Company, "Unit History"; Meade, *Military History*, p. 175.
40. "HMGK" 3: 327.
41. Ibid., p. 316.
42. 45th MG Company, "Unit History."
43. Ibid.
44. Ibid.
45. In an earlier reorganization of the Posŏng PC in November, it was stated that the PC had taken the wrong side in landlord-tenant disputes and had to be eliminated ("HMGK" 3: 286).
46. 45th MG Company, "Unit History."
47. 45th MG Company reports of December 22, 1945, and January 5, February 9, March 4, 1946.
48. 45th MG Company, "Unit History."
49. 45th MG Company reports of December 29, 1945, and January 19, March 23, March 30, 1946.
50. G-2 "Weekly Report," no. 20, January 20-27, 1946.
51. "HMGK" 3: 318.
52. Franz Neumann, "Approaches to the Study of Political Power," in Roy C. Macridis and Bernard E. Brown, eds., *Comparative Politics*, 4th ed. (Homewood, Ill.: Dorsey Press, 1972), p. 58.
53. G-2 "Weekly Report," no. 24, February 17-24, 1946.
54. "HMGK" 3: 269. Meade wrote that in Mokp'o, "with but few exceptions the Committee had taken over the city government lock, stock, and barrel" (*Military Government*, p. 170).
55. "HMGK" 3: 268, 271; G-2 "Weekly Report," no. 19, January 13-20, 1946.
56. "HMGK" 3: 268.

57. Ibid., p. 282.
58. Ibid., p. 280.
59. Ibid., p. 290.
60. Translation in 28th MG Company report of November 15, 1945.
61. 28th MG Company report of December 16, 1945.
62. 64th MG Company, "Unit History," dated January 7, 1946 (most unit histories are undated).
63. 56th MG Company, "Unit History."
64. "HMGK" 3: 209, 215-217.
65. 48th MG Company report of March 15, 1946.
66. "HUSAFIK," vol. 3, ch. 3, pp. 48, 51; and ch. 4, p. 34.
67. 28th MG Company, "Unit History."
68. "HMGK" 3: 197.
69. "HUSAFIK," vol. 3, ch. 3, p. 51. See a similar statement in "HMGK" 3: 198.
70. "HUSAFIK," vol. 3, ch. 4, p. 34. City level police affairs were directed by people like Yi Chin-ha, a member of the secret police before liberation, police chief in Kunsan and later Chŏnju, and arrested in March 1949 for pro-Japanese offenses (see cable, Drumwright to Secretary of State; in RG 59, decimal file, 895.00/3-2149, March 21, 1949).
71. "HUSAFIK," vol. 3, ch. 3, pp. 53-54.
72. 28th MG Company, "Unit History."
73. 28th MG Company reports of December 16 and 29, 1945.
74. Ibid., report of December 16, 1945.
75. Ibid., report of December 8 and 29, 1945.
76. Ibid., report of January 12, 1946.
77. Ibid., report of February 1, 1946.
78. Ibid.
79. "HMGK" 3: 217, 222.
80. Ch'oe Hyŏn-sik et al., *Chŏngŭp kunji* [History of Chŏngŭp County] (Kwangju: Mudŭng kyoyuk ch'ulp'an chusik hoesa, 1957), pp. 422-426, 457, 462; and *Chōsen nenkan 1943* [Korea Yearbook 1945] (Seoul: Keijo nippo-sha, 1945), p. 409. It is worth noting that in the various county histories that I have consulted, nearly always the names of people's committee leaders who functioned as county magistrates, police chiefs, and so on, for some period of time have simply been expunged from the historical record; so too, in many cases, we cannot find listings of Korean local officials in the period 1937-1945.
81. G-2 "Weekly Report," no. 12, November 25-December 2, 1945.
82. G-2 "Periodic Report," no. 64, November 11-12, 1945.
83. "HMGK" 3: 195.
84. 28th MG Company report of December 23, 1945.
85. Ibid., report of January 19, 1946.
86. Ibid., report of February 1, 1946.
87. Ibid., report of February 5, 1946.
88. Hoon K. Lee, *Land Utilization and Rural Economy in Korea* (Shanghai: Kelly & Walsh, 1936), p. 163.
89. See provincial breakdowns on participants in Frank Baldwin, "The March 1 Movement: Korean Challenge and Japanese Response" (Ph.D. dissertation, Columbia University, 1969).
90. G-2 "Weekly Report," no. 27, March 10-17, 1946.
91. "HUSAFIK," vol. 1, ch. 6, p. 10.
92. Ibid., pp. 10, 57; G-2 "Periodic Report," no. 22, October 1-2, 1945.

93. Yun Il was arrested, allegedly for burning down a courthouse at Hyŏpch'ŏn (G-2 "Periodic Report," no. 59, November 6-7, 1945), and was apparently replaced as province PC leader by O Tŏk-jun. See also 98th MG Company, "Unit History." This report said, "Worker's committees in some instances seized plants and operated them themselves or hired Korean managers. Certain Koreans in turn bid for worker managerships [or] . . . for worker's committee support."
94. G-2 "Periodic Report," no. 22, October 1-2, 1945.
95. "History of the 40th Infantry Division in Korea," no date; in XXIV Corps Historical File.
96. "HUSAFIK," vol. 3, ch. 3, pp. 63, 66.
97. 50th MG Company, "Unit History."
98. 98th MG Company, "Unit History."
99. Memorandum of October 9, 1945; quoted in "History of the 40th Infantry Division in Korea."
100. Ibid.
101. G-2 "Weekly Report," no. 174, March 11-12, 1946.
102. Ibid. See also cable, Drumwright to Secretary of State, March 21, 1949; in RG 59, decimal file, 895.00/3-2149.
103. 40th Infantry Division, "Operations Report," October 20, 1945.
104. G-2 "Periodic Report," no. 63, November 10-11, 1945. But a Korean informant who wishes not to be identified told me that his wife's uncle, chief of the Haman PC, was a landlord and that the entire extended family was landed as well. The informant explained that landlords were the only Koreans who could afford to educate their sons; the process of education, however, often led sons to radicalism. Thus many Korean radicals, the informant thought, were from landed backgrounds.
105. 40th Infantry Division, "Operations Report," October 10, 1945.
106. G-2 "Periodic Report," no. 183, March 21-22, 1946.
107. G-2 "Periodic Report," no. 39, October 17-18, 1945 (document reproduced therein).
108. G-2 "Weekly Report," no. 6, October 14-21, 1945.
109. "HUSAFIK," vol. 1, ch. 6, p. 61.
110. "HUSAFIK," vol. 3, ch. 3, p. 35.
111. 40th Infantry Division, "Operations Reports," October 10, 12, 24, and 25, 1945.
112. Ibid., October 12 report.
113. "HUSAFIK," vol. 1, ch. 6, pp. 58-60.
114. "HUSAFIK," vol. 3, ch. 3, p. 67.
115. 98th MG Company, "Unit History."
116. "HMGK" 3: 185.
117. Interview with Col. Francis E. Gillette (American provincial governor), April 23, 1946; memorandum in XXIV Corps Historical File.
118. "HMGK" 3: 189.
119. Interview with Col. Francis Gillette, April 23, 1946. Gillette later stated that the purge occurred because "a great many governmental functions were already in the hands of Communists, who had been sent down by the Russians," when the Americans arrived. He also stated that elections held under American supervision "usually resulted in an 80% vote for the conservatives, while those held without such supervision usually resulted in an 80% vote for the Communists." The latter occurred, he thought, because of "Communist threats and blackmail." (See memorandum of conversation between Col. Gil-

lette and several State Department officials, July 2, 1946; in RG 59, decimal
file, 740.0019/7-246.)
20. "HMGK" 3: 190-191.
21. 63rd MG Company reports of March 16 and July 6, 1946.
22. Ibid., reports of May 25 and June 15, 1946.
23. Ibid., report of February 23, 1946.
24. Ibid., report of May 18, 1946.
25. On the Constabulary detachment in North Kyŏngsang, see chapter five.
26. Kim Tae-u was listed as provincial governor in North Chŏlla from 1943 to
1944 in *Chōsen nenkan 1945*, p. 376; presumably he was switched to North
Kyŏngsang before the Americans arrived.
27. "HUSAFIK," vol. 1, ch. 6, p. 51.
28. Ibid., pp. 51-53, based on interviews with Henn in 1945 and 1946.
29. Ibid., vol. 3, ch. 4, p. 35.
30. 99th MG Company, "Unit History"; and ibid. On September 16 the North
Kyŏngsang *ch'iandae* organization sent a letter to provincial military government, saying: "According to your instructions, the former policemen . . . who
disarmed themselves after the thunderclap of Aug 15 and who have been
regarded for thirty-five years as a malignant cancer in the heart of the people,
are now to reorganize as members of the military government" (translation
in USFIK 11071 file, box 62/96).
31. Kim's appointment is recorded in USAMGIK, *Official Gazette*, appointment
no. 73. See also "HMGK" 3: 163. Kim was a leader in the KDP when it was
inaugurated on September 16, 1945 (see Kim Chun-yŏn, ed., *Han'guk minjudang so-sa* [A Short History of the Korean Democratic Party] [Seoul: Han'guk
minju-dang sŏnjŏn-bu, 1948], p. 16.
32. Public Opinion Bureau, raw reports, March 29, 1946.
33. "HUSAFIK," vol. 1, ch. 6, p. 53; 63rd MG Company reports of January 5 and
26, 1946.
34. "HMGK" 3: 139.
35. Ibid.
36. Ibid., p. 181.
37. Zaichikov, *Geography of Korea*, p. 128.
38. 68th MG Company reports of January 12 and February 2, 1946.
39. Ibid., report of January 12, 1946.
40. Ibid., report of March 10, 1946. The fighting in Kudam-dong provides a fascinating glimpse of politics at the lowest level, about which more will be said
in volume two of this study. Kudam-dong apparently had about 250 families,
of which 110 were from the Sunch'ŏn Kim clan and 75 were from the Kwangsan Kims. After liberation, the Kwangsan Kims joined *Chŏnnong* local peasant
unions, while the Sunch'ŏn Kims joined an *Aeguk tongji-hoe* (Patriotic Comrades Association), a rightist group. On March 1 the *Aeguk* group, with police
aid, attacked some 1,500 peasant union demonstrators (see the account in
Seoul sinmun, March 18, 1946). It was often the case that, at the village level,
Left-Right splits were isomorphic to clan splits. This was to be expected in
the absence of modern political organization and in the Korean village milieu
where an entire clan could be disadvantaged for centuries.
41. 68th MG Company report of March 29, 1946.
42. Ibid., report of May 11, 1946.
43. Ibid., report of August 17, 1946.
44. Public Opinion Bureau, raw reports, March 29, 1946.

145. On February 25 and March 7, 1946, the P'ohang people's committee and peasant union offices were raided, leading to the arrests of thirty-one people (G-2 "Periodic Report," no. 179, March 10, 1946).

146. Ibid. See also Richard Robinson's Public Opinion Bureau report of July 1946.

147. Robinson, Public Opinion Bureau report.

148. 68th MG Company reports of January 5 and March 16, 1946.

149. Ibid., report of March 30, 1946.

150. 63rd MG Company report of January 5, 1946.

151. Ibid.

152. Yŏngyang kunji p'yŏnch'an wiwŏnhoe, *Yŏngyang kunji* [Local History of Yŏngyang] (Taegu: Chungwoe ch'ulp'an-sa, 1970), pp. 211-212.

153. *Yŏngyang kunji*, pp. 291, 421, 428, 435; and Kim, ed., *Han'guk minjudang so-sa*, p. 15. Cho Jun-yŏng became provincial governor of North Kyŏngsang Province in 1960.

154. *Chosŏn kyŏngje nyŏnbo* [Annual Economic Review of Korea] (Seoul: Chosŏn unhaeng chosa-bu, 1948), provincial section, pp. 56-57.

155. See table XIX-8, "Korean Volunteers for Japanese Army Enlistment, by Province, 1938-1940," in Chong-sik Lee, ed., *Statistical Profile of Korea under Japanese Rule*, forthcoming. I wish to thank Professor Lee for providing me with a copy of this table.

156. "HUSAFIK," vol. 1, ch. 6, pp. 26, 49.

157. "HMGK" 3: 64; 27th MG Company, "Unit History."

158. "HUSAFIK," vol. 3, ch. 3, p. 29.

159. Ibid., p. 40.

160. Ibid., p. 30; 27th MG Company, "Unit History."

161. Republic of Korea, Naemu-bu ch'ian'guk, *Taehan kyŏngch'al chŏn-sa* [Military History of the Korean National Police] (Seoul: Hŭng'guk yŏn'gu hyŏphoe, 1952), 1: 86.

162. "HUSAFIK," vol. 1, ch. 6, p. 48.

163. Ibid., vol. 3, ch. 3, pp. 35-36.

164. Ibid., p. 37.

165. Ibid., p. 37-38.

166. Account in 67th MG Company report of December 20, 1945. This is the only indication that there may have been PCs in Koesan, Ŭmsŏng, and Chinch'ŏn.

167. Ibid.

168. Ibid.

169. Ibid., report of May 15, 1946.

170. Ch'ungju Counter-Intelligence Corps report, January 10, 1946.

171. G-2 "Periodic Report," November 1, 1945.

172. Ch'ungju CIC report, October 10, 1946.

173. 67th MG Company report of May 15, 1946.

174. Both quoted in ibid., report February 15, 1946.

175. Ibid.

176. "HUSAFIK," vol. 3, ch. 3, p. 30; G-2 "Periodic Report," no. 39, October 17-18, 1945.

177. G-2 "Periodic Report," no. 35, October 13-14, 1945.

178. "HUSAFIK," vol. 3, ch. 3, pp. 30-31.

179. Ibid., ch. 4, p. 36.

180. Ibid., pp. 36-37; G-2 "Weekly Reports," nos. 9, 12, 15, November 4-11, November 25-December 2, December 16-23, 1945.

181. "HMGK" 3: 83.
182. G-2 "Periodic Report," no. 39, October 17-18, 1945. On February 11, 1946, eight persons associated with the Ch'ŏnan PC were arrested and charged with plotting the murder of local officials (see G-2 "Periodic Report," no. 153, February 13-14, 1946).
183. G-2 "Weekly Report," no. 24, February 17-24, 1946.
184. "HMGK" 3: 90-91, 93.
185. "HUSAFIK," vol. 3, ch. 3, pp. 38, 40.
186. "HMGK" 3: 42.
187. "HUSAFIK," vol. 1, ch. 3, p. 23. See also G-2 "Periodic Report," no. 140, February 8-11, 1946.
188. "HUSAFIK," vol. 1, ch. 3, p. 23.
189. Ibid., pp. 9, 21.
190. Ibid., p. 22.
191. 48th MG Company, various reports, 1945-1946.
192. In January 1946 the Samch'ŏk PC was reported to be the only political group operating, with associated labor, peasant, and women's unions (the last was 2,000 strong); county officials were PC members as well (see G-2 "Periodic Report," no. 115, January 3-4, 1946).
193. Public Opinion Bureau, raw reports, March 29, 1946.
194. Ibid., July 30, 1946.
195. "HUSAFIK," vol. 3, ch. 3, p. 12.
196. USAMGIK, *Official Gazette*, appointment no. 87.
197. "HUSAFIK," vol. 3, ch. 3, p. 12.
198. Ibid., ch. 4, p. 38; 68th MG Company, "Unit History."
199. 60th MG Company, "Unit History."
200. G-2 "Weekly Report," no. 12, November 25-December 2, 1945.
201. "The Korean People's Republic," undated; in XXIV Corps Historical File.
202. 68th MG Company report of May 13, 1946.
203. Ibid., report of June 10, 1946.
204. Public Opinion Bureau, raw reports, February 23, 1946.
205. Kim Pong-hyŏn and Kim Min-ju, *Cheju-do inmindŭl ŭi '4-3' mujang t'ujaeng-sa* [History of the Cheju Island People's 'April 3' Armed Struggle] (Osaka: Munu-sa, 1963), p. 16.
206. "HUSAFIK," vol. 1, ch. 7, p. 49.
207. Kim and Kim, *Cheju-do inmindŭl t'ujaeng-sa*, p. 17.
208. Ibid., p. 17; and Meade, *Military Government*, p. 185.
209. "HUSAFIK," vol. 1, ch. 6, pp. 27-28, 40. In fact, the 59th gave much support to the PCs, according to Meade, *Military Government*, pp. 185-186.
210. Public Opinion Bureau, raw reports, December 9, 1946.
211. Kim and Kim, *Cheju-do inmindŭl t'ujaeng-sa*, pp. 26, 33.
212. Public Opinion Bureau, raw reports, May 6 and December 9, 1946.
213. Ibid., report of December 9, 1946.
214. Kim and Kim, *Cheju-do inmindŭl t'ujaeng-sa*, p. 46.
215. Ibid., pp. 21-22; USAMGIK, *Official Gazette*, appointment no. 107.
216. Public Opinion Bureau, raw reports, December 9, 1946.
217. An excellent study of this insurgency is John Merrill, "The Cheju-do Rebellion" *Journal of Korean Studies* 2 (1980), pp. 139-198.

NOTES TO CHAPTER TEN

Autumn Harvest Uprisings

1. General Hodge wired General MacArthur on October 28, 1946, saying, "evidence is growing that Russians are planning an invasion of South Korea after gathering of rice crop this fall" (see State Department, *FRUS* [1946], 8: 750). This marked the first of many subsequent warnings of attack from the north leading up to June 25, 1950.
2. Richard Robinson, "Betrayal of a Nation," Manuscript at Massachusetts Institute of Technology, p. 162. Mark Gayn was in Korea during the uprisings and wrote, "[it was] a full-scale revolution, which must have involved hundreds of thousands, if not millions of people" (see *Japan Diary* [New York: William Sloane Associates, 1948], p. 388). Gayn's account of the rebellion was for years the only extant one in English; formerly classified documents show how accurate it was.
3. "HUSAFIK," Manuscript in the Office of the Chief of Military History, Washington, D.C. (Tokyo and Seoul, 1947, 1948), vol. 2, pt. 2, p. 2; USAMGIK, G-2 "Weekly Report," no. 55, September 22-29, 1946; and no. 56, September 29-October 6, 1946.
4. Counter-Intelligence Corps report, Seoul, September 30, 1946.
5. G-2 "Weekly Report," no. 56, September 29-October 6, 1946.
6. *Chosŏn yŏn'gam 1948* [Korea Yearbook 1948] (Seoul: Chosŏn t'ongsin-sa, 1948), p. 258.
7. Ibid., p. 257.
8. G-2 "Weekly Report," no. 55, September 22-29, 1946.
9. *Chosŏn yŏn'gam 1948*, pp. 257-258; *Seoul Times*, September 23-30, 1946; *Chwaik sakŏn sillok* [Record of the Left-wing Incidents] (Seoul: Tae'gŏmch'al-ch'ong, susa-guk, 1964), pp. 361-375; *Siwŏl inmin hangjaeng* [The October People's Resistance] (Seoul: Haebang-sa, 1947), p. 6.
10. *Chosŏn yŏn'gam 1948*, pp. 257-258; *Chwaik sakŏn sillok*, p. 354.
11. G-2 "Weekly Report," no. 55, September 22-29, 1946.
12. G-2 "Weekly Report," no. 56, September 29-October 6, 1946. Numerous petitions calling for transfer of power to the committees and saying, "long live the Korean People's Republic," some signed in blood, are available in the original Korean in an attachment to cable from Langdon to Secretary of State, February 2, 1947; in State Department, RG 59, decimal file, 740.0019/2-1147.
13. *Seoul Times*, September 24, 1946.
14. Ibid., September 28, 1946.
15. CIC report, Seoul, September 28, 1946.
16. *Seoul Times*, October 1, 1946.
17. G-2 "Weekly Report," no. 56, September 29-October 6, 1946.
18. *Seoul Times*, October 2, 1946.
19. Ibid., October 3, 1946.
20. Stewart Meacham, *Korean Labor Report* (Seoul: USAFIK, 1947), p. 24.
21. *Seoul Times*, October 4, 1946.
22. CIC report, October 12, 1946.
23. *Seoul Times*, August 5, 1946.
24. *Chwaik sakŏn sillok*, p. 376; and *Siwŏl inmin hangjaeng*, p. 6.
25. *Chwaik sakŏn sillok*, p. 376.

26. "HUSAFIK," vol. 2, pt. 2, p. 3; 99th MG Company, "Unit Journal," entry for October 1, 1946; in XXIV Corps Historical File.
27. In "HUSAFIK," vol. 2, pt. 2, p. 3, it is stated that the death came in the evening; another source stated that it occurred in the morning. See also Maj. Gen. Albert Brown, "Report on an Investigation of Disorders in Kyongsang Province," October 5, 1946; in XXIV Corps Historical File (note the similarity in the title to Mao Tse-tung's famous "Report on an Investigation into the Peasant Movement in Hunan").
28. In G-2 "Weekly Report," no. 56, September 29-October 6, 1946, the figure is put at 2,000; Brown, "Report on an Investigation," puts it at 1,000. American sources said the slain demonstrator had been "dressed up" to look like a student.
29. Thomas E. Campbell, "The Taegu Riots: One of the U.S. Prosecutors Tells of the First Soviet-inspired Attempt to Take Over all Korea," *Commonweal* 54, no. 22 (September 7, 1951), pp. 519-522. Campbell also reported that another demonstration leader from a village near Taegu was a respected local elder, Buddhist leader, and doctor of Chinese medicine who opposed the MG because he thought its policy was "to force Christianity upon Korea."
30. "HUSAFIK," vol. 2, pt. 2, pp. 3-4; 99th MG Company, "Unit Journal," entry for October 2; G-2 "Weekly Report," no. 56, September 29-October 6, 1946; and Brown, "Report on an Investigation."
31. G-2 "Weekly Report," no. 56, September 29-October 6, 1946.
32. See "HUSAFIK," vol. 2, pt. 2, pp. 11-12. Numerous pictures of slain policemen are available in XXIV Corps Historical File.
33. Naemubu ch'ian'guk, *Taehan kyŏngch'al chŏn-sa* [Military History of the Korean National Police], vol. 1, "Minjok ŭi sŏnbong" [Spearhead of the Nation] (Seoul: Hŭng'guk yŏn'gu hyŏp-hoe, 1952), pp. 55.
34. Mao Tse-tung, "Report on an Investigation into the Peasant Movement in Hunan," *Selected Works* 1 (New York: International Publishers, 1954): 21-59. It may be that the combination of a poor and local peasantry and a national police unresponsive to local pressure has much to do with such extremes of violence. This was also the case in Spain; on unrestrained violence against the Guardia Civil, see Edward E. Malefakis, *Agrarian Reform and Peasant Revolution in Spain* (New Haven: Yale University Press, 1970), pp. 310-312.
35. Quoted in "HUSAFIK," vol. 2, pt. 2, p. 12.
36. 99th MG Company, "Unit Journal," entry for October 2, 1946. The original martial law declaration is included in Brown, "Report on an Investigation."
37. G-2 "Weekly Report," no. 56, September 29-October 6, 1946; "HUSAFIK," vol. 2, pt. 2, p. 5; *Taehan kyŏngch'al chŏn-sa*, p. 55; and *Siwŏl inmin hangjaeng*, p. 11.
38. Interview with a missionary priest in Yongch'ŏn, cited in CIC report, Taegu, November 5, 1946.
39. *Siwŏl inmin hangjaeng*, pp. 11, 39-40, 45-46.
40. CIC report, Taegu, October 11, 1946.
41. CIC report, Taegu, October 14, 1946.
42. 63rd MG Company report, October 12, 1946.
43. *Taehan kyŏngch'al chŏn-sa*, p. 56.
44. "HUSAFIK," vol. 2, pt. 2, p. 5; and CIC report, Taegu, October 14, 1946.
45. 99th MG Company, "Unit Journal," entry for October 3, 1946.
46. Ibid., October 3 and 4, 1946.
47. *Taehan kyŏngch'al chŏn-sa*, p. 54; and *Siwŏl inmin hangjaeng*, pp. 11-12.

48. CIC report, Taegu, September 26, 1946.
49. 99th MG Company, "Unit Journal," October 3, 1946.
50. Ibid., October 4, 1946.
51. CIC report, Pusan, October 31, 1946.
52. Leftist and communist organizers later called for more planning, less violence, and "organized, well thought-out guidance" of the masses—who were, they thought, more aroused than the organizers (see the summing-up in *Siwŏl inmin hangjaeng*, pp. 49-50).
53. "HUSAFIK," vol. 2, pt. 2, p. 6.
54. Ibid.
55. 63rd MG Company report, October 5, 1946.
56. Ibid., October 12, 1946.
57. Ibid., October 5 and 12 reports. A leftist source, however, claimed that 44 police, officials, and "reactionaries" and some 45 insurgents were killed in Yech'ŏn (see *Siwŏl inmin hangjaeng*, p. 11).
58. 63rd MG Company report, October 19, 1946.
59. *Siwŏl inmin hangjaeng*, pp. 43-44.
60. G-2 "Weekly Report," no. 57, October 6-13, 1946.
61. CIC report, Chinju, October 24, 1946.
62. G-2 "Weekly Report," no. 57, October 6-13, 1946; and *Siwŏl inmin hangjaeng*, p. 12.
63. G-2 "Weekly Report," no. 57, October 6-13, 1946; and "HUSAFIK," vol. 2, pt. 2, pp. 6-7.
64. 6th Infantry Division report, December 31, 1946; in XXIV Corps Historical File. See also CIC report, Chinju, October 16, 1946.
65. CIC report, Pusan, October 9, 1946; *Seoul Times*, October 9, 1946.
66. G-2 "Weekly Report," no. 58, October 13-20, 1946.
67. Ibid.; and CIC report, Seoul, October 21, 1946.
68. *Chwaik sakŏn sillok*, p. 389. "HUSAFIK," vol. 2, pt. 2, p. 11, reported that one policeman was killed and a police warehouse burned down in Susaeng-ni.
69. *Chwaik sakŏn sillok*, pp. 389-390; "HUSAFIK," vol. 2, pt. 2, pp. 9-10.
70. CIC reports, Seoul, October 22 and 24, 1946.
71. CIC report, Inch'ŏn, October 26, 1946.
72. "HUSAFIK," vol. 2, pt. 2, pp. 8-9; G-2 "Weekly Report," no. 58, October 13-20, 1946.
73. 41st MG Company report, November 29, 1946.
74. CIC report, Taejŏn, October 22, 1946.
75. CIC report, Taejŏn, November 1, 1946.
76. CIC report, Taejŏn, October 10, 1946.
77. CIC report, Taejŏn, October 13, 1946.
78. CIC report, Taejŏn, October 31, 1946.
79. "Cholla-South Communist Uprising of November 1946," December 31, 1946, United States 6th Infantry Division headquarters; in XXIV Corps Historical File.
80. Day & Zimmerman, Inc., *Report No. 5002 to His Excellency, Syngman Rhee, President, on the Conditions, Rehabilitation, and Further Development of Certain Elements in the Industry of the Republic of Korea* (Seoul, 1949), pp. 47-48.
81. On August 15, 1946, about 1,000 miners marched toward Kwangju, calling for the return to power of the people's committees. American tactical forces used tanks to block the marchers and even buzzed them with seven army P-51s.

Three demonstrators and five policemen died. (See the accounts in G-2 "Periodic Report," August 15, 1946; *Seoul Times,* August 17, 1946; and *Chosŏn inmin-bo,* August 22, 1946.)

82. CIC report, Kwangju, October 31, 1946.
83. "HUSAFIK," vol. 2, pt. 2, p. 15.
84. Ibid., pp. 15-16.
85. "Cholla-South Communist Uprising."
86. Ibid. See also "HUSAFIK," vol. 2, pt. 2, pp. 13-14.
87. "HUSAFIK," vol. 2, pt. 2, p. 14; and *Seoul Times,* November 4 and 5, 1946.
88. "Cholla-South Communist Uprising."
89. Ibid.
90. Ibid.
91. Ibid.
92. Ibid.
93. All information drawn from ibid. This report stated that "the 'People's Committee' has a superb organization reaching down into the smallest villages and a chain of Command upward through the myon, gun, and province to Seoul." I think this is an exaggeration of the strength of PC organization in the autumn of 1946.
94. *Siwŏl inmin hangjaeng,* pp. 1-4, passim.
95. "HUSAFIK," vol. 2, pt. 2, p. 16.
96. CIC report, Chŏnju, November 24, 1946. See also covering XXIV Corps headquarter's memorandum.
97. Robinson, "Betrayal of a Nation," p. 163 (based on eyewitness CIC accounts).
98. CIC reports, Ch'unch'ŏn, October 22 and 29 and November 6, 1946.
99. 32nd Infantry Company "K" headquarters, report, November 1, 1946; in XXIV Corps Historical File.
100. *Pi'p'an sinmun,* October 28, 1946; translation in G-2 "Periodic Report," November 5, 1946. See also *Siwŏl inmin hangjaeng,* p. 1.
101. "HUSAFIK," vol. 2, pt. 2, p. 16.
102. Ibid., pp. 7, 9, quoting an NSRRKI propaganda leaflet.
103. Handbill in original Korean, enclosed in 63rd MG Company report, October 12, 1946.
104. See, for example, ibid. See also *Taehan kyŏngch'al chŏn-sa,* p. 57.
105. Minutes of the Korean-American Conference, November 19, 1946; in XXIV Corps Historical File.
106. Brown, "Report on an Investigation."
107. "HUSAFIK," vol. 2, pt. 2, p. 13.
108. 99th MG Company, "Unit Journal."
109. 63rd MG Company report, October 5, 1946.
110. "HUSAFIK," vol. 2, pt. 2, p. 23.
111. Ibid., p. 24.
112. Memorandum, Cho Pyŏng-ok to William Maglin, October 20, 1946; in XXIV Corps Historical File.
113. "HUSAFIK," vol. 2, pt. 2, p. 29.
114. Meacham, *Labor Report,* p. 24.
115. Quoted in ibid., p. 24.
116. "HUSAFIK," vol. 2, pt. 2, p. 24.
117. Ibid., p. 25.
118. Ibid., p. 27.
119. Memorandum, Cho to Maglin, October 20, 1946.

120. G-2 "Weekly Report," no. 56, September 29-October 6, 1946.
121. Robinson, "Betrayal of a Nation," p. 163. On November 14, 1946, American CIC headquarters prepared a report, "Statement of Outside Influences upon the Recent Unrest and Civil Disturbances in South Korea." The data contained therein demonstrates that local issues and local radicals fueled the uprisings. (See XXIV Corps Historical File.)
122. G-2 "Weekly Report," no. 56, September 29-October 6, 1946; and SKILA materials, enclosures nos. 6 and 7, anonymous memorandum of conversation with Yŏ Un-hyŏng; in XXIV Corps Historical File.
123. G-2 "Weekly Report," no. 58, October 13-20, 1946.
124. SKILA materials, enclosure no. 22, letter of November 29, 1946; in XXIV Corps Historical File.
125. *Chwaik sakŏn sillok*, p. 354.
126. Meacham, *Labor Report*, pp. 23-24.
127. *Taehan hyŏngch'al chŏn-sa*, pp. 50-57; and *Chwaik sakŏn sillok*, p. 380.
128. American delegation to the United States-Soviet Joint Commission, memorandum on interview with the Korean governor of North Kyŏngsang Province, October 14, 1946; in XXIV Corps Historical File.
129. "HUSAFIK," vol. 2, ch. 6, p. 52.
130. Derived from Meacham, *Labor Report*, p. 19.
131. James Shoemaker, *Notes on Korea's Postwar Economic Position* (New York: Institute of Pacific Relations, 1947), p. 12.
132. Bank of Korea, *Monthly Economic Statistics*, no. 23 (Seoul, June 1949), p. 1.
133. Meacham, *Labor Report*, p. 18. Another source claimed that Korean workers' real wages were lower in the period May-July 1946 than at any time in the years 1938-1945 (see Minjujuŭi minjok chŏnsŏn, *Chosŏn haebang illyŏn-sa* [History of the First Year of Korean Liberation] [Seoul: Munu insŏ'gwan, 1946], pp. 315-316).
134. Meacham, *Labor Report*, p. 13.
135. *Seoul Times*, September 17, 1946. There were numerous newspaper reports in September 1946 of Koreans attempting to return to Japan.
136. American delegation to the United States-Soviet Joint Commission, memorandum on interviews with nineteen North Kyŏngsang Province officials, October 14, 1946; in XXIV Corps Historical File.
137. National Economic Board, "Survey of Food Distribution in South Korea" (Seoul: USAMGIK headquarters, 1947), pp. 3-4; and "Survey of Grain Collections in South Korea 1946," p. 4; both attached to "History of the National Food Administration" (Seoul, 1948), XXIV Corps Historical File. See also *Siwŏl inmin hangjaeng*, pp. 39-40.
138. CIC report, Seoul, September 25, 1946.
139. Memorandum of interviews with nineteen North Kyŏngsang officials.
140. "HUSAFIK," vol. 3, ch. 4, p. 52.
141. CIC report, Seoul, September 25, 1946. The Military Government's public reaction to Korean charges that rice was being smuggled to Japan expressed the opinion that such charges represented sheer madness.
142. CIC report, Taegu, November 9, 1946.
143. Interviews with nineteen North Kyŏngsang officials.
144. "HUSAFIK," vol. 2, pt. 2, p. 23.
145. *Chwaik sakŏn sillok*, p. 388.
146. *Chosŏn yŏn'gam 1948*, p. 258.

NOTES TO CHAPTER ELEVEN

The North Wind

1. Karl Polanyi, *The Great Transformation* (New York: Beacon Press, 1967 ed.), pp. 182-183. See also Immanuel Wallerstein, "The Rise and Future Demise of the Capitalist World System," *Journal of Comparative Studies in Society and History* 16 (1974): 387-415.

2. George Alexander Lensen, *The Strange Neutrality: Soviet-Japanese Relations During the Second World War, 1941-1945* (Tallahassee, Fla.: Diplomatic Press, 1972), p. 156. On the importance of Soviet entry in the final Japanese capitulation, see pp. 194-195.

3. Ibid., p. 168. Lensen gives the date as August 12, but a North Korean source says the attacks at Ŭnggi and Najin began on August 10 (see *Chosŏn kŭndae hyŏngmyŏng undong-sa* [History of Korea's Modern Revolutionary Movement] [P'yŏngyang: Kwahakwŏn yŏksa yŏn'gu-so, 1962], p. 422). American intelligence later reported that the attacks at Ŭnggi and Najin began on August 10, with the Soviets successfully occupying Ŭnggi without a shot and Najin with few losses. But on August 12 the Soviets lost 30 men at Ch'ŏngjin and were "badly mauled" the next day before capturing the city. (See "Intelligence Summary, North Korea," no. 37, May 31, 1947; in RG 319, Intelligence [G-2] Library "P" File, 1946-1951.)

4. *Chosŏn kŭndae hyŏngmyŏng undong-sa*, p. 422. Baik Bong says that Kim Il Sung and his allies aided the Soviet attacks, but no dates are given (see *Kim Il Sung: A Political Biography* [New York: Guardian Books, 1970], 1: 512-513). This is an official biography of Kim that has been translated into several languages. Until recently, North Korean accounts made no mention of Kim's participation in Soviet landings in northern Korea, and Baik Bong carefully avoids saying Kim personally was involved; he only suggests that his "units" did battle at this time.

5. Hodge, monologue to visiting congressional delegation, October 4, 1947; in USAFIK, USFIK 11071 file, box no. 62/96.

6. William Zimmerman, "Choices in the Postwar World (1): Containment and the Soviet Union," in Charles Gati, ed., *Caging the Bear: Containment and the Cold War* (New York: Bobbs-Merrill Co., 1974), p. 102; and Isaac Deutscher, *Stalin: A Political Biography*, 2d ed. (New York: Oxford University Press, 1966), pp. 573-581.

7. There is some evidence that in 1947-1949 the Soviets hoped to enroll Manchuria and North Korea into a Soviet-dominated sphere, a matter to be dealt with in the second volume of this study. Even then, however, the Soviets did not dominate North Korea in typical satellite fashion, nor was Kim Il Sung "a puppet of a foreign power to an extent unmatched by any individual's relationship to a foreign power during this period [1945-1948]." This judgment by Robert A. Scalapino and Chong-sik Lee (*Communism in Korea* I [Berkeley: University of California Press, 1972]: 381) is not supported by their own evidence and so remains polemic.

8. Max Beloff, *Soviet Policy in the Far East, 1944-1951* (London: Oxford University Press, 1953), p. 156.

9. *Chosŏn inmin-bo* [Korean People's Report], September 8, 1945.

10. *Taejung* [The Masses], September 30, 1945.

11. *Haebang ilbo* [Liberation Daily], November 27, 1945.
12. George McCune, *Korea Today* (Cambridge: Harvard University Press, 1950), p. 51.
13. *Nodongja sinmun* [Worker's News], September 22, 1945.
14. Dae-sook Suh states that "300 Russian Koreans" accompanied Soviet forces into Korea, but includes Kim Il Sung's forces among that total (*The Korean Communist Movement 1918-1948* [Princeton: Princeton University Press, 1967] p. 317). Scalapino and Lee say only that "a large number" of "Russianized Koreans" came in with Soviet troops (*Communism in Korea* I: 318). Other sources tend to inflate greatly the numbers of "Russian Koreans" in the northern regime, mixing Kim's forces in with the total, but there is no good evidence on the total numbers involved. Some important leaders in the subsequent regime had lived most of their adult lives in the Soviet Union, and some were born there. In much of the existing literature there is the none-too-subtle assumption that "Russian Koreans" were the nefarious carriers of a Soviet bacillus and therefore not quite Korean. The fact is that the Soviet Union absorbed a large part of the dispossessed migrant diaspora of the Japanese colony and remained from 1917 to 1941 the one power that consistently backed Korean independence—often with funds and organization. Moreover, why should a Korean who lived for decades in Russia be anymore a "Russian Korean" than Syngman Rhee was an "American Korean"? Koreans tended to remain Korean wherever they lived, and the foreign-linked labels provide little guide to their behavior, or to the likelihood that they would do foreign bidding once back in Korea.
15. See, for example, T'ak Ch'ang-dŏk, "*Naega pon samp'al-do ibuk sajŏng*" [The Situation that I Saw North of the Thirty-eighth Parallel], in *Chungsŏng* [Voice of the Masses] (February 1946), pp. 27-32. After hearing many reports of Soviet pillage, American intelligence suggested that "it is doubted that the Russians intend to remain in northern Korea" (see "Intelligence Summary, North Korea," no. 1, December 1, 1945).
16. Interview with Han, cited in USAMGIK, G-2 "Weekly Report," no. 9, November 4-11, 1945.
17. G-2 "Weekly Report," no. 20, January 20-27, 1946; and no. 24, February 17-24, 1946.
18. Interview with Father Hopple, cited in U.S. Ambassador to Korea John Muccio to Secretary of State; in State Department, RG 59, decimal file, 740.0019/1-649, January 10, 1949. Hopple also stated that there were only a few "Soviet-Koreans" in the north; no "Soviet-Korean" troops were ever quartered there; Russian-speaking Koreans tended to come from Manchurian and Korean border regions near or in Russia.
19. *Report on Japanese Assets in Soviet-Occupied Korea to the President of the United States* (Washington, D.C., June 1946), submitted by Edwin W. Pauley, orig. classification, "restricted." This report found that the Soviets, instead of stripping north Korean industry, had with them technical personnel whose function was to aid in the rapid rebuilding of industry, to get the plants "producing at a maximum scale as early as possible" (p. 12). It noted the presence in many plants of Japanese technicians and said that control of the plants was said to be under workers' and people's committees and that most plant managers were Koreans. At the Mitsui Light Metals Company, renamed the Pukjong Electro-Metallurgical Plant, a Korean manager supervised 800 employees of whom fully 500 appeared to be Japanese in military uni-

form; Japanese technicians also were in evidence, while no Soviet personnel or supervisors were observed (pp. 58-60).

20. G-2 "Weekly Reports," no. 41, June 16-23, 1946; and no. 53, September 8-15, 1946.

21. See, for example, Scalapino and Lee, *Communism in Korea* I: 315; and Robert R. Simmons, *The Strained Alliance: Peking, P'yŏngyang, Moscow and the Politics of the Korean Civil War* (New York: Free Press, 1975), p. 21.

22. "HUSAFIK," Manuscript in the Office of the Chief of Military History, Washington, D.C. (Tokyo and Seoul, 1947, 1948), vol. 2, pt. 1, ch. 4, pp. 25-29; also "XXIV Corps Journal," March 9, 1946 entry; in XXIV Corps Historical File. On American looting in South Chŏlla Province, see E. Grant Meade, *American Military Government in Korea* (New York: King's Crown Press, Columbia University, 1951), p. 82.

23. See 68th MG Company reports of May 20, May 27, and June 17, 1946.

24. David L. Olmsted, "Two Korean Villages: Culture Contact at the 38th Parallel," *Human Organization* 10, no. 3 (Fall 1951): 33-36. I am indebted to Allen S. Whiting for putting me in touch with Dr. Olmsted.

25. *Han'guk inmyŏng tae sajŏn* [Dictionary of Korean Biography] (Seoul: Sin'gu munhwa-sa, 1967), p. 872.

26. Republic of Korea, Kukpang-bu p'yŏnch'an wiwŏn-hoe, *Han'guk chŏnjaeng-sa* [History of the Korean War], I (Seoul: Kukpang-bu, 1967): 51, 26.

27. *Chosŏn inmin-bo*, September 8, 1945.

28. *Han'guk chŏnjaeng-sa* I: 53; O Yŏng-jin, *Hana ŭi chŭng'ŏn* [One Witness] (Pusan, 1952), pp. 111-114; and Scalapino and Lee, *Communism in Korea* I: 315-316.

29. *Chosŏn inmin-bo*, September 8, 1945.

30. Scalapino and Lee, *Communism in Korea* I: 320-321. On Hyŏn's student activities, see Suh, *Korean Communist Movement*, p. 195.

31. *Chosŏn inmin-bo*, September 8, 1945; *Han'guk chŏnjaeng-sa* I: 53. Other members of the P'yŏng'an committee included the husband-wife team of Kim Yong-bŏm and Pak Chŏng-ae; for their activities in the 1930s, see Suh, *Korean Communist Movement*, p. 196.

32. "Intelligence Summary, North Korea," no. 1, December 1, 1945. This was, of course, the time when Hodge and Langdon were planning a separate southern government.

33. Suh, *Korean Communist Movement*, p. 315.

34. "Intelligence Summary, North Korea," no. 4, January 18, 1946.

35. *Nodongja sinmun*, September 22, 1945.

36. Philip Rudolph, *North Korea's Political and Economic Structure* (New York: Institute of Pacific Relations, 1959), p. 10.

37. G-2 "Weekly Report," no. 33, April 21-28, 1946; information based on an intercepted letter to the head of a people's committee in Kangwŏn Province. In cities over 200,000 there were six sections with 60 staff in each; the numbers of staff decreased according to population, with 15 staff members in cities of 50,000 or less. The five sections were: general affairs, finance, industry, vital statistics, welfare.

38. G-2 Translation Documents, no. 337, February 27, 1946; and no. 359, March 20, 1946; also G-2 "Periodic Report," no. 183, March 21-22, 1946 (all in USFIK 11071 file). See also *P'yŏngbuk sinbo* [North P'yŏng'an News], February 1 and 2, 1946.

39. G-2 "Periodic Report," no. 183, March 21-22, 1946.

40. G-2 "Weekly Report," no. 24, February 17-24, 1946.

41. *P'yŏngyang minbo* [P'yŏngyang People's Report], October 23, 1945.

42. See Chŏng T'ae-sik's comments in a roundtable discussion in *Ch'unch'u* [Spring and Autumn], no. 1 (February 1946), p. 27.

43. Chong-sik Lee, "Stalinism in the East: Communism in North Korea," in Robert Scalapino, ed., *The Communist Revolution in Asia: Tactics, Goals and Achievements*, 2d ed. (Englewood Cliffs, N.J.: Prentice-Hall, 1969), pp. 120-121.

44. See G-2 Translation Documents, no. 353, March 14, 1946.

45. McCune, *Korea Today*, p. 45.

46. G-2 "Periodic Report," December 1, 1945.

47. State Department, *North Korea: A Case Study in the Techniques of Takeover* (Washington, D.C.: United States Government Printing Office, 1961), p. 6.

48. Teodor Shanin, *The Awkward Class: Political Sociology of the Peasantry in a Developing Society, Russia 1910-1925* (Oxford: Clarendon Press, 1972), p. 146.

49. See Bruce Cumings "Kim's Korean Communism," *Problems of Communism* 23, no. 2 (March-April 1974): 31-33.

50. *Miscellany of Mao Tse-tung Thought, 1949-1968* (Washington, D.C.: Joint Publications Research Service, 1974), pt. I, p. 106. Mao made this statement in 1958.

51. In English, see Baik Bong, *Kim Il Sung*, vols. 1 and 2. The exaggeration and mythology about Kim that is prevalent in the north bespeaks several needs: (1) the need of a people for affirmation that resistance to the Japanese continued to the end and that Korea was, in some small measure, liberated by the Koreans themselves; (2) the reaction of an isolated people to the refusal in South Korea, the United States, and elsewhere to give Kim the slightest measure of what, in fact, is due him; and (3) the needs of Kim's monumental ego, which seems to require constant nourishment. There is no justification in socialist theory for such a personality cult, but there is justification in Korean tradition. Hagiography is prevalent, past and present; Syngman Rhee, for example, was termed "the leader," "the prophet," even "the messiah," in Yang U-chong, *Yi taet'ongnyŏng t'ujaeng-sa* [History of President Rhee's Struggle] (Seoul: Yŏnhap sinmun-sa, 1949), pp. 38, passim.

52. See, for example, *Han'guk chŏnjaeng-sa* I: 50, where it is argued that the "real" Kim Il Sung would have made a good leader of postwar Korea.

53. Suh, *Korean Communist Movement*, pp. 228-229.

54. Typically this literature, like that on Kim, refers to mysterious dark periods, with the whereabouts of the leader unknown, and to the miniscule number of followers. Hoang Van Chi, for example, proposes as a reasonable theory for Ho Chi Minh's activities between 1933 and 1941 the idea that he was "secretly hidden in the Soviet Union—somewhere far from Moscow." (*From Colonialism to Communism* [New York: Praeger, 1964], p. 52.) For a representative attack on Tito's partisan activities, see N. J. Klones, "Tito and the Yugoslav Partisan Movement," in Gary K. Bertsch and Thomas W. Ganschow, eds., *Comparative Communism: The Soviet, Chinese, and Yugoslav Models* (San Francisco: W. H. Freeman and Co., 1976), pp. 121-128.

Castro offers the best comparison with Kim, in that Castro had about 100 men with him when he attacked the Moncada Barracks in 1953, and the attack failed; in 1956 he landed in the ship *Granma* with but 82 men. Kim's record was far superior to this, however. Castro also was "alien" to the Cuban communist mainstream going back to the 1920s, a charge also leveled at Kim. Finally, it simply stretches credulity to argue that Kim, who spent at most four years in Russia and did not speak the language well, would be a "Russian-Korean," whereas Syngman Rhee, with four decades in the United States, an Austrian wife, and fluent English, remained the patriotic father of his country. Yet much of the South Korean literature has it this way.

55. See, for example, Wilfred Burchett, quoted in *The People's Korea*, June 19, 1974.

56. *Haebang-hu samnyŏn-gan ŭi kungnae-oe chungyo ilgi* [Chronology of Important Events Within and Without Korea in the Three-Year Period since Liberation] (P'yŏngyang: Minju Chosŏn-sa, 1948), pp. 1-2 (volume to be found in RG 242, Captured Enemy Documents, SA 2005, item 2/9). On this point, see also *Chosŏn kŭndae hyŏngmyŏng undong-sa*, pp. 420-422.

57. Kwangju-bu ch'ongmu-gwa kongbo-gye, *Haebang chŏn-hu hoego* [Reflections before and after Liberation] (Kwangju: Kwangju-bu, 1946), p. 6.

58. "Kim Il-sŏng changgun pudae wa Chosŏn ŭiyonggun ŭi chunggyŏn kanbu chwadam-hoe," [Discussion between General Kim Il Sung's Unit and Leading Cadres of the Korean Volunteer Army] *Sin Ch'ŏnji* [New Realm], I, no. 3 (March 1946): 230-237. See also Suh, *Korean Communist Movement*, p. 318.

59. See "Intelligence Summary, North Korea," no. 30, February 16, 1947.

60. Far East Command, "History of the North Korean Army" (hereafter designated "HNKA"), Manuscript in the Office of the Chief of Military History, Washington, D.C. (Tokyo: G-2 Section, 1952), p. 9. A fascinating account in the magazine *Amerasia*, published in October 1945 and obviously based on Chinese sources of information, said that Kim and his army (wrongly estimated at 15,000 strong) also established contact with the Eighth Route Army around the time of liberation. (See "Korea—The Crossroads of Asia," *Amerasia* 9, no. 17 [October 1945], p. 277.)

61. *Haebang-hu chungyo ilgi*, p. 2. A handwritten Japanese police report, dated June 1945, now in the possession of K. P. Yang, head of the Korean Section at the Library of Congress, quotes two captured Koreans as saying that Kim Il Sung was then sending agents into Korea and expected Korea to be liberated in August 1945.

62. See, for example, Scalapino and Lee, who quote freely from O Yŏng-jin's anticommunist account: Kim's youth, combined with his "haircut like a Chinese waiter" and his "monotonous, plain, and duck-like voice," left the people gathered at the meeting with "an electrifying [*sic*] sense of distrust, disappointment, discontent, and anger" (*Communism in Korea* I: 324-325). I heard similar accounts from Koreans in the south who claimed to have attended the same meeting; there is no way to verify such impressions. Similar things were said about other exile leaders, especially Kim Ku, who was said to have a singsong voice and to have waddled like a duck. These things belong in gossip columns.

63. *P'yŏngyang minbo*, October 21, 1945.

64. *Chŏnsŏn* [Battle Front], October 27, 1945.

65. *Tongnip sinmun* [Independence News] November 11, 1945; *Haebang ilbo*, November 5, 1945.

66. Most interesting here are the minutes of the November 24-25, 1945 meeting of people's committee representatives in Seoul. Cho Tu-wŏn, an ally of Yŏ Un-hyŏng, referred in his speech at the meeting to Kim and his forces as follows: "After 1931 one ardent wing of the anti-Japanese struggle was en-

gaged in direct armed battle [with the Japanese], during the [Japanese] aggression against Manchuria, the Sino-Japanese War, and the Second World War; this was the righteous armed movement [*ŭibyŏng undong*] with General Kim Il Sung at the center." Cho then referred in similar fashion to KVA forces in Yenan led by Mu Chŏng and to forces in central China led by Kim Wŏn-bong and Yi Ch'ŏng-ch'ŏn. However, a delegate from South Hamgyŏng Province, Kim Pyŏng-hu, referred to three individuals—Yi Chu-ha, O Ki-sŏp, and Cho Hun—as "our great leaders," or *uri widaehan chidoja*. This delegate did not mention Kim Il Sung, although the *widaehan chidoja* term was already being used for him. (See these minutes in RG 242, Captured Enemy Documents, SA 2006, item 13/65.)

67. "HUSAFIK," vol. 2, ch. 4, p. 315.

68. USAMGIK, "Political Trends," no. 16, January 12, 1946.

69. "HNKA," p. 90. This study claims that Kim was a captain in the Soviet army. If the date in the quotation in the text is correct (October 3), this would be a meeting in a restaurant in P'yŏngyang (see Scalapino and Lee, *Communism in Korea* I: 323). Since the quotation refers to a crowd being present, however, it probably refers to the October 10 welcome for Kim (Cho Man-sik introduced Kim at both meetings).

70. See the report by Gregory Henderson of his conversation with Kim Kyu-sik; included in Embassy to Secretary of State, RG 59, decimal file, 895.00/6-2949, June 6, 1949. Kim Kyu-sik also stated that he thought Kim Il Sung was being misled by the Russians and other Koreans.

71. Suh, *Korean Communist Movement*, p. 319.

72. Cho Man-sik was removed from office because of his opposition to trusteeship. According to an American intelligence report, the Soviets asked Cho to support the Moscow accords three separate times, on January 2, 4, and 5, 1946. After his third refusal he resigned and was kept confined to a hotel in P'yŏngyang for months thereafter. (See "Intelligence Summary, North Korea," no. 4, January 18, 1946.)

73. Han Kŭn-jo told American intelligence officers in early November (when planning for a separate southern government had begun in the south) that only provincial administrations existed in the north; he thought, however, that the Russians hoped to set up a central northern government. (See G-2 "Weekly Report," no. 9, November 4-11, 1945.)

74. Kim Il Sung, "On the Work of the Organizations at all Levels of the Communist Party of North Korea," *Selected Works* (P'yŏngyang: Foreign Languages Publishing House, 1971): 10-22.

75. See Cumings, "Kim's Korean Communism," p. 33; and Charles Bettleheim, "The Great Leap Backward," *Monthly Review* 30, no. 3 (July-August 1978): 43-63.

76. There is some question, as we have seen in earlier chapters, whether any real center existed at all in the southern party. There was no center at this time in the sense of an authoritative body at the top of a disciplined hierarchy, the lower reaches of which could be counted upon to carry out orders.

77. Kim Il Sung, "Concerning the Organization of a Communications Net," March 21, 1946; translation in G-2 "Weekly Report," no. 34, April 28-May 5, 1946.

78. NKCP Central Committee directives, April 7, 1946, and April 11, 1946; translated in ibid. There had been several anticommunist student demonstrations in the north, including a violent one in Sinŭiju.

79. Baik, *Kim Il Sung* 2: 102-103. Baik can criticize Pak Hŏn-yŏng because of his subsequent purge and execution after the Korean War. Pak and other southern leaders were full of criticism for the organization of the KPR, however (Minjujuǔi minjok chŏnsŏn, *Chosŏn haebang illyŏn-sa* [History of the First Year of Korean Liberation] [Seoul: Munu insŏ'gwan, 1946], p. 81 and passim).

80. *P'yŏngyang minbo*, February 12, 1946; translated in G-2 Translation Documents, no. 351, March 13, 1946. See also the special edition of *Chongno* published at the time of the establishment of the NKIPC, dated February 10, 1946; in G-2 Translation Documents, no. 331, February 21, 1946.

81. *P'yŏngyang minbo*, February 12, 1946.

82. Kim Il Sung, "Report Concerning the Present Korean Political Situation and the Problems of Organization of the People's Committee of North Korea"; in G-2 Translation Documents, no. 331.

83. See *Chongno*, January 27, 1946; in G-2 Translation Documents, no. 337, February 27, 1946.

84. *Chongno*, February 1, 1946; in G-2 Translation Documents, no. 332, February 21, 1946.

85. Many northern newspapers noted the timing of the establishment of the NKIPC, especially that it occurred after Shtikov returned to P'yŏngyang from the Joint Conference (see various translations in G-2 Translation Documents, no. 329, February 20, 1946).

86. Suh, *Korean Communist Movement*, pp. 319-321.

87. G-2 "Periodic Report," March 15, 1946.

88. Glenn D. Paige, "North Korea and the Emulation of Russian and Chinese Behavior," in A. Doak Barnett, ed., *Communist Strategies in Asia* (New York: Praeger, 1963), p. 246.

89. *P'yŏngbuk sinbo*, February 2, 1946.

90. Baik, *Kim Il Sung* 2: 99, 103.

91. *Chongno*, February 10, 1946; in G-2 Translation Documents, no. 331, February 21, 1946.

92. *Chongno*, February 24, 1946; in G-2 Translation Documnts, no. 368, March 29, 1946.

93. *Wŏnsan ilbo*, February 22, 1946; in G-2 Translation Documents, no. 359, March 20, 1946. A similar report said that in a flux plant in North P'yŏng'an, run by its 300 Korean employees after liberation, the NKIPC took control in March 1946—although it continued in office the plant manager who had been selected by the workers ("Intelligence Summary, North Korea," no. 37, May 31, 1947).

94. Ibid.

95. G-2 "Weekly Report," no. 41, June 16-23, 1946.

96. *Chosŏn haebang illyŏn-sa*, pp. 163, 172-176. For a list of northern peasant union leaders by province, see p. 172.

97. State Department, *North Korea: A Case Study*, p. 87. See also "HNKA," pp. 8-9.

98. "HNKA," p. 8.

99. G-2 "Weekly Report," no. 34, April 28-May 5, 1946; and Scalapino and Lee, *Communism in Korea* I: 332.

100. "HNKA," pp. 8-9. See also "Intelligence Summary, North Korea," no. 39, June 30, 1947.

101. "HNKA," pp. 8-9. See also "Intelligence Summary, North Korea," no. 1, December 1, 1945.
102. G-2 "Weekly Report," no. 24, February 17-24, 1946.
103. Kim O-sŏng, ed., *Chidoja kunsang* [The Leaders] (Seoul: Taesŏng ch'ulp'an-sa, 1946), p. 181.
104. G-2 "Weekly Report," no. 29, March 24-31, 1946.
105. G-2 "Weekly Report," no. 34, April 28-May 5, 1946.
106. See "HNKA," pp. 8-12; ibid.; and Henry Chung, *The Russians Came to Korea* (Seoul: Korean Pacific Press, 1947), pp. 70-71.
107. G-2 "Weekly Report," no. 33, April 21-28, 1946.
108. *North Korea: A Case Study*, p. 87. See also "HNKA," p. 10.
109. *North Korea: A Case Study*, pp. 87-90.
110. Baik, *Kim Il Sung* 2: 225-226.
111. "HNKA," p. 11. See also "Intelligence Summary, North Korea," no. 39, June 30, 1947.
112. G-2 "Weekly Report," no. 34, April 28-May 5, 1946.
113. Scalapino and Lee, *Communism in Korea* I: 390-391n. The authors cite the account of "a prominently placed defector," but he is not named, nor is there an indication of where or when the account was taken.
114. Suh, *Korean Communist Movement*, pp. 320-321, passim.
115. "HNKA," pp. 6, 11-13; "Intelligence Summary, North Korea," no. 30, February 16, 1947.
116. In Korean, see Kim Ch'ang-sun, *Puk-Han sip'onyŏn-sa* [Fifteen-Year History of North Korea] (Seoul: Chimun-gak, 1961), p. 63; in English, see Scalapino and Lee, *Communism in Korea* I: 333.
117. Kim, *Sip'onyŏn-sa*, pp. 61-65; "HNKA," p. 6; also "Intelligence Summary, North Korea," no. 46, October 18, 1947.
118. "HNKA," p. 6; also "Intelligence Summary," no. 46.
119. G-2 "Weekly Report," no. 34, April 28-May 5, 1946. See also Scalapino and Lee, *Communism in Korea* I: 334. Yenan veterans made up as much as 80 percent of the total officer corps, according to "Intelligence Summary, North Korea," no. 30, February 16, 1947.
120. Kim Il Sung, "The Results of the Agrarian Reform and Future Tasks," *Selected Works* I: 35-55; Hankum Tralim (pseud.), "Land Reform in North Korea," *Amerasia* 11, no. 2 (February 1947): 55-60; *Chosŏn haebang illyŏn-sa*, pp. 332, 431. For a comparison with Chinese land reforms in Manchuria in the late 1940s, which had considerable similarity to the North Korean reform pattern, see Steven Levine, "Political Consolidation in Manchuria, 1945-49" (Ph.D. dissertation, Harvard University, 1973), ch. 7.
121. G-2 "Weekly Report," no. 27, March 10-17, 1946; and *North Korea: A Case Study*, p. 57.
122. *Haebang illyŏn-sa*, pp. 431-445; On Ak-jung, ed., *Puk-Chosŏn kihaeng* [North Korean Journey] (Seoul: Chosŏn chung'ang ilbo ch'ulp'an-sa, 1948), pp. 29-30; see also Tralim, "Land Reform in North Korea."
123. "Intelligence Summary, North Korea," no. 42, August 18, 1947.
124. The account here is taken from *Chosŏn haebang illyŏn-sa*, pp. 431-432, 439-440; for the land reform law, see p. 424. The law is translated in Hankum Tralim, "Land Reform in North Korea."
125. *North Korea: A Case Study*, p. 57.
126. G-2 "Weekly Report," no. 27, March 10-17, 1946. See also Public Opinion Bureau report, April 14, 1946; in XXIV Corps Historical File.

127. Kim, "The Results of the Agrarian Reform and Future Tasks," p. 37.
128. Baik, *Kim Il Sung* 2: 128.
129. In 1956 and 1958 Mao termed this North Korean practice "favor-ism," that is, bestowing "graceful favors" on the masses from on high (see *Miscellany of Mao Tse-tung Thought*, pt. 1, pp. 34, 106).
130. Belden, *China Shakes the World*; and Hinton, *Fanshen*.
131. Kim, "The Results of the Agrarian Reform and Future Tasks," pp. 39-41.
132. *North Korea: A Case Study*, p. 57; and Public Opinion Bureau report, April 14, 1946.
133. G-2 "Weekly Report," no. 53, September 8-15, 1946; Baik, *Kim Il Sung* 2: 134, 187; and Pauley, *Report on Japanese Assets*, p. 12 and passim.
134. G-2 "Weekly Report," no. 52, September 1-8, 1946. Workers in the north got a 25 percent pay boost in August 1946.
135. Suh, *Korean Communist Movement*, p. 321. American intelligence sources bore out Suh's argument that Kim Il Sung had to struggle and maneuver to overcome the opposition of Kim Tu-bong, Mu Chŏng, and other leaders (see G-2 "Weekly Report," no. 50, August 18-25, 1946).
136. See the speeches by Kim Il Sung and Kim Tu-bong in *Chosŏn haebang illyŏn-sa*, pp. 456-458; also Koon Woo Nam. *The North Korean Communist Leadership, 1945-1965* (University, Ala.: University of Alabama Press, 1974), pp. 50-51; also Scalapino and Lee, *Communism in Korea* I: 355-358.
137. *Puk Chosŏn nodongdang ch'angnip taehoe* [Founding Meeting of the North Korean Worker's Party] (P'yŏngyang: Puk Chosŏn nodongdang chung'ang ponbu, 1946); in RG 242, Captured Enemy Documents, SA 2005, item no. 2/64. Note that these figures do not always add up to 801; probably information was not available on all delegates for all categories.
138. Ibid., pp. 41-42.
139. Ibid., p. 36.
140. See Baik, *Kim Il Sung* 2, p. 154, which calls this practice "creatively defining the qualifications of a party member."
141. Scalapino and Lee, *Communism in Korea* I: 375.
142. Kim and Kim, *Haebang chŏn-hu*, p. 209; Kim O-sŏng, *Chidoja kunsang*, pp. 51-59; Suh, *Korean Communist Movement*, p. 228n.
143. Kim Chong-bŏm and Kim Tong-un, *Haebang chŏn-hu ŭi Chosŏn chinsang* [The True Situation of Korea Before and After Liberation] (Seoul: Chosŏn chŏnggyŏng yŏn'gu-sa, 1945), pp. 208-209; Kim O-sŏng, *Chidoja kunsang*, pp. 71-80; Suh, *Korean Communist Movement*, p. 221n; "HNKA," p. 98.
144. See *Nodongja sinmun*, September 22, 1945; also "HNKA," p. 98.
145. Kim, *Chidoja kunsang*, p. 71.
146. "HNKA," p. 99.
147. Ibid., p. 99.
148. *Chosŏn inmin-bo*, March 28, 1946; in G-2 Translation Documents, no. 369, March 30, 1946. Something may have been lost in this translation, but the original is unavailable.
149. *Puk Chosŏn nodongdang ch'angnip taehoe*, p. 39.
150. "Report of the Visit of Arthur C. Bunce with Chancellor Balasanov in P'yongyang," October 16, 1946; in XXIV Corps Historical File. Bunce interviewed both Cho Man-sik and Kim Il Sung. He found Cho in good health and living in a room at the P'yŏngyang railroad hotel and found Kim to have "a good sense of humor, pleasant manner, and ready grin."
151. Article by An Ki-sŏng, in *Kŭnyŏk chubo* [Korea Weekly], November 26, 1945.

151. On Ak-jung, ed., *Puk-Chosŏn kihaeng*, p. 19. The XXIV Corps liaison officer in P'yŏngyang, Lt. Col. Walter F. Choinski, argued that the Soviets had administered the north directly in the first few months after liberation. In the fall of 1946, however, he remarked, "It is quite apparent that the Soviet command is retiring from all military government functions and forcing the Provisional People's Committee [NKIPC] to the front. Matters of an administrative or economic nature heretofore regulated by the Russians have now been turned over to the Peoples Committee." (See his "Report on Current Events in North Korea," November 14, 1946; in RG 59, decimal file, 895.00/7124.) In fact, the Soviets never set up a military government, but it may be that in the fall of 1946 they turned over more responsibilities to the committees. Southern leftists and communists were also highly laudatory in their comments on the northern situation, which might go without saying except for the many conflicts that existed between the southern and northern Left. (See, for example, *Chosŏn haebang illyŏn-sa*, pp. 390-446.

152. See, for example, G-2 "Weekly Report," no. 27, March 10-17, 1946.

153. *Seoul Times*, November 21, 1947.

154. In November 1945 an American reporter, Robert P. Martin, said that more Koreans were moving north than south (New York *Post*, November 20, 1945). American intelligence reports from 1945/46 contain scattered evidence of northward movement, with no figures provided on the numbers involved. The most significant migration to the north was from Japan, with some 370,000 Koreans, many of them native southerners and most of them peasants and workers, going to the north in the late 1940s. This is probably the largest group of voluntary émigrés to a socialist country on record and is usually unmentioned in accounts of refugees leaving the north. More movement of Koreans from Japan to North Korea occurred in 1959 and thereafter, involving hundreds of thousands.

155. The official State Department study of the north stated that "the USSR was able to supervise developments in north Korea with a relatively small number of strategically placed Russian personnel" (*North Korea: A Case Study*, p. 3). A Korean who worked in the northern Agricultural and Forestry Department told American intelligence that only three Soviet advisors were assigned to the department and that they knew and did little. A Korean electrical engineer said that at the plant where he worked Japanese served as technicians, with the few Soviet advisors present only at the highest levels of plant management. (See G-2 "Weekly Report," no. 53, September 8-15, 1946; also "HUSAFIK," vol. 3, ch. 6, pp. 433-434.)

156. Wartime interviews with north Koreans indicated that many of them were put off by "the persistent excesses of Soviet troops" but that "most of the population seemed to have been grateful for land reform, increased industrialization, and the facade of popular participation in government" (see William G. Bradbury, Samuel M. Meyers, and Albert G. Biderman, eds., *Mass Behavior in Battle and Captivity: The Communist Soldier in the Korean War* [Chicago: University of Chicago Press, 1968], p. 226).

157. "Notes on the Pattern of Sovietization in North Korea," based on interviews with 125 north Korean POWs and refugees, in *A Preliminary Study of the Impact of Communism Upon Korea*, Psychological Warfare Research Report No. 1 (Maxwell AFB, Ala.: Air University Human Resources Research Institute, 1951), pp. 207-209, 214, 224-225, 247, 254.

NOTES TO CHAPTER TWELVE

Liberation Denied

1. From Karl Marx, *The Eighteenth Brumaire of Louis Bonaparte* (1852, reprint ed.; New York: International Publishers, 1963), the words mean "Here is Rhodes, leap here! Here is the rose, dance here!" As Robert Tucker put it, one of Aesop's fables referred to a braggart who claimed he could produce a witness to prove he had once made a remarkable leap to Rhodes, whereupon the listeners said, "Here is Rhodes, leap here"—why cite witnesses? (See Tucker, ed., *The Marx-Engels Reader* [New York: W. W. Norton & Co., 1972], p. 440n.)

2. "HUSAFIK," Manuscript in the Office of the Chief of Military History, Washington, D.C. (Tokyo and Seoul, 1947, 1948), v. 3, pt. 2, p. 1.

3. In 1947 the United States Central Intelligence Agency lamented, "there are apparently no articulate proponents of capitalism among the Koreans" (see Central Intelligence Agency, "Korea," SR 2 [Washington, D.C., 1947], orig. classification "secret," pp. I 7-8).

4. F. G. Bailey, "The Peasant View of the Bad Life," in Teodor Shanin, ed., *Peasants and Peasant Societies* (Baltimore: Penguin Books, 1971), p. 315.

5. Barrington Moore, Jr., *Social Origins of Dictatorship and Democracy: Lord and Peasant in the Making of the Modern World* (Boston: Beacon Press, 1966), p. 505.

6. Here we are concerned with Hodge's "Comments" of January 8 and Meacham's rejoinder in a memorandum of February 20, 1948; both in USAFIK, XXIV Corps Historical File.

7. Hodge conversation with General Albert Wedemeyer, August 27, 1947, in ibid.

8. Undated, untitled study by David E. Mark, enclosed in American Ambassador to Korea, John Muccio to State Department, May 23, 1949; in State Department, RG 59, decimal file, 740.0019/5-2349.

I. Official Sources

Unpublished

Counter-Intelligence Corps reports, 1945-1947, are all to be found in United States Armed Forces in Korea, Record Group 332, XXIV Corps Historical File.

Military Government Company reports, 1945-1946, are all to be found in United States Army, Record Group 407, "World War II Operations Reports." Entry no. 427.

United States Air Force. "A Preliminary Study of the Impact of Communism Upon Korea," Psychological Warfare Research Report No. 1. Maxwell Air Force Base, Ala.: Air University Human Resources Research Institute, 1951.

United States Armed Forces in Korea. "History of the United States Armed Forces in Korea." Compiled under the supervision of Harold Larsen, chief historian. Tokyo and Seoul, 1947, 1948. Manuscript in the Office of the Chief of Military History, Washington, D.C.

————. Record Group 332, forty-four boxes, XXIV Corps Historical File. Suitland, Md.: Federal Records Center Annex.

————. USFIK 11071 File. Suitland, Md.: Federal Records Center Annex.

United States Army. Record Group 319, "Intelligence Summaries, North Korea" (Army Staff), no. 739, Intelligence (G-2) Library, "P." File, 1946-1951.

————. Record Group 407, entry 427, "World War II Operations Reports." Suitland, Md.: Federal Records Center Annex.

United States Army Military Government in Korea. Record Group 319 "G," "Biographies." Suitland, Md.: G-2 Section, Federal Records Center Annex.

————. "History of the United States Army Military Government in Korea." Seoul: Office of Administrative Services, Statistical Research Division, 1946. Manuscript in the Office of the Chief of Military History, Washington, D.C.

————. "Memorandum, Political Parties" Seoul, Department of Public Opinion, 1948.

————. "Opinion Trends," periodic. Seoul: Department of Public Information, 1945-1946.

————. "Political Trends," periodic. Seoul: Department of Public Information, 1945-1946.

————. Record Group 319, G-2 (intelligence) weekly and periodic reports. Suitland, Md.: Federal Records Center Annex.

United States Army Military, etc. "Report on the Occupation of South Korea." Seoul: Administrative Services Division, September 1947.

———. "Who's Who in the South Korean Interim Government." Seoul, 1947.

United States Central Intelligence Agency. "The Current Situation in Korea," ORE 15-48, March 18, 1948, "secret."

———. "Korea." SR 2. Washington, D.C., 1947.

United States, Far East Command. "History of the North Korean Army." Tokyo: G-2 Section, 1952. Manuscript in the Office of the Chief of Military History, Washington, D.C.

———. Record Group 242, "Captured Enemy Documents." Suitland, Md.: Federal Records Center Annex.

United States, Joint Chiefs of Staff. Record Group 218, Geographic File 1945-1947, 383.21 Korea (3-19-45).

United States, Office of Strategic Services. "Joint Army-Navy Intelligence Study—Korea-75," 2 vols. (JANIS 75), 1945.

———. 1942-1946 File. Modern Military Branch, National Archives.

United States, State Department. "Biographic Reports on the Cabinet of the Korean Republic." Washington, D.C.: Office of Intelligence, 1948.

———. "Draft Trusteeship Agreement for Korea," November 8, 1945. Copy in possession of John Kotch.

———. Record Group 9, "Messages, Japanese Government, Incoming and Outgoing." 1945.

———. Record Group 43, "U.S.-U.S.S.R. Joint Commission on Korea." 1946-1947.

———. Record Group 59, Decimal File, 895.00 category. 1942-1949.

———. Record Group 59, Decimal File, 740.0019 Control (Korea). 1945-1946.

———. Record Group 353, State-War-Navy Coordinating Committee. "SWNCC 101." 1945.

———. Record Group 353, "SWNCC-SANACC." 1946-1947.

United States War Department. Record Group 165, ABC Decimal File—Korea. 1944-1946.

———. Record Group 319, Plans and Operations Division Decimal File, "Korea 1946-1950, 091 Korea." 1945-1947.

United States, Supreme Command, Allied Powers. Record Group 5, "Japanese Surrender File," no. 2. 1945.

Published

American Delegation to the United States-Soviet Joint Commission. "Report on the Occupation Area of South Korea Since Termination of Hostilities." Seoul, 1947.

Bank of Korea. *Monthly Economic Statistics*. Seoul, 1948-1949.

Chosŏn kyŏngje nyŏnbo [Annual Economic Review of Korea]. Seoul: Chosŏn unhaeng chosa-bu, 1948.

A Chronicle of Principal Events Relating to the Korean Question, 1945-1954. Peking: World Culture, 1954.

Chwaik sakŏn sillok [Record of the Left-Wing Incidents]. Seoul: Tae'gŏmch'-al-ch'ong, susa-guk, 1964.

Coles, Harry L., and Weinberg, Albert K. *Civil Affairs: Soldiers Become Governors*. Washington, D.C.: Office of the Chief of Military History, 1964.

Facts About South Korea, 1945-1960. P'yŏngyang: Foreign Languages Press, 1960.

Government-General, Korea. *Annual Report on the Administration of Chōsen*. Keijo: Korean Government-General, 1928-1930.

———. *Annual Report on the Administration of Tyosen* [sic] *1937-1938*. Seoul: Government-General, 1938.

Han'guk inmyŏng tae sajŏn [Dictionary of Korean Biography]. Seoul: Sin'gu munhwa-sa, 1967.

Kungnae kanhaengmul kisa saeg'in [Korean Periodicals Index]. Seoul: National Assembly Library, 1960.

Meacham, Stewart. *Korean Labor Report*. Seoul: USAFIK, 1947.

National War College. *Korea: Problems of United States Army in Occupation, 1945-1947*. Washington, D.C.: Department of the Army, 1948.

Pauley, Edwin W. *Report on Japanese Assets in Soviet-Occupied Korea to the President of the United States*. Washington, D.C., June 1946.

Political Advisory Group. "Handbook of the Democratic People's Front and Associate Organizations." Seoul: XXIV Corps Headquarters, January 1948.

Republic of Korea. Kukpang-bu p'yŏnch'an wiwŏn-hoe. *Haebang kwa kŏn'-gun* [Liberation and the Establishment of the Army]. *Han'guk chŏnjaeng-sa* [History of the Korean War], vol. 1. Seoul: Kukpang-bu, 1967.

———. Kuksa p'yŏnch'an wiwŏn-hoe. *Taehan min'guk-sa* [History of the Republic of Korea]. Seoul: 1970.

———. Naemu-bu ch'ian'guk. *Minjok ŭi sŏnbong* [Spearhead of the Nation]. *Taehan kyŏngch'al chŏn-sa* [Military History of the Korean National Police], vol. 1. Seoul: Hŭng'guk yŏn'gu hyŏp-hoe, 1952.

Sawyer, Robert K. *Military Advisors in Korea: KMAG in Peace and War*. Edited by Walter G. Hermes. Washington, D.C.: Office of the Chief of Military History, 1962.

Schnabel, James F. *Policy and Direction: The First Year*. Washington, D.C.: Office of the Chief of Military History, 1972.

South Korean Interim Government. *Activities*. Seoul, 1947.

———. *Chosŏn t'onggye. yŏn'gam 1943* [Korean statistics yearbook, 1943]. Seoul, 1948.

Stalin's Correspondence with Churchill, Attlee, Roosevelt, and Truman, 1941-1945. New York: E. P. Dutton & Co., 1958. Originally published by USSR Ministry of Foreign Affairs, 1957.

State Statistical Bureau. *China: Ten Great Years*. Peking: Foreign Languages Press, 1960.

Sudo kwan'gu kyŏngch'al ch'ong. *Haebang ihu sudo kyŏngch'al paltal-sa* [His-

tory of the Development of the Metropolitan Police after Liberation].
Seoul: Sudo kwan'gu kyŏngch'al ch'ong, 1947.

Tewksbury, Donald. *Source Materials on Korean Politics and Ideologies.* New
York: Institute of Pacific Relations, 1950.

United States Army Military Government in Korea, Department of Agriculture. *Present Agricultural Position of South Korea.* Seoul, 1947.

————, Department of Justice. *Selected Legal Opinions of the Department of
Justice.* Seoul. 1948.

————, Department of Public Opinion. "Memorandum: Political Parties."
Seoul, 1948.

————, Headquarters. "Historical Summation, Department of Public Health
and Welfare, September 1945-May 1947." Seoul, 1947.

————, Office of Administration. *Manual of Military Government Organization and Function.* Seoul, n.d.

————. *Official Gazette.* Seoul, 1945-1946.

————. *Population of Korea by Geographic Divisions and Sex.* Seoul, 1946.

United States, Defense Department. *The Entry of the Soviet Union into the
War Against Japan: Military Plans, 1941-1945.* Washington, D.C., 1955.

————. *United States-Vietnam Relations, 1945-1967.* Washington, D.C., 1971.

United States, Office of Strategic Services. *Expressions of Korean Attitudes
Toward Post-War Problems.* Washington, D.C., 1945.

————. *The Korean Independence Movement.* Washington, D.C., 1945.

————. *Questions on Korean Politics and Personalities.* Washington, D.C.,
1945.

United States, State Department. *Department of State Bulletin.* Washington,
D.C.: U.S. Government Printing Office, 1945-1947.

————. *Foreign Relations of the United States.* 8 vols. Washington, D.C.,
1943-1946.

————, Foreign Relations of the United States, Diplomatic Papers. *The Conference of Berlin, 1945.* Washington, D.C., 1960.

————, Foreign Relations of the United States, Diplomatic Papers. *The
Conferences at Cairo and Teheran, 1943.* Washington, D.C., 1961.

————, Foreign Relations of the United States, Diplomatic Papers. *The Conferences of Malta and Yalta, 1945.* Washington, D.C., 1955.

————. *Korea, 1945-1948.* Washington, D.C.: 1948.

————. *North Korea: A Case Study in the Techniques of Takeover.* Washington, D.C.: 1961.

————. *The Record on Korean Unification 1943-1960.* Washington, D.C.:
1960.

United States, Supreme Command, Allied Powers. *Summation of Non-Military Activities in Japan and Korea.* Tokyo, 1945-1946.

United States, War Department, Military Intelligence Division, *Terrain
Handbook: Korea.* Washington, D.C.: 1945.

Wedemeyer, Albert C., "Report to the President: Korea, September 1947."
Washington, D.C.: U.S. Government Printing Office, 1951.

II. Books

Korean and Japanese Language

An Chae-hong. *Han minjok ŭi kibon chillo* [The Fundamental Path of the Korean Nation]. Seoul: Choyang-sa ch'ulp'an-bu, 1949.

——. *Sin minjokjuŭi wa sin minjujuŭi* [New Nationalism and New Democracy]. Seoul: Minu-sa, 1945.

An Yŏng-sŏp. *Chosŏn minjok ŭi sal'kil* [The Livelihood of the Korean Nation]. Seoul: Chosŏn-ŏ yŏn'gu-hoe, 1946.

Chae-Mi Hanjok yŏnhap wiwŏn-hoe. *Haebang Chosŏn* [Liberated Korea]. Hawaii: Chae-Mi Hanjok yŏnhap wiwŏn-hoe, 1948.

Chang Pok-sŏng. *Chosŏn kongsandang p'ajŏng-sa* [History of the Factional Struggles of the Korean Communist Party]. Seoul: Taeryuk ch'ulp'an-sa, 1949.

Ch'in-Il p'a kunsang [The Pro-Japanese Groups]. Keijo: Samsaeng munhwa-sa, 1948.

Cho Ki-jun. *Han'guk kiŏpga-sa* [History of Korean Entrepreneurs]. Seoul: Pag'yŏng-sa, 1973.

Cho Pyŏng-ok. *Minjok unmyŏng ŭi kiro* [The Nation's Future at the Crossroads]. Seoul: Kyŏngmu-bu kyŏngch'al kongbo-sil, 1948.

——. *Na ŭi hoegorok* [My Recollections]. Seoul: Min'gyo-sa, 1959.

Cho Yŏng-am. *Ko Dang Cho Man-sik* [Cho Man-sik]. Seoul, 1953.

Ch'oe Hyŏn-sik et al. *Chŏngŭp kunji* [History of Chŏngŭp County]. Kwangju: Mudŭng kyoyuk ch'ulp'an chusik hoesa, 1957.

Chŏn Sŏk-dam, Hŏ Chong-ho, and Hong Hŭi-yu. *Chosŏn esŏ chabon chuŭi chŏk kwangye ŭi palsaeng* [The Growth of Capitalist Relationships in Korea]. P'yŏngyang, 1970.

Chŏng Han-jo. *Samsan isu* [Three Mountains, Two Rivers]. Seoul, 1965.

Chŏng Si-u, ed. *Tongnip kwa chwa-u hapjak* [Independence and Left-Right Coalition]. Seoul: Sammi-sa, 1946.

Chōsen nenkan 1945 [Korea Yearbook 1945]. Seoul: Keijo nippo-sha, 1945.

Chōsen shōkō taikan [Commerce and Industry in Korea]. Seoul, 1929.

Chosŏn inmindang. *Inmindang ŭi nosŏn* [The Program of the People's Party]. Seoul: Sin munhwa yŏn'gu-so ch'ulp'an-bu, 1946.

Chosŏn kŭndae hyŏngmyŏng undong-sa [History of Korea's Modern Revolutionary Movement]. P'yŏngyang: Kwahakwŏn yŏksa yŏn'gu-so, 1962.

Chosŏn yŏn'gam 1948 [Korea Yearbook 1948]. Seoul: Chosŏn t'ongsin-sa, 1948.

Chungguk kongsandang kwa minjok t'ongil chŏnsŏn [The Chinese Communist Party and the Path to (Korean) National Unification]. Seoul: Uri munhwa-sa, 1945.

Haebang hu samnyŏn-gan ŭi kungnae chungyo ilgi [Chronology of Important Events within Korea in the Three-year Period since Liberation]. P'yŏngyang: Minju Chosŏn-sa, 1948.

Haebang ihu Chosŏn-nae chuyo ilgi [Chronology of Important Events in Korea after Liberation]. Seoul, 1946.

Haebang nyusŭ [Liberation News]. Seoul: T'ongsin-sa, 1945.

Haebang yŏnji 1946 [Record of Liberation, 1946]. Tokyo: Haebang sinmun-sa, 1946.

Han Chae-dok. *Kim Il-sŏng ŭl kobal handa* [I Indict Kim Il Sung]. Seoul, 1965.

Han T'ae-su. *Han'guk chŏngdang-sa* [A History of Korean Political Parties]. Seoul: Sin t'aeyang-sa, 1961.

Hong Sŭng-myŏn et al. *Haebang isimnyŏn* [Twenty Years of Liberation]. Seoul: Semun-sa, 1965.

In Chŏng-sik. *Chosŏn nongch'ŏn munje sajŏn* [Dictionary of Korean agriculture]. Seoul: Sinhak-sa, 1948.

———. *Chosŏn nong'ŏp kyŏngje ron* [On the Korean Agricultural Economy]. Seoul: Pangmun ch'ulp'an-sa, 1949.

———. *Chosŏn ŭi t'oji munje* [Korea's Land Question]. Seoul: Ch'ŏngsu-sa, 1946.

Kang Man-gil. *Chosŏn hugi sangŏp chabon ŭi paltal* [The Development of Commercial Capital in the Late Yi]. Seoul: Koryŏ taehakkyo ch'ulp'an-bu, 1973.

Kim Ch'ang-sun. *Puk-Han sip'onyŏn-sa* [Fifteen-Year History of North Korea]. Seoul: Chimun-gak, 1961.

Kim Chong-bŏm, and Kim Tong-un. *Haebang chŏn-hu ŭi Chosŏn chinsang* [The True Situation of Korea Before and After Liberation]. Seoul: Chosŏn chŏnggyŏng yŏn'gu-sa, 1945.

Kim Chun-yŏn, ed. *Han'guk minjudang so-sa* [A short history of the Korean Democratic Party]. Seoul: Han'guk minjudang sŏnjŏn-bu, 1948.

———. *Tongnip nosŏn* [The Path of Independence]. Seoul: Hŭnghan chae-dan, 1947.

Kim Ki-sŏk, *Puk Chosŏn ŭi hyŏnsang kwa changnae* [North Korean Present and Future]. Seoul: Chosŏn chŏnggyŏng yŏn'gu-sa, 1947.

Kim O-sŏng, ed. *Chidoja kunsang* [The Leaders]. Seoul: Taesŏng ch'ulp'an-sa, 1946.

Kim Pong-hyŏn, and Kim Min-ju. *Cheju-do inmindŭl ŭi '4.3' mujang t'ujaeng-sa* [History of the Cheju Island People's 'April 3' Armed Struggle]. Osaka: Munu-sa, 1963.

Kim Sam-gyu. *Minjok ŭi yŏmyŏng* [Dawn of the Nation]. n.p., 1949.

Kim Sa-rim, ed. *Kija such'ŏp* [Reporter's Notebook]. Seoul: Tonga ilbo-sa, 1947.

Kim Yong-jin, ed. *Pan-minja tae kongp'an-gi* [Court Record of the Traitors]. Seoul: Hanp'ung ch'ulp'an-sa, 1949.

Kim Yong-mo. *Hanmal ŭi chibae-ch'ŭng* [The Ruling Stratum at the End of the Yi Dynasty]. Seoul: Han'guk munhwa yŏn'gu-so, 1972.

Kim Yŏng-sŏp. *Chosŏn hugi nong'op-sa yŏn'gu: nongch'ong kyŏngje sahoe pyŏndong* [Studies in the Agrarian History of the Late Yi Dynasty: The Peasant Economy and Social Change]. Seoul: Ilcho-gak, 1971.

Kim Yun, ed. *Chuŭi haesŏl* [Commentary on Ideology]. Seoul: Sahoe palchon-sa, 1945.

Kobayakawa, Kurō, ed. *Chōsen nōgyo hattatsu-shi* [History of the Development of Korean Agriculture]. 2 vols. Keijo: Chōsen nōkai, 1944.

Ko Ha sŏnsaeng chŏn'gi p'yŏnch'an wiwŏn-hoe. *Ko Ha Song Chin-u sŏnsaeng chŏn* [Collection on Ko Ha, Song Chin-u]. Seoul: Tonga ilbo ch'ulp'an-guk, 1964.

Ko Wŏn-byŏn, ed. *Panminja choejang-gi* [Record of the Crimes of the Traitors]. Seoul: Paeg'yŏp munhwa-sa, 1949.

Ko Yŏng-hwan. *Kŭmil ŭi chŏnggaekdŭl* [Today's Politicians]. Seoul: Tonga ilbo-sa, 1949.

Kohŭng kun hyangt'o-sa [A Local History of Kohŭng County]. Kohŭng: Kohŭng kun hyangt'o-sa p'yŏnch'an wiwŏnhoe, 1971.

Kohŭng kun-sa [History of Kohŭng County]. Kwangju: Chŏllam taehakkyo ch'ulp'an-bu, 1969.

Kŏn'guk simnyŏn-ji [Ten Years of Independence]. Seoul: Kŏn'guk simnyŏn-ji kanhaeng-hoe, 1956.

Kwangju-bu ch'ongmu-gwa kongbo-gye. *Haebang chŏn-hu hoego* [Reflections Before and After Liberation]. Kwangju: Kwangju-bu, 1946.

Minjujuŭi minjok chŏnsŏn. *Chosŏn haebang illyŏn-sa* [History of the First Year of Korean Liberation]. Seoul: Munu insŏ'gwan, 1946.

O Yŏng-jin. *Hana ŭi chŭng'ŏn* [One Witness]. Pusan, 1952.

On Ak-jung et al. *Minjujuŭi ŭi sibi kang* [Twelve Speeches on Democracy]. Seoul: Munu insŏ'gwan, 1946.

———, ed. *Puk Chosŏn kihaeng* [North Korean Journey]. Seoul: Chosŏn chungang ilbo ch'ulp'an-sa, 1948.

Pae Sŏng-nyŏng. *I hondong ŭl ottok'e susŭp halga* [How Will We Deal with This Chaos]. Seoul: Chŏn'guk chŏngch'i undongja huwŏn-hoe, 1945.

Paek Nam-un. *Chosŏn minjok ŭi chillo* [The Path of the Korean Nation]. Seoul: Sin'gŏn-sa, 1946.

Pak T'ae-wŏn. *Yaksan kwa ŭiyŏldan* [Yaksan (Kim Wŏn-bong) and the Patriotic Fighter's Corps]. Seoul: Paeg'yang-dang, 1947.

Puk-Chosŏn nodongdang ch'angnip taehoe [Founding Meeting of the North Korean Worker's Party]. P'yŏngyang: Puk-Chosŏn nodongdang chung'-ang ponbu, 1946.

Puk Han isimnyŏn [Twenty-Year (History) of North Korea]. Seoul: Kongbo-bu, chosa-guk, 1965.

Siwŏl inmin hangjaeng [The October People's Resistance]. Seoul: Haebang-sa, 1947.

Sŏbuk ŭi aegukja [Patriots of the Northwest]. Seoul: P'yŏng'an ch'ŏngnyŏn-hoe, 1946.

Sŏl Ŭi-sik. *Haebang ihu* [After the Liberation]. Seoul: Tonga ilbo-sa, 1947.

Song Chong-ik. *Samch'ŏnman ŭi sŏwŏn* [The Vow of the Thirty Millions]. Seoul: Hŭngsadan munsa-bu, 1946.

Taehan min'guk chŏngdang-sa [History of Political Parties in the Republic of Korea]. Seoul: Chungang sŏn'go kwalli wiwŏn-hoe, 1964.

Taehan tongnip undong kwa imsi chŏngbu t'ujaeng-sa [The Korean Independence Movement and the Struggle of the Korean Provisional Government]. Seoul: Kyerim-sa, 1946.

Tobata, Seiichi, and Toshitaro, Morinaga, eds. *Beikoku keizai no kenkyu* [Studies on the Rice Economy]. Tokyo, 1939.

Wŏlchu Sanin, pseud. ed. *Chosŏn tongp'o ege koham* [To the Korean Brethren]. Seoul: Cho'gwang-sa, 1945.

Yang U-chong. *Yi taet'ongnyŏng t'ujaeng-sa* [History of President Rhee's Struggle]. Seoul: Yŏnhap sinmun-sa, 1949.

Yi Chae-hun. *Minjok ŭisik kwa kyegŭp ŭisik* [National Consciousness and Class Consciousness]. Seoul: Tongyang kongsa ch'ulp'an-sa, 1946.

Yi Chŏng-sik (Chong-sik Lee). *Kim Kyu-sik ŭi saengae* [The career of Kim Kyu-sik]. Seoul: Sin'gu munhwa-sa, 1974.

Yi Hyŏk, ed. *Aeguk ppira chŏnjip* [Collection of Patriotic Handbills]. Seoul: Cho'guk munhwa-sa, 1946.

Yi Kang-guk. *Minjujuŭi ŭi Chosŏn kŏnsŏl* [The Construction of Democratic Korea]. Seoul: Chosŏn inminbo-sa husŏng-bu, 1946.

Yi Ki-ha. *Han'guk chŏngdang paltal-sa* [History of the Development of Korean Political Parties]. Seoul: Ŭihoe chŏngch'i-sa, 1961.

Yi Kŏn-hyŏk. *Kŏn'guk kwa kungmin kyŏngje* [National Construction and the National Economy]. Seoul: Hansŏng sanghoe, 1946.

Yi Man-gyu. *Yŏ Un-hyŏng t'ujaeng-sa* [History of Yŏ Un-hyŏng's Struggle]. Seoul: Ch'ongmun-gak, 1946.

Yi Pŏm-sŏk. *Han'guk ŭi punno* [Korea's Indignation]. Translated from the Chinese by Kim Kwang-ju. 2d ed. Seoul: Kwangch'ang-gak, 1945.

———. *Minjok kwa ch'ŏngnyŏn* [Youth and the Nation]. Seoul: Paeksu-sa, 1948.

Yi Sŭng-man (Syngman Rhee). *Ilminjuŭi kaesul* [Outline of the One People's Principle]. Seoul: Ilminjuŭi po'gŭp-hoe, 1949.

Yi Yŏng-hyŏp. *Han'guk hyŏndae t'oji chaedo-sa yŏn'gu* [Studies on the History of the Modern Land System in Korea]. Seoul: Pomun-gak, 1962.

Yŏ Un-hong. *Mongyang: Yŏ Un-hyŏng.* Seoul: Ch'ongha-gak, 1967.

Yŏ Un-hyŏng sŏnsaeng e taehan p'an'gyŏl-so [The Judicial Record of Mr. Yŏ Un-hyŏng]. Seoul: Kunsŏdang sŏjŏm, 1946.

Yŏngyang kunji p'yŏnch'an wiwŏnhoe. *Yŏngyang kunji* [Local History of Yongyang County]. Taegu: Chungwoe ch'ulp'an-sa, 1970.

Yu Kwang-yŏl, ed. *Mi-Su sangguk kwa kŭkdong p'ungun* [American-Soviet Rivalry and the Far Eastern Situation]. Seoul: Kukje munhwa hyŏphoe, 1947.

English Language

Acheson, Dean. *Present at the Creation: My Years in the State Department.* New York: Signet Books, 1970.

Aitken, Hugh G. J., ed. *The State and Economic Growth.* New York: Social Science Research Council, 1959.

Allen, Richard (pseud.). *Korea's Syngman Rhee: An Unauthorized Portrait.* Rutland, Vermont: Charles E. Tuttle Co., 1960.

Alperovitz, Gar. *Atomic Diplomacy: Hiroshima and Potsdam.* New York: Simon and Schuster, 1965.

Anderson, Perry. *Lineages of the Absolutist State.* London: New Left Books, 1974.

Asiatic Research Center, ed. *International Conference on the Problems of Modernization in Asia.* Seoul, 1965.

Baik, Bong. *Kim Il Sung: A Political Biography.* 3 vols. New York: Guardian Books, 1970.

Bailey, Sidney D. *The Korean Crisis.* London: National Peace Council, 1950.

Balazs, Etienne, *Chinese Civilization and Bureaucracy.* New Haven: Yale University Press, 1964.

Bartz, Patricia M. *South Korea.* London: Oxford University Press, 1972.

Beer, George Louis. *African Questions at the Paris Peace Conference.* New York: Macmillan Co., 1923.

Belden, Jack. *China Shakes the World.* New York: Monthly Review Press, 1949, 1970.

Beloff, Max. *Soviet Policy in the Far East, 1944-1951.* London: Oxford University Press, 1953.

Blum, Jerome. *The End of the Old Order in Rural Europe.* Princeton: Princeton University Press, 1978.

Borton, Hugh. *Japan Since 1931: Its Political and Social Developments.* New York: Institute of Pacific Relations, 1940.

Bradbury, William C., Samuel M. Meyers, and Albert D. Biderman, eds. *Mass Behavior in Battle and Captivity.* Chicago: University of Chicago Press, 1968.

Brandt, Vincent. *A Korean Village Between Farm and Sea.* Cambridge: Harvard University Press, 1971.

Bree, Germaine, and George Bernauer, eds. *Defeat and Beyond.* New York: Pantheon Books, 1970.

Brenan, Gerald. *The Spanish Labyrinth.* Cambridge: Cambridge University Press, 1943.

Burns, James MacGregor. *Roosevelt: The Soldier of Freedom, 1940-1945.* New York: Harcourt Brace Jovanovich, 1970.

Byas, Hugh. *Government by Assassination.* New York: Alfred A. Knopf, 1942.

Byrnes, James F. *Speaking Frankly.* New York: Harper & Bros., 1947.

Caldwell, John C. *The Korea Story.* Chicago: Henry Regnery Co., 1952.

Cameron, Rondo, ed. *Banking in the Early Stages of Industrialization.* New York: Oxford University Press, 1967.

Chirot, Daniel. *Social Change in the Twentieth Century.* New York: Harcourt Brace Jovanovich, 1977.

Cho, Soon Sung. *Korea in World Politics, 1940-1950.* Berkeley: University of California Press, 1967.

Chung, Henry. *The Russians Came to Korea.* Seoul: Korean Pacific Press, 1947.

Chung, Kyung Cho. *Korea Tomorrow.* New York: Macmillan Co., 1956.

Clemens, Diane Shaver. *Yalta.* New York: Oxford University Press, 1970.

Cohen, Jerome B. *Japan's Economy in War and Reconstruction.* Minneapolis: University of Minnesota Press, 1949.

Cohen, Warren I. *America's Response to China.* New York: John Wiley & Sons, 1971.

Conroy, Hilary. *The Japanese Seizure of Korea, 1868-1910.* Philadelphia: University of Pennsylvania Press, 1960.

Collins, J. Lawton. *War in Peacetime: The History and Lessons of Korea.* Boston: Houghton Mifflin Co., 1969.

Cynn, Hugh Heung-woo. *The Rebirth of Korea.* New York: Abingdon Press, 1920.

Day & Zimmerman, Inc. *Report No. 5002 to His Excellency, Syngman Rhee, President, on the Conditions, Rehabilitation, and Further Development of Certain Elements in the Industry of the Republic of Korea.* Seoul, 1949.

Dahrendorf, Ralf. *Class and Class Conflict in Industrial Society.* Stanford: Stanford University Press, 1959.

Dallek, Robert. *Franklin D. Roosevelt and American Foreign Policy, 1932-1945.* New York: Oxford University Press, 1979.

Deuchler, Martina. *Confucian Gentlemen and Barbarian Envoys: The Opening of Korea, 1875-1885.* Seattle: University of Washington Press, 1977.

Deutscher, Isaac. *Stalin: A Political Biography.* New York: Oxford University Press, 1949.

Dobb, Maurice. *Studies in the Development of Capitalism.* New York: International Publishers, 1947, 1963.

Eckstein, Alexander. *China's Economic Development.* Ann Arbor: University of Michigan Press, 1975.

Eden, Anthony. *Memoirs: The Reckoning.* Boston: Houghton Mifflin Co., 1965.

Facts About Korea, 1945-1960. P'yŏngyang: Foreign Languages Publishing House, 1960.

Fanon, Franz. *The Wretched of the Earth.* Preface by Jean-Paul Sartre. New York: Grove Press, 1966.

Feis, Herbert. *The Atomic Bomb and the End of World War II.* Princeton: Princeton University Press, 1966.

———. *Between War and Peace: The Potsdam Conference.* Princeton: Princeton University Press, 1960.

———. *Churchill, Roosevelt, Stalin: The War They Waged and the Peace They Sought.* Princeton: Princeton University Press, 1957.

———. *Contest Over Japan.* New York: W. W. Norton, 1967.

Fraenkel, Ernst. *Military Occupation and the Rule of Law: Occupation Government in the Rhineland, 1918-1923.* New York: Oxford University Press, 1944.

Freeland, Richard M. *The Truman Doctrine and the Origins of McCarthyism.* New York: Alfred A. Knopf, 1972.

Friedrich, Carl J. et al. *American Experiences in Military Government in World War II.* New York: Rinehart & Co., 1948.

Gaddis, John Lewis. *The United States and the Origins of the Cold War, 1941-1947.* New York: Columbia University Press, 1972.

Gann, L. H., and Peter Duignan, eds. *Colonialism in Africa, 1870-1960,* vol. 2, *The History and Politics of Colonialism, 1914-1960.* New York: Cambridge University Press, 1970.

Gardner, Lloyd. *Architects of Illusion.* Chicago: Quadrangle Books, 1970.
———. *Economic Aspects of New Deal Diplomacy.* 2d ed. Boston: Beacon Press, 1971.
Gati, Charles, ed. *Caging the Bear: Containment and the Cold War.* New York: Bobbs-Merrill Co., 1974.
Gayn, Mark. *Japan Diary.* New York: William Sloane Associates, 1948.
Geertz, Clifford. *Agricultural Involution: The Process of Ecological Change in Indonesia.* Berkeley: University of California Press, 1966.
Gerschenkron, Alexander. *Economic Backwardness in Historical Perspective.* Cambridge: Harvard University Press, 1962.
Gitovich, A., and B. Bursov. *North of the 38th Parallel.* Shanghai: Epoch Publishing Co., 1948.
Grajdanzev, Andrew J. *Modern Korea.* New York: Institute of Pacific Relations, 1944.
Green, A. Wigfall. *The Epic of Korea.* Washington, D.C.: Public Affairs Press, 1950.
Gunther, John. *The Riddle of MacArthur.* New York: Harper & Bros., 1950.
Hailey, Foster. *Half of One World.* New York. Macmillan Co., 1950.
Hall, John W., and Marius B. Jansen, *Studies in the Institutional History of Early Modern Japan.* Princeton: Princeton University Press, 1968.
Halliday, Jon. *A Political History of Japanese Capitalism.* New York· Pantheon Books, 1975.
Halperin, Morton H. *Bureaucratic Politics and Foreign Policy.* Washington: The Brookings Institution, 1974.
Han, Sungjoo. *The Failure of Democracy in South Korea.* Berkeley: University of California Press, 1974.
Harriman, W. Averell and Elie Abel. *Special Envoy to Churchill and Stalin 1941-1946.* New York: Random House, 1975.
Hartz, Louis. *The Liberal Tradition in America.* New York: Harcourt, Brace & World, 1955.
Hatada, Takashi. *A History of Korea.* Translated and edited by Warren Smith and Benjamin Hazard. Santa Barbara, California: American Bibliographical Center, 1969.
Hechter, Michael. *Internal Colonialism: The Celtic Fringe in British National Development, 1536-1966.* Berkeley: University of California Press, 1975.
Henderson, Gregory. *Korea: The Politics of the Vortex.* Cambridge: Harvard University Press, 1968.
Herz, Martin F. *Beginnings of the Cold War.* Bloomington: Indiana University Press, 1966.
Hinton, William. *Fanshen: A Documentary of Revolution in a Chinese Village.* New York: Vintage Books, 1966.
Hirschman, Albert. *The Passions and the Interests: Political Arguments for Capitalism before its Triumph.* Princeton: Princeton University Press, 1977.
Hobsbawm, Eric J. *Industry and Empire.* London: Penguin Books, 1969.
———. *Primitive Rebels.* 2d ed. New York: W. W. Norton, 1965.

Hull, Cordell. *Memoirs*. New York: Macmillan Co., 1948.

Huntington, Samuel. *Political Order in Changing Societies*. New Haven: Yale University Press, 1968.

Ienaga, Saburo. *The Pacific War: World War II and the Japanese, 1931-1945*. Translated by Frank Baldwin. New York: Pantheon Books, 1978.

Japan Times. *Economic Development of Korea and Manchuria*. Tokyo: Japan Times Publishing Co., 1923.

Johnson, E.A.J. *American Imperialism in the Image of Peer Gynt*. Minneapolis: University of Minnesota Press, 1971.

Jones, F. C. *Manchuria Since 1931*. New York: Oxford University Press, 1949.

Kawai, Kazuo. *Japan's American Interlude*. Chicago: University of Chicago Press, 1960.

Kim, Bong-gi. *Brief History of the Korean Press*. Seoul: Korea Information Service, 1965.

Kim, Changsoon, ed. *The Culture of Korea*. n.p. Korean-American Culture Association, 1945.

Kim Il Sung. *Selected Works*, vol. I. P'yŏngyang: Foreign Languages Publishing House, 1971.

Kim, Richard. *Lost Names*. Seoul: Sisayongo Publishing Co., 1970.

Kim, Se-jin. *The Politics of Military Revolution in Korea*. Chapel Hill: University of North Carolina Press, 1971.

Kimm, Kiusic (Kim Kyu-sik). *The Far Eastern Situation*. Shanghai: Sino-Korean People's League, 1933.

Klein, Sidney. *Land Tenure Reform in East Asia After World War II*. New York: Bookman Associates, 1958.

Koen, Ross. *The China Lobby in American Politics*. New York: Macmillan Co., 1960.

Kolko, Gabriel. *The Politics of War: The World and United States Foreign Policy, 1943-1945*. New York: Random House, 1968.

Kolko, Joyce, and Gabriel Kolko, *The Limits of Power: The World and United States Foreign Policy, 1945-1954*. New York: Harper & Row, 1972.

Koo, Jae Suh. *A Study of the Regional Characteristics of Korean Agriculture*. Seoul: Korea University, 1967.

Korea and the Pacific War. n.p. United Korean Committee in America, Planning and Research Board, 1943.

Korean Liberty Conference. Los Angeles: United Korean Committee in America, 1942.

Kramer, Irving I. *Japan in Manchuria*. Tokyo: Foreign Affairs Association of Japan, 1954.

Ladejinsky, Wolf. *Chosen's Agriculture and Its Problems*. Washington, D.C.: Department of Agriculture, 1940.

LaFeber, Walter. *America, Russia, and the Cold War, 1945-1966*. New York: John Wiley & Sons, 1967.

Langer, William. *Japan Between East and West*. New York: Council on Foreign Relations, 1957.

Lasswell, Harold. *Power and Personality*. New York: W. W. Norton, 1948.

Lauterbach, Richard. *Danger From the East.* New York: Harper & Bros., 1947.

Lee, Chong-sik. *Counterinsurgency in Manchuria: The Japanese Experience, 1931-1940.* Santa Monica, Calif.: The RAND Corporation, 1967.

———. *Materials on Korean Communism, 1945-1947.* Honolulu: University of Hawaii Press, 1977.

———. *The Politics of Korean Nationalism.* Berkeley: University of California Press, 1963.

Lee, Hoon K. *Land Utilization and Rural Economy in Korea.* Shanghai: Kelly & Walsh, 1936.

Lee, Man-gap, and Herbert R. Barringer, eds. *A City in Transition: Urbanization in Taegu, Korea.* Seoul: Hollym Publishers, 1971.

Lensen, George Alexander. *The Strange Neutrality: Soviet-Japanese Relations During the Second World War, 1941-1945.* Tallahassee, Fla.: Diplomatic Press, 1972.

Levin, Gordon, Jr. *Woodrow Wilson and World Politics.* London: Oxford University Press, 1968

Lloyd, Peter C. *Classes, Crises, and Coups: Themes in the Sociology of Developing Countries.* London: MacGibbon & Kee, 1971.

Lockwood, William W. *The Economic Development of Japan: Growth and Structural Change.* 2d ed. Princeton: Princeton University Press, 1968.

———, ed. *The State and Economic Enterprise in Japan.* Princeton: Princeton University Press, 1965.

McAlister, John T., Jr. *Vietnam: The Origins of Revolution.* Garden City, N.Y.: Doubleday Anchor Books, 1971.

McCune, George. *Korea Today.* Cambridge: Harvard University Press, 1950.

———. *Korea's Postwar Political Problems.* New York: Institute of Pacific Relations, 1947.

McCune, Shannon. *Korea's Heritage: A Regional and Social Geography.* Rutland, Vt.: Charles E. Tuttle, 1956.

McNeill, William Hardy. *America, Britain, and Russia: Their Cooperation and Conflict, 1941-1946.* Reprint ed. New York: Johnson Reprint Corp., 1970.

Malefakis, Edward E. *Agrarian Reform and Peasant Revolution in Spain.* New Haven: Yale University Press, 1970.

The Manchoukuo Yearbook, 1942. Hsinking, Manchuria: Manchoukuo Yearbook Co., 1942.

Mao, Tse-tung. *Miscellany of Mao Tse-tung Thought, 1949-1968.* 2 vols. Washington, D.C.: Joint Publications Research Service, 1970.

Marr, David G. *Vietnamese Anticolonialism.* Berkeley: University of California Press, 1971.

Marx, Karl. *Capital.* 3 vols. New York: International Publishers, 1967 ed.

———. *The Eighteenth Brumaire of Louis Bonaparte.* Reprinted. New York: International Publishers, 1963.

———. *Pre-Capitalist Economic Formations.* Introduction by Eric J. Hobsbawm. New York: International Publishers, 1965.

Materi, Irma. *Irma and the Hermit.* New York: W. W. Norton and Co., 1949

May, Ernest. *Lessons of the Past.* New York: Oxford University Press, 1973

May, Ernest, and James C. Thomson, Jr., eds. *American-East Asian Relations: A Survey.* Cambridge: Harvard University Press, 1972.

Mayer, Arno J. *Dynamics of Counterrevolution in Europe, 1870-1956: An Analytic Framework.* New York: Harper Torchbooks, 1971.

Meade, E. Grant. *American Military Government in Korea.* New York: King's Crown Press, Columbia University, 1951.

Michels, Robert. *Political Parties.* Reprint ed. New York: Dover Publications, 1959.

Migdal, Joel S. *Peasants, Politics and Revolution.* Princeton: Princeton University Press, 1974.

Millis, Walter, ed. *The Forrestal Diaries.* New York: Viking Press, 1951.

Mills, C. Wright. *The Sociological Imagination.* New York: Oxford University Press, 1959.

Mitchell, C. Clyde. *Final Report and History of the New Korea Company.* Seoul: National Land Administration, 1948.

——. *Korea: Second Failure in Asia.* Washington, D.C.: Public Affairs Institute, 1951.

Moore, Barrington, Jr. *Reflections on the Causes of Human Misery and upon Certain Proposals to Eliminate Them.* Boston: Beacon Press, 1970.

——. *Social Origins of Dictatorship and Democracy: Lord and Peasant in the Making of the Modern World.* Boston: Beacon Press, 1966.

Morris, Ivan. *Nationalism and the Right Wing in Japan.* New York: Oxford University Press, 1960.

Moulder, Frances V. *Japan, China, and the Modern World-Economy.* New York: Cambridge University Press, 1977.

Myrdal, Gunnar. *Asian Drama: An Inquiry into the Poverty of Nations.* 3 vols. New York: Pantheon Books, 1968.

Nam, Koon Woo. *The North Korean Communist Leadership, 1945-1965.* University, Ala.: University of Alabama Press, 1974.

Nathan, Robert R., Associates. *An Economic Programme for Korean Reconstruction.* New York: United Nations Reconstruction Agency, 1954.

Neumann, Franz. *The Democratic and the Authoritarian State.* Glencoe, Ill.: Free Press, 1957.

Norman, E. H. *Origins of the Modern Japanese State.* Edited by John Dower. New York: Pantheon Books, 1975.

Oliver, Robert T. *Korea: Forgotten Nation.* Washington, D.C.: Public Affairs Press, 1944.

——. *Syngman Rhee and American Involvement in Korea, 1942-1960.* Seoul: Panmun Books, 1979.

——. *Syngman Rhee: The Man Behind the Myth.* Cornwall, N.Y.: Cornwall Press, 1955.

Paige, Jeffrey M. *Agrarian Revolution.* New York: Free Press, 1975.

Pak Induk. *September Monkey.* New York: Harper & Bros., 1954.

Pak Ki-hyuk et al. *A Study of Land Tenure System in Korea.* Seoul: Korea Land Economics Research Center, 1966.

Pak Ki-hyuk et al. *Three Clan Villages in Korea.* Seoul: Yonsei University Press, 1963.

Palais, James B. *Politics and Policy in Traditional Korea.* Cambridge: Harvard University Press, 1976.

Park, Chung Hee. *Our Nation's Path.* Seoul: Kwangmyong Publishing Co., 1960.

Pihl, Marshall, ed. *Listening to Korea.* New York: Praeger Publishers, 1973.

Polanyi, Karl. *The Great Transformation.* Reprint ed. New York: Beacon Press, 1967.

Popkin, Samuel L. *The Rational Peasant.* Berkeley: University of California Press, 1979.

Range, Willard. *Franklin Delano Roosevelt's World Order.* Athens: University of Georgia Press, 1959.

Redfield, Robert. *Peasant Society and Culture.* 2d ed. Chicago: University of Chicago Press, 1960.

Rosenman, Samuel, ed. *Public Papers and Addresses of Franklin D. Roosevelt, 1942.* New York: Harpers, 1942.

Rudolph, Philip. *North Korea's Political and Economic Structure.* New York: Institute of Pacific Relations, 1959.

Sansom, Robert. *The Economics of Insurgency in the Mekong Delta of Vietnam.* Cambridge: MIT Press, 1970.

Scalapino, Robert A., and Chong-sik Lee. *Communism in Korea.* 2 vols. Berkeley: University of California Press, 1972.

Schattschneider, E. E. *The Semi Sovereign People.* New York: Holt, Rinehart, Winston. 1960.

Schumpeter, E. B., ed. *The Industrialization of Japan and Manchukuo, 1930-1940.* New York: Macmillan Co., 1940.

Schurmann, H. Franz. *Ideology and Organization in Communist China.* Berkeley: University of California Press, 1968.

————. *The Logic of World Power: An Inquiry into the Origins, Currents and Contradictions of World Politics.* New York: Pantheon Books, 1974.

Sebald, William J., and Russell Brines. *With MacArthur in Japan: A Personal History of the Occupation.* New York: W. W. Norton and Co., 1965.

Selden, Mark. *The Yenan Way in Revolutionary China.* Cambridge: Harvard University Press, 1971.

Sherwood, Robert E. *Roosevelt and Hopkins: An Intimate History.* 2d ed. New York: Harper & Bros., 1950.

Shanin, Teodor. *The Awkward Class: Political Sociology of the Peasantry in a Developing Society, Russia 1910-1925.* Oxford: Clarendon Press, 1972.

————, ed. *Peasants and Peasant Societies.* Baltimore, Md.: Penguin Books, 1971.

Shen, Mo. *Japan in Manchuria: An Analytical Study of Treaties and Documents.* Manila, 1960.

Sherwin, Martin. *A World Destroyed: The Atomic Bomb and the Grand Alliance.* New York: Alfred A. Knopf, 1975.

Shoemaker, James. *Notes on Korea's Postwar Economic Position.* New York: Institute of Pacific Relations, 1947.

Shoup, Laurence H., and William Minter. *Imperial Brain Trust: The Council on Foreign Relations and United States Foreign Policy.* New York: Monthly Review Press, 1977.

Simmons, Robert R. *The Strained Alliance: Peking, P'yŏngyang, Moscow, and the Politics of the Korean Civil War.* New York: Free Press, 1975.

Smith, R. Harris. *OSS: The Secret History of America's First Central Intelligence Agency.* Berkeley: University of California Press, 1972.

Smith, Thomas C. *The Agrarian Origins of Modern Japan.* Stanford: Stanford University Press, 1959.

————. *Political Change and Industrial Development in Japan: Government Enterprise, 1868-1880.* Stanford: Stanford University Press, 1955.

Sohn Pow-key, Kim Chol-choon, and Hong Yi-sup. *The History of Korea.* Seoul: Korean National Commission for UNESCO, 1970.

South Manchurian Railway Company. *Sixth Report on Progress in Manchuria, to 1939.* Dairen, 1939.

Stavenhagen, Rudolfo. *Social Classes in Agrarian Societies.* New York: Anchor Press/Doubleday, 1975.

Stettinius, Edward R., Jr. *Roosevelt and the Russians: The Yalta Conference.* Edited Walter Johnson. New York: Doubleday & Co., 1949.

Suh, Dae-sook. *Documents of Korean Communism, 1918-1948.* Princeton: Princeton University Press, 1970.

————. *The Korean Communist Movement, 1918-1948.* Princeton: Princeton University Press, 1967.

Suh, Sang Chul, *Growth and Structural Changes in the Korean Economy, 1910-1945.* Cambridge: Council on East Asian Studies, distributed by Harvard University Press, 1978.

Sun, Kungtu C. *The Economic Development of Manchuria in the First Half of the Twentieth Century.* Cambridge: Harvard University East Asian Center Monographs, 1969.

Taeuber, Irene B. *The Population of Japan.* Princeton: Princeton University Press, 1958.

Tawney, R. H., *Land and Labor in China.* Reprint ed. Boston: Beacon Paperback, 1966.

Thorne, Christopher. *Allies of a Kind: The United States, Britain, and the War Against Japan.* New York: Oxford University Press, 1978.

Truman, Harry S. *Year of Decisions.* Reprint ed. New York: Signet Books, 1965.

————. *Years of Trial and Hope.* Reprint ed. New York: Signet Books, 1965.

Tuchman, Barbara W. *Stilwell and the American Experience in China, 1911-1945.* New York: Macmillan Co., 1971.

Tucker, Robert, ed. *The Marx-Engels Reader.* New York: W. W. Norton, 1972.

Van Buskirk, James Dale. *Korea: Land of the Dawn.* New York: Missionary Education Movement, 1931.

Wagner, Edward Willett. *The Korean Minority in Japan, 1904-1950.* Vancouver: University of British Columbia, 1951.

——, *The Literati Purges: Political Conflict in Early Yi Korea.* Cambridge: Harvard University East Asian Research Center, 1974.

Wales, Nym and Kim San. *Song of Ariran: A Korean Communist in the Chinese Revolution.* 1941. Reprint. San Francisco: Ramparts Press, 1973.

Wallerstein, Immanuel. *The Modern World-System: Capitalist Agriculture and the Origins of the European World-Economy in the Sixteenth Century.* New York: Academic Press, 1974.

——, ed. *Social Change: The Colonial Situation.* New York: John Wiley & Sons, 1966.

Williams, William Appleman. *The Tragedy of American Diplomacy.* 2d rev. ed. New York: Dell Publishing, 1972.

Wolf, Eric. *Peasants.* Englewood Cliffs, N.J.: Prentice-Hall, 1966.

——. *Peasant Wars of the Twentieth Century.* New York: Harper & Row, 1969.

Wright, Gordon. *Rural Revolution in France: The Peasantry in the Twentieth Century.* Stanford: Stanford University Press, 1964.

Yamamura, Kozo. *A Study of Samurai Income and Entrepreneurship.* Cambridge: Harvard University Press, 1974.

Yergin, Daniel. *Shattered Peace: The Origins of the Cold War and the National Security State.* Boston: Houghton Mifflin Co., 1978.

Yim, Louise. *My Forty-Year Fight for Korea.* Seoul: Chungang University, International Culture Research Center, 1951.

Zaichikov, V. T. *Geography of Korea.* Translated by Albert Parry. New York: Institute of Pacific Relations, 1952.

III. ARTICLES AND PERIODICALS

Korean Language

Ch'unch'u (Spring and Autumn), no. 1 (Seoul, February 1946).

Chungsŏng [Voice of the Masses], no. 1 (Pusan, February 1946).

Hong Kyung-hi. "Han'guk ŭi toshiwha" [Korean Urbanization], pts. 1 and 2. *Kyŏngbuk University Theses* 6-7 (Seoul, 1962): 287-325, 355-381.

Kim Yŏng-sŏp. "Yang'an ŭi yŏn'gu Chosŏn hugi ŭi monka kyŏngje" [A Study of the Land Registers: The Economy of Peasant Households in the Late Yi Dynasty], pts. 1 and 2. *Sahak yŏn'gu* (Seoul, May and November 1960).

Minju kyŏngch'al [The Democratic Policeman]. Seoul: Kyŏngch'al kyoyuk-kuk, 1946-1947.

O Ki-su. "Yŏ Un-hyŏng sŏnsaeng-ron" [On Yŏ Un-hyŏng]. *Paengmin* 2 (White People), no. 1 (Seoul, January 1947).

Sin Ch'ŏnji (New Realm), nos. 1-12 (Seoul, 1946).

Yi Kang-guk. "P'asijŭm' kwa sint'ak munje" [Fascism and the Trusteeship Question]. *Inmin kwahak* [People's Science] (Seoul, March 1946).

Yibuk t'ongsin [News from the North]. Seoul: Sambal-sa, 1947-1948.

English Language

Alavi, Hamza. "Peasants and Revolution: Russia, China, India." *Socialist Register*. New York: Monthly Review Press, 1965.

Balbus, Isaac C. "The Concept of Interest in Pluralist and Marxian Analysis." *Politics and Society* 1, no. 2 (February 1971): 151-177.

Bix, Herbert P. "Japanese Imperialism and the Manchurian Economy, 1900-1931." *China Quarterly*, no. 51 (July-September 1972).

Borton, Hugh. "American Pre-Surrender Planning for Postwar Japan." In *Occasional Papers of the East Asian Institute*. New York: Columbia University, 1967.

Butler, Paul. "A Korean Survey." *International Affairs* (July 1946), pp. 361-375.

Campbell, Thomas E. "The Taegu Riots: One of the U.S. Prosecutors Tells of the First Soviet-inspired Attempt to Take Over All Korea." *Commonweal* 54, no. 22 (September 7, 1951): 519-522.

Chandra, Vipin. "The Independence Club and Korea's First Proposal for a National Legislative Assembly." *Occasional Papers on Korea*, no. 4. Seattle: University of Washington, 1975.

Cho, Soon-sung. "The Failure of American Military Government in Korea." *Korean Affairs*, vol 2, no. 3 (Seoul, 1963).

Coulter, John W., and Bernice Bong Hee Kim. "Land Utilization Maps of Korea." *The Geographical Review* (July 1934), pp. 418-422.

Cumings, Bruce. "Is Korea a Mass Society?" *Occasional Papers on Korea*, no. 1. Seattle: University of Washington, 1973.

———. "Kim's Korean Communism." *Problems of Communism* 23, no. 2 (March-April 1974): 27-41.

Deane, H. "Korean Diary." *Nation* (November 1, 1947), pp. 469-471.

Deutsch, Karl. "Social Mobilization and Political Development." *American Political Science Review* 55, no. 3 (September 1961): 493-514.

Eastman, Lloyd. "Fascism in Kuomintang China." *China Quarterly*, no. 49 (January-March 1972), pp. 1-31.

Eckstein, Harry. "On the Etiology of Internal War." *History and Theory*, vol. 4, no. 2 (1965).

Foster, George M. "Peasant Society and the Image of Limited Good." *American Anthropologist*, no. 67 (April 1965), pp. 239-315.

Grey, Arthur L. "The Thirty-eighth Parallel." *Foreign Affairs*, vol. 29, no. 3 (April 1951).

Haimson, Leopold. "The Problem of Social Stability in Urban Russia, 1905-1917." *Slavic Review* 13, no. 4 (December 1964): 619-642.

Halliday, Jon. "The Korean Communist Movement." *Bulletin of Concerned Asian Scholars* 2, no. 4 (Fall 1970): 98-107.

———. "The Korean Revolution." *Socialist Revolution* 1, no. 6 (November-December 1970): 95-134.

Hamlin, W. [pseud.]. "Korea: An American Tragedy." *Nation* (March 1, 1947), pp. 245-247.

Hankum Tralim [pseud.]. "Land Reform in North Korea." *Amerasia* 11, no. 2 (February 1947): 55-60.

Hofheinz, Roy. "The Ecology of Chinese Communist Success." In A. Doak Barnett, ed. *Chinese Communist Politics in Action*. Seattle: University of Washington Press, 1969, pp. 3-77.

Johnson, U. Alexis. "Farming Households, Holdings, Ownership and Tenant Status in Chosen." (Keijo, 1939).

Jones, Gareth Stedman. "The History of U.S. Imperialism." In Robin Blackburn, ed. *Ideology in Social Science*. New York: Vintage Books, 1973, pp. 207-237.

Juhn, Daniel. "Nationalism and Korean Businessmen under Japanese Colonial Rule." *Korea Journal*, vol. 17, no. 1 (January 1977).

Kim, Doo Young. "Labor Legislation in North Korea." *Amerasia* 11, no. 4 (May 1947): 156-160.

Kim, Yong-mo. "Social Background and Mobility of the Landlords under Japanese Imperialism in Korea." *Journal of Social Sciences and Humanities*, no. 31 (Seoul, June 1971).

"Korea—the Crossroads of Asia." *Amerasia*, vol. 9, no. 17 (October 1945).

Korea Economic Digest. New York: Economic Society, 1944-1945.

Korean Research Bulletin. Los Angeles: Korean Research Council, 1943-1944.

LaFeber, Walter. "Roosevelt, Churchill, and Indochina: 1942-1945." *American Historical Review*. vol. 80, no. 5 (December 1975).

Lauterbach, Richard E. "Hodge's Korea." *Virginia Quarterly Review* 23, no. 3 (Summer 1947): 349-368.

Lee, Chong-sik. "Stalinism in the East: Communism in North Korea." In Robert Scalapino, ed. *The Communist Revolution in Asia: Tactics, Goals, and Achievements*. 2d ed. Englewood Cliffs, N.J.: Prentice-Hall, 1969.

Lee, Won-sul. "The Embryo of Korean Bureaucracy in 1945." *Koreana Quarterly* 7, no. 3 (Autumn 1965): 32-49.

Mao, Tse-tung. "Report on an Investigation into the Peasant Movement in Hunan." *Selected Works* 1: 21-59. New York: International Publishers ed., 1954.

McColl, Robert. "The Oyüwan Soviet Area, 1927-1932." *Journal of Asian Studies* (November, 1967).

———. "A Political Geography of Revolution: China, Vietnam, and Thailand." *Journal of Conflict Resolution* (June, 1967).

McCune, George M. "Korea: The First Year of Liberation." *Pacific Affairs* (March 1947), pp. 3-17.

———. "Occupation Politics in Korea." *Far Eastern Survey*, vol. 15, no. 3 (February 13, 1946).

McCune, Shannon. "Regional Diversity in Korea." *Korean Review* (September 1949), pp. 3-13.

Meisner, Maurice "Leninism and Maoism: Some Populist Perspectives on Marxism-Leninism in China" *China Quarterly* (January-March 1971).

Merrill, John. "The Cheju-do Rebellion," *Journal of Korean Studies*, no. 2 (1980), pp. 139-198.

Mitchell, Edward J. "Inequality and Insurgency: A Statistical Study of South Vietnam." *World Politics* (April 1968), pp. 421-438.

———. "Some Econometrics of the Huk Rebellion." *American Political Science Review* 63, no. 4 (December 1969): 1,159-1,171.

Morrock, Richard. "Heritage of Strife: The Effects of Colonial 'Divide and Rule' Strategy Upon Colonial Peoples." *Science and Society* 37, no. 2 (1973): 129-151.

Moskowitz, Karl. "The Creation of the Oriental Development Company." *Occasional Papers on Korea*, no. 2. Seattle: University of Washington, 1975.

Neumann, Franz. "Approaches to the Study of Political Power" in Roy C. Macridis and Bernard E. Brown, eds. *Comparative Politics: Notes and Readings*. Homewood, Ill.: The Dorsey Press, 1972, 4th ed.

Noble, Harold J. "Our Most Dangerous Boundary." *Saturday Evening Post* (August 31, 1946).

Olmsted, David L. "Two Korean Villages: Culture Contact at the 38th Parallel." *Human Organization*, vol. 10, no. 3 (Fall 1951).

"Our Record in Korea in the Light of the Increasing Hostility of the Korean People to our Military Government." *Amerasia* (November 1946), pp. 141-146.

Paige, Glenn D. "North Korea and the Emulation of Russian and Chinese Behavior." In A. Doak Barnett, ed. *Communist Strategies in Asia*. New York: Praeger, 1963.

Palais, James B. "Political Participation in Traditional Korea." *Journal of Korean Studies*, no. 1 (1979).

———. "Stability in Yi Dynasty Korea: Equilibrium Systems and Marginal Adjustment." *Occasional Papers on Korea*, no. 3. Seattle: University of Washington, 1975.

"Pattern of Reconquest." *Amerasia* (October 1945), pp. 271-279.

Portes, Alejandro. "Migration and Underdevelopment." *Politics and Society* 8, no. 1 (1978): 1-48.

Pyle, Kenneth B. "Advantages of Followership: German Economics and Japanese Bureaucrats, 1890-1925." *Journal of Japanese Studies* 1, no. 1 (Autumn 1974): 127-164.

Quinones, Kenneth. "The Impact of the Kabo Reforms upon Political Role Allocation in Late Yi Korea, 1884-1902." *Occasional Papers on Korea*, no. 4. Seattle: University of Washington, 1975.

Race, Jeffrey. "Toward an Exchange Theory of Revolution." In John W. Lewis, ed. *Peasant Rebellion and Communist Revolution in Asia*. Stanford: Stanford University Press, 1974.

Roth, Andrew. "Cross-Fire in Korea." *Nation*, vol. 162, no. 8 (February 23, 1946).

———. "Korea's Heritage." *Nation*, vol. 162, no. 5 (February 2, 1946).

Sarafan, Bertram D. "Military Government: Korea." *Far Eastern Survey* (November 20, 1946).

Schivelbusch, Wolfgang. "Railroad Space and Railroad Time." *New German Critique*, no. 14 (Spring 1978).

Shin, Susan S. "Some Aspects of Landlord-Tenant Relations in Yi Dynasty Korea." *Occasional Papers on Korea*, no. 3. Seattle: University of Washington, 1975.

Shin, Yong-ha. "Landlordism in the Late Yi Dynasty I." *Korea Journal* 18, no. 6 (June 1978): 25-32.

Smith, Thomas C. "Pre-Modern Economic Growth: Japan and the West." *Past and Present*, no. 60 (August 1973), pp. 127-160.

Stinchcombe, Arthur L. "Agricultural Enterprise and Rural Class Relations." *American Journal of Sociology*, no. 67 (September 1961), pp. 165-176.

Stone, Lawrence. "Theories of Revolution." *World Politics* (January 1966).

Strong, Anna Louise. "A Visit to North Korea." *New Statesman and Nation* (January 17, 1948).

Taeuber, Irene B. "Korea in Transition: Demographic Aspects." *Population Index* 10, no. 4 (October 1944): 229-242.

———. "The Population Potential of Postwar Korea." *Far Eastern Quarterly*, vol. 5, no. 3 (May 1946).

Tilly, Charles. "Does Modernization Breed Revolution?" *Comparative Politics* 5, no. 3 (April 1973): 429-447.

Trewartha, Glenn, and Wilbur Zelinsky. "Population Distribution and Change in Korea, 1925-1949." *The Geographical Review*, vol. 45, no. 1 (January 1955).

Vetterling, Philip W., and James J. Wagy. "China: The Transportation Sector, 1950-1971." In *People's Republic of China: An Economic Assessment*. Washington, D.C.: Joint Economic Committee, Congress of the United States, 1972.

Wallerstein, Immanuel. "The Rise and Future Demise of the Capitalist World-System." *Journal of Comparative Studies in Society and History*. Vol. 16 (1974).

Wilkie, Mary E. "Colonials, Marginals, and Immigrants: Contributions to a Theory of Ethnic Stratification." *Comparative Studies in Society and History* 19, no. 1 (January 1977): 67-96.

Zagoria, Donald. "Asian Tenancy Systems and Communist Mobilization of the Peasantry." In John W. Lewis, ed. *Peasant Rebellion and Communist Revolution in Asia*. Stanford: Stanford University Press, 1974.

IV. Unpublished Dissertations and Studies

Baldwin, Frank. "The March 1 Movement: Korean Challenge and Japanese Response." Ph.D. dissertation, Columbia University, 1969.

Benesch, Ralph Keating. "Kim Ku: A Study of a Nationalist." M.A. thesis. University of Washington, 1964.

Chang, Paul Timothy. "Political Effect of World War II on Korea: With Special Reference to the Policies of the United States." Ph.D. dissertation, University of Notre Dame, 1952.

Chen, I-te. "Japanese Colonialism in Korea and Formosa: A Comparison of Its Effects upon the Development of Nationalism." Ph.D. dissertation, University of Pennsylvania, 1968.

Cho Jae-hong. "Post-1945 Land Reforms and Their Consequences in South Korea." Ph.D. dissertation, Indiana University, 1964.

Cumings, Bruce. "The Politics of Liberation: Korea, 1945-1947." Ph.D. dissertation, Columbia University, 1975.

Dong, Wonmo. "Japanese Colonial Policy and Practice in Korea, 1905-1945: A Study in Assimilation." Ph.D. dissertation, Georgetown University, 1965.

Gragert, Edwin H. "Some Reflections on the Land Survey of 1910-1918 and its Treatment in Korean Historiography." Paper, Columbia University Faculty Seminar on Korea, December 1973.

Han Yung Chul. "Traditionalism and the Struggle for Political Modernization in Contemporary Korea: With Special Reference to the Development of Political Parties." Ph.D. dissertation, New York University, 1966.

Hoag, C. Leonard. "American Military Government in Korea: War Policy and the First Year of Occupation, 1941-1946." Draft manuscript prepared under the auspices of the Office of the Chief of Military History, Department of the Army, 1970.

Kang, Han-mu. "The United States Military Government in Korea, 1945-1948: An Analysis and Evaluation of its Policy." Ph.D. dissertation, University of Cincinnati, 1970.

Karl, Hongkee. "A Critical Evaluation of Modern Social Trends in Korea." Ph.D. dissertation, University of Chicago, 1934.

Knez, Eugene Irving. "Sam Jong Dong: A South Korean Village." Ph.D. dissertation, Syracuse University, 1959.

Koh Kwang-il. "In Quest of National Unity and Power: Political Ideas and Practices of Syngman Rhee." Ph.D. dissertation, Rutgers University, 1962.

Lee, Won-sul. "The Impact of United States Occupation Policy on the Socio-Political Structure of South Korea, 1945-1948." Ph.D. dissertation, Western Reserve University, 1961.

Levine, Steven. "Political Consolidation in Manchuria, 1945-1949." Ph.D. dissertation, Harvard University, 1973.

McMahon, John E. "Antecedents, Character, and Outcome of the Korean Elections of 1948." M.A. thesis, University of California, 1954.

Matray, James J. "The Reluctant Crusade: American Foreign Policy in Korea, 1941-1950." Ph.D. dissertation, University of Virginia, 1977.

Merrill, John. "The Cheju-do Rebellion." M.A. thesis, Harvard University, 1975.

Morris, William George. "The Korean Trusteeship, 1941-1947: The United States, Russia and the Cold War." Ph.D. dissertation, University of Texas, 1974.

Perry, Elizabeth. "From Rebels to Revolutionaries: Peasant Protest in Huaibei." Draft manuscript to be published by Stanford University Press, 1980.

Robinson, Richard. "Betrayal of a Nation." Manuscript, Massachusetts Institute of Technology.

Sloane, Justin. "The Communist Effort in South Korea, 1945-1948." M.A. thesis, Northwestern University, 1949.

Suh Sang Chul. "Growth and Structural Change in the Korean Economy, 1910-1945." Ph.D. dissertation, Harvard University, 1967.

Yoo Sae Hee. "The Korean Communist Movement and the Peasantry Under Japanese Rule." Ph.D. dissertation, Columbia University, 1974.

V. NEWSPAPERS

Korean Language

Chayu sinmun [Free News]. Seoul, 1945-1946.

Chŏlla minbo [Cholla People's Report]. Kwangju, November 1945.

Chŏn'guk nodongja sinmun [National Worker's News]. Seoul, November 1945-April 1946.

Chŏnsŏn. [Battle Front]. Seoul, nos. 1-4, October 1945.

Chosŏn inmin-bo [Korean People's Report]. Seoul, 1945-1946.

Chosŏn minjung ilbo [Korean Masses Daily]. Seoul, November 1945.

Chung'ang ilbo [Central Daily]. Seoul, 1945-1946.

Hanmin ilbo [Koreans' Daily]. Seoul, September 1945.

Haebang ilbo [Liberation Daily]. English translation by Chong-sik Lee. Seoul, September-December 1945.

Han'guk minjudang t'ŭkbo [Korean Democratic Party Special Report]. Seoul, December 1945-February 1946.

Hyŏngmyŏng sinmun [Revolution News]. Seoul, September-October 1945.

Kongop sinmun [Industrial News]. Seoul, October-November 1945.

Kŭnyŏk chubo [Korea Weekly]. November 1945.

Maeil sinbo [Daily News]. August-November 1945.

Minjung ilbo [The Masses Daily]. Seoul, 1945-1946.

Munhwa chŏnsŏn [Cultural Front]. Seoul, November-December 1945.

Nodongja sinmun [Worker's News]. Seoul, September-October 1945.

P'yŏngbuk sinbo [N. P'yŏng'an News]. Sinŭiju, January 1946.

P'yŏngyang minbo [P'yŏngyang People's Report]. P'yŏngyang, January-April 1946.

Seoul sinmun [Seoul News]. Seoul, November 1945-1946.

Tonga ilbo [East Asia Daily]. Seoul, December 1945-1946.

Tongbang sinmun [Eastern News]. Seoul, September-October 1945.

Tongnip sinmun [Independence News]. Seoul, November-December 1945.

Tongsin ilbo [New East Daily]. Seoul, 1945-1946.

English language

Korea Times. Seoul, September-December 1945.

Korean Independence. Los Angeles, 1946.

New York Times. New York, 1945-1947.

The People's Korea. Tokyo, 1972-1978.

Seoul Press. Keijo, 1937.

Seoul Times. Seoul, 1945-1948.

Star Exponent. Los Angeles, 1944.

Stars and Stripes. Washington, D.C. and Tokyo, 1946.
Voice of Korea. Washington, D.C., 1945-1948.

OTHER

Dean Acheson Papers, Truman Library.
Eben A. Ayers Papers, Truman Library.
Interview with Leonard Bertsch. Akron, Ohio, May 19, 1973.
Matthew J. Connelly Papers, Truman Library.
Interviews in Seoul with various informants. 1971-1972.
Interview with Professor Han T'ae-su. Seoul, June 1972.
M. Preston Goodfellow, private papers, accession no. 69085-8.37, boxes 1 and 2. Stanford, California: The Hoover Institution Archives.
"Miscellaneous File, Korea," Accession no. TS Korea U58, The Hoover Institution Archives.

The Ladder of Success in Imperial China, by Ping-ti Ho. New York: Columbia University Press, 1962.

The Chinese Inflation, 1937-1949, by Shun-hsin Chou. New York: Columbia University Press, 1963.

Reformer in Modern China: Chang Chien, 1853-1926, by Samuel Chu. New York: Columbia University Press, 1965.

Research in Japanese Sources: A Guide, by Herschel Webb with the assistance of Marleigh Ryan. New York: Columbia University Press, 1965.

Society and Education in Japan, by Herbert Passin. New York: Teachers College Press, Columbia University, 1965.

Agricultural Production and Economic Development in Japan, 1873-1922, by James I. Nakamura. Princeton: Princeton University Press, 1966.

Japan's First Modern Novel: Ukigumo of Futabatei Shimei, by Marleigh Ryan. New York: Columbia University Press, 1967.

The Korean Communist Movement, 1918-1948, by Dae-Sook Suh. Princeton: Princeton University Press, 1967.

The First Vietnam Crisis, by Melvin Gurtov. New York: Columbia University Press, 1967.

Cadres, Bureaucracy, and Political Power in Communist China, by A. Doak Barnett. New York: Columbia University Press, 1967.

The Japanese Imperial Institution in the Tokugawa Period, by Herschel Webb. New York: Columbia University Press, 1968.

Higher Education and Business Recruitment in Japan, by Koya Azumi. New York: Teachers College Press, Columbia University, 1969.

The Communists and Chinese Peasant Rebellions: A Study in the Rewriting of Chinese History, by James P. Harrison, Jr. New York: Atheneum, 1969.

How the Conservatives Rule Japan, by Nathaniel B. Thayer. Princeton: Princeton University Press, 1969.

Aspects of Chinese Education, by C. T. Hu. New York: Teachers College Press, Columbia University, 1969.

Documents of Korean Communism, 1918-1948, by Dae-Sook Suh. Princeton: Princeton University Press, 1970.

Japanese Education: A Bibliography of Materials in the English Language, by Herbert Passin. New York: Teachers College Press, Columbia University, 1970.

Economic Development and the Labor Market in Japan, by Koji Taira. New York: Columbia University Press, 1970.

The Japanese Oligarchy and the Russo-Japanese War, by Shumpei Okamoto. New York: Columbia University Press, 1970.

Imperial Restoration in Medieval Japan, by H. Paul Varley. New York: Columbia University Press, 1971.

Japan's Postwar Defense Policy, 1947-1968, by Martin E. Weinstein. New York: Columbia University Press, 1971.

Election Campaigning Japanese Style, by Gerald L. Curtis. New York: Columbia University Press, 1971.

China and Russia: The "Great Game," by O. Edmund Clubb. New York: Columbia University Press, 1971.

Money and Monetary Policy in Communist China, by Katherine Huang Hsiao. New York: Columbia University Press, 1971.

The District Magistrate in Late Imperial China, by John R. Watt. New York: Columbia University Press, 1972.

Law and Policy in China's Foreign Relations: A Study of Attitudes and Practice, by James C. Hsiung. New York: Columbia University Press, 1972.

Pearl Harbor as History: Japanese-American Relations, 1931-1941, edited by Dorothy Borg and Shumpei Okamoto, with the assistance of Dale K. A. Finlayson. New York: Columbia University Press, 1973.

Japanese Culture: A Short History, by H. Paul Varley. New York: Praeger, 1973.

Doctors in Politics: The Political Life of the Japan Medical Association, by William E. Steslicke. New York: Praeger, 1973.

Japan's Foreign Policy, 1868-1941: A Research Guide, edited by James William Morley. New York: Columbia University Press, 1973.

The Japan Teachers Union: A Radical Interest Group in Japanese Politics, by Donald Ray Thurston. Princeton: Princeton University Press, 1973.

Palace and Politics in Prewar Japan, by David Anson Titus. New York: Columbia University Press, 1974.

The Idea of China: Essays in Geographic Myth and Theory, by Andrew March. Devon, England: David and Charles, 1974.

Origins of the Cultural Revolution, by Roderick MacFarquhar. New York: Columbia University Press, 1974.

Shiba Kōkan: Artist, Innovator, and Pioneer in the Westernization of Japan, by Calvin L. French. Tokyo: Weatherhill, 1974.

Embassy at War, by Harold Joyce Noble. Edited with an introduction by Frank Baldwin, Jr. Seattle: University of Washington Press, 1975.

Rebels and Bureaucrats: China's December 9ers, by John Israel and Donald W. Klein. Berkeley: University of California Press, 1975.

House United, House Divided: The Chinese Family in Taiwan, by Myron L. Cohen. New York: Columbia University Press, 1976.

Insei: Abdicated Sovereigns in the Politics of Late Heian Japan, by G. Cameron Hurst. New York: Columbia University Press, 1976.

Deterrent Diplomacy, edited by James W. Morley. New York: Columbia University Press, 1976.

Cadres, Commanders and Commissars: The Training of the Chinese Commu-

nist Leadership, 1920-45, by Jane L. Price. Boulder, Colorado: Westview Press, 1976.

Sun Yat-sen: Frustrated Patriot, by C. Martin Wilbur. New York: Columbia University Press, 1976.

Japanese International Negotiating Style, by Michael Blaker. New York: Columbia University Press, 1977.

Contemporary Japanese Budget Politics, by John Creighton Campbell. Berkeley: University of California Press, 1977.

The Medieval Chinese Oligarchy, by David Johnson. Boulder, Colorado: Westview Press, 1977.

Escape from Predicament: Neo-Confucianism and China's Evolving Political Culture, by Thomas A. Metzger. New York: Columbia University Press, 1977.

The Arms of Kiangnan: Modernization in the Chinese Ordnance Industry, 1860-1895, by Thomas L. Kennedy. Boulder, Colorado: Westview Press, 1978.

Patterns of Japanese Policymaking: Experiences from Higher Education, by T. J. Pempel. Boulder, Colorado: Westview Press, 1978.

The Chinese Connection, by Warren Cohen. New York: Columbia University Press, 1978.

Militarism in Modern China: The Career of Wu P'ei-fu, 1916-1939, by Odoric Y. K. Wou. Folkestone, England: Wm. Dawson & Sons, 1978.

A Chinese Pioneer Family: The Lins of Wu-feng, by Johanna Meskill. Princeton: Princeton University Press, 1979.

Perspectives on a Changing China: Essays in Honor of Professor C. Martin Wilbur, edited by Joshua A. Fogel and William T. Rowe. Boulder, Colorado: Westview Press, 1979.

The Memoirs of Li Tsung-jen, by T. K. Tong and Li Tsung-jen. Boulder, Colorado: Westview Press, 1979.

Subject Index

Library of Congress Cataloging in Publication Data

Cumings, Bruce, 1943-
    The origins of the Korean War.

    (Studies of the East Asian Institute, Columbia
University)
    "The first of a planned two-volume study."
    Bibliography: p.
    Includes index.
    1. Korea—History—Allied occupation, 1945-1948.
2. Korean War, 1950-1953—Causes. I. Title.
II. Series: Columbia University. East Asian Institute.
Studies.
DS917.55.C85   951.9′042   80-8543
ISBN 0-691-09383-0
ISBN 0-691-10113-2 (pbk.)